*Promoting Academic Competence
and Literacy in School*

Promoting Academic Competence and Literacy in School

Edited by

Michael Pressley, Karen R. Harris, and John T. Guthrie

College of Education
University of Maryland at College Park
College Park, Maryland

Academic Press, Inc.
Harcourt Brace Jovanovich, Publishers

San Diego   New York   Boston   London   Sydney   Tokyo   Toronto

Academic Press, Inc.
1250 Sixth Avenue, San Diego, California 92101-4311

United Kingdom Edition published by
Academic Press Limited
24–28 Oval Road, London NW1 7DX

Library of Congress Cataloging-in-Publication Data

Promoting academic competence and literacy in school / Michael
    Pressley, Karen R. Harris, and John T. Guthrie, [editors].
        p.   cm.
    Conference held at the University of Maryland, College Park, May
10-11, 1990
    Includes bibliographical references and index.
    ISBN 0-12-564438-8
    1. Reading--United States--Congresses.   2. English language-
-Composition and exercises--Study and teaching--United States-
-Congresses.   I. Pressley, Michael.   II. Harris, Karen R.
III. Guthrie, John T.
LB1573.P78   1992
428.4'07--dc20   92-4971
                                                                        CIP

PRINTED IN THE UNITED STATES OF AMERICA

92 93 94 95 96 97   QW   9 8 7 6 5 4 3 2 1

Contents

I. ACADEMIC COMPETENCE IN CLASSROOMS

1. *In Search of Student Expertise in the Classroom: A Metacognitive Analysis*
Donald Miechenbaum and Andrew Biemiller

2. *Understanding How Students Learn in Classrooms*
Graham Nuthall and Adrienne Alton-Lee

II. READING

3. Skilled and Not-So-Skilled Reading: Good Information Processing and Not-So-Good Information Processing

Michael Pressley, Pamela Beard El-Dinary, and Rachel Brown

4. Reading Comprehension as a Conversation with an Author

Timothy Shanahan

5. Improving Reading and Thinking: From Teaching or Not Teaching Skills to Interactive Interventions

Cathy Collins

6. *Developing Self-Sufficient Learners in Reading and Mathematics through Self-Instructional Training*
Gloria E. Miller and Mary Ellen Brewster

7. *Collaborative Instruction for Reading Comprehension: The Role of Discourse and Discussion*
Margaret A. Gallego

8. *Guiding Students' Cognitive Processing of Scientific Information in Text*
Richard E. Mayer

III. Writing

IV. DEVELOPMENT OF TEACHERS WHO PROMOTE ACADEMIC COMPETENCE, SKILLED READING, AND GOOD WRITING

Contributors

Numbers in parentheses indicate the pages on which the authors' contributions begin.

Adrienne Alton-Lee (57), Department of Education, University of Canterbury, Christchurch 1, New Zealand

Patricia L. Anders (457), College of Education, University of Arizona, Tucson, Arizona 85721

Andrew Biemiller (3), Institute of Child Study, University of Toronto, Toronto, Ontario, Canada M5R 2X2

John G. Borkowski (477), Department of Psychology, University of Notre Dame, Notre Dame, Indiana 46556

Candace S. Bos (457), College of Education, University of Arizona, Tucson, Arizona 85721

Mary Ellen Brewster (169), Department of Psychology, University of South Carolina, Columbia, South Carolina 29208

Rachel Brown (91), College of Education, University of Maryland at College Park, College Park, Maryland 20742

Beverly A. Busching (311), Department of Instructional and Teacher Education, College of Education, University of South Carolina, Columbia, South Carolina 29208

Cathy Collins (149), School of Education, Texas Christian University, Fort Worth, Texas 76129

Elizabeth A. Cunicelli (407), Benchmark School, Media, Pennsylvania 19063

Donald D. Deshler (361), University of Kansas, Institute for Research in Learning Disabilities, Lawrence, Kansas 66045

Pamela Beard El-Dinary (91), College of Education, University of Maryland at College Park, College Park, Maryland 20742

Jill Fitzgerald (337), School of Education, University of North Carolina at Chapel Hill, Chapel Hill, North Carolina 27599

Margaret A. Gallego (223), Department of Teacher Education, Michigan State University, East Lansing, Michigan 48824

Irene W. Gaskins (407), Benchmark School, Media, Pennsylvania 19063

Steve Graham (277), Department of Special Education, University of Maryland at College Park, College Park, Maryland 20742

Anne Graves (261), College of Education, San Diego State University, San Diego, California 92182

Karen R. Harris (277), Department of Special Education, University of Maryland at College Park, College Park, Maryland 20742

Frank M. Kline (361), Department of Curriculum and Instruction, Wichita State University, Wichita, Kansas 67208

Richard E. Mayer (243), Department of Psychology, University of California, Santa Barbara, Santa Barbara, California 93106

Christine B. McCormick (311), Department of Educational Psychology, College of Education, University of South Carolina, Columbia, South Carolina 29208

Donald Miechenbaum (3), University of Waterloo, Waterloo, Ontario, Canada N2L 3G1

Gloria E. Miller (169), Department of Psychology, University of South Carolina, Columbia, South Carolina 29208

Marjorie Montague (261), College of Education, University of Miami, Coral Gables, Florida 33124

Nithi Muthukrishna (477), Department of Psychology, University of Notre Dame, Notre Dame, Indiana 46556

Graham Nuthall (57), Department of Education, University of Canterbury, Christchurch 1, New Zealand

Ellen F. Potter (311), Department of Educational Psychology, College of Education, University of South Carolina, Columbia, South Carolina 29208

Michael Pressley (91), College of Education, University of Maryland at College Park, College Park, Maryland 20742

Laura R. Roehler (427), College of Education, Michigan State University, East Lansing, Michigan 48824

Eric Satlow (407), Benchmark School, Media, Pennsylvania 19063

Jean B. Schumaker (361), University of Kansas, Institute for Research in Learning Disabilities, Lawrence, Kansas 66045

Timothy Shanahan (129), College of Education, University of Illinois at Chicago, Chicago, Illinois 60680

Preface

On May 10, 1990, the University of Maryland at College Park hosted a conference on "Cognitive Research for Instructional Innovation" sponsored by the Center for Educational Research and Development, College of Education. Despite ten hours of torrential rain, over 500 visitors attended the conference in the University's student union. John Borkowski, Irene Gaskins, Donald Meichenbaum and Andrew Biemiller, Michael Pressley, and Laura Roehler made presentations throughout the day. All the presenters had previously agreed that their talks would be translated into a conference volume—a small volume that would simply present the talks and provide a brief commentary about them.

On May 11, 1990, the presenters and selected members of the audience met for more intimate discussion of the issues that motivated the conference. Participants in this discussion included Donald Deshler, Jean Schumaker, Gloria Miller, Karen Harris, Steve Graham, and Anne Graves. By the end of this long and productive dialogue, the participants were convinced that a larger book than originally envisioned should grow out of the two day's talks and deliberations. It was agreed that Pressley, Harris, and Guthrie, the conference organizers, would edit it. Deshler and Schumaker, Miller, Harris, Graham, and Graves were recruited for contributions before they departed for home. A "wish" list of other contributors was drawn up by the editors in collaboration with the presenters and others who attended the private session.

Promoting Academic Competence and Literacy in School is the result of those efforts as well as many exchanges between the editors and authors. The editors wanted the authors to pursue their main interests but encouraged complementary themes and discussions. The contributors responded enthusiastically to the feedback. This volume addresses contemporary knowledge of literacy development in classrooms and challenges to be met if theoretical and research-based understandings are to be translated into practice.

The editors gratefully acknowledge the many staff, faculty, and students of the College of Education at Maryland who made the conference a success, with special thanks to Stan Bennett of the Department of Human Development. The publicist for the conference was Patricia O. Duffy from the College of Education's Center for Educational Research and Development. Robert Reid, Kathy Boyer-Schick, and Pam El-Dinary were a three-member student committee who did all they could to keep the editors sane as they responded to the demands of putting on a major conference.

Mike Pressley extends a special thanks to Tim Pressley. As the youngest attendee at the conference—not yet 3 at the time—his rapt attention during Irene Gaskin's talk and his good behavior and enthusiasm during dinner were especially appreciated. And then there were those Saturdays and Sundays when Tim read picture books and played with *Reader Rabbit* on the computer as Daddy edited chapters. Father appreciated it, confident that what was contained in this book would translate into educational practice that would promote the literacy of Timmy and his future classmates.

Part I

ACADEMIC COMPETENCE IN CLASSROOMS

Many, many volumes have been written that decry the state of education, presenting the message that classroom learning is often not efficient or reaching its potential. The competent teaching and learning that occurs in classrooms every day is too rarely the focus of media or researcher attention. Often studies of children's learning have focused on artificial tasks or artificial settings that permit strong experimenter control of stimulation and input. The work reported in this part of this volume is very different from traditional work because the researchers are applying powerful observational methodologies in actual school settings in order to understand how children manage themselves and regulate their learning during the school day.

Meichenbaum and Biemiller report a landmark investigation in which children who were high and low in self-direction were studied intensely; they relate their findings to the growing literature on expertise. Their premise is that it is very easy for teachers to identify highly competent and less competent students. Their question is how such distinctions are made, that is, what behaviors distinguish self-directed students from those who lack direction. A panorama of differences emerges; self-directed children are task-engaged and competent compared with their non-self-directed classmates. In particular, Meichenbaum and Biemiller observe a great deal of self-directive language in self-directed students, supportive of Meichenbaum's theory that self-directed speech and language supports behavioral regulation in general, and that it is an essential part of planning and monitoring behavior and learning.

Nuthall and Alton-Lee use a similar methodology, attempting to capture as much information as possible about the academic experiences of target children during the school day. They plot these experiences against what students learn in school, using procedures that permit them to relate the probability that particular pieces of information would be acquired given particular experiences. In a series of studies, they demonstrate how students construct new schemata; this work reveals powerful formal (i.e., public) and informal (i.e., private and student interactive) learning mechanisms operating in the classroom. The chapter by Nuthall and Alton-Lee summarizes the construction of a theory, the development of methods that permit such theory construction, and the initial validation and cross-validation of the theory.

In short, these two chapters provide outstanding examples of how real classroom learning can be studied to determine its dynamics while capturing individual differences in learning. These ambitious new studies display the type of innovative research and data-informed theorizing this book is intended to stimulate.

1

In Search of Student Expertise in the Classroom: A Metacognitive Analysis

Donald Meichenbaum and Andrew Biemiller

INTRODUCTION

A brief description of how the present research program evolved will provide a useful framework to better appreciate our present progress and our
future research agenda. As for many research projects, a confluence of
interests and fortuitous events contributed to the present project. Meichenbaum's interests revolved around the dual concerns of trying (1) to develop
ways to assess metacognitive or executive self-regulatory processes in
children who evidenced behavioral or academic difficulties and (2) to develop ways to enhance the generalization and maintenance of cognitive-
behavioral intervention procedures with children. Research has indicated
that cognitive-behavioral intervention procedures were often effective in
improving children's classroom behavior and academic performance in the
short run, but that they were not as successful in producing permanent
changes. There was thus a need to leave the confines of both the lab and
the clinic in the search for generalization in the classroom. There was also
a need to develop more natural means of assessing "metacognitive processes" in classroom settings.

This chapter is based on a paper presented at the Conference on Cognitive Research for
Instructional Innovation at the University of Maryland, College Park, Maryland, on May 10,
1990.

Fortunately, Biemiller and his colleagues at the Institute of Child Study (ICS) in Toronto had already begun naturalistic classroom observations in their attempt to identify and study children who displayed no difficulties, namely, "competent" children. When Meichenbaum was invited to present his work at ICS, a follow-up meeting with the ICS Lab School teachers led to an intriguing discussion of what distinguished the more "competent" from the less "competent" children in their classrooms. Over the course of several meetings with ICS teachers, as well as in meetings with teachers from the Waterloo (Ontario) County School Board, a character sketch of the "competent" child emerged. The teachers tended to equate the concept of competence with "self-direction," namely, the ability of a child to "know what to do in class, and do it, without even having to be told." Some teachers labeled these children as "experts," since they efficiently anticipated and negotiated both classroom demands and teacher expectations.

These discussions led us to follow two paths. First, we decided to spend time in classrooms observing teacher-nominated "self-directed" children. We wanted to determine what self-directed children did, what they said to others as well as to themselves, and what others (peers and teachers) said to them. We enlisted the help of student teachers in Biemiller's classes at the University of Toronto. We were able to observe 140 teacher-nominated children (rated high and low in "self-direction") in several schools. Ages ranged from 3 to 12 years. Based on these informal naturalistic accounts, we have developed a reliable coding scheme of social- and self-discourse as a means of explicating the nature of expertise in the classroom.

The second path we took was to summarize the literature on expertise in order to determine specific behaviors to look for in self-directed children. We begin our report with a brief consideration of this literature and then turn our attention to our classroom observations.

The Nature of Expertise

An examination of the extensive literature on expertise in adults may afford some suggestions of what to look for in children's classroom behaviors. We emphasize the word "suggestions", since we fully recognize that developmental and competence (knowledge and skill) variables will contribute the differences between adult "experts" and children.

The literature on expertise is quite extensive, in terms of both the variety of experts studied and the diverse research approaches employed (e.g., naturalistic observations, analysis of performance on laboratory tasks, "think aloud" samples, self-report accounts, biographical analyses). The following list of experts studied indicates the level of investigatory activity. The experts studied (and this is likely to be an incomplete list) include

1. players of chess, bridge, go
2. high level musicians (e.g., violinists and pianists) and people expert in music notation and composition
3. people expert in science, writing, reading (prose and maps), solving algebraic and physics word problems and math calculations (exceptional recall of calendar dates)
4. athletes expert in such sports as basketball, field hockey, baseball, tennis, volleyball, figure skating, and karate
5. experts in computer programming, electronic circuit designs, and medical diagnoses
6. experts in such specialties as typing, Morse code operators, and skilled memorizers (e.g., waiters who are exceptional in recall of patrons' dinner orders)

Two challenging questions for our research efforts emerge when previewing this extensive list of experts. First, what do these various experts have in common? Second, what, if anything, can we learn from this literature on adult experts that will help us more readily understand children's expertise in the classroom?

The search for common characteristics among experts does *not* overlook the fact that obvious domain-specific skills are required in each area. For example, research on expert typists illustrates the specific fashion in which they coordinate incoming input (namely, expert typists look ahead faster than they type). The work on expert runners indicates that their extensive practice routine can cause bodily changes and adaptations that are unique to this sports area. Although we do not ignore domain-specific features of expertise, we begin by considering those common factors that emerge under three general headings: (a) knowledge, (b) strategies, and (c) motivation. Let us consider each of these factors[2] and then explore how to incorporate these concepts in our classroom observation task.

Knowledge Differences

The literature is consistent in highlighting that, relative to novices, experts differ in terms of *the amount of knowledge they possess* and *how that*

---

[2]These observations are based on findings reported, among others, by Abelson, 1981; Allard & Barnett, 1985; Anderson, 1982; Bereiter & Scardamalia, 1986; Charness, 1989; Chase & Simon, 1978; Chi, Feltovich, & Glaser, 1981; Chiesi, Spilich, & Voss, 1979; Dawson, Zeitz, & Wright, 1989; deGroot, 1965; Elstein, Shulman, & Sprafka, 1978; Engle & Bukstel, 1978; Ericsson, 1985; Ericsson & Smith, 1989; Ericsson, Tesch-Romer, & Krampe, 1990; Glaser, 1984; Larkin, McDermott, Simon, & Simon, 1980; Prawat, 1989; Rabinowitz & Glaser, 1989; Reitman, 1976; Scardamalia & Bereiter, 1989; Starks & Deakin, 1984; and Sternberg, 1981.

knowledge is structured (Bereiter & Scardamalia, 1986). More specifically:

1. Experts possess a more extensive, systematized, and organized domain of knowledge in their area of expertise. In other words, experts
   have a larger storage of information in long-term memory and a
   greater availability of meaningful relationships, as reflected by a richer
   domain-specific vocabulary and more developed associative networks.
2. Whereas novices tend to use "surface knowledge," experts use a
   "deeper understanding" to solve problems. For instance, experts make
   better use of what they know by organizing their knowledge in a more
   coherent fashion (around a more central set of concepts and understandings). In contrast, novices tend to deal with information as
   isolated fragments, only vaguely related to higher related principles.
3. Experts have access to multiple alternative theories; this access
   contributes to their tendency to formulate more flexible and numera-
   ble hypotheses.
4. Experts have a more developed representation of the task. This
   contributes to a better pattern recognition since they can integrate
   task characteristics into a whole.
5. Experts are able to retrieve solution methods as part of their attempt
   to immediately comprehend the problem. This is in contrast to the
   novice's step-by-step appraisal. Experts frequently go beyond what the
   immediate situation or problem requires.
6. Experts are more active in creating and nurturing their knowledge
   base (e.g., they practice more and they are more experimental and
   curious, as illustrated by their pursuit of "why" questions).
7. Experts have a faster response time or more ready access to relevant
   knowledge (minimal search time). Experts map incoming domain-
   specific information faster and more efficiently.
8. Experts are able to recall more information more efficiently from their
   area of expertise, as well as access relevant tacit knowledge. For
   example, experts are more likely to use normative or base-rate data
   in formulating decisions.
9. Experts have more generic and abstract problem types and more
   complete solution procedures stored in memory and can use these
   instead of thinking out each step. This contributes to their ability to
   solve problems in their area of expertise more quickly and efficiently.

Experts and novices differ not only in the knowledge they bring to a task,
but in how they organize and use that knowledge, as Bereiter and Scardamalia (1986) observe. Experts also differ with respect to the strategies
they employ.

Strategy Differences or Responses to Problems

As Ericsson and Smith (1989) observe, experts have more efficient scripted strategies and they engage in more developed effortful behaviors when the automatic nature of their behavior or script is interrupted or blocked. More specifically:

1. Experts have a more varied, flexible, and efficient set of strategies with which to perform the domain-specific task.
2. Experts explore more *relevant* alternative combinations. The word "relevant" is highlighted because experts usually do not consider all options. Experts usually restrict their search space to a limited range of possible choices. This efficient search strategy is in part due to the fact that experts have superior recall of domain-relevant stimuli. Experts more readily discriminate relevant from irrelevant cues and use these in inferring relationships, in identifying feasible options, and in developing hypotheses that direct decision making in a forward fashion, with an accompanying appreciation of the implications of their decisions.
3. Experts alter their search strategy depending on the level of task difficulty. For example, experts tend to engage in more forward search (formulate hypotheses), whereas novices tend to work backward from problem statements using a form of means–ends analysis. Experts tend to engage in more self-explanations of the problem at hand and, moreover, monitor these explanations.
4. Experts tend to organize their strategies and performance over the course of a task. For example, experts tend to pause and reflect after solving problems.
5. Finally, experts are more likely to employ *metacognitive* executive skills (that is, planning; self-monitoring, as evident in their noting inconsistencies and engaging in revisions of their goals and methods; more efficient and developed inferential procedures, fix-up strategies, and problem-solving skills). Most important, experts exert voluntary control over these executive or metacognitive processes. As Lefebvre-Pinard and Pinard (1985) observe, experts have the capacity to "take charge" of their own cognitive functioning. Brown (1982) has high-lighted that becoming an expert is largely the process of acquiring explicit knowledge about the strategies and goals needed for efficient performance.

In the same way that experts are active in developing their knowledge base, they are also active in exercising their strategic and metacognitive skills. Experts advance their own competence and build personal knowledge. A key ingredient in this self-advancement process is the expert's ability to select or be assigned tasks at a difficulty level that helps exercise strategic skills and further develops a knowledge base. (See Chapter 3 for an example of expert reading compared with novice reading.)

Belmont and Mitchells (1987) have highlighted the importance of the difficulty level of tasks in nurturing expertise in their concept of the "optimum perceived difficulty level" *as judged by the learner*. They propose that tasks can be placed on a continuum from being so easy that the individual does not have to work (produce effortful strategies) to master it to being so hard that the individual feels that all attempts would prove futile. There is, however, a moderate level of task difficulty at which strategic behaviors are employed and exercised. It is proposed that experts seek out and work in this moderate or optimal level of difficulty more often than novices, continuously challenging and extending their strategic skills.

Motivation and Personal Striving

We know that experts are not only better at doing the same things that novices do, but they also do these things differently. The picture of experts that is emerging is beginning to sound too mechanical and lacking in emotion. The portrayal, thus far, seems to convey that experts are just more efficient computer-like machines who can be measured in terms of the size of their knowledge base, the speed of their information processing, the size of their mental chunks, and the efficiency of their selected strategy. Where is the "person in the machine?" Where is the interest, the passion, and the determination that leads to the many, many hours of practice that are required to become an expert? A major characteristic that distinguishes experts from others is the sheer amount of practice in which experts engage. This finding is underscored by Bloom (1985) and Ericsson, Tesch-Romer, and Krampe (1990), who reported on experts in the areas of chess, music, and sports. Their conclusions are informative in highlighting the important role of motivation in the development of expertise. They found that experts in the areas of chess, music, and sports

1. began their activities at an earlier age
2. demonstrated a higher level of sustained practice for their age and worked harder on their selected tasks
3. evidenced interest in their respective activities before they began systematic practice
4. engaged in systematic practice that was most often initiated by their parent(s), who actively supported and rewarded their practice habits
5. continued to practice throughout adolescence in response to the efforts of an advanced teacher or coach

6. reduced leisure time activities during adolescence as more time was devoted to their area of expertise
7. reached maximal or optimal levels of practice by age 20

In short, the analysis of expertise needs to include a consideration of the motivational factors (e.g., learning or mastery goals versus performance goals, attributional style in response to failure and success, and the nature of social supports available to develop expertise) that sustain the level of commitment and practice required for the development of expertise.

As Dweck (1986) and Borkowski, Johnson, and Reid (1987) argue, motivational beliefs, particularly those related to the perceived causes of failure and success, should be considered in any explanation of expertise. Affective and motivational components can energize or hinder the use of one's knowledge and strategies, one's level of practice, and one's performance. Thus, we need to consider what motivates individuals (1) to invest their effort in becoming expert, (2) to develop the commitment to the autonomous pursuit of learning, and (3) to cope with their failures and successes.

Summary

In summary, we see that expertise is a complex and dynamic process that involves knowledge, strategy, and motivational components. How do these characteristics of experts express themselves in classroom settings? Our attempt to answer this question began with extensive discussions with classroom teachers (preschool to Grade 6). We asked them how expertise (or, as they preferred to call it, "competence") expresses itself in their classrooms. The discussions soon shifted to specific exemplary children. In the same way that we might nominate Julia Child or Craig Claiborne in the cooking area, or Martina Navratilova or Ivan Lendl in tennis, our teachers kept referring to specific children in their classes. We searched for the attributes these children shared and, moreover, for an appropriate label for our would-be experts. Jointly, we decided on the label "self-directed child."

CLASSROOM OBSERVATIONS 1988–1989: CHARACTERISTICS OF SELF-DIRECTED BEHAVIOR

A Study of Self-Directed Children

The teachers were consistent in suggesting that the self-directed child was one who "knows what needs to be done and does it without having to be told." With this as a central tenet, a number of additional specific features emerged. Based on the discussion with the teachers, the following character sketch was developed.

> By self-directed (SD) we mean a child who apparently knows what needs to be done and does it, often without having to be asked or told. The SD child deals with problems on her/his own as much as possible. The SD child seems able to "read the teacher's mind," anticipating what is expected. The SD child often keeps the teacher "on her/his toes" by correcting or giving the teacher feedback.
>
> The SD child moves through routines with a certain directedness, rarely manifesting boredom. For instance, the SD child can usually find something to do on his/her own (rarely expressing, "I don't know what to do"). The SD child is a self-starter at the beginning of class or at transition periods ("not at loose ends"), finishing one task and beginning another. When asked to do something, the SD child seems to have an idea about the goals of the task, behaves confidently as if she/he has a plan, and follows a series of steps to conduct the task. The SD child does not get unduly upset by errors and failures.
>
> The SD child tends to ask appropriate questions at appropriate times. For instance, if instructions are inadequate, the SD child asks for clarification. The child tends to be more interested and curious than other children. If the teacher has difficulty soliciting an answer from the class, the teacher knows she/he can depend on the SD child for an answer.
>
> SD children are more likely to be chosen by teachers and peers to help other pupils or younger children. If the teacher is going to be absent and needs to give the substitute teacher the name of a child who can explain the routine and related items, the SD child would be nominated. The SD child is the type of child teachers might wish to duplicate. Teachers would usually like more such SD children in their classes.

Using this multifaceted complex portrayal, we asked teachers to nominate children who fit the SD sketch. The next step was to "track" SD children and their non-SD counterparts, in order to determine how they negotiate classroom activities. The naturalistic observations consisted of recording descriptive narrative accounts of classroom behavioral samples (usually 10–30 min). We wanted to know how SD children (1) spent their time (how they behaved); and (2) interacted with their teachers and peers, and in turn, how their peers and teachers interacted with them.

This initial phase of research was quite descriptive in nature, as observers situated themselves in preschool to Grade 6 classrooms, close enough (not more than a few feet from the child) to observe and record all behaviors, as well as all verbalizations, in a written running commentary. In short, observers recorded (1) what the SD child did; (2) what the SD child said to self, peers, teacher; and (3) what the peers and teacher said to the SD child.

An interesting picture soon began to emerge from the more than 140 observations obtained, as summarized by Biemiller and Meichenbaum (1989).

What Self-Directed Children Did

- Initiated work quickly
- Made transitions smoothly
- Were on task a relatively high percentage of the time
- Retrieved needed materials quickly
- In group work, took charge by organizing and distributing tasks and responsibilities (e.g., dispensing materials and assignments to peers)
- Were organized in getting ready for next school activity (e.g., seat work, note taking)
- Persevered even when a solution to a problem was not immediately apparent, as illustrated by their lingering at the task even when others were done or gone to recess
- Were more likely to say to the teacher, "Don't tell me the answer, I can figure it out myself!"

What Self-Directed Children Say to Themselves

Children in classrooms emit a fair amount of overt private speech (that is, verbalizations not ostensibly directed at any one else). The private speech we observed could be classified into such categories as self-interrogative, self-monitoring, and self-retrieval activities. The following verbalizations were commonly evidenced by SD children.

1. Overt self-interrogative: "How can I do this?"; "What does . . . (capital J look like?). I know."
2. Overt self-monitoring: "Let me check this."; "I'm almost finished."; "Erase this. Okay now I got it."; "I better slow down here."; "There is something strange about this."
3. Self-retrieval activities using analogical problem solving: "This reminds me . . . "; "Remember when we . . . "; "This is like . . . ".

These self-regulatory activities that generally have been subsumed under the heading "metacognition" were not limited to the SD child's private speech, but were also evident in interactions with other children and the teacher. Let us consider illustrative examples of the types of verbalizations SD children direct at others.

What Self-Directed Children Say to Others

1. Verbalizations that suggest that the SD child has a goal representation and accompanying procedural script of how a task or activity should be conducted: "You don't do it that way."; "You forgot to shuffle the cards."; "No, it's John's turn."; "This one goes first."; "You forgot to mark it down."; "Mrs. (teacher), do you want us to do A or B?" (the child lists alternative activities).
2. Verbalizations that reflect SD child's anticipation of problems, the

need for more information, or the desire to move the task along: "Becky, don't forget you have to cut a little further so be sure to leave room."; "You shouldn't write so big. You will run out of space."; Mrs. X, did you want us to do six or seven words?" (when in fact teacher did not specify the number of words to be completed); "Today is Tuesday, Miss Z; we don't have gym."; "Don't they have a dance in the gym tonight, so we can't practice?"; Peer states, "I'm done." SD child comments, "That is because you didn't cut along the lines."; "If you make noise then we won't be able to go to recess."

In short, the SD children not only are more prone to monitor their own behavior, but often monitor and comment on others' behaviors. In some ways, SD children act like "mini-teachers". As one SD child, Jessica, commented to an observer in the classroom:

Jessica to D.M.:   "What are you doing?"

    D.M.:   "I am here to watch how teachers teach and how children learn. So I am taking some notes."

Jessica: "Okay."

After several minutes of observing Jessica, Jessica looked over at D.M. in a concerned fashion. D.M. felt that perhaps his observational effort was too obtrusive, so he discontinued recording and just watched the teacher.

Jessica asks D.M.:   "What are you doing now?"

    D.M.:   "I'm resting."

Jessica: "Oh, you can't rest. This is school!"

In a similar vein, one teacher reported that an SD child would occasionally remind her that she was talking too loudly, thus disturbing the SD child and other children who were working quietly in their small groups.

Interestingly, these corrective comments do not usually appear to be offered in a "bossy" directive fashion, but are offered in an observational tone. The SD child also tends to offer a fair amount of praise, complimenting other children ("I like yours.", "You did a good job."). SD children provide support and encouragement to other children. For instance, a peer says, "I can't do this." (referring to cutting with scissors). A third grade SD child says, "Yes, you can." Peer says, "I can't do it!" SD child says to her classmate, "Remember yesterday, when you said you couldn't do the pottery wheel and you were able to do it anyway? Maybe the cutting is just like that." This is a quite sophisticated form of giving help. In another situation, when an SD child was being bossed about by another child, the SD child turned to the other child and said, "Is it okay if I do it myself, your highness?"

How Self-Directed Children Use Their Teachers

SD children use their teachers in interesting ways. First, they tend to use them as resources or as consultants, rather than as mere repositories of knowledge and solutions. When SD children seek help they tend to present teachers with alternative ways of doing something, rather than simply asserting, "I can't . . . " or "What do you want me to do next?" For example, an SD child comments to his teacher (about a worksheet) "I've got a space here and a space here. Should I go across or down?"

SD children also often answer the questions they direct at teachers, peers, and themselves. By articulating their ideas aloud in the form of questions, SD children tend to formulate thoughts into communicable representations. As Piaget (1964) noted, these thoughts become objects for reflection: "Speech provides a means of bringing knowledge to light and controlling it." (p. 14)

We were struck by the number of occasions on which SD children approached a teacher and, in the midst of asking questions, worked out their own answers: "Oh, I get it! You don't have to tell me." Out of their effort to seek help, they developed an awareness of what they knew. These interpersonal exchanges may be the forerunner of internalized self-explanations and monitoring the experts evidence (Chi & Bassok, 1989). As Vygotsky ([1934] 1962) highlighted, such social discourse provides children with the means of developing and internalizing "private speech."

The SD children take great pride in conveying (often announcing) to others, especially their teachers, that they are done. "I'm done!" "I did it!" "Can I now do X?" "I did five. I only have three more to do."

How Peers and Teachers Interact with Self-Directed Children

Our fascination in watching SD children was further heightened when we recorded how others (peers and teachers) interacted with them. We observed that SD children are frequently approached by peers for assistance (or have peers directed to them for help by teachers). For example, peers often asked SD children "Which one goes first?"; "How many words do we have to do?"; "Which one do you think is better?". Teachers also tend to ask SD children to help other children: "Will you show Jane what to do next?"; "Perhaps, you can explain to Dan how we show books in class."

Most interestingly, when teachers ask the class or group of students questions that require sequential descriptions of activities (procedural knowledge), SD children are selected to answer more frequently: "Who can tell the class how we did this the last time?"; "Who can tell us what we do when we go to the library?" SD children tend to volunteer and are more frequently called on to answer such questions. Parenthetically, it is worth noting that some teachers indicated that they are aware of SD children's ability to dominate or voluntarily answer such questions. Teachers stated that occasionally they will intentionally not call on SD children, or comment publicly or privately that the SD child should let others answer. However, not all children who were nominated as SD by teachers were outgoing, volunteering answers, providing comments to peers and teachers, calling attention to their work, or emitting private speech. Instead, some SD children evidenced a "quiet competence." They just went about the task at hand in an organized, seemingly planned manner, often eliciting praise from the teacher or requests for them to share with other students descriptions of how they did the task.

Whatever the specific form of expression of SD, such children are provided with multiple opportunities to exercise their metacognitive skills. In short, SD children have the ability to create learning opportunities in which they can exercise and nurture their metacognitive abilities and develop their personal knowledge.

Finally, teacher–SD child interactions are noted for the relative infrequency of teacher-compliance requests. Teachers are less likely to instruct SD children to "pay attention," or remind them to "get going" or "finish their work." In contrast, we observed that teachers tend to be much more instructive, directive, and intrusive with low SD impulsive children. With such SD children, the teacher frequently monitors their behavior (almost with a "third eye") and asks questions or gives directions that act as metacognitive prosthetic devices. Consider the following directions teachers offered low SD impulsive children: "Johnny, what are you doing?" "Have you started yet?" "What are you supposed to be doing?" "What are you going to do next?" "Is there enough room for you and Bobby to sit at the table?" "Come over here, so we can work together." "Let's get going." "Listen carefully!" "You are having difficulty concentrating on your work." "You have to do all of them." "It is twenty past ten and you have hardly done anything."

Thus, in an effort to help Johnny (and other low SD children), the teacher provides prompts, cues, probes, and directives. These observations are consistent with the research findings on parent and teacher interactions with impulsive hyperactive children (Barkley, 1981). Adults, when interacting with hyperactive children, tend to be directive, intrusive, and negative. We hypothesize that the nature of these interactions reflect the hyperactive children's self-regulatory deficits and the adult's efforts to provide metacognitive supports. Thus, the children who need most practice in developing such executive skills receive the fewest practice trials. Instead, others (teachers, parents, peers) seem to conduct many of the thinking processes for low SD children.

Contrast the directive teacher–low SD children interactions with those verbalizations offered by teachers of high SD children. Illustrative teacher comments included: "Show me your work. How did you do that?" "Tell the class what we are working on and why?" "Tell us how you used your mind in solving this one." "Remember when you did one like this before. Is this like that?" Our observations revealed that high SD children received many more teacher inquiries that "pulled for" procedural, declarative, and elaborative knowledge, or what Sigel (1982) describes as distancing strategies. Such teacher verbalizations stimulate SD children to project themselves into the past or into the future, transcending the immediate present. Such communicative acts nurture the development of representational thought (Sigel & Olmsted, 1971), and we propose that they also foster the development of SD metacognitive skills. In contrast, the low SD children "pull for" teacher directives and specific probes that reduce the likelihood of their engaging in self-monitoring, planning, reflecting, and the like. Teachers are more prone to produce metacognitive statements for low SD children. In short, the teacher becomes a "metacognitive prosthetic device" for the low SD children.

Variations in Self-Directed Behaviors as a Function of the Task

One other interesting set of findings emerged as we followed children from activity to activity in the classroom. It soon became evident that the SD children manifested variability in their self-directed behaviors across academic settings, and even within the same settings over time. Thus, our research focus shifted from studying so-called SD children to examining the characteristics of self-directed behaviors that children evidence under varied conditions.

For instance, in one class we observed children doing classwork, and then going to an art room with a different teacher. We found that some children who made few task-related verbalizations in the regular classroom and appeared not to know what to do often became quite vocal in producing task-directive planning and monitoring verbalizations in the art room, about both their own work and that of others.

In another small study, we invited third and fourth grade children to choose their own math "worksheets" from exercises and problem sheets that varied considerably in difficulty. When given a chance to choose their own levels of task difficulty, having previously received some guidance concerning appropriate choices (selecting a mix of "easy" or "review" tasks and "hard-for-me" or "thinking" tasks), two aspects of the children's work were especially noticeable. First, under the choice condition, the level of motivation was very high. We observed a minimum of task-avoiding, daydreaming, and alternative activities (e.g., task-irrelevant talk). The children stated that they liked "choosing math." In fact, the amount of work accomplished increased. Second, when children were given choice in selecting difficulty levels, overt metacognitive statements (e.g., planning, monitoring), directed at both self and others, were more frequent, especially among the less mathematically skilled children. For example, self-interrogation and other forms of problem-solving self-talk increased under the "choice" condition. Children seeking assistance specified alternatives that they were considering, rather than simply saying, "I can't!"

Our observational studies of children across academic settings led us to revise our concept of self-direction. Rather than be a characteristic of an individual child, self-direction seems to be the *fit* between the level of the task demands (i.e., difficulty and interest levels) and the child's abilities (i.e., knowledge, strategy, motivation). Rather than a "trait-like" individual difference dimension, self-direction (or expertise) should be viewed as a *transactional* concept reflecting the *fit* between the perceived task difficulty level and the child's perceived and actual abilities to perform the task.

Summary

Our informal study of self-directed children—or, more appropriately, self-directive behaviors—highlighted many similarities with the literature on adult expertise. When children manifested self-directive behaviors, they were more likely to·

1. access and employ declarative, procedural, and elaborative knowledge
2. evidence metacognitive behaviors (defining or labeling tasks, planning, monitoring, and evaluating)
3. emit more preparatory, deliberate, and sustained scripted behaviors
4. be motivated to achieve, compared with what Scardamalia and Bereiter (1989) called a "do it and be done with it" approach
5. have others (teachers and peers) interact with them in ways that nurture, exercise, and reinforce their metacognitive skills

CLASSROOM OBSERVATIONS 1989–1990: DEVELOPMENT OF A TAXONOMY OF TASK-DIRECTIVE LANGUAGE

In the summer of 1989, we reviewed our observational data with the objectives of developing a taxonomy of metacognitive behaviors and of identifying and understanding the nature of expertise in children. As we read the narrative observations of the children's behaviors from preschool through grade 6, it became apparent that social- and self-discourse provided important clues about how children employ their mental processes to negotiate classroom demands. An analysis of the 140 narrative protocols led us to focus, once again, on the children's and the teacher's verbalizations. We also continued to record the children's behaviors, since these data provided a context for understanding the functional role of their verbalizations.

Thus, this phase of our research was designed to go beyond the initial impressionistic data and develop an objective reliable coding system of children's verbalizations, in particular, the children's task-directive language. This chapter provides both a progress report of our observational efforts and a preliminary discussion of their pedagogical implications, as we strive to better understand self-directive behavior and expertise in the classroom.

The Functions of Language about Tasks

Before detailing our coding system, it is useful to reflect on the functions of language about tasks. When talking to another person about a task, a child can *state* a procedure that needs to be done (e.g., "You need a period at the end of the sentence.").[3] The other child can carry this out (assuming he/she "knows how"). In other words, the effect of the statement in this case is to access the other's *plan* or procedure for "putting a period at the end of the sentence," and carry it out. The function of overt verbal task statements seems to be analogous to reading a program statement or reading program output. By verbalizing statements about the task, the child accesses plans or subplans (*defining*), moves elements of plans from verbal storage to readiness for action (*planning*), notes progress or problems requiring action (*monitoring*), and facilitates storage of information about the results of the task (*evaluating*). (These distinctions will be elaborated subsequently in our discussion of a model of classroom tasks.)

The first child could also *ask* what should be done next (e.g., "How do I do X?"). The second child can provide a statement (or several statements) in reply. In asking what should be done next, the first child was *asking for a statement* (verbal input) about the plan of the task. One can ask others for oneself about the task as a whole (defining), the sequence of subplans or components of a subplan (planning), progress within a plan (monitoring), conditions that influence action choices (conditional planning), or various aspects of the results of the task (evaluating).

The Knowledge Context of Task-Directive Language

In the preceding examples, our target child was either producing statements about the current task or asking for statements about the current task from the other child. The context of knowledge being expressed about the task is current.

We also have observed examples of a child stating relationships between

---

[3]Statements can be seen as "directives." Essentially they function like statements in a computer program—asserting the next action to be taken.

a current task and some prior task or classification of tasks (e.g., "This is like what we did yesterday."). The effect of this statement on a second child might be to *access stored information* about "yesterday's" task. Statements of this sort *elaborate* information about the current task, making other relevant information available (as in the "yesterday" example). Children can also elaborate information by categorizing it (e.g., "Some people would call this editing."). Categorizing may both access existing stored information and render the current task (or object) more retrievable in future situations.

A child or teacher might also seek or ask for elaborative statements from others. Thus, we can have *elaborative statements* and *elaborative questions.*

Self-Directed Task Language

Everything that we have just said about dialogue between two children can also be said of self-directed dialogue; children can make task-directive statements to themselves, and ask for task information from themselves (ask themselves questions; see Chapter 6 for a review of related research). They can also elaborate task information by noting similarities between the current task and other tasks and by categorizing tasks, thus rendering task information more accessible for future purposes. Finally, children can ask for elaborative statements from themselves. In fact, the observations of 1988–1989 have convinced us that many children overtly do some or all of these things.

Recording Task-Directive Language

Basically, the 1989–1990 research strategy was the same as that in 1988–1989. We asked teachers to nominate high SD and low SD children in their class. Then we recorded a narrative description of the child's behaviors and all verbalizations emitted by or directed to the child. The coding scheme focused on the recorded verbalizations, using the behavioral descriptions as background information to provide a context for classifying each speech unit. Once again, observers situated themselves close enough to the children so they could record both verbalizations and behaviors. In most instances, the recording was conducted in open classroom settings as children worked. The children were free to move from one activity setting to another as they saw fit. In four trial sessions with pairs of observers, agreement in recording the children's verbalizations was very high (over 85%). When the observers did disagree, it was mainly because one observer did not hear what was being said or the speed of the verbal interchange among several children was so rapid that some portion of the verbalizations was missed. Nevertheless, we feel confident that, in spite of the crudity of our observational efforts,[4] we obtained representative samples of children's and teacher's verbalizations in the classroom.

A Coding System for Task-Directive Language

The observational team[5] developed a system for coding each of the child's task-directive sentences as well as those verbalizations directed to the child. Although verbalizations were coded, information about nonverbal behavior and the situational context was also crucial to reliable coding.

1. First, record all verbalizations and the accompanying behavior emitted by the target child and all verbalizations that are directed to the target child.
2. Second, unitize the social- and self-discourse, using the sentence (either statements or questions) as the basic unit, and identifying specifically task-directive language.
3. Third, code each unit of task-directive language for a number of dialogue features and task features.

A long tradition of recording classroom discourse has resulted in many diverse coding systems (see Cazden, 1986). Our decision to simultaneously code each task-directive sentence for several dialogue and task features is unique to our present system.

Identifying Task-Directive Language

Task-directive statements and questions are those verbalizations that explicitly concern the target child's or another's task. These were coded for dialogue features and task features as described next.

Two other categories of verbalizations, social speech and verbal products, were not coded. Social speech refers to discourse that primarily serves an interpersonal function such as fostering affiliation ("Can you come over to my house after school?"), exchanging information ("Who won the baseball game?"), or compliance ("Don't push!"). Verbal products refer to those verbalizations that are the product or result of an activity. They may take the form of the child counting out loud, naming the result of a computation, or reading or spelling out loud. These verbalizations are by-products of the child thinking aloud while performing a specific task.

---

[4]We have experimented with videotape. Our experience has been that careful recording of the child's verbalizations is crucial. Classroom videotape records are not as useful as observer records because they often do not pick up the target child's verbalizations as he or she moves about the room. We are now experimenting with remote microphones and video cameras.

[5]The 1989–1990 team included Donald Meichenbaum, Andrew Biemiller, Elizabeth Morley, Jennifer Motha, Janet McCarroll-Spiers, Casey Pugh, Lisa Semandeni, and Louise Webb-Ingle.

Coding Dialogue Features

The dialogue features describe the social context in which the sentence occurred. These include the following characteristics:

1. *initiation:* whether the target child initiated the sentence spontaneously or whether the sentence was emitted in response to a teacher or peer
2. *direction:* to whom the sentence was directed (to a specific peer, group of peers, teacher, or self)
3. *mode:* whether the verbalization was a statement or a question
4. *ownership:* whether the task being discussed belonged to the target child, a peer, or was shared
5. *knowledge context:* whether the context conveyed by the verbalization was strictly current (refers only to the immediate situation) or whether it was elaborated to include reference to other settings (e.g., "This is like what we did at recess.") or reference to categories (e.g., "Some people would call this editing."). Note, that "elaborated" is only coded when there is an explicit reference to another setting or category.

The first three categories (initiation, direction, and mode) are quite straightforward to code. However, task ownership and knowledge context bear further comment. Task ownership is designed to provide an indication of the child's general attentional focus or "ownership" as reflected in his or her verbalization. For instance, the verbal unit is coded for whether the target child is commenting on his or her own task, on someone else's task that may be related or unrelated to the target child's task, or on a shared task. A prototype of this category was a high SD child who not only was verbalizing to himself about his *own* writing task, but would interrupt his performance by commenting to his fellow students about a chess game they were playing. This category permits an analysis of the general attentional focus of children as they negotiate classroom tasks. A more specific measure of attention, in terms of the specific components of the task that was attended to, will be described subsequently under task features.

Knowledge context reflects the observation that children often comment on the relationship between a current task and some prior or future task, or that children may classify or categorize the present task. These elaborative verbalizations reflect representational thought that goes beyond the immediate context. Elaborative verbalizations are often analogical, taking the form of a "like" statement (e.g., "This is *like* our making the Indian hat."). The effect of this verbalization on a second child might be to access stored information about the "hat-making" task. Such elaborative statements place information in a context, making other relevant procedural information available. Elaborations may also code current information into categories that will render it accessible for future use. Offering such connections ("like" statements) and categorizations facilitates identification of what J. J. Gibson (1979) called "affordances." E. J. Gibson (1982) noted that Kofka's description of his chimpanzee Sultan demonstrating "insight" by putting two sticks together to reach a desired banana was an example of such an affordance. We have observed SD children who engage in similar behaviors. For instance, one SD child retrieved blocks as counting objects from a nearby table to facilitate work on paper-and-pencil subtraction problems. His elaborative statements to his peer reflected his perception of the availability and usefulness (affordance) of the blocks to solve his arithmetic problem.

Appendix A offers other examples of current and elaborative sentences. Once again, the child's verbalizations are used to infer her or his mental processes. Such inferences provide the basis for scoring social- and self-discourse in terms of the task features.

Task Features

The task features describe the "metacognitive" or self-regulatory features of each sentence. These included (1) task functions or metacognitive acts, (2) task content or objects of metacognitive acts, and (3) task affect or feeling about the task, the product, or the child's abilities. Before summarizing these coding categories, we will outline the rationale behind them.

A Model of Classroom Tasks

In order to better understand the task feature categories, it is first helpful to consider the model of classroom tasks that we developed. A classroom task may be thought of as a "program" or list of instructions for carrying out actions with specified materials, usually leading to an expected outcome. Such a list has a *definition,* a title or phrase that serves to identify the list (and retrieve it from storage). Most components of this list of instructions are a sequence of procedures or "subtasks" to be executed in order. The sequence of procedures is the *plan* of the task. Checking or *monitoring* progress on a procedural (subtask) outcomes or external conditions may be a necessary part of the task.[6] Sometimes the sequence of procedures is conditional on monitoring the outcomes of previous procedures or the availability of materials or other conditions. This constitutes a *conditional plan.* (Generally speaking, "strategic" issues, or choices between alternative plans for accomplishing the same end, involve conditional plans of an "if . . . then . . . " variety.) The final component of the list may be a test or *evaluation* of the result of the task, usually comparing the actual out-

[6]Note that, when a task is well practiced, some procedures are usually *not* monitored. However, when problems are encountered (e.g., unexpected outcomes), "experts" are frequently able to identify the procedure generating the problem, monitor, and "repair" it.

come with the expected outcome or goal.[7] The results of evaluations are often stored, becoming part of the knowledge the child has about the plan. Evaluation usually leads to a decision to (a) repeat or continue the task; (b) modify and continue the task; or (c) change tasks. These five components—defining, planning, conditional planning, monitoring, and evaluating—are what we call task functions, reflecting the child's metacognitive activity.

Coding Task Functions   Each task-directive sentence is coded for one task function.[8] The task functions or metacognitive acts include:

1. *defining:* "It's John's game." "That's red paint". Verbalization reflects the speaker's attempt to label a task, procedure, or object. It may also involve noting features of tasks, procedures, and objects. Note that the task labels may be in the form of phrases (e.g., "writing a paper"), task names (e.g., "chess", "spelling charades"), or any other label that serves to identify (access) a stored task (e.g., "John's game") or stored information about an object.
2. *planning:* "Can I do X?" "Mix some soap in the paint." "Where are the sparkles?" A planning statement or planning question concerns the sequence of procedures or what will or might happen next. A planning verbalization reflects the speaker's intention, and may be in the form of a statement, request,[9] or desire (e.g., "I need . . . "), as well as in the form of a question. Planning statements or queries conveying sequence are made before the action is carried out.
3. *monitoring* (ongoing task): "You're going too fast." "I need to slow down." "That's the right one." "I can't do this!" "This is fun!" Monitoring refers to statements or questions that denote progress, or lack thereof, in the task, commenting on actions, objects, or task quality. Monitoring conveys that the child is comparing her/his own or other's on-going performance with some implicit criterion or goal representation.
4. *conditional planning:* "If we make noise, then we won't have recess." "If I want yellow, should I mix green and red?" Conditional planning statements or questions relate a plan to a condition or specify the basis for choosing among alternative plans. These statements or questions combine monitoring and planning. Many have an

---

[7]Note that each procedure or subtask specified in the list can have the components of a task—a definition, a plan, and monitoring and evaluating procedures.

[8]If the sentence has more than one function, it should be broken into two verbalizations and each should be coded. This has not occurred in the instances coded to date.

[9]Note that requests for permission to carry out specific procedures or tasks are coded as statements rather than questions. On the other hand, if a child asks what the next step should be (e.g., "Now what should I do?"), the sentence is coded as a question.

"if . . . then . . . " quality. Other conditional modifiers are also used (e.g., "Suppose that . . . ").

5. *evaluating* (completed or aborted task): "This is my best one so far!" "I can't do it!" "The math squares are fun." Evaluating statements or questions concern conclusions after ending the task, regarding the product, the child's ability, or the experience of doing the task. Sometimes the result of evaluation will be a return to the task.

It is important for observers to record not only the verbalizations, but also when they occur in the flow of behavioral activity. If a verbalization precedes the action referred to, it is considered planning. If it occurs during the action or before completion, it will be coded as monitoring. If the verbalization follows completion of the task, it will be coded as evaluation. Thus, information about the context and timing are important.

Coding Task Content   The contents or objects of the metacognitive acts include:

1. *task:* "It's John's game." Verbalization refers to the task as a whole rather than to any specifiable component of the task.
2. *procedure:* "Can I do X?" "Mix some soap in the paint." "If we make noise, then we won't have recess." "You're going too fast." Verbalization specifies a component action. Note that statements or questions coded for procedures may include action only (e.g., "You have to push hard.") or an object(s) as well (e.g., "I'm hammering a nail.").
3. *object:* "Where are the sparkles?" "This is my best one so far!" (referring to a product) "That's red paint." Verbalization specifies an object, object characteristic, or symbol (e.g., "Do I use an *a* here?"). Note that this category is only used when action is not specified in the statement.
4. *ability:* "I can't do it!" Verbalization specifies ability to perform the task or procedure. This may refer to the speaker's ability or to someone else's.[10] Note that "can" statements regarding own ability on own task are also coded for positive affect, whereas "can't" statements are coded for negative affect.
5. *task quality:* "The math squares are fun!" "This is boring!" "Painting is easy!" Verbalization specifies the quality of the experience of doing the task. Most task quality statements will also receive a positive or negative affective tone coding.

---

[10]During analysis, the dialogue features are used to discriminate statements about the target child's ability on her/his own task from ability-related statements about others' performance.

Task Affect   Finally, in order to tap the emotions that accompany performance, each verbal unit was coded for affective tone (positive, neutral, or negative).

1. *neutral:* No identifiable affective tone.
2. *positive:* "The math squares are fun!" "This is cinchy!" Verbalization directly implies positive affect (e.g., ". . fun!") or observer directly notes affect (e.g., *smiles*). All positive ability statements are coded as positive affective tone.
3. *negative:* "This is boring!" "I can't do this." Evidence of negative affect.

Summary

This comprehensive coding system was designed to use the children's verbalizations as a "window onto their cognitive, metacognitive, and affec-

Table 1
Summary of Dialogue Features and Task Features

Dialogue features	Task features
1. Initiation	1. Task functions
S self (target child)	D defining
C other child	P planning
T teacher	M monitoring
O other (specify)	C conditional planning
2. Mode	E evaluating
S statement	2. Task content
Q question	T task as a whole
3. Direction	P procedure
S self	O object(s)
P peer (specify name)	A ability
G group at large	Q task quality
T teacher	3. Affective tone
O other	P positive (includes "can" statements
4. Ownership	about own task)
O own task	N negative (includes "can't" state-
S shared task	ments about own task)
R other's related task	O neutral
U other's unrelated task	
5. Knowledge context	
C current situation only	
E elaborative	
Co connects current task with	
other situation	
Ca categorizes current task	

tive components of expertise." All the child's verbalizations are initially recorded, along with everything that is said to the child. Sentences are then categorized as social, verbal products (e.g., reading out loud or counting), and task directive. Task-directive verbalizations are further coded on a number of dialogue features and task features, as summarized in Table 1. Appendix A illustrates the coding system. Some illustrative findings using this coding system will be presented in the next section.

INITIAL APPLICATIONS OF THE CODING SYSTEM

In order to assess the usefulness of the present coding system, three preliminary analyses were conducted. In each analysis, the basic objective was to examine the task-directive speech of children perceived to differ in "self-direction." In the first study, 28 protocols that were obtained from our initial observations were analyzed according to the task-directive language coding system. The children were chosen from grades 1–6,[11] including equal numbers of teacher-nominated high self-directed and low self-directed children. In the second study, four children (two high and two low self-directed children, as nominated by their teacher) were observed on three separate occasions in the same classroom. Their own task-directive speech and verbalizations directed to them were analyzed in terms of dialogue and task features.

The third and final study to be reported extends the coding system into a laboratory context. The coding of social- and self-discourse is not only applicable to classroom settings, but could be applied to social interactions in any setting. As an initial test of this proposition, the coding system was applied to the analysis of a pair of boys (one diagnosed as hyperactive and the other a nonhyperactive same-age peer) who engaged in a cooperative Lego building task in a laboratory setting. Once again, we recognize that caution is required in drawing specific conclusions from such a limited analysis, but for illustrative purposes the analysis does highlight the potential of the present coding system. This analysis can also be extended to other pair (or group) interaction combinations (e.g., groups of more than two children, parent–child interactions, family interactions, and the like). Let us now consider the specific sensitivity of the coding system in identifying so-called "experts," or children with self-directive behaviors in classroom settings.

---

[11]We have a substantial number of observations of 3-, 4-, and 5-year-old children. They will be the subject of a future study.

Table 2
Distribution of Observations by Grade
and Self-Direction Status

Self-Direction	Grade				
	1	2	3	4–6[a]	All
High					
N	4	2	5	3	14
sentence/hour	37	47	34	34	37
SD	9	22	22	20	17
Low					
N	4	2	5	3	14
sentence/hour	38	27	17	33	28
SD	19	13	13	3	15

[a]Combines one child in each of grades 4, 5, and 6.

Study 1: Analysis of Task-Directive Sentences from 28 Grade 1 to Grade 6 Children

The first study involved applying the coding system to selected observations obtained in several Toronto schools during the past 2 years. Observations were made by project staff and by graduate students as part of course assignments. Coding was done by one of the investigators (A.B.) and a research assistant who is an experienced teacher. Observations to be coded were selected on the basis of (1) choice of setting in which self-directed activity was likely to emerge (e.g., "free activity," art room, "independent work"), (2) equal numbers, per grade, of teacher-nominated children who were identified as high SD and low SD, and (3) completeness of the recorded observation. Fourteen observations of high SD children and fourteen observations of low SD children were analyzed using the self-direction taxonomy. Coding reliability was over 90% on all categories except task functions for which reliability was 79%. (Problems in coding task functions are discussed in Appendix B.) The composition of the sample by grade is shown in Table 2. From the high SD group, 253 task-directive sentences were obtained in 459 min of observation. The high SD group's average rate of sentences per hour was 37.[12] From the low SD group, 126 task-directive sentences were obtained in 306 min, or an average rate of 28 sentences per hour. Differences in observation time reflect the fact that low

[12]This figure is based on determining each child's rate of sentences per hour [60 (number of sentences/number of min observed)] and averaging these rates, since the length of time each child was observed varied. Thus, data from each child is equally weighted. The same approach is used for rates of sentences per hour within each category as reported later in this section.

Table 3
Dialogue Features: Mean Sentences per Hour by Category for High
and Low Self-Directed Children

Self-direction	Dialogue features[a]									
	Initiation		Mode		Direction		Task ownership		Knowledge context	
High										
N = 14 children	self	27	stm.	31	self	6	own	29	cur.	36
	peer	5	que.	6	peer	21	rel.	7	ela.	1
	tea.	5			tea.	10	unr.	1		
	tot.	37	tot.	37	tot.	37	tot.	37	tot.	37
Low										
N = 14 children	self	19	stm.	19	self	4	own	24[b]	cur.	27
	peer	2	que.	9	peer	9	rel.	3	ela.	1
	tea.	8			tea.	15	unr.	1		
	tot.	28	tot.	28	tot.	28	tot.	28	tot.	28

[a]Abbreviations: stm., statement; que., question; tea., teacher; rel., related; unr., unrelated; cur., current; ela., elaborated; tot., total.
[b]Includes both *own* tasks and *shared* tasks.

SD children tended to spend less time on a single task. The overall rate of sentences per hour did not differ significantly by self-direction group or grade, nor was there a significant relationship between SD group and grade.

Dialogue Features

The frequencies of sentences with each of the five dialogue features are shown in Table 3. There were no significant differences between high SD and low SD children in the initiation of sentences. However, there were differences in the mode of expression; the high SD children emitted significantly more statements than low SD children (31 versus 19 sentences per hour; t = 2.48, $p < .05$). There were also differences in direction; high SD children directed more of their task-directive language to peers (21 versus 9 sentences per hour; t = 2.32, $p < .05$). The low SD children directed more sentences to teachers but not significantly more (15 versus 10 sentences per hour). Consistent with the high SD children's greater tendency to speak to peers was the fact that they generated more sentences about related tasks (7 versus 3 sentences per hour; t = 2.33, $p < .05$). Virtually all sentences produced by both groups concerned current rather than elaborated contexts.

In summary, compared with low SD children, the task-directive language of high SD children included significantly more statements, was more frequently directed to peers, and more often concerned peer's tasks that were

Table 4

Task Features: Mean Sentences per Hour by Category
for High and Low Self-Directed Children
(Self-Initiated Statements Only)

	Task features[a]					
Self-direction	Task function		Task content		Affective tone	
High						
N = 14 children	def.	2	task	5	pos.	3
	plan.	8	proc.	9	neg.	1
	c. pl.	2	obj.	7	neut.	18
	mon.	9	abil.	1		
	eval.	1	qual.	0		
	tot.	22	tot.	22	tot.	22
Low						
N = 14 children	def.	1	task	1	pos.	1
	plan.	3	proc.	5	neg.	1
	c. pl.	0	obj.	3	neut.	9
	mon.	6	abil.	1		
	eval.	1	qual.	1		
	tot.	11	tot.	11	tot.	11

[a]Abbreviations: def., defining; plan., planning; c. pl., conditional planning; mon., monitoring; eval., evaluation; tot., total; proc., procedure; obj., object; abil., ability; qual., task quality; pos., positive; neg., negative; neut., neutral.

similar to the high SD child's. There were no significant grade differences or relationships between grade and self-direction.[13]

Task Features

When the task features of all sentences (with statements and questions) are examined, no significant differences between high SD and low SD children emerged. However, when only self-initiated statements are considered, some important differences can be seen (Table 4). Overall, the high SD children initiated more statements than the low SD children (22 versus 11 sentences per hour; t = 2.70, $p = .01$). Analysis of the task function category reveals that high SD children initiated significantly more planning (8 versus 3 sentences per hour, t = 2.31, $p < .05$) and conditional planning (2 versus 0 sentences per hour, t = 2.40, $p < .05$) statements. Differences in the other categories are not statistically significant. There were no significant grade effects or interactions.

There were no significant differences between high SD and low SD children in numbers of self-initiated statements per hour in the task content

[13]In the analysis of grade effects, Grades 4–6 were collapsed into one group because of small sample size.

categories nor in the affect categories (Table 4). However, when all sentences with positive or negative affect that concern the child's own task are examined, 89% of 27 high SD sentences were positive, as opposed to 59% of 17 low SD sentences. This difference is significant (Fisher exact test, $p < .05$).

These analyses illustrate the importance of dialogue features in understanding task features. It is not surprising that self-initiated statements play an important role in self-direction. Such statements reflect active knowledge on the part of the child about her/his own and related tasks. Although our low SD children, in fact, talked quite a bit about planning activities, much of this talk was in the form of questions directed at others (e.g., "How do you . . . ?) or statements elicited by others [e.g., Teacher: "What do you need to do next?" Child: (answers)]. Since low SD children often can provide such answers, it appears that an environment that leads them to use their knowledge spontaneously is needed. Possible ways of doing this will be discussed in the subsequent section "Implications for Education."

Study 1: Conclusions

This preliminary application of the coding system to children who varied widely in age, specific tasks observed, observers, and coders shows that important differences in task-directive language of children perceived by teachers as high or low in self-direction can be reliably demonstrated. The task-directive language of high SD children included more statements than questions, and was directed more often to peers. High SD children initiated more planning and conditional planning statements. Low SD children emitted most of the sentences expressing negative affect. These data indicate the feasibility and usefulness of the coding scheme and substantiate qualitative observations reported previously in this chapter.

Study 2: Analysis of Social- and Self-Discourse in Four Third Graders

As part of her undergraduate honors thesis at the University of Waterloo, Louise Webb Ingle conducted observations in a Grade 3 classroom consisting of 23 students. The teacher nominated children she considered self-directed and also chose low self-directed counterparts. The teacher was asked to carefully review the names of the students in her class and identify those who best fit and least fit the character sketch of self-directive behavior that had been developed.[14]

---

[14]In order to further corroborate the teacher's global impressions of self-direction, she was asked at a later date to fill out questionnaires in hyperactivity–impulsivity and self-direction. The two low SD children averaged 20.5 out of 30 on the hyperactivity scale and 3 out of 15 on the self-direction scale. Conversely, the two high SD children averaged 1.5 on the hyperactivity scale and 12 on the self-direction scale.

Reliability

In order to further assess the reliability of the coding system, observations were conducted by two independent observers on several children, yielding 204 codable sentences. There was an interjudge agreement of 91% on recording the children's verbalizations, a 95% agreement regarding the coding of sentences, and a range of 90–99% agreement on all categories except task functions. On this category, agreement was 80%. Problems generally occurred in discriminating planning from monitoring, which depended on noting whether statements were made prior to or while behaving. Further details of reliability are given in Appendix B.

Dialogue Features

We begin our analysis with a consideration of the children's verbalizations as emitted or elicited over three separate occasions. The length of observation was determined by the children as they began and completed a given activity (e.g., math, spelling, art work). The observer recorded all verbalizations emitted by the target child as well as all verbalizations directed at the target child from the beginning to the end of a given activity. The two high SD children were observed for a total 81 and 72 min, respectively, whereas the low SD children were observed for a total of 78 and 57 min cumulatively over the three observational occasions. The rate of verbalizations emitted by the high SD children was substantially higher than that of the low SD children (65 versus 41 sentences per hour).

Table 5 indicates to whom the children directed their self-initiated speech (to self, peers, and teacher), and the distribution of childrens', classmates', and teacher's speech directed to them. Several interesting differences emerge. First, high SD children talk to themselves more frequently (an average of 13% of all self-initiated verbalizations were self-directed as opposed to only 3% for the low SD children). The high SD children talked to their peers twice as much (average of 44 sentences per hour) as the low SD

Table 5

Rate of Self-Initiated Sentences per Hour That the Target Child Directs to Self, Peers, and Teacher and Rate of Sentences per Hour Directed to Target Child by Peers and Teacher

Child	Target child (TC) to other				Other to target child		
	Self	Peer	Teacher	All	Peer	Teacher	All
High self-direction							
1	6	54	2	62	11	1	12
2	8	34	3	45	7	3	10
Low self-direction							
1	1	16	13	30	9	10	19
2	1	26	15	42	11	26	37

Table 6

Examples of Verbal Exchanges for LSD and HSD Children with Their Teacher and Peers

LSD Children	HSD Children
Teacher to LSD child	Teacher to HSD child
What are you doing?	You did research about Terry Fox.
What do you have to do first?	This is just like that.
Did you check your assignment?	Look it up in your book. You can find
You will have to clean up your desk	the answer.
after you're finished.	Tell me how you solved that?
Peer to LSD child	Peer to HSD child
You forgot to loop again.	What are we supposed to do?
You can't have two the same.	Should I . . . ?
Did you ask 32 people yet?	How did you do that?
You have already done that.	
If you do X, then Y will happen.	
(Several sentences offered of an	
"If . . . then . . . variety.)	
LSD child to peer	HSD child to peer
Can you help me?	You don't cut each one individually.
What do they mean by . . . ?	You cut the whole thing.
Do you know what I'm supposed to	That glue goes this way.
do here?	You've done that already, haven't you?
My card is missing.	

children (21 sentences per hour). The most substantial difference between low and high SD children is the frequency of verbal exchanges with their teacher. High SD children infrequently initiate verbalizations to their teacher (average of 2.5 sentences per hour) and rarely receive teacher-initiated verbal encounters (average of 2 sentences per hour). High SD children seem to "do their own thing" with respect to the teacher, and interact more frequently with their classmates. Peers often ask them questions seeking procedural information. In contrast, the low SD children not only initiate more verbalizations to their teacher (average of 14 self-initiated sentences per hour), but receive many teacher-initiated verbalizations (average of 18 sentences per hour).

Moreover, the content and quality of these verbal exchanges with both teacher and peers are quite different. Consistent with the findings reported earlier from our informal observations, Table 6 conveys the differences in these verbal exchanges.

Another very significant difference that emerged in dialogue features was the proportion of the children's verbalizations that were elaborations (namely, the child going beyond the immediate situation referring to either the past or future, often in the form of a "like" statement). Of the high SD children's verbalizations, 25% involved elaborative context, compared with only 3% for the low SD children. Illustrative elaborative comments offered by the high SD children are: "It looks like a slipper." "For instance, we traded because it won't show up." (referring to a prior event) "Come here Liz. You are the only one who can spell Elizabeth Manley's name." "Remember the garden we made last time? Yours should be outside the castle." These comments illustrate how the high SD child readily calls on prior knowledge and future expectations to guide both own and peer behavior.

Finally, in regard to the last two dialogue features, mode (statements versus questions) and ownership (focus on one's own or other's task), there were no major differences between the low and high SD children. The percentage of questions asked and statements offered were comparable among the four children, as were the percentages of sentences about own, related, or unrelated tasks.

In part, the absence of differences in focus on unrelated tasks between high SD and low SD children reflects the very active and directive style of the teacher and peers in this classroom. Both teacher and peers acted as "metacognitive prosthetic devices," helping the low SD children at each juncture of the task, keeping the low SD children "on task" as conveyed in Table 6. These prompts, reminders, and directives to low SD children reduced the likelihood of differences in attention to tasks emerging in this particular setting. In an important sense, the low SD children's teacher and peers are doing their thinking for them. For instance, when the teacher asked a low SD child a question that he could not answer ("What center are you at?"), the high SD child answered for him. However, the teacher's and peers' interactional style did not preclude differences in task features and affective tone emerging.

Task Features

The major task function differences to emerge are the higher incidence of self-initiated planning (18 versus 6 sentences per hour) and self-initiated monitoring (14 versus 5 sentences per hour) statements by the high SD children. The high SD children emitted many more verbalizations to both themselves and peers about what they intended to do next, as well as many more verbalizations reflecting an ongoing monitoring of performance. The low SD children more frequently defined objects and activities.

Another coding category that provides interesting data is that of the children's affective tone. As noted earlier, an analysis of children's classroom performance must not only attend to cognitive, but also to affective (emotional, attributional) processes. Differences between high and low SD children emerged in the affective tone. Whereas the high SD children evidenced more positive emotional expressions (average of 11% of their verbal units compared with 4% for the low SD children), the low SD children were much more likely to include negative expressions of affect, conveying both their inability to perform tasks and general negative emotions (11% negative expressions of affect for low SD children versus 1% for high SD children). For example, low SD children made the following statements to themselves, peers, and teachers: "I am not going to do it. I just get confused."; "I made a mistake again."; "I thought I could do it. I can't."; "She is going to get lots of pluses." (conveying that he is not).

Study 2: Conclusions

Thus, a general picture emerges of low SD children who have difficulty negotiating classroom activities; who are kept on task by the "hovering" directives, prompts, and probes of both their teacher and peers; and who rarely spontaneously plan, monitor, or elaborate. The low SD children do evaluate performance, but this evaluation tends to be more negative in tone, conveying an attributional style of "I can't do it." The major impression conveyed is that the low SD children have helped to create or are in learning environments in which they turn to others for—or others readily offer—directives, probes, and information. The low SD children have little opportunity to practice or receive constructive feedback about their thinking processes. In short, low SD children can count on others to think for them or act as "metacognitive prosthetic devices;" thus, they do not readily learn to spontaneously engage in such self-directive mental activities themselves. Although these children need the most practice developing such self-regulatory activities, they actually receive the fewest trials. A vicious cycle develops in which teachers and peers come to expect (in part, justifiably) that low SD children will not be able to do things on their own, nor follow through on instructions, so they provide low SD children with help. In response to such direct teacher and peer probes and directives, the low SD child often responds in a more metacognitive fashion, but providing such help by thinking for the children precludes their developing and exercising the very self-regulatory activities they need. Thus, the cycle continues.

The high SD children are also part of an interactional cycle, but in their case the cycle is designed to nurture and strengthen their impressive self-regulatory metacognitive skills. Perhaps this process is best illustrated by the example of a teacher who told some children to check with a high SD child because the child knew more than the teacher about the topic. The teacher often directed peers to the high SD children, who were called on repeatedly to employ elaboration, planning, and monitoring skills. High SD children not only employ their metacognitive skills when called on to do so, but also spontaneously employ these skills with others and with themselves. Consider one high SD child who told herself, "This is cinchy! Everything is cinchy! I can spell except that I did a g for a p . . . I think I'm going to need a longer line."

The "rich get richer" (Walberg & Tsai, 1983) as the high SD children help create a learning environment that provides them with innumerable trials to develop, test, and refine their metacognitive skills. This is surely the budding environment for the development of self-directed behavior and "expertise." We will discuss the need for maintaining such an environment for *all* children in the subsequent section, "Implications for Education."

Study 3: Application to Laboratory Study of Hyperactivity

The previous two studies examined the usefulness of the task-directive language coding system for social- and self-discourse as recorded in natural classroom settings. Whereas such naturalistic observations provide ecological validity, they give up both the precision of recording and the control of environmental factors that can influence language behavior. An opportunity to assess the potential usefulness of the coding system for laboratory-derived data was offered by Alison Day, a graduate student at the University of Waterloo who is conducting her doctoral dissertation under the supervision of Richard Steffy and Chuck Cunningham. Alison arranged for hyperactive boys to interact with same-age and same-sex nonhyperactive peers in a laboratory setting. Alison also arranged for the diagnosed hyperactive children to be taken off stimulant medication prior to the time of testing. The two boys, both seated at the same table, were given the task of making the same Lego design (e.g., a truck). Each boy, however, had some pieces the other needed to complete the task (e.g., wheels of the car). The instruction given to the two boys was that they would have 15 minutes to complete the task, they would be left alone, and they should "cooperate or get along as much as possible." Two subsequent 15-min trials under slightly different instructional sets used different Lego designs to investigate interactions. The interactions between the two boys were videotaped and all verbalizations were recorded. Although Alison's research focus was on the boys' social behavior, it was apparent to us that the experimental task lent itself to analysis of the children's task-related discourse.

In order to highlight the potential of the present coding system, a detailed analysis will be offered of two 11-year-old boys (one hyperactive boy with a nonhyperactive male peer). Let us now consider the dialogue and task features, and accompanying expressions of affect, of each boy's task-directive speech. The coders were blind to the diagnostic classification of each child.

Overall Language

The first feature to be examined is the number of language units (sentences) each boy emitted. Interestingly, the respective rates of verbalization were comparable. Overall the total number of verbalizations across the three trials was 157 for the hyperactive child and 177 for his nonhyperactive peer. When social speech (18% for the hyperactive and 20% for the nonhyperactive child) was subtracted from the total number of language units, 128 task-directive language units (sentences) over the three 15-min trials were emitted by the hyperactive child, and 140 by the nonhyperactive boy, or 171 and 187 sentences per hour, respectively.[15] These verbalizations were quite evenly distributed over the three trials. These rates of verbalization are markedly higher than those obtained in the first two studies, and reflect the task demands and varied situational contexts.

Social Speech

There was a striking difference in language units in terms of which child initiated social speech (that is, speech not directed at performing the assigned Lego task). The hyperactive child initiated 71% of such social speech units (e.g., "I bet they are watching us from the other room." "Are you hyper?" "What's your marks?"), and in 55% of those instance the non-hyperactive child responded in a social manner.

Dialogue Features

We can now examine the dialogue features of the mode, direction, ownership, and knowledge contexts of the two boys' task-directive speech. In terms of mode of expression, the hyperactive child asked more questions (23 versus 17 per hour), but made fewer statements (135 versus 169 per hour). The amount of speech directed at self was comparable for both children (11% and 13% for the hyperactive and nonhyperactive child, respectively).

Perhaps the most substantial and striking difference in dialogue features is the attentional focus of the child while doing the Lego tasks. The category of ownership, which determines whether the child's verbalization is directed or focused on his own task or on the other child's task or on something task irrelevant, was most clearly distinguishable. Whereas 24% of the hyperactive child's verbalizations concerned his own task over each of the three Lego trials, the nonhyperactive child's verbalizations about his own task increased over the three trials, going from 46% on Trial 1, to 75% and 85% on Trials 2 and 3, respectively. These numbers reflect the non-hyperactive child's tendency to comment on specific aspects of his task (e.g., number of pieces, missing pieces, what is to be done, and the like). Thus, the children's social- and self-discourse is distinguishable.

---

[15]These rates were obtained by dividing the number of task-directive language units (128 and 140 for the hyperactive and nonhyperactive boy, respectively) by 45 min (total observation time for each) and multiplying by 60 min.

As in Study 1, the final dialogue feature of knowledge context (namely, going beyond the immediate circumstance of the task, tapping either prior knowledge or outside information) was only marginally different. The hyperactive child emitted 6% elaborations and his nonhyperactive counterpart emitted 11% elaborations. In most instances, the nonhyperactive child was more likely to spontaneously offer associative linkages. Thus, when his Lego design dropped on the floor but did not break, the nonhyperactive child promptly commented, "Takes a licking and it keeps on ticking," a reference to a Timex® commercial. The associative nature of the nonhyperactive child's discourse accounted for the slight different in percentage of elaborations. The more consistent finding is that the incidence of elaborations on the Lego tasks is quite low for both children.

Task Features

We now turn to the metacognitive aspects of the children's speech: to the task functions they describe, to the content these functions are applied to, and to the expression of accompanying affect.

Task Functions

We have seen in Studies 1 and 2 that it is desirable to look at self-initiated statements when examining the task functions children talk about. In Study 3, the nonhyperactive boy emitted more planning (45 versus 32 sentences per hour), conditional planning (12 versus 3 sentences per hour), and monitoring (73 versus 40 sentences per hour) statements and fewer defining (9 versus 27 sentences per hour) statements that the hyperactive boy. This pattern resembles that found in Studies 1 and 2. We remain encouraged by the diagnostic power of the system for coding task-directive speech.

On the other hand, it is important to note that, in this laboratory context, the hyperactive child initiated roughly six to eight times as many planning and monitoring statements per hour as low self-directed children in classrooms. To put it simply, the hyperactive child was far from incapable of generating task-directive speech! This finding has positive implications for fostering task-directive language in less self-directed children.

In a qualitative analysis of the observations, the major difference that emerges in task functions is that the nonhyperactive boy spent a good deal of his effort monitoring the hyperactive boy's performance (44 language units, as opposed to 24 language units for the hyperactive child). The nonhyperactive boy seemed to hold a picture or goal representation of what the final product should look like and the proper procedures to achieve that objective, and he was prone to comment to the hyperactive child when his performance deviated. These comments were offered in a helpful spirit and were, in part, a response to the hyperactive child's tendency to ask for help. The nonhyperactive child was acting as a "metacognitive prosthetic device," helping the hyperactive boy by monitoring and guiding his performance. In some sense, the nonhyperactive child was doing the hyperactive child's thinking for him. Consider the following examples: "I think you might need that."; "Notice that the parts of these are already put together."; "Watch, I'll show you." Each of these statements serves a planning function. "I think you're putting the wheels on backwards."; "It would be a better idea to dump everything out."; "You got that one upside down." These statements serve a monitoring function for the hyperactive child. "You figured something out right. Good."; "They look more the same now." These comments serve evaluative (reinforcing) functions.

The hyperactive child is not completely lacking in self-monitoring ability, but tended to be more global and evaluative than specifically task-directive in his comments. ("I'll never be able to make this."; "Not too good a memory."; "This doesn't make sense.") On occasion the hyperactive child would comment to the nonhyperactive child about what he needed to do or on his ongoing performance ("Now you need the fire thing."; "Now snap this guy, together."), but such verbalizations were rarely spontaneously offered to his peer or to himself. Rather, the hyperactive child tended to globally define the task ("I'm copying you."; "I'm building."), and also tended to make global, often negative, evaluations of his performance.

Task Content

This difference is further highlighted when we consider the category of task content, namely, does the child's verbalization reflect whether the child is focusing on the whole task or on a specific procedure, object, ability, or task quality? Approximately one-third of the time both childrens' verbalizations were about a specific object or procedure, with slightly more frequent references to the task as a whole by the nonhyperactive child (39%). The hyperactive child had a 25% frequency of references to the task as a whole. These individual differences were largely due to the higher frequency of interpersonal monitoring of the hyperactive child by the nonhyperactive child, conveying how he should do the task. For example, the nonhyperactive child said: "No, that won't work." or "Yeah, that's right." Another difference is that the hyperactive child's verbalizations reflected 8% comments about ability to perform the task, compared with 0% for the nonhyperactive child, who seemed to just do the task, not having to comment on his ability. The nonhyperactive child spent the most time commenting on specific procedures (33%) or on specific objects required to do the task (28%).

Affective Tone

The most impressive differences to emerge between the hyperactive and nonhyperactive child were in the affective tone or emotional expression evident when verbalizing either to themselves or to each other. Of the hyperactive child's sentences, 9% were positive. In contrast, 20% of the nonhyperactive child's sentences were positive. These expressions of positive affect were evident in the nonhyperactive child taking pride in his performance ("Okay, that's right!"; "Yeah, that's pretty good."; "That's more like it."; "Now, this is getting easier."; "I've figured this out!"; "Now, this is interesting."). Although such expressions were occasionally evident in the verbalizations of the hyperactive child, they occurred much less frequently.

The hyperactive child was clearly more frequent in generating verbalizations of negative affect. Whereas the nonhyperactive child evidenced a remarkable 0% negative affect across all three trials, 23% of the hyperactive child's sentences conveyed negative affect. In other words, of the 128 task-directive language units, the hyperactive child expressed a negative emotional tone in 29 of them. What is the hyperactive child saying to himself and his peer? "I'll never be able to make this."; "It's stupid!"; "I don't care anyway."; "I don't care if I get this right."; "I can't do this."; "I hate this thing!" These negative expressions not only reflect the child's frustration, but also reduce the likelihood that the child engaging in the cognitive and metacognitive activities will improve performance. Affect, thinking, and behavior are reciprocally interdependent in affecting performance. As the child began to develop skills on the Lego task (Trial 3), the incidence of negative expressions of affect was reduced from 30% (Trial 2) to 11% (Trial 3).

The complete absence of negative expression by the nonhyperactive boy in 140 task-directive language units is indeed impressive. The nonhyperactive youth also experienced frustration and failures at the Lego task, but invariably had an immediate compensatory verbalization. For instance, "I have no idea what I'm doing, I'm putting down whatever looks good."; "Oh well, it doesn't have to make sense."; "Whoops! Oh, I put it on the wrong side. Oh well, mine is looking more like it should."; "It's not right! But, I know I didn't use every piece."; "This makes no sense whatsoever, but oh well!". Such compensatory self-statements kept the nonhyperactive child on target, persisting at the Lego task. In contrast, the hyperactive child conveyed that he "was finished" much earlier in the sequence and would "attentionally exit" from the task, focusing his attention on task-irrelevant items, social interchanges, and the like.

Study 3: Conclusions

Obviously, we must be cautious when drawing conclusions about hyperactivity from an analysis of one pair of students. The objective was to demonstrate the potential usefulness of the present observational scheme when conducting a microanalytic analysis of social- and self-discourse. The language analysis, when scored for dialogue and task features and accompanying affect, was quite sensitive in revealing important differences. More sophisticated analyses are possible by using conditional probability time-lag analyses. For now, a number of research questions emerge. For instance, the differences reported occurred when the hyperactive child was removed from stimulant medication. What would happen to social- and self-discourse if the hyperactive child were put back on medication? Perhaps we have developed a sensitive new index that could be used to assess the effects of interventions other than medication, for example, cognitive-behavioral interventions. If cognitive-behavioral training is designed to teach children to "stop and think" before they act, to plan, monitor, and evaluate their behavior, then these changes should be evident when analyzing children's performance and the accompanying task-directive language, for example, while doing Lego tasks. Finally, it would be interesting to examine these same data on tasks in which the child develops and experiences success. At what point and on which tasks do metacognitive indices appear (that is, when does the child define, plan, monitor, conditionally plan, evaluate, elaborate)? Moreover, what interferes with the child's use of metacognitive skills that may be in his repertoire?

Illustrative Studies: Summary

Individually, each of these mini-studies using the new coding scheme would be unconvincing. Even together, they simply hint at hypotheses about the kinds of task-directive speech teachers might seek. They do suggest, however, that task-directive speech is relatively common, that it differentiates children who are perceived as self-directed from those who are not, and that, specifically, self-initiated planning and monitoring statements may well be facilitators of effective performance. Further analysis of the numerous observations now available to us, and an increased emphasis on active roles teachers can play to facilitate effective mastery of tasks, will be needed to determine how useful these approaches can be. These concepts will be discussed in a subsequent section, "Implications for Education."

In Search of Elementary Expertise

We began this chapter with an analysis of expertise in adults. Studies of "experts" in many domains suggested differences in the knowledge they had and used about their field of expertise, in the organization of that knowledge, in the strategies they employed when solving problems, and in their motivation and personal striving. Our "elementary experts" (children functioning in a self-directed manner as manifested in their social- and self-discourse) evidenced many of these same features. In terms of knowledge and its organization, the high SD children spontaneously verbalized their activities to a considerably greater extent, to both themselves and others, than did low self-directed children; they also offered advice to others. This advice was primarily in the form of planning and monitoring statements. These differences imply the presence of verbal (or verbalizable) scripts or plans with accompanying goal representations for the tasks in question, in other words, verbal knowledge about the tasks. This knowledge is more readily accessed in the form of elaborations (analogical thinking of a "like" variety) by the high SD children (see Study 2). Although few instances of elaborative organizational efforts were evident, we suggest that verbalizing tasks and offering connective elaboratives is a necessary precursor to constructing verbal organizations of task information. The use of overt organization is generally seen in Piaget's stage of "formal operational development," which typically begins near the end of the elementary school age range.

The higher frequency of self-initiated planning, conditional planning, and monitoring statements in the task-directive discourse of high SD children is consistent with much of the description of the strategy differences observed in experts (see discussion by Pressley *et al* (1990b) of the nature of strategies). The high SD children's higher rate of conditional planning statements (or explicit choices between alternative plans) is important for the development of a "strategic" approach to academic tasks. Finally, in terms of motivation and striving; the self-directed children tended to spend more time on task (until completed) and to verbalize more positive ability content and more positive affect, with relatively infrequent instances of negative affective tone.

We stress again our observation that some children perceived as less self-directed could also demonstrate these same characteristics (1) when prompted or guided by others, (2) in other task domains (e.g., art), or (3) when task difficulty was better matched to their abilities (e.g., when given choice of task difficulty). In short, it appears that many children have the potential of evidencing self-initiated regulatory metacognitive activity if given the correct "fit" between task demands and the child's abilities and interests. This is consistent with the conclusions of many theorists such as Belmont and Mitchells (1978), Good and Brophy (1980), Rohwer (1973), and Vygotsky (1978). Our taxonomy of children's task-directive language provides an effective window on the identification of that fit and on the development of elementary expertise in classrooms.

IMPLICATIONS FOR EDUCATION: THE DISTINCTION BETWEEN PERFORMANCE AND "CLASSROOM EXPERTISE"

In her 1989 address to the American Educational Research Association, Nancy Cole (1990) noted that there are two different conceptions of educational achievement—essentially, basic skills and expertise (Cole calls these "higher order skills and knowledge"). She suggested that there has been little progress in the past 30 years in reconciling these views, and called for a conceptual framework in which to do this, as well as a curriculum in which both basic skills and expertise could be fostered.

We share her viewpoint. In our study of expertise in classrooms, we have learned to see educational growth in a particular skill (e.g., reading, mathematics) as having two dimensions. One of these is the traditional "curriculum sequence": new skills are acquired and eventually become the foundation on which additional new skills are built (Gagne & Briggs, 1979). This is the "basic skills" dimension of educational growth. However, as Cole suggested, there is an additional dimension of educational growth. As we initially observed, when children in classrooms are working on tasks that they can complete competently, they demonstrate some of the characteristics of expertise. In other words, they overtly define, plan, monitor, and evaluate their own and other's work. They question themselves and others. In some cases, they actively elaborate their mental representations of tasks or task-related information. This is the second dimension of educational growth: "classroom expertise" (aptly described by Zimmerman, 1989). Our observations clearly indicate that some children now develop well in this expertise dimension. To foster growth in this dimension in other children, we hypothesize that greater attention must be paid to the pacing of skills taught and consolidated, to the labeling of task functions, and to the modeling and explicit teaching of the use of task-directive language in carrying out tasks and solving problems. We will elaborate these ideas in this section.

The distinction between performance and expertise is hardly novel. For 10 years researchers in cognition and instruction have been concerned with the difference between skill performance and expertise or understanding.[16] Educational theorists have been making the distinction for much longer (e.g., Vygotsky, 1978; Dewey, 1916; and others). Our contribution lies in identifying criteria by which growth in "expertise" in particular skills can be observed in normal classroom environments, and in identifying the roles of task complexity and aspects of classroom settings and instructional style as conditions for fostering "expertise."

Individual Differences and Teaching for Expertise

Educators display a strong tendency to perceive children whose skills (performance) are advanced relative to the rest of the class as more capable of "expertise" or understanding. When observed carrying out a specific task that is quite "difficult" for much of the class, children tend to confirm

---

[16]This issue has been recently summarized by Bereiter and Scardamalia (1989) and Brown and Palincsar (1989), as well as in Cole's (1990) address.

this perception. However, our observations suggest that many children can behave "like experts" when task demands or complexity do not exceed their grasp. One fundamental implication of this observation is the need for classroom learning activities to vary considerably in complexity in the major domains taught. This is particularly true when the acquisition of new skills is involved.

The Range of Individual Differences

The range of individual differences in basic educational skills tends to be very large. For example, by the end of the third grade, children at the 90th percentile on the Wide Range Achievement Test can solve problems such as multidigit multiplication with regrouping and can read words such as "emphasis" and "aeronautic." Average fifth graders can handle these tasks. On the other hand, at the end of third grade, children at the 10th percentile solve problems such as two-digit adding without regrouping and read words such as "cliff" and "lame." Average second graders can handle these tasks. The range differences in ability is even greater by the end of sixth grade, and presumably continues to increase in the high school years (Jastak & Wilkinson, 1984). Similar comparisons can be made for reading comprehension and math problem solving.

Differences of these magnitudes suggest that if most children in the same grade with a normal range of abilities are to have opportunities to experience expertise or understanding, they must have some opportunities to work on tasks that vary as widely in complexity demands as those just illustrated. In other words, teachers must adjust task difficulty for individual students. This is true of reading, writing, and math skills, as well as of other areas of "knowledge." On the basis of our observations and those of many others (Belmont and Mitchells, 1987; Fisher *et al.*, 1980), we believe that excessive complexity inhibits the child's ability to "talk to himself" metacognitively or to talk to others about a task. If the immediate cognitive demands of a task occupy the child's complete attentional capacity, there is no capacity remaining for "metacognition" or conscious talk *about* the task.[17] If the task can be made less demanding, that is, less complex, it is more likely that the child will "reflect" or talk to himself or others about the plan, monitor progress, and the like. Our findings about self-directed children suggest that they are frequently in a position to do this. Children not perceived as self-directed are less likely to engage in such self-regulatory activities. We infer from these observations that reducing complexity will increase task-directive self-regulatory speech. Our preliminary observations of children's task-directive speech in different domains and under

---

[17]The concept of limitations of cognitive capacity is discussed at length in Case (1985) and in LaBerge and Samuels (1974).

circumstances that allowed children to control task difficulty support this conclusion. In summary, "fostering classroom expertise" means, among other things, individualizing activities in terms of levels of difficulty, so that all children may experience tasks ranging from less to more demanding and complex for them.

Behavior Settings That Foster Expertise and Understanding

Educational programs consist of sequences of "behavior settings."[18] Behavior settings are environmental units defined by space, time, and specific action patterns and purposes (Barker, 1968; Schoggen, 1989). For example, a reading instructional group is a common behavior setting in elementary school classes. So is "independent work," when children are expected to complete assignments with minimal teacher assistance. (The amount of approved peer assistance varies greatly across classrooms and philosophies.) Work on "projects" and "themes," often in cooperative groups, is another common educational behavior setting.[19]

We suggest that most educational behavior settings fall into three categories: direct instruction, consolidation, and application. Descriptions of these types of settings, and suggestions for nurturing expertise in each of them, follow.

Direct Instruction Settings

These settings are primarily concerned with the direct transfer of skills from "expert" (teacher) to "novice" (student). This transfer can be effected by teachers through direct instruction, modeling, coaching, scaffolding, and explanation, or what Collins, Brown, and Newman (1989) call "cognitive apprenticeship." Direct instruction settings are usually highly teacher centered. Direct instruction usually emphasizes the process of the task being taught (i.e., the plan and how to monitor it) rather than the product of the task.

Fostering Expertise in Direct Instruction Settings　When introducing and demonstrating new tasks and skills, teachers can explicitly label task functions and specific procedures so that such instructions can be readily recalled and discussed. In doing so, teachers can also model task-directive language, both self-directed statements and questions (see

---

[18]Children in the same classroom do not necessarily follow the same sequence of settings.

[19]Educational "philosophies" are, to a large extent, actualized through the behavior settings teachers establish, and through decisions about how much time to devote to different types of settings and about certain details of the operation of such settings (e.g., who decides what is to be done with whom).

Meichenbaum & Goodman, 1971; Meichenbaum, 1977; and others). Teachers frequently model elaborations of task functions.[20] In a current mini-study in a Grade 2 classroom at the Institute of Child Study, teaching task-directive language has been accomplished to a considerable degree in spelling, math, and handwriting work.[21] Costa (1984) and Palincsar and Brown (1984) have suggested many other means of directly using and labeling task and strategy terms. We have found that teaching teachers to use the present coding system sensitizes them to how they can more effectively nurture their pupil's metacognitive activity and not think for them.

Consolidation Settings

These settings are primarily concerned with the consolidation of recently acquired skills, with or without expert guidance from teachers or more skilled peers. This consolidation is usually thought to occur through "practice" on tasks (e.g., worksheets) selected by the teacher. Consolidation settings are often called "independent work." There is usually some emphasis on both the process (how the child carries out tasks) and the product (are the results correct or acceptable for public consumption?). Historically, the amount of guidance or assistance permitted from peers has varied widely. At present, one of the consequences of the "open education" (Good & Brophy, 1986) movement has been an increase in permitted peer assistance, and reorganization of the classroom environment to encourage consultation among children.

Fostering Expertise in Consolidation Settings   We are particularly concerned about the role of consolidation settings that occupy half or more of children's time in typical elementary school classrooms (Denham & Lieberman, 1980). Consolidation settings are primarily where the "ownership" of tasks shifts from teacher to child. However, when consolidation activities are thought of as primarily concerned with increasing skill through practice (or "automatizing" skills), there is often little concern for growth in expertise. To foster expertise in addition to skill, the teacher's role in designing or selecting appropriate tasks is especially important. A mix of consolidation activities including some that are relatively easy or low in complexity for the child is important if each child is to have the opportunity to apply his or her expertise. This condition is often not met. Other tasks may be more difficult, but none should be beyond the reach of the child given some support by other children or by the teacher. As the

---

[20]It is possible that elaborations should be de-emphasized until the basic task functions are well established. More research is needed on this idea.

[21]We wish to thank Robin Ethier for her work in developing this approach.

child becomes more competent at the specific skill in question, we believe that he or she begins to provide many of the task-related verbal prompts that were formerly supplied by the teacher or by more skilled peers. Thus, the child's self-initiated task-directive speech is a crucial indicator of progress in acquiring expertise in consolidation settings.

Expertise-fostering consolidation activities require establishment of appropriate rules permitting peer consultation and self-talk. We suspect, from some of our observations, that avoiding too large a working group may be desirable.[22] Direct instruction to children regarding getting and giving appropriate assistance may be necessary (see Brown & Palincsar, 1989).

In addition to setting appropriate tasks, and monitoring growth in task-directive speech, teachers may have to take a more active role in consolidation activities. Primarily, this means interacting with children as they carry out their tasks.[23] This interaction would initially involve high levels of prompts, questions provoking planning responses,[24] and other "scaffolding" approaches. As children gain in skill, it is essential that the teacher gradually reduce her or his level of support. Diaz (1989) and Diaz, Neal, and Amaya-Williams (1990) have emphasized the importance of an "interactive," as opposed to an instructional, role for teachers wishing to nurture self-direction. Collaboratively evaluating the usefulness of alternative strategies by means of sensitive probes following consolidation work can be particularly valuable. The reciprocal teaching model of Palincsar and Brown (1984) illustrates an active process of moving skill "ownership" from expert to novice. Essentially this involves directly teaching and coaching children to take on the role of teacher as they go about their tasks and to develop self-regulatory skills. As part of the reciprocal teaching process, teachers fade supports (remove scaffolds) in order to nurture the students' metacognitive and self-regulatory activities.[25]

---

[22]In a replication of our experiment involving children's choices of task complexity, we observed that a consolidation setting with 23 children yielded less task-directive language than one with 10 children. To what extent this resulted from classroom rules and to what extent it was a function of the size of the total group was unclear.

[23]We recognize that this imposes a difficult program-design burden on teachers. Typically, "independent work" is just that—a period permitting the teacher to teach *someone else*. We suspect that part of the answer lies in relative balance of time needed for actual instruction (conveying of new skills or concepts) and the time needed for guided consolidation (supporting children's efforts to consolidate skills). For example, much of what occurs in "reading groups" could be described as "consolidation" activity. Proportionately, much more time should be spent providing beginning readers with opportunities for scaffolded reading practice than instructing new sight words or decoding strategies.

[24]See Haywood, 1986, and Costa, 1984, for illustrations of such questions.

[25]We think it would prove revealing to score both children's and instructor's task-directive speech as they go through reciprocal teaching à la Palincsar and Brown's (1984) procedure.

Application Settings

These settings are primarily concerned with the application of skills, recently acquired or otherwise developed. Application settings often demand the integration of a number of skills and areas of knowledge. For example, projects, such as the building of a castle or planning and conducting of a trip, call on many different skills. These settings are often partially or highly child-centered, that is, children play an active role in choosing or designing tasks, implicitly selecting task complexity (difficulty) or determining what products or results should be achieved. They may also have some or complete say in social groupings. In application settings, there is often more of an emphasis on the creation of public "products" (e.g., "published" stories, letters that are actually sent, dramatic presentations to be given to an audience, posters to be displayed publicly). Thus, there is a legitimate concern for the quality of performance (being correct, clear, or neat).

Fostering Expertise in Application Settings   Well-designed applications or projects provide opportunities to use skills (tasks) that are already reasonably well consolidated. This use of skills should occur in meaningful contexts, that is they should involve outcomes that the children deem desirable. If possible, children should be able to see for themselves what skills to use. If not, questions from the teacher or other children should be sufficient for a child to recall needed skills. In planning or designing application activities, it is important for teachers to consider how children with different skill levels will be able to participate in the project. Otherwise, such activities will involve application for some and consolidation for others. Task-directive language should continue to be emphasized and monitored as a means of solving problems.

Much of what teachers do in supporting children's consolidation and application work consists of elaborating skills and knowledge. Categorizing tasks, and noting similarities to other relevant situations, helps the process of extending expertise. Obviously, teachers must not only do this for students, but they must also lead students to elaborate task knowledge for themselves.

Concluding Note

Following these suggestions will mean accepting that children will not all come out the same at the end of the year or at the end of 12 years. Of course, this is the way things are now. If educators would attend more carefully to mastery and expertise, and less to grade level curricula and norms, we believe the level of effective school skills would rise noticeably. There would be a substantially larger group of truly literate and numerate graduates. Many might be exposed to fewer subjects or topics, but they truly would be able to use what they had learned for purposes they value, rather than perceiving schooling as a series of irrelevant hoops to be jumped through on the road to adulthood.

Appendix A

Scoring a Narrative Record for Dialogue and Task Features

	Dialogue features					Task features		
Record	Initiation	Mode	Direction	Ownership	Knowledge context	Task function	Task content	Affective tone
(S. enters art room)								
S. "What am I doing?"	S	Q	T	O	C	D	T	O
T. (Teacher) "This is what you're doing." Hands S. his mobile pieces from last week.								
T. "Do you remember what your plans were?"								
S. "Um . . ." (hesitates)								
T. "Were you cutting?"								
S. "Yeah." (S. goes and gets scissors and begins cutting a tape out of cardboard. He is standing at a table with 3 boys.)	T	S	T	O	E	M	P	O
P. (Peer) "What did the teacher say to you?" (Refers to disciplinary action upstairs.)								
S. "Not much." (not coded-social)								
P. "Boy, once I was sent to the principal's office."								
S. "Oh, not me, not much." (not coded-social) (S.'s hands never stop moving. He is cutting quickly and efficiently. Finishes cutting.)								
S. (to T.) "Okay, I need paints." (T. gets S. a paint tray.)	S	S	T	O	C	P	O	O
T. "Now, for that shiny surface, you'll need soap in the paint."								
S. "I was using blue and white."	S	S	T	O	C	M	O	O
T. "Okay." (T. goes to get his supplies for him.)								
T. "You have to mix colors if you want a different color."								

(*continues*)

Scoring a Narrative Record (*Continued*)

Record	Dialogue features					Task features		
	Initiation	Mode	Direction	Ownership	Knowledge context	Task function	Task content	Affective tone
S. (to peers at table) "Do you know what mine's going to be like?"	S	Q	P	O	C	D	O	O
S. "It'll have wings. They're going to be wide like the last time."	S	S	P	O	E	D	O	O
S. "D., how did you make sparkles stick to yours?"	S	Q	P	R	C	P	P	O
D. "I put them on wet paint."								
P. "I'm a double mixer." (with paints)								
S. "Don't mix white and don't mix black." (S. is painting his shape very quickly.)	S	S	P	R	C	M	P	O
S. (to all?) "Finished!"	S	S	P	O	C	M	T	O
S. (to T.) "Hey, finished!"	S	S	T	O	C	E	T	P
T. "S., you have to think . . . in mobiles both sides show, so you have one side all white, but what about this side?" (S. goes back to work.)								
C. (peer to S.) "Is there soap in here or something?"								
S. "Yes, so it will stick to shiny paper like one's we did last time." (S. is painting with black.)	P	S	P	O	E	C	P	O
S. "Okay, C. I'm out of black."	S	S	P	O	C	M	O	O
S. "I'll get the soap, you get the black." (C. doesn't go.) (T. helps. S. gets black bottle and pushes past the kids around the paint tray.)	S	S	P	O	C	P	P	O
P. "S.!"								
C. "S., you put enough soap in this!"								
S. "Let's put more in!" (He does.) (S. paints the whole back black. Then he sprinkles red glitter all over it.)	P	S	P	O	C			
S. (to T.?) "Look!" (T. hangs it up to dry.)	S	S	T	O	C	E	T	P

(*continues*)

Scoring a Narrative Record (*Continued*)

Record	Dialogue features					Task features		
	Initiation	Mode	Direction	Ownership	Knowledge context	Task function	Task content	Affective tone
S. (to P.) "I'm going to make a big escape pod now." (S. searches in box of materials.)	S	S	P	O	C	P	T	O
S. (to P.) "No, I'm making 5 mini flying saucers." (He lifts out 5 paper plates.)	S	S	P	O	C	D	T	O
D. (peer) "Oh God, look at S.'s! Look at the sparkes side." (D. indicates S.'s work hanging to dry.) (S. smiles.) (S. sets out 5 paper plates and quickly paints each into a flying saucer.)								
S. (to self) "This is my best so far." (C. is trying to open the paint.)	S	S	S	O	C	E	A	P
S. "I think you've made a mistake."	S	S	P	R	C	M	P	O
S. "You've closed that flip top, not opened it." (S. goes and takes paints and opens the top, gives it back.)	S	S	P	R	C	M	P	O
S. "Now you can do it." (S. mixes all colors in his paint tray together and dumps it all over his flying saucers.)	S	S	P	R	C	M	A	O
T. "S., you've got an awful lot of paint there."								
S. "I need gray." T. (to group at table) "You know you use a little bit of paint if you're mixing."	T	S	T	O	C	P	O	O
T. "S., how are you going to hang these flying saucers? This way or this way?" (demonstrates)								
S. "This way." (demonstrates) D. (peer to S.) "God, you've got so much paint!" T. (to S.) "Yes, that's a terrible waste of paint."	T	S	T	O	C	P	P	O

(*continues*)

Scoring a Narrative Record   (*Continued*)

Record	Dialogue features					Task features		
	Initiation	Mode	Direction	Ownership	Knowledge context	Task function	Task content	Affective tone
S. "Okay." (S. has found another piece of cardboard.)	T	S	T	O	C	P	P	O
S. "Hey, (T.), is this stiff enough for a mobile?" T. "Sure." (S. paints it.)	S	Q	T	O	C	M	O	O
S. (to peers?) "Oh cool. Look at this!"	S	S	P	O	C	E	O	P
S. "This is my USA rocket—my purple rocket."	S	S	P	O	C	D	O	P
S. (to peers) "Hey, wouldn't this be cool? Put sparkles on this color? (Note—this is coded as one sentence, stating a plan with affect.) D. "Like I did on mine."	S	S	P	O	C	P	P	P
S. "Yeah, look at mine." (indicates first project hanging up) (S. sprinkles sparkles.)	P	S	P	O	C	M	O	O
S. "Hey, cool, eh?" P. "See how many sparkles S. used." [T2 (second teacher) enters.]	S	S	P	O	C	E	O	P
S. (to T2) "Hey, look at this!" (really proud) (He has produced 7 items for a mobile. The average production by others is 2.)	S	S	T	O	C	E	O	P
S. (to self) "I'm going to make one more thing." (Quickly makes another flying saucer.) (S. goes to wash up.)	S	S	S	O	C	P	P	O

Scoring Sample Sentences for Dialogue and Task Features

Record	Dialogue features					Task features		
	Initiation	Mode	Direction	Ownership	Knowledge context	Task function	Task content	Affective tone
(S. enters art room)								
S. "What am I doing?"	S	Q	T	O	C	D	T	O
S. (to peers at table) "Do you know what mine's going to be like?"	S	Q	P	O	C	D	O	O
S. "It'll have wings. They're going to be wide like the last time."	S	S	P	O	E	D	O	O
S. "D., how did you make sparkles stick to yours?"	S	Q	P	R	C	P	P	O
S. "Don't mix white and don't mix black."	S	S	P	R	C	M	P	O
C. (peer to S.) "Is there soap in here or some-thing?"								
S. "Yes, so it will stick to shiny paper like the one's we did last time."	P	S	P	O	E	C	P	O
S. (to P.) "I'm going to make a big escape pod now." (searches in box of materials)	S	S	P	O	C	P	T	O
S. (to self) "This is my best so far."	S	S	S	O	C	E	A	P
S. (to peers?) "Oh cool. Look at this!"	S	S	P	O	C	E	O	P
S. (to self) "I'm going to make one more thing." (quickly makes an-other flying saucer)	S	S	S	O	C	P	P	O

APPENDIX B: RELIABILITY

Three classes of reliability need to be considered. The first form of reliabili-ty addresses the question, "Are observers able to adequately record the children's and teacher's verbalizations as they negotiate their classroom activities?" As reported, they are. In classrooms in both Study 1 and Study 2, we determined that two independent observers were able to agree on 90% of both the target child's verbalizations and those verbalizations di-rected toward the target child.

The second form of reliability concerns the need to unitize the verbal productions in terms of sentences. When the initial records were typed, a 95% agreement was obtained in demarcating language units that could be coded for dialogue and task features. Very strict criteria were used to determine what constituted a given sentence unit. Disagreements emerged over compound sentences, when the speaker's intonation and pausing dic-tated the length of the language unit. If observers narratively record the data, it is important for them to score their observations immediately after the session in order to reduce the likelihood of such disagreements. (In Study 2, whenever disagreements emerged between raters, the judgment of the rater who had conducted the observation was employed. This rule also applied to the third class of reliability, namely, the scoring of the dialogue and task features.)

The third estimate of interjudge reliability concerned the various categories of the task-directive language coding system. In Study 1, 100 sentences were coscored. Of 800 judgements, there were 90 disagreements (11%). In Study 2, the verbal protocols of two children (one high, one low in self-direction) were scored. Of a total possible 1020 joint judgments of 204 language units made by two independent raters, there were disagreements on 122 occasions (12%). We conducted a detailed examination of the errors in Study 2. The ratings were based on the scoring of typed transcripts; one of the judges did not conduct the actual observations. In terms of dialogue features, there was 1% disagreement in initiation, 10% disagreement in direction, and similar rates (5–10%) for the other dialogue feature categories—mode, ownership, and knowledge context. Disagreements were 10% or lower for affective tone and task content, as well. The major area of difficulty in obtaining interjudge agreement occurred in the case of scoring task functions (defining, planning, monitoring, and evaluating). The level of interjudge disagreement reached 25% in Study 1 and 20% in Study 2, mainly because the narrative observational account was not of sufficient detail to determine whether the child's verbalization occurred prior to an act (planning), accompanying an act (monitoring), or following an act (evaluating). Most rater disagreements occurred in discriminating between planning and monitoring functions. Note that errors in discriminating these categories would not change the basic findings that both of these categories were more common among high SD children.

Thus, there is a need for observers to provide specific comments about *when* such verbalizations occur in the flow of ongoing activity. When the children's behavior was videotaped, as in Study 3, these rating difficulties concerning task functions were significantly reduced.

ACKNOWLEDGMENTS

We gratefully acknowledge the support of the Laidlaw Foundation without which the research described in this paper could not have been accomplished. The senior author is also indebted to the Izaak Killam Fellowship award that supported his research efforts. The teachers and children at the Laboratory School of the Institute of Child Study, University of Toronto, and at Smithson School in Kitchener, Ontario, were actively involved in this study. We especially thank Anne Marie Sinclair, Shirley Kondo, and Robin Ethier for collaborative projects in the Laboratory School. Last but not least, we thank our research associate, Elizabeth Morley, whose observations, diplomacy, and insights have greatly enriched our efforts.

REFERENCES

Abelson, R. (1981). Problem solving and the development of abstract categories in programming languages. *Memory and Cognition, 9,* 422–433.

Allard, F., and Barnett, N. (1985). Skill in sport. *Canadian Journal of Psychology, 39,* 294–312.

Anderson, J. R. (1982). Acquisition of cognitive skill. *Psychological Review, 89,* 369–406.

Atcheson, J. W. (1964). *An introduction to motivation.* Princeton, New Jersey: Van Nostrand.

Baldwin, A. (1980). *Theories of child development* (2 ed.) New York: Wiley.

Barker, R. (1968). *Ecological psychology: Concepts and methods for studying the environment of human behavior.* Stanford, California: Stanford University Press.

Barkley, R. (1981). *Hyperactive children.* New York: Guilford Press.

Belmont, J., and Mitchells, D. (1987). The general strategies hypothesis as applied to cognitive theory in mental retardation. *Intelligence, 11,* 91–105.

Bereiter, C., and Scardamalia, M. (1986). Educational relevance of the study of expertise. *Interchange, 17,* 10–19.

Bereiter, C., and Scardamalia, M. (1989). Intentional learning as a goal of instruction. In L. Resnick (Ed.), *Knowing, learning, and instruction* (pp. 361–392). Hillsdale, New Jersey: Erlbaum.

Biemiller, A., and Meichenbaum, D. (1989). *Self-direction in the classroom.* Paper presented at the Canadian Society for the Study of Education, Quebec City, Quebec, Canada.

Biemiller, A., and Morley, E. (1986). *Self direction in the classroom.* Unpublished manuscript.

Bloom, B. S. (Ed.) (1985). *Development of talent.* New York: Ballantyne Books.

Borkowski, J. G. (1985). Signs of intelligence: Strategy generalization and metacognition. In S. Yussen (Ed.), *The development of reflection in children* (pp. 105–144). San Diego: Academic Press.

Borkowski, J. G., Johnson, M. B., and Reid, M. K. (1987). Metacognition, motivation, and controlled performance. In S. J. Ceci (Ed.), *Handbook of cognitive, social, and neuropsychological aspects of learning disabilities* (Vol. 2). Hillsdale, New Jersey: Erlbaum.

Brown, A. L. (1982). Learning and development: The problem of compatibility, access, and induction. *Human Development, 25,* 89–115.

Brown, A. L., and Campione, J. C. (1986). Psychological theory and the study of learning disabilities. *American Psychologist, 41,* 1059–1068.

Brown, A. L., and Palincsar, A. S. (1989). Guided, cooperative learning and individual knowledge acquisition. In L. Resnick (Ed.), *Knowing, learning, and instruction* (pp. 393–450). Hillsdale, New Jersey: Erlbaum.

Carroll, J. (1989). The Carroll model: A 25-year retrospective and prospective view. *Educational Researcher, 18 (January-February),* 26–31.

Case, R. (1985). *Intellectual development: Birth to adulthood.* New York: Academic Press.

Cazden, C. B. (1986). Classroom discourse. In M. C. Wittrock (Ed.), *Handbook of research on teaching* (3 ed.). London: Collier MacMillan.

Charness, N. (1989). Expertise in chess: The balance between knowledge and search. In A. Ericsson and J. Smith (Eds.), *The study of expertise: Prospects and limits.*

Chase, W. G., and Simon, H. A. (1973). Perception in chess. *Cognitive Psychology, 4,* 55–81.

Chi, M. T., and Bassok, M. (1989). Learning from examples via self-explanations. In L. B. Resnick (Ed.), *Knowing, learning, and instruction.* Hillsdale, New Jersey: Erlbaum.

Chi, M. T., Feltovich, P. J., and Glaser, R. (1981). Categorization and representation of physics problems by experts and novices. *Cognitive Science, 5,* 121–152.

Chiesi, H., Spilich, G., and Voss, J. F. (1979). Acquisition of domain-related information in relation to high and low domain knowledge. *Journal of Verbal Learning and Verbal Behavior, 18,* 257–273.

Cole, N. (1990). Conceptions of educational achievement. *Educational Researcher, 19(3),* 2–7.

Collins, A., Brown, J. S., and Newman, S. E. (1989). Cognitive apprenticeship: Teaching the crafts of reading, writing, and mathematics. In L. Resnick (Ed.), *Knowing, learning, and instruction* (pp. 453–493). Hillsdale, New Jersey: Erlbaum.

Costa, A. (1984). Mediating the metacognitive. *Educational Leadership, 22,* 57–60.

Dawson, V. L., Zeitz, C. M., and Wright, J. C. (1989). Expert–novice differences in person perception: Evidence of experts' sensitivities to the organization of behavior. *Social Cognition, 7,* 1–30.

de Groot, A. (1965). *Thought and choice in chess.* The Hague: Mouton.

Denham, C., and Lieberman, A. (Eds.) (1980). *Time to learn.* Washington, D.C.: National Institute of Education.

Dewey, J. (1916). *Democracy and education.* New York: MacMillan.

Diaz, R. (1990). *Acceleration through self-regulation: Promoting self-regulated learning in educationally at risk students.* Unpublished manuscript.

Diaz, R., Neal, C. J., and Amaya-Williams, M. (1990). The social origins of self-regulation. In L. Mole (Ed.), *Vygotsky and education.* Cambridge: Cambridge University Press.

Dweck, C. S. (1986). Motivational processes affecting learning. *American Psychologist, 41,* 1040–1048.

Elstein, A. S., Shulman, L. S., and Sprafka, S. A. (1978). *Medical problem solving.* Cambridge, Massachusetts: Harvard University Press.

Engle, R. W., and Bukstel, L. (1978). Memory processes among bridge players of differing expertise. *American Journal of Psychology, 91,* 673–689.

Ericsson, K. A. (1985). Memory skill. *Canadian Journal of Psychology, 39,* 188–231.

Ericsson, K. A., and Smith, J. (1989). *The study of expertise: Prospects and limits.* Hillsdale, New Jersey: Erlbaum.

Ericsson, K. A., Tesch-Romer, C., and Krampe, R. M. (1990). The role of practice and motivation in the acquisition of expert-level performance in real life: An empirical evaluation of a theoretical framework. In M. J. Howe (Ed.), *Encouraging the development of exceptional abilities and talents.* Leicester: British Psychological Society.

Fisher, C., Berliner, D., Filby, N., Marliave, R., Cahen, L., and Dishaw, M. (1980). Teaching behaviors, academic learning time, and student achievement: An overview. In C. Denham and A. Lieberman (Eds.), *Time to learn.* Washington, D.C.: National Institute of Education.

Gagne, R., and Briggs, L. (1979). *Principles of instructional design* (2nd ed.). New York: Holt, Rinehart, and Winston.

Garner, R., and Alexander, P. A. (1989). Metacognition: Answered and unanswered questions. *Educational Psychologist, 24,* 143–158.

Gibson, E. J. (1982). The concept of affordances in development. The renascence of functionalism. In W. A. Collins (Ed.), *The concept of development.* Hillsdale, New Jersey: Erlbaum.

Gibson, J. J. (1979). *The ecological approach to visual perception.* Boston: Houghton-Mifflin.

Glaser, R. (1984). Education and thinking: The role of knowledge. *American Psychologist, 39,* 93–104.

Good, T. L., and Brophy, J. E. (1986). *Looking in classrooms.* New York: Harper & Row.

Harter, S. (1983). Developmental perspectives on the self-system. In E. M. Hetherington (Ed.), *Handbook of child psychology: Socialization, personality and social development* (Vol. 4, 4th ed., pp. 275–386). New York: Wiley.

Haywood, C. (1986). Teachers as mediators. *Human Intelligence International Newsletter, 7,* 3.

Jastak, S., and Wilkinson, G. S. (1984). *Wide range achievement test.* Wilmington, Delaware: Jastak Association.

LaBerge, D., and Samuels, J. (1974). Towards a theory of automatic information processing in reading. *Cognitive Psychology, 6,* 293–323.

Larkin, A. M., McDermott, J., Simon, D. L., and Simon, H. A. (1980). Expert and novice performance in solving physics problems. *Science, 208,* 1335–1342.

Lefebvre-Pinard, M., and Pinard, A. (1985). Taking charge of one's cognitive activity: A moderator of competence. In E. D. Neimark, R. DeLisi, and J. L. Newman (Eds.), *Moderators of competence.* Hillsdale, New Jersey: Erlbaum.

Meichenbaum, D. (1977). *Cognitive-behavior modification: An integrative approach.* New York: Plenum Press.

Meichenbaum, D., and Goodman, J. (1971). Teaching impulsive children to talk to themselves. *Journal of Abnormal Psychology, 77,* 115–126.

Palincsar, A. S., and Brown, A. L. (1984). Reciprocal teaching of comprehension-fostering and comprehension-monitoring activities. *Cognition and Instruction, 1,* 117–175.

Piaget, J. (1964). Development and learning. In T. R. Ripple and V. Rockcastle (Eds.), *Piaget rediscovered.* Ithaca, New York: Cornell University Press.

Prawat, R. S. (1989). Promoting access to knowledge, strategy and disposition in students: A research synthesis. *Review of Educational Research, 59,* 1–41.

Pressley, M., Borkowski, J. G., and Schneider (1990a). Good information processing: What it is and how education can promote it. *International Journal of Educational Research, 5,* 857–867.

Pressley, M., Woloshyn, V., Lysynchuk, L. M., Martin, V., Wood, E., and Willoughby, T. (1990b). A primer of research on cognitive strategy instruction: The important issues and how to address them. *Educational Psychology Review, 2,* 1–58.

Rabinowitz, M., and Glaser, R. (1985). Cognitive structure and process in highly competent performance. In F. D. Horowitz and M. O'Brien (Eds.), *The gifted and talented: A developmental perspective.* Washington, D.C.: American Psychological Association.

Reitman, J. S. (1976). Skilled perception in Go: Deducing memory structures from inter-response times. *Cognitive Psychology, 9,* 336–356.

Ryan, T. (1970). *Intentional behavior: An approach to human motivation.* New York: Ronald Press.

Scardamalia, M., and Bereiter, C. (1989). Literate expertise. In A. Ericsson and J. Smith (Eds.), *The study of expertise: Prospect and limits.*

Schoggen, P. (1989). *Behavior settings: A revision and extension of Roger G. Barker's Ecological Psychology.* Stanford, California: Stanford University Press.

Schank, R. C., and Abelson, R. D. (1977). *Scripts, plans, goals, and understanding: An inquiry into human knowledge structures.* Hillsdale, New Jersey: Erlbaum.

Sigel, I. E. (1982). The relationship between parental distancing strategies and the child's cognitive behavior. In L. M. Laosa and I. E. Sigel (Eds.), *Families as learning environments for children.* New York: Plenum Press.

Sigel, I. E., and Olmsted, P. (1971). The development of classification and representational competence. In I. J. Gordon (Ed.), *Readings in research in developmental psychology.* Glenview, Illinois: Scott, Foresman.

Simon, D. P., and Simon, H. A. (1978). Individual differences in solving physics problems. In R. Siegler (Ed.), *Children's thinking: What develops?* Hillsdale, New Jersey: Erlbaum.

Starks, J. L., and Deakin, J. M. (1984). Perception in sport: A cognitive approach to skilled performance. In W. F. Straub and J. M. Williams (Eds.), *Cognitive sport psychology.* Lansing, New York: Sport Science Association.

Sternberg, R. J. (1981). Intelligence and nonentrenchment. *Journal of Educational Psychology, 73,* 1–16.

Vygotsky, L. S. [1934](1962). *Thought and language.* Reprint. Cambridge, Massachusetts: MIT Press.

Vygotsky, L. S. (1978). *Mind in society: The development of higher psychological processes.* Cambridge, Massachusetts: Harvard University Press.

Walberg, H. J., and Tsai, S. (1983). Matthew effects in education. *American Educational Research Journal, 20,* 359–379.

Weiner, B. (1986). *An attributional theory of motivation and emotion.* New York: Springer-Verlag.

Whitehead, A. N. (1916). *Address to the British Mathematical Society.* Manchester, England.

Zimmerman, B. J. (1989). A social cognitive view of self-regulated academic learning. *Journal of Educational Psychology, 81,* 329–339.

2

Understanding How Students Learn in Classrooms

Graham Nuthall and Adrienne Alton-Lee

Of what kind are the causes and the principles, the knowledge of which is wisdom.
—Aristotle

INTRODUCTION

One of the most important and recurrent questions that teachers ask is "How do students learn?" It is a question that arises from a teacher's need to understand and make sense of what is happening in the classroom, why some techniques work and others don't, why some students succeed when others don't, and why programs that work one year seem not to work the next.

Finding the answer to this question, in terms that relate directly to teacher's classroom experience, is one of the most important and most difficult undertakings in educational research. In this chapter we would like to describe a series of research studies designed to answer this question that have been undertaken at the University of Canterbury (New Zealand).

Our purpose in focusing on student learning was to produce results that teachers could use to understand and improve their own classroom experience and practices. To us, this meant providing teachers with an explanatory theory of student learning that was grounded in both teachers' and students' experiences of classroom events and that explained both the short-term and long-term effects of those events. We wanted this theory to be both descriptive of the cognitive reality of student learning and predictive of the outcomes that teachers could expect from the different ways in which they tried to manage students' learning experiences.

We were also concerned that the theory should be cross-disciplinary, bringing together the cognitive, social, and cultural processes that influence student learning and make up the "lived culture" of the classroom (cf. Apple & Weiss, 1983).

THE DESIGN OF THE STUDIES

The first study in the series was designed as an open-ended study of selected fourth-grade students, in which as much information as possible was gathered about all aspects of their experience during the course of a 7-wk (42-hr) integrated curriculum unit on land conservation and endangered species (Alton-Lee, 1984). Focusing on learning meant developing extensive tests of knowledge and skill acquisition and attitude change. These tests were developed in close collaboration with the teacher to cover all aspects of the intended curriculum outcomes. The tests were administered before the unit began, immediately afterward, and a third time 12 months later.

To obtain as much information as possible about each student's experience, continuous observations (one observer per student) and audiorecordings were made of classroom process, teacher and students were interviewed, and records were made of all teacher and student work (writing, artwork, etc.).

The need to record the continuous experience of each individual student made it difficult to study more than three students (this number was raised to four in later studies). In traditional terms, this is a small number of subjects. However, the purpose of this first study was not to reach universal conclusions about the nature of student learning but to discover whether it was possible to record and explain exactly how an individual student experienced a curriculum unit and learned from that experience. A small amount of information about a large number of students had been replaced by a large amount of continuous information about a small number of students. The ability to draw general conclusions, we have argued, is a matter of finding out first what is true for an individual student, and later finding out if the same things are true for other students in other classes (cf. Alton-Lee, 1984; Alton-Lee & Nuthall, 1990). For this reason, a series of consecutive studies involving different classes in different schools was planned.

It was also our intention, as we planned the later studies, that the design of the studies should be evolutionary. The design of the second study was modified to take into account the findings from the first study; this process was repeated with the third and fourth studies. Details of each of the studies are set out in Table 1.

Table 1
The Structure of the Four Studies

Number of days	Number of target pupils	Age of pupils (yrs)	Content of unit	Number of data intervals
Study One				
31	3	9–10	Conservation, erosion, and endangered animals	15,480 (1/2 min)
Study Two				
21	3	9–10	Middle Ages in England	37,704 (1/4 min)
Study Three				
5	4	11	New York City: a study of cultural differences	6,176 (1/4 min)
Study Four				
8	4	9–10	Weather: observation and forecasting	6,784 (1/4 min)

ANALYZING THE DATA

The data from the first study was analyzed by creating item files. A file containing all of the information relevant to a student's experience of the content of an item was created for each student for each item in the outcome test. This involved identifying every half-minute of class time during which anything relevant to the test item occurred. Each half-minute consisted of a transcript of any public talk by teacher or students, a record of any resources being used or referred to, any written or art work being done by the students, and the observer's records of the student's behavior (see Table 2).

Item files were classified according to whether the item was already known by the student before the unit (already known), learned during the unit but forgotten 12 months later (forgotten), learned during the unit and remembered 12 months later (remembered), or not learned during the unit (not learned). Quantitative analyses were carried out by counting the number of half-minute intervals and the number of times different behaviors occurred for items that were not learned compared with items that were learned and forgotten or remembered 12 months later. In addition to these simple frequencies, rates of occurrence per hour of class time were also calculated, to identify the most effective behaviors and activities with time held constant. Findings from these quantitative analyses were related back to the descriptive accounts in the item files to illuminate processes

Table 2
A Half-Minute Interval (Day 1, Time: 2.21′30″) from the Item File for a Test Item on "The Sea as an Agent of Erosion" from Study 1

Item	Students required to identify "sea" as one of the "agents of erosion" in a list containing 16 possible alternatives.
Context	Students have previously been given a definition of erosion and set a task in small groups to identify whether or not each item on a given list (e.g., glacier, snow, sea, river) is an example of erosion. The teacher has brought the groups back to discuss, in the whole class group, the reasons for their choices.

Public transcript

Teacher:	Can you explain how waves cause erosion? What is being eroded?
Pupil:	The rocks
Teacher:	The rocks are being eroded. How?
Pupil:	The waves come in so fast . . . (inaudible)
Teacher:	Right. Now a couple of girls over here said it can't be right. Why? What was your reason for thinking Dave was wrong?
Amy:	I thought the rocks would stay hard.

Behaviors

Gus:	Apparently listening to teacher
Diane:	Hand raised, apparently listening to teacher, fiddling with eraser
Amy:	Apparently listening to teacher; public response "I thought the rocks would stay hard.

that might have been going on or to identify any critical incidents that occurred during the learning process (see Alton-Lee, 1984, for details).

Findings From the First Study

Several important findings emerged from the first study that guided how we approached data from the subsequent studies.

Student Classroom Experience and Learning Is Unique

Our belief that student experience varies significantly from student to student within the same classroom was confirmed. Most of the test items learned by each case study student were not learned by the other two case study students, that is, the case study students learned an average of 22 items each, but only 4 of these items were learned by all three students.

Opportunity to Learn and Context Structures the Learning Process

Exposure to relevant content (opportunity to learn) was strongly related to learning. This was true for the total amount of time, for the number of separate occasions on which opportunity to learn relevant content occurred, and for the number of different task contexts.

Misconceptions Play an Important Role in Understanding Student Learning

An analysis of the exceptions to the general principle that opportunity to learn was strongly related to learning showed that, in almost all cases, the students had acquired misconceptions about significant concepts. These misconceptions were largely hidden from the teacher and resulted in students misunderstanding or misinterpreting relevant experiences.

The Teaching of Attitudes Can Be Counterproductive

The "opportunity to learn" principle did not operate with the learning of attitudes. For example, although the teacher intended the students to become more concerned about environmental pollution, their attitudes shifted in the opposite direction. Interviews with the students suggested that the more they learned about pollution, the more powerless they felt to influence the problem, and the less concerned they felt about it.

Developing a Three-Variable Model of Learning

Behaviors and activities that showed significant relationships with learning outcomes (e.g., involvement in teacher–student discussion, erasing own work, talking to peer) were incorporated with the qualitative analysis into a grounded theory of the learning process. According to this theory, learning was the product of the interaction between three variable clusters. These variable clusters were:

1. *Opportunity to learn.* Effective opportunity involved sufficient length and spread of exposure to relevant content in both teacher-directed and individual task contexts. A misconception required experiences that challenged and displaced the misconception.
2. *Engaging in facilitative behaviors.* These behaviors consisted of overt involvement with relevant curriculum content through activities such as reading, drawing illustrations, and interacting with the teacher during lessons, and covert processes signaled by relevant talking to self and peers, fiddling, and erasing.
3. *Resource access.* Relevant resources consisted of relevant background knowledge, out-of-school experiences (e.g., family discussions, vacations), and classroom skills, status, and equipment (e.g., reading skills, negotiating information and help from peers, pens).

The process of acquiring new knowledge required the student to go through three stages. First, the student became aware of a lack of relevant knowledge or of a problem to be solved. Second was a stage of processing new information by integrating it with related concepts and restructuring previous knowledge. Finally, the student developed a fully structured schema in the process of using and applying the new knowledge.

WHAT WE LEARNED FROM THE INITIAL ANALYSIS OF STUDY 3 DATA

It was clear from Study 1 that the interactions that took place between students were an important part of their experience, and we needed better ways to record that experience. We tried using individual broadcast microphones to record the private interactions taking place between the case study students for part of the time during Study 2, but the quality of the recordings was not good enough to use these data in any systematic way. By the time we began Study 3, we had been able to obtain better quality equipment and arranged for the pupils in that class to wear individual broadcast microphones throughout the unit.

Because of our concern to understand the role that private interactions play in student learning experiences, we have delayed completing the detailed analysis of the data from Study 2 and moved directly to completing the analysis of the data from Study 3.

In Study 3, we followed the experience of four sixth-grade students through an integrated unit on life in New York. The same sources of data were used as in Study 1, with the addition of transcripts of the recordings from the individual broadcast microphones. We used the same procedure of sorting the data into item files, but for this study used quarter-minute intervals and developed much more detailed systems for coding the data. The item-relevant information to which the students were exposed was classified by source (teacher, student, blackboard, demonstration, or worksheet), by validity (correct, incorrect, corrected, synonym, or analogy), and by type of content (explicit item answer, part of item answer, or example of concept, reason, background information). Student behaviors and activities were divided into more specific categories and the student utterances recorded off the individual microphones were classified by relevance, type of content, experience referred to, and language forms.

Two conclusions emerged from the initial analyses of the very detailed data that we had obtained in Study 3 (see Nuthall & Alton-Lee, 1990b). The first was the multidimensional nature of the processes taking place in the classroom. Powerful cultural processes were evident in the individual microphone transcripts and in the interviews. For instance, it became apparent that the girls in the class inhabited a different world than the boys and, during the teacher-directed lessons, the boys played a major part in the construction of the curriculum as it unfolded in the classroom (Alton-Lee & Nuthall, 1991).

The second conclusion was that quantitative analysis was not providing the same pattern of findings as the pattern that emerged from the first study. We had hoped that the greater detail and completeness of the data would help strengthen some of the findings of the first study and clarify some of the ambiguities. Specifically, we hoped that, by taking into account details of the contexts in which behaviors and activities occurred and by looking at the combined effects of several different variables at once, we would get a better insight into the underlying learning processes. Instead, the more complex the quantitative analysis, the more complex the results.

We solved this problem by reminding ourselves that the explanatory theory rather than the detailed findings ought to have been carried forward from the first study. The theory that had been developed from Study 1 claimed that student learning was a process of schema construction (Alton-Lee, 1984). Specifically, as the student was exposed to successive opportunities to learn item-relevant content, the student was able to build on past experience to construct a new schema that could then be used to answer the test item. What we needed to do in Study 3 was develop new data analysis procedures based directly on this model of student learning.

PREDICTING STUDENT LEARNING IN STUDY 3

We began the reanalysis of the data from Study 3 with the idea that it should be possible to construct a model of the schema construction process that would allow us to tell, from our data, which outcome test items a student would learn and which items the student would not learn. This model would need to specify exactly what kinds of experiences the student needed, in what sequence, and over what period of time. The model would also need to specify how to determine, from the data, the student experiences that were affecting schema construction and the ones that were not.

Exploratory analyses of the sequences of item-relevant content the students were exposed to when they learned and did not learn the items led to the development of the following set of formal data analysis steps for predicting if and when schema construction would occur.

Step 1. Identify the type of knowledge required to answer the test item. Five types have been distinguished: knowledge of a general or abstract concept, visual/pictorial knowledge, knowledge of names and word meanings, knowledge of a procedure, and knowledge of specific information.

Table 3
The Information Content Coding Categories

1. Explicit Spoken	Item answer or paraphrase of item answer spoken
2. Explicit Visual	Item answer or equivalent presented visually or by demonstration, drawing, or coloring activity
3. Explicit Procedural	Item answer procedure carried out or practiced, or instructions given for carrying out item answer procedure
4. Explicit Written	Item answer or paraphrase of item answer written or copied by student
5. Partial Item Information	Part of an item answer or information from which it is possible to deduce item answer
6. Reasons and Examples	Examples, instances, analogies, underlying processes, explanations
7. Verbal Background and Related Information	Additional contextual, and background information related to item answer, including student personal experiences
8. Visual Background Information	Additional contextual or explanatory information related to item answer, presented visually or by student drawing or coloring activity
9. Procedural Background Information	Additional or indirectly related information about item-relevant procedures, or review of item-relevant procedures
10. Occurrence of Key Word or Concept	Reference made to key word or concept in context that does not contain item-relevant information
11. Peripheral Resource	Item answer or part of item answer visually present (e.g., on blackboard, wall map) but not explicitly attended to

Step 2. Identify the item-relevant knowledge and beliefs the student has prior to the unit.

Step 3. Identify the stream of item-relevant information the student is exposed to from all sources (teacher, other students, worksheets, books, activities, pictures) during the unit and code it using the content codes listed in Table 3.

Step 4. Identify, from observer and video records, from student writing and artwork, and from private utterance data, how the student is interacting with each piece of information and tag it accordingly.

Step 5. Apply the schema construction rules appropriate to the type of knowledge required (see Step 1) to the stream of information identified in Step 3 to determine if and when schema construction occurs. These rules define the schema construction model and are reported in detail in Nuthall and Alton-Lee (1991).

Step 6. Cross-validate the results of Step 5 by examining the parallel student utterance and behavior data for evidence of the state of the student's knowledge during the course of the unit.

The first four of these steps involve preparing the data for the application of the model of schema construction, which is applied as a set of analysis rules in Step 5. Step 6 involves cross-validating the model's prediction.

The model is based on two underlying principles. First, it presumes that, under ideal circumstances, the student will actively engage in making sense of experience. "Making sense of experience" involves bringing together or integrating (Bransford & Franks, 1971) into a structured and coherent whole (or schema) all the experiences relevant to a particular topic or idea and any related prior knowledge.

Second, this process of schema construction must work against the problems of forgetting and confusion. In the normal course of classroom experience, relevant information is interspersed with irrelevant information and with potentially contradictory or misleading information. Individual pieces of information or experience must be held in a temporary store and will be forgotten unless they occur in temporal proximity to further pieces of relevant information or become associated with relevant prior knowledge. There is a critical mass of related information needed to form a viable cognitive structure that can be retained in long term memory and used in later cognitive processing.

Analyzing the Item File for Item #6 for Jon

In order to illustrate how the analysis procedure works, we will analyze an actual item file from Study 3. The item to which the students responded in the outcome test was:

Item #6. Puerto Rico is   (a) the capital of Peru

(b) a Caribbean island

(c) a state of America

(d) an American port

(e) I don't know

On the pretest, Jon and Mia picked "the capital of Peru," Joe picked "I don't know," and Ann picked "an American port." Jon and Mia's response suggests they know something of Spanish-American names. Ann appeared to have no relevant prior knowledge and to have based her answer on the pronunciation of "Puerto" (the test was read aloud to them).

The item file for this item was relatively brief. For Jon it consisted of only 9 quarter-minute intervals dispersed over 4 days. The first four of these quarter-minutes are reproduced in Table 4.

Table 4
Item File for Jon for Item 6

Day 1   Time 169   Content code 8   (Jon only)
   Context   Pupils were set the task of identifying New York, Hudson River, Atlantic Ocean, Mexico, etc., on blank printed map of North America. Jon is working with a peer with an atlas
   Transcript
     Pupil: Atlantic ocean, Caribbean
     Jon: Atlantic Ocean is here. Mexico. Mehico
     Pupil: Mekico
   Behaviors
     Jon talking to peer, looking at atlas, writing on map worksheet

Day 2   Times 89, 90   Content codes 5, 1, 7   (Jon, Joe, Ann, Mia)
   Context   Teacher–student discussion with whole class; the teacher displays this transparency on a screen

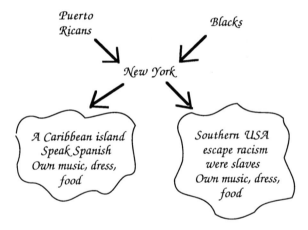

   Behaviors (Time 89)
     Jon is watching teacher, watching screen, fiddling hands. Joe has chin on hands, calls out "Caribbean, Caribbean." Ann is glancing around, swinging legs, talking to self: "South America?" Mia is watching screen, talking to self: (inaudible).
   Transcript (Times 89, 90)
     Teacher: More recently the folk who have immigrated to New York have come from mainly two different areas, one suburb being Puerto Ricans who came from Puerto Rico which is?
     Pupil: Mexico
     Pupil: The Caribbean
     Teacher: An island in the Caribbean. In Puerto Rico they speak Spanish, they have neat music . . .
   Behaviors (Time 90)
     Jon is watching screen, fiddling with hands. Joe is watching screen, talking to self: "Carib-

---

(*continued*)

Table 4   *Continued*

bean." Ann is watching screen, swinging legs, talking to per "Puerto Ricans. Oh, I put something different again." Peer: "I put the (port?) of New York." Mia is watching screen, glancing down.

Day 3   Time 44   Content code 7   (Jon, Joe, Ann, Mia)
   Context   Teacher–student discussion with whole class. Teacher has asked children to nominate questions they would like answered about New York.
  Transcript
  Pupil: . . . or something, and where Puerto Rico was.
  Behaviors
   Jon is glancing around. Joe has head on hands. Ann is smiling, watching teacher. Mia is watching teacher, glancing at camera operator.

The subsequent five quarter-minutes of Jon's item file contained the following information:

Day 3, Time 81	Jon reads worksheet statement: Puerto Rico is a Caribbean island associated with the United States. (Jon is reading, turning pages.)
Day 4, Time 22	Teacher asks group (including Jon) where Puerto Rico is. Peer says it is near Mexico in the Caribbean. Teacher confirms it is in the Caribbean Sea. (Jon is talking to self "My cousin's called Ricky," watching teacher, fiddling with mouth.)
Day 4, Times 30, 31	Teacher points out the location of Puerto Rico on sketchmap of North America drawn on blackboard. Teacher says "Puerto Rico . . . is an island here," (pointing to map). (Jon raises hand tentatively, watches teacher, fiddling with knee.)
Day 4, Time 196	Teacher says that the boy in a story read by pupils is a Puerto Rican boy "which means that he comes from Puerto Rico." (Jon, working on artwork, overhears this discussion with another group.)

The first steps in the analysis involve determining what prior knowledge Jon has that relates to the item content. His pretest response suggests that he makes some association between Puerto Rico and South America. Other pretest and interview answers suggest that Jon knows something about the Spanish background of Middle and South America.

Jon's first exposure to item-relevant content occurs in the context of a task in which he and a peer are asked to identify the Caribbean Sea on a map of the Americas. This provides visual background information (content code 8, Table 3). On the next day, Jon is provided with an explicit item answer (content code 1): ". . . Puerto Rico which is? . . . an island in the Caribbean." At the same time, the overhead transparency provides further partial information (code 5), that is, it shows "Puerto Ricans" connected by arrows to "a Caribbean island." On the same transparency is additional related information (code 7): "speak Spanish, own music, dress, food."

At this stage, three pieces of information (codes 1, 5, and 7) have been added to the information that Jon experienced on the previous day (code 8). On the next day (Day 3/81), Jon reads information on a worksheet that provides him with the item answer (code 1) a second time (". . . Puerto Rico is a Caribbean island associated with the United States. . . ").

The following day (Day 4/22), Jon hears a discussion with the teacher in his group in which the teacher confirms the item answer ("Where is Puerto Rico? . . . it was an island . . . The Caribbean Sea"). The schema construction rules identify this as the point at which Jon has experienced sufficient relevant information for schema construction to occur.

Later that day (Day 4/30), Jon hears a discussion in which the teacher identifies the location of Puerto Rico on a sketch map on the blackboard, and he also learns that the hero of a story he will be reading is a boy from

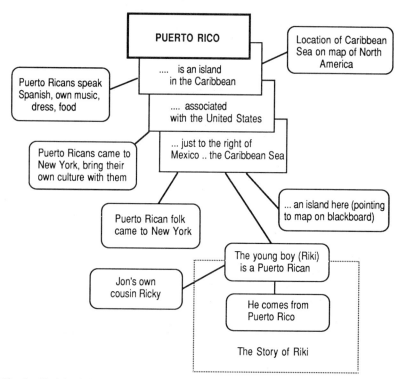

Fig. 1 Model of the schema constructed by Jon about the location of Puerto Rico (Study 3).

Puerto Rico. This information should be added directly to the schema about Puerto Rico that now exists in memory, as should the association he makes to his own cousin, Ricky.

In general, schema construction depends on the student experiencing two or three instances of explicit item answer information (e.g., code 1) and additional partial or illustrative information (codes 5 and 6) within a limited period of time. Additional visual or procedural information is required for items requiring visual or procedural information (see Nuthall & Alton-Lee, 1991).

Figure 1 represents the content of the schema that Jon constructed in long-term memory. The schema was formed on Day 3 and supplemented with further information on the following day.

In applying the analysis to this example we have omitted Steps 4 and 6. We have made the assumption that Jon was actively engaged with the information (i.e., actively engaged in reading and comprehending the information in the worksheet referred to on Day 3, Time 81). Applying Steps 4 and 6 requires a detailed analysis of the behaviors and utterances that the student is engaged in at the time the student is exposed to the relevant information. When the behaviors and utterances indicate active involvement (for example, when Jon refers to his cousin Ricky when the teacher is talking about a story about a Puerto Rican boy named Riki, Day 4, Time 22), the information is given a positive tag. When the behaviors and utterances indicate that the student's attention is focused elsewhere, the information is given a negative tag. Information with a negative tag is discarded from the schema construction analysis.

THE RESULTS OF APPLYING THE SCHEMA CONSTRUCTION ANALYSIS

When the analysis procedures just described were applied to all the item files for each of the four case study pupils, the actual learning outcome was predicted for 83% of the item files. The details of these predictions are set out in Table 5. Prediction of items learned was more successful than prediction of items that were not learned. The predictions were most successful for Jon and Mia, and least successful for Ann. In particular, it was the prediction of the outcomes for items that Ann did not learn that was least successful. Comparing the different types of items, it is clear that the prediction of learning for the visual items was the least successful. The number of items involved in this category was small, so failing to predict the outcome of one item (#2: locating New York on a map of North America) for three of the pupils made a substantial difference in the average prediction success in this category.

Table 5
Frequency of Item Learning Outcomes Predicted for Study 3

Type of item	Outcome predicted					Outcome not predicted					% Predicted
	Jon	Joe	Ann	Mia	Total	Jon	Joe	Ann	Mia	Total	
Items learned											
Specific information	6	6	9	14	35		1	2	3	6	85
General concept	2	3	2	2	9		1			1	90
Word meaning	1	4	4	5	14		1			1	93
Visual	3	2	2	3	10			1	1	2	83
Items not learned											
Specific information	1	6	8	6	21			3		3	88
General concept	1	1	2	2	6			1		1	86
Word meaning	2	2	3	4	11	1	1	1	1	4	73
Visual		1	1	1	3		2	1	1	4	43
Totals	16	25	31	37	109	1	6	9	6	22	83.2

Since the analysis procedures have been developed on the data from Study 3, we needed to test them on further data in order to find out how general the principles were that had been used as the basis for the analysis procedures. The data from Study 4 provided the first test of the procedures.

Study 4 was carried out in a fourth-grade classroom in a school in a working class area with a high percentage of Polynesian and Asian residents. Two of the four case study students were of Maori ancestry. The continuous experience of these four case study students was recorded using the same methods that we had used in Study 3. The curriculum unit was an integrated science unit on weather that lasted about 28 hr spread over 8 days. The same item file preparation and coding procedures were used.

The schema construction analysis procedures described here were formalized and Steps 4 and 5 were written as a set of formal decision rules that could be applied to data that had been coded using our content, behavior, and utterance codes. These procedures were applied to the item files from Study 4 and predictions were made for each item for each case study student. The results of these predictions have been reported in Table 6. On this new set of data, the learning outcomes of 79% of the item files were successfully predicted. This is essentially the same level of prediction as we had obtained on the data from Study 3. Only one item lowered the prediction rate. This was an item involving skill learning (how to read a thermometer). Since there were no examples of this type of item in Study 3, the analysis procedures used were those developed for items involving visual content, and they proved inadequate.

Although we had achieved considerable success with the formal analysis procedures, the data we had available for the items we failed to predict suggested that explanations for these exceptions would not be hard to find. When we failed to predict that a student would learn an item, there were some instances in which the students appeared to have deduced the answer from related knowledge that was not strictly relevant to the item according to the criteria that we were using. There were other instances in which the source of relevant information was from outside the unit or from information available to the students in the classroom during the unit, but we had no record of the students actually attending to it.

Failure to learn an item when our procedures predicted that the student should have learned it was sometimes due to the student being exposed to contradictory information from the teacher and other sources, and sometimes due to student misconceptions. For example, Ann did not learn Item #6 (described earlier) despite sufficient exposure to relevant content. She began the unit with the misconception that Puerto Rico was a port of New York. This misconception was sustained by the further misconception that immigration and commuting were the same thing. In this way, she trans-

Table 6
Frequency of Item Learning Outcomes Predicted for Study 4

Type of item	Outcome predicted					Outcome not predicted					% Predicted
	Jan	Pam	Rata	Tui	Total	Jan	Pam	Rata	Tui	Total	
Items learned											
Specific information	6	10	8	6	30	1	2	3		6	83
Word meaning			1	1	2			2		2	50
Visual	3	2	2	7	14		1	1		2	88
Skill							1			1	0
Items not learned											
Specific information	9	21	14	20	64	1	2	2	8	13	83
Word meaning	1	1	1	3	6					0	100
Visual		1	1		2		1			1	67
Skill						1	1	2	2	6	0
Totals	19	35	27	37	118	3	8	10	10	31	79

formed the information that Puerto Ricans were immigrants to New York into the idea that they commuted each day to work in New York.

STUDENT ENGAGEMENT WITH CONTENT

The schema construction analysis described so far was successful at predicting, for each student, whether learning would occur, and more or less precisely when it did occur. We did not yet, however, have a clear picture of exactly what students were doing and how they were engaging with the curriculum content during the process of schema construction.

Public Involvement with the Construction of the Curriculum

First we analyzed the way students were participating in the construction of the public content during class lessons. We identified who was participating and when, during the first major teacher-directed lesson sequence of the unit. This initial segment began with the teacher conducting three brainstorms in which the students were asked to answer the questions: What does New York make you think of? What do you know about New York? What would it be like to live in New York? Then followed a series of short lessons in which the teacher described and discussed the European settlement of New York, its location, development, major landmarks, and boroughs. Interspersed through these lessons were several reviews of the previous lesson content. The whole segment lasted 36 min.

Another way to describe this segment is as a series of tasks, each of which was initiated by the teacher asking a question or giving an instruction (Doyle, 1983). Students normally responded by raising their hands and waiting for the teacher to name them. Occasionally they called out answers without being named. The two boys, Jon and Joe, responded most, Jon because he was asked most often by the teacher and Joe because he called out most often. Mia was asked to respond by the teacher as often as Joe, but almost never called out an answer. Ann was asked least by the teacher, but reacted to this by calling out more often.

As Doyle indicates, there are risks involved in responding to teacher requests during class discussions. The level of risk is determined by the likelihood that a student can supply an answer and by the accountability system set up by the teacher and other pupils (Doyle, 1983). In our data, the risks appeared to be lower for boys than for girls. Although Joe's usual level of achievement in class was lower than average, he received unusually positive feedback from the teacher. This seemed to encourage his calling out, although occasionally his responses were quite inappropriate. Mia's usual level of achievement in class was higher than average, but she gave tentative answers that were likely to receive neutral or negative feedback, as the following example illustrates.

Teacher: What do you know about the Empire State Building

Mia: Um, its the tallest building in the world, isn't it?

Teacher: Ah, no, it's not.

Mia (talking to self):   I thought it was.

Mia was clearly strongly influenced by the teacher's response and remembered this particular incident in our interview with her 12 months later.

Interviewer: Do you remember quite well when you said something in class?

Mia: Yeah, 'cause I was wrong (laughs). So I remember that.

The Utterance Data and the Private Student Engagement with Curriculum

Next we examined in detail the transcripts of the student utterances that were recorded on the individual microphones. These utterances provided a window on the private world of student interaction in the classroom that is not normally available to teachers or observers. For example, in the opening 36-min segment of Study 3, the majority (about 60%) of the utterances recorded on the individual microphones was not recorded by the observers, although these observers focused continuously on individual students.

The amount of private talk students engaged in varied considerably from student to student. In Study 3, Jon and Joe were talking privately about 40% of the time during teacher-directed class lessons, Ann was talking privately about 30% of the time, and Mia about 14% of the time. During other contexts, the amount of private talk was considerably higher. During small group tasks, Jon talked 87% of the time and Mia, at the other extreme, talked 52% of the time. During individual tasks, Joe talked about 71% of the time, and Mia talked least, at 16% of the time.

Table 7 provides a comparison between the amount of public talk (re-

Table 7
Average Number of Utterances during the Time Spent on Each Item

	Ann	Joe	Jon	Mia
Utterances in public discourse	1.1	2.3	2.4	0.5
Private student-to-peer utterances	8.2	8.1	8.2	2.9
Listening to peer	4.7	3.8	6.5	1.8
Talking to self	1.5	2.6	2.4	1.0
Other	0.5	0.5	0.7	0.1

sponding to teacher questions, calling out during class lessons) and the different kinds of private verbal interactions that the students engaged in during Study 3. The numbers in the table show the relative frequency with which the different kinds of talk occurred during the time spent on the content of each of the test items (i.e., within each item file).

Talking and Listening to Peers

Table 7 indicates that talking and listening to peers was the most common form of verbal interaction that students engaged in during Study 3. This was true during teacher-directed lessons as well as during group and individual tasks. The first response of many observers and researchers is to treat this private discourse as off-task. However, for the unit as a whole, between 50 and 55% of the private verbal interactions of the case study students was related to the content of the public curriculum and a further 12 to 22% was related to the nature of the task or to concurrent curriculum-related activities.

What were the students talking about to each other? During the opening teacher-directed segment (described previously), Ann communicated almost exclusively with her best friend. The two of them helped each other with the answers to the teachers questions, articulating their reasons for answers and their misconceptions.

Joe communicated primarily with Ricky, sharing verbal associations and wordplay related to the public discussion. Many of these comments were humorous or involved sexual innuendos. Later in this task sequence, Joe became verbally and physically abusive, calling Ricky names.

Jon interacted with his two preferred workmates, Neil and Bart. He dominated these interactions, providing answers, explaining the reasons for his answers, making content related jokes, and demonstrating his additional knowledge. He kept up a running commentary on the adequacy of other students' responses and the teacher's statements.

Mia was the exception. Although she interacted frequently with her peers during small group tasks, she rarely interacted verbally with other students during teacher-directed activities.

Talking to Self

The second most frequent type of utterance was talking to self (see Table 7). These were audible comments that were not directed to anyone in particular and were almost always related to the content of the public discussion. They consisted of answering or repeating the teacher's questions, repeating the answer given by another student, making associations with the public content, referring to related personal experience, or making puns or wordplays. Occasionally the public content would cue quiet singing or humming of a phrase or two from a popular song.

These data clearly indicate that much of a student's experience of the curriculum comes from, or is accompanied by, private talk, either individually or in interaction with peers. To try to understand student learning without taking this private talk into account would be to omit a substantial proportion of the student's classroom experience.

The Relationship of Private Student Utterances to Engagement with Content and with Learning

As part of our initial quantitative analysis of the data from Study 3, we examined the frequencies and rates of content-related utterances for items that were learned and items that were not learned. Four kinds of utterances occurred more frequently during the time spent on content that was learned and remembered, for three of the four students. The exception was usually Mia, who, as we have indicated already, rarely spoke during teacher-directed lessons.

The four types of utterance were private responses to the teacher, making a verbal association with the public content, expanding on the public content, and giving reasons for, or justifying an answer. The following examples of these types of utterances are from the opening teacher-directed segment of the unit.

Giving an Answer Privately

Teacher: What ocean would it be?

Mia (whispering to self):   Pacific.

Student: Atlantic.

Teacher: Correct.

Making a Verbal Association: Relating to Own Experience

Teacher: . . . Peter Stuyvesant. Name of a cigarette. . . .

Joe (talking to peer):   My father smokes that!

Peer (to Joe):   So does mine.

Joe (to peer):   They're yummy!

Teacher: Henry Hudson . . .

Ann (talking to self):   Hudson. Hudson. Moro bar.[1]

---

[1]In New Zealand, Hudson is the name of a manufacturer of chocolate and Moro is the trade name of a chocolate bar.

Extends or Modifies Public Content

Teacher: . . . The English took over from the Dutch, and they said, "We'll blow you up if you don't give us the island!"

Jon (talking to self): Threatened them!

Gives Reasons or Justifies Answer

Student: Eight million.

Teacher: What made you say eight million?

Ann (talking privately to peer): I guessed that because I just thought that New Zealand is three million and New York's bigger than that.

These utterances show the many different ways in which the students were making connections between their personal experience and the content of the public discussion. They indicate that schema construction in the classroom is not the creation of a new and separate structure containing a single fact or concept. Instead it involves the restructuring or reorganization of existing knowledge in test-item relevant ways as new experiences become attached to existing knowledge. This reorganization produces a schema that is used as a memory search and utilization device for answering relevant test questions. Our analysis of interview data on the ways in which students used their knowledge to answer test items indicates that the test-answering process is itself highly complex (see Nuthall & Alton-Lee, 1986). Even apparently simple factual items may, and usually do, involve students in complex memory search and deduction processes that make use of a network of related information and stored experience. The following excerpt from an interview from Study 1 illustrates this process. The student is responding to a question about how he answered a test item on why flightless birds need to find food at ground level.

Gus: We had to draw a picture of a kiwi, and the person sitting next to me drew a kiwi, and . . . he drew the body about half the size of a piece of paper, and then really big legs. And I said, "That doesn't look right." And then the next day I went up and asked the teacher and he said, "That's not right, they're meant to have short legs." So . . . seeing they have short legs, I thought . . . you know . . . they're going to have to have food near the ground to be able to reach it.

The schema that students do construct contains not only the semantic or informational content of class experiences but also the episodic or surface features of those experiences. Our data indicate that woven into students' memories for the curriculum content are many unexpected details of the social and physical dimensions of life in the classroom.

Table 8

Learning Outcomes of Items for the Case Study Students
in Study 3

Number of items	Ann	Joe	Jon	Mia
Already known	42	46	64	40
Not learned	22	16	7	16
Learned and forgotten	3	8	3	3
Learned and remembered	17	12	10	27

UNDERSTANDING INDIVIDUAL DIFFERENCES IN STUDENT EXPERIENCE AND LEARNING

Our model of the students' schema construction process and our analysis of the ways in which students were interacting with the curriculum have thrown light on how the learning process takes place in the classroom, but this analysis has not yet accounted for the differences in the amount that each student learned.

There were clearly substantial differences between the students in the prior knowledge they brought to the unit and the amount they learned from it. Table 8 documents these differences. It is clear from this table that, in relation to the intended curriculum, Jon knew the most to begin with and ended up knowing the most, although the amount he learned during the unit was limited because of his high level of prior knowledge. Ann, Mia, and Joe started the unit with lower levels of prior knowledge, but Mia ended up learning the most during the unit. Ann and Joe learned considerably less and Joe forgot more than the other three students.

Table 8 does not make it clear that there was very little overlap in the prior knowledge each student brought to the unit. Not only did the students start with different levels of prior knowledge, but each came with different kinds of knowledge.

We felt that, before we could provide a full account of how students learned, we needed to know how these individual differences in prior knowledge related to other differences among the students in their experiences and ways of interacting with each other. Again, we returned to the utterance data, supplementing it this time with the transcripts of our interviews, and with other data we obtained on the social status and personal relationships among students.

HOW DOES STUDENT STATUS AFFECT ENGAGEMENT WITH CONTENT?

We first considered each student's status and the roles she or he played in the class. Because each student's interaction with the content frequently took place in the context of peer interaction, it seemed important to find out how this interaction was structured. What were the students' perceptions of their own and other students' status and abilities? How was status structured and established? How did status and role affect the way students engaged with the content and obtained help and information from the teacher and from each other? The data from interviews and a sociometric questionnaire provided an initial picture of the way the students perceived each other's status and roles.

Ann was 14th (of 21 positions among 29 students) in the class hierarchy of friendship, working partner, and leadership choices. She was only chosen by girls and was valued for her friendship, personality, humor, and because she was perceived as being good to work with.

Joe was 17th in the class hierarchy. He was chosen by only two others (both boys). One of those who chose him was also chosen by Joe. The other was Ricky who selected Joe as his best friend. The conflict between these two reflected a pattern characteristic of male students with low achievement (cf. Huesmann & Eron, 1986).

Jon was the second most popular and respected student in the class, but he was chosen only by boys. His choices for friend and working partner were reciprocated. He was valued by other boys for his friendship, humor, knowledge, sensible attitude toward work, and his ability to "get work done."

Mia was the fifth most popular and respected student in the class. She was' one of only two girls in the class to be selected by boys. She was described by other students as kind, friendly, good at leadership, responsible, a person with good ideas, and able to keep others in order without being bossy.

The relative social positions of the students in the class were closely related to their level of achievement in class work. As the later analysis of the "lived culture" of the classroom will show, Jon's role in the class reflected his position as a highly popular, high-achieving male student whose cultural position was central and highly valued. For example when the teacher set groups to work to identify the major racial groups living in New York, Jon assumed his role as a source of knowledge.

Peer (reading instructions):   Racial groups.

Jon: That doesn't mean racist groups, that means racial groups.

Peer: I know.

Jon: As in a whole bunch of whites living together and a whole bunch of Spanish living together.

Peer: I know.

Jon: Well, Joe thinks it means racist, cause he says "Ku Klux Klan."

Peer: . . . Ku Klux Klan?

Jon: That's racial groups, not racist groups.

Mia was also popular and high achieving, but as a female her assimilation to the central male-dominated culture of the classroom was highly problematic (see the next section). In the security of a small all-girl group, she was friendly and helpful. In the following example, the group was identifying the occupations referred to in a tourist pamphlet.

Mia: In the elevators, if they break down.

Peer: Wouldn't that be horrible.

Mia: I read this book, and they got stuck in the elevator. In the Empire Strikes Back, I mean, the Empire State Building.

Joe was frequently in conflict with another low-achieving boy who selected Joe as his best friend. His aggressive reactions seemed to be stimulated by his awareness of his own lack of knowledge, and may well have prevented him from access to the knowledge his peers could have given him (Huesmann, Eron, & Yarmel, 1987). Arguments over ignorance and dumbness were frequent. In the following example, Joe and the other student are identifying racial groups living in New York.

Joe: Buddhas live there.

Peer: People don't live in museums.

Joe: God, you're dumb.

Peer (as he writes on worksheet):   . . . Europeans, Indians . . .

Joe: I don't know . . . I don't know what you're even talking about.

Ann was aware of her lack of knowledge and her utterances indicated that she tried hard to keep up with a curriculum that was racing past her as the boys eagerly contributed to the class discussion and the teacher ignored her own hand raises.

Teacher: What ocean would that be?

Peer: Atlantic.

Ann (to self):   Atlantic.

Teacher: Correct. The Atlantic Ocean. The name of the island which is the one we talk about all the time?

Ann (to self): Long Island.

    Peer: Manhattan Island?

Teacher: Manhattan Island. Today in the middle of Manhattan Island we have Central Park . . .

Ann (to self): Park . . . (to peer) I'll have to learn all this (laughs).

Unlike the boys, whose interaction was usually competitive, Ann shared with her friend (Julia) her lack of knowledge and her anxieties about having to remember everything.

CULTURAL PROCESSES IN THE CLASSROOM: "I ONLY THINK OF MEN. I DON'T THINK OF WOMEN."

The further we pursued this analysis of individual differences, the clearer it became that there were significant cultural processes being played out in the classroom. Differences in race, class, and gender were reflected in the ways in which the teacher and the students interacted with each other. The gender differences that occurred in Study 3 illustrate how these cultural processes were working. As we have already indicated, we found that girls were less likely to respond publicly and less likely to talk or respond to each other privately. Their private interactions were different from those of the boys. They were more likely to be friendly and cooperative toward each other and less likely to be competitive or abusive.

We attempted to identify the processes and structures that were creating and sustaining these gender differences. We carried out a gender analysis of the actual curriculum as it occurred in the unit. A count was made of all the people mentioned in the public and private utterances during the opening 36-min teacher-directed segment of the Study 3 unit, which set the scene for the rest of the unit. We found an almost complete absence of females in both the public and private discourse of the teacher and the students during this opening segment. This result paralleled the analysis we have done of the public discourse for both Studies 2 and 3 (see Alton-Lee, Densem & Nuthall, 1991). References to females made up no more than 3.9% (Study 3) and 2.4% (Study 2) of all references to persons.

The gender bias in the experienced curriculum has at least two sources. One is the absence of references to females in the curriculum resources available to teachers, and the other is the curriculum construction process that takes place in the interaction between teachers and students. Those who participate most play a more dominant role in the process. Their knowledge becomes the content of the experienced curriculum.

In Study 3, it was clear during the unit, and from interviews with the students, that television was a significant source of relevant information for understanding and participating in the discussions about New York. Boys at this age watch more television than girls (cf. Huston, Wright, Rice, Kerkman, & St. Peters, 1990). In order to assess the case study student's access to this resource, we had included in the outcome test an additional seven items on the content of recently broadcast television programs that contained content relevant to New York. Jon and Joe scored significantly higher on these items than Ann and Mia. During the interviews, Jon and Joe indicated that they watched 10 of the programs that had relevant content, whereas Ann and Mia indicated that they had watched 4 and 5 such programs. Jon made frequent reference, in the interviews, to television programs as the source of his knowledge, whereas Mia indicated that the few programs she watched (mainly sitcoms) were more misleading than helpful.

Interviewer: Have you ever seen anything on television about crime in New York?

Mia: Crime in New York?

Interviewer: Or gangs or violence?

Mia: Mmm. . . I don't think so . . . No . . . Dad doesn't like television much and especially he doesn't like American programs, so we don't watch them.

This indication of gender bias in the domain-specific prior knowledge the students brought to the unit provides part of the explanation for the omission of women from the curriculum. The teacher also played a role by identifying, albeit unconsciously, with a white male perspective. He used the occasional football metaphor ("Let's boot off . . . ") and, during his discussion of the European settlement of New York, slipped into the use of the pronoun "we" when referring to the male English settlers.

Teacher: . . . Before we, or the Dutch people, could get this island, where we wanted to build our city . . .

This raises an important question about how—in this almost totally male-centered curriculum which girls entered with very limited domain-specific knowledge, in which girls were chosen to participate in class discussion less frequently than boys, in which sexual innuendoes formed part of the banter of boys, and in which the teacher worked hardest to maintain the attention and good behavior of the boys—girls like Mia managed to learn as much as they did. The data already discussed show that she was relatively quiet in the classroom. Unlike the others, she revealed little through her private or public utterances. One of her ways of coping, however, appeared to be an unconscious identification with the dominant male perspective.

Mia: I think its the Indians. I think they were the first people to have it [Manhattan] . . . Indians came before . . . sort of wearing all them facepaints and things and you sort of think of them being first there because they're before us . . .

Interviewer: Where do you get those images from, those pictures from?

Mia: Um, just from pictures you've seen or books.

Interviewer: Yeah. And you say, you don't think of them—you think of them being there before us?

Mia: Mmm.

Interviewer: And do you feel, when you say us, do you mean that the people who came to settle New York after the Indians were people like us?

Mia: Mmm. Mmm. (nods)

Interviewer: How were they like us?

Mia: Well, they didn't wear, um, warpaint and carry weapons around. They just sort of had, they wore clothes like us, sort of (laughs) civilized clothes.

Interviewer: When you say "us" do you think of women or men?

Mia: I think of men, really, cos, like, sort of early Canterbury,[2] you have visions of people wearing sort of long suits and things. You know I don't really, yeah, that's right! I only think of men (giggles). I don't think of women (giggles).

THE RELATIONSHIP OF TEACHING TO STUDENT LEARNING

At the time of writing this chapter we have just begun to identify the ways in which the activities of the teachers formed part of, and structured, the students' experience. The data in our studies came from the classrooms of reasonably skilled and experienced teachers. They varied in their styles and ways of interacting with their students, but they all used carefully planned and integrated tasks and management techniques they had presumably learned from years of experience.

It is not easy to unravel the ways in which teachers structure and encourage student interactions with the curriculum. Our analyses so far have shown that students themselves play a significant role in constructing the experienced curriculum, especially when they are engaged in small group

[2]The city of Christchurch in which this study took place was settled by English colonists as the province of Canterbury in 1850. It was inhabited at that time by indigenous Maori people. Mia will have been taught about this settlement and is making the connection to the European settlement of New York.

and individual tasks. Teachers and students participate in the "lived culture" of the classroom, playing out personal and social roles, constrained and shaped by the structures of the larger culture outside the classroom. Clearly, what the teachers intend and what the students experience can be very different things.

Preliminary analyses of the relationships between students' content-related utterances and teacher behaviors during teacher-directed lessons suggest that tasks like brainstorms and reviews produce a high frequency of student responses that involve making connections between public content, prior knowledge, and personal experiences. Reviews may also require students to search memory and check their recall against a publicly verified answer.

Teacher (reviewing lesson on history of New York):   1664?

Students (raising hands and calling out):   Aah . . . Ooh . . . I know . . .

Teacher: Great happenings. 1664? Chris?

Ann (talking to self):   American revolution?

Chris: Ah, um, the English took over from the Dutch, and they said . . .

Ann (exclaiming to self):   Ohh!

The questions teachers use and the ways in which they encourage and manage student responses to their questions are the major techniques for structuring the cognitive processes of students during lessons. Considerable research already exists on the effects of teacher questions. Question characteristics such as difficulty level, cognitive demand, clarity, wait-time, and method of selecting the respondent have been related to learning (cf. Brophy & Good, 1986). As we proceed with our analysis, we hope to be able to identify how these variables relate to student engagement with content and to the underlying schema construction processes that determine learning.

During small group and individual tasks, different variables operate to engage and sustain student involvement with the content. The difficulty level and clarity of the teacher's instructions and the difficulty level of the materials appear to determine how much time students spend on task process rather than on task content. The following example is from two consecutive quarter-minute intervals in Study 3 during the time the students were engaged in the task of filling in names and geographical features on a blank map of the New York area. Each case study student was working in a small group with three or four other students

Joe's group	*Ann's group*	*Mia's group*
Joe: Manhattan isn't on this map.	Ann: Are you definitely doing pencil? . . . I'll tell you	(Mia has attracted the teacher's attention to her group.)

Peer: Yes it is.

Joe: Where? Oh! over on this one. (other map)

Peer: I've got that one. That one there. I've done them all.

which blue I did . . . I'm not going to take long. Remember we had to do that map in Social Studies? . . . Its not going to take as long as that. . .

Mia (to teacher): And does the Hudson River, . . . do I draw it across there?

Teacher: The Hudson River is about here. That's all you need.

Mia: Is that it?

In this excerpt, Joe is getting confused information from a peer about what map he is supposed to be working on. Ann is talking to a peer about how she is going to color her map. Mia is getting content-relevant information from the teacher. The differences between the students reflect the interacting effects of each student's understanding of the task requirements (Ann colored her map but did not write in any names) and their ability to use the available resources (teacher or peers).

CONCLUSIONS

In this chapter we have attempted to describe the progress we have made in analyzing the data from a series of studies of students' learning in the classroom. The question that guided the design of these studies was "How do students learn?" We undertook to obtain as much information as we could about the experience of individual students throughout the course of integrated curriculum units and to relate that experience in a systematic way to measures of the intended outcomes of the units.

Although we started by using traditional methods of analyzing our data by looking for direct associations between classroom experiences and learning outcomes (see Nuthall & Alton-Lee, 1990a), we ended by developing a predictive model of the schema construction processes that underlie student learning. This model provides an account of the cognitive processing of content-relevant experiences in which students engage. Specifically, the model describes the learning process as one in which the students associate incoming experience with prior knowledge, and integrate and reorganize that knowledge into a structure that can be used to answer relevant outcome test items.

We then attempted to use the data we had from individual broadcast microphones and interviews with teachers to explore further how the students were engaging with the curriculum content, both in the public classroom context and in the equally important private worlds of peer interaction and talking to self. Here we discovered that the students in our studies were constantly engaged in exchanging, developing, and discussing relevant information.

We also discovered that the cognitive processes and engagement with the curriculum that we had uncovered took place in the context of significant individual differences between the students and an even stronger context of a "lived culture" structured by dimensions such as gender and race (Alton-Lee, Nuthall, & Patrick, 1987). The interactions between teachers and students played out roles determined by the larger culture.

We have yet to find a more formal way of describing the ways in which the cognitive, social, and cultural processes interact with each other in the classroom, and how task processes structure and constrain this interaction. We have also yet to look at the generalizability of our analyses. As we indicated at the beginning of this chapter, we see the ability to generalize as a matter of understanding the specific and the individual first, and then determining how, and in what ways, this understanding can be applied to other individuals in other circumstances.

We are trying to achieve a description of student learning processes, based on our model of schema construction, that teachers can use to understand how and when students are learning the formal curriculum content. As we understand more of the "lived culture" of the classroom, we plan to integrate our description of the learning process with an equally useful description of the cultural and social processes that determine students' well-being and enculturation into the structures of our society. Our concern for the usefulness and generalizability of our explanatory theory has led us to become involved in two further studies in which we are looking at how teachers can restructure the gender processes in their classroom. Looking at the effects on learning processes of a change in gender bias in the curriculum and in teacher interactions with students will further our understanding of the role that teachers do and can play in determining the outcomes of schooling.

REFERENCES

Alton-Lee, A. G. (1984). *Understanding learning and teaching: An investigation of pupil experience of content in relation to immediate and long term learning.* Unpublished doctoral dissertation. University of Canterbury, Christchurch.

Alton-Lee, A. G., and Nuthall, G. A. (1990). Pupil experiences and pupil learning in the elementary classroom: An illustration of a generative methodology. *Teaching and Teacher Education, 6,* 27–45.

Alton-Lee, A. G., and Nuthall, G. A. (1991). *What children's comments, call-outs, conversations and whispers reveal about learning processes within the lived culture of the classroom.*

Paper presented at the annual meeting of the American Educational Research Association, Chicago.

Alton-Lee, A. G., Nuthall, G. A., and Patrick, J. M. (1987). Take your brown hand off my book: Racism in the classroom. *SET Research Information for Teachers, 1,* 8.

Alton-Lee, A. G., Densem, P. A., and Nuthall, G. A. (1991). Imperatives of classroom research: Understanding what children learn about gender and race. In J. Morss and T. Linzey (Eds.), *Growing up: Lifespan development and the politics of human learning.* Auckland, New Zealand: Longmans Paul.

Apple, M. W., and Weiss, L. (1983). Ideology and practice in schooling: A political and conceptual introduction. In M. W. Apple and L. Weiss (Eds.), *Ideology and practice in schooling,* (pp. 3–33). Philadelphia: Temple University Press.

Bransford, J., and Franks, J. (1971). The abstraction of linguistic ideas. *Cognitive Psychology, 2,* 331–350.

Brophy, J. E., and Good, T. L. (1986). Teacher behavior and student achievement. In M. Wittrock (Ed.), *Handbook on research on teaching* (3rd ed., pp. 328–375). London: Collier Macmillan.

Doyle, W. (1983). Academic work. *Review of Educational Research, 53,* 159–199.

Huesmann, L. R., and Eron, L. D. (1986). The development of aggression in American children as a consequence of television violence viewing. In L. R. Huesmann and L. D. Eron (Eds.), *Television and the aggressive child: A cross national comparison* (pp. 45–80). Hillsdale, New Jersey: Erlbaum.

Huesmann, L. R., Eron, L. D., and Yarmel, P. W. (1987). Intellectual functioning and aggression. *Journal of Personality and Social Psychology, 52,* 232–240.

Huston, A. C., Wright, J. C., Rice, M. L., Kerkman, D., and St.Peters, M. (1990). Development of television viewing patterns in early childhood: A longitudinal investigation. *Developmental Psychology, 26(3),* 409–420.

Nuthall, G. A., and Alton-Lee, A. G. (1986). *Children's test-answering processes and classroom learning.* Paper presented at the annual Conference of the Australian Association for Research in Education, Melbourne.

Nuthall, G. A., and Alton-Lee, A. G. (1990a). Research on teaching and learning: Thirty years of change. *The Elementary School Journal, 90,* 547–570.

Nuthall, G. A., and Alton-Lee, A. G. (1990b). *Understanding learning and teaching project: Study three. First report focussed on quantitative data.* Christchurch, New Zealand: University of Canterbury, Education Department.

Nuthall, G. A., and Alton-Lee, A. G. (1991). Making the connection between teaching and learning. Paper presented at the annual meeting of the American Educational Research Association, Chicago.

Part II

READING

The six chapters in this section provide alternative perspectives on the nature of skilled and not-so-skilled reading as well as insights on how to improve reading. Pressley, El-Dinary, and Brown directly confront this issue, detailing studies that establish that adult readers often fail to read as efficiently as good readers should read. These authors also report a study of the extremely skilled reading of advanced scholars studying articles in their areas of expertise. Shanahan provides an indictment of some modern conceptions of skilled reading, claiming that these ideas disregard that skillful readers can and do consider the sources of text and authorial intentions. An especially interesting facet of this chapter is that the author explicitly discusses how his perspective on social communicative aspects of text results in a model of reading that is different from the one proposed in the chapter by Pressley, El-Dinary, and Brown. These two chapters present complementary views of how knowledge, strategies, metacognition, and motivation contribute to competent reading.

The chapters in this section also summarize important research programs concerned with the instructional development of competent reading. Pressley, El-Dinary, and Brown discuss instructional programs at Benchmark School (see Chapter 14). Collins reports on her work with strategy instructional programs that emphasize thinking skills as well as traditional comprehension strategies, summarizing striking outcomes already obtained as well as studies that are now being initiated. Her work is especially impressive in its developmental breadth, spanning the elementary and secondary school years. Miller and Brewster provide a state-of-the-art summary of self-instructional strategy interventions. Although they are optimistic about the effectiveness of these interventions and recognize the importance of self-instruction as part of instructional packages, they are also realistic about the size of effects produced by self-instruction per se. Miller and Brewster provide important insights into what can be expected from teaching students self-instruction.

Most of the interventions proposed in this section involve social-collaborative activities and some extent of dialogue between students and teachers. Gallego, however, particularly focuses on the power of dialogue and collaborative discourse as an instructional tool, presenting an initial study of how students working as a group can be taught to construct semantic maps of texts. The data to date suggest that this form of instruction increases comprehension of social science texts.

This part of this volume concludes with Mayer's discussion of his work on comprehension of scientific text. He specifically considers ways in which scientific texts can be prepared and presented to increase the probability that students will understand it, as well as strategies (e.g., generative note taking) that students can be taught to increase their learning from scientific texts.

State-of-the-art commentary on child and adult readers' competencies and their needs is presented in Part II. Some of the most comprehensive and up-to-date interventions for increasing reading comprehension are detailed by their developers and evaluators. Important theoretical and practical thinking about reading and its improvement is represented.

3

Skilled and Not-So-Skilled Reading: Good Information Processing and Not-So-Good Information Processing

Michael Pressley, Pamela Beard El-Dinary, and Rachel Brown

Pressley, Borkowski, and Schneider (1987a, 1989a) presented a detailed conception of how a really skilled mind operates. Such minds possess extensive knowledge about how to do important things (i.e., they have strategies), know when and where to use the strategies they possess (i.e., they have metacognitive knowledge about the strategies they know), possess extensive knowledge about the world and a variety of specific content domains, and are motivated to use their strategies, metacognition, and world knowledge as they take on new challenges. Good information processing consists largely of articulated use of strategies and world knowledge appropriate to a task at hand. Such processing is highly motivated and informed by extensive metacognitive knowledge about tasks and the capabilities of one's own mind. In this chapter, this model is applied to some recent reading data.

Four specific claims are developed in this chapter: (1) The reading and studying of "good" adult readers (e.g., university undergraduates) is often unsophisticated in important ways, and such reading is not good information processing. (2) The research community is beginning to understand reading at its very best, and it resembles good information processing. (3) Much of the comprehension instruction inspired by the theory and research of the 1980s does not promote good information processing. (4) More positively, a few educators are already offering instruction that mirrors the information processing of really good readers. Thus, the tone of this chapter alternates between gloom and optimism in addressing whether good reading comprehension is possible. The short answer is that skilled comprehension sometimes happens already but probably does not happén as often as we would like; more positively, substantial progress is being made in determining how to increase reading comprehension.

Consistent with the invitation to the Maryland Literacy Conference, the work of Pressley and his colleagues is highlighted in supporting these claims. Nonetheless, because the complex problems covered in this chapter are ones being addressed by a number of investigators, a fair discussion requires review of other research. It is heartening that most of the important conclusions presented here can be supported both with work generated in our own laboratory and in the laboratories of others.

ADULT READING AND STUDYING IS OFTEN UNSOPHISTICATED

During the latter half of the 1980s, Pressley and his associates conducted a number of investigations of adult reading, studying, and text processing. In general, this work was designed to elucidate the processing used by adult readers as they read and studied expository materials (i.e., strategies adults use to understand and remember text, and to monitor comprehension and learning). In addition, processes that might be taught to adults to improve their memory of information encountered in text were identified (e.g., richer elaborative processing than students use on their own). Pressley's group did not expect to come to the generally pessimistic outlook developed in this section. The popular perspective when this work was initiated was that adult reading, at least that of university students, was strategic and well regulated (e.g., Baker & Brown, 1984). That viewpoint has faded with the accumulation of data during the 1980s and early 1990s.

Use of Restudy Opportunities

Snyder and Pressley (1990) studied how university students process university-level textbook material. The participants were enrolled in an introductory psychology course. These students were asked to read a 12-page section of their course text, a part not yet assigned. They read this section one time from the beginning to end and were then informed about an upcoming fill-in-the-blank quiz and were asked to continue studying the text until they felt they could get 80% on the quiz. They were informed that the quiz questions would be roughly as difficult as practice questions given to them throughout the course.

The hypotheses in this study included (1) that these university students would be selective and strategic during the study period, and (2) that they might be able to monitor how well they had learned the text as they studied it (i.e., they would be aware of whether they were ready to achieve at the 80% level on the criterion test). If so, they should get at least 80% correct on the criterion test.

Our hypotheses turned out to be wrong. First, the students were anything but selective and strategic during the study period. Almost all students relied on a single strategy to prepare for the quiz, rereading the text from beginning to end, doing this an average of two times. This effortful and time-consuming approach did not produce especially impressive learning. Most students scored well below 80%, although all indicated they were certain they were ready to score at least 80% on the test. Their monitoring of test preparedness was far from perfect.

Text Search Failures

Symons and Pressley (1990) asked introductory psychology students to search for particular pieces of information that could be found in a psychology text, one not used in their own course. For example, one question "Why do children think that accidentally breaking 15 cups is worse than intentionally breaking one cup?" Some of these students were tested at the beginning of the course, when they knew little about the content of introductory psychology. Others were tested halfway through the course, when they were expected to be familiar with some introductory psychology content, but not all. A third group was tested after completing introductory psychology. The hypothesis was that increasing familiarity with the domain would show increasing success at search.

In general, this main hypothesis was supported. In particular, once the section in which the answer could be found was identified, prior knowledge facilitated identification of it. Those high in prior knowledge found the answer more quickly than those low in prior knowledge. Most relevant here, however, is that students often failed to find the correct answers. When searching a familiar domain question, they found the correct answers about half the time; they found fewer answers for unfamiliar domain questions. Even when students narrowed search to the correct page, they often failed to find the information they were seeking. Our confidence in these data is bolstered by other reports of search inefficiency in adults, most notably the work of Guthrie and Dreher (e.g., Dreher & Guthrie, 1990; Guthrie, 1988; Guthrie & Mosenthal, 1987).

Monitoring Failures

Whether or not readers use comprehension strategies when they are needed depends to a large extent on whether they monitor well their comprehension and learning of text. If they do not, they are unlikely to activate comprehension and memory strategies. Unfortunately, adults' monitoring of comprehension is often far from perfect.

Pressley, Ghatala, Woloshyn, and Pirie (1990a; Experiment 1) required university students to read a series of passages from the verbal section of the Scholastic Aptitude Test (SAT). These covered literary, scientific, and social scientific content. Each was accompanied by a comprehension question, which was attempted immediately after reading the passage one time. Then the subjects were given an opportunity to reread the passage if they were unsure of their answer. The students were nearly as likely to reread when they were right as when they were wrong; this tendency was especially striking when the question covered a main idea in the text rather than a detail. Students were poor at monitoring whether or not they understood the main messages in the text.

Pressley, Ghatala, Pirie, and Woloshyn, (1991c) conducted a follow-up study aimed at assessing more directly how well university students monitor their comprehension of main ideas in text. Again, subjects read SAT passages. Each was followed by a question requiring understanding of the main idea of the passage (e.g., the author's primary purpose, a good title for the text). After attempting each question, the participants rated their confidence in their answers. Readers were confident in their answers, regardless of the correctness of an answer. They did not recognize when they were wrong. Moreover, Pressley and co-workers (1990a) did not obtain any dependable correlation between reading ability and monitoring competence (see also Pressley & Ghatala, 1988; Pressley *et al.,* 1991c). Poor monitoring was observed at all ability levels. [For additional data documenting monitoring deficiencies in adults, see Epstein, Glenberg, and Bradley (1984); Glenberg and Epstein (1985); Glenberg, Wilkinson, and Epstein (1982); Maki and Berry (1984); and Pressley, Snyder, Levin, Murray, and Ghatala (1987c).]

Failure to Activate and Use Relevant Prior Knowledge Completely

Prior knowledge often affects understanding and memory of content that is read. For example, Voss and his colleagues (e.g., Chiesi, Spilich, & Voss, 1979; Spilich, Vesonder, Chiesi, & Voss, 1979; Voss, Vesonder, & Spilich, 1980) presented passages about baseball to baseball experts and novices. Adult baseball experts understood and remembered baseball-relevant content better than did baseball novices.

Even so, failure to relate prior knowledge to text while reading and studying is a very common occurrence. For instance, Woloshyn, Willoughby, Wood, and Pressley (1990; Experiment 2) asked Canadian university students to learn information about universities in their homeland; the material was presented in factually dense text. Thus, each student was presented 5 paragraphs to study, each about a different university and each containing 6 facts.

Two instructional conditions in the study are particularly relevant here. In the reading control condition, the participants read the material aloud under instruction to make certain they understood what was being read. In the second condition, participants were given an elaboration instruction. They were instructed to determine why it made sense that the fact would be true of the university in question. Because elaborations occur in response to such "why" questions, this procedure is known as elaborative interrogation.

There was a clear main effect for elaborative interrogation—matching of facts with the appropriate schools was substantially better in the elaborative interrogation condition than in the reading-to-understand control condition. These data, as well as other outcomes (Martin & Pressley, 1991; Pressley, McDaniel, Turnure, Wood, & Ahmad, 1987b; Pressley, Symons, McDaniel, Snyder, & Turnure, 1988; Wood, Pressley, & Winne, 1990; for reviews, see Pressley, Wood, & Woloshyn, 1990b; Pressley, Wood, Woloshyn, Martin, King, & Menke, 1992b), make obvious that elaborative interrogation improves learning of potentially confusing factual relationships. Most critical here, the impact of elaborative interrogation suggests that reading control participants are not automatically elaborating facts as they read them or, at least, they are not doing so as completely as they could. [See Martin and Pressley (1991) for additional data that are relevant to this point.]

Closing Comment

Other recent data on university undergraduates are a bit more positive than the results reported in this section. For instance, Wade, Trathen, and Schraw (1990) found that some undergraduates in their study were much more complete and sophisticated in their apparent use of strategies to process expository text than were other students. Particularly impressive, some students purposely used a diversity of study tactics, consistent with Pressley *et al.*'s (1989a) good information processor. Unfortunately, less than 10% of the total sample fell into this category. Moreover, about a third of their sample relied principally on rote strategies. That is, even though the subjects of Wade *et al.* (1990) seemed more strategic than Snyder and Pressley's (1990) students; a large proportion was still content to try to "pound it in!" Even their good information processors remembered only 16% more content than did the rote learners; the good information processors' recall of the text was far from complete. Thus, although the findings of Wade *et al.* (1990) are a bit more positive than most of the outcomes reported in this section, their undergraduates still fell far short of what could be considered highly competent reading.

There can be little doubt that this is a pessimistic beginning to a discussion of literacy. More positively, some adult reading is good information processing; the next section covers reading that is exceptionally able.

READING AT ITS BEST

One of the most conspicuous characteristics of the work reviewed thus far is that the readers in those studies processed texts from domains in which they lacked expertise. On many occasions, the topics featured in texts were probably not particularly interesting to the readers. Perhaps it should not be surprising that readers were not particularly active when reading uninteresting material in unfamiliar domains.

Good information processing during reading might be more likely when readers are operating in domains in which they possess expert prior knowledge and when they are interested in what they are reading. Lundeberg (1987) studied such reading. She analyzed how lawyers (8 law professors, 2 practicing attorneys) read legal cases. Their task was to read a law case and explain to the researcher how they did it. Some prompts were provided by the researchers as reading proceeded: "What are you looking at?"; "What are you smiling at?"; "What caused you to say 'Aha'?" The researcher recorded both verbal and nonverbal reactions by the lawyers as well as reading times. The lawyers knew they were to read the case so that they could answer the kinds of questions posed to first-year law students as part of their education in case law: What are the relevant facts in this case? What is the issue? What is the rule of the case? What is the rationale (i.e., the judge's reasoning)? The study behaviors reported by the lawyers were compared with study behaviors of high-ability novices in the law (i.e., people holding master's degrees in some other field) as they read cases.

Lundeberg (1987) identified five strategies used more by experts than by notices. (1) Experts *used context clues,* directing attention to headings, the parties in the case, the type of court in which the case was tried, the date, and the name of the judge. (2) Experts *overviewed* the case before reading it through, noting length, the decision, actions taken, and important facts about the case. (3) Experts *reread analytically,* focusing on key terms, facts, and rules of the case. (4) Experts *synthesized* in order to increase cohesion, merging relevant facts, issues, rules, and rationales. They also hypothesized about outcomes if the facts had been different. (5) Experts *evaluated* whether they agreed with the court's approach, and they commented on the cleverness and sophistication of the jurisprudence in the case—on the quality of the court's decision.

The novices also exhibited behaviors counterproductive to good comprehension, including addition of incorrect information to the case. Whereas experts spent more time on the first page than on the remainder of the case, novices evenly distributed their reading time across the pages of the document. Particularly striking, extremely unimportant asides were processed slowly and carefully by novices; experts tended to skip these irrelevancies. The only strategic behavior that the novices and experts had in common was that both underlined as they read.

In short, the experts were extremely active and selective in their reading of the cases. Experts used strategies; they applied prior knowledge during the analyses of the cases; and they seemed to monitor while they read, comparing what was in the case with their expectations based on their knowledge and predilections. In contrast, the novices behaved much like the university students described in the first section of this chapter. Tedious front-to-back reading of cases was the norm, rather than sophisticated strategic processing. Instead of making sense of the materials in light of prior knowledge, prior knowledge was actually an obstacle in some cases. For example, rather than attempting to determine the meanings of legal terms by relating them to natural English, they simply expressed confusion if the context did not support their personal interpretation exactly. Thus, to the phrase, "One of the supposed parties is *wanting,*" one novice responded, "Wanting? Only one party has to want a contract?" Lundeberg's (1987) results are consistent with the conclusion that skilled reading exists, although it may be limited to domains in which one has substantial experience and prior knowledge.

In reviewing Lundeberg's (1987) work, Pressley and his students at Maryland (including Pamela Beard El-Dinary, Rachel Brown, Peter Evans, Shelley Stein, & David Wyatt) concluded that her basic paradigm held great promise for providing information about the nature of skilled adult reading. Nonetheless, they also felt that Lundeberg may not have gone far enough in maximizing the likelihood of seeing reading at its best. For instance, the participants in that study had no say in what they read. Thus, Pressley and his students had experts in the social sciences read articles of their own choosing, instucted only to select research-based articles of interest and of importance to them. As participants read, they were asked to tell what they were doing. If there was a long period of silence (i.e., a minute and a half), they were cued to provide commentary. Their comments and nonverbal behaviors were recorded.

Without exception, all these readers displayed a rich mixture of strategies, accompanied by substantial use of prior knowledge. Although they generally read articles from front to back, they sometimes skipped forward and backward during reading. They read some sections more carefully than others, ignoring some information entirely. Participants tended to be aware of specific information they were seeking in the article and to evaluate whether specific information in the article was meeting their needs. They were planful, watching for particular information as they read, predicting what might be in the text, and noting parts of the text to be reread later. These readers monitored whether content was difficult, easy, puzzling, not understood, not worth knowing, already known, not already known, or taken from another source. They critiqued the literature reviews in the paper, theoretical perspectives offered by authors, methods, analyses, results, novelty of findings, conclusions, and writing style. They integrated across units of text and across text and tables or figures. They constructed conclusions as they read, made paraphrases, generated examples, and offered interpretations. They placed many types of notes in the text. They reacted on the basis of personal prior knowledge, attempting to relate the content to their own theory, research, writing, or teaching. They showed affective reactions to text, both positive and negative: surprise, anger, and fatigue. Our readers noted when the text contained information conflicting explicitly with their prior knowledge. Perhaps the way to best make the point is by presenting the reactions of a typical participant.

Professor Edward Fink of the University of Maryland is an expert in human communications who elected to read an article from the *Journal of Personality and Social Psychology,* a piece strongly recommended by a colleague as highly relevant to a mutual research project. The paper was 11 pages long and included two experiments, reported in normal APA format. Professor Fink required 1 hr 23 min to complete the reading.

He began by reading the references for a minute and a half, marking references to papers not encountered before. Dr. Fink made marginal notes to the reference list to highlight which authors were cited in the paper. Fink would return to the references several times while reading the article and then again after completing it.

He spent 2 min 20 sec reading the abstract line by line, attempting to draw out the design of the study based on the abstract. Later Fink returned to this drawing, elaborating and correcting it based on information encountered in text. He remarked that it was a difficult abstract; thus, he read it twice. Dr. Fink made few notes in the body of the abstract. At the 3 min 50 sec point, he began reading the actual article from the beginning. Fink marked key issues as he encountered them. He went back a few times while reading the introduction to seek clarification. Many such rereadings for clarification were observed throughout the reading. Professor Fink noted that one point made in the introduction was similar to a question he had put on a recent examination. On reflection, he thought his explanation to the class was simpler than the explanation in the article. He was puzzled once while reading the introduction. He noted that this article about problem solving was probably related in some way to previous work he had done on riddles.

Edward Fink carefully read and processed footnotes. For instance, for the first footnote encountered in text, he monitored that it was difficult to understand but consciously decided he wanted to understand it. In reading the methods, Fink paid particular attention to some surprising methodology in Experiment 1 and what he considered a cleverly conceived condition in the second experiment. He paid particular attention to figures when reading the results. Dr. Fink made extensive notes on them and relabeled some parts of them, rereading several points in the results so that they would be more comprehensible and memorable to him. He alternated between texts and figures throughout reading of the results, marking key results. He ended by carefully reading the discussion, marking an interesting metaphor in it, checking some references that were cited, and outlining in the margin a model covered near the end of the discussion.

In summary, when adults read in areas of expertise, sophisticated reading can occur. In addition to the work already cited, two recent reports have provided prominent data substantiating that use of reading strategies in an area of expertise is different than in an area of nonexpertise. Afflerbach (1990) reported much more reliance on prior knowledge strategies in the construction of main ideas from text when chemistry and anthropology doctoral students read in their areas of expertise than when they read in an area of nonexpertise (i.e., anthropology and chemistry, respectively). Pritchard (1990) observed many more prior-knowledge-based strategies and generally more strategically sophisticated reading when readers read information pertaining to their own culture rather than to another culture. When reading culturally relevant material, Pritchard's participants read ahead, related new sentences to previous sentences, extrapolated from text, made intertextual associations, visualized the text content, related what they were reading to previous experience, and speculated beyond the text. Sometimes adult reading is good information processing.

SINGLE STRATEGY INSTRUCTION AND RAPID TEACHING OF MANY STRATEGIES

One reaction to the poor reading reviewed in the first section of this chapter is that poor strategy use, search, monitoring, and use of prior knowledge reflect deficient educational practices that are now past or passing. A number of investigators (e.g., Applebee, 1984, 1986; Durkin, 1979; Moely *et al.*, 1986; Thompson, 1985) have documented that the current cohort of university students was not explicitly taught many strategies in school. Nonetheless, given a great deal of research during the 1980s on strategy instruction and, particularly relevant here, the teaching of comprehension strategies (Pressley, Johnson, Symons, McGoldrick, & Kurita, 1989c), perhaps more teaching of strategies is going on now than occurred in the past. If that is so, reading comprehension might be considerably better in future assessments of reading than it has been in previous assessments. Such a possibility might seem especially likely because many of the new reading curricula specify teaching of strategies (e.g., *Health Reading*, Alvermann *et al.*, 1988; *Open Court Reading and Writing*, Bereiter *et al.*, 1989; *Journeys*, Tuinman, Newman, & Rich, 1988). Even so, there are reasons to be skeptical that reading comprehension research or curricular innovations based on that research will really make an impact on reading efficiency.

One of the main reasons for this skepticism is that strategy instruction studied to date and currently being implemented is not like the processing of skilled readers. The information processing taught in most studies of strategy instruction pales in comparison to the processing exhibited by really skilled adult readers. A typical experiment includes one group of subjects, all of whom are instructed to use a particular strategy, and a second group of participants, all of whom are left to their own devices. Thus, there have been studies in which students have been taught to analyze fiction in terms of story grammar components (e.g., Idol, 1987; Nolte & Singer, 1985; Short & Ryan, 1984), experiments in which students were taught specific schemes for summarizing text (e.g., Armbruster, Anderson, & Ostertag, 1987; Baumann, 1984; Bean & Steenwyk, 1984; Berkowitz, 1986; Jenkins, Heliotis, Stein, & Haynes, 1987; Rinehart, Stahl, & Ericson, 1986; Taylor, 1982; Taylor & Beach, 1984), and investigations of various types of imagery instructions on memory and comprehension of text (e.g., Gambrell & Bales, 1986; Peters & Levin, 1986; Pressley, 1976).

A typical finding in single-process studies was that teaching the single process in question boosted comprehension as measured in the short-term with some conventional measure of memory for text. A steady stream of such findings during the last decade was largely responsible for the introduction of single-strategy teaching in many of the new basal reader series. These materials contain many examples of lessons on story-grammar analysis, summarization, and imagery generation, as well as on other single strategies. However, the logic of these innovations may have a terrible flaw, a problem that is obvious when the processing of really skilled readers at their best is considered.

Why Single Strategy Instruction Does Not Encourage Processing Like That of Skilled Readers

Expert readers do not rely on a single strategy to comprehend on article. They use a variety of on-line strategic processes, each deployed briefly to accomplish a small part of comprehending an entire piece of text (e.g., Afflerbach, 1990; Pritchard, 1990; in progress Maryland study of social scientists described earlier). Use of single strategies not only contrasts with what skilled adult readers do when reading at their best, it also makes no sense conceptually.

Contemporary models of reading specify comprehension as the product of a number of factors, including strategies, prior knowledge, metacognition, and motivation (e.g., Pressley *et al.* (1989a), Good Information Processor model); the weightings of these components vary depending on the emphasis of the model (e.g., contrast Baker & Brown, 1984, with Oakhill & Garnham, 1988). Moreover, contemporary models make the following assumptions: strategies will vary as a function of text characteristics both across and within texts; prior knowledge will be stimulated differently in different parts of text; and inferential activities in reaction to particular pieces of information in text will occur as new information is processed.

How can such analyses of skilled reading be translated into instruction of single strategies, each taught one at a time? Duffy (1990) offered an analysis that we find telling. For many years educators have conceived of reading as a set of articulated skills. Thus, decoding was decomposed into auditory and visual discriminations, sound-symbol associations, and segmentation skills (e.g., Harris & Sipay, 1985; see also Chapter 12). The assumption was that, given a lot of practice with individual skills, students eventually would be able to coordinate all of them into fluid decoding. The problem is that sometimes this integration does not happen. The student can execute the skill when required to do so on a workbook page but either cannot or does not use the skill as part of fluent reading. Duffy (University of South Carolina, Aiken; October 28, 1989) provided a memorable example. As part of one of Duffy's studies, a student was interviewed about some reading instruction that was just completed.

Interviewer: What was your teacher teaching you today?

Third-grade Student: Prefixes and suffixes.

Interviewer: Why do you think your teacher taught you about prefixes and suffixes?

Student: Cause when you get in junior high school and other grades you have to know that stuff to pass.

Interviewer: Why do you have to know that stuff?

Student: In order to pass . . . you have to know your divisions, your times, your prefixes, your suffixes, your base words, and your pluses and your minuses in order to pass . . .

Interviewer: All that stuff, huh? Well, where would you use your prefixes, suffixes, and your base words?

Student: You use the base word on a word . . . and she teaches us compounds, too.

Interviewer: Compounds, huh?

Student: Yeah.

Interviewer: When you're reading, how would you get a chance to use what you learned today? If you were in a book for instance, when would you a get a chance to use prefixes, suffixes, and base words in a book?

Student: In a book?

Interviewer: Yeah, in a book.

Student: Well, I wouldn't use them in a book, but you would use them when she says write a word, circle the prefix, underline the suffix, and draw a square around the base word.

This student clearly had learned a skill, but had no idea how to apply it when reading. Duffy (1990) believes, and we concur, that much of comprehension strategy instruction seems similar to traditional skill instruction. The assumption is that, if enough practice is given with the individual strategies, the reader will somehow pull it all together to produce fluid comprehension. What might such teaching produce? It is somewhat easy to imagine the following interview with a student:

Student: We learned about imagery today.

Interviewer: When you're reading a pleasure book, how might you get a chance to apply what you learned today?

Student: With a pleasure book?

Interviewer: Yeah, a pleasure book.

Student: You wouldn't use it with a pleasure book. You use it when the teacher tells you to make up images about what is going on in the story . . . you know, the story in the reader. In a pleasure book? That's really silly.

These results may continue to appear if teaching single strategies is the only possible intervention. Fortunately, there are alternatives. Not all are effective, however, as will become obvious from the following text.

Instruction of a Large Number of Strategies in a Short Period of Time

Many efforts have been made to teach a large number of strategies in a short period of time (Dansereau, 1985; Jones, Amiran, & Katims, 1985; Weinstein & Underwood, 1985). For example, the study skills classes that are now common on university campuses are instances of this approach. More often than not, evaluations of these interventions do not clarify whether the strategy instruction produced real reading gains (e.g., uncontrolled pretest–posttest data are collected; for commentary, see Mayer, 1986; also Pressley, Cariglia-Bull, & Snyder, 1984). When interpretable evaluations are provided, the effects produced by the interventions are usually small or nonexistent, a fact that even supporters of this approach acknowledge (e.g., Dansereau, 1985). Rarely do the skills learned in these courses transfer to study of material encountered in other courses (see Schallert, Alexander, & Goetz, 1988).

There are several candidate hypotheses to explain the low transfer of learned skills. Relatively little metacognitive information is provided about where and when to use the procedures. When provided, it is not emphasized. Little is done to motivate use of strategies that are taught, except to point out that they can aid particular types of performances. Practice of the strategies, especially with respect to actual school materials, is often left to the discretion of the student or the course instructor.

A reasonable hypothesis was that these interventions would more certainly produce general effects on cognition if more information about where and when to use the strategies was provided, if more attention was given to motivating use of the strategies taught, and if more structured practice with realistic texts was included as part of the instruction. Paris and his associates at Michigan (Jacobs & Paris, 1987; Paris & Jacobs, 1984; Paris & Oka, 1986; Paris, Cross, & Lipson, 1984) tried to do so, designing a set of materials, Informed Strategies for Learning (ISL), to supplement regular elementary reading instruction. Their goals were to promote awareness of reading strategies and encourage use of strategies by elementary school students.

A series of 20 lessons was devised, each intended for presentation in three 30-min sessions; the 20 lessons were spread over the course of much of an academic year. A number of comprehension and comprehension monitoring strategies were covered in the lessons, including elaboration, inference, integration, activation of prior knowledge, summarization, rereading, self-questioning, checking consistencies, and paraphrasing. A metaphor was devised for each lesson (e.g., hunt for reading treasure, be a reading detective); a bulletin board display illustrated each metaphor. Teacher guidance and support was faded as the student progressed through each lesson from the first to the third session.

The first two lessons introduced the metaphor, described the strategy, and explained how to use the strategy while reading. Practice and feedback were provided for the whole class. The third lesson was referred to as a "bridging" lesson because the reading material was to be taken from other parts of the teachers' curriculum such as social studies or science so that students could learn directly that these strategies should be transferred to content area reading. Worksheets and passages accompanied all 60 lessons, making more than 300 pages of material. (Paris & Oka, 1986, p. 32)

Two evaluations of ISL have been reported, one small in scale (8 classrooms, Grade 3 and Grade 5 students) and the other much larger (71 Grade 3 and Grade 5 classrooms). In both studies, some classrooms received ISL and others did not (i.e., control classrooms). The results in both studies were extremely similar. The main findings included (1) small gains in performance on a homemade metamemory scale, consisting of multiple-choice questions tapping knowledge of memory strategies and metamemory content, most of which was explicitly covered in the ISL curriculum; (2) small gains on a cloze task similar to cloze tasks included as part of instruction in the ISL conditions but not in the control condition; (3) small gains on a task requiring detection of errors in prose (Markman, 1985), again a task experienced as part of instruction in the ISL condition but not in the control condition; and (4) no significant difference between ISL and control students on standardized comprehension measures.

Nothing in these results suggested that teaching a large number of strategies over the course of an academic year enhanced performance on reading tasks not practiced extensively as part of the ISL curriculum. Although interpreting null effects is always dangerous, the larger study was very large (i.e., more than 1300 degrees of freedom in the error terms of the test statistics), so power to detect significant effects was very high, especially given the analysis options elected by Paris and his colleagues. Our interpretation is that Paris and his associates did whatever possible to increase the likelihood of finding treatment effects. That their largest effects were moderate in size (Cohen, 1988) at best is powerful evidence that providing a large number of strategies in a small amount of instructional time probably does not increase reading comprehension dramatically.

Summary

The teaching of single strategies was studied intensely and extensively during the 1980s. This work produced a set of strategies that improve some aspects of comprehension and memory of text when they are executed alone on demand. These successes stimulated the development of curricula involving the teaching of large numbers of single strategies. For the most part, these multiple-strategy curricula are untested, although the evaluations that have been done suggest that such interventions often do not produce large effects on comprehension and memory of text.

Still it is extremely important to continue research on this type of intervention, if for no other reason than that it is the only possibility of strategy instruction for many students. Millions of college students arrive on campus annually inadequately prepared for the academic demands that will be made on them. Single semester courses that teach study skills do fit into the undergraduate curriculum and may be an only hope for such students. In addition, although we believe that elementary, middle-school, and high-school students would be much better off with processing instruction that is integrated with the regular curriculum and distributed across the content areas, this alternative does not seem likely for the vast majority of students, at least not in the foreseeable future. Independent courses on how to study are much more likely in these contexts. Given the inevitability of such interventions, every effort should be made to develop high quality courses that have maximum impact.

This section can end on a positive note because of a recent example of such a course having a huge impact on reading achievement during the middle-school years. Collins (1991) taught reasoning skills to students in Grades 5 and 6. Lessons were provided 3 days a week for a semester. The competencies taught during the lessons included seeking clarification when uncertain; looking for patterns and principles; analyzing decision-making that occurs in text content; problem-solving including the use of backward reasoning and visualization; summarizing; predicting; adapting, rearranging, modifying, and substituting parts of ideas in text, especially as part of summarization and prediction; and negotiating interpretations of text in groups.

Although there were no significant differences among experimental and control participants on Iowa test performances before the intervention, there were large differences on a postinstruction administration of the test. For instance, comprehension performance on the test was 3 standard deviations greater for the strategy-instructed students than for the controls. An intervention that produces such a striking effect certainly deserves additional evaluation, especially since this type of short-term instruction does match the scheduling ecology of middle and high schools. If Collins' (1991) outcome can be replicated, we would have reason to be much more optimistic about short-term intervention than most other results suggest. In contrast, all that follows is more optimistic.

BEYOND SHORT-TERM SCAFFOLDING TO LONG-TERM DIRECT EXPLANATION

The approaches to instruction covered in this section were motivated by some common assumptions about strategy use and strategy instruction that follow from contemporary theories of teaching and performance, such as the good information processor model (Pressley *et al.,* 1987a, 1989a): Good reading involves coordination of multiple strategies; the good reader knows, at least tacitly, when and where to use the strategies he or she possesses. Some students do not acquire comprehension strategies on their own, nor the metacognitive knowledge required to use the strategies proficiently. Scaffolded instruction of strategies encourages acquisition of both strategies and supporting metacognition . . . and more.

Scaffolded Instruction

Since the 1978 translation of *Mind in Society* (Vygotsky, 1978), there has been a surge of interest in North America in the work of Vygotsky. Of special interest were his claims that much transmission of information occurs in adult–child dyads in which more knowledgeable adults, such as parents and teachers, adjust their interactions with children to match the young-sters' understanding of the concepts being taught. At first the adult models and explains new skills and concepts and is largely responsible for control of the intellectual activity in the dyad. Control is gradually ceded to the child as he or she increases in competence; additional adult intervention is provided whenever the child falters. Hints and subtle cues can be provided if the child forgets to carry out some aspect of a procedure being learned; more complete reinstruction can be provided if the child has forgotten entirely the to-be-learned procedure or concept. Eventually the child can perform without assistance.

The metaphor of a scaffold has been proposed to describe this process, since a scaffold is erected at the outset of construction and gradually withdrawn as a building becomes self-supporting (Wood, Bruner, & Ross, 1976). Eventually, the entire scaffold is eliminated and no external support is required for the building to remain upright. [See Day, Cordon, and Kerwin (1989) for a clear explanation of this process.]

A large number of instructional interventions (Newman, Griffin, & Cole, 1989; Rogoff, 1990; Tharp & Gallimore, 1988) has been developed or in-terpreted in light of this Vygotskian analysis. The most prominent of these was reciprocal teaching of reading comprehension strategies.

Reciprocal Teaching

Reciprocal teaching includes instruction about four reading comprehen-sion strategies (questioning, prediction, summarizing, and clarifying), taught in a group including a teacher and students (Palincsar & Brown, 1984). The teacher and students take turns leading a discussion about a text they are reading. The leader begins by asking a question about the content of the text and later offers a summary. Discussion centers on dis-agreements about the content of summaries and clarification needs of the participants. Leaders conclude their turns by predicting future content. The teacher provides prompting and feedback throughout the process, responding as needed.

Presumably a lot of metacognitive information about when and where to use strategies occurs during the dialogues between participants. The social cooperative nature of the intervention is assumed to be especially motivating. The fact that other members of the group can provide help on an as-needed basis reduces frustration and increases task persistence.

Most of the evaluations of the method have been generated with populations of children (middle-school in the Palincsar & Brown studies; 4th grade and 7th grade in Lysynchuk, Pressley, & Vye, 1990) who are experiencing reading comprehension problems. The outcomes have been consistent across studies. A month of reciprocal teaching produces consistent moderate effects on comprehension (Rosenshine & Meisner, 1991), as long as care has been taken to make certain that students know how to execute the processes orchestrated in the package. A minority of children experience large gains (e.g., 15 or more percentile points on a standardized reading test); almost as many control children experience large gains (Brown & Palincsar, 1989; Lysynchuk *et al.,* 1990).

Interactive Teaching and Learning

The great visibility of reciprocal teaching as well as other interventions (e.g., Kamehameha School in Hawaii; Tharp & Gallimore, 1988) interpretable via Vygotskian theory has prompted a great deal of thinking about how instruction can occur in social situations and how scaffolding can be exploited to enhance various types of learning, including acquisition of strategies. One such attempt has been dubbed "interactive learning and teaching" by its developers.

Gallego and her colleagues (e.g., Chapter 7; Gallego, Duran, & Scanlon, 1990) are teaching children how to most benefit from discussions that can accompany reading. Gallego *et al.*'s approach promises to fit well into classroom settings because there are often opportunities to discuss material that is read, material students are expected to understand and remember.

In Gallego *et al.* (1990), students learned how to carry out dialogue to produce a semantic map of text being read. They were taught to use general-level questions to stimulate group comprehension processes (e.g., "Does this make sense?"). This amounted to teaching the coordinated use of a number of comprehension strategies aimed at relating prior knowledge to new ideas and identifying relationships between ideas.

> Students were encouraged to (a) activate prior knowledge by prompting each other to recall related past experiences; (b) tie new knowledge to old knowledge by connecting their related prior knowledge and experience to each

other and to new information provided by their peers or by the text; (c) predict relationships by hypothesizing how their ideas and those of the text related and prompted each other to identify alternatives; (d) utilize cooperative knowledge sharing by using others in their group as resources for information and consensus building; (e) teach concepts to their peers in relation to the organization of the semantic map or the passage; (f) justify relationships between and among concepts by explaining underlying reasons for their responses; and (g) confirm understanding by questioning their understanding to resolve misconceptions. (p. 6)

Semantic maps were constructed for five different social studies passages; one was presented for each of 5 wk. The students met for 40 min each day of the week to carry out the four parts of semantic mapping: brainstorming, constructing a clue list, constructing a map relating clues, and confirming their understanding of the map (Stahl & Vancil, 1986). The title of the passage was presented as a stimulus for the brainstorm; students were instructed to think of personal experiences and prior knowledge related to the topic of the passage. The group reviewed each candidate idea to determine its relevance to the topic. Students skimmed the passage to identify clue words (important vocabulary and concepts in the text). Students then predicted relationships between these clues; justifications of these predictions were generated by the students. Once there was agreement on predictions, students constructed the semantic map. The confirmation phase consisted of reading the passage, followed by review and revision of the semantic map by the group.

At first the group of 6 learning disabled children who participated in the study observed the teacher modeling strategies during construction of a semantic map. There was a gradual shift of control of the strategies from teacher to students. As expected, both the amount and quality of student communicative interactions increased from the beginning to the end of the instruction. In particular, the proportion of interactions related to the procedures being taught as part of the strategy increased substantially. The proportion of off-task behavior decreased. In addition, there was evidence of increased comprehension of passages as instruction proceeded. At the end of each week, students were required to generate individual essays about the passage read that week. Students were encouraged to put all they knew about the topic in the passage and not to be overly concerned with writing mechanics. The holistic quality of these essays improved from the first to the fifth week of the intervention.

Although not yet evaluated in true experiments, Gallego *et al.*'s (1990) treatment is conceptually interesting. In many ways the teaching resembles reciprocal teaching: a teacher models and explains a strategy at first and releases control of the strategy to students as they become more proficient with it. Multiple strategies are taught in groups of students. There is an emphasis on cooperative interaction in the group. Unlike reciprocal teaching, however, Gallego is trying to teach comprehension when interacting in a group and is explicitly concerned with understandings of text that develop via group processing. (In contrast, the goal in reciprocal teaching is autonomous comprehension of text by internalizing the processes once executed in a group.) Contemporary interest in group communicative processes should stimulate additional research on this intervention (e.g., O'Flahavan, 1989).

Meichenbaum's Self-Instructional Approach

Meichenbaum and Asarnow (1979) described a study conducted by Bommarito in which children were taught to instruct themselves to use particular comprehension strategies to process text. The self-instructions were in the form of questions posed to oneself to cue strategy use and performance monitoring. The students were also taught to reinforce themselves when they did well. Long-term use of instructed strategies and the associated comprehension increases in strategy-instructed children were assumed to be due to acquisition of the strategies in the context of a routine that focused students' attention on the performance gains produced by the strategies.

Although cognitive self-instruction interventions have been shown to facilitate acquisition of a variety of complex cognitive strategies relevant to both academic (e.g., writing) and clinical (e.g., anxiety reduction) goals, there has been surprisingly little study of them with respect to text processing, despite the promising start made by Bommarito. The work that has been done, however, suggests great potential for the approach.

Elliott-Faust and Pressley (1986) asked Grade 3 children to listen to stories, some of which contained inconsistencies. Their task was to spot these inconsistencies when they occurred. The students were taught two text processing strategies for this purpose: to compare adjacent sentences in the stories for consistency and to compare the meaning of the sentence just heard with the overall meaning of the passage. Students in a self-instructional condition were taught to orient themselves to the task by asking "What am I supposed to do?" They were taught to self-cue use of comparison strategies with "What's my plan?" and to ask themselves "Am I using my plan?" as they executed the strategies. This was to stimulate evaluation of their implementation of the procedures taught. Self-evaluation was encouraged by the self-question "How did I do?"

Elliott-Faust and Pressley's (1986) hypothesis was that teaching the two comparison strategies would increase detection of inconsistencies in text, but that maintenance of these strategies (i.e., using them 2 wk later on an occasion when they were not cued to do so) would be more likely for the group with the self-instructional intervention. The results were as expected.

Miller (1987) produced a very similar result when Grade 5 students read text in search of inconsistencies. The self-instructional condition participants in her study were provided instructions similar to the most instructionally complete condition in Elliott-Faust and Pressley (1986). As in the previous study, students taught to self-instruct detected more of the inconsistencies both immediately following instruction and after a delay (this time of 1 wk).

Borkowski and his colleagues have demonstrated that children with intellectual disabilities can be taught to self-instruct use of text-processing strategies. Borkowski and Varnhagen (1984) taught retarded children to use self-instruction with a paraphrase strategy applied to learning sentences. They were taught to begin a task by asking themselves "What am I supposed to do here?" and answer "I have to think of a way to remember these sentences." This instruction was followed by a self-probe designed to remind them to think of relevant strategies that might be applied to the task: "Okay, how can I do that?" They then responded by reiterating the direction to restate the sentences in their own words. Students constructed the paraphrase; self-generated reinforcement concluded the execution of the strategy (e.g., "Hey, that's very good"). Throughout instruction, the utility of the strategy was emphasized, with provision of a great deal of feedback about recall accuracy. As practice proceeded, adult cuing of the strategies decreased; students increasingly executed the strategies silently rather than overtly. In general, children so taught remembered more sentences both during instruction and on maintenance tests than did control children who did not receive the strategy instruction. Perhaps most critical is the result that, given the hypothesized effects of self-instruction on long-term and general use of strategies, 2 of the 6 children taught to paraphrase indicated that they used the strategy on a generalization task. This involved reading an entire story in preparation for a recall test; the self-instructional students reported attempting to paraphrase sentences in the story that was read.

A very impressive self-instructional intervention that combined strategy teaching, provision of metacognitive information, and input designed to enhance motivation to use strategies was developed by Kurtz and Borkowski (1987). Impulsive children were taught how to summarize text. This included analyzing the prose to identify a topic sentence and then constructing a summary around the main themes of the prose. The students were taught to ask themselves "What is this story (paragraph) about? What is the main idea in one word? What is the most important thing about the main idea? Why is that the main idea?" The children were also provided instruction about how the mind works. They learned that strategies are flexible, that strategy appropriateness is task specific, and that working slowly is often more important than completing a task quickly. Monitoring of strategy execution and strategy effects on performance were emphasized throughout instruction. Such extended teaching of summarization strategies improved prose recall more than a no-instruction control condition and a condition in which students received summarization instruction that was not embellished with self-instructional, metacognitive, or motivational components.

Graham (1986) also provided a study in which self-instruction of strategies improved performance on a complex reading task. Grades 5 and 6 poor and average readers participated in a true experiment that included a condition in which students were taught to self-instruct, a didactic teaching condition, and a no-instruction control group. The criterion task for all conditions was responding appropriately to comprehension questions requiring responses based on content explicitly stated in the text ("here" questions), information implicit in the text ("hidden" questions), or information that could be constructed on the basis of prior knowledge ("in-my-head" questions). Both of the instructed groups were taught explicitly to identify a question as either a "here," "hidden," or "in-my-head" question. Students in the self-instructional condition also learned to pose three self-questions to guide their answering of comprehension questions. The first focused attention on the task: How will I answer this question? The second reminded the student to categorize the question: What type of question is this? The third reminded students to check their answers: is my answer correct? Answering comprehension questions was clearly improved by self-instruction relative to the no-instruction control condition. Although the effect was not large, performance in the self-instruction condition also exceeded performance in the didactic condition, a significant main effect (i.e., collapsing over populations).

In short, reading interventions that include teaching children to self-instruct using questions have consistently improved performance on a variety of reading tasks. Studies analytical enough to isolate effects produced by self-questioning (Elliott-Faust & Pressley, 1986; Graham, 1986) have generally provided evidence that self-questioning per se is an active part of the self-instructional intervention mix. Teaching children to execute a sequence of self-questions permits coordination of several different processes—attention to the task, identification of the goal, use of one or more coding strategies, checking and monitoring—each of which contributes to skilled reading.

Summary

A great deal of progress has been made in identifying short-term interventions that encourage effective processing of text. All of these interventions encourage greater student activity. All of these treatments are based on models of cognitive development. Vygotskian and related Soviet positions have especially stimulated development and study of reciprocal teaching, interactive learning, and self-instruction. In all three approaches, operations that were originally social (i.e., involving teacher and student interaction) and external eventually are internalized and carried out covertly.

One view is that development of the full repertoire of skilled strategies that constitute skilled reading cannot be accomplished with short-term interventions. Thus, there has been increasing recognition and development of models of cognitive development and change that are decidedly long term in their emphasis. Scaffolding is at the heart of these interventions; the emphasis in these models is on how very long scaffolding must continue for internalization to occur. Effective long-term scaffolding involves long-term explanations of strategies.

LONG-TERM DIRECT EXPLANATION OF STRATEGIES

Multiple-year approaches to strategy instruction are now being developed and implemented in actual school settings (e.g., Bergman & Schuder, 1992; Gaskins & Eliott, 1991; Pressley, Goodchild, Fleet, Zajchowski, & Evans, 1989). These interventions usually involve explicit instruction of strategies; only a few are taught at a time. Explanations of each strategy are provided as their use is modeled for students. The explanations are rich in information about where and when to use the procedures taught; modeling and teacher commentaries are complemented by student practice of the strategies with materials similar to those to which students are expected to apply the newly learned strategies. Successful use of the strategies is expected to make the utility of the procedures obvious and to increase motivation to use them.

Duffy and Roehler's Direct Explanation of Strategies Using Mental Modeling

Duffy and colleagues (1987) generated an extremely well designed study (see Lysynchuk, Pressley, d'Ailly, Smith, & Cake, 1989) of the effects produced on Grade 3 reading performances by direct explanation of reading strategies. They taught Grade 3 teachers to explain directly the strategies and processes that are part of Grade 3 reading. Direct explanations included an initial explanation of the strategy, followed by mental modeling of the strategy being taught. Mental modeling entailed showing the students exactly how good readers would apply the strategy to reading (Duffy & Roehler, 1989). That is, the teacher revealed his or her reading processes in applying the strategy.

Thus, when teaching about story structures, students might be told, "When reading this story, I first look at setting, characters, and problem. I see that it is about . . ." (Duffy & Roehler, 1989, p. 221) Explanations were followed by guided student practice of the strategy. The students initially carried out the strategy overtly so that the teacher could monitor better their success with the strategy being taught. At first, the teacher provided a lot of assistance to students as they attempted to execute the strategy. This included re-explanations tailored to particular student difficulties. As the student gained proficiency in executing a strategy, control of strategy execution by the teacher was gradually released. That is, instruction was scaffolded.

Once students learned how to apply the strategies with materials used in reading class, they were explicitly instructed about transfer of the newly learned strategies. They were provided reminders to use the new strategies in other reading situations; information was provided by the teacher about tasks that would call for use of the strategies. When a strategy could be used in the school day, the teacher made obvious its relevancy. For example, story-structure strategies are useful not only during reading but when composing narratives as well. Their utility for composition would be explained and students would be cued to transfer story-structure strategies to composition tasks. Cuing and prompting of strategy use was continued until students readily applied the strategies that had been taught to appropriate tasks naturally encountered during the school day.

Duffy *et al.* (1987) found that a year of this type of instruction did have an impact on Grade 3 students. Students taught by teachers in the direct explanation condition were more aware of lesson content and of the strategic nature of reading than were students taught by teachers in a control condition in which teachers were taught classroom management strategies not directly related to reading comprehension. Most important, students in direct explanation classrooms outperformed students in classroom-management control classrooms on a variety of reading measures, including standardized reading achievement tests. Correlational data consistent with the experimenter outcomes were also reported; all evidence in the report converged on the conclusion that a full year of direct explanation of Grade 3 reading strategies and skills can have important consequences for reading achievement.

Benchmark School Approach

Gaskins and her colleagues at Benchmark School (e.g., Chapter 14; Gaskins & Elliott, 1991) have developed a multiple-year, multistrategy instructional intervention. This intervention has been under development for almost two decades as part of the instructional program for bright underachievers, the target population of this Philadelphia-area private school. Although there never has been a true experimental study of the curriculum, and probably never could be, it is easy to accept that the school is successful. For instance, most of their students arrive at the school not able to read at all, usually after experiencing 1 to 2 years of failure in regular education (i.e., most begin between age 7 and 9). Such students are at extremely high risk for long-term school failure, including eventual school dropout (e.g., Wagner, 1990). After an average of 4 years at Benchmark, most return to regular education and typically achieve at levels well within the normal range of achievement, with almost all eventually graduating from high school.

All of the comprehension strategies that have been validated as effective during the elementary years are represented in the curriculum. In general, teaching new strategies occurs a few at a time. The introduction of a strategy can take from 1 to 3 months; many opportunities to practice the strategy throughout the curriculum follow its introduction. The principle method of teaching is direct explanation; Duffy and Roehler's (1989) influence is apparent.

During 1989–1990, Pressley, Gaskins, and the research staff and teachers of Benchmark School collaborated on research designed to elucidate the nature of strategy instruction provided at the school. An extremely extensive interview study was completed (Pressley *et al.,* 1991a) as were several observational studies. The Benchmark approach proved to be similar to classical direct explanation instruction with some important differences. The differences are critical in explaining how strategy instruction can be adapted to classrooms.

One of the most important findings in Pressley *et al.*'s (1991a) interview study (involving the 31 academic teachers at Benchmark) was that teachers reported using all the components associated with direct explanation and scaffolded instruction of strategies. They model, explain, re-explain, fade instructional cuing, and encourage flexible use and transfer of strategies that are taught. It is very interesting, however, that teaching of a new strategy in the classroom does not proceed in a linear fashion from explicit instruction and modeling to reduced cuing to no cuing, a type of progression frequently observed when individual teachers interact with individual students (e.g., Rogoff, 1990). Rather, teachers report cuing during all phases of instruction. Teachers seem to attempt to respond to the needs of all children in the class. Since some students require explicit instruction and modeling throughout instruction, there is always some cuing of the strategies.

Instruction of a new strategy is always in the context of continuing instruction of other strategies. The teachers model how to use a new procedure in coordination with other procedures already introduced into the curriculum. It would be all but impossible to spend 30 min in a Benchmark

Table 1
A Benchmark School Teacher–Student Interaction about Task Analysis[a]

Teacher: Look at your grade first. That's the natural thing to do. Find out what you've got wrong. Look at it. Why? Because number one, if you're going to take a makeup, you don't want to make the same mistakes all over again. Alright, so if I was somebody who didn't like my grade, I'm going to circle the question, circle the part of the question I didn't understand or I didn't know the answer to, and I'm going to go home this weekend and . . . study that question specifically so that I do better the next time. Number two reason to find the right answer . . . we'll talk about the Pilgrims and Puritans again because we like to compare things. It makes everything easier if you understand Pilgrims, Puritans, and Jamestown real well. It's going to make the whole next chapter easier to understand . . . You want to be sure you understand as much as you can before you move on . . . What should you be thinking about?

Student: . . . you should write down on a piece of paper what you have wrong and work on it.

Student: You should really learn another way to study.

Teacher: Even I have had Fs. I didn't live with those Fs long because I analyzed things. Maybe I asked the teacher what I could be doing better . . . he's the guy giving me the test. He might have some insight on how to do well on his or her tests. So what I mainly have to do is find out why I didn't do as well as I should have. And, it probably has to do not with something wrong in my brain but with how I am studying. Do you think a person who didn't do very well . . . Is it because they didn't study long enough?

Student: No.

Teacher: Sure it could. Some of you may not have studied at all and that's why you did bad . . . What's the other possibility you didn't do well? . . .

Student: Because you didn't write it down.

Teacher: That could be part of it. Some people though took twenty pages of notes . . . and still . . . did badly. Why? What's another possible reason?

Student: Because you never understood. You never put it in your own words.

Teacher: It's possible you didn't put it in your own words. Another thing that could go wrong? . . . How can you tell if you really understand something?

Student: Well, when you ask yourself questions or you quiz yourself and you don't know all the answers.

Teacher: That's part if it . . .

---

[a]Benchmark School teacher is Jim Benedict.

classroom without observing at least one salient instance of this type of instruction. How this is accomplished is best described using an example.

The student-teacher interaction in Table 1 occurred while the teacher, Jim Benedict, was trying to teach students to analyze tasks they were attempting. Much of the discussion was about justifying task analysis but, as part of that discussion, Benedict mixed in discussion of comparing and contrasting strategies, note taking, paraphrasing, and seeking information from others. Student replies included mention of still other strategies including self-questioning.

Table 2
Strategies Covered by Mary Lee Bass in her January 16, 1990,
Reading Lesson at Benchmark School[a]

Organizing thinking while reading a text (including reorganizing a text as
    it is read)
Root word analysis of new vocabulary
Use of sentence context to infer meaning of new vocabulary
Flexibility in thinking
Surveying text before reading
Prior knowledge activation before reading a text
Prior knowledge activation while reading a text
Identifying the main ideas of text
Note taking, especially using key words
Predicting text content
Paying attention and being involved with text even when text is boring

---

[a]Processes are listed roughly in the order of introduction in the lesson.

How much process instruction can occur during a reading lesson can be appreciated by considering a group lesson led by Mary Lee Bass on January 16, 1990. The reading group studied an article on sneakers that day. The strategies covered as part of processing the text are summarized in Table 2. Although the main purpose of the lesson was to learn how to reorganize and reconceptualize text, a number of other processes were covered in response to demands of understanding the text. Thus, the students and teacher coordinated the use of a number of strategies as part of the lesson. One of the concerns frequently voiced by critics of strategy instruction is that content suffers when there is instructional emphasis on process. The fact that that is not the case with the type of strategy instruction conducted at Benchmark School can be appreciated by the summary of vocabulary covered during Ms. Bass' lesson (see Table 3). Moreover, vocabulary was not covered in isolation but as part of a discussion of interrelated concepts. Thus, heat-sensitive was covered both in the context of designing tennis shoes and with reference to the space shuttle. Commentary on the space shuttle permitted a minilesson on why heat-sensitive materials are needed on the space shuttle when it re-enters the atmosphere. In short, there is a rich mixture of strategy teaching, content coverage, and instruction of metacognition during strategy instruction at Benchmark School.

Recurring information about when strategies can be employed profitably should do much to increase the likelihood that students will understand when and where the strategies they are learning can be used. Practice using a strategy and variations of the strategy across the curriculum might be expected to be even more beneficial. Some Benchmark faculty are making special efforts to teach the same strategies with a variety of contents;

Table 3
Vocabulary Covered by Mary Lee Bass
during the January 16, 1990, Reading Lesson

identical	heat sensitive
mirror image	Olympians
absorb (two definitions)	Carl Lewis
cushioning	waste (as euphemism for
evaporate	foolish use of resources)

such demonstrations have high potential for convincing students that strategies can have general utility for them.

For example, Pressley, Gaskins, Wile, Cunicelli, and Sheridan (1991b) studied one head teacher (Deborah Wile) and her co-teacher (Jacqueline Sheridan) as they taught text-structure strategies (e.g., compare–contrast, cause–effect) as part of writing instruction, reading comprehension, and social studies. Thus, one school day in spring 1990 started with a half-hour of writing instruction. The students were in the midst of producing essays based on compare–contrast arguments. Most had completed first drafts and were spending the half-hour in interaction with a classmate who provided feedback about the adequacy of the essay. Those students who were experiencing difficulties producing a first draft were receiving additional instruction about compare and contrast argument structures and how to generate them. During reading class, each reading group read an expository article from *My Weekly Reader,* analyzing the article into a series of cause–effect arguments resulting in a semantic mapping of the article's content. During social studies, students constructed a compare–contrast chart for the colonies of Maryland and the Carolinas, one capturing the role of religion in the founding of colonies, the reasons colonies were established, the location of cities, the types of soil, the settlers in Maryland and the Carolinas, and the sizes of the grants establishing the two colonies.

Throughout the instructional day there was emphasis on the flexible application of the text-structure strategies. Thus, students were taught that many different essays could result from comparisons and contrasts, that many different cause-and-effect semantic mappings were possible for any text, and that modifications could be made to the chart about the colonies as the students saw fit. Students were provided many reminders about when and why they should use the text structure strategies (e.g., so that expository text would be remembered better, so that the similarities and differences in the colonies would be apparent).

In addition, throughout the day, other strategies were reviewed when the context permitted it. Thus, when a difficult word was encountered in the social studies reading, students strategically decoded it using a word identification strategy taught in another class. The room was filled with reminders about the strategies being learned, including wall posters detailing strategy components and the utility of each strategy. The process and content covered the previous day was probed explicitly at the start of each class. Classroom management was extremely efficient; transitions from task to task were very smooth. Disciplinary encounters were handled quickly and quietly.

Rather than rigidly following some particular set of materials, these teachers exploited materials as they were relevant to the instructional goals of the day. Thus, the *Weekly Reader* was only used on this day because it contained articles that could be analyzed using the text structures being taught.

Students were reinforced for their efforts. Teachers attributed successful performances to the strategies used by the students. The future usefulness of the procedures was highlighted whenever teachers had an opportunity to do so.

The Benchmark faculty believe that daily exposure to strategies, daily exposure to information about when and where and how to use strategies, and consistent strategy-mediated success are likely to lead to long-term commitments to the advanced processing approaches being taught at the school (Gaskins & Elliott, 1991). A day in Ms. Wile's class makes apparent that at least some strategies can be taught in the context of the ongoing curriculum and that teachers and students can work cooperatively to adopt strategies to different demands during the school day.

That instruction at Benchmark is very different from instruction in most other schools was especially obvious in a recent analysis of the discourse patterns in Benchmark classes (Gaskins, Anderson, Pressley, Cunicelli, & Satlow, 1991). Typical discussions in American classrooms are predominated by one discourse structure: the teacher initiates the interaction in the form of a question, a student responds, and the teacher evaluates (i.e., IRE cycles; Cazden, 1988; Mehan, 1985). In contrast, such cycles are rarely seen in Benchmark classrooms. Rather, the teachers stimulate the students to apply one or more of the strategic processes to the content being covered. When a student responds, the teacher's reaction is additional cuing to keep the processing going until the student successfully completes the original teacher request. There can be a number of turns in such cycles; scaffolding is provided by teachers as well as by students. These process–content cycles account for 70% of classroom interaction time in Gaskins *et al.* (1991).

Summary and Discussion

At the beginning of the 1980s, there was already work in which strategies were taught in packages that included metacognitive and motivational components. For example, Palincsar and Brown's initial studies of reciprocal teaching had been completed. At Benchmark and in other schools with process-oriented instruction (see Pressley *et al.,* 1991d), much more ambitious curriculum efforts were developed subsequently. Many more than four strategies were taught in these settings. Rather than using rigid sequences of strategies (e.g., invariant sequences of predicting, questioning, clarifying, and summarizing as during reciprocal teaching), at Benchmark there is great emphasis on flexible adaptation of the strategic repertoire. In short, direct explanation models of strategies instruction are strongly favored because they are designed to deliver a repertoire of strategies; instruction is conceived as extending over several academic years. Direct explanations emphasize that strategies are modifiable and should be modified by students. Teaching of strategies is also flexible; adjustments are made depending on student difficulties and needs. Metacognitive and motivational components are prominent in direct explanation. Moreover, direct explanation is proving to be a method that can be operationalized in school; Duffy and Roehler's work and the teaching at Benchmark School provide striking evidence that real teachers in real classrooms can come to understand direct explanation and teach in a direct explanation fashion.

Making a claim in favor of direct explanation does not discount the possibility of incorporating other procedures reviewed in this subsection into direct explanation instruction. For instance, Gallego *et al.*'s (1990) interactive learning and teaching has a direct explanation component and would be incorporated into curricula based on direct explanation rather easily. In all studies of self-instruction to date, this approach has been taught using direct explanation. It is easy to imagine such teaching fitting into settings like Benchmark School.

Our support of direct explanation should not be construed to mean that we are completely comfortable with the state of knowledge concerning the effects of direct explanation on academic performance. First, very little research has been aimed at elucidating the effects of direct explanation on long-term performance in school. In part, this is because most of these interventions are implemented over a very long period of time, making true experiments either expensive or impossible (e.g., family mobility alone makes it difficult to maintain samples of research participants in classrooms for periods of up to several years; schools require flexibility in shuffling students into new programs from time to time, so that it is impossible to maintain samples intact for long periods of time without infringing on the authority of schools to make the decisions they need to make to best serve their clients). Second, when research has been conducted, it usually has been by the developers of the particular approach being evaluated. Although we believe these researchers are honest and have no reason to doubt the data they have produced, evaluations by researchers other than the developers are desirable. Potential questions and issues that might be addressed in such research are considered in the general discussion that follows.

GENERAL DISCUSSION

This chapter has provided an overview of some of what is known about proficient reading, instruction that might promote proficient reading, and instruction that probably does not do so. Many suggestions for future research were presented.

The Nature and Prevalence of Proficient Reading

Our point of view is that much text processing, even that of well-educated adult readers, is less efficient and proficient than it could be. It has proven rather easy to document failures to use reading strategies and monitoring failures. More positively, some readers (e.g., our social scientist sample) are extremely strategic, at least some of the time. Much more needs to be known in order to establish who becomes strategic and who does not. Moreover, little is known about within-reader differences in strategy deployment, although studies like those of Pritchard (1990) are exceptions to this generalization. How readers approach different types of materials deserves intensive study. The highly strategic processing of exceptionally competent reading is generally unstudied.

Instruction That Increases Reading Proficiency

Can reading comprehension be improved through strategy teaching? During the last decade, a number of single strategies were identified that promote performance when taught alone, at least shortly after teaching has occurred. Nonetheless, it has become apparent that single strategy teaching is not well matched to the demands of complex reading, so single strategy teaching does not seem appropriate. The current hypothesis is that comprehension packages should include instruction of powerful strategies along with metacognitive information about where, when, and how to use the strategies. Attention to motivation is critical as well. Extended teaching across the curriculum and across years of schooling seems to be more successful than shorter-term, more narrow instruction.

Methods in Reading Proficiency Research

A major challenge for the 1990s will be to provide realistic and meaningful assessments of complex reading instruction. In the best of all possible worlds, these would be true experiments. When true experiments are not possible, other relevant comparisons must be considered. For instance, formal comparisons between Benchmark clients at the beginning and end of their Benchmark careers and groups of normally achieving students at corresponding points in their schooling could be very informative about the amount of academic gain produced by the Benchmark intervention. If the gap between normal and Benchmark students is much smaller in Grades 7 and 8 than in Grades 2 and 3, as informal analyses suggest, this would be powerful evidence in favor of the Benchmark process.

These multiple-year studies would be extremely expensive, but their cost seems worthwhile given the very high cost of implementation of such programs. In addition, such assessments can (and, in our view, should) include detailed analyses and descriptions of the components of these effective treatments. This type of information is critical if treatments are to be implemented at places other than their development sites. Thus, there are complementary roles for qualitative and quantitative research here.

In closing, we note that much of the way the argument was made in this chapter might be surprising to some readers, especially since one author has generally used experimental methodologies throughout most of his career. A pure experimental approach to reading instruction would be hard to defend in the 1990s, however. The experimental psychology of reading during the 1980s consisted largely of analyses of single strategies or single components (e.g., monitoring); not surprisingly, the instructional recommendations that followed from these analyses focused on the teaching of single strategies. A frequent observation was that strategy use did not transfer following teaching of single strategies. In retrospect, the failings of single strategy and single component instruction should not be surprising since skilled reading is definitely not the execution of single strategies. Skilled reading that reflects good information processing is a complex mix of procedures that operates in combination with prior knowledge. Skilled readers are interpretive while they read and experience affective reactions to the content of text.

Instruction mirroring skilled reading is possible. Again, qualitative analyses have been revealing on this point: the Benchmark faculty are constantly modeling complex interactions between strategies and prior knowledge. One big question is whether such instruction can produce the type of sophisticated reading that highly knowledgeable people perform when they are reading something interesting. That question will return us to experimental methodologies.

The critical point here is that we are contemplating such exciting experiments only because of the qualitative research experiences discussed in this chapter. The qualitative studies have both informed us about potential problems with models of reading inspired by the experimental analyses of the 1980s and inspired us to conduct experiments on potentially more adequate models of reading instruction. Such research is well worth doing. Be assured that the qualitative methodologies will occupy a prominent place in our methodological tool box, along with the experimental methodologies that have resided there for so long, as we seek ways to understand and advance good information processing.

REFERENCES

Afflerbach, P. P. (1990). The influence of prior knowledge on expert readers' main idea construction strategies. *Reading Research Quarterly, 25,* 31–46.

Alvermann, D. E., Bridge, C. A., Schmidt, B. A., Searfoss, L. W., Winograd, P., Bruce, B., Paris, S. G., Priestley, M., Priestley-Romero, M., and Santeusanio, R. P. (1988). *Heath reading.* Lexington, Massachusetts: Heath.

Applebee, A. N. (1984). *Contexts for learning to write.* Norwood, New Jersey: Ablex.

Applebee, A. N. (1986). Problems in process approaches: Toward a reconceptualization of process instruction. In A. R. Petrosky, D. Bartholomae, and K. J. Rehage (Eds.), *The teaching of writing: Eighty-fifth yearbook of the National Society for the Study of Education* (pp. 95–113). Chicago: University of Chicago Press.

Armbruster, B. B., Anderson, T. H., and Ostertag, J. (1987). Does text structure/summarization instruction facilitate learning from expository text? *Reading Research Quarterly, 22,* 321–346.

Baker, L., and Brown, A. L. (1984). Metacognitive skills and reading. In D. Pearson, R. Barr, M. Kamil, and P. Mosenthal (Eds.), *Handbook of reading research* (pp. 353–394). New York: Longman.

Baumann, J. E. (1984). Effectiveness of a direct instruction paradigm for teaching main idea comprehension. *Reading Research Quarterly, 20,* 93–108.

Bean, T. W., and Steenwyk, F. L. (1984). Effect of three forms of summarization instruction on sixth graders' summary writing and comprehension. *Journal of Reading Behavior, 16,* 297–306.

Bereiter, C., Scardamalia, M., Brown, A. L., Anderson, V., Campione, J. C., and Kintsch, W. (1989). *Open court reading and writing.* Lasalle, Illinois: Open Court.

Bergman, J., and Schuder, R. T. (1992). Teaching at-risk elementary school students to read strategically. *Educational Leadership.*

Berkowitz, S. J. (1986). Effects of instruction in text organization on sixth-grade students' memory for expository reading. *Reading Research Quarterly, 21,* 161–178.

Borkowski, J. G., and Varnhagen, C. K. (1984). Transfer of learning strategies. A contrast of self-instructional and traditional formats with EMR children. *American Journal of Mental Deficiency, 88,* 369–379.

Brown, A. L., and Palincsar, A. S. (1989). Guided, cooperative learning and individual knowledge acquisition. In L. B. Resnick (Ed.), *Knowing, learning, and instruction: Essays in honor of Robert Glaser* (pp. 393–451). Hillsdale, New Jersey: Erlbaum.

Cazden, C. B. (1988). *Classroom discourse.* Plymouth, New Hampshire: Heinemann Books.

Chiesi, L., Spilich, G. J., and Voss, J. F. (1979). Acquisition of domain-related information in relation to high and low domain knowledge. *Journal of Verbal Learning and Verbal Behavior, 18,* 257–273.

Cohen, J. (1988). *Statistical power analysis for the behavioral sciences* (2nd ed.). Hillsdale, New Jersey: Erlbaum.

Collins, C. (1991). Reading instruction that increases thinking abilities. *Journal of Reading, 34,* 510–516.

Dansereau, D. F. (1985). Learning strategy research. In J. W. Segal, S. F. Chipman, and R. Glaser (Eds.), *Thinking and learning skills* (Vol. 1, pp. 209–240). Hillsdale, New Jersey: Erlbaum.

Day, J. D., Cordon, L. A., and Kerwin, M. L. (1989). Informal instruction and development of cognitive skills: A review and critique of research. In C. B. McCormick, G. E. Miller, and M. Pressley (Eds.), *Cognitive strategy research: From basic research to educational applications* (pp. 83–103). New York: Springer-Verlag.

Dreher, M. J., and Guthrie, J. (1990). Cognitive processes in textbook search tasks. *Reading Research Quarterly, 25,* 323–339.

Duffy, G. G. (1990). *Creating authentic strategy learning.* Unpublished manuscript.

Duffy, G. G., and Roehler, L. R. (1989). *Improving classroom reading instruction: A decision-making approach* (2nd ed.). New York: Random House.

Duffy, G. G., Roehler, L. R., Sivan, E., Rackliffe, G., Book, C., Meloth, M., Vavrus, L., Wesselman, R., Putnam, J., and Bassiri, D. (1987). The effects of explaining the reasoning associated with using reading strategies. *Reading Research Quarterly, 22,* 347–368.

Durkin, D. (1979). What classroom observations reveal about reading comprehension instruction. *Reading Research Quarterly, 14,* 481–538.

Elliott-Faust, D. J., and Pressley, M. (1986). How to teach comparison processing to increase children's short- and long-term listening comprehension monitoring. *Journal of Education Psychology, 78,* 27–33.

Epstein, W., Glenberg, A. M., and Bradley, M. (1984). Coactivation and comprehension: Contributions of text variables to the illusion of knowing. *Memory & Cognition, 12,* 355–360.

Gallego, M. A., Duran, G. Z., and Scanlon, D. J. (1990). *Interactive teaching and learning: Facilitating learning disabled students' transition from novice to expert.* Paper presented at the annual meeting of the National Reading Conference, Austin, Texas.

Gambrell, L. B., and Bales, R. J. (1986). Mental imagery and the comprehension-monitoring performance of fourth- and fifth-grade poor readers. *Reading Research Quarterly, 21,* 454–464.

Gaskins, I. W., and Elliott, T. T. (1991). *The Benchmark model of strategy instruction: A manual for teachers.* Cambridge, Massachusetts: Brookline Books.

Gaskins, I. W., Anderson, R. C., Pressley, M., Cunicelli, E., and Satlow, E. (1991). *The moves and cycles of cognitive process instruction at Benchmark School.* Technical Report. Media, Pennsylvania: Benchmark School.

Glenberg, A. M., and Epstein, W. (1985). Calibration of comprehension. *Journal of Experimental Psychology: Learning, Memory, and Cognition, 11,* 702–718.

Glenberg, A. M., Wilkinson, A. C., and Epstein, W. (1982). The illusion of knowing: Failure in the self-assessment of comprehension. *Memory & Cognition, 10,* 597–602.

Graham, L. J. (1986). *The comparative effectiveness of didactic teaching and self-instructional training of a question-answering strategy in enhancing reading comprehension.* Master's thesis. Simon Fraser University, Department of Education, Burnaby, British Columbia.

Guthrie, J. T. (1988). Locating information in documents: Examination of a cognitive model. *Reading Research Quarterly, 23,* 178–199.

Guthrie, J. T., and Mosenthal, P. (1987). Literacy as multidimensional: Locating information and reading comprehension. *Educational Psychologist, 22,* 279–297.

Harris, A. J., and Sipay, E. R. (1985). *How to increase reading ability: A guide to developmental and remedial methods.* New York: Longman.

Idol, L. (1987). Group story mapping: A comprehension strategy for both skilled and unskilled readers. *Journal of Learning Disabilities, 20,* 196–205.

Jacobs, J. E., and Paris, S. G. (1987). Children's metacognition about reading: Issues in definition, measurement, and instruction. *Educational Psychologist, 22,* 255–278.

Jenkins, J. R., Heliotis, J., Stein, M. L., and Haynes, M. (1987). Improving reading comprehension by using paragraph restatements. *Exceptional Children, 54,* 54–59.

124   *Michael Pressley* et al.

Jones, B. F., Amiran, M., and Katims, M. (1985). Teaching cognitive strategies and text structures within language arts programs. In J. W. Segal, S. F. Chipman, and R. Glaser (Eds.), *Thinking and learning skills. Relating instruction to research* (Vol. 1, pp. 259–295). Hillsdale, New Jersey: Erlbaum.

Kurtz, B. E., and Borkowski, J. G. (1987). Metacognition and the development of strategic skills in impulsive and reflective children. *Journal of Experimental Child Psychology, 43,* 129–148.

Lundberg, M. A. (1987). Metacognitive aspects of reading comprehension: Studying understanding in legal case analysis. *Reading Research Quarterly, 22,* 407–432.

Lysynchuk, L. M., Pressley, M., d'Ailly, J., Smith, M., and Cake, H. (1989). A methodological analysis of experimental studies of comprehension strategy instruction. *Reading Research Quarterly, 24,* 458–470.

Lysynchuk, L. M., Pressley, M., and Vye, N. J. (1990). Reciprocal instruction improves standardized reading comprehension performance in poor grade-school comprehenders. *Elementary School Journal, 90.*

Maki, R. H., and Berry, S. L. (1984). Metacomprehension of text material. *Journal of Experimental Psychology: Learning, Memory, and Cognition, 10,* 663–679.

Martin, V. L., and Pressley, M. (1991). Elaborative interrogation effects depend on the nature of the question. *Journal of Educational Psychology, 83,* 113–119.

Mayer, R. E. (1986). Teaching students how to think and learn: A look at some instructional programs and the research: A review of J. W. Segal, S. F. Chipman, & R. Glaser's (1985) *Thinking and learning skills.* Vol. 1: *Relating instruction to research* and S. F. Chipman, J. W. Segal, & R. Glaser's (1985) *Thinking and learning skills.* Vol. 2: *Research and open questions. Contemporary Psychology, 31,* 753–756.

Mehan, H. (1985). The structure of classroom discourse. In T. A. van Dijk (Ed.), *Handbook of discourse analysis. Discourse and dialogue* (Vol. 3, pp. 120–131). Orlando, Florida: Academic Press.

Meichenbaum, D., and Asarnow, J. (1979). Cognitive-behavior modification and metacognitive development: Implications for the classroom. In P. Kendall and S. Hollon (Eds.), *Cognitive behavioral interventions: Theory, research, and procedures* (pp. 11–35). New York: Academic Press.

Miller, G. E. (1987). The influence of self-instruction on the comprehension monitoring performance of average and above average readers. *Journal of Reading Behavior, 19,* 303–317.

Moely, B. E., Hart, S. S., Santulli, K., Leal, L., Johnson, T., Rao, N., and Burney, L. (1986). How do teachers teach memory skills? *Educational Psychologist, 21,* 55–72.

Newman, D., Griffin, P., and Cole, M. (1989). *The construction zone: Working for cognitive change in school.* New York: Cambridge University Press.

Nolte, R. Y., and Singer, H. (1985). Active comprehension: Teaching a process of reading comprehension and its effects on reading achievement. *The Reading Teacher, 39,* 24–31.

Oakhill, J., and Garnham, A. (1988). *Becoming a skilled reader.* Oxford: Blackwell.

O'Flahavan, J. F. (1989). *Second graders' social, intellectual, and affective development in varied group discussions about literature: An exploration of participation structure.* Ph.D. Thesis. University of Illinois Department of Early Childhood and Elementary Education, Champaign.

Palincsar, A. M., and Brown, A. L. (1984). Reciprocal teaching of comprehension-fostering and -monitoring activities. *Cognition and Instruction, 1,* 117–175.

Paris, S. G., and Jacobs, J. E. (1984). The benefits of informed instruction for children's reading awareness and comprehension skills. *Child Development, 55,* 2083–2093.

Paris, S. G., and Oka, E. R. (1986). Children's reading strategies, metacognition, and motivation. *Developmental Review, 6,* 25–56.

Paris, S. G., Cross, D. R., and Lipson, M. J. (1984). Informed strategies for learning: A program to improve children's reading awareness and comprehension. *Journal of Educational Psychology, 76,* 1239–1252.

Peters, E. E., and Levin, J. R. (1986). Effects of a mnemonic imagery strategy on good and poor readers' prose recall. *Reading Research Quarterly, 21,* 179–192.

Pichert, J. A., and Anderson, R. C. (1977). Taking different perspectives on a story. *Journal of Educational Psychology, 69,* 309–315.

Pressley, M. (1976). Mental imagery helps eight-year-olds remember what they read. *Journal of Educational Psychology, 68,* 355–359.

Pressley, M., and Ghatala, E. S. (1988). Delusions about performance on multiple-choice comprehension tests. *Reading Research Quarterly, 23,* 454–464.

Pressley, M., Cariglia-Bull, T., and Snyder, B. L. (1984). Are there programs that can really teach thinking and learning skills? A review of Segal, Chipman, & Glaser's *Thinking and learning skills,* Vol. 1, *Relating instruction to research. Contemporary Education Research, 3,* 435–444.

Pressley, M., Borkowski, J. G., and Schneider, W. (1987a). Cognitive strategies: Good strategy users coordinate metacognition and knowledge. In R. Vasta and G. Whitehurst (Eds.), *Annals of child development* (Vol. 5, pp. 89–129). New York: JAI.

Pressley, M., McDaniel, M. A., Turnure, J. E., Wood, E., and Ahmad, M. (1987b). Generation and precision of elaboration: Effects on intentional and incidental learning. *Journal of Experimental Psychology: Learning, Memory, and Cognition, 13,* 291–300.

Pressley, M., Snyder, B. L., Levin, J. R., Murray, H. G., and Ghatala, E. S. (1987c). Perceived readiness for examination performance (PREP) produced by initial reading of text and text containing adjunct questions. *Reading Research Quarterly, 22,* 219–236.

Pressley, M., Symons, S., McDaniel, M. A., Snyder, B. L., and Turnure, J. E. (1988). Elaborative interrogation facilitates acquisition of confusing facts. *Journal of Educational Psychology, 80,* 268–278.

Pressley, M., Borkowski, J. G., and Schneider, W. (1989a). Good information processing: What it is and how education can promote it. *International Journal of Educational Research, 13,* 857–867.

Pressley, M., Goodchild, F., Fleet, J., Zajchowski, R., and Evans, E. D. (1989b). The challenges of classroom strategy instruction. *Elementary School Journal, 89,* 301–342.

Pressley, M., Johnson, C. J., Symons, S., McGoldrick, J. A., and Kurita, J. (1989c). Strategies that improve memory and comprehension of what is read. *Elementary School Journal, 90,* 3–32.

Pressley, M., Ghatala, E. S., Woloshyn, V. E., and Pirie, J. (1990a). Sometimes adults miss the main ideas in text and do not realize it: Confidence in responses to short-answer and multiple-choice comprehension questions. *Reading Research Quarterly, 25,* 232–249.

Pressley, M., Wood, E., and Woloshyn, V. (1990b). Elaborative interrogation and facilitation of fact learning: Why having a knowledge base is one thing and using it quite another. In W. Schneider and F. E. Weinert (Eds.), *Interactions among aptitudes, strategies, and knowledge in cognitive performance* (pp. 200–221). New York: Springer-Verlag.

Pressley, M., Gaskins, I. W., Cunicelli, E. A., Burdick, N. J., Schaub-Matt, M., Lee, D. S., and Powell, N. (1991a). Strategy instruction at Benchmark School: A faculty interview study. *Learning Disability Quarterly, 14,* 19–48.

Pressley, M., Gaskins, I. W., Wile, D., Cunicelli, E. A., and Sheridan, J. (1991b). Teaching literacy strategies across the curriculum: A case study at Benchmark School. In S. McCormick and J. Zutell (Eds.), *40th yearbook of the National Reading Conference.* Chicago: National Reading Conference.

Pressley, M., Ghatala, E. S., Pirie, J., and Woloshyn, V. E. (1991c). Being really, really certain you know the main idea doesn't mean you do. In J. Zutell and S. McCormick (Eds.), *39th yearbook of the National Reading Conference* (pp. 249–256). Chicago: National Reading Conference.

Pressley, M., El-Dinary, P. B., Gaskins, I. W., Schuder, T. L., Bergman, J. L., Almasi, J., and Brown, R. (1991d). Direct explanation done well: Transactional instruction of reading comprehension strategies. *Elementary School Journal.*

Pressley, M., Wood, E., Woloshyn, V. E., Martin, V., King, A., and Menke, D. (1992b). Encouraging mindful use of prior knowledge: Attempting to construct explanatory answers facilitates learning. *Educational Psychologist.*

Pritchard, R. (1990). The effects of cultural schemata on reading processing strategies. *Reading Research Quarterly, 25,* 273–295.

Rinehart, S. D., Stahl, S. A., and Ericson, L. G. (1986). Some effects of summarization training on reading and studying. *Reading Research Quarterly, 21,* 422–438.

Rogoff, B. (1990). *Apprenticeship in thinking: Cognitive development in social context.* New York: Oxford University Press.

Rosenshine, B., and Meisner, C. (1991). *Ten experimental studies which used reciprocal teaching: A review of research.* Paper presented at the annual meeting of the American Educational Research Association, Chicago.

Schallert, D. L., and Tierney, R. J. (1980). *Learning from expository text: The interaction of text structure with reader characteristics* (Report No. 79-0167, ERIC Document Reproduction Services No. ED 221 833). Washington, D.C.: National Institute of Education.

Schallert, D. L., Alexander, P. A., and Goetz, E. T. (1988). Implicit instruction of strategies for learning from text. In C. E. Weinstein, E. T. Goetz, and P. A. Alexander (Eds.), *Learning and study strategies: Issues in assessment, instruction, and evaluation* (pp. 193–214). Orlando, Florida: Academic Press.

Short, E. J., and Ryan, E. B. (1984). Metacognitive differences between skilled and less skilled readers: Remediating deficits through story grammar and attribution training. *Journal of Educational Psychology, 76,* 225–235.

Snyder, B. L., and Pressley, M. (1990). *What do adults do when studying for a test with unpredictable questions?* Technical Report. London, Canada: University of Western Ontario, Department of Psychology.

Spilich, G. J., Vesonder, G. T., Chiesi, H. L., and Voss, J. F. (1979). Text-processing of domain-related information for individuals with high and low domain knowledge. *Journal of Verbal Learning and Verbal Behavior, 18,* 275–290.

Stahl, S. A., and Vancil, S. J. (1986). Discussion is what makes semantic maps work in vocabulary instruction. *The Reading Teacher, 40,* 62–67.

Symons, S., and Pressley, M. (1990). *Evaluation of Guthrie's model of search in a text domain.* Paper presented at the annual meeting of the American Educational Research Association, Boston.

Taylor, B. M. (1982). Text structure and children's comprehension and memory for expository material. *Journal of Educational Psychology, 74,* 323–340.

Taylor, B. M., and Beach, R. W. (1984). The effects of text structure instruction on middle-grade students' comprehension and production of expository prose. *Reading Research Quarterly, 19,* 134–146.

Tharp, R. G., and Gallimore, R. (1988). *Rousing minds to life: Teaching, learning, and schooling in social context.* New York: Cambridge University Press.

Thompson, A. G. (1985). Teachers' conceptions of mathematics and the teaching of problem solving. In E. A. Silver (Ed.), *Teaching and learning mathematical problem solving* (pp. 281–294). Hillsdale, New Jersey: Erlbaum.

Tuinman, J. J., Newman, M., and Rich, S. (1988). *Journeys.* Toronto: Ginn.

Voss, J. F., Vesonder, G. T., and Spilich, G. J. (1980). Text generation and recall by high-knowledge and low-knowledge individuals. *Journal of Verbal Learning and Verbal Behavior, 19,* 651–667.

Vygotsky, L. S. (1978). *Mind in society: The development of higher psychological processes.* Cambridge, Massachusetts: Harvard University Press.

Wade, S. E., Trathen, W., and Schraw, G. (1990). An analysis of spontaneous study strategies. *Reading Research Quarterly, 25,* 147–166.

Wagner, M. (1990). *School programs and school performance of secondary students classified as learning disabled: Findings from the national longitudinal transition study of special education students.* Menlo Park, California: SRI International.

Weinstein, C. E., and Underwood, V. L. (1985). Learning strategies: The *how* of learning. In J. W. Segal, S. F. Chipman, and R. Glaser (Eds.), *Thinking and learning skills. Relating research to instruction* (Vol. 1, pp. 241–258). Hillsdale, New Jersey: Erlbaum.

Woloshyn, V. E., Willoughby, T., Wood, E., and Pressley, M. (1990). Elaborative interrogation and representational imagery facilitate adult learning of facts presented in paragraphs. *Journal of Educational Psychology.*

Wood, D., Bruner, J. S., and Ross, G. (1976). The role of tutoring in problem-solving. *Journal of Child Psychology and Psychiatry, 17,* 89–100.

Wood, E., Pressley, M., and Winne, P. H. (1990). Elaborative interrogation effects on children's learning of factual content. *Journal of Educational Psychology, 82,* 741–748.

4

Reading Comprehension as a Conversation with an Author

Timothy Shanahan

Marley was dead, to begin with. There is no doubt whatever about that. The register of his burial was signed by the clergyman, the clerk, the undertaker, and the chief mourner. Scrooge signed it. And Scrooge's name was good upon 'Change for anything he chose to put his hand to.
Old Marley was as dead as a door-nail. . . . How could it be otherwise?

A Christmas Carol
Charles Dickens

There are texts and readers, to begin with. There is no doubt whatever about that. The warrant of this was signed by the cognitive psychologist, the curriculum designer, the education professor, and the basal reader publisher. The International Reading Association proclaimed it. And its name was good upon 'Change for anything it chose to put its hand to.

There are texts and there are readers. . . . How could it be otherwise?

Yet in Dicken's tale, Marley isn't dead, not in the common sense of the word; at least his spirit walks the land. In our tale, the one about reading comprehension, there may be more to it than texts and readers; maybe we need to consider the role of authors, too. This chapter will explore the idea that reading comprehension instruction should foster a sense of reading as a conversation between readers and authors.

For most of the past two decades, reading researchers have pursued a number of worthwhile cognitive questions about how individuals comprehend text. These studies have most often pursued comprehension from a problem-solving framework (Anderson & Pearson, 1984; McNamara, Miller, & Bransford, 1991). Such studies have explored the role of reader's topic knowledge (Anderson & Pearson, 1984), issues of memory (Loftus, 1979), problem-solving strategies (Tierney & Cunningham, 1984), and so on, or they have explored the implications of various structural features of text, such as organization (Graesser, Golding, & Long, 1991), coherence (Halliday & Hasan, 1976), and vocabulary (Beck & McKeown, 1991). The empirical problem of reading comprehension has been treated largely as one in which active learners analyze and manipulate linguistic or textual objects with little, if any, regard for the sources of texts or for authors' intentions.

As a result of these approaches, researchers and educators have made a number of claims about the nature of the psychological act of reading and the goals of instruction that omit considerations of the person creating the text. The Aristotelian triangle (author, audience, topic) has been reduced effectively to a straight line! It is my contention that this reduction has led to a conception of reading comprehension that is woefully inadequate, as well as to the neglect of some effective reading comprehension strategies.

A SOCIAL CONCEPTION OF READING COMPREHENSION

Pressley, El-Dinary, and Brown (Chapter 3) posited a framework for thinking about reading comprehension and comprehension instruction. That framework included strategies, metacognition, motivation, and knowledge. How would these components be conceptualized in a social communications approach to reading comprehension? This chapter will explore each of these components of the reading process from a social communication stance. Before doing so, however, it would be useful to redefine reading comprehension from a social communication perspective and to consider some of the problems inherent in such an approach.

The nature of reading comprehension has long been a topic of debate. The controversies generally have turned on the different conceptions of meaning. Is meaning contained in a text (Richards, 1929), is it constructed by individual readers (Anderson & Pearson, 1984), or is it the creation of discourse communities (Fish, 1980)? Is it synonymous with authors' intentions (Hirsch, 1967)? Although such disputes are far from resolution, recent treatments of reading comprehension have proceeded as though meaning were the result of some type of interaction between reader and text.

One way to think about these controversies is to consider what a person would need to know about a text to understand it fully. Consider the following paragraph, for instance.

> I am keeping this journal because I believe myself to be in some danger and because I have no other way of recording my fears. I cannot report them to the police, as you will see, and I cannot confide in my friends. The losses I have recently suffered in self-esteem, reasonableness, and charity are conspicuous, but there is always some painful ambiguity about who is to blame. I might be to blame myself. Let me give you an example. Last night I sat down to dinner with Cora, my wife, at half past six. Our only daughter has left home,

and we eat, these days, in the kitchen, off a table ornamented with a goldfish bowl. The meal was cold ham, salad, and potatoes. When I took a mouthful of salad I had to spit it out. "Ah, yes," my wife said. "I was afraid that would happen. You left your lighter fluid in the pantry, and I mistook it for vinegar." (Cheever, 1978, p. 567)

What would constitute an understanding of this text? Some readers might be satisfied with a factual repetition of the information contained in it. "It is about a man and his wife Cora. The man keeps a journal. He is afraid, but he is uncertain of the source of his fear." Others might require some kind of factual inference. "This is about a man who thinks his wife might be trying to kill him, but he isn't sure. He is too embarrassed to tell anyone what's going on." Still others might desire some type of personal response or interpretation. "I've felt just like he does. Once I thought my boss really hated me and wanted me to quit, but then I figured out he was just gruff with everybody and that he didn't mean anything by it. . . . Who would eat with a goldfish bowl on the table? That's disgusting."

Each of these readings, although different, is quite acceptable. What happens, though, if we ask readers to consider the author as well as the propositional information in the text and their own background knowledge? "I think this is probably meant to be a story. . . . Wouldn't it be horrible if this was true? . . . The author is using this paragraph to tell me about the main character, but I don't think he really wants me to believe that the character is in real danger; the example is too ludicrous." Another response: "Oh, I love Cheever. His first paragraphs are always grabbers. I prefer him to Updike because I always feel, like in this paragraph, that there is some suspense . . . that something might actually happen to these people; that his wife might actually kill him or he might kill himself."

These author-oriented interpretations of the text seem as adequate and useful as the textually or personally oriented interpretations presented earlier. Consideration of author intentions, craft, and voice are fruitful interpretive tools that help us look deeper into a text to construct a richer meaning. Evaluations of an author's truthfulness and prejudices are useful as well.

Of course, there are many good philosophical reasons to "kill off" the author when considering reading comprehension. Literary theorists (Brooks & Warren, 1938; Rosenblatt, 1978), hermeneuticists (Gadamer, 1975), and deconstructionists (Foucault, 1979) have striven long and hard to free "meaning," or at least interpretation, from the bonds of author intentions. Texts, of course, can carry meanings for a reader that never occurred to the author. Text, because of the life that goes on around it, can end up with historical, literary, and social implications deeper and more complex than any the author possibly could have conceived (Warnke, 1987).

Certainly, to confuse "meaning" for author's intentions would be a mistake. That neither prevents readers from considering authors nor limits the value of such considerations. This chapter will not attempt to resolve the ancient philosophical issues concerning the nature of meaning and the role of author intentions. Instead, it will describe how readers use their conceptions of author strategically and metacognitively in ways that can enhance comprehension and interpretation, and it will suggest how conceptualizing reading as a dialogue between reader and author can increase understanding and appreciation.

THE CONTEXT OF READING AND AWARENESS OF AUTHORS

Before considering the issues of knowledge, strategy, metacognition, and motivation it would be useful to briefly think about how author awareness might be instantiated with different types of texts or under a variety of reader purposes. Although there are many ways of classifying texts, for our purposes I will focus only on the most general, and consequently the most widely used, divisions: fiction and fact.

Authors of fiction have attempted over the last century to obscure their appearances in their works (Booth, 1983). Stories can "tell," but novels and short stories have increasingly attempted to show rather than tell; reading has become an act of entering into a world that seems to offer direct experiences without noticeable author intervention. However, as Booth (p. 149) points out, an "author cannot choose to avoid rhetoric; he can choose only the kind of rhetoric he will employ." Authors may be less likely to pose themselves as narrators or to provide direct commentary on what they are doing in their stories, but they still use various author-revealing devices for communicating voice, tone, and point of view.

Booth provides what remains the best analysis of the devices that authors use to speak directly to readers. He indicates four important personages involved in the creation and interpretation of any story: the author, the implied author, the reader, and the implied reader. The author is the real flesh-and-bones person who composed the story. The implied author refers to the writer's persona that is created and communicated in the story. The reader is a real person, whereas the implied reader is the audience that must have been assumed by the writer in laying out the tale. The author and reader are real and the implied author and reader are fictions created to communicate a story effectively. Booth indicates that the reader must be positively inclined affectively toward the implied author if the text is to be viewed positively or sympathetically. According to this view, one of the reader's most central responsibilities is to recognize the implied author and his or her points of view, attitudes, and biases. It is not essential that the reader consider the actual author (although, at least in some cases, this may be necessary), but to understand the art of the story fully the reader must develop some sense of the relationship between the real and implied authors, that is, the reader should try to understand how the implied author is having an effect on the readers. "As we read any literary work, we necessarily create a fiction or metaphor of its author. The author is perhaps our myth, but the experience of literature partly depends on that myth" (Rosenberg & Bloom, 1990).

Rabinowitz (1987) extends this formulation by considering the notion of implied readers or "authorial audiences" more thoroughly. He, too, rejects the notion that readers should seek the real author's private psyche through the text, but he argues that it is essential that we consider the author's decisions in our reading. "We can experience the ebb and flow of a text—its resolutions and surprises, its climaxes and anticlimaxes—only if we assume while reading that the author has control over its shape" (p. 118). He demonstrates the importance of considering the assumptions that the author made about who we are, what we know, and what we believe if we are to resist the ideological or political influence of the text.

Fiction, of course, *can* be read with only an eye to the plot and characters and little (conscious) consideration of the author. However, a sense of the author, real and implied, permits the reader to analyze how a text is exerting its influence. Readers who recognize text as a set of author's choices are more likely to appreciate the craft of the story. Readers who can effectively distinguish author, narrator, and characters are more likely to be aware of stance and tone and to recognize irony and other literary tools. Readers who are aware of the author's position and the sources of the author's information (such as interior views of characters, information from omniscient sources, and so on) are better able to evaluate the qualities of characters and to appreciate the twists of plot.

Exposition works differently in detail, but not in substance. Readers look to the author in different ways and for somewhat different purposes, but they look to the author, nevertheless. Contrary to this assertion, it has been claimed (Gibson, 1969) that the author's persona is not an issue when reading expository works. Gibson suggests that little or no sense of authorship is needed when reading newspaper articles or social science research studies. He bases his view on the fact that, in such texts, the author adopts a corporate voice of authority that provides the illusion that there is no author. However, although authorship is obscured in such sources, its importance is not diminished.

When reading factual material from a newspaper article or a research journal, it is important to consider whether the implied authority is appropriate or whether it is a mask used to hide ignorance or bias. These authors do not do away with a persona; they simply attempt to "join" in a powerful voice that can appear to be beyond question. Obviously, effective readers of the columns that appear on the op–ed page of the *New York Times* consider carefully whether an author is a liberal or conservative, a Democrat or Republican, a representative of a special interest group, or a man or woman. In such cases, readers are trying to understand why the author is taking a particular position. This behavior is to be expected when reading editorials. However, the best readers must consider similar issues when reading news stories as well. Although such stories might attempt to be accurate representations of facts, the facts that are used and how they are assembled can be shaped by author bias and belief. The effective reader wonders why the author has selected these points or chosen to talk with these informants. Examining the author in such a case is a test of prejudice and veracity. The reader of fiction seeks author persona and attitude to interpret the work, whereas the reader of fact considers an author's bias and authority part of critical reading. Both readers consider who has constructed the text and the choices that person made in doing so, although they do this in different ways and toward different ends.

Type of text is only one aspect of the context of reading; reader purpose is a central issue, too. A reader *can* obviously read without thinking about author; such thinking will not help much with some goals. I can immerse myself in reading a novel, focusing entirely on the characters and story line, and I can read a feature in the newspaper with no consideration of who wrote it. Of course, reading in that way, I might not grasp the significance of the novel fully or appreciate its art, or gain a feeling of social connection through the author's voice, or I might be misled by the author's bias.

"We care a lot about the authorship in a confession, but we care little about it in a catalog" (J. T. Guthrie, personal communication). Certainly authorship does not matter equally with all types of reading. Some texts are even produced to appear as if there were no authors at all. "In summer there are hosts of small books or pamphlets giving information on cheap holidays, camping sites, farmhouse accommodations, and so on; some of these publications do not even have a named author." (Mann, 1982, p. 50) I wonder if these reading experiences are as authorless as they first appear and, if so, at what cost. Certainly, many compendiums attempt to provide a very personal authorship (such as a Julia Child or "Frugal Gourmet" cookbook); critics have noted the power and effectiveness of gardening catalogs that speak with a clear authorial voice (White, 1979). When I want to follow a recipe or place an order, I care very little about authorship and I certainly do not use it for interpretive purposes (although, by this point, I have accepted or taken for granted the author's accuracy and authority). However, the cookbooks that I languor over are those that give me some sense of the author's joy in discoveries and accomplishment, rather than those that simply specify the ingredients and directions.

For the purposes of this chapter, it is assumed that there are a variety of reasons for considering the author and a variety of useful ways to do so. Author awareness can be a tool of interpretation, a method of critical analysis, a source of appreciation, or an avenue to enjoyment. We are not necessarily interested in the actual author as much as in the author's voice and place in the text, although considering the relationship of real and implied authors can be a useful technique for gaining a deeper understanding of a text. Children might need to think about real authors before they can deal with their mythical counterparts. The ways in which author awareness is used will vary according to circumstances including types of text read and reader's purposes.

Knowledge

Many studies of reading comprehension have focused on the role of reader knowledge. Readers use their knowledge to disambiguate confusion (Rumelhart, 1980), to generate necessary inferences (Clark & Haviland, 1977), to guide the use of cognitive resources (Goetz, Schallert, Reynolds, & Radin, 1983), and to facilitate the storage and retrieval of information in memory (Pichert & Anderson, 1977). One type of knowledge, domain knowledge or knowledge of the world (Perfetti, 1985), has been the focus of many of these studies. Typically, such research has shown the facilitative effects of knowledge about such topics as baseball, physics, Indian wedding ceremonials, and clothes washing on the ability to read and remember texts written on these topics. When readers know about the topic of a text, their reading comprehension is affected, usually positively (Anderson & Pearson, 1984).

The consideration of author intentions obviously requires a knowledge of people, their motives, and social interactions. However, the role of such social knowledge in reading has rarely been emphasized in empirical studies. Generally, the few studies that have been conducted have demonstrated that those people with the greatest awareness of human intentions and the most complex understandings of social interaction are the most sophisticated readers. These studies, however, have usually considered character intentions rather than author purposes. For example, Gruenich and Trabasso (1981) found that, as readers grow older, they increasingly consider characters' intentions, instead of their behaviors, in interpretations of text. Golden and Guthrie (1986), in an examination of ninth graders, found that empathy for characters was positively implicated in interpretation. If fact, they found that those who empathized with the narrator interpreted the story's theme differently than did those who empathized with the main character.

In another study, it was found that the cognitive complexity of reader judgments of the interpersonal aspects of characters was related to similar judgments of their peers (Hynds, 1989). Also, those with the greatest knowledge of interpersonal relationships read the most (Hynds, 1985). "An understanding of characters' motives and underlying psychological states is related to social cognitive knowledge formed through interactions in the social world. As readers develop interpersonal knowledge through their relationships with others, they learn to make attributions about the psychological states and behaviors of literary characters" (Beach & Hynds, 1991, pp. 466–467).

Some evidence suggests that such interpersonal knowledge and awareness of psychological states is used by readers when thinking about authors, too. McGee (1983) found that, with development, readers learned more reasons that authors write and developed more thorough conceptions of author intentions to communicate social information. The awareness of potential intentions is an important interpretive tool.

Consider, for example, the interview I conducted with my own daughter, Meagan, when she was 5 years old. At that point she had been read to almost daily since birth; she herself could read books at a high first-grade level. On the day of the interview she brought home a big stack of books from the local library including one expository text about baby wolves and how they live, and a storybook in which two best friends fight and make up. I read these books to her and conducted the interview printed in Table 1.

Initially, she had difficulty even understanding the question about why authors do what they do. Instead of answering the question, she provided propositional information from the text. When she finally understood the purpose of the question, like McGee's younger students (her's were second graders), she offered nonsocial reasons for the author—he writes it for himself, not for the reader. Eventually, through the consideration of *Little Red Riding Hood,* a story that she knows quite well, she was able to arrive at some general social communications reasons for writing, and ended up with a richer interpretation at least of that storybook. Reading comprehension, certainly of something like the thematic statement that she ended up with, is closely allied with an understanding of author intentions (what is the author trying to accomplish and why?).

Knowing why authors write, that they have intentions, obviously can help with thematic understandings and critical reading, but the higher level appreciations of craft demonstrated in the author-oriented readings of the Cheever text, for example, when the readers compared authors or evaluated their own appreciation of Cheever's writing, require a knowledge of the stylistic inventions that characterize author voice or persona. Hayes (1992) has demonstrated that skilled readers, because of their knowledge of personality traits, are able to come to highly similar interpretations of who wrote the text and the personality that was communicated. This study used naturally occurring texts that were written to convey author personality

Table 1
Interview with Child about Authorship

Adult: (read an informational picture book aloud) Why did the author write that?
Child: About baby wolves.
Adult: But why did the author write it?
Child: So he told about the baby and what the mom and dad could do like.
Adult: Why did the author tell that?
Child: Maybe he like a story about wolves.
Adult: (read a fictional storybook aloud) What did the author want you to know?
Child: About children.
Adult: (indicated information book, again) What did the author want you to know?
Child: About wolves.
Adult: Why did the author write the book about children?
Child: Probably wanted like the people . . . he wanted all the people to know what the people do in the story.
Adult: (indicated each storybook) Is it real or make-believe?
Child: (correctly categorized both books)
Adult: Why does the author make up a story?
Child: They like to make up stories for kids so that they'd have fun to read them.
Adult: Why write the other one?
Child: Kids might want to know what is real.
Adult: (showed informational book) Can you learn from this?
Child: Yes.
Adult: (indicated the storybook) And from this one?
Child: No.
Adult: Like what could you learn?
Child: About baby wolves.
Adult: Could they make this fun?
Child: Make it not real.
Adult: How?
Child: Put people in it and they will come up to them. Pet them. Just be nice to them.
Adult: Where could they live?
Child: Woods . . . forest.
Adult: Where if it was just for fun?
Child: House.
Adult: (told the story "Little Red Riding Hood," a story with which the child was familiar) Anything you could learn from that?
Child: No, . . . Strangers could capture you!
Adult: Why would an author write about that?
Child: They don't want anybody to get killed or anything.
Adult: (reread the storybook) What could you learn from that?
Child: Kids can know that kids are best friends and then when they talk about it the other person is their friend again. People can get mad and be buddies again.
Adult: So why do authors write?
Child: So you can learn or have fun.
Adult: Did you know that's why authors wrote books?
Child: No.

(college admissions applications), and the readers (college admissions officers) were highly skilled at inferring author traits. However, some useful demonstrations of the efficacy of "reading for persona" are drawn from literary studies in which the interpretation of narrative texts is enhanced by a consideration of author personality traits as communicated in the text (Booth, 1983; Gibson, 1969).

Green and Laff (1980) have shown that even kindergarten children have sufficient knowledge to recognize common authorship on the basis of style among a collection of texts. It is doubtful that these kindergartners would have recognized the commonalities if the texts had employed more subtle style differences. The awareness of author voice, however, does seem to increase with learning. Another study, of second and fifth graders, found a significant positive relationship between ability to establish a personal voice through one's own writing and reading comprehension ability (Cox, Shanahan, & Sulzby, 1990); the relationship was strongest for the older and more mature readers. The reading abilities of mature readers can even be indexed successfully in terms of awareness of authors (Stanovich & West, 1989).

Having social and stylistic knowledge is not enough, of course. In order for this knowledge to benefit reading comprehension, the reader must recognize the relevance and usefulness of such information and apply it to interpretation. Studies show that, when text encourages readers to be aware of authorial voice, for example, through the use of metadiscourse, reading comprehension and recall of information improves, even with college level students (Beauvais, 1989; Crismore, 1985). Metadiscourse provides readers with a clear notion that someone is behind the text and that it would be useful to think about this person and what he or she is doing (Brandt, 1990). In exposition, the type of text that usually has been the focus of metadiscourse studies, the author might draw attention to himself or herself by describing the purpose for the discourse ("This is a book for readers and for those who wish to become readers. Particularly, it is for readers of books. Even more particularly, it is for those whose main purpose in reading books is to gain increased understanding."); by sharing value judgments ("For teachers and children alike, the most important feature of classroom instruction is the fact that it is a *collective* social enterprise."); or by highlighting the organizational structure of the text ("This chapter presents and discusses the findings of studies of the reading, writing, and oral language requirements of the occupations and related training programs described in Chapter 2.") Each of these metadiscourse devices reminds the reader that an author is behind the text making decisions.

Fiction, too, has rhetorical devices that permit an author to remind the reader of his or her existence (Booth, 1983). In fiction, this might take the form of narrative commentary, as is used at the beginning of *Huckleberry*

Finn ("Persons attempting to find a motive in this narrative will be prosecuted; persons attempting to find a moral in it will be banished; persons attempting to find a plot in it will be shot. By order of the author."), or it can be *implied* in the structure of a text (Booth, 1983), as when each chapter is told from a different character's perspective (Toni Morrison's *Beloved*) or when the title lets us know that the story will borrow the episodic form of another work (James Joyce's *Ulysses*).

These metadiscourse devices or rhetorical features of text direct the readers' attention and allow them to access the author's approach or biases. They reveal that an author is making conscious choices to direct our attention and to influence our thinking, choices of which we want to be aware. Poorer readers, and those learning to read, would seem most likely to benefit from such author revealing devices, since they might have difficulty imagining an author and that author's choices without at least some help. The *best* readers might not benefit as much from metadiscourse because their rich knowledge of author motives, interpersonal relationships, and stylistic inventions could be applied to the text without such signaling.

Strategies

Similar to other popular approaches to reading comprehension, social conceptions of reading posit an active purposeful reader who interprets, rather than simply accesses, information in the text (Anderson, Hiebert, Scott, & Wilkinson, 1985). However, the essence of the reader's actions are characteristically different in social models from those proposed in problem-solving ones. For instance, in problem-solving approaches, readers might review what they know about a topic and generate predictions about the direction the text might take (Stauffer, 1969), or they might examine the text organization in order to ascertain how the topic is explored (Bean, Singer, Sorter, & Frazee, 1986). Alternatively, after reading they might summarize the text to make sure that it is understood and remembered in a well-organized manner (Brown & Day, 1983). Each active step guides the reader's interaction with the text in a manner that increases the possibility of grasping the information included there.

Social approaches are no less active, but require a more conscious consideration of the author's role. Text has meaning, but it also has purpose. Text has structure, but it has voice, too. Readers can operate on text as if on an object, or they can interact with the voice in the text as if it were a human being. Social strategies induce dialogues with the text.

Martin (1987), in a study of high school seniors identified as good readers, found that making connections with authors was a major strategic response to text. In this study, students read two texts and engaged in a think-aloud activity during their reading/comprehending. These students not only made connections with the authors and author intentions during the reading, but used this strategy more frequently than they did some of the most recommended comprehension strategies (i.e., questioning). Students consciously inferred authors more frequently when they were reading abstract, difficult-to-understand texts than when reading easier ones.

In a similar study with adult proficient readers (Flower, 1987), this tendency to strategically infer authors was even more marked. Flower described such strategic behaviors as "rhetorical inferences." She reports that rhetorical inferences were made 60% of the time in order to resolve difficulties of interpretation. That is, as in the Martin study, readers were more likely to consider authors when they were having trouble making sense of a text; thinking about authors in this way is an interpretive act that is engaged in during difficulty.

It is possible to construct factual information from a text without consideration of an author, but critical evaluation of text seems to benefit from the use of such strategic considerations. In one study, it was found that children who were enrolled in classes that emphasized author awareness had higher recall of text information, but also were more critical of the logic and clarity of what they read (Tierney, LaZansky, Raphael, & Cohen, 1987). In this study, author awareness was heightened through writing and conferencing activities, in which children regularly carried on a dialogue with their classmates about texts that they had authored.

Gibson (1969) wrote: "To catch the particular accent of the speaking voice in a piece of writing is . . . one of our primary obligations as readers." He suggested a number of strategic approaches that readers might use in order to become aware of an author's voice and to use this knowledge interpretively. One of the strategies that he recommends for fiction is an active consideration of the relationship between author, protagonist, and narrator. Studies show that children often are confused about these relationships, and clarification of them seems to be useful for understanding (Hade, 1990).

To clarify such relationships, Edmiston (1990) recommended the use of reader's logs and a strategy in which symbolic representations of reader, author, narrator, and characters are physically manipulated in order to analyze the meaning of a text. Such acts led her students to consider issues such as author craft and intentions more thoroughly. The fourth and fifth graders in her study engaged in the reading of literature by taking actions such as considering author attitude toward certain characters or situations.

Tierney, Soter, O'Flahavan, and McGinley (1989), in a study of reading–writing relationships, described the interpretations of factual text that resulted when students read a newspaper editorial and then wrote "letters to the editor." Interpretations became increasingly rich, personal, and critical when they moved back and forth between a text and their own dialogue with the person behind the text.

Unfortunately, there is no experimental data on the types of activities recommended by Gibson (1969), Edmiston (1990), and Tierney *et al.* (1989), although their illustrations of interpretation are persuasive. Two studies, both emphasizing somewhat simpler strategies, in which readers tried to consider possible author purposes while they read, have indicated the effectiveness of such approaches in experimental settings, however, Mosenthal (1983) with college students and LaZansky & Tierney (1985) with children in upper elementary grades found that training students to consider author intentions increased recall, especially for difficult texts.

Clearly, there is still a great deal of work to be accomplished in this area. However, it is equally clear that when students actively converse with authors—inferring author motives and relationships to texts—better comprehension results. Students need to learn to ask authorship questions while they read, for example:

- Why is the author telling me this?
- What does he/she want me to know? Why?
- What does the author think of the protagonist or subject matter? What does he/she want me to think about this?
- What else should the author have told me?
- What is the author's attitude toward me?
- Why is the author writing in this manner and not in some other one?

When students engage strategically in active considerations of the author, better and more critical understanding appears to be the result.

Metacognition

Metacognition refers to the understanding and regulation of cognitive activity. Baker and Brown (1984) stress that this usually includes two types of mental processing. The first, an awareness of one's own cognitive resources and strategies, is used to generate plans and approaches to cognitive problems such as reading. The second aspect of metacognition refers to being self-critical and self-aware of one's own progress in proceeding with a cognitive problem. Thus, a reader might decide to make predictions while reading a text (an example of the first aspect of the definition of metacognition), but as the activity proceeds the reader might decide that he or she isn't really understanding the text completely enough (an example of the second aspect of the definition) so a new strategy might be considered (back to the first aspect).

For purposes of discussion, I will only emphasize the role of author awareness in a reader's oversight of the efficacy of the reading process. The idea that readers can and do use author awareness in order to engage a text more effectively has already been demonstrated in the section of this chapter on strategy. Unfortunately, many of the metacognitive issues concerning the use of such strategies (e.g., Under what conditions should authors be considered? At what points in the process do such considerations help? What kinds of problems can be resolved with specific approaches to dialoguing with authors?) have not been addressed empirically; one can only speculate on these issues at this time.

Treatments of metacognition in reading have usually considered self-monitoring (that is, watching to see if one's comprehension is making sense) and critical reading as separate phenomena. This is unfortunate because, immediately upon recognition of an interpretive problem, the reader cannot possibly know whether the text or the reading is in error. Self-monitoring implies that the problem is with the processing, whereas critical reading suggests that the difficulty lies in the text itself. Of course, in reading both types of problems occur: the reader might misread something or forget some critical information, but the source of the confusion or difficulty might be an error of printing or author logic as well. For the sake of this discussion, I will consider the role of author awareness of any kind, textually based or reader based, in monitoring activity.

The idea that readers consider authors when a text is not making sense usually has not been highlighted in cognitive approaches to reading comprehension. So, for example, when Collins and Smith (1980) discussed comprehension processes, they suggested that readers who were having difficulty understanding ignore the problem and read on, suspend judgment, guess, reread, or ask an expert. Consider Kintsch & van Dijk's (1978) model of comprehension, which attempted to describe the system of mental operations that underlie the processes occurring in text comprehension. Their system accounted for local and global organization of text, substantive knowledge of the world, summarization, inference, the forming of micro- and macro structures, and long-term memory for text information, but no attention is given to readers' attempts to address issues of who created the text and to what purpose. Even more recent treatments of comprehension processes and instruction that go beyond these "processing" variables (Winograd & Johnston, 1987) often do so with little regard for the reader–writer social dimension.

The Flower (1987) and Martin (1987) studies noted earlier stand in stark contrast to these models of fix-up strategies. Both demonstrated that readers increasingly attempt dialogues with authors as text becomes more difficult and abstract; in fact, they apparently do so with greater regularity than they perform some of the actions emphasized in the other popular models. However, the fact that readers consider authors when the "going gets tough" does not mean that readers become more aware of the fallibility of reading and texts as a result of such discourse.

The limited research on this issue does indicate that those who are most aware of authors are also those with the greatest sensitivity to the accuracy and effectiveness of the reading process. That is, students who know the most about authoring seem to be most able to monitor the accuracy of their own reading comprehension.

Shanahan (1989), in an examination of seven elementary school classrooms, found great differences in author consideration during instruction. This study used teacher diaries supplemented with observations to describe a plethora of instructional activities, including author mentions, author discussion, participation in author conferencing, and so on. A significant relationship was found between the incidence of such activities in the classroom and students' ability to recognize various errors that had been made in a text. At all grade levels, 1–6, and with both narrative and expository texts, students who had experienced the greatest number of author awareness activities in classroom instruction were consistently better at noticing errors in logic, fact, syntax, and spelling that appeared in a grade-level-appropriate text.

In a similar vein, Tierney and colleagues (1987) found that students with the most awareness of authors evidenced the greatest critical interpretation of text. These elementary grade students evidenced more criticism of author logic and clarity than was characteristic of those with less author awareness. Students who became critical of their own writing later were able to transfer this ability to the texts of others. Learning to monitor one's own writing by being an author seems to be an important, and possibly essential, influence on one's ability to respond critically to the texts of others.

Both the Shanahan (1989) and Tierney *et al.* (1987) studies found the greatest author awareness in classrooms in which students were writing and participating in conferences about their writing and that of their peers. It is possible that such students do better because of the practice in being critical rather than because of any increased awareness of authors. This will be difficult to sort out, however, since Shanahan found that authors were discussed markedly more often when a text was written by one of the children than when it was from a basal reader, textbook, or tradebook. More than 80% of the discussions of student writing included consideration of authors, whereas such considerations occurred in less than 15% of the discussions of published texts. Thus, there appear to be few nonwriting activities in classrooms that encourage children to be aware of authors, and the most popular writing activities have a tendency to encourage children to read critically *"like writers"* (Smith, 1984).

Motivation

Finally, what is the role of author awareness in motivation for reading? This discussion will necessarily be the briefest, most speculative, and most theoretical of the various sections in this chapter. This role of author awareness in motivation, as opposed to interpretation, has rarely been the topic of empirical study. Motivation has often been treated as a force emanating from the usefulness of the topical information in a text, or exerted on some contextual feature separate from text–reader relationships, such as home influences (Wigfield & Asher, 1984). Thus, if I am interested in baseball, it is expected that I will understand or remember more when I read about this subject. If my parents like to read I will try to read well to be like them. Contrary to this view, Fitzgerald (1990) suggests that even more basic motives are inherent in the reading process. Readers have a "disposition to 'meet' minds, a desire for some degree of union or communion with the other minds." (p. 84)

Fitzgerald challenges the idea that readers use text to isolate themselves from society. In fact, the stereotype of the friendless bespectacled bookworm (such as Marian the Librarian in *The Music Man*) is rejected by her formulation. Readers and writers are actually hypersocial in this model of literacy or in that proposed by Brandt (1990). Readers try to reach across texts to other human beings, having to be *more* consciously aware of what is taking place on the other side of the communication than is necessary when the discourse is oral. Readers read not to separate from others, but to reach out to them. The motive for reading is to find other minds. Useful recommendations for encouraging children to think about authors as a tool for motivating them to read have been made (Clary, 1991).

Lain (1986), in a large-scale survey of the reading of adults, has provided a description of reader's purposes that concurs with Fitzgerald's contention. That study found three purposes for reading, one of them companionship. Readers indicated that they used reading in order to overcome loneliness and to create feelings of companionship. Of the three reasons provided, companionship was the only one that was consistently emphasized at all age levels. Similar results have come from much smaller scale observational studies conducted with very different adult (Health, 1980) and child populations (Janiuk & Shanahan, 1988; Tierney, 1986).

Readers certainly use authorship as a feature of selection in helping them determine what to read. Mann (1982) reports a study by Spiller that focused on reasons why adults selected particular books from the library. It was found that 54% of the books were selected solely on the basis of author, and that the author figured at least partially in the selection 89% of the time. It has also been found that children who read multiple books by the same author do best on comprehension tests (Shanahan, 1987), although this could simply be the result of the best readers doing more reading of all types.

Although it has not been studied, to my knowledge, it seems likely that those who read for companionship and social need would be most aware of authors. It is the consideration of the author—voice, style, intention, oeuvre—that makes reading an activity of social interaction. If the desire for such interaction is a basic drive or highly valued possibility for human beings, then the ability to converse with authors would be a highly motivational action. Our social (Tierney & LaZansky, 1980) and ethical responsibilities (Hirsch, 1976) to authors should encourage us to seek a negotiated meaning with text; it should motivate us to understand rather than just to know.

CONCLUSIONS

Since Moses brought the tablets down from the mountain, author awareness in interpretation has been a significant issue. Although it has been shown that text can be understood and interpreted without consideration of authors, empirical research has shown that a knowledge of authorship has a positive impact on reading and learning to read. It has been shown that author awareness can be used strategically during reading through active consideration of author purposes and author relationships to text. Author awareness was also found to have a positive influence on the metacognitive activity inherent in critical reading and in motivation.

REFERENCES

Anderson, R. C., and Pearson, P. D. (1984). A schema-theoretic view of basic processes in reading. In R. Barr, M. L. Kamil, P. Mosenthal, and P. D. Pearson (Eds.), *Handbook of reading research* (Vol. II, pp. 255–292). New York: Longman.

Anderson, R. C., Hiebert, E., Scott, J., and Wilkinson, I. (1985). *Becoming a nation of readers.* Washington, D.C.: National Institute of Education.

Baker, L., and Brown, A. (1984). Metacognitive skills and reading. In R. Barr, M. L. Kamil, P. Mosenthal, and P. D. Pearson (Eds.), *Handbook of reading research* (Vol. II, pp. 353–394). New York: Longman.

Beach, R., and Hynds, S. (1991). Research on response to literature. In P. D. Pearson (Ed.), *Handbook of reading research* (pp. 453–489). New York: Longman.

Bean, T. W., Singer, H., Sorter, J., and Frazee, C. (1986). The effect of metacognitive instruction in outlining and graphic organizer construction on students' comprehension in a tenth-grade world history class. *Journal of Reading Behavior, 15,* 153–169.

Beauvais, P. (1989). A speech act theory of metadiscourse. *Written Communication, 6,* 3–10.

Beck, I., and McKeown, M. (1991). Conditions of vocabulary acquisition. In P. D. Pearson (Ed.), *Handbook of reading research* (pp. 789–814). New York: Longman.

Booth, W. C. (1983). *The rhetoric of fiction* (2nd ed.). Chicago: University of Chicago Press.

Brandt, D. (1990). *Literacy as involvement: The acts of writers, readers, and texts.* Carbondale, Illinois: Southern Illinois University Press.

Brooks, C., and Warren, R. P. (Eds.) (1938). *Understanding poetry.* New York: Holt.

Brown, A. L., and Day, J. D. (1983). The development of plans for summarizing texts *Journal of Verbal Learning and Verbal Behavior, 22,* 1–14.

Cheever, J. (1978). The Ocean. In J. Cheever, *Stories* (pp. 567–583). New York: Knopf.

Clark, H. H., and Haviland, S. E. (1977). Comprehension and the given-new concept. In R. O. Freedle (Ed.), *Discourse production and comprehension.* Norwood, New Jersey: Ablex.

Clary, L. M. (1991). Getting adolescents to read. *Journal of Reading, 34,* 340–345.

Collins, A., and Smith, E. (1980). *Teaching the process of reading comprehension* (Technical Report No. 182). Champaign, Illinois: Center for the Study of Reading, University of Illinois at Urbana-Champaign.

Cox, B. E., Shanahan, T., and Sulzby, E. (1990). Good and poor readers' use of cohesion in writing. *Reading Research Quarterly, 25,* 47–65.

Crismore, A. (1985). *Metadiscourse as rhetorical act in social studies text: Its effect on student performance and attitude.* Unpublished Ph.D. thesis. University of Illinois, Urbana-Champaign.

Edmiston, P. E. (1990). *From onlooker to activist: The nature of readers's participation in stories.* Paper presented at the National Reading Conference, Miami.

Fish, S. (1980). *Is there a text in this class?* Cambridge, Massachusetts: Harvard University Press.

Fitzgerald, J. (1990). Reading and writing as "mind meeting." In T. Shanahan (Ed.), *Reading and writing together* (pp. 81–98). Norwood, Massachusetts: Christopher-Gordon.

Flower, L. (1987). *Interpretive acts: Cognition and construction of discourse* (Occasional Paper No. 1). Berkeley: Center for the Study of Writing, University of California.

Foucault, M. (1979). What is an author? In J. V. Harari (Ed.), *Poststructuralist criticism* (pp. 141–160). Ithaca, New York: Cornell University Press.

Gadamer, H. (1975). *Truth and method* (translated by J. C. B. Mohr). New York: Seabury Press.

Gibson, W. (1969). *Persona: A style study for readers and writers.* New York: Random House.

Goetz, E. T., Schallert, D. L., Reynolds, R. E., and Radin, D. I. (1983). Reading in perspective: What real cops and pretend burglars look for in a story. *Journal of Educational Psychology, 75,* 500–510.

Golden, J. M., and Guthrie, J. T. (1986). Convergence and divergence in reader response to literature. *Reading Research Quarterly, 21,* 408–421.

Graesser, A., Golding, J. M., and Long, D. L. (1991). Narrative representation and comprehension. In R. Barr, M. L. Kamil, P. Mosenthal, and P. D. Pearson (Eds.), *Handbook of reading research* (Vol. II, pp. 171–205). New York: Longman.

Green, G. M., and Laff, M. O. (1980). Five-year-olds' recognition of authorship by literacy style. (Technical Report No. 181). Urbana: University of Illinois, Center for the Study of Reading.

Gruenich, R., and Trabasso, T. (1981). The story as social environment: Children's comprehension and evaluation of intentions and consequences. In J. Harvey (Ed.), *Cognition, social behavior, and the environment* (pp. 265–287). Hillsdale, New Jersey: Erlbaum.

Hade, D. D. (1990). *The reader's stance as event.* Paper presented at the National Reading Conference, Miami.

Halliday, M. A. K., and Hasan, R. (1976). *Cohesion in English.* New York: Longman.

Hayes, J. R. (1992). A psychological perspective applied to literacy studies. In R. Beach, R. J. Green, M. L. Kamil, and T. Shanahan (Eds.), *Multidisciplinary perspectives on literacy research.* Urbana: National Conference of Research on English.

Heath, S. B. (1980). The functions and uses of language. *Journal of Communication, 30,* 123–133.

Hirsch, E. D. (1967). *Validity in interpretation.* Chicago: University of Chicago Press.

Hirsch, E. D. (1976). *The aims of interpretation.* Chicago: University of Chicago Press.

Hynds, S. (1985). Interpersonal cognitive complexity and the literary response processes of adolescent readers. *Research in the Teaching of English, 19,* 386–404.

Hynds, S. (1989). Bringing life to literature and literature to life: Social constructs and contexts of four adolescent readers. *Research in the Teaching of English, 23,* 30–61.

Janiuk, D. M., and Shanahan, T. (1988). Applying adult literacy practices in primary grade instruction. *Reading Teacher, 41,* 880–887.

Kintsch, W., and van Dijk, T. A. (1978). Towards a model of text comprehension and production. *Psychological Review, 85,* 363–394.

Lain, L. (1986). Steps toward a comprehensive model of newspaper readership. *Journalism Quarterly, 63,* 69–74.

LaZansky, J., and Tierney, R. J. (1985). *The themes generated by fourth-, fifth-, and sixth-graders in response to stories.* Paper presented at the National Reading Conference, San Diego.

Loftus, E. F. (1979). The malleability of human memory. *American Scientist, 67,* 312–320.

Mann, P. (1982). *From author to reader.* London: Routledge & Kegan Paul.

Martin, S. (1987). *The meaning-making strategies reported by proficient readers and writers.* Paper presented at the meeting of the National Reading Conference, St. Petersburg, Florida.

McGee, L. (1983). Perceptions of author's intentions: Effects on comprehension. In J. A. Niles and L. A. Harris (Eds.), *Searches for meaning in reading/language processing and instruction* (pp. 148–157). Rochester, New York: National Reading Conference Yearbook.

McNamara, T. P., Miller, D. L., and Bransford, J. (1991). Mental models and reading comprehension. In R. Barr, M. L. Kamil, P. Mosenthal, and P. D. Pearson (Ed.), *Handbook of reading research* (Vol. II, pp. 490–511). New York: Longman.

Mosenthal, J. (1983). Instruction in interpretation of a writer's argument: A training study. Unpublished Ph.D. thesis. University of Illinois, Urbana-Champaign.

Perfetti, C. A. (1985). *Reading ability.* New York: Oxford University Press.

Pichert, J. W., and Anderson, R. C. (1977). Taking different perspectives on a story. *Journal of Educational Psychology, 69,* 309–315.

Rabinowitz, P. J. (1987). *Before reading.* Ithaca, New York: Cornell University Press.

Richards, I. A. (1929). *Practical criticism.* New York: Harcourt, Brace & World.

Rosenberg, D., and Bloom, H. (1990). *The book of J.* New York: Grove Weidenfeld.

Rosenblatt, L. (1978). *The reader, text, the poem.* Carbondale: Southern Illinois University Press.

Rumelhart, D. E. (1980). Schemata: The building blocks of cognition. In R. J. Spiro, B. C. Bruce, and W. F. Brewer (Eds.), *Theoretical issues in reading comprehension* (pp. 33–58). Hillsdale, New Jersey: Erlbaum.

Shanahan, T. (1987). A survey of student literacy experiences in a large scale assessment. In J. Readence and S. Baldwin (Eds.), *Research in literacy: Merging perspectives.* (36th yearbook of the National Reading Conference, pp. 35–44). Rochester, New York: National Reading Conference.

Shanahan, T. (1989). *Authorship and critical reading.* Paper presented at the National Reading Conference, Austin, Texas.

Smith, F. (1984). Reading like a writer. In J. M. Jensen (Ed.), *Composing and comprehending.* Urbana, Illinois: National Council of Teachers of English.

Stanovich, K., and West, R. F. (1989). Exposure to print and orthographic processing. *Reading Research Quarterly, 24,* 402–433.

Stauffer, R. G. (1969). *Directing reading maturity as a cognitive process.* New York: Harper & Row.

Tierney, R. J. (1986). Functionality of written literacy experiences. In M. Sampson (Ed.), *The pursuit of literacy* (pp. 108–115). Dubuque, Iowa: Kendall-Hunt.

Tierney, R. J., and Cunningham, J. W. (1984). Research on teaching reading comprehension. In P. D. Pearson (Ed.), *Handbook of reading research* (pp. 609–656). New York: Longman.

Tierney, R. J., and LaZansky, J. (1980). The rights and responsibilities of readers and writers: A contractual agreement. *Language Arts, 57,* 606–613.

Tierney, R. J., LaZansky, J., Raphael, T., and Cohen, P. (1987). Author's intentions and reader's interpretations. In R. J. Tierney, P. Andes, and J. Mitchell (Eds.), *Understanding readers' understanding.* Hillsdale, New Jersey: Erlbaum.

Tierney, R. J., Soter, A., O'Flahavan, J., and McGinley, W. (1989). The effects of reading and writing upon thinking critically. *Reading Research Quarterly, 24,* 134–173.

Warnke, G. (1987). *Gadamer: Hermeneutics, tradition, and reading.* Cambridge, England: Polity Press.

White, K. S. (1979). *Onward and upward in the garden.* New York: Farrar Straus Giroux.

Wigfield, A., and Asher, S. R. (1984). Social and motivational influences on reading. In P. D. Pearson (Ed.), *Handbook of reading research,* (pp. 423–452). New York: Longman.

Winograd, P., and Johnston, P. (1987). Some considerations for advancing the teaching of reading comprehension. *Educational Psychologist, 22,* 213–230.

5

Improving Reading and Thinking: From Teaching or Not Teaching Skills to Interactive Interventions

Cathy Collins

My problems seem less complicated now that I know problem-solving techniques. I did not expect to list my problems on paper and figure out an answer, but I do. Because of you [my reading teacher] I make decisions now instead of beating around the bush. Thank you very much! Thank you for teaching me how to think.

—Jason, a seventh grader (unsolicited note to a research teacher in our study)

WHERE OUR WORK BEGAN

In 1988 we read and agreed with a National Assessment of Educational Progress report that concluded that reading programs should (1) emphasize critical thinking, (2) build students' elaboration skills, (3) advance readers' abilities to interpret, and (4) afford opportunities to form opinions with reasoned support (Applebee, Langer, & Mullis, 1988). We also discovered that, although high school students' reasoning abilities had increased through infusion of thinking development strategies in science, mathematics, and social science (Baron & Sternberg, 1987; deBono, 1970), relatively few studies had analyzed the impact of lessons to expand thinking development during reading, writing, and language arts (Collins & Mangieri, 1992; Resnick, 1989).

As we began our studies, a second need was obvious. With every passing year comes a greater necessity to enhance students' complex cognitive processes, since acceptable levels of literacy in the past are unlikely to satisfy the demands of life beyond the 1990s (AACTE, 1989; Langman, 1989; NCTE, 1989; NEA, 1989; *Reading Today,* 1989). Future reading instruction will have to do more than build a value for reading as a self-selected leisure and information-gathering activity, since merely reading and applying facts will not be sufficient for future success. To be literate soon will require that students know how to identify problems in, and reason effectively with, printed information; recognize writing formats and authors' thinking patterns; and use reading to solve life's problems. By the time of graduation from high school, students have not learned all the vocabulary, decoding, and comprehension skills necessary to be successful in life. In our rapidly changing society, the intellectual demands on citizens have increased; information is made obsolete daily; vocabulary and knowledge increase continually; and all present technology represents only a fraction of what will be available to today's kindergartners when they are adults (Brock, 1987; Duffy, 1991).

A third need is that today's students have more responsible decisions to make earlier in their lives than did past generations. Instead of a "sweet sixteen and never been kissed" society (in which most researchers grew up), today's youth, by ages 10–15, reach a point at which they "have their last best chance to choose paths toward productive and fulfilled lives" (Carnegie Council on Adolescent Development, 1989, p. 20). As Hahn, Dansberger, and Lefkowitz (1987) found, significant correlations exist between students' inabilities to think on high levels and their use of destructive means to fulfill a need for power and importance. Better thinking skills may permit them to avoid poor choices with harmful consequences (Blos, 1979; Brozo, 1990; Dorman & Lipsitz, 1981; Drash, 1980; Eichhorn, 1966; Irvin, 1990; Johnston & Markle, 1986; Worell & Danner, 1984).

Inability to think and communicate is easy to spot in schools. Very early in school, many students have difficulty maintaining eye contact, making requests of others, and stating preferences or independent thoughts. Likewise, when work is too difficult, these same students mask their inabilities by faking disinterest or trying to convince teachers that the information to be learned is "beneath them" (Collins, 1990b; Epstein & MacIver, 1991; Siegler, 1988).

PAST STUDIES

With these needs in mind, we reviewed taxonomies and descriptions of thinking competencies (Baron & Sternberg, 1987; Beyer, 1987; Collins, 1989a, 1990a, 1992; deBono, 1970; Marzano, Jones, & Brandt, 1988; Paul, 1990). The thinking abilities in these taxonomies were categorized into eight dimensions, or domains, of thinking ability that were amenable to instruction. As depicted in Figure 1, each dimension is a distinct set of thinking competencies.

Once these abilities were identified, we selected a target age at which to begin our work. Although we spent a few months field-testing lessons with children in kindergarten through Grade 11, we selected eleventh graders for

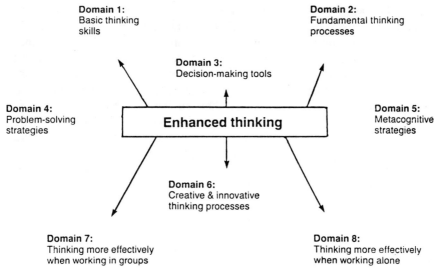

Fig. 1 Thinking dimension amenable to instruction.

several reasons. First, many high school students reported that their courses were not as challenging as they desired. It was our original intent to create a course entitled "Thinking Development" that (eventually and ideally) all students in the eleventh grade would take. This course would contain 1 month's study of each competency of thought so, by year's end, graduates would have advanced all dimensions of their thinking. Although the field-test results from self-reports and ethnographic data were promising, it became increasingly clear that thinking abilities develop slowly and have limited transfer when taught as a separate subject or skill. It also became painfully apparent that developing higher level thinking in students would require more than 1 year's instruction (Collins, 1989b).

Several important findings from this study guided construction of future lessons. One of the most significant findings stemmed from asking students what they needed in order to think better. The attributes most frequently expressed were less external supervision, stimulation of intellect through cognitive challenges, advanced information on topics, positive thinking models/instruction, decision-making tools, and a classroom environment that offered autonomy (Collins, 1990a).

Two quantitative tests were made before and after instruction. We assessed the experimental subjects' ability to generate ideas as well as their reflectivity. Experimental subjects significantly increased their ability to generate plausible solutions to a problem after instruction (6 ideas per group of 4 in a 7-min period prior to instruction; 15 ideas per group of 4 in a 7-min period after instruction). Likewise, experimental subjects significantly increased their reflectivity after instruction. Subjects were asked to read a first-person narrative, in which the narrator was identified only as "I". As soon as subjects identified the narrator, they noted the time and wrote the narrator's name. They could change their mind before receiving the true identity, which was given on a separate sheet of paper at any point during the reading that subjects requested. Once a subject received the true identity, they could not change their choice of narrator.

On the pretest, 34 of 42 subjects were unsuccessful in identifying the narrator. The reflection time (time elapsed between beginning to read and selecting narrator) of the subjects was 1 min 14 sec. Of the 8 subjects who eventually identified the narrator, all made one inaccurate identification within the same 1 min 14 sec reflection time.

On the posttest, 40 of 42 subjects identified the narrator correctly on their first attempt, with an average reflection time of 3 min 46 sec.

Our high school students went on to describe that our best research lessons were informal; had dense but sequential information; allowed high-level, small group discussions; and, included individual goal setting activities or assessments that pushed them to exceed their past performances. They also reported that the best teachers praised specifically and modeled their own "hard-won" thinking habits by think-alouds. Our high school students believed that these lessons gave them the directions, autonomy, and courage to think through their own problems (Collins, 1989b).

We conducted a second study with 208 middle school subjects. We taught thinking skills in conjunction with reading and writing lessons. All groups read the same selections of children's literature and textbooks. Thinking strategy lessons were taught on Mondays, Wednesdays, and Fridays from the second week in January through the last week in April, as described in greater detail in Collins (1991a,b). When lessons designed to build eight dimensions of thinking were incorporated into one period of a traditional middle school program, experimental subjects significantly outscored control subjects on several measures. Although pretests of experimental and control groups showed no significant differences between groups, experimental subjects scored significantly higher (by a wide margin) on the reading comprehension posttest of the Iowa Test of Basic Skills. The experimental group also scored significantly higher than the control group on the vocabulary subtest and total battery scores.

Following instruction, experimental subjects also significantly outscored the control group on four measures of self-esteem, using the Harter Self-Perception Profile for Children (Harter, 1985). Experimental subjects scored significantly higher than control subjects on social competence, behavior in groups, confidence in appearance, and physical competence.

Two measures of students' self-initiated thinking were also taken in the study. The first occurred in postexperimental writing samples, completed 2 wk after the study's end. Without being told that their writing samples were a part of the study, subjects were asked to "describe some important things [they had] learned this year." An in-depth description of these writing samples appears in Collins (1992a), but two new pieces of evidence are reported here. As shown in Figure 2, experimental subjects included 13 types of thinking in their unprompted writing. Their statements represented all eight domains of thought. Conversely, all but 3 of the 195 statements from control subjects' writings represented only first-dimensional

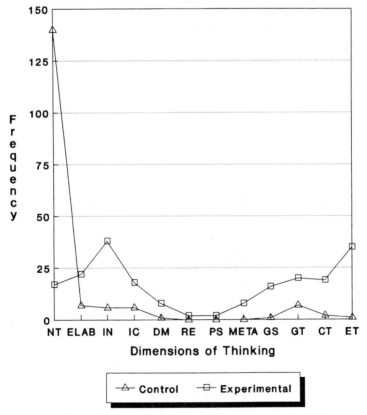

Fig. 2 Dimensions of thinking reflected in free recall. NT, notetaking (Level 1—recall); ELAB, elaboration (Level 1—clarifying); IN, producing inferences (Level 2—processing and producing new interpretations); IC, interpreting content (Level 2—making comparisons and analyzing concepts); DM, decision making (Level 3—selecting information to use in life); RE, research (Level 4—establishing criteria and solving problems); PS, problem solving (Level 4—judging credibility of sources); META, metacognitive thinking (Level 5—assessing one's own knowledge relative to tasks); GS, goal setting and establishing redirection when alone (Level 8—ability to think productively when alone); GT, thinking effectively in groups (Level 7—using talents interactively); CT, creative and innovative thinking (Level 6—specific actions for improving); ET, evaluating one's own thinking ability (Level 5—metacognitive thinking).

factual thinking. A clear association existed between thought categories and experimental group.

In a reanalysis of these data, we uncovered another interesting outcome. Although the difference in recall between groups was statistically significant, differences between experimental and control groups in Dimension 3 (decision making) and Dimension 4 (problem solving) thinking were not significant. These data can be interpreted in three ways.

First, our lessons (one-fourth of the treatment) may need to be redesigned. Perhaps we have not yet identified specific strategies that significantly increase decision-making and problem-solving abilities. Second, students may not initiate decision-making or problem-solving thoughts when they are not prompted to do so. This seems reasonable since, in prompted assessments, specific incidents of their use were cited (see page 153). Third, decision making and problem-solving may be two dimensions of thinking that need longer than 11 wk to develop. Some research indicates that students may need 9 yr of instruction in decision making and problem solving before proficiency is attained (Baron & Sternberg, 1987; Collins, 1991c; Collins & Mangieri, 1992; Lockhead & Whimbey, 1987; Ogle, 1992).

This may occur because, as Graves and Stuart (1985) report, many things in and out of school convince students that there is only one correct answer, and that answers to problems should be simple. For example, students view television episodes in which "all you need is one grand shootout at the O. K. Corral . . . and all this complex fuss that they have watched for three hours will be over." (p. 32) Similarly, before children begin school, when they go to cut a string, they cut it wherever they wish. After they come to school, they begin to realize that there is only *one* middle and they work feverishly to cut each string exactly where "it's supposed to be cut" (P. Messier, U.S. Department of Education, personal communication).

Thus, in our new lessons, students are asked to generate, instead of shun, alternatives as they work. We invite more than one solution, and summon alternative paths to answers.

Our second measure of self-initiated higher-level thinking was a posttest of prompted recall. To analyze whether students transferred thinking abilities to life, subjects answered the question "Have you used anything you learned at school this month to help you with problems outside of school?" Although none of the control subjects answered affirmatively, 95% of the experimental group said they had used their new thinking tools. Of these students, 62% stated very specific incidents of use, as cited in Collins (1991b).

Similarly, when five raters conducted blind reviews of videotapes of the last lesson in experimental and control classes, each ranked the four experimental tapes as more thoughtful classes than the four control tapes. Raters identified 11 differences between interactions that occurred in experimental versus control groups:

- experimental subjects did not interrupt the person talking
- they asked each other questions
- they made fewer random comments during discussion
- they built on each others' answers
- they volunteered ideas, evidence, and rationale to help classmates' thinking
- they gave each other sufficient time to answer questions
- students were more interested in the class and its tasks until the end of the period
- students used terms to describe their thinking
- they used jargon less frequently
- the noise level was lower
- teachers engaged greater number of students in discussions (Collins, 1991b)

We reasoned that positive results from our second study, which emanated from 33 days of instruction, justified research to incorporate thinking intervention lessons into a year-long curriculum. This is our present project. We are collecting data for the first year of a 5-yr longitudinal study that will follow some students after they graduate from high school.

PRESENT STUDY

We are testing new lessons to develop thinking during reading instruction. Before beginning, we interviewed and surveyed 17 teachers that were selected as outstanding in eight school districts. Our present study involves students in kindergarten through Grade 8. We seek answers to several questions: Can we teach basic decoding and comprehension strategies simultaneously with thinking abilities (past subjects were already strong decoders)? What aspects of the interactive nature of our lessons are effective? Why? At what ages can students initiate and build their own thinking? Although we are convinced that interactive interventions are the key to developing higher level thinking/reading/writing abilities, what were the weaknesses in the third and fourth lessons of our last study? In our present study, we are using several types of interactive intervention (as described subsequently). Is "too much of a good thing" wonderful, or is too much of anything bad?

Interactive Interventions in Present Work

Several types of interactive interventions are used in our present study. The first is a prompted intervention in students' thinking. We ask students to conduct two types of thinking during reading. Students are taught a specific thinking strategy and a general thinking ability (e.g., in the illustrative lesson in Appendix A, structural analysis is the specific skill and how to frame thoughts and ask questions to clarify is the broader thinking ability).

Second, instruction uses four communication modalities. We hypothesize that practicing thinking/reading objectives through speaking, listening, reading, and writing in every lesson will be advantageous. To implement this intervention, each lesson is designed for students to use thinking strategies while they read, write, speak, and listen.

Third, we build specific abilities in authentic ways. To do so, we teach strategies that adults use to read and think. For example, as you will see in the sample lesson, we do not introduce structural analysis by teaching the meanings of "pre", "un", and "tion". This is because, as adults, we do not apply structural analysis skills in that sequence. What we, as expert readers, do is to look at long words and break them into smaller parts. We then ask if we know any of these parts, and we compare spelling patterns to familiar words that help decode meaning (Gaskins, Gaskins, and Gaskins, 1991).

Fourth, students interact with the material. They choose which segments of the lesson are most important for them. This self-selection occurs at three points in each lesson: before students begin to read, at one point during the reading, and after the reading is complete.

Fifth, direct explanation and student-directed activities are included in each lesson. Part I provides direct explanation of strategies; Part II extends responsibility to students to apply the strategy they learned to meet their own needs.

Sixth, teachers do not wait for students to "discover" how to read and think, yet teachers do not tell students how to read or think. We accomplish this by designing lessons consistent with what Langer (1991) discovered in her work to advance literacy understandings.

> Teacher's interactions are carefully structured so that they are not so tight a scaffold that they offer more praise for their answers than for students' original thinking . . . a contrast from the former discovery models where scaffolding was limited, and potential "teachable" moments were lost, well-meaning teachers do not become too "invisible", failing to provide guidance when needed. (p. 34)

In our lessons, teachers follow a script and, within divisions of the plan, they select among alternative explanations that vary in depth. We hypothesize that such a flexible scripting will overcome a problem Langer (1991) observed in her research.

> Although teachers mean to encourage student thinking, sometimes support and control are confused . . . in an attempt to be noncontrolling, opportunities for guidance are lost. [Alternatively], teacher-sanctioned responses are sometimes kept as a hidden goal. (p. 35)

Seventh, the second part of each lesson is collaborative group work.

In summary, we hypothesize that when students encounter various forms of knowing operating together in a natural situation, when they see accomplished teachers moving back and forth spontaneously among these forms, when students are engaged in their own rich and engaging projects that call upon a variety of modes of representation, when they have the opportunity to interact and communicate with individuals who evidence complementary forms of thinking, they will learn to think better (Brown, Collins, & Duguid, 1989; Gardner, 1990; Resnick, 1987).

Lesson Format for Present Studies

Part 1: Introduction to Readings

Introductions contain *Prerequisites* (decoding strategies to be used in the lesson are described), *Prelesson Vocabulary Teaching Strategies* (strategies to build students' abilities to increase their reading/speaking/listening/writing vocabularies independently), and *Reading/Thinking Objectives*. Objectives state goals, provide rationale, and describe methods of instruction as well as evaluation. By stating what the objectives are, how they will be studied, and how students will know they have learned them, direct explanation and prompting of reading/thinking processes, strategies, and products occurs (a prompting that has been demonstrated to substantially increase learning by Duffy & Roehler, 1986; Pressley, Goodchild, Fleet, Zajchowski, & Evans, 1989; Chapter 3).

Immediately after the prompting of reading/thinking strategies, students are encouraged to dispel misconceptions (Beck & Dole, 1992; Eichinger & Roth, 1990; Glaser, 1986). As Beck and Dole discussed, in the face of reading evidence contradictory to their beliefs, many students refuse to engage in thinking and learning. In addition, by dispelling misconceptions, students have a more positive attitude toward reading and thinking. Through this positive attitude, students more easily integrate the affective and cognitive domains (Collins & Mangieri, 1992; Glaser, 1986; Vygotsky, 1978). For example, misconceptions relative to the sample lesson in Appendix A included (1) students discussing inaccurate statements that former students made concerning structural analysis, and asking questions (e.g., "It takes too long to break words into parts, so I just skip all the long words I don't

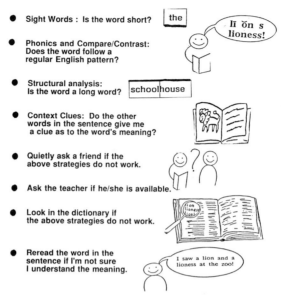

Fig. 3   When I don't know a word. Created by Sandra Hines, Elementary Education Major, Texas Christian University, 1990.

know."); (2) students listening to an audiotaped testimonial of a student who believed that asking questions causes people to think "you are stupid," and how completing this lesson taught him that this isn't true "when you learn to ask really good questions, like those on the strategy sheet;" and (3) students stating their strongest beliefs about the lesson objectives as questions that will be answered at the end of the lesson (e.g. "I believe I'm too bashful to ask questions in front of the whole class." is rewritten to "In the past, why was I too shy to ask questions? What can I learn today to improve my thinking and my ability to ask questions in groups?").

Thinking/Reading Strategy Charts

The third part of the lesson consists of the Thinking/Reading Strategy Sheets. We found that thinking/reading strategy instruction is more effective if inserted before reading than if it appears as an after-reading enrichment/extension activity (Collins, 1989a). Such "after-lesson grafting" is less effective because it is difficult to strengthen reading comprehension in retrospect; instruction to build reading/thinking strategies is likely to be viewed by teachers and students as an add-on; and reading/thinking strategies detached from content do not develop self-initiated thinking while reading (Beck and Dole, 1991; Collins, 1992; McGrane and Sternberg, 1991). Each strategy is charted on a single page (see Figure 3). Each names and differentiates the strategy so students can discuss it in the course of their work. Many strategy charts contain graphics, as shown in Appendix A, so students can imagine and retrieve each strategy with less effort.

Students Selection of Goals, Sample Objectives, and Assessments

After the strategy charts are introduced, students read three or four examples of how to use the strategies during reading. Examples come from peers who have used the strategy effectively in prior research studies. These examples engage student desires to think deeply about their reading, and initiate their motivation to set their own purpose for reading/thinking. Because purpose setting and motivation precede thinking and reading in real life, students practice thinking as it will be practiced in life, making transfer of instruction easier (J. Mangieri, personal communication).

By selecting or creating their own objectives for thinking and reading, students also take a risk and invest themselves before they read. Selection also places students in charge of their depth of thinking, what they will think during reading, and how they will use a thinking/reading strategy to reach their objective. Objectives from which students choose are specifically designed to appeal to different learning modalities and personality types.

At this point in each lesson, students read and complete their objectives. What they learned in the process is evaluated through unplanned and planned assessments. Unplanned assessments are incidents in which students use the reading/thinking strategies without being asked to do so. When students initiate a strategy's use, it is noted and dated on the Unplanned Assessment Classroom Monitor. The monitor is used once a week for the course of the study. This way, students have 40 wk to demonstrate that the strategies in the study are used. Planned assessments are criterion-based and transpire at this point in each lesson for both control and experimental groups.

Part 2: Rethink, Reread, and Reformulate Comprehensions

Hansen (1991) and teachers in our interviews and surveys discovered that the aspect of literature-rich classrooms most appreciated by students is the ability to select what they want to read. In Part 2 of our lessons, students select their own reading material and plan demonstrations of what they have learned relative to lesson objectives. Through this rethinking step, students construct more mature mental patterns and assess their abilities to do so. For example, students can choose to practice prediction strategies (in Lesson 6.1) and use the information in the reading from Part 1 to forecast an ending for their selected reading in Part 2. Students' success in completing this objective, however, rests both on the correctness in using prediction strategies, and on whether or not they identified comparable or distinct thinking patterns between themselves and the author that led to similarities and dissimilarities in the endings they created for the story or book. We hypothesize that activities in Part 2 will increase students' abilities to generate alternatives and reconsider opinions.

Self-Selected Assessment

Lessons close with students' self-assessment of the reading/thinking objectives under study. Students choose methods to demonstrate that they have learned a reading/thinking strategy. They also answer the question "What have I learned from this lesson that I will use later in life?" Sample student self-selected assessments include (1) generating back-up strategies to rely on in reading/thinking relative to lesson objectives; (2) characterizing an unplanned insight they gained through the lesson; (3) planning, with a classmate, a way to extend and share what they learned with the class; (4) reporting pleasurable/effective experiences outside of the classroom in which they have used the objectives successfully; (5) reporting which things in the lesson helped them to improve their reading and thinking, and why these methods most enhanced their learning; (6) completing exercises in applied citizenship, using problems that exist in the world today; and (7) making tests or diagrams for themselves and others concerning lesson objectives.

FUTURE ANALYSES AND STUDIES

All grade levels will be taught all dimensions of thinking, and analyses will be made between and within groups and grade levels. Throughout the present study we will analyze nine types of data. First, planned assessments will be given each week to experimental and control groups. Second, analyses will be made of student self-reports (e.g., answers they give to "What have I learned that I will use in my life?"). Third, we will do qualitative analyses of the increased reasoning abilities demonstrated in student answers (e.g., why they chose the objectives they did in Part 1 of lessons and the self-assessments they did in Part 2). Fourth, analyses will be made to compare data from the Class Monitor concerning the groups' self-initiated use of thinking strategies. Fifth, analyses will be made between experimental and control group scores on the Iowa Test of Basic Skills. Sixth, comparisons will be made between groups on the Texas minimal reading/writing objectives, relative to higher level thinking. Seventh, comparisons will be made between subjects on the Ennis–Weir Critical Thinking Essay Test for Grades 7 and 8, and on written statements for younger subjects. Videotapes, teacher journals, and case studies will also be collected and analyzed. To assess the aspects of the intervention that were most effective, beginning in January, 1992, we will randomly omit one type of interaction in the lessons until each type has been removed from three different lessons.

SUMMARY AND CONCLUSIONS

The main purpose of this chapter was to recount the successes and failures in our work to develop students' thinking and reading abilities, and to outline present work. We have become more convinced that thinking abilities can be increased, and that reading and language arts programs are viable segments in the curriculum in which such instruction can occur. What we know now is that teacher direction and student selection interact to expand thinking. We also know that teacher scaffolding in a lesson that provides opportunities for prompted and unprompted use of thinking and reading strategies increases thinking and reading abilities, as well as self-esteem.

We are in the process of discovering (1) whether two types of thinking/reading objectives interact to produce greater gains than instruction to build one at a time; (2) what effects activities that purposely integrate reading and thinking objectives with listening, writing, and speaking can have on thinking and reading development; (3) whether authentic instruction, as we have defined it, will enhance thinking and reading abilities; (4) whether engaging students in purposeful thinking before, during, and after lessons will strengthen their abilities to think and to use the materials they read in their lives better; and (5) what contribution group work makes to thinking and reading development?

We look forward to exploring these and other hypotheses in our present and future work. Our goal is to assist students to contribute more productively to our world through their thoughts, words, and deeds. We believe that the first step is to help them read and think more effectively. Perhaps this chapter on the present state of our research will assist others to advance instruction in higher level thinking and reading abilities.

APPENDIX A

Excerpts from a Third Grade Lesson on Structural Analysis and Asking Questions for Clarification

To illustrate the experimental program, I share excerpts from one lesson. It demonstrates the interactive interventions we follow. These excerpts are as they appear in prototypical scripts, in which teachers closely follow directives.

Prerequisites: Review of Decoding Strategies

Introduce Reading/Thinking Strategy Sheet 1 (as shown in Figure 3). You may wish to spend one day teaching each of the decoding strategies listed on Strategy Sheet 1. If you do, use the following examples. . . . If your students already use these strategies, do the following "think-alouds" to model how they can use them in this reading lesson.

Prelesson Vocabulary Development Strategy

Students turn to page 1 in their notebooks where the following words are printed, followed by a sentence from the historical nonfiction reading used in Lesson 1.1: . . . Students identify the decoding strategy that should be used first if they don't know one of these words (structural analysis, due to word length).

Lesson 1.1 Reading Objective

"When you read and a long word appears that you don't know, you break it into parts. By breaking it into parts you've seen before, you can locate root words/prefixes/suffixes more quickly, which give clues to meaning. Today, you will know you have improved your reading ability when you break one word you do not know into parts, and define its meaning. (Teachers do a think-aloud at this point in the lesson.)

Lesson 1.1 Thinking Objective

"Today you will also learn how to reduce confusion when you read, listen, speak, and write. You will do so by asking questions. At the end of our work, you will see how much you have improved your ability to ask good questions. Scientists have discovered that successful people ask questions when something confuses them. Because they do this, they better understand others, and others better understand them. When you learn to ask questions, you will not misunderstand as many things. (Teachers continue the rationale for this objective.)

Dispelling Misconceptions

This is described on page 157.

Thinking/Reading Strategy Sheet

Ask students to take out Thinking/Reading Strategy Sheet 1.1 entitled "Asking Questions to Clarify Thinking and Reading" (see Figure 4). Tell them to lay it beside their notebooks for reference as they read. (Teachers teach each question on the sheet here.)

Student Selection of Goals, Sample Objectives, and Assessments

"There are several ways you can improve your reading and thinking abilities today. Suggested objectives (as shown here) are on page 1 of your

1. Why?

2. What is the most important point?

3. What do you mean by "_____"?

4. To help me understand, could you give me an example?

5. Can you tell me where the point you are making will not apply?

6. If your idea is accepted, what is the biggest change that will occur?

7. Would you say more about_____?

8. What is the main difference between _____ and _____?

9. Is this what you mean: "_____"?

Fig. 4 Thinking/reading strategy sheet 1.1. Asking questions to clarify, and the types of questions to ask.

notebook. Select the one that will help you the most, or submit your own objective. With either choice, write why this objective will benefit you the most. When you've written your reason, raise your hand if you wrote your own objective. I'll discuss it with you. If you selected an objective from page 1, you may begin reading page 2 as soon as you've written your reason for selecting your objective."

Suggested objectives are:

1. If you have trouble reading big words, practice breaking these words into smaller parts as you read today. Circle the big words you read and use structural analysis to decode them. Place a check mark above the word if structural analysis helped you decode it and understand its meaning. If structural analysis did not help you enough, use context clues. If, by using structural analysis and context clues together, you determine a word's meaning, place two check marks above that word. If you tried all that you know and you still did not understand a word, place three checkmarks above that word. When you finish reading, go back over your reading and look at your pattern of check marks. In the space labeled "After Reading Thoughts" on page 1, write what you think about structural analysis. Is it a useful strategy for you? Why or why not? When and when not?

2. Today's story is true. If you enjoy comparing your thinking to other

people's, pretend you are the reporter in the story, and describe what you would have done had you been the reporter. You will then read what the reporter actually did and, in the space marked "After Reading Thoughts" on page 1, analyze why your actions were the same or different from those of the reporter (using the thinking strategy you select). Describe two thinking strategies that could be used to defend your decisions. (Two other objective options appear at this point in the lesson.)

Students read. (Students read a story about President Roosevelt and a reporter who used questions for clarification. At one point in the reading, students must write what they think the reporter did, which was to ask a question for clarification.)

"In the space marked 'After Reading Thoughts' on page 1, write to the objective and to the goal you set for yourself at the beginning of our lesson. If you finish before I pull the group together, answer this question also: "What did you learn in this lesson that will help you in your life? Why will this help you?"

At this point, conduct a discussion about what the students learned. You add that the reporter, when confused, chose to ask a question. He chose not to remain silent and confused, or to reject the President's offer. He knew if he remained confused he could misinterpret the President's action. Instead he turned his confusion into an opportunity to learn and grow. By asking for clarification, the reporter more closely understood the actions of the President. Students who selected objective 3 ask their questions of the class and describe their thinking.

Part 1: Planned Assignment

Students watch Video Tape Segment 1.1. The tape is of a group of students their age who are discussing a problem at their school that they wanted to solve. As they watch, students write the questions of clarification that students on the tape asked, as well as the effects of these questions. In addition, they list questions that could have been asked to improve the discussion. When the videotape is over, students grade their work, with you, using Master 1. At the bottom of their sheet is the question "What have you learned about using structural analysis and asking questions when you read? What have you learned about what asking questions can do to help you listen and think better?"

As the last question on the planned assessment, students who have not yet answered the question "What have I learned that I will use in my life?" do so.

Part 2: Rethink, Reread, and Reformulate Comprehensions

(Four suggestions for self-assessment are cited to spur students' creative thinking.) Students design their own product and process objectives for the second half of the lesson. Students tell why they made the selection they did.

REFERENCES

AACTE (1989). Resolution to include methods of advancing students' thinking in teacher preparation coursework. Resolution passed in the 1989 Business Meeting of the American Association of Colleges of Teacher Education, April.

Applebee, A., Langer, J. N., and Mullis, A. (1988). Report of the National Assessment of Educational Progress. Washington, D.C.: U.S. Department of Education.

Baron, J., and Sternberg, R. (1987). *Teaching thinking skills: Theory and practice.* New York: Freeman.

Beck, I., and Dole, J. (1992). Reading and thinking with history and science text. In C. Collins and J. Mangieri (Eds.), *Teaching Thinking: An agenda for the twenty-first century* (pp. 2–17). Hillsdale, New Jersey: Erlbaum.

Beyer, B. (1987). *Practical strategies for the teaching of thinking.* Boston: Allyn and Bacon.

Blos, P. (1979). *The adolescent passage: Developmental issues.* New York: International Universities Press.

Brock, W. (1987). *Workforce 2000.* Washington, D.C.: United States Department of Labor.

Brown, J. S., Collins, A., and Duguid, P. (1989). Situated cognition and the culture of learning. *Educational Researcher, 18*(1), 32–42.

Brozo, W. G. (1990). Hiding out in secondary content classrooms: Coping strategies of unsuccessful readers. *Journal of Reading, 33*(5), 324–328.

Carnegie Council on Adolescent Development (1989). Turning points: Preparing American youth for the 21st century. New York: Carnegie Foundation.

Collins, C. (1989a). *A new approach to middle school reading: Expanded thinking.* Paper presented at the annual conference of the National Reading Conference, Austin, Texas.

Collins, C. (1989b). Administrators hold the key to thinking development. *REACH, 3,* 139–147.

Collins, C. (1990a). *Reasoning through reading: Vignettes that produce engagement.* Paper presented at the annual conference of the International Reading Association, Atlanta, Georgia.

Collins, C. (1990b). Administrators can promote higher level thinking skills. *NASSP Bulletin, 74* (526), 102–109.

Collins, C. (1991a). Reading instruction that increases thinking abilities. *Journal of Reading, 34* (7), 510–516.

Collins, C. (1991b). Don your critical thinking caps. *The School Administrator, 48*(1), 8–14.

Collins, C. (1992a). Thinking development through intervention: Middle school students come of age. In C. Collins and J. Mangieri (Eds.) *Teaching Thinking: An agenda for the twenty-first century* (pp. 67–83). Hillsdale, New Jersey: Erlbaum.

Collins, C. (1992b). *Expanding thinking through the language arts.* Boston: Allyn and Bacon.

Collins, C., and Mangieri, J. (Eds.) (1992). *Teaching Thinking: An agenda for the twenty-first century.* Hillsdale, New Jersey: Erlbaum.

deBono, E. (1970). *Lateral thinking.* New York: Harper and Row.

Dorman, G., and Lipsitz, J. (1981). Early adolescent development. In G. Dorman (Ed.), *Middle grades assessment program.* Carrboro, North Carolina: Center for Early Adolescence.

Drash, A. (1980). Variations in pubertal development and the school system: A problem and a challenge. In D. Ster (Ed.), *The emerging adolescent characteristics and educational implications.* Columbus, Ohio: National Middle School Association.

Duffy, G. G., and Roehler, L. (1986). *Improving classroom reading instruction: A decision-making approach.* New York: Random House.

Duffy, J. (1992). Business partnerships to build a thinking populist. In C. Collins and J. Mangieri (Eds.), *Teaching Thinking: An agenda for the twenty-first century* (pp. 289–303). Hillsdale, New Jersey: Erlbaum.

Eichhorn, D. (1966). *The middle school.* New York: The Center for Applied Research in Education.

Eichinger, D., and Roth, K. J. (1990). *Critical analysis of an elementary science curriculum.* Paper presented at the annual meeting of the American Educational Research Association, Boston.

Epstein, J. L., and MacIver, D. J. (1991). *Education in the middle grades: Overview of national practices and trends.* Columbus, Ohio: The National Middle School Association.

Gardner, H. (1990). *Art education and human development.* Los Angeles: The Getty Center for Education in the Arts.

Gaskins, R. W., Gaskins, J. C., and Gaskins, I. W. (1991). A decoding program for poor readers— and the rest of the class, too! *Language Arts, 68,* 213–225.

Glaser, W. (1986). *Control theory in the classroom.* New York: Harper and Row.

Graves, D., and Stuart, V. (1985). *Teachers who write.* Portsmouth, Heineman.

Hahn, A., Dansberger, J., and Lefkowitz, B. (1987). *Dropouts in America: Enough is known for action.* Washington, D.C.: Institute for Educational Leadership.

Hansen, J. (1991). *Portfolios.* Paper presented at the annual meeting of the International Reading Association, Las Vegas.

Harter, D. (1985). *Harter self-perception profile for children.* Boulder: University of Colorado.

Irvin, J. L. (1990). *Reading and the middle school student.* Boston: Allyn and Bacon.

Johnston, J. H., and Markle, G. C. (1986). *What research says to the middle level practitioner.* Columbus, Ohio: National Middle School Association.

Langer, J. A. (1991). *Literary Understanding and Literature Instruction.* Report Series 2.11. Albany, New York: Center for the Learning and Teaching of Literature.

Langman, J. (1989). *NBO's youth in Pittsburgh: Initial observations.* Preliminary report of the Spencer Foundation/Stanford University Grant entitled Language, Socialization, and Neighborhood Organizations.

Lockhead, J., and Whimbey, A. (1987). Teaching analytic reasoning through thinking aloud pair problem solving. In J. Stice (Ed.), *Developing critical thinking and problem solving abilities* (pp. 237–256). San Francisco: Jossey-Bass.

Marzano, R., Jones, B., and Brandt, R. (1988). *Dimensions of thinking.* Alexandria, Virginia: Association for Supervision & Curriculum.

McGrane, P., and Sternberg, R. (1992). Fatal vision—The failure of the schools in teaching children to think. In C. Collins and J. Mangieri (Eds.), *Teaching Thinking: An agenda for the twenty-first century* (pp. 386–403). Hillsdale, New Jersey: Erlbaum.

NCTE (1989). Report on basal readers by the Commission on Reading. Urbana, Illinois: National Council of Teachers of English.

NEA (1989). *Newsbriefs.* Washington, D.C.: National Education Association.

Ogle, D. (1992). Developing problem solving through language arts instruction. In C. Collins and J. Mangieri (Eds.), *Teaching Thinking: An agenda for the twenty-first century.* Hillsdale, New Jersey: Erlbaum.

Paul, R. (1990). *Critical thinking: What every person needs to survive in a rapidly changing world.* Rohnert Park, California: Sonoma State University.

Pressley, M., Goodchild, F., Fleet, J., Zajchowski, R., and Evans, E. D. (1989). The challenges of classroom strategy instruction. *Elementary School Journal, 89,* 301–342.

Reading Today (1989). Resolutions concerning basal readers. September–October 1989, 1 and 7.

Resnick, L. (1987). Learning in school and out. *Educational Researcher, 16*(1), 19–26.

Resnick, L. (1989). *Education and learning to think.* Washington, D.C.: National Academic Press.

Siegler, R. S. (1988). Individual differences in strategy choices: Good students, not-so-good students, and perfectionists. *Child development, 59,* 833–851.

Siegler, R. S. (1989). Strategy diversity and cognitive assessment. *Educational Researcher, 18* (9), 15–19.

Worell, J., and Danner, F. (1984). *The adolescent as decision maker: Applications to development and education.* San Diego: Academic Press.

Vygotsky, L. S. (1978). *Mind in society: The development of higher psychological processes.* Cambridge: Harvard University Press.

6

Developing Self-Sufficient Learners in Reading and Mathematics through Self-Instructional Training

Gloria E. Miller and Mary Ellen Brewster

The challenge of developing self-sufficient learners who can fulfill their academic potential has driven more than a decade of research on cognitive strategy instruction. Characteristics that distinguish successful and unsuccessful learners were outlined (Pressley, Borkowski, & Schneider, 1987a) and recently expanded in the "Good Information Processor" model by Pressley, Borkowski, and Schneider (1989a). According to this model, self-sufficient learners know about the parameters that affect cognition, know how to control cognitive endeavors, and have a sense of efficacy about their own cognition. In essence, self-sufficient learners exhibit efficient behavioral, cognitive, and motivational processes that enhance their performance of complex tasks (Zimmerman, 1986, 1989). These processes include effective problem analysis and problem-solving skills, as well as the metacognitive abilities to reflect on personal attributes and background knowledge related to a problem, to devise plans for solving problems in light of this information, and to monitor efforts and progress toward a solution (Brown, 1978). Further, self-sufficient learners are motivated to be strategic, are challenged to tackle new problems (Pressley *et al.*, 1989a), and exhibit what Rosenbaum (1983) refers to as "learned resourcefulness" or the ability to minimize the effects of internal or external events that interfere with task execution.

PROMOTING ACADEMIC COMPETENCE AND LITERACY IN SCHOOLS

Educational researchers agree that meeting this challenge requires multicomponent interventions that emphasize self-regulation processes (Brown, Campione, & Day, 1981; Harris, Graham, & Pressley, 1992; Ryan, Weed, & Short, 1986b; Wong, 1985; Zimmerman, 1989). One such intervention, called self-instructional training (SIT), was originally conceived by Meichenbaum and Goodman (1971) to improve task performance in children exhibiting severe attention deficits. During SIT, children actively employ self-guidance, self-monitoring, and self-motivation processes. SIT has been hypothesized as a desirable instructional procedure because it overcomes children's reliance on external agents, discourages rote repetition, stresses active collaboration and dialogue between a student and a tutor, and fosters independence, greater self-awareness, and positive personal attributes (Asarnow & Meichenbaum, 1979; Harris, 1990; Kendall & Braswell, 1985; Lennox & Polling, 1984; Meichenbaum, 1977).

The conceptual foundation for SIT (Meichenbaum & Goodman, 1969, 1971) was heavily influenced by the work of three divergent forces: (1) cognitive theorists (Flavell, 1977; Reese, 1962), who focused on the role of verbal mediation and production deficiencies in the learning performances of young children (Craighead, 1982; Pressley, 1979); (2) Soviet theorists (Luria, 1961; Vygotsky, 1962), who emphasized the central role of internal speech and mediated social interactional experiences on the development of self-regulated behavior (Wertsch, 1979; Zivin, 1979); and (3) social learning theorists (Bandura, 1977), who stressed the role of performance rehearsal, observation, and modeling in fostering optimal self-control and problem-solving skills (Craighead, Wilcoxin-Craighead, & Meyers, 1978). Verbal mediation, self-speech, and the notion that self-regulation processes develop through direct observation of and interaction with a sophisticated other are integral to SIT (Harris, 1990).

During SIT, novices (i.e., children) are taught to internalize performance strategies by observing, interacting, and receiving direct feedback from sophisticated (i.e., adult) tutors. Through such mediational experiences, children learn to adopt a series of personally worded statements (or interrogatives). These personal dialogues help the learner (1) analyze a task and recognize a desired goal (What do I have to do?), (2) formulate a specific plan of action (How should I do it?), (3) evaluate ongoing progress toward goal attainment (How am I doing?), (4) reinforce performance (That's good work.), and (5) employ corrective actions and cope with obstacles that impede task completion (That's not quite right. Keep cool; I will try again.). The self-statements can include global content-free statements that generalize across a variety of problems as well as task-specific statements that apply directly to the current problem (Meichenbaum, 1977, 1980). Children are encouraged to internalize the self-statements as part of SIT through a five-phase instructional sequence. In the first phase, the novice observes as the tutor models and verbalizes a personalized task approach and evaluation process. In the second phase, the tutor provides guided instruction while completing the task with the child. In the third phase, the child independently vocalizes a task approach strategy and receives directive feedback. In the fourth phase, the child performs the task with minimal guidance or feedback from the tutor and reduces vocalizations to a whisper. Finally, in the fifth phase, the child uses private speech or subvocalizations while independently performing the task.

Early work evaluating SIT effectiveness was conducted with behavior-disordered clinical populations using nonacademic perceptual–motor tasks to improve attention, persistence, and other general on-task behaviors. (See Hobbs, Moguin, Tyroler, & Lahey, 1980; Kazdin, 1982; Kendall, 1977, for excellent reviews of this literature). SIT has been used to a lesser extent to foster academic performances and skills, although SIT often is identified as a promising cognitive-behavioral intervention for academic remediation (Harris, 1982; Meichenbaum, 1980; Meichenbaum & Asarnow, 1979; Meichenbaum & Burland, 1979; Wong, 1985). Evidence is accumulating that a variety of cognitive-behavioral interventions successfully promote a range of academic behaviors (Abikoff, 1979; Cole & Kazdin, 1980; Craighead, Meyers, Wilcoxon-Craighead, & McHale, 1982; Harris, 1982; Lloyd, 1980; Pressley, Forrest-Pressley, Elliot-Faust, & Miller, 1985), but few reviews have focused specifically on the efficacy of SIT procedures. The purpose of this chapter is to review critically SIT effectiveness within two academic domains receiving increased attention from educational researchers: reading and mathematics.

To accomplish this goal, several inclusionary and exclusionary criteria were delineated. Empirically based SIT studies published since 1971 were included if reading and mathematics skills were targeted during SIT and evaluated as outcome variables. Also acceptable were studies that targeted academic domains in addition to reading and mathematics (i.e., spelling; Swanson, 1985; Swanson & Scarpati, 1984) or emphasized general attentional skills using reading and math problems (Brown & Alford, 1984). Moreover, studies were chosen without regard to learner characteristics to examine SIT effects across a wide range of student ability levels. (For a review of SIT with mentally retarded populations, see Lennox & Polling, 1984; Whitman, 1987; with learning disabled populations, see Harris, 1982; Wong, 1985; with hyperactive populations, see Abikoff, 1985).

Excluded from this review were SIT studies that focused solely on improvements in other academic areas (e.g., listening, handwriting, written composition; Elliot-Faust & Pressley, 1986; Graham & Harris, 1987, 1989a,b; Grinder, 1988; Harris & Graham, 1985; Schmidt, Deshler, Schumaker, & Alley, 1988), affective states or motivational processes (e.g., anxiety, self-worth; effort, attributions; Reiher & Dembo, 1984), or in general cognitive, attention, or perceptual–motor skills (e.g., rehearsal, serial recall, attention to details; Asarnow & Meichenbaum, 1979; Bornstein & Quevillon, 1976; Bryant & Budd, 1982; Douglas, Parry, Marton, & Garson, 1976; Evangelisti, Whitman, & Johnston, 1986; Jackson & Calhoun, 1982; Kendall & Wilcox, 1980). Finally, studies were eliminated if the training regimen did not incorporate components designated as critical to self-instructional training paradigms. This excluded studies in which mediated instruction was not part of the training regimen (e.g., Beck, Matson, & Kazdin, 1982; Wong, Wong, Perry, & Sawatsky, 1986) or in which talk-aloud or modeling procedures were employed as the sole intervention (e.g., Lloyd, Kneedler, & Cameron, 1982; Schunk, 1981).

The remainder of this chapter is divided into four sections. In the first section, a general description of the targeted studies is provided, followed by an overview of immediate, long-term, and generalized SIT outcomes, and a review of several important methodological shortcomings. Since few differences were detected across the reading and mathematics domains, outcomes apply to both academic areas unless otherwise noted. In the second section, critical student pretreatment characteristics are reviewed with respect to their impact on SIT effectiveness. Critical training components and parameters that can affect SIT outcomes are presented in the third section. Finally, specific conclusions and recommendations for improving the efficacy of SIT interventions in educational settings are offered.

GENERAL OVERVIEW
AND METHODOLOGICAL ANALYSIS

Thirty-six SIT treatment studies that met the previously described criteria were located through Psychological Abstracts or ERIC. Individual experiments in a study were considered independently, as were the three studies that targeted both reading and math skills. A total of 17 reading and 20 mathematics studies formed the basis of this review (see Tables 1–4). A broad range of reading skills was targeted for intervention: oral reading performance, decoding ability, sight word recognition, recall of story information, error detection, and comprehension of factual and inference questions. Math skills included: one-to-one correspondence or counting; addition and subtraction with or without regrouping; multiplication with numbers, decimals, and fractions; simple and long division problems; and completion of word problems. These academic skills primarily were evaluated through informal and formal measures of performance accuracy (i.e., the number or proportion of correctly solved items) although indices of rate (i.e., the number of items correctly completed with a designated period of time) were included in several math studies.

A variety of experimental designs were represented. Pretest/posttest control group designs with 2–5 treatment conditions were employed in 10 reading and 11 math studies; 3 of the 11 math studies included an additional treatment or subjects factor. Posttest-only group designs were employed in 2 reading studies, which included an additional subjects factor. Single-subject designs constituted the remaining 5 reading and 9 math studies, most of which were some variation of a multiple-baseline-across-subjects design. A reversal design was employed in 1 math study.

Overall Findings

Significant academic improvements were found in 12 of the 17 reading and 18 of the 20 math studies immediately following SIT relative to the results obtained from control training or baseline procedures, providing clear evidence of SIT effectiveness. SIT benefits were noted across both individual and small group administration formats; group sizes ranged from 3 (Schunk & Rice, 1984) to 12 (Johnston & Whitman, 1987) students. Moreover, the largest groups worked equally well across both academic domains and worked with younger and older students. Sustained SIT benefits were found in the 5 (of 7) reading and 6 (of 8) math studies that examined maintenance, over delay periods that ranged from 1 week to 6 months. Transfer was assessed in 15 reading and 16 math studies, most frequently across tasks that assessed near generalization. However, several studies assessed transfer to other skills, behaviors, and affective domains or across settings. Favorable SIT outcomes were reported on at least one index of transfer in 10 reading and 12 math studies. Overall, these findings appear to support the efficacy of SIT procedures for improving reading and mathematics performances in young children. Unfortunately, such favorable general conclusions are limited by a number of important methodological shortcomings.

Strength of Control Comparisons

A closer inspection of the control comparisons made in each study revealed an unflattering picture of SIT benefits relative to comparable didactic strategy instruction. Significant SIT effects were most often found compared with "weak" no-treatment or minimal training control conditions, whereas nonsignificant SIT benefits often were reported relative to stringent control comparisons. In a representative group study with educable mentally retarded (EMR) students (Borkowski & Varnhagen, 1984), SIT provided no further performance benefits over that obtained with an equivalent didactic strategy instruction procedure (but both training conditions outperformed a no-treatment control). Similar conclusions were drawn from a multiple-baseline study (Roberts, Nelson, & Olson, 1987). Moreover,

Table 1
Reading—Group Studies

Study	Subject information[a]	Independent variables[b]	Duration of treatment	Design[c]	Dependent variables[d]	Immediate results	Follow-up
Abikoff et al. (1988)	N = 33; x̄ = 9.5 yrs; Hyp	(i) SIT + med (ii) CD + med (iii) C + med	32 Ts @ 1 hr = 32 hr (16 wk)	Pre, post, 6-mo FU	SAT		
					word study	nsd	nsd
					reading comprehension	nsd	nsd
					Gilmore		
					acc	nsd	nsd
					comp	nsd	nsd
					rate	nsd	nsd
					Gen meas		
					P & T ratings	−G	+G
					self-concept	−G	−G
					self-eff	−G	−G
					MFF	−G	−G
					20 Q	−G	−G
					other SAT	−G	−G
Borkowski & Varnhagen (1984)	N = 18; x̄ = 11–7 yrs; EMR	(i) SIT (ii) CD (iii) CAP	6 @ ? = ? (1 wk)	Pre, post, 1-wk FU, 3-wk FU	Free recall, sentence	SIT, CD > CAP	SIT, CD > CAP
					Serial recall	SIT, CD > CAP	SIT, CD > CAP @ 1 wk, 3wk
					Gen meas		
					Free recall, story	−G	−G
Brown & Alford (1984)	N = 20; x = 12–7 yrs; LD/att	(i) SIT (ii) C	16 Ts @ 1 hr = 16 hr (2 mo)	Pre, post, 3-mo FU	WRAT read	SIT > C	SIT > C
					Gen meas		
					task—WRAT, spell	−G	−G
					DTA	+G	+G
					MFF	+G	+G

Eastman & Rasbury (1981)	N = 11; Gr. 1; Hyp	(i) SIT (ii) CAP	3 @ 20 min = 1 hr (approx. 1 wk)	Pre, post	Ginn acc Gen meas on T	nsd −G	
Friedling & O'Leary (1979)	N = 8; x̄ = 7-7 yrs; Gr. 2 & 3; Hyp	(i) SIT (ii) CAP	1 @ 90 min & 2 @ 40 min = 2 hr, 50 min (?)	Pre, post	Sullivan acc # Gen meas task—math on T	nsd nsd −G +G when re-inf.	
Glenwick & Barocas (1979)	N = 40; Gr. 5 & 6; Imp/Beh	(i) SIT—parents & teachers (PT) (ii) SIT—teachers (T) (iii) SIT—parents (P) (iv) SIT—experimenters (CH) (v) C	8 Ts @ 50 min = 6 hr, 40 min (4 wk)	Pre, post, 5-wk FU	WRAT read Gen meas MFF PPVT WISC Porteus maze P & T ratings task—WRAT, spell	PT, T, P, CH > C +G −G −G −G −G −G	PT, T, P, CH > C
Malamuth (1979)	N = 33; Gr. 5; BA	(i) SIT (ii) CM	4 @ 30 min = 2 hr (2 wk)	Pre, post	Story and sentence completion # Gen meas audiovis task omission err commission err	SIT > CM +G +G	

(continued)

Table 1 (*Continued*)

Study	Subject information[a]	Independent variables[b]	Duration of treatment	Design[c]	Dependent variables[d]	Immediate results	Follow-up
Miller (1985)	N = 44; x̄ = 9–4 yrs; Gr. 4; A	(i) SIT (s) (ii) SIT (g) (iii) CD (s) (iv) CAP	3 @ 45 min = 2 hr, 15 min (1 wk)	Pre, post, 3-wk FU	Err detect	SIT(s), SIT(g) > CAP; SIT(g) > CD(s)	SIT(s), SIT(g) > CD (s), CAP
Miller (1987)	N = 52; x̄ = 11–1 yrs; Gr. 5; A & AA	(i) SIT (ii) CD	1 @ 40 min = 40 min (1 day)	Pre, post, 1-wk FU, X 2 (ability)	Err detect	SIT(AA) > CD(AA)	SIT(AA) > CD(AA)
Miller, Giovenco, & Rentiers (1987)	N = 48; Gr. 4 & 5; BA & AA	(i) SIT (ii) CAP	3 @ 45 min = 2 hr, 15 min (1 wk)	Post, X 2 (ability)	Err detect contradictory; Gen meas; Err detect cohesion	SIT(AA) > SIT(BA) > CAP(AA) > CAP(BA); +G	
Miller & Rentiers (1991)	N = 45; Gr. 4 & 5; BA & A	(i) SIT (BA) (ii) CD (A) (iii) CD (BA)	3 @ 30 min = 1 hr, 30 min (1 wk)	Post	Err detect; Text recall	CD(A) > SIT(BA) > CD(BA); CD(A), SIT(BA) > CD(BA)	

Schunk & Rice (1984)	N = 42; Gr. 2, 3, & 4; Lang def	(i) SIT (ii) CM	8 @ 30 min = 4 hr (4 wk)	Pre, post	Gen meas rdg attitudes anx enj	+G +G
					SRA list acc	SIT > CM for Gr. 3 & 4
					Gen meas self-eff	+G

[a]A, average; AA, above average; Att, attention problems; BA, below average; Beh, behavior problems; C, competent; CD, conduct disorder; ED, emotionally disturbed; EMR, educable mentally retarded; FMA, females/math anxiety; HI, hearing impaired; Hyp, hyperactive; Imp, impulsive; Lang def, language deficiency; LC, less competent; LD, learning disabled; Off T, off task; Schiz, schizophrenic; Sev ed han, severely educationally handicapped.

[b]C, control (nothing); CA, control attention; CAP, control attention and practice; CD, control didactic or remedial tutoring; CF, control plus feedback; CM, control modeling; med, medication; R, reinforced for SIT; Ac, reinforced for accuracy; (s), specific; (g), general.

[c]MB, multiple baseline (across subject unless otherwise specified).

[d]#, number completed; acc, accuracy; Comp Q, comprehension questions; Err detect, error detection; Gen meas, generalization measures; on T, on task in classroom; Rdg Q, reading questions; Self-eff, self-efficacy judgments; DTA, Attention Tests from Detroit Tests of Learning Aptitude; Gilmore, Gilmore Oral Reading; Ginn, Ginn Series Reading Worksheets; MFF, Matching Familiar Figures; SAT, Stanford Achievement Test; SATA, Scholastic Achievement Test; SDMT, Stanford Diagnostic Math Test; SRA List, SRA Listening Comprehension Test; Sullivan, Sullivan Reading Program; PIAT, Peabody Individual Achievement Test; PPVT, Peabody Picture Vocabulary Test; WISC, Wechsler Intelligence Scale for Children; WRAT, Wide Range Achievement Test.

Table 2
Math—Group Studies[a]

Study	Subject information	Independent variables	Duration of treatment	Design	Dependent variables	Immediate results	Follow-up
Abikoff et al. (1988)	N = 33; x̄ = 9.5 yrs, Hyp	(i) SIT + med (ii) CD + med (iii) C + med	32 Ts @ 1 hr = 32 hr (16 wk)	Pre, post, 6-mo FU	SAT		
					concepts	nsd	nsd
					comp	nsd	nsd
					app	nsd	C +med CD + med
					Gen meas		
					P & T ratings	−G	+G
					self-concept	−G	−G
					self-eff	−G	−G
					MFF	−G	−G
					20 Q	−G	−G
					other SAT	−G	−G
Barling (1980)	N = 138; x̄ = 10 yrs; A	(i) SIT (ii) self-monitoring (SM) (iii) self-standards (SS) (iv) CF (v) C	1 T @ 20 min = 20 min (1 day)	Pre, post	SATA		
					acc	SS > SM > SIT > CF, C	
					Gen meas		
					PPVT	−G	
Brown & Alford (1984)	N = 20; x̄ = 12–7 yrs; LD/att	(i) SIT (ii) C	16 Ts @ 1 hr = 16 hr (2 mo)	Pre, post, 3-mo FU	WRAT		
					math	SIT = C	SIT = C
					Gen meas		
					task—WRAT, spell	−G	−G
					DTA	+G	+G
					MFF	+G	+G

178

Study	Sample	Groups	Duration	Design	Measures	Results	
Genshaft & Hirt (1980)	N = 36; Gr. 7; F/MA	(i) SIT (ii) CD (iii) C	16 Ts @ 40 min = 10 hr, 40 min (8 wk)	Pre, post	SDMT comp app; Gen meas math attitudes, locus of control	SIT > CD, C; nsd; +G; −G	
Glenwick & Barocas (1979)	N = 40; Gr. 5 & 6; Imp/Beh	(i) SIT—parents & teachers (PT) (ii) SIT—teachers (T) (iii) SIT—parents (P) (iv) SIT—experimenters (CH) (v) C	8 Ts @ 50 min = 6 hr, 40 min (4 wk)	Pre, post, 5-wk FU	WRAT math; Gen meas MFF, PPVT, WISC, Porteus maze, P & T ratings, task—WRAT, spell	PT > T, P, CH, C; +G; −G; −G; −G; −G; −G	PT > T, P, CH, C; +G; —; —; −G; —; −G
Johnston & Whitman (1987)	N = 44; x̄ = 7–0 yrs; Gr. 1; C & LC	(i) SIT (s) (ii) SIT (g & s) (iii) CD (s) (iv) CD (g & s)	7 Ts @ 30 min = 3 hr, 30 min (1 wk)	Pre, post, 1-day FU, 1-wk FU, 1-mo FU, X 2 (content)	Add probs acc; #; Gen meas complex probs acc; #	SIT (g & s) > CD (g & s) for LC; SIT(s) = CD(s); s > g & s; CD > SIT; −G; −G	g & s > s; s > g & s

a See Table 1 for legend.

(continued)

Table 2 (*Continued*)[a]

Study	Subject information	Independent variables	Duration of treatment	Design	Dependent variables	Immediate results	Follow-up
Keogh et al. (1988)	N = 38; x̄ = 7.2 yrs; Gr. 1; A; N = 16; x̄ = 10.6 yrs; EMR	(i) SIT (ii) external instruction (EI)	7 Ts @ 30 min = 3 hrs; 30 min (2 wk)	Pre, post, 1-wk FU, X 2 (subject)	Add probs acc	EMR: SIT > EI A: SIT = EI nsd	EMR: SIT > EI A: SIT = EI
					#		EI: A > EMR
					Gen meas complex probs acc	−G	
					#	−G	−G −G
Leon & Pepe (1983)	N = 37; x̄ = 10.2 yrs; LD & EMR	(i) SIT (ii) CAP	35 Ts @ 15 min = 8 hr, 45 min (7 wk)	Pre, post	Key math oper content app	SIT > CAP SIT = CAP SIT = CAP	
					Gen meas # units passed	+ G	
Roberts et al. (1987)	N = 12; Gr. 1 & 2; BA	(i) SIT – R (ii) SIT – Ac (iii) SIT– R + A (iv) C – Ac	10 Ts @ ? = ? (?)	MB within each group	Add & subtract probs acc	SIT – R, SIT – Ac, SIT – R + Ac > C – Ac	
Schleser et al. (1983)	N = 48; Gr. 3 & 4; Imp	(i) SIT (s) (ii) SIT (g) (iii) directed discovery (DD) (iv) CD	4 Ts @ 45 min = 3 hr (4 wk)	Pre, post	Add Probs acc	SIT(s), DD > CD, DD > SIT (g)	
					PIAT math	SIT(s), DD > SIT(g), CD	

Study	Sample	Conditions	Design	Gen meas	Results
Schunk (1982)	N = 44; x̄ = 10-7 yrs BA	(i) strategy verb (SV) (ii) free verb (FV) (iii) SV & FV (iv) CAP	Ts @ 45 min = 1 hr, 30 min (2 days) Pre, post, 2 (SV v no SV) × 2 (FV v no FV)	MFF task—PIAT, read task—PIAT, spell task—PIAT, info Div probs acc persist #	+G −G (+G for DD) +G +G FV, SV & FV > SV, CAP nsd nsd
Spates & Kanfer (1977)	N = 45; x̄ = 6.4 yrs; Gr. 1; BA	(i) Grp 1—self-monitoring (SM) (ii) Grp 2—criterion setting (CS) (iii) Grp 3—SM + CS (iv) Grp 4— SM + CS + self eval + self reinf (v) CA	1 T @ ? = ? (1 day) Pre, post	Gen meas self-eff Add probs acc	+G Grp 2, 3, 4 > Grp 1 = CA

[a]See Table 1 for legend.

Table 3
Reading—Single Subject Designs[a]

Study	Subject information	Independent variables	Duration of treatment	Design	Dependent variables	Immediate[c] results	Follow-up
Guevremont, Osnes, & Stokes (1988)	N = 4; preschool; off T	SIT	8 Ts @ 20 min[b] = 2 hrs, 40 min (2–3 wk)	MB	Decoding acc	SIT > BL for 3/4 subjects	
					time	SIT > BL	
					Gen meas on T	+G	
Smith & Van Biervliet (1986)	N = 6; x̄ = 11-6 yrs; Gr. 6; BA	SIT	6 Ts @ 30 min = 3 hr (approx. 2 wk)	MB, FU for 3 wk	Comp Q	SIT > BL	SIT > BL
					Gen meas setting—classrm	+G	
					oral read	–G	

Study	Subjects	Treatment	Sessions	Design	Measure	Result
Swanson (1985), Exp. 1	N = 1; 13 yrs; HI/ED	SIT	9 Ts @ 45 min = 6 hr, 45 min (approx. 2 wk)	MB, task & setting	Comp Q	SIT > BL
					Gen meas	
					Rdg Q	+G
					setting—classrm	+G
Swanson & Scarpati (1984), Exp. 1	N = 2; 14-6, 13-8 yrs; LD/Beh	SIT	10 Ts @ 45 min = 9 hr (approx. 2 wk)	MB	Comp Q	SIT > BL
					Gen meas	
					Rdg Q	+G
					setting—classrm	-G
Varni & Henker (1979)	N = 3; 8, 10, 10 yrs; Hyp/LD	SIT	3 Ts @ 30 min = 1 hr, 30 min (approx. 1 wk)	MB	Sullivan	
					#	nsd
					acc	nsd
					Gen meas	
					task—math	-G
					setting—classrm	-G
					on T	-G

[a]See Table 1 for legend.
[b]Estimates averaged across subjects.
[c]BL = Baseline.

183

Table 4
Math—Single Subject Designs[a]

Study	Subject information	Independent variables	Duration of treatment	Design	Dependent variables	Immediate results	Follow-up
Cameron & Robinson (1980)	N = 3; 8.0, 7.7, 8.0 yrs; Hyp	SIT	12 Ts @ 30 min = 6 hr (approx. 3 wk)	MB, FU for 6 days	Add & subtract probs acc	SIT > BL	SIT > BL
					Gen meas on T		
					# wds. read	+G	+G
					# self-correct	+G	+G
						+G	+G
Case et al. (1991)	N = 4; 11–8, 11–1, 11–1, 11–2 yrs; Gr. 5 & 6; LD	SIT	8 Ts @ 35 min[b] = 4 hr, 40 min (2–3 wk)	MB, 10–13-wk FU	Add & subtract word probs acc	SIT > BL	SIT > BL for 2/4 subjects
					Gen meas setting—classrm self-eff	+G −G	
Davis & Hajicek (1985)	N = 7; x̄ = 12 yrs; 6 CD, 1 Schiz	SIT	11 Ts @ 20 min[b] = 3 hr, 40 min (approx. 3 wk)	MB	Multi probs rate of acc	SIT > BL	
					Gen meas on T	+G	

Study	Subjects	Treatment	Training	Design	Dependent measure	Results
Johnston et al. (1980)	N = 3; 9–9, 9–10, 10–3 yrs; EMR	SIT	12 Ts @ 30 min[b] = 6 hr (approx. 3 wk)	MB	Add & subtract probs acc #	SIT > BL SIT < BL
Murphy et al. (1984)	N = 9; preschool handicapped	SIT	10 Ts @ ? = ? (approx. 2 wk)	MB, 3 grps 6-mo FU	Count blocks Gen meas count objects	SIT > BL +G
Swanson (1985), Exp. 2	N = 3; x̄ = 9.7 yrs; ED	SIT	10 Ts @ 30 min[b] = 5 hr (approx. 2 wk)	MB	Add & subtract probs acc Gen meas word probs	SIT > BL +G
Swanson & Scarpati (1984), Exp. 2	N = 1; 13 yrs; Sev ed han	SIT	23 Ts @ 30 min[b] = 11 hr, 30 min (approx. 5 wk)	ABAB	Math probs Gen meas setting—classrm	SIT > BL +G
Whitman & Johnston (1983)	N = 9; x̄ = 11–10 yrs; EMR	SIT	27 Ts @ 30 min[b] = 13 hr, 30 min (approx. 6 wk)	MB, 3 grps	Add & subtract probs acc #	SIT > BL SIT < BL

[a] See Table 1 for legend.
[b] Estimates averaged across subjects.
[c] BL = Baseline.

several well-designed and comprehensive SIT studies revealed less impressive or nonsignificant immediate and long-term outcomes (Abikoff *et al.,* 1988; Borkowski & Varnhagen, 1984; Eastman & Rasbury, 1981; Friedling & O'Leary, 1979; Varni & Henker, 1979). In fact, Abikoff and colleagues (1988) failed to find any clear immediate or delayed SIT benefits following 32 sessions of training over a 16-wk period, although the severity of students' pretreatment disorders may have been a factor in these outcomes.

Contribution of Reinforcement Contingencies

The literature debates the relative contribution of behavioral contingency and self-management procedures on SIT effectiveness (Roberts & Dick, 1982). That reinforcement contingencies alone can influence academic performances in children raises the question of the independent contributions of SIT in a large number of studies reviewed here. Concomitant external reinforcement beyond social praise or self-management techniques (i.e., self-monitoring, self-reinforcement) were employed in almost half the studies reporting either immediate, sustained, or generalized SIT facilitation (e.g., Cameron & Robinson, 1980; Smith & Van Biervliet, 1986; Swanson & Scarpati, 1984). Moreover, only one study reported successful SIT transfer to a classroom setting without the use of such additional procedures (Guevremont, Osnes, & Stokes, 1988). Considerable variation was seen also regarding when reinforcement was administered (i.e., during training or following training), the behaviors targeted for reinforcement (i.e., academic responding, social appropriateness, attention, or use of self-instructions), and whether external- or self-management procedures were employed (e.g., Abikoff *et al.,* 1988; Johnston, Whitman, & Johnson, 1980; Swanson, 1985; Whitman & Johnston, 1983).

One study was designed specifically to assess the additive and differential benefits of tangible reinforcement on SIT effectiveness. Roberts and coworkers (1987) randomly assigned first- and second-grade children to one of three SIT conditions in which token reinforcement was administered by an external agent during training contingent either on math performance accuracy, on appropriate use of the self-verbalization procedure, or on both accuracy and use of self-instructions. Children's math performance improved in all three SIT contingency conditions relative to baseline performance and to a no-training control condition that simply received reinforcement for accurate responses. However, all SIT conditions led to performances equivalent to those observed in a didactic strategy instruction condition combined with accuracy reinforcement. These authors concluded that optimal learning processes might be best obtained through combined SIT and external reinforcement procedures, regardless of the format of such contingencies. A similar conclusion was forwarded by Cameron and Robinson (1980), who suggested that SIT combined with self-management procedures gives children "the skill and the will" to perform. The fact that children only improved from SIT following the addition of self-management techniques in Varni and Henker (1979) also supports this conclusion. Thus, the work reviewed here suggests that behavioral contingencies or self-management techniques may be required to foster long-term and generalized SIT improvements.

Performance Rates and Accuracy

Another shortcoming is that SIT can lead to initial reductions in rate of responding. That is, SIT benefits often were obtained on measures of math performance accuracy but not on indices of rate (Keogh, Whitman, & Maxwell, 1988; Johnston & Whitman, 1987; Johnston et al., 1980; Schunk, 1982; Whitman & Johnston, 1983). Slower workrates (Guevremont et al., 1988) and a reduced quantity of completed items (Friedling & O'Leary, 1979) also were indirectly reported in two reading studies. Similar rate reductions have been found in previous work on nonacademic tasks (Meichenbaum & Goodman, 1971). Although one might argue that substantial reductions in children's rate of completion could interfere with classroom progress, the average rate reduction found in these studies was minimal in comparison with the average increases in performance accuracy. Also, the lower rates of completion found in SIT students immediately following training were not evident at a 1 week or a 1 month follow-up (Johnston & Whitman, 1987). In another study, two SIT children who evidenced a slower workpace displayed greater on-task behavior, presumably because of the more careful responding (Guevremont et al., 1988).

Such findings indicate that students may need time to practice the self-verbalization strategies inherent in SIT, especially when consolidating them in the context of newly acquired academic skills (Eastman & Rasbury, 1981). The extra expenditure of effort necessary to employ a heavily verbal strategy such as SIT may initially result in less time for complex cognitive processes (Borkowski & Varnhagen, 1984), the impact of which is particularly evident in the mathematics domain. Several researchers have suggested that initial reductions in performance rate should be expected until children internalize and automatically apply their self-verbalization strategies (Johnston et al., 1980; Keogh et al., 1988). The potential drawback of performance rate reductions may be minimized if recognized as a necessary by-product of SIT, if seen as a more conscientious or cautious mode of responding, and if outcome evaluations are based on rates of correct responding rather than on simple response rates (e.g., Case, Harris, & Graham, 1991).

Restricted Evidence of Maintenance and Generalization

An important criterion for any educational intervention ultimately is whether it insures sustained and generalized improvements in performance. Unfortunately, neither durability nor generalizability of SIT performance gains has been well substantiated. First, assessments of maintenance were conducted in less than half the studies and follow-up rarely entailed periods of more than a few weeks. When a 6-month delay was used, long-term SIT benefits were not obtained in one study (Abikoff *et al.*, 1988) and maturation and schooling may have contributed to sustained benefits in the other study (Murphy, Bates, & Anderson, 1984).

Second, although generalization across tasks was evaluated in a large proportion of studies, transfer most typically was examined through a narrow framework using tasks or measures that closely overlapped with those skills targeted during training; for example, slightly more complex word problems (Johnston & Whitman, 1987; Leon & Pepe, 1983; Swanson, 1985), from addition to subtraction tasks (Case *et al.*, 1991), slightly different text errors (Miller, Giovenco, & Rentiers, 1987), or recall of stories instead of sentences (Borkowski & Varnhagen, 1984). Rarely was generalization assessed across multiple modalities (i.e., cognitive, behavioral, or affective), multiple settings (i.e., home, school, or community), or from the perspective of more than one respondent (i.e., teacher, parent, or child). Unfortunately, in the three studies in which transfer was assessed using a broader range of procedures, limited SIT effects were found in one study (Abikoff *et al.*, 1988), chance findings may have contributed to the favorable outcomes obtained in the second study (Glenwick & Barocas, 1979), and equivocal generalization effects were found in the third study (Case *et al.*, 1991). That is, Case and co-workers (1991) found positive generalization on arithmetic word problems in the classroom but small improvements in self-efficacy and mixed results in transferring from addition to subtraction problems.

Third, attempts to assess SIT effects across alternative behavioral and cognitive skill domains produced equivocal results. SIT benefits transferred from training on academic tasks to tasks requiring general attentional skills [e.g., Matching Familiar Figures Test (MFFT)] (e.g., Brown & Alford, 1984; Schleser, Meyers, Cohen, & Thackwray, 1983) but not to stable indices of intelligence or verbal abilities (e.g., Abikoff *et al.*, 1988; Glenwick & Barocas, 1979). Furthermore, SIT applied to math tasks led to improvements in oral reading (Cameron & Robinson, 1980) and on standardized measures of spelling, reading, and general information (Schleser *et al.*, 1983). SIT applied to reading tasks did not result in improvements on math tasks, however (Friedling & O'Leary, 1979; Varni & Henker, 1979). Such results indicate that training in one academic domain may not automatically lead to improvements in other skill domains or on general intellectual skills. That transfer is more evident when SIT is applied to academic skill domains other than mathematics possibly reflects the greater emphasis on task-specific skills during mathematics remediation.

Fourth, in the few cases in which transfer was obtained across settings (i.e., to academic or behavioral performances in the classroom), concomitant self-management procedures were employed (Cameron & Robinson, 1980; Smith & Van Biervliet, 1986; Swanson & Scarpati, 1984) in all but two studies (Case *et al.,* 1991; Guevremont *et al.,* 1988). Moreover, in several studies SIT fostered neither academic gains (Swanson, 1985; Varni & Henker, 1979) nor on-task behavior (Eastman & Rasbury, 1981; Friedling & O'Leary, 1979; Varni & Henker, 1979) in the classroom, even with additional self-management procedures.

Finally, interactive treatment procedures like SIT, involving corrective feedback, mediated instruction, and modeling, have been postulated to lead to posttreatment motivational improvements because children can better monitor personal performances and thereby increase their sense of personal control (Bandura, 1977, 1986; Schunk, 1981). However, equivocal results have been reported regarding generalized motivational and affective improvements following SIT (Keogh *et al.,* 1988). More positively, junior high school girls who received SIT as opposed to didactic instruction evidenced reductions in self-reported math anxiety and greater internal locus of control (Genshaft & Hirt, 1980). Similarly, reading anxiety reductions and increased reading enjoyment were reported following SIT in fifth-grade below-average readers (Miller & Rentiers, 1991). Improvements in self-concept and self-efficacy have also been reported (Schunk, 1982; Schunk & Rice, 1984), although significant effects are not obtained consistently (Abikoff *et al.,* 1988; Case *et al.,* 1991; Keogh *et al.,* 1988).

In general, the qualifications surrounding SIT maintenance and generalization are consistent with the well-documented difficulty of obtaining sustained and generalized performance gains following other strategy training and cognitive-behavioral interventions (Cole & Kazdin, 1980; Kendall, Borkowski, & Cavanaugh, 1980; Meichenbaum & Asarnow, 1979; Stokes & Baer, 1977; Whalen, Henker, & Hinshaw, 1985). This body of data makes it obvious that more research is required to identify means of increasing the durability and generalization of SIT effects.

Minimal Evidence of Social Validity

Another methodological drawback was the lack of attention given to the notion of social validity (Kazdin, 1977). As defined by Wolf (1978), social validity refers to the significance of targeted treatment goals, treatment procedures, and treatment outcomes. Such concepts have recently been incorporated into clinical treatment research as subjective consumer judgments about the fairness, reasonableness, and appropriateness of a chosen treatment and associated client outcomes (Kazdin, 1980, 1981). A growing body of literature supports the idea that such consumer perceptions also significantly impact treatment use in educational settings (Elliot, 1988; Martens, Peterson, Witt, & Cirone, 1986; Witt & Elliot, 1985). Teachers (Witt & Elliot, 1985) and children (Elliot, 1986; Elliot, Turco, & Gresham, 1987) are less apt to continue or promote the use of interventions that are viewed as cumbersome, less effective, or resource demanding. Only one study directly considered consumers' acceptance of SIT and its associated performance outcomes through informal posttreatment interviews. The four students and the one teacher in this study were asked to provide feedback on the effectiveness and value of the SIT procedures (Case *et al.,* 1991).

One way to assess the practical significance of SIT effects is to include a comparison peer control group to determine if academically deficient children who receive SIT function at the same level as normally achieving peers who receive no extra instruction. This was the case in one study, in which SIT-instructed below-average readers evidenced greater sensitivity to text errors than nontrained above-average readers (Miller *et al.,* 1987). Similarly, SIT-instructed EMR students performed at a level commensurate to normal peers who received no math remediation training (Keogh *et al.,* 1988). However, performance equivalency was not observed in cases in which skilled learners received didactic strategy instruction (Miller & Rentiers, 1991). These results provide only limited evidence that SIT can lead to practically significant academic performance improvements in less-skilled students.

Cost-effectiveness analyses require that the resources and negative side-effects associated with SIT be weighed against its accrued benefits (Wong, 1985). Moreover, SIT outcomes should be contrasted against those obtained through other accepted intervention procedures, since carefully conceived strategy training may suffice to produce academic improvements in some children (Burger, Blackman, & Clark, 1981). Again, few attempts were made to assess SIT on either of these social validity dimensions. However, in two studies, alternative training procedures were found to suffice in producing academic performance gains. Borkowski and Varnhagen (1984) reported equivalent recall performances in EMR students who received SIT or equivalent didactic strategy instruction. A long-term medication regimen, accompanied by external reinforcement procedures, also was more effective in producing lasting educational gains in attention-deficit disorder children than 32 hr of intensive one-to-one tutoring in SIT (Abikoff *et al.,* 1988). Such findings suggest that the observed behavioral and academic improvements following SIT may not always justify the required expenditures of time and effort. Thus, future recommendations regarding SIT effectiveness for academic remediation must be based on more comprehensive considerations of treatment acceptability, consumer satisfaction, practical significance, and cost-effectiveness.

Limited Consideration of Treatment Fidelity

Treatment fidelity is another important methodological consideration that focuses on the degree to which an intervention is taught and used as intended and whether designated treatment changes are linked to hypothesized performance outcomes (Kazdin, 1981, 1986; Yeaton & Sechrest, 1981). In the educational treatment literature, such issues have been referred to as intervention integrity, and include determinations of whether an intervention is taught with similar levels of enthusiasm, flexibility, and efficacy (Harris, 1982, 1988; Wong, 1985). Treatment fidelity is often overlooked in evaluating the efficacy of clinical or academic interventions (Moncher & Prinz, 1991). However, fidelity documentation is necessary if we wish to gain a better understanding of limited treatment outcomes or to conclude that a specific treatment directly affects performances (Cavanaugh & Borkowski, 1979). Without appropriate treatment fidelity assessments, less than optimal SIT effects could be attributed to inappropriate or incomplete applications of self-verbalization strategy rather than to any functional failure of SIT. In fact, cognitive researchers have found that students often modify or simplify trained strategies over time (Wong et al., 1986).

Unfortunately, less than half the SIT studies reviewed here provide clear evidence that any consideration was given to treatment fidelity. Only a few attempts were made to insure that designated SIT procedures were followed during training, through the use of scripts, manuals, checklists, or direct observations (e.g., Cameron & Robinson, 1980; Case et al., 1991; Miller, 1985, 1987; Schunk, 1982; Schunk & Rice, 1984; Smith & Van Biervliet, 1986). Moreover, only a few attempts were made to establish the quality of SIT presentations or to determine whether students employed the SIT intervention as planned during task performances (Barling, 1980; Case et al., 1991; Johnston & Whitman, 1987; Miller, 1985, 1987; Roberts et al., 1987; Schunk, 1982). In fact, students in one negative outcome study determined "whether or not to work on any given day" (i.e., use the SIT procedures), presumably as an attempt to minimize adult control (Varni & Henker, 1979, pp. 89). Formal analyses of lip movements (i.e., subvocalizations) were conducted in five studies to assess students' continued use of self-instructions (Cameron & Robinson, 1980; Eastman & Rasbury, 1981; Roberts et al., 1987; Smith & Van Biervliet, 1986; Whitman & Johnston, 1983). Other efforts to document children's use of the SIT procedures following training included: interviews in which children were asked to articulate the SIT procedures (Keogh *et al.,* 1988), direct recall assessments of SIT (Miller, 1987; Schunk, 1982), or observations of a child instructing a peer to use the SIT procedures (Malamuth, 1979). Direct links were established between children's use of the SIT self-verbalization strategy and performance accuracy in only one math study (Keogh *et al.,* 1988).

Although greater consideration of treatment fidelity was observed in the studies published after 1980, comprehensive analyses were rarely conducted to address all essential fidelity issues. Such evaluations would necessitate specific documentation of how the SIT procedure was taught and implemented during training, whether children employed the strategy as planned following training, and if strategy use was predictive of performance outcomes. Thus, more complete fidelity analyses are recommended in future evaluations of SIT effectiveness.

Summary

These methodological shortcomings, and the conflicting reports of maintenance and generalization following SIT, have led researchers and educators to focus on parameters that contribute to less than optimal SIT outcomes (Cole & Kazdin, 1980; Harris, 1982, 1985; Lloyd, 1980; Meichenbaum & Asarnow, 1979; Wong, 1985). One model for conceptualizing factors that impact on the efficacy of SIT proposed by Cohen and Meyers (1984) includes a thorough consideration of pretreatment student characteristics and instructional variables. Issues in each area are considered separately in the next two sections with respect to SIT-mediated math and reading outcomes.

STUDENT PRETREATMENT CHARACTERISTICS

Students in the review studies ranged in age from 4 to 14 years, covering the preschool to middle school grades. Moreover, a broad range of clinical subject populations was represented (i.e., hyperactive, impulsive, ADDH, conduct disorder, learning disabled, EMR). The majority of subject populations evidenced reading or mathematics skill deficiencies, typically determined on the basis of standardized test performance and teacher reports.

Cognitive Maturity and Verbal Ability

The complex verbal nature of SIT has led to the assumption that young children or less intellectually mature students may not evidence benefits because of less sophisticated cognitive and language abilities (Harris, 1982; Kendall, 1990). In particular, the application of a highly verbal strategy like

SIT might be expected to impede the decoding, comprehension, and retention processes critical for reading performances in less verbally skilled children. Such an assumption was supported by Schunk and Rice (1984), who found significant SIT effects with older (third and fourth grade) but not younger (second grade) children on story comprehension tasks. Similarly, Eastman and Rasbury (1981) reported minimal SIT facilitation with preschoolers on reading tasks.

On the other hand, SIT has led to significant performance benefits with lower verbal ability children in various cognitive and academic task domains (Copeland, 1981; Evangelisti, Whitman, & Maxwell, 1987; Whitman, 1987). Such was the case in two multiple-baseline studies conducted with handicapped preschoolers (i.e., reading, Guevremont *et al.,* 1988; math, Murphy *et al.,* 1984), in which immediate and generalized benefits were reported. Substantial SIT benefits also were found in three math studies conducted with EMR populations (Johnston *et al.,* 1980; Keogh *et al.,* 1988; Whitman & Johnston, 1983). In each case, an emphasis was placed on training children to self-instruct overtly and care was taken to insure that children mastered the self-statements. One especially striking outcome involved EMR students who, after receiving overt SIT, performed at a level commensurate with normal first-grade students (Keogh *et al.,* 1988).

Such results suggest that less cognitively mature children can evidence improvements in both reading and math skills following SIT when additional practice is provided and overt self-verbalization strategies are emphasized. Whitman (1990b) argued that overt SIT may encourage children to focus attention specifically on the problem to be solved and may foster active and optimal task performance strategies. Also, overt self-instructions are more easily prompted and reinforced by external agents. Even with such training modifications, however, it is clear that not all young children will benefit equally from SIT, since a good deal of performance variability was observed across these studies. Also, challenges have been raised about the adequacy of simple markers of a student's age and IQ as pretreatment indices of cognitive status (Cohen & Meyers, 1984). Assessments of Piagetian cognitive preskills (i.e., conservation, concrete operational thinking) have been recommended as alternative predictors of whether a child can profit from SIT (Borden, Brown, Wynne, & Schleser, 1987; Cohen & Meyers, 1984; Schleser, Meyers, & Cohen, 1981).

Learning and Attentional Deficits

Training procedures such as SIT, that stress self-controlled behavior and active problem-solving processes, might be expected to benefit children known to be inattentive (Abikoff, 1985) or inactive nonstrategic learners (Torgensen, 1982; Torgensen & Licht, 1983; Wong, 1985). Some support for this assumption has been found previously with learning disabled and EMR students (Harris, 1986; Steele & Barling, 1982) and was also seen in several studies reported here (Case *et al.,* 1991; Leon & Pepe, 1983; Swanson & Scarpati, 1984). The coexistence of severe attention and academic deficiencies, however, was likely to impede SIT outcomes across both academic domains. That is, all subjects in the negative or minimally effective SIT studies were characterized by moderate to extreme attention deficit disorders (with and without concomitant conduct difficulties) (e.g., Friedling & O'Leary, 1979). Of particular relevance is that no SIT benefits were found with children who had a long-standing diagnosis of ADDH in the most comprehensive and thorough study reviewed here (Abikoff *et al.,* 1988). When significant SIT gains were observed with children evidencing hyperactive or impulsive behaviors, either the population was judged not to be as severe or behavioral contingency programs were integrated into the SIT regimen (e.g., Brown & Alford, 1984; Cameron & Robinson, 1980; Glenwick & Barocas, 1979). Thus, SIT treatment modifications may be required to foster academic remediation in students who evidence severe pretreatment attentional deficits.

Prior Knowledge and Skill in an Academic Domain

Although there is much support for the efficacy of SIT in promoting cognitive processes, there is debate about the role played by students' prerequisite knowledge and skills in a targeted academic domain (Wong, 1985). One hypothesis is that SIT will be most effective in fostering the academic performances of students with severe academic deficiencies, because students are encouraged to employ active problem-solving processes and to focus on critical task components (Whitman, 1987, 1990a,b). Alternatively, students may require a standard repertoire of task entrance skills before SIT benefits can be realized (Kendall, 1990; Lloyd, Saltzman, & Kaufman, 1981). A third hypothesis is that SIT training may have the greatest impact with students who have the capacity (i.e., possess some rudimentary skills) but for some reason do not spontaneously employ their academic skills and strategies (Harris, 1982, 1986; Meichenbaum, 1980; Wong, Harris, & Graham, 1992).

That the majority of both reading and math studies reported positive outcomes with academically deficient populations supports the latter hypothesis. It appears that SIT is most effective with students who are not spontaneously strategic during learning. For example, below-average readers evidenced significant comprehension monitoring benefits following an extended SIT regimen (i.e., 3 as opposed to 1 training session) (Miller *et al.,* 1987). Further support that SIT is effective with less sophisticated subjects was demonstrated by the fact that EMR students with few prerequisite math skills displayed greater SIT benefits than their more knowledgeable normal peers (Keogh *et al.,* 1988). The critical role of prior knowledge was supported in this same study by the fact that pretreatment academic test scores significantly predicted math problem-solving accuracy over and above any other variable entered into the multiple regression equation, including treatment condition, language skill, and personal attributions.

Another hypothesis regarding pretreatment skill levels is that SIT may not benefit students who have high abilities in an academic domain. In fact, Peterson and Swing (1984) concluded that, in some instances, a resource-demanding cognitive strategy intervention such as SIT may actually interfere with learners who already possess and automatically apply critical cognitive and metacognitive processes. Minimal support for this idea was found in one study in which children with above-average math skills were not found to benefit any more from SIT than from learning how to set personal criteria and to apply a self-monitoring procedure (Barling, 1980). Such findings stress the importance of adequate learner analyses, since skilled learners may not require the self-mediational and self-control benefits inherent in SIT. Similar conclusions have been drawn from past work in the general cognitive literature, where overt verbalizations were found to interfere with the memory performances of high achieving children (Denny & Turner, 1979).

Unfortunately, only minimal attention was given to the impact of pretreatment academic abilities on SIT effectiveness, making it difficult to draw accurate conclusions. It is clear that such variables do play a role in SIT responsiveness, although mixed results were reported regarding the direction of such influences. There was also some suggestion that training environment variables, such as the extent of instruction, are a factor in determining SIT effectiveness with skill deficient populations. Much more work is needed to assess how critical prerequisite academic skills differentially impact on SIT outcomes across various academic domains.

Affective or Motivational Characteristics

Meichenbaum (1977, 1980) and others (Harris, 1982; Kendall & Braswell, 1985) have routinely proposed that careful attention be paid to identifying students' pretreatment maladaptive behaviors, cognitions, and feelings that can affect the success of SIT. Until recently, there have been few attempts to examine the latter group of affective and motivational characteristics. Such variables include self-efficacy perceptions that one has the capability to perform a task (Bandura, 1977, 1986; Bandura & Adams, 1977); outcome expectations or judgments that a given behavior will lead to a certain outcome (Rotter, Chance, & Phares, 1972); and causal attributions or beliefs that one's increased efforts can produce success whereas a lack of effort will predict failure (Weiner, 1979). Deficits in such motivational processes have been postulated to lead to less than optimal half-hearted performances, less persistence in the face of performance obstacles (Schunk, 1981, 1986), and less positive assessments of one's worth (Covington & Beery, 1976; Covington & Omelich, 1979). Accumulating evidence suggests that such motivational characteristics are frequently seen in students with learning difficulties and have a strong influence on the success of academic remediation procedures (Borkowski, Johnston, & Reid, 1987; Harris *et al.,* 1992; Kurtz & Borkowski, 1984; Pearl, 1985; Ryan, Short, & Weed, 1986a).

That motivational pretreatment characteristics function as important mediators of SIT outcomes was demonstrated in an early study by Bugenthal, Whalen, and Henker (1977), in which attributive orientation was shown to determine children's performance on general cognitive tasks following SIT. Similar conclusions were drawn in several studies here. Johnston and Whitman (1987) found that attributions of personal causation regarding successful math performance affected whether students evidenced greater math performances following SIT or didactic instruction. Students with external attributive styles benefitted more from a self-instruction regimen than from didactic instruction, but no such SIT facilitation was noted for students with internal attributions. Such differential effectiveness was ascribed to the fact that the active strategic processing and self-regulation promoted through SIT was more beneficial for those students who were known to be passive in their approach to problem-solving. Pretreatment self-efficacy perceptions and ratings of task persistence also were found to account for a significant proportion of math performance variance (Schunk, 1982). These findings were contradicted, however, by the results of another study in which attributive style was not found to significantly add to a regression model in predicting math performance over that obtained with preskill knowledge alone (Keogh *et al.,* 1988).

The mixed outcomes regarding the influence of pretreatment motivational characteristics on SIT effectiveness may be attributed to the fact that such variables also are postulated to be affected by interactive treatment procedures such as SIT (Bandura, 1977; Schunk, 1981). In fact, after reviewing the child psychotherapy literature, Braswell, Koehler, and Kendall (1985) concluded that motivational variables such as self-efficacy judgments, performance expectations, and causal attributions should be regarded both as mediators and as targets of treatment outcomes. Thus, although firm conclusions cannot yet be drawn regarding the differential impact of unique student motivational characteristics, these results contribute to the growing body of literature that calls for more careful examinations of the role of motivational variables in designing future SIT regimens.

Summary

In general, the results reviewed here support the call for more careful assessments of students' incoming characteristics and abilities in order to more fully assess the efficacy of SIT for academic remediation. Not all students should be expected to benefit from one SIT paradigm (Schleser, Cohen, Meyers & Rodick, 1984). Cognitive, behavioral, academic, and motivational individual differences at pretest were found to affect SIT responsiveness, supporting previous work in other cognitive domains (Cole & Kazdin, 1980; Craighead, Meyers, & Craighead, 1985; Harris, 1986; Pearl, 1985). It appears that different SIT procedures may be necessary for students with varying attentional capacities, academic preskills, and motivational attributes (Bornstein, 1985). Moreover, Kendall (1977) asserts that a child's pretraining failure experiences and the quality of past adult relationships also impact on SIT success. Such characteristics may affect whether SIT is directed toward the development of basic academic skills or toward the promotion of preexisting skills (Wong, 1985). It is also clear that task complexity is another parameter that interacts with pretreatment characteristics to affect children's performances (Evangelisti et al., 1986). Unfortunately, not nearly enough research has been done to adequately address the multitude of questions about the mediational role of individual difference variables on SIT effectiveness. Further documentation of pretreatment characteristics is essential to designing SIT interventions that match critical student deficits and treatment goals to affect greater SIT outcomes.

INSTRUCTIONAL VARIABLES

There have been numerous requests for more careful conceptualizations and componential analyses of SIT regimens (Cohen & Meyers, 1984; Harris, 1982, 1990), yet rarely are SIT procedures described in enough detail to allow for accurate assessments of the authors' adherence to the original SIT regimen (Meichenbaum, 1977; Meichenbaum & Goodman, 1971), and few studies are adequately designed to assess the separate contributions of various treatment components inherent in SIT. The available literature, nonetheless, permits some preliminary conclusions about the relative contributions of the components constituting SIT.

Nature of the Self-Verbalization Intervention

As originally proposed, a complete self-verbalization intervention involves (1) task analysis or criterion-setting statements that identify variables related to a desired performance goal; (2) planning statements that specify a specific plan of action; (3) evaluative statements that encourage ongoing monitoring of progress toward goal attainment; (4) reward statements to reinforce ongoing performances; and (5) corrective or coping statements for dealing with obstacles to problem solution or task completion. Although it is assumed that each of these strategy components is necessary to effect optimal outcomes, questions have arisen about whether certain components are more critical than others to improving academic performances (Cole & Kazdin, 1980; Meichenbaum, 1980).

The relative contribution of the early criterion-setting and task-focused statements was directly assessed in one math study (Spates & Kanfer, 1977). First-grade students were randomly assigned to one of five experimental conditions in which various components were progressively added to the SIT regimen. Improvements in math accuracy and rate were obtained only when criterion-setting components (i.e., task analysis and planning self-statements) were incorporated into the self-verbalization strategy. These improvements were relative to two control conditions in which children either read numbers from a math problem sheet or verbalized each problem in a left to right progression. Further improvements were not observed with the addition of self-reinforcement or coping statements, suggesting that the task-analysis and planning verbalizations are critical to SIT regimens, at least in the domain of mathematics.

An informal examination of the self-verbalization content in the math studies reporting positive SIT outcomes provided further support for this conclusion. Early problem-focused components were included and the latter motivational components (i.e., reward statements and corrective or coping statements) were often omitted from the SIT regimen in these studies. A similar examination of the successful reading outcome studies did not reveal such omissions, however. In fact, more complete SIT regimens were found in the reading- than in the math-focused studies. Thus, the inclusion of the two motivational components may be especially critical for promoting outcomes in the reading but not in the math domain.

Content of the Self-Verbalization Strategy

The content of the self-verbalizations used in a SIT regimen has been posed as another possible moderator of SIT effectiveness (Kendall, 1977; Swanson & Kozleski, 1985). Self-statements can apply to a broad range of tasks across domains or can be specific to the task at hand. These distinct categories are respectively labeled as task-approach and task-specific statements (Harris, 1982). Task-approach statements typically are structured as interrogatives (i.e., What do I need to do here?) that guide general problem-solving and regulatory processes (i.e., attention, monitoring, and motivation). Task-specific statements provide critical academic skills and usually are structured as direct task-performance steps.

Global task-approach statements have been hypothesized to promote greater generalization of skills than task-specific self-statements, an assumption that has received some confirmation in past studies assessing general cognitive skills (Kendall & Wilcox, 1980; Schleser et al., 1981). Little support for this assumption was obtained across the academic domains reviewed here, however. In fact, no facilitative differences were noted between the two self-verbalization strategies relative to didactic instruction on assessments of comprehension monitoring during reading (Miller, 1985). Moreover, there was some suggestion that specificity of the self-verbalizations was a critical determinant of math improvements. That is, Schleser and colleagues (1983) found a task-specific SIT approach to be significantly more effective than a global SIT approach in facilitating generalized math performances in behavior-disordered third- and fourth-graders. More importantly, however, neither self-verbalization strategy facilitated generalization as broad as that obtained through a "directed discovery" SIT approach in which children were led to discover appropriate self-verbalization strategies through a question-and-answer Socratic dialogue.

An important advantage of the directed discovery SIT procedure used by Schleser and co-workers (1983) is that it fosters a systematic combination of both global task-approach and task-specific problem-solving strategy statements. Such combined approaches have been hypothesized to optimize SIT outcomes and to facilitate generalization (Swanson & Kozleski, 1985; Whitman, 1987, 1990a,b). That a majority of the positive outcome studies reviewed here involved such a combined approach lends support to this assumption. Further affirmation of the combined approach was reported by Johnston and Whitman (1987), who found significantly greater improvements in first-graders' math accuracy after a combined SIT strategy over either a task-specific SIT strategy or an equivalent didactic instruction. Moreover, greater facilitation was observed in students who evidenced the lowest pretreatment math ability, leading these researchers to suggest that a combined self-verbalization strategy is especially facilitative for less competent students.

One conclusion to be drawn, although not directly tested here, may be that recommendations regarding the optimal content of the self-instructions should depend on critical student pretreatment characteristics. General task-approach SIT may be best suited to students with less efficient self-regulation or attentional capacities but with some prior academic skills and background knowledge. Task-specific SIT may be best suited to students with poorly organized or deficient task strategies necessary for academic performances. Alternatively, combined SIT approaches may always lead to the greatest facilitation for less competent students, regardless of their academic deficits (Brown & Alford, 1984; Case et al., 1991; Swanson, 1985; Swanson & Scarpati, 1984). Thus, future work is needed to determine more accurately how student factors interact with the content of the self-verbalization strategies inherent in SIT.

Procedures to Foster Internalization

As originally conceptualized, the internalization of a self-verbalization strategy was to be accomplished by teaching children to fade the self-verbalizations first to a whisper and eventually to a covert subvocalization level. The critical role of such an internalization procedure and the specific role of covert speech has been the focus of much debate (Harris, 1990; Roberts, 1979). Although modeling and overt verbalization procedures have been postulated as critical instructional components for enhancing self-regulated learning in young children (Jackson & Calhoun, 1982; Schunk, 1986), overt verbalizations also have been found to interfere with timed, reflexive, or automatic cognitive processes (Harris, 1982; Robin, Armel, & O'Leary, 1975). Indeed, a mixed picture was also presented here regarding the overall importance of internalizing the self-verbalization regimens.

The relative effect of successively adding the modeling, overt verbalization, and covert procedures into a SIT regimen was indirectly assessed in two multiple-baseline studies. In one study, the greatest improvements in children's math performance accuracy were obtained following the addition of modeling and overt self-verbalization phases; no further improvements were noted after the children learned to covertly apply the SIT procedures (Swanson, 1985). Similarly, in another study with severely behaviorally disordered children, only minimal improvements were noted in children's math performance accuracy following the addition of a faded self-verbalization procedure (Davis & Hajicek, 1985). The findings in two other group studies also ran counter to the notion that verbal mediation influences self-controlled behavior. That is, only weak (Roberts *et al.,* 1987) or negative (Eastman & Rasbury, 1981) associations were found between children's documented use of a self-verbalization strategy and subsequent behavioral and academic improvements.

One explanation for these equivocal results is that the necessity of employing covert self-verbalizations may differ depending on the academic skills targeted for remediation. In fact, approximately 75% of the reading and 50% of the math studies that reported positive outcomes employed all phases of the SIT procedure. Possibly, the internalization phases of SIT are more essential for fostering reading than math performances, whereas the modeling and overt utilization of a self-verbalization strategy are enough to lead to increased math performances. The further facilitation noted on attentional but not math indices following the addition of a faded SIT procedure in Davis and Hajicek (1985) lends support to this idea. Another explanation is that the internalization of the SIT procedure may interact with children's cognitive maturity (Fuson, 1979). Greater math accuracy was found in EMR students relative to children exhibiting normal or below-average math skills during overt applications of SIT. No such group differences were noted during internalized SIT procedures (Koegh et al., 1988; Whitman & Johnston, 1983), indicating that covert self-verbalization strategies may not be as effective with less-competent students. Similar outcomes on general cognitive tasks have been reported for normal preschool-aged children (Jackson & Calhoun, 1982). A final explanation provided by Guevremont and co-workers (1988) is that children who benefit most from SIT are those who evidence adequate mastery of the self-verbalization procedure at an overt level. Perhaps young children need to meet a criterion level of SIT performance at an overt level before positive effects are obtained from internalization procedures. Unfortunately, none of these hypotheses regarding the contribution of internalization procedures was tested fully here.

Intensity of the SIT Regimen

Training intensity most often refers to the duration and time frame in which a treatment is provided. However, it can also refer to the amount of time devoted specifically to the skills targeted for improvement, to the variety of examples used during training, and to the number of settings across which a treatment is administered (Stokes & Baer, 1977). In many cases, the intensity of a provided treatment is difficult to ascertain because of incomplete treatment descriptions or because a variety of training tasks is employed. More critically, cross-study comparisons are tricky because the extent of training across studies varies widely. Between 1 and 35 training sessions were administered in the studies reviewed; total training contact ranged from 20 min to 32 hr, spanning periods of 1 day to 6 months.

Training intensity has been found to strongly affect the generalizability of clinical outcomes with children (Kazdin, 1982). Such a conclusion was supported here in several ways. A contributing factor in the cases in which limited evidence of SIT generalization was reported may have been the use of low intensity training procedures. With the exception of one study (Abikoff et al., 1988), more intense SIT regimens (i.e., several sessions spanning at least 2 wks) were represented in the majority of favorable outcome studies. It should be noted, however, that the average time devoted to SIT in any of the positive outcome studies was extremely limited. Moreover, the intensity of a SIT regimen appeared to be a critical determinant of less-abled students' performance and of reading versus math performances. Eastman and Rasbury (1981) noted an increased trend toward SIT facilitation on reading performances only after several training sessions, leading them to conclude that less verbally skilled students may require more time to consolidate SIT skills. Indirect support for this idea was also found in two other studies in which SIT benefits were observed on comprehension monitoring performances in less capable readers after three sessions (Miller *et al.,* 1987) but not after one session of SIT (Miller, 1987). On the whole, it appeared that more successful outcomes in math than in reading were obtained after shorter training regimens, suggesting that the intensity of SIT treatment may differentially impact performances in reading and math domains. Such a conclusion deserves further empirical validation, however.

Another aspect of treatment intensity is whether various people in the child's major life environments are involved in administering the SIT regimen. The specific impact of various change agents on SIT effectiveness was directly addressed by Glenwick and Barocas (1979). In that study, 40- fifth- and sixth-grade impulsive students were randomly assigned to a no-treatment control or to one of four experimental SIT conditions in which an experimenter, a teacher, a parent, or both a parent and a teacher implemented the SIT regimen. Keeping in mind several important drawbacks (i.e., the inflated chance for error, the lack of verification that training was given consistently across the conditions, the significant pre- to posttest improvements in all experimental conditions), sustained and generalized SIT benefits (especially on math tasks) were more evident when SIT was implemented and monitored by both teachers and parents.

Thus, more work is needed to further assess how factors related to treatment intensity impact upon SIT effectiveness. From the work reviewed here, it appears that more successful immediate and generalized outcomes will be obtained when SIT is administered during multiple sessions, over expanded periods of time, using a variety of training tasks, and by various change agents within a child's major life environments. However, students' pretreatment characteristics and the academic skills targeted for remediation also may be factors in designing maximally efficient SIT procedures.

Addition of Metacognitive Training Components

A growing body of literature points to the critical importance of metacognitive information during cognitive-behavioral (Loper, 1982; Meichenbaum, 1980, 1986; Meichenbaum & Asarnow, 1979; Tharp & Gallimore, 1985) and other strategy instruction models (Borkowski & Cavanaugh, 1979; Garner & Alexander, 1989; Symons, Snyder, Cariglia-Bull, & Pressley, 1989). Such information goes beyond explanations of how to apply a strategy and includes explanations of why a strategy is useful, when and where a strategy may be most effective, and routines to promote active performance regulation (Brown, 1978; Brown *et al.,* 1981; Pressley *et al.,* 1987a, 1989a; O'Sullivan & Pressley, 1984; Reeve & Brown, 1985). Pressley, Borkowski, and O'Sullivan (1984) have argued that students could be taught directly to attend to such critical strategy information through metacognitive acquisition procedures (MAPs), such as self-testing and comparing one's performance using a newly learned procedure with previous performance. Direct training of MAPs is intended to highlight the value of a newly learned strategy by getting students to monitor the effects of the strategy on personal performances. Such metacognitive procedures are hypothesized to enhance self-regulatory processes that contribute to sustained and generalized outcomes. (See Ghatala, 1986, and Pressley & Ghatala, 1989, for reviews of relevant evidence.)

Surprisingly, neither metacognitive information nor MAPs were incorporated as a goal of training here. In fact, only seven studies even minimally attended to these issues (Abikoff *et al.,* 1988; Borkowski & Varnhagen, 1984; Cameron & Robinson, 1980; Case *et al.,* 1991; Miller *et al.,* 1987; Miller & Rentiers, 1991; Swanson & Scarpati, 1984). In all cases, metacognitive information was provided by the instructor through explanations about the purpose, usefulness of, or best place to employ the SIT strategy. For example, Cameron and Robinson (1980) explained why SIT would be useful in the classroom and actually had children pretend they were doing classroom tasks during training. Swanson and Scarpati (1984), provided a rationale for the use of overt verbalizations not only to the target child but also to the child's classmates, who were administered tokens for appropriately ignoring the target child's self-talk. The children in Case and co-workers (1991) were reminded directly at the end of each training session of appropriate times to use SIT and also were encouraged to discuss SIT with their teacher. In most cases, however, few details were given in regard to the frequency or the exact incorporation of such information in the SIT regimen. Also, there were no attempts made to encourage independent strategy comparisons, before and after SIT performance contrasts, or any other active MAPs. Nevertheless, in all but one case (Abikoff *et al.,* 1988) the outcomes for these studies clearly supported previous hypotheses regarding the facilitative effects of such information on children's sustained and generalized use of the SIT strategy.

The work reviewed here clearly suggests that SIT procedures should be augmented with more comprehensive metacognitive details about the rationale and usefulness of the strategy, as well as with specific procedures that emphasize the comparative benefits of SIT and link SIT efforts to improved performances. Although successful transfer was observed in most studies in which such information was directly provided, the independent contribution of such training components has not been adequately addressed. Further assessments also are needed of the incremental performance effects obtained when attention is given to the intentional training of MAPs during SIT, especially in regard to fostering generalization to new task domains and to new settings.

Summary

There is little doubt that critical instructional parameters can influence the success of SIT interventions. In fact, self-instructional training components were shown to promote durable use of a listening-comprehension strategy (Elliot-Faust & Pressley, 1986). Variations in the nature and inclusion of major SIT components, the intensity of training, and the provision of meta-cognitive information and routines have led to the recognition that much more work is needed to clarify the aspects of SIT intervention that affect broader academic performance gains. Future work is also required to assess the effect of specific treatment components for children with various behavioral, cognitive, and motivational characteristics. There is reason to believe that differential treatment effects found in past studies are due in part to the ways SIT is designed, presented, and practiced (Harris, 1988). A greater analysis of instructional variables that contribute to children's performances will increase teachers' instructional repertoires by enabling them to flexibly select and vary SIT interventions to best fit their own and their students' needs and preferences (Joyce & Weil, 1986).

CONCLUSIONS AND RECOMMENDATIONS

Self-instructional training is a multifaceted intervention technique that encourages active self-regulation processes and promotes self-sufficient learners. Clearly, the studies reviewed here suggest that SIT procedures can lead to improvements in children's performances on a variety of academic skills across the domains of reading and mathematics. Moreover, SIT procedures appear to be applicable for children evidencing a wide range of cognitive, behavioral, and motivational deficits. These encouraging results add to the growing consensus that self-instruction is an academic remediation technique worthy of continued empirical investigation (Harris, 1982; Lloyd, 1980; Meichenbaum, 1985, 1986; Meichenbaum & Burland, 1979; Swanson & Kozleski, 1985; Wong *et al.,* 1992).

Several reasons have been given for the apparent success of SIT as an effective academic remediation technique. First, the verbalization and fading procedure inherent in SIT may provide a natural developmental training sequence to enhance children's verbal mediational strategies during cognitive tasks (Day, Cordan, & Kerwin, 1989; Fuson, 1979; Harris, 1986; Palincsar, 1986; Wertsch, 1980). Second, the incorporation of a problem-solving self-verbalization strategy serves to focus attention on critical task features, promote more active encoding and retrieval processes, and foster executive control processes such as the ability to plan, monitor, and evaluate ongoing cognitive processes (Asarnow & Meichenbaum, 1979; Brown *et al.*, 1981; Ryan *et al.*, 1986; Wong, 1980). Third, the modeling, self-monitoring, and self-reinforcement components inherent in SIT have been hypothesized to elicit improved coping responses and motivational constructs (Bandura, 1986; Pearl, 1985; Schunk, 1981, 1986; Zimmerman, 1989). Finally, the explicit teaching, modeling, elaboration, and feedback contained in SIT procedures and the gradual removal of such instructional supports provides the scaffolding that enables students to become independent self-sufficient learners (Bruner, 1984; Duffy & Roehler, 1989; Pearson & Fielding, 1991).

Nevertheless, the findings reviewed here also suggest that SIT interventions for academic remediation are still at a preliminary stage. Several important methodological reservations were noted, making it difficult to accurately determine the components of SIT that are necessary or sufficient to further academic performances or to fully assess whether SIT promotes socially valid, sustained, and generalized benefits. Such observations have direct implications for enhancing the design of future SIT interventions and for broadening the scope of SIT instruction.

Enhancing the Design of Future SIT Interventions

Match SIT with Student Characteristics

The strong interrelationship of behavioral, cognitive, and motivational systems in strategy instruction research (Borkowski, Weyhing, & Turner, 1986; Copeland, 1981) points to the need for comprehensive assessments of critical individual differences in each of these domains. At a minimum, pretreatment assessments should focus on general attentional, intellectual, and verbal capacity, cognitive and metacognitive processes, academic knowledge and abilities, and motivational characteristics (Harris, 1982; Ryan *et al.*, 1986). The latter might involve appraisals of self-efficacy, outcome expectations, and attributions toward the academic skills under consideration as well as toward the effort required to apply a verbal mediation strategy like SIT (Harris, 1990).

More careful documentation of students' incoming abilities and characteristics should directly influence the form, content, and rate of self-instructional training regimens (Kendall, 1977; Meichenbaum 1977, 1980). Students should not be expected to benefit equally from one type of SIT paradigm (Reeve & Brown, 1985; Schleser *et al.*, 1984). Knowledge of student individual differences is crucial for making decisions about SIT modifications (e.g., overt versus covert verbalizations) and for determining under what conditions to append alternative remedial approaches to SIT procedures. For example, it appears that cognitive and behavioral improvements in children with severe attention deficits may best be obtained when SIT is combined with external reinforcement contingencies, self-management, relaxation, or psychostimulant medication (Abikoff, 1985; Horn, Chatoor, & Conners, 1983). In addition, task-specific deficits should be determined before training is designed to maximize treatment benefits (e.g., Case *et al.,* 1991). Decisions concerning SIT design also must be made in conjunction with critical task requirements and targeted treatment goals, to insure optimal performance benefits (Harris, 1982). Thus, differential SIT regimens should be designed only after careful consideration of a child's pretreatment characteristics, various criterion tasks, and desired performance goals (Guevremont *et al.,* 1988; Stokes & Osnes, 1986).

Conduct Componential Analyses and Fidelity Assessments

Future SIT evaluations are needed to uncover the aspects of training that play a critical role in improved performances. As it stands now, it is impossible to adequately analyze factors that mediate the efficacy of SIT. Componential analyses of SIT such as those employed in Barling (1980) or Elliot-Faust and Pressley (1986) are needed to further assess the independent contribution of specific instructional processes (e.g., explicit instruction, modeling, covert internalization), the nature of the self-verbalization strategy (e.g., task-analysis, goal setting, monitoring, coping self-statements), and the additive contributions of reinforcement contingencies, self-management procedures, and other instructional adjuncts. Future work also is required to assess the interrelationship of specific treatment components and children's pretreatment individual differences. A more precise account of training features responsible for changes in children with different needs and backgrounds is needed to design the most effective SIT arrangements (Harris, 1985).

Treatment fidelity concerns must be addressed in future evaluations of SIT effectiveness. Such procedures, at a minimum, should include assessments of how the SIT procedure was taught and implemented during training, efforts to document children's use of SIT strategies following training, and analyses of hypothesized links between strategy use and performance outcomes (Borkowski & Cavanaugh, 1979; Harris, 1985, 1988; Moncher & Prinz, 1991). Greater efforts are recommended to program environmental cues that remind children to use SIT and help them overcome potential memory errors (e.g., cue cards). However, as Asarnow and Meichenbaum (1979) have cautioned, care must be taken to avoid inflexible adherence to a strict set of standardized self-verbalizations during any procedure designed to monitor children's application of a self-verbalization strategy. Thus, it is recommended that future fidelity assessments allow for both instructor and student individuality in order to avoid overly rigid applications of SIT.

Expand Outcome Evaluations of SIT

Kendall and Braswell (1982) stressed the importance of treatment evaluations that allow for greater specification of exactly what changed and broader determinations of the value and impact of treatment outcomes in a child's life. In regard to the former, comprehensive evaluations of post-treatment changes are recommended for longer follow-up periods and across multiple performance domains (i.e., cognitive, behavioral, and affective), settings, and respondents to further our knowledge of the durability and generalization of SIT effects. Also, broader academic measures are needed to detect changes in basic knowledge, skills, and processes. Procedures to assess treatment fidelity also must be embedded in all future SIT evaluations to establish that SIT functions as expected (Harris, 1985). Such comprehensive evaluations are necessary to demonstrate that SIT leads to more than just superficial changes on a limited number of tasks (Craighead *et al.,* 1982).

Expanded evaluation procedures are needed to track sequential changes in children's use of the self-verbalization strategy over time and to document individual differences in SIT generalization. For example, at different points during and following training, Borkowski and Varnhagen (1984) interviewed children about the strategies employed when performing a generalization task. Individual response analyses were conducted to determine which children demonstrated transfer of skills. The two children who evidenced the earliest transfer and who reported the most complex strategies were in the SIT instruction condition (rather than the didactic instruction condition), suggesting that SIT led to differential transfer across subjects. Such detailed evaluations will allow for more accurate determinations of how children progress from conscious and deliberate applications to automatic and effortless implementation of SIT procedures (Harris, 1985; Harris & Pressley, 1992). Continued assessments over prolonged time periods will also enable specification of how students modify and uniquely adapt SIT strategies for use in new settings and with new tasks (Harris *et al.,* 1992; Wong *et al.,* 1986). Knowing more about the course of students' SIT application should help guide future SIT design and evaluations.

Social validity considerations are integral to Kendall and Braswell's (1982) second recommendation for expanding treatment evaluations. Routine assessments of consumer's acceptance of and satisfaction with SIT outcomes should be conducted. Further, determinations are needed to assess the practical significance of SIT outcomes, possibly through the inclusion of comparison control conditions to assess whether less-skilled students perform at a level commensurate with that of normally achieving peers after training. Finally, cost-effectiveness issues must be directly considered and conditions under which SIT may not be the most effective means of improving students academic behaviors should be identified.

Broadening the Scope of Future SIT Interventions

Enrich SIT Instructional Contexts

Recommendations to broaden the scope of SIT interventions are inspired by the cogent challenges that have been raised in regard to effective academic strategy instruction (Pearson & Fielding, 1991; Pressley, Snyder, & Cariglia-Ball, 1987b; Pressley, Goodchild, Fleet, Zajchowski, & Evans, 1989b). Wong and colleagues (1992) have recently called for a greater consideration of ecological, systems, and agent factors to improve cognitive-behavioral interventions in educational domains. Significantly greater performance outcomes can be expected from more intense SIT training regimens that involve a greater number of change agents and deliver treatment across more than one major life environment (i.e., home, school, and community) (Hughes & Hall, 1989; Ryan *et al.,* 1986). Optimally, the context of training should closely resemble the environments in which improvements are intended. Parents, siblings, teachers, and peers could be taught to implement, model, and encourage SIT procedures during daily routines. In fact, Whalen and co-workers (1985) suggest that students learn to arrange their own environments to facilitate transfer and that peers be incorporated routinely into SIT programs. It is also likely that lengthier treatments will be required to maximize practically significant outcomes (Kendall, 1985).

Another recommendation is to create self-instructional routines that allow for greatest individual flexibility and generalizability across tasks (Meyers, Cohen, & Schleser, 1989). SIT should be geared to relevant classes of behaviors that apply to a wide variety of academic situations (Fish & Pervan, 1985). This change could be accomplished by combining both task-approach and task-specific self-verbalizations in the SIT regimen (Swanson, 1985; Whitman & Johnston, 1983). Rosenthal and Downs (1985) have endorsed the use of cognitive aids in teaching and treating children. Such aids would serve to (1) prepare or orient students to critical aspects of new information, (2) enhance the vividness or personal salience of new information, (3) stimulate encoding and interpretive processes during learning, and (4) organize new information in ways that would facilitate retrieval. In regard to SIT, multiple instructional modes and formats are recommended (i.e., analogies, illustrations, diagrams, visualization) that enhance clarity, actively involve the learner, and make the self-verbalization process more appealing and personally meaningful (e.g., use favorite imaginary heros who learn to use SIT steps). Importantly, the most facilitative adjunctive cognitive aids are those designed to be clear and simple and to match the needs of the learner (Rosenthal & Downs, 1985).

Instructional researchers also have begun to stress the importance of the situational context in affecting students' ability and motivation to generalize newly learned strategies (Brown, Collins, & Duguid, 1989). Two major ideas arising from this work have direct relevance for enriching the instructional context in which SIT is delivered. Students are hypothesized to develop an understanding of instructional goals through the work tasks they are assigned (Doyle, 1983). Also, students develop more usable strategy knowledge when the tasks and procedures employed during instruction are embedded in naturalistic rather than contrived learning activities (Dole, Duffy, Roehler, & Pearson, 1991). For example, SIT applied to "getting the right answers" on a series of workbook exercises may give students the impression that comprehension involves the static employment of a self-verbalization strategy to be used only during classroom seatwork assignments. Alternatively, when SIT is employed flexibly across multiple naturalistic tasks and settings, students learn that self-verbalization strategies are adaptable to accomplish a variety of learning goals. The latter training context insures that students develop accurate conceptions of the comprehension processes critical for successful reading and mathematics performances. Thus, closer attention should be paid to selecting SIT activities that lead to appropriate student representations of academic goals.

In a similar vein, researchers have consistently acknowledged that the quality of instructor–child relationships and instructional dialogue also affects intervention outcomes (Kendall, 1985; Palincsar, 1986). SIT routines should be presented in a supportive and enthusiastic environment and must be implemented in ways that allow students to play an interactive and collaborative role (Harris & Pressley, 1992; Meichenbaum, 1977; Reeve & Brown, 1985). A guided discovery SIT approach in which children are encouraged to formulate personalized self-instructional routines through a Socratic dialogue with the instructor may be optimal in this regard (Cohen & Meyers, 1984; Schleser et al., 1984). Moreover, Meichenbaum (1986) has stressed that SIT must not be viewed as a stilted regimented procedure. He further recommends that instructors model self-instructions in a natural and spontaneous fashion and discourage students' rote repetition of the self-verbalization strategy.

Add Metacognitive and Motivational Adjuncts

One fruitful area of research addresses how to insure that students develop a metacognitive understanding of the self-regulatory strategies inherent in SIT. It is likely that optimal outcomes will be obtained only if children understand the value of SIT procedures in fostering greater learning outcomes. Such information could be explicitly provided before, during, and after SIT by instructing children when and why to use SIT strategies. More recently, instructional researchers have stressed the importance of training children to acquire such essential strategy information on their own through metacognitive acquisition procedures (Pressley *et al.,* 1984). Children could be taught to predict and to chart their performances both before and after SIT to highlight the power of the newly learned self-verbalization strategy (Ghatala, 1986; Pressley & Ghatala, 1989). Alternatively, children could be instructed in SIT and in another less effective strategy, after which children could be allowed to freely choose one strategy for future tasks (Ghatala, Levin, Pressley, & Goodwin, 1986). Enhanced immediate and generalized performances are best obtained when metacognitive training adjuncts are embedded in strategy training procedures (Pressley *et al.,* 1987).

Increased attention has been given to motivational factors that impact on children's learning and academic achievement (Borkowski *et al.,* 1987; Kukla, 1972; Nicholls, 1983; Weiner, 1985). In fact, instructional researchers have begun to recommend that adjunctive strategy training procedures may be necessary to affect changes in children's motivational beliefs, attributions, and perceptions as a means of fostering academic achievement (Cecil & Medway, 1986; Fowler & Peterson, 1981; Ryan *et al.,* 1986). Although most of the work regarding motivational training procedures has been conducted relative to general cognitive performances, similar results might be expected for cognitive-behavioral interventions focused on academic remediation (Pearl, 1985). In fact, Harris (1985) has suggested at least three critical motivational mediators of cognitive-behavioral treatment outcomes, namely, students' perceptions and attributions concerning the academic domain under study, the effort involved in applying the strategy, and the potential of the strategy to affect worthwhile personal benefits.

These findings translate into direct recommendations for motivational adjuncts to SIT that alter children's causal attributions, self-efficacy perceptions, and outcome expectancies. Such adjuncts are expected to increase students' propensity to use SIT procedures and might include consistent instructional feedback to highlight performance success (and failure) as a function of students' expended effort rather than as a function of innate ability (Borkowski *et al.,* 1986; Borkowski, Weyhing, & Carr, 1988; Shunk, 1983; Short & Ryan, 1984). For example, instructors could constantly point out that students are responsible for the successful implementation of SIT (e.g., "You worked hard at thinking through that problem using all of the steps and it looks like it paid off for you."). Moreover, students could be encouraged to incorporate explicit effort attribution statements into the SIT self-verbalization routine (e.g., "OK, I really want to apply myself here and try really hard.") (Reiher & Dembo, 1984). Pearl (1985) has cautioned, however, that such procedures may not be appropriate for students who suffer from real ability deficits since an emphasis on personal effort attributions and on "working harder" may still result in failure. Modeling procedures in SIT could be enhanced through the inclusion of a variety of training examples, explicit cues to focus students' attention toward targeted problem-solving processes, and constant modeling by instructors of attributional performance statements during demonstrations (Bandura, 1986; Schunk, 1985). Metacognitive adjuncts, such as those mentioned earlier, that involve detailed descriptions of expected SIT consequences as well as direct attempts to increase the salience of SIT performance outcomes also might be helpful for motivating children to continue using the SIT procedures and to increase outcome expectancies.

Much more work is necessary to clarify how motivation adjunctive procedures can be optimally incorporated into SIT. It is likely that a complex interrelationship exists between metacognitive and motivational factors that can impact on instructional effectiveness (Reeve & Brown, 1985). Neither adjunctive approach may suffice to sustain children's use of newly learned strategies (Short & Ryan, 1984), since some children have not developed a personal appreciation of the value of school success (Wong *et al.*, 1986). In such cases, further attention will be needed to help students develop a "possible theory of self" that is in concert with the SIT goal of enhancing academic self-sufficiency (Markus & Nurius, 1987; Markus & Wurf, 1987; McCombs, 1989). Similarly, Kendall (1985) has proposed that adjunctive efforts may be needed to correct children's misinterpretations and alter their representation of therapeutic experiences such as SIT.

Attend to Consumer Expectations

Pretreatment assessments are recommended to determine whether all affected consumers (i.e., child, teachers, parents) perceive SIT as a logical, reasonable, and appropriate intervention for academic remediation. Consideration also should be given to the client's (and other consumers') expectations regarding his or her role in the intervention process (Sweet, 1984). Before a SIT procedure is implemented, it is recommended that pretreatment discussions be held to provide a conceptual framework for SIT, a rationale for using SIT, and a preview of what to expect from SIT (Reiher & Dembo, 1984; Rosenthal & Downs, 1985). At a minimum, all involved consumers should be fully informed and accepting of the following potential SIT limitations: (1) Intense and extended SIT procedures are required before generalized academic improvements across a variety of tasks or behaviors can be expected. (2) The effects of a complex and comprehensive instructional procedure such as SIT may not lead to obvious performance improvements until delayed posttests. (3) The verbal mediational aspects of SIT (i.e., talking outloud) could interfere with other classroom procedures and possibly lead to ridicule from peers (Craighead *et al.,* 1978). Greater attention to consumer perceptions and expectations through pretreatment consultation has been hypothesized to increase engagement during treatment, to insure later treatment adherence, and to lead to greater performance outcomes (Franks, 1972; Kazdin, 1981; Miller & Prinz, 1990).

Final Thoughts

SIT represents a remarkably successful instructional option for academic remediation because it encourages active, self-sufficient, and strategic learners who are capable and motivated to meet new and challenging tasks (Fox & Kendall, 1983; Harris *et al.,* 1992; Pressley *et al.,* 1989a). However, the potential usefulness of this procedure will only be realized from broader documentation of its effectiveness in educational settings (Meichenbaum, 1986; Meichenbaum & Asarnow, 1979). In fact, Bornstein (1985) has called for a halt to research that solely focuses on whether SIT is effectual and recommends that further attention be given to a new set of questions regarding the parameters of effective SIT implementation. One of the most challenging problems facing SIT researchers is whether SIT procedures can be readily adapted for classroom use.

Instructional researchers have long believed that children generalize newly learned strategies to the extent that teachers are responsive to students' individual needs, encourage a gradual transfer of strategy ownership, and establish an atmosphere of support for independent and strategic learning (Brown, Palincsar, & Armbruster, 1984; Duffy & Roehler, 1989; Pressley *et al.,* 1985, 1989b; Wood, Bruner, & Ross, 1976). Similar suggestions have also been raised regarding the effective application of SIT interventions in classroom settings (Meichenbaum, 1979). Teachers not only must show students how to employ SIT, but also must support students by providing means and opportunities to apply SIT and by emphasizing the personalized value of SIT on a continual basis.

The guidelines proposed by Tierney (1982) for enhancing reading instruction also have direct relevance for the design of SIT regimens in classroom settings. He recommends that (1) the instructional strategy be clearly beneficial to improving task-relevant performance, (2) students know why, when, where, and how to use the strategy, (3) the instructional strategy be adaptable to a variety of student learning styles and needs, (4) the instructional strategy encourage independence and self-reliance, and (5) students be given numerous opportunities to put the instructional strategy into action. Examinations are needed of how SIT procedures can best be integrated into the ongoing curriculum and how teachers can most effectively implement, reinforce, and assist children in using SIT procedures in classroom settings. Hopefully, future research will continue to demonstrate SIT as a viable classroom intervention for developing self-sufficient learners and fostering greater academic performances.

REFERENCES

Abikoff, H. (1979). Cognitive training interventions in children: Review of a new approach. *Journal of Learning Disabilities, 12,* 65–77.

Abikoff, H. (1985). Efficacy of cognitive training interventions in hyperactive children: A critical review. *Clinical Psychology Review, 5,* 479–512.

Abikoff, H., Ganeles, D., Reiter, G., Blum, C., Foley, C., and Klein, R. G. (1988). Cognitive training in academically deficient ADDH boys receiving stimulant medication. *Journal of Abnormal Child Psychology, 16,* 411–432.

Asarnow, J., and Meichenbaum, D. (1979). Verbal rehearsal and serial recall: The mediational training of kindergarten children. *Child Development, 50,* 1173–1177.

Bandura, A. (1977). Self-efficacy: Toward a unifying theory of behavioral change. *Psychological Review, 84,* 191–215.

Bandura, A. (1986). *Social foundations of thoughts and action: A social cognitive theory.* Englewood Cliffs, New Jersey: Prentice-Hall.

Bandura, A., and Adams, N. E. (1977). Analysis of self-efficacy theory of behavioral change. *Cognitive Therapy and Research, 1,* 287–310.

Barling, J. (1980). A multistage multidependent variable assessment of children's self-regulation of academic performance. *Child Behavior Therapy, 2,* 43–54.

Beck, S., Matson, J. L., and Kazdin, A. E. (1982). An instructional package to enhance spelling performance in emotionally disturbed children. *Child & Family Behavior Therapy, 4,* 69–77.

Borden, K. A. Brown, R. T., Wynne, M. E., and Schleser, R. (1987). Piagetian conservation and response to cognitive therapy in attention deficit disordered children. *Journal of Child Psychology, 28,* 755–764.

Borkowski, J. G., and Cavanaugh, J. C. (1979). Maintenance and generalization of skills and strategies by the retarded. In N. R. Ellis (Ed.), *Handbook of mental deficiency, psychological theory and research* (2nd ed., pp. 569–617). Hillsdale, New Jersey: Erlbaum.

Borkowski, J. G., and Varnhagen, C. K. (1984). Transfer of learning strategies: Contrast of self-instructional and traditional training formats with EMR children. *American Journal of Mental Deficiency, 88,* 369–379.

Borowski, J. G., Weyhing, R. S., and Turner, L. A. (1986). Attributional retraining and the teaching of strategies. *Exceptional Children, 53,* 130–137.

Borkowski, J. G., Johnston, M. B., and Reid, M. K. (1987). Metacognition, motivation, and controlled performance. In S. J. Ceci (Ed.), *Handbook of cognitive, social, and neuropsychological aspects of learning disabilities,* Vol. 2 (pp. 147–173). Hillsdale, New Jersey: Erlbaum.

Borkowski, J. G., Weyhing, R. S., and Carr, M. (1988). Effects of attributional retraining on strategy-based reading comprehension in learning disabled students. *Journal of Educational Psychology, 80,* 46–53.

Bornstein, P. H. (1985). Self-instructional training: A commentary and state-of-the-art. *Journal of Applied Behavior Analysis, 18,* 69–72.

Bornstein, P., and Quevillon, R. (1976). Effects of a self-instructional package on overactive preschool boys. *Journal of Applied Behavior Analysis, 9,* 179–188.

Braswell, L., Koehler, C., and Kendall, P. C. (1985). Attributions and outcomes in child psychotherapy. *Journal of Social and Clinical Psychology, 3,* 458–465.

Brown, A. L. (1978). Knowing when, where, and how to remember: A problem in metacognition. In R. Glaser (Ed.), *Advances in instructional psychology,* Vol. 1 (pp. 77–165). Hillsdale, New Jersey: Erlbaum.

Brown, A. L., Campione, J., and Day, J. D. (1981). Learning to learn: On training students to learn from texts. *Educational Researcher, 10,* 14–21.

Brown, A. L., Palincsar, A. S., and Armbruster, B. B. (1984). Instructing comprehension-fostering activities in interactive learning situations. In H. Mandl, N. L. Stein, and T. Trabasso (Eds.), *Learning and comprehension of text* (pp. 255–286). Hillsdale, New Jersey: Erlbaum.

Brown, J. S., Collins, A., and Duguid, P. (1989). Situated cognition and the culture of learning. *Educational Researcher, 18,* 32–42.

Brown, R. T., and Alford, N. (1984). Ameliorating attentional deficits and concomitant academic deficiencies in learning disabled children through cognitive training. *Journal of Learning Disabilities, 17,* 20–26.

Bruner, J. S. (1984). Vygotsky's zone of proximal development: The hidden agenda. In B. Rogoff and J. V. Wertsch (Eds.), *Children's learning in the "zone of proximal development"* (pp. 93–97). San Francisco: Jossey-Bass.

Bryant, L. E., and Budd, K. S. (1982). Self-instructional training to increase independent work performance in preschoolers. *Journal of Applied Behavior Analysis, 15,* 259–271.

Bugenthal, D. B., Whalen, C. R., and Henker, B. (1977). Causal attributions of hyperactive children and motivational assumptions of two behavior change approaches: Evidence for an interactionist position. *Child Development, 48,* 1874–1884.

Burger, A. L., Blackman, L. S., and Clark, H. T. (1981). Generalization of verbal abstraction strategies by EMR children and adolescents. *American Journal of Mental Deficiency, 85,* 611–618.

Cameron, M. I., and Robinson, V. M. J. (1980). Effects of cognitive training on academic and on-task behavior of hyperactive children. *Journal of Abnormal Child Psychology, 8,* 405–419.

Case, L. P., Harris, K., and Graham, S. (1991). Improving the mathematical problem solving skills of students with learning disabilities: Self-instructional strategy development.

Cavanaugh, J. C., and Borkowski, J. G. (1979). The metamemory—memory "connection": Effects of strategy training and maintenance. *Journal of General Psychology, 101,* 161–174.

Cecil, M. A., and Medway, F. J. (1986). Attribution retraining with low-achieving and learned helpless children. *Techniques: A Journal for Remedial and Counseling, 2,* 173–181.

Cohen, R., and Meyers, A. W. (1984). The generalization of self-instructions. In B. Gholson and T. L. Rosenthal (Eds.), *Applications in cognitive-developmental theory* (pp. 95–112). New York: Academic Press.

Cole, P. M., and Kazdin, A. E. (1980). Critical issues in self-instruction training with children. *Child Behavior Therapy, 2,* 1–21.

Copeland, A. P. (1981). The relevance of subject variables in cognitive self-instructional programs for impulsive children. *Behavior Therapy, 12,* 520–529.

Covington, M. V., and Beery, R. G. (1976). *Self-worth and school learning.* New York: Holt, Rinehart, & Winston.

Covington, M. V., and Omelich, C. L. (1979). Are causal attributions causal? A path analysis of the cognitive model of achievement motivation. *Journal of Personality and Social Psychology, 37,* 1487–1504.

Craighead, W. E. (1982). A brief clinical history of cognitive-behavior therapy with children. *School Psychology Review, 11,* 5–13.

Craighead, W. E., Wilcoxon-Craighead, L., and Meyers, A. W. (1978). New directions in behavior modification with children. *Progress in Behavior Modification, 6,* 159–201.

Craighead, W. E., Meyers, A. W., Wilcoxon-Craighead, L., and McHale, S. M. (1982). Issues in cognitive-behavior therapy with children. In M. Rosenbaum, C. M. Franks, and Y. Joffe (Eds.), *Perspectives on behavior therapy in the eighties* (pp. 234–261). New York: Springer-Verlag.

Craighead, W. E., Meyers, A. W., and Craighead, L. W. (1985). A conceptual model for cognitive-behavior therapy with children. *Journal of Abnormal Child Psychology, 13,* 331–342.

Davis, R. W., and Hajicek, J. O. (1985). Effects of self-instructional training and strategy training on a mathematics task with severely behaviorally disordered students. *Behavioral Disorders, 10,* 211–218.

Day, J. D., Cordan, L. A., and Kerwin, M. L. (1989). Informal instruction and development of cognitive skills: A review and critique of research. In C. McCormick, G. Miller, and M. Pressley (Eds.), *Cognitive strategy research: From basic research to educational applications* (pp. 83–103). New York: Springer-Verlag.

Denny, N. W., and Turner, M. C. (1979). Facilitating cognitive performance in children: A comparison of strategy modeling and strategy modeling with overt self-verbalization. *Journal of Experimental Child Psychology, 28,* 119–131.

Dole, J. A., Duffy, G. G., Roehler, L. R., and Pearson, P. D. (1991). Moving from the old to the new: Research in reading comprehension instruction. *Review of Educational Research, 61,* 239–264.

Douglas, V., Parry, P., Marton, P., and Garson, C. (1976). Assessment of a cognitive training program for hyperactive children. *Journal of Abnormal Child Psychology, 4,* 389–410.

Doyle, W. (1983). Academic work. *Review of Educational Research, 53,* 159–199.

Duffy, G. G., and Roehler, L. R. (1989). Why strategy instruction is so difficult and what we need to do about it. In C. McCormick, G. Miller, and M. Pressley (Eds.), *Cognitive strategy research: From basic research to educational applications* (pp. 133–154). New York: Springer-Verlag.

Eastman, B. G., and Rasbury, W. C. (1981). Cognitive self-instruction for the control of impulsive classroom behavior: Ensuring the treatment package. *Journal of Abnormal Child Psychology, 9,* 381–387.

Elliot, S. N. (1986). Children's ratings of the acceptability of classroom interventions for misbehavior: Findings and methodological considerations. *Journal of School Psychology, 24,* 23–35.

Elliot, S. N. (1988). Acceptability of behavioral treatments in educational settings. In J. C. Witt, S. N. Elliot, and F. M. Gresham (Eds.), *Handbook of behavioral therapy in education* (pp. 121–150). New York: Plenum Press.

Elliott, S. N., Turco, T. L., and Gresham, F. M. (1987). Consumers' and clients' pretreatment acceptability ratings of classroom-based group contingencies. *Journal of School Psychology, 25,* 145–154.

Elliott-Faust, D. J., and Pressley, M. (1986). How to teach comparison processing to increase children's short- and long-term listening comprehension monitoring. *Journal of Educational Psychology, 78,* 27–33.

Evangelisti, D. B., Whitman, T., and Johnston, M. B. (1986). Problem-solving and task complexity: An examination of the relative effectiveness of self-instruction and didactic instruction. *Cognitive Therapy and Research, 10,* 499–508.

Evangelisti, D. B., Whitman, T. L., and Maxwell, S. E. (1987). A comparison of external and self-instructional formats with children of different ages and tasks of varying complexity. *Cognitive Therapy and Research, 4,* 419–436.

Fish, M. C., and Pervan, R. (1985). Self-instruction training: A potential tool for school psychologists. *Psychology in the Schools, 22,* 83–92.

Flavell, J. H. (1977). *Cognitive development.* Englewood Cliffs, New Jersey: Prentice-Hall.

Fowler, J. W., and Peterson, P. L. (1981). Increasing persistence and altering attributional style of learned helpless children. *Journal of Educational Psychology, 73,* 251–260.

Fox, D. E., and Kendall, P. C. (1983). Think through academic problems: Application of cognitive-behavior therapy to learning. In T. Kratochwill (Ed.), *Advances in school psychology* (pp. 269–301). Hillsdale, New Jersey: Erlbaum.

Franks, J. D. (1972). *Persuasion and healing.* Baltimore: Johns Hopkins Press.

Friedling, C., and O'Leary, S. G. (1979). Effects of self-instructional training on second- and third-grade hyperactive children: A failure to replicate. *Journal of Applied Behavior Analysis, 12,* 211–219.

Fuson, K. C. (1979). The development of self-regulating aspects of speech: A review. In G. Zivin (Ed.), *The development of self-regulation through private speech* (pp. 135–217). New York: Wiley.

Garner, R., and Alexander, P. A. (1989). Metacognition: Answered and unanswered questions. *Educational Psychologist, 24,* 143–158.

Genshaft, J. L., and Hirt, M. L. (1980). The effectiveness of self-instructional training to enhance math achievement in women. *Cognitive Therapy and Research, 4,* 91–97.

Ghatala, E. S. (1986). Strategy-monitoring training enables young learners to select effective strategies. *Educational Psychologist, 21,* 43–54.

Ghatala, E. S., Levin, J. R., Pressley, M., and Goodwin, D. (1986). A componental analysis of the effects of derived and supplied strategy-utility information on children's strategy selections. *Journal of Experimental Child Psychology, 22,* 199–216.

Glenwick, D. S., and Barocas, R. (1979). Training impulsive children in verbal self-control by use of natural change agents. *Journal of Special Education, 13,* 387–398.

Graham, S., and Harris, K. R. (1987). Improving composition skills of inefficient learners with self-instructional strategy training. *Topics in Language Disorders, 7,* 66–77.

Graham, S., and Harris, K. R. (1989a). Components analysis of cognitive strategy instruction: Effects on learning disabled students' compositions and self-efficacy. *Journal of Educational Psychology, 81,* 353–361.

Graham, S., and Harris, K. R. (1989b). Improving learning disabled students' skills at composing essays: Self-instructional strategy training. *Exceptional Children, 56,* 201–214.

Grindler, M. (1988). Effects of cognitive monitoring strategies on the test anxieties of elementary students. *Psychology in the Schools, 25,* 428–436.

Guevremont, D. C., Osnes, P. G., and Stokes, T. F. (1988). The functional role of preschoolers' verbalizations in the generalization of self-instructional training. *Journal of Applied Behavior Analysis, 21,* 45–55.

Harris, K. R. (1982). Cognitive-behavior modification: Application with exceptional students. *Focus on Exceptional Children, 15,* 1–16.

Harris, K. R. (1985). Conceptual, methodological, and clinical issues in cognitive-behavioral assessment. *Journal of Abnormal Child Psychology, 13,* 373–390.

Harris, K. R. (1986). The effects of cognitive-behavior modification on private speech and task performance during problem solving among learning-disabled and normally achieving children. *Journal of Abnormal Child Psychology, 14,* 63–67.

Harris, K. R. (1988). Learning disabilities research: The need, the integrity, and the challenge. *Journal of Learning Disabilities, 21,* 267–270, 274.

Harris, K. R. (1990). Developing self-regulating learners: The role of private speech and self-instruction. *Educational Psychologist, 25,* 35–49.

Harris, K. R., and Graham, S. (1985). Improving learning disabled students' composition skills: Self-control strategy training. *Learning Disabled Quarterly, 8,* 27–36.

Harris, K. R., and Pressley, M. (1992). The nature of cognitive strategy instruction: Interactive strategy construction. *Exceptional Children.*

Harris, K. R., Graham, S., and Pressley, M. (1992). Cognitive-behavioral approaches in reading and written language: Developing self-regulating learners. In N. Singh and I. Beale (Eds.), *Current perspectives in learning disabilities: Nature theory and treatment.* New York: Springer-Verlag.

Hobbs, S. A., Moguin, L. W., Tyroler, M., and Lahey, B. B. (1980). Cognitive behavior therapy with children: Has clinical utility been demonstrated? *Psychological Bulletin, 87,* 147–165.

Horn, W. F., Chatoor, I., and Conners, C. K. (1983). Additive effects of Dexedrine and self-control training: A multiple assessment. *Behavior Modifications, 7,* 383–402.

Hughes, J. N., and Hall, R. J. (1989). *Cognitive-behavioral psychology in the schools: A comprehensive handbook.* New York: Guilford Press.

Jackson, J. L., and Calhoun, K. S. (1982). A comparison of cognitive self-instructional training and externally administered instructions in preschool children. *Child Study Journal, 12,* 7–20.

Johnston, M. B., and Whitman, T. (1987). Enhancing math computation through variations in training format and instructional content. *Cognitive Therapy and Research, 11,* 381–397.

Johnston, M. B., Whitman, T. L., and Johnson, M. (1980). Teaching addition and subtraction to mentally retarded children: A self-instruction program. *Applied Research in Mental Retardation, 1,* 141–160.

Joyce, B., and Weil, M. (1986). *Models of teaching.* New York: Academic Press.

Kazdin, A. E. (1977). Assessing the clinical or applied significance of behavior change through social validation. *Behavior Modification, 1,* 427–452.

Kazdin, A. E. (1980). Acceptability of alternative treatments for deviant child behavior. *Journal of Applied Behavior Analysis, 13,* 259–273.

Kazdin, A. E. (1981). Acceptability of child treatment techniques: The influence of treatment efficacy and adverse side effects. *Behavior Therapy, 12,* 493–506.

Kazdin, A. E. (1982). Current developments and research issues is cognitive-behavioral interventions: A commentary. *School Psychology Review, 11,* 75–82.

Kazdin, A. E. (1986). The evaluation of psychotherapy: Research, design and methodology. In S. L. Garfield and A. E. Bergin (Eds.), *Handbook of psychotherapy and behavior change* (3rd ed., pp. 23–68). New York: Wiley.

Kendall, P. C. (1977). On the efficacious use of verbal self-instruction procedures with children. *Cognitive Therapy and Research, 1,* 331–341.

Kendall, P. C. (1985). Toward a cognitive-behavioral model of child psychopathology and a critique of related interventions. *Journal of Abnormal Child Psychology, 13,* 357–372.

Kendall, P. C. (1990). Challenges for cognitive strategy training: The case of mental retardation. *American Journal on Mental Retardation, 94,* 365–367.

Kendall, P. C., and Braswell, L. (1982). Assessment for cognitive behavioral interventions in the schools. *School Psychology Review, 11,* 21–31.

Kendall, P. C., and Braswell, L. (1985). *Cognitive-behavioral therapy for impulsive children.* New York: Guilford.

Kendall, P. C., and Wilcox, L. (1980). A cognitive-behavioral treatment for impulsivity: Concrete versus conceptual training in non-self-controlled problem children. *Journal of Consulting & Clinical Psychology, 48,* 80–91.

Kendall, P. C., Borkowski, J. G., and Cavanaugh, J. C. (1980). Maintenance and generalization of an interrogative strategy by EMR children. *Intelligence, 4,* 255–270.

Keogh, D. A., Whitman, T. L., and Maxwell, S. E. (1988). Self-instruction versus external instruction: Individual differences and training effectiveness. *Cognitive Therapy and Research, 12,* 591–610.

Kukla, A. (1972). Attributional determinants of achievement-related behavior. *Journal of Personality and Social Psychology, 21,* 166–174.

Kurtz, B. E., and Borkowski, J. G. (1984). Children's metacognition: Exploring relations among knowledge, process, and motivational variables. *Journal of Experimental Child Psychology, 37,* 335–354.

Lennox, D., and Polling, A. (1984). Self-instructional training with mentally retarded individuals: A review of the literature. *The Mental Retardation and Learning Disability Bulletin, 12,* 30–38.

Leon, J. A., and Pepe, H. J. (1983). Self-instructional training: Cognitive behavior modification for remediating arithmetic deficits. *Exceptional Children, 50,* 54–60.

Lloyd, J. (1980). Academic instruction and cognitive behavior modification: The need for attack strategy training. *Exceptional Education Quarterly, 1,* 53–63.

Lloyd, J. W., Kneedler, R. D., and Cameron, N. A. (1982). Effects of verbal self-guidance on word reading accuracy. *Reading Improvement, 19,* 84–89.

Lloyd, J., Saltzman, N., and Kaufman, J. (1981). Predictable generalization in academic learning as a result of preskills and strategy training. *Learning Disabilities Quarterly, 4,* 203–216.

Loper, A. B. (1982). Metacognitive training to correct academic deficiency. *Topics in Learning and Learning Disabilities, 2,* 61–68.

Luria, A. (1961). *The role of speech in the regulation of normal and abnormal behavior.* New York: Liveright.

Malamuth, Z. N. (1979). Self-management training for children with reading problems: Effects on reading performance and sustained attention. *Cognitive Therapy and Research, 3,* 279–289.

Markus, H., and Nurius, P. (1987). Possible selves: The interface between motivation and the self-concept. In K. Yardley and T. Honess (Eds.), *Self and identity: Psychosocial perspectives* (pp. 157–172). New York: Wiley.

Markus, H., and Wurf, E. (1987). The dynamic self-concept: A social psychological perspective. *Annual Review of Psychology, 38,* 299–337.

Martens, B. K. Peterson, R. L., Witt, J. C., and Cirone, S. (1986). Teacher perceptions of school-based intervention: Ratings of intervention effectiveness, ease of use, and frequency of use. *Exceptional Children, 53,* 213–223.

McCombs, B. L. (1989). Self-regulated learning and academic achievement: A phenomenological view. In B. J. Zimmerman and D. H. Schunk (Eds.), *Self-regulated learning and academic achievement: Theory, research, and practice* (pp. 51–82). New York: Springer-Verlag.

Meichenbaum, D. H. (1977). *Cognitive behavior modification.* New York: Plenum.

Meichenbaum, D. H. (1979). Teaching children self-control. In B. B. Lahey and A. E. Kazdin (Eds.), *Advances in clinical child psychology* (pp. 1–33). New York: Plenum Press.

Meichenbaum, D. H. (1980). Cognitive behavior modification with exceptional children: A promise yet unfulfilled. *Exceptional Education Quarterly, 1,* 83–88.

Meichenbaum, D. H. (1985). Teaching thinking: A cognitive behavioral perspective. In S. Chipman, J. Segal, and R. Glaser (Eds.), *Thinking and learning skills* (Vol. 2, pp. 407–426). Hillsdale, New Jersey: Erlbaum.

Meichenbaum, D. H. (1986). Metacognitive methods of instruction: Current status and future prospects. *Special services in the schools* (Vol. 3, pp. 23–32). New York: Haworth Press.

Meichenbaum, D., and Asarnow, J. (1979). Cognitive behavioral modification and metacognitive development: Implications for the classroom. In P. C. Kendall and S. D. Hollon (Eds.), *Cognitive-behavioral interventions: Theory, research, and procedures* (pp. 11–35). New York: Academic Press.

Meichenbaum, D., and Burland, S. (1979). Cognitive behavior modification with children. *School Psychology Digest, 8,* 426–433.

Meichenbaum, D., and Goodman, J. (1969). The development of control of operant motor responding by verbal operants. *Journal of Experimental Child Psychology, 7,* 553–565.

Meichenbaum, D., and Goodman, J. (1971). Training impulsive children to talk to themselves: A means of developing self-control. *Journal of Abnormal Psychology, 77,* 115–121.

Meyers, A. W., Cohen, R., and Schleser, R. (1989). A cognitive-behavioral approach to education: Adopting a broad-based perspective. In J. Hughes and R. Hall (Eds.), *Cognitive behavioral psychology in the schools: A comprehensive handbook* (pp. 62–86). New York: Guilford Press.

Miller, G. E. (1985). The effects of general and specific self-instruction training on children's comprehension monitoring performances during reading. *Reading Research Quarterly, 20,* 616–628.

Miller G. E. (1987). The influence of self-instruction on the comprehension monitoring performance of average and above average readers. *Journal of Reading Behavior, 19,* 303–317.

Miller, G. E., and Prinz, R. J. (1990). Enhancement of social learning family interventions for childhood conduct disorder. *Psychological Bulletin, 2,* 291–307.

Miller, G. E., and Rentiers, K. A. (1991). Self-instructional effects of fifth grade children's monitoring, comprehension, and reading attitudes (submitted).

Miller, G. E., Giovenco, A., and Rentiers, K. A. (1987). Fostering comprehension monitoring in below average readers through self-instruction training. *Journal of Reading Behavior, 19,* 379–394.

Moncher, F. J., and Prinz, R. J. (1991). Treatment fidelity in outcome studies. *Clinical Psychology Review, 11,* 247–266.

Murphy, J., Bates, P., and Anderson, J. (1984). The effect of self-instruction training of counting skills by preschool handicapped students. *Education and Treatment of Children, 7,* 247–257.

Nicholls, J. G. (1983). Conceptions of ability and achievement motivation: A theory and its implications for education. In S. G. Paris, G. M. Olson, and H. W. Stevenson (Eds.), *Learning and motivation in the classroom* (pp. 211–239). Hillsdale, New Jersey: Erlbaum.

O'Sullivan, J. T., and Pressley, M. (1984). Completeness of instruction and strategy transfer. *Journal of Experimental Child Psychology, 38,* 275–288.

Palincsar, A. S. (1986). The role of dialogue in providing scaffolded instruction. *Educational Psychologist, 21,* 73–98.

Pearl, R. (1982). LD children's attribution for success and failure: A replication with a labeled LD sample. *Learning Disability Quarterly, 5,* 379–398.

Pearl, R. (1985). Cognitive-behavioral interventions for increasing motivation. *Journal of Abnormal Child Psychology, 13,* 443–454.

Pearson, P. D., and Fielding, L. (1991). Comprehension instruction. In R. Barr, M. Kamil, P. Mosenthal, and P. D. Pearson (Eds.), *Handbook of reading research* (Vol. 2, pp. 815–860). New York: Longman.

Peterson, P. L., and Swing, S. R. (1984). Problems in classroom implementation of cognitive strategy instruction. In M. Pressley and J. R. Levin (Eds.), *Cognitive strategy research: Educational applications* (pp. 267–287). New York: Springer-Verlag.

Pressley, M. (1979). Increasing children's self-control through cognitive interventions. *Review of Educational Research, 49,* 319–370.

Pressley, M., and Ghatala, E. S. (1989). Metacognitive benefits of taking a test for children and young adolescents. *Journal of Experimental Child Psychology, 47,* 430–450.

Pressley, M., Borkowski, J. G., and O'Sullivan, J. T. (1984). Memory strategy instruction is made of this: Metamemory and durable strategy use. *Educational Psychologist, 19,* 84–107.

Pressley, M., Forrest-Pressley, D. L., Elliot-Faust, D., and Miller, G. (1985). Children's use of cognitive strategies, when to teach strategies and what to do if they can't be taught. In M. Pressley and C. Brainard (Eds.), *Cognitive approaches to memory development* (pp. 1–37). New York: Springer-Verlag.

Pressley, M., Borkowski, J. G., and Schneider, W. (1987a). Cognitive strategies: Good strategy users coordinate metacognition and knowledge. In R. Vasta and G. Whitehurst (Eds.), *Annals of child development* (Vol. 5, pp. 89–129). New York: JAI Press.

Pressley, M., Snyder, B., and Cariglia-Ball, T. (1987b). How can good strategy use be taught to children? Evidence of six alternative approaches. In S. Cormier and J. Hagman (Eds.), *Transfer of learning: Contemporary research and applications* (pp. 81–120). Orlando, Florida: Academic Press.

Pressley, M., Borkowski, J. G., and Schneider, W. (1989a). Good information processing: What it is and how education can promote it. *International Journal of Educational Research, 13,* 857–867.

Pressley, M., Goodchild, F., Fleet, J., Zajchowski, R., and Evans, E. D. (1989b). The challenges of classroom strategy instruction. *The Elementary School Journal, 89,* 301–342.

Reese, H. (1962). Verbal mediation as a function of age. *Psychological Bulletin, 59,* 502–509.

Reeve, R. A., and Brown, A. L. (1985). Metacognition reconsidered: Implications for intervention research. *Journal of Abnormal Child Psychology, 13,* 343–356.

Reiher, R. H., and Dembo, M. H. (1984). Changing academic task persistence through a self-instructional attribution training program. *Contemporary Educational Psychology, 9,* 84–94.

Roberts, R. N. (1979). Private speech in academic problem-solving: A naturalistic perspective. In G. Zivin (Ed.), *The development of self-regulation through private speech* (pp. 295–324). New York: Wiley.

Roberts, R. N., and Dick, M. L. (1982). Self-control in the classroom: Theoretical issues and practical applications. In T. Kratochwill (Ed.), *Advances in school psychology* (Vol. 2, pp. 275–314). Hillsdale, New Jersey: Erlbaum.

Roberts, R. N., Nelson, R. O., and Olson, T. W. (1987). Self-instruction: An analysis of the differential effects of instruction and reinforcement. *Journal of Applied Behavior Analysis, 20,* 235–242.

Robin, A., Armel, S., and O'Leary, K. D. (1975). The effects of self-instruction on writing deficiencies. *Behavior Therapy, 6,* 178–187.

Rosenbaum, M. (1983). Learned resourcefulness as a behavior repertoire for self-regulation of internal events: Issues and speculations. In M. Rosenbaum, C. M. Franks, and Y. Joffe (Eds.), *Perspectives on behavior therapy in the eighties* (pp. 54–73). New York: Springer-Verlag.

Rosenthal, T. L., and Downs, A. (1985). Cognitive aids in teaching and treating. *Advances in Behavior Research and Therapy, 7,* 1–53.

Rotter, J. B., Chance, J. E., and Phares, E. J. (1972). *Applications of a social learning theory of personality.* New York: Holt, Rinehart, & Winston.

Ryan, E. B., Short, E. J., and Weed, K. A. (1986a). The role of cognitive strategy training in improving the academic performance of learning disabled children. *Journal of Learning Disabilities, 19,* 521–529.

Ryan, E. B., Weed, K. A., and Short, E. J. (1986b). Cognitive behavior modification: Promoting active, self-regulatory learning styles. In J. K. Torgesen and B. Y. L. Wong (Eds.), *Psychological and educational perspectives on learning disabilities* (pp. 367–397). New York: Academic Press.

Schleser, R., Meyers, A., and Cohen, R. (1981). Generalization of self-instructions: Effects of general versus specific content, active rehearsal, and cognitive level. *Child Development, 52,* 335–340.

Schleser, R., Cohen, R., Meyers, A. W., and Rodick, J. D. (1984). The effects of cognitive level and training procedures on the generalization of self-instruction. *Cognitive Therapy and Research, 8,* 187–200.

Schleser, R., Meyers, A. W., Cohen, R., and Thackwray, D. (1983). Self-instruction interventions with non-self-controlled children: Effects of discovery versus faded rehearsal. *Journal of Consulting and Clinical Psychology, 51,* 954–955.

Schmidt, J. L., Deshler, D. D., Schumaker, J. B., and Alley, G. R. (1988). Effects of generalization instruction on the written language performance of adolescents with learning disabilities in the mainstream classroom. *Journal of Reading, Writing, & Learning Disabilities, 4,* 291–309.

Schunk, D. H. (1981). Modeling and attributional effects on children's achievement: A self-efficacy analysis. *Journal of Educational Psychology, 73,* 93–105.

Schunk, D. H. (1982). Verbal self-regulation as a facilitator of children's achievement and self-efficacy. *Human Learning, 1,* 265–277.

Schunk, D. H. (1983). Ability versus effort attributional effort: Differential effects on self-efficacy and achievement. *Journal of Educational Psychology, 75,* 848–856.

Schunk, D. H. (1985). Self-efficacy and classroom learning. *Psychology in the Schools, 22,* 208–223.

Schunk, D. H. (1986). Verbalization and children's self-regulated learning. *Contemporary Educational Psychology, 11,* 347–369.

Schunk, D. H., and Rice, J. M. (1984). Strategy self-verbalization during remedial listening comprehension instruction. *Journal of Experimental Education, 53,* 49–54.

Short, E. J., and Ryan, E. B. (1984). Metacognitive differences between skilled and less skilled readers: Remediating deficits through story grammar and attribution training. *Journal of Educational Psychology, 76,* 225–235.

Smith, A. M. B., and Van Biervliet, A. (1986). Enhancing reading comprehension through the use of a self-instructional package. *Education and Treatment of Children, 9,* 40–55.

Spates, C. R., and Kanfer, F. H. (1977). Self-monitoring, self-evaluation, and self-reinforcement in children's learning: A test of a multistage self-regulation model. *Behavior Therapy, 8,* 9–16.

Steele, K., and Barling, J. (1982). Self-instruction and learning disabilities: Maintenance, generalization, and subject characteristics. *The Journal of General Psychology, 106,* 141–154.

Stokes, T. F., and Baer, D. M. (1977). An implicit technology of generalization. *Journal of Educational Psychology, 10,* 349–367.

Stokes, T., and Osnes, P. (1986). Programming the generalization of children's social behavior. In P. Strain, M. Guralnick, and H. Walker (Eds.), *Children's social behavior: Development, assessment, and modification* (pp. 407–443). New York: Academic Press.

Swanson, H. L. (1985). Effects of cognitive-behavioral training on emotionally disturbed children's academic performance. *Cognitive Therapy and Research, 9,* 201–216.

Swanson, H. L., and Kozleski, E. B. (1985). Self-talk and handicapped children's academic needs: Applications of cognitive behavior modification. *Techniques: A Journal for Remedial Education and Counseling, 1,* 367–379.

Swanson, H. L., and Scarpati, S. (1984). Self-instruction training to increase academic performance of educationally handicapped children. *Child & Family Behavior Therapy, 6,* 23–39.

Sweet, A. A. (1984). The therapeutic relationship in behavior therapy. *Clinical Psychology Review, 4,* 253–272.

Symons, S., Snyder, B. L., Cariglia-Bull, T., and Pressley, M. (1989). Why be optimistic about cognitive strategy instruction? In C. B. McCormick, G. E. Miller, and M. Pressley (Eds.), *Cognitive strategy research: From basic research to educational applications* (pp. 3–32). New York: Springer-Verlag.

Tharp, R. G., and Gallimore, R. (1985). The logical status of metacognitive training. *Journal of Abnormal Child Psychology, 13,* 455–466.

Tierney, R. J. (1982). Essential considerations for developing basic reading comprehension skills. *School Psychology Review, 11,* 299–305.

Torgesen, J. K. (1982). The learning disabled child as an inactive learner: Educational implications. *Topics in Learning and Learning Disabilities, 2,* 45–52.

Torgesen, J. K., and Licht, B. G. (1983). The learning disabled child as an inactive learner: Retrospects and prospects. In J. D. McKinney and L. Feagans (Eds.), *Current topics in learning disabilities* (Vol. 1, pp. 3–31). Norwood, New Jersey: Ablex.

Varni, J. W., and Henker, B. (1979). A self-regulation approach to the treatment of three hyperactive boys. *Child Behavior Therapy, 1,* 171–192.

Vygotsky, L. S. (1962). In E. Hanfman and G. Vakar (Eds.), *Thought and language.* Cambridge: MIT Press.

Weiner, B. (1979). A theory of motivation for some classroom experiences. *Journal of Educational Psychology, 71,* 3–25.

Weiner, B. (1985). An attributional theory of achievement motivation. *Psychological Review, 92,* 548–573.

Wertsch, J. (1979). From social interaction to higher psychological processes: A clarification and application of Vygotsky's theory. *Human Development, 22,* 1–22.

Wertsch, J. (1980). The significance of dialogue in Vygotsky's account of social, egocentric, and inner speech. *Contemporary Educational Psychology, 5,* 150–162.

Whalen, C. K., Henker, B., and Hinshaw, S. P. (1985). Cognitive-behavioral therapies for hyperactive children: Premises, problems, and prospects. *Journal of Abnormal Child Psychology, 13,* 391–410.

Whitman, T. L. (1987). Self-instruction, individual differences, and mental retardation. *American Journal of Mental Deficiency, 92,* 213–223.

Whitman, T. L. (1990a). Development of self-regulation in persons with mental retardation. *American Journal of Mental Retardation, 94,* 373–376.

Whitman, T. L. (1990b). Self-regulation and mental retardation. *American Journal of Mental Retardation, 94,* 347–362.

Whitman, T., and Johnston, M. B. (1983). Teaching addition and subtraction with regrouping to educable mentally retarded children: A group self-instructional training program. *Behavior Therapy, 14,* 127–143.

Witt, J. C., and Elliott, S. N. (1985). Acceptability of classroom management strategies. In T. R. Kratochwill (Ed.), *Advances in School Psychology* (Vol. 4, pp. 251–288). Hillsdale, New Jersey: Erlbaum.

Wolf, M. M. (1978). Social validity: The case for subjective measurement or how applied behavior analysis is finding its heart. *Journal of Applied Behavior Analysis, 11,* 203–214.

Wood, D., Bruner, J. S., and Ross, G. (1976). The role of tutoring in problem solving. *Journal of Child Psychology and Psychiatry, 17,* 89–100.

Wong, B. Y. L. (1980). Activating the inactive learner: Use of questions/prompts to enhance comprehension and retention of implied information in learning disabled children. *Learning Disability Quarterly, 3,* 29–37.

Wong, B. Y. L. (1985). Issues in cognitive-behavioral interventions in academic skill areas. *Journal of Abnormal Child Psychology, 13,* 425–442.

Wong, B. Y. L., Wong, R., Perry, N., and Sawatsky, D. (1986). The efficacy of a self-questioning summarization strategy for use by underachievers and learning disabled adolescents in social studies. *Learning Disabilities Focus, 2,* 20–35.

Wong, B. Y. L., Harris, K. R., and Graham, S. (1992). Cognitive-behavioral procedures: Academic applications with students with learning disabilities. In P. C. Kendall (Ed.), *Child and adolescent therapy: Cognitive-behavioral procedures.* New York: Guilford Press.

Yeaton, W. H., and Sechrest, L. (1981). Critical dimensions in the choice and maintenance of successful treatments: Strength, integrity, and effectiveness. *Journal of Consulting and Clinical Psychology, 49,* 156–167.

Zimmerman, B. J. (1986). Development of self-regulated learners: Which are the key subprocesses? *Contemporary Educational Psychology, 16,* 307–313.

Zimmerman, B. J. (1989). Models of self-regulated learning and academic achievement. In B. J. Zimmerman and D. H. Schunk (Eds.), *Self-regulated learning and academic achievement: Theory, research, and practice* (pp. 1–25). New York: Springer-Verlag.

Zivin, G. (Ed.). (1979). *The development of self-regulation through private speech.* New York: Wiley.

7

Collaborative Instruction for Reading Comprehension: The Role of Discourse and Discussion

Margaret A. Gallego

INTRODUCTION

Classroom discourse has been a seminal area of recent research. This research has produced a wealth of information regarding the consistent and often reticent nature of classroom interaction, loosely referred to as classroom discussion (Alvermann & Hayes, 1989). Classroom discourse has been characterized by the sequence of teacher's initiation, students' response, and teacher's provision of feedback or some type of evaluation (Mehan, 1979). Researchers concur that the type of discourse primarily taking place in classrooms is not discussion at all, but teacher-controlled recitation (Alvermann & Hayes, 1989; Alvermann, O'Brian, & Dillon, 1990; Green, 1983).

The purpose of this chapter is to describe the influence of a collaborative instructional strategy in enabling students with learning disabilities to move beyond recitation toward involvement in discussion. The strategy introduced students to verbal discourse prompts used to stimulate and maintain discussion regarding social studies concepts. Increases in student content comprehension support the use of this strategy for text understanding and vocabulary growth. The individual participant roles that emerged from the employment of this strategy provide insights regarding the possible constraints in students' discussion engagement. Further, the strategy prompted collaborative interactions that induced the development of collaborative cognition (i.e., collective knowledge generated by group members engaged in a joint activity).

TRADITIONAL CLASSROOM DISCOURSE

The importance of communication has been documented in a variety of social settings (Heath, 1983; Wells, 1986). One setting paramount in a child's life is the classroom. Schools are likely to be the first structured environment in which students not only are present but are also expected to participate (Cazden, 1986). Teachers and students participate in the act of schooling by communicating among themselves and with each other through classroom discourse.

Research (Edwards & Furlong, 1978; Stubbs, 1983) has documented that classroom discourse is quite different from other types of talk, noting that when everyday conversation is recorded and transcribed its apparent confusion is surprising. Utterances trail off, overlap, and are interrupted. There are frequent false starts, hesitations, and repetitions. When unedited, the results are tedious to read and often impossible to follow. In contrast, unedited transcriptions of talk recorded in traditional classrooms often read like play scripts. Most utterance are completed and speakers instinctively seem to remember their lines and their turn to speak.

Dialogue generated in traditional classrooms reflects unyielding classroom recitation practices in which the "actors" know all too well how the script should read. The unspoken rules for classroom interaction are indicative of the unequal communicative rights held by teacher and pupils. In traditional classrooms, teachers have the right to talk first, talk last, control the content, and regulate the allocation of turns at speaking. Sacks, Schegloff, and Jefferson (1974) were quite candid in their description of such interaction as "teacher-owned."

The teacher's prerogative in classroom interaction has been documented in a variety of studies from the one classroom examined by Mehan (1979) to the many classrooms studied by Sinclair and Coulthard (1975). The pervading discourse structure identified by these and other investigations (c.f. Cazden, 1986) is characterized by a three-part interaction sequence of (1) teacher initiation, (2) compiled with a student response, and (3) followed by the teacher's evaluation (IRE; Mehan, 1979). The IRE interaction pattern illustrates the teacher's privilege to make the decisions necessary to secure orderly interaction.

CLASSROOM DISCOURSE AND READING INSTRUCTION

Although oral language ability is considered an important factor for successful reading (Holdaway, 1979), students are given few opportunities to actively engage in oral language activities (Sirotnik, 1983). Durkin (1979) found that teacher-directed reading lessons consisted primarily of teacher-posed questions. Students' contributions during these lessons were usually limited to responses to teacher-posed questions, requiring brief and literal text-based responses. Recent studies investigating classroom discourse document similar findings. Gambrell (1987) reported that most questions raised during reading lessons were teacher-initiated student talk was restricted to responses to teacher-initiated questions. O'Flahaven, Hartman, and Pearson (1988) conducted a comparison study and reported that elementary teachers practicing 20 years ago overwhelmingly relied on the use of literal level questioning as their primary means of appraising students' understanding. Their comparison indicated that contemporary teachers continue to rely on posing questions for assessing student's content comprehension. When high school teachers were asked to describe activities that constitute a classroom discussion, most recounted question-and-answer sessions in which students reviewed their assigned reading and teachers were major participants (Alvermann & Hayes, 1989). These recollections characterize recitation more than dialogue. However, teachers also expressed their feeling that the greater the student participation, the better.

Investigations such as these document that much of the communicative work is normally done by teachers, and that pupils' participation is restricted. There is a critical need to restructure classroom discourse to be more student centered, involve more give-and-take between participants, and encourage students to participate in classroom discussion actively, spontaneously, and constructively.

CLASSROOM DISCOURSE: A MOVE TOWARD DISCUSSION

Learning has been characterized as an active process that requires cognitive and social collaboration (Anderson, 1984; Rumelhart, 1980; Vygotsky, 1978). Classroom discourse greatly influences learning and social collaboration in school. The knowledge an individual acquires, accesses from memory, and applies to aid further acquisition is interactive. Socially, students can achieve learning tasks beyond their independent performance when collaborating with peers. Cazden (1986) refers to this phenomenon as performance before competence. Therefore, research suggests that learning is facilitated when students are allowed to interact with each other (Au, 1980; Palinscar & Brown, 1984) and such interaction is beneficial for students of various abilities (Moll & Diaz, 1985).

In the advent of new definitions for learning requiring students' active participation and collaboration, researchers contend that traditional classroom discourse must change if true discussion and rich learning is to occur. From this perspective, effective instruction is marked by new roles for teachers and students.

Dillon (1981) identified three criteria for distinguishing recitation from true discussion. First, the discussion participants must present multiple points of view and be ready to change their minds after hearing convincing arguments. Second, the participants must interact with one another as well as with the teacher. Finally, a majority of the verbal contributions must be longer than the typical two or three word phrases found in recitation.

Langer (1992) considers three areas for instructional change: (1) control of interaction, (2) pedagogical function, and (3) participants' contributions. Several options exist for determining control of the interaction. The interaction may be (1) regulated by the teacher, (2) shared by teacher and student, or (3) controlled by the students.

Instructional interaction can serve a variety of different pedagogical functions, depending on the goals of the teacher and the needs of the students. For instance, it may (1) motivate participants to engage in the activity, (2) reassure and encourage risk taking and decision making, or (3) model, instruct, or question.

The nature of contributions is also important. Contributions may be organized around (1) demonstration, with students observing while the teacher or other students demonstrate how to complete the task, (2) direct instruction with explicit presentation of information or procedure for the learner to assimilate, (3) posing of more open ended problems and search for appropriate solutions, or (4) mutual reflection and task definition around shared problems or interests.

In response to such recommendations, classroom dialogue is beginning to move beyond traditional teacher-laden recitation practices toward students' active participation in the selection of discussion topics and the navigation of discussion content. Two such strategies, the Experience–Text–Relationship (ETR) method (Au, 1979) developed as part of the Kamehameha Early Education Program (KEEP) (Au, 1979, 1980) and Reciprocal Teaching (Palincsar & Brown, 1984) which is an approach primarily used with less capable readers, influenced the development of the strategy.

CLASSROOM DISCUSSION: SPECIAL CONSIDERATIONS

Although researchers promote student participation for active learning, it is difficult to achieve given the constraints of traditional classroom recitation. Active participation may be more problematic for students with learning disabilities who frequently lack appropriate social interaction skills (Bryan, Wheeler, Felcan, & Henek, 1976) and are often unaware of their comprehension failures (Torgeson & Licht, 1983). Specifically, students with learning disabilities may lack awareness of (1) their limitations as problem solvers, (2) compensatory strategies to overcome such limitations, or (3) self-management techniques for monitoring and checking their own progress (Brown, 1982). These poor learner behaviors may cause the students to be inactive or ineffective participants in the discussion.

More positively, students with learning disabilities are capable of employing these strategies when cued to do so by teachers or peers (Bos & Filip, 1984; Wong, 1980). Thus, I was optimistic that, with teacher support, students with learning disabilities would be able to use a semantic mapping strategy, especially if taught in a peer group situation that permitted and encouraged students to cue one another to participate (Scanlon, Duran, Reyes, & Gallego, 1992a,b). Initially the teachers in this study modeled and demonstrated the semantic mapping strategy, then progressively faded instruction. They became more like coaches than group leaders. Student participation incrementally increased as teacher support decreased. The students were strongly encouraged to prompt each other to use prior knowledge, to share their ideas with others, and to form relationships among ideas and concepts during the construction of maps depicting text meaning. In this way, the interactive semantic mapping strategy encouraged student participation in a joint dialogue for organizing social studies content.

INTERACTIVE SEMANTIC MAPPING

Mapping strategies (Armbruster & Anderson, 1980) encourage students to represent important relationships in a text in interconnected diagrams. Students do so by analyzing text content in light of their prior knowledge (Rumelhart, 1980). In general, such semantic mapping was expected to improve learning from text (Stahl & Vancil, 1986), including the development of new vocabulary (Jones, 1984) and improved reading comprehension (Johnson, Toms-Bronowski, & Pittleman, 1982; Johnson, Pittleman, Toms-Bronowski, & Levin, 1984). The visual display constructed by the

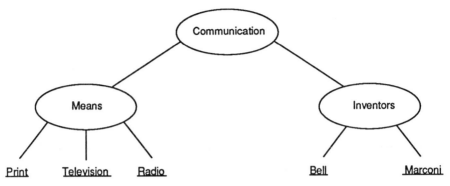

Fig. 1   Semantic map.

group represented relationships between both the content vocabulary and concepts identified by the students from the text *and* supplemental vocabulary and concepts generated by the students during the group discussion (Scanlon, Duran, Reyes, & Gallego, 1992a) (see Figure 1).

Seven components of interactive teaching and learning were used as discussion prompts (Bos & Anders, 1987; Gallego, 1989; Gallego & Anders, 1988). These included (1) activating prior knowledge by prompting each other to recall related past experiences; (2) tying new knowledge to old by connecting related prior knowledge and experience to new information provided by peers or by text; (3) predicting relationships by hypothesizing how their ideas and those of the text relate and prompt each other to identify alternatives; (4) sharing knowledge by using others in the group as resources for information and consensus building; (5) teaching concepts to peers in relation to the organization of the semantic map or the passage; (6) justifying relationships between and among concepts by explaining responses; and (7) confirming comprehension by discussing potential misconceptions. These prompts were embedded in the pre-, during-, and postreading discussions. The teacher initially modeled the prompts and then coached their use. Eventually students were able to use the prompts on their own as part of group functioning.

METHOD

Participants

The student participants were six bilingual (Spanish/English) 11- and 12-year-old girls identified as having learning disabilities (LD) according to school district criteria. The school district criteria used for identifying students as LD included (1) a severe discrepancy between intellectual functioning and academic achievement and (2) one or more deficits in cognitive processing as determined by district pupil evaluation teams. Subjects with a standard score of 85 or higher on the Wechsler Intelligence Scale for Children Revised (WISC-R; Wechsler, 1974) and with a disability in reading were selected for this study. Subjects' reading grade scores on Woodcock–Johnson Psychoeducational Battery (Woodcock, 1977) ranged from 1.4 to 2.7. No standardized measure of students' writing ability was available.

These students were a representative subsample of subjects who participated in a larger 3-year intervention study for the improvement of content area comprehension. The present study draws from data collected during the final intervention weeks in which students employed the strategy with little or no direct assistance from the teacher.

Procedures

The students learned and rehearsed interactive semantic mapping (Scanlon, Duran, Reyes, & Gallego, 1990) using five nonconsecutive related passages from a third-grade-level social studies text over a 5-wk period. A single chapter of approximately 8–10 pages was studied over 3–4 days during each week. Students were engaged in the activity for approximately 40 min each day. Each week, students participated in four lesson phrases: (1) brainstorm, (2) clue list, (3) relationship map construction, and (4) confirm understanding.

Students began the lesson by brainstorming concepts related to a content area passage. The title of the chapter was presented as the central idea for the brainstorm. As a guide for brainstorming, students were instructed to think of personal experiences and previous knowledge related to the topic. Ideas offered by students were deliberated for their relevancy by the group. Group consensus deemed an idea appropriate or inappropriate and therefore accepted or not accepted. Second, students generated a clue list by skimming the text to identify key vocabulary and concepts in the chapter. The sources for clues included pictures, titles, subheadings, and words in bold print. Third, students made predictions regarding the relationships among the concepts generated in the brainstorm and those presented in the text, and prompted each other to justify those predictions. After reaching consensus concerning the proposed relationships, students organized and displayed their predicted relationships among concepts by creating a semantic map. During the fourth phase, students read the passage to confirm their hypothesized relationships and conferred with each other to review and possibly change their map accordingly.

Data Sources

Three data sources were collected and analyzed: (1) videotaped classroom interactions recorded during the implementation of the semantic mapping activity, (2) multiple-choice comprehension quizzes collected at the conclusion of weekly lessons, and (3) student-written summaries, also collected weekly.

The 1st, 3rd, and 5th weeks of the intervention were videotaped. Three bilingual (Spanish/English) coders observed 15-min segments of each of the four phases of each lesson. Each coder was assigned two students to observe. Coders recorded all verbal contributions made by their assigned students. Students' verbal contributions were coded according to interaction using four categories: (1) interactive, (2) noninteractive, (3) off task, and (4) procedural. During training sessions, coders collectively observed two target subjects at two separate times for 20 min each (5 min per lesson phase). After each lesson phase, coders compared their coding. When coding was not in agreement, coders discussed their decisions until consensus was reached. An interrater reliability of 86% was attained.

Each student utterance was coded as interactive, noninteractive, off task, or procedural. Interactive utterances, such as "What else might go with this?" or "What made you think of that?" reflected interactive components (Bos & Anders, 1987; Gallego, 1989). Noninteractive utterances consisted of statements that reflected a directive or noncollaborative approach, such as "I'll do it myself" or "That's a dumb idea". Statement coded as off task were utterances that did not pertain to the procedures nor to the lesson content, such as "Hey, pizza for lunch" or "Teacher, are we going to recess today?" Procedural utterances reflected statements that referred to the management and set up of the lesson, such as "Now what do we do?" or "Is this part of the clue list?". Students' interaction patterns were recorded according to the frequency of initiations and responses directed to each group member (Gallego, 1989). Utterances directed to the teacher as well as those directed to the group as a whole were recorded and tallied.

Two comprehension measures were used to document students' content understanding. An eight-item multiple-choice comprehension quiz was administered weekly and scored for the percentage of correct responses. Test items consisted of an equal number of conceptual items, requiring students to draw relationships among concepts, and vocabulary items, requiring definitional knowledge. At the conclusion of the 5th week, a similar multiple-choice comprehension test consisting of 20 items was administered. This test was also administered 3 weeks later as a follow-up.

A second comprehension measure was also collected each week. Students were asked to individually generate a written summary of lesson content. Researchers encouraged students to write all they knew about the topic and assured them that their ideas, not their writing mechanics, were of primary importance. The purpose of the summaries was to identify student knowledge not identified by the multiple-choice quiz. The written summaries were scored as part of the larger study. Six coder were trained to use a holistic scoring procedure (Irwin & Mitchell, 1983).

During holistic rating training, coders were instructed to rate the same subset of 10 summaries from 1 to 5 (5 being the best). Through discussion, coders established a collective set of criteria reflective of a range of writing characteristics including organization, application, and accuracy of information. Summaries rated during training were used as references for the rating of the complete data set. The remaining summaries were rated independently by two coders. If ratings were the same or were adjacent scores, they were summed. If not, coders discussed the reasons for their score and deliberated to reach a consensus; then the two scores were summed. Reliability of 92% was achieved.

Although recent studies have documented the benefits of teacher support and increased student participation in classroom discussion, few have investigated autonomous student interpretation and implementation of discourse prompts for guiding and maintaining group discussion. The present study investigates group interaction according to (1) student reading comprehension and understanding of social studies concepts and (2) student self-defined discussion roles and responsibilities.

RESULTS

The results of this intervention are described in two categories: (1) group data, documenting student understanding of social studies concepts and student participation in group discussion, and (2) individual data, documenting target contributions by students, specifically the quality and the quantity of the interaction patterns among group members.

Group Contributions across Time

As a group, students gained in their understanding of social studies concepts and in their employment of the discourse prompts (Gallego, Duran, & Scanlon, 1990). Contributions generated by the total group during week 1, week 3, and week 5 were examined. There was a significant increase in the number of student contributions made over the 5-wk period, from an average of 6.4 contributions per student in week 1 to 23.8 turns per student in week 3.

Correlational analyses revealed a significant positive relationship between total group student contributions with the holistic ratings ($r = .68$,

$p < .003$). However, the total amount of student interaction was not significantly correlated with the comprehension quiz scores ($r = .06$)

Teacher Contributions across Time

Although teacher contributions varied slightly from week to week, these fluctuations were not statistically significant. The total number of teacher contributions during the 5 weeks was not correlated to the holistic ratings for the written summaries nor to the comprehension quiz scores.

Group Written Summaries across Time

Holistic scores assigned to written summaries were examined. There was a positive (and statistically significant) trend for summaries across the 5-wk period. There was no difference for the holistic scores recorded for week 5 and those recorded for the follow-up 3 weeks later.

Nature of Group Contributions

Proportional data provided further information regarding the nature of the group contributions. The quality of contributions improved over the 5 weeks. The percentage use of interactive, noninteractive, procedural, and off-task utterances revealed a consistent use of interactive statements and an increased use of procedural statements over the 5-wk period. A decrease in off-task contributions was also documented across the intervention weeks (see Table 1).

Individual Data

There was varied use of the discourse prompts among group members; all students participated in different ways at different times. Case study investi-

Table 1
Percentage of Use of Interactive, Noninteractive, Procedural, and Off-Task Contributions across Weeks 1, 3, and 5

Week	Type of interaction				Total
	Interactive	Noninteractive	Procedural	Off-task	
1	44.5%	0%	18.5%	36.0%	146
3	39.0%	2.0%	34.0%	25.0%	366
5	34.0%	0.1%	43.0%	19.0%	304

gation was employed to further examine target students' discussion participation. The case study approach allowed for inquiry regarding possible relationships between a student's overall discussion participation, specific interaction patterns, and comprehension performance. Three case study descriptions portray target students as distinctive group members.

Target Students' Performance

The three target students selected represent highest, median, and lowest achievement for the six students. Performance was measured by raw scores obtained on the multiple choice quiz and on the holistic ratings for each written summary. Target students' performance and preintervention reading comprehension scores are summarized in Table 2.

Target student contributions generated during week 1, week 3, and week 5 were categorized according to utterance type. Although there was variability in the amount and nature of involvement in discussion, all target students increased their use of procedural utterances during week 3. Frequency counts for each target student are summarized in Table 3.

Various interaction patterns among students were recorded. Discussions included talk among select group members, off-task dialogue, and conversations with their teacher. Case study summaries illustrate each target student's participation.

Table 2

Target Students Performance on Repeated Multiple Choice Quiz and Written Summary at Post-test and Follow-up, and Pre-intervention Woodcock–Johnson Reading Scores[a]

	Target student		
Measure	A	B	C
Comprehension quiz			
Post-test	13	15	14
Follow-up	18	15	10
Written summary			
Post-test	8	7	2
Follow-up	10	8	6
Woodcock–Johnson	2.4	1.4	1.7

[a]Raw score performance on 20-item quiz; Holistic score range 0–10 on written summary; Woodcock–Johnson grade equivalents.

Table 3

Target Students Use of Interactive, Noninteractive, Procedural, and Off-Task Utterances across Weeks 1, 3, and 5[a]

	Week		
Utterance	1	3	5
Student A			
Interactive	36	21	22
Noninteractive	0	3	1
Procedural	13	39	38
Off-task	25	20	11
Total	74	83	72
Student B[b]			
Interactive	0	5	16
Noninteractive	0	0	0
Procedural	0	31	22
Off-task	0	3	5
Total	0	39	43
Student C			
Interactive	10	37	20
Noninteractive	0	1	0
Procedural	5	15	9
Off-task	10	25	11
Total	25	78	40

[a] Raw frequency counts
[b] Student B was absent the entire first week.

CASE STUDIES

Target Student A

Overall Participation

Relative to other group members, student A was an active participant (see Table 3). Virtually no noninteractive contributions were recorded. Off-task utterances progressively decreased over time. Initially student A predominantly used interactive statements (many initiations directed to the teacher). As the responsibility shifted from the teacher to the students (weeks 3 and 5), more interactions regarding the procedure for executing the task were recorded.

Interaction Patterns

During week 1, responses (43) outnumbered initiations (31). Many were replies to the teacher. In part, this occurred because the teacher initially played a significant role in modeling the activity. During subsequent weeks, the teacher relinquished control of and responsibility for the task to the students. In addition to the interaction with the teacher, a few comments were directed to the total group; the remaining interactions were between students A and D.

During the third week, a decrease in teacher-directed initiations (from 19 to 14) and responses (from 34 to 17) was recorded. A marked decrease in teacher-directed responses suggested the teacher's decreased involvement. Less teacher interaction freed students to interact with each other; this is reflected in interactions between student A and all other group members, except student B. During week 5, there was a decrease in initiations (from 43 to 23) and responses (from 37 to 19). However, responses directed to the teacher increased (from 17 to 22). The teacher's persistence is interesting considering that the student initiated interactions with the teacher only 6 times but responded to 22 teacher initiations. A postintervention interview with the teacher explained this imbalance. The interview revealed the teacher's overriding concern that the students "do it right." Further comments alluded to the teacher's committment to assure that "the researchers get what they need." Although student A conversed with every group member except for student B, these contributions did not necessarily aid the group's completion of the task (off-task utterances).

Target Student B

Overall Participation

Student B's overall verbal contributions slightly increased from week 3 to week 5 (see Table 3). No noninteractive statements were recorded for this student. Off-task utterances slightly increased from week to week, although very few were recorded. A consistent number of initiations (21 during week 3 and 23 during week 5) and an increase in responses (13 during week 3 and 19 during week 5) were recorded. The student's absence during the first week partially explains the student's frequent involvement in procedural interactions during week 3 (39) and during week 5 (22).

Interaction Patterns

During the third week, this student's initiations (21) outnumbered responses (13) by approximately 3 to 2. However, responses were most often directed to the teacher. Nonetheless, this student initiated interaction with all but one group member, student C. Student B self-initiated and self-responded several times during week 3. Student B may have tried to be self-reliant, since she did not participate during week 1.

During week 5, an increase in initiations directed to the total group was recorded, which suggested that student B prodded other students to provide information to the group. Although this student interacted with every group member (frequently with student A during week 3 and student F during week 5), she was most likely to initiate interactions with the total group. The student made no initiation toward the teacher. However, more teacher responses were directed to her than to any other student. The teacher's involvement may have an effort to assure the students' "correct" completion of the task as well as an attempt to integrate the student into the group.

Target Student C

Overall Participation

Utterances recorded for student C fluctuated both in amount and type (see Table 3). For the first week 25 utterances were recorded; the number tripled (78 utterances) during week 3 and declined during the last week (40 utterances). A similar fluctuating pattern was recorded for off-task utterances (10, then 25, then 11). Virtually no noninteractive statements were recorded. A plausible reason for the increase in off-task utterances is the increased responsibility granted students for the activity during the third week. Student C may have become frustrated and decided to ignore the charge, preferring to occupy time in off-task conversation. Although this student most often used interactive statements, many of these interactions involved the teacher, particularly during the third week.

Interaction Patterns

During week 1, more responses (14) than initiations (11) were recorded. The interaction occurred almost exclusively between student C and the teacher. In part, this occurred because the teacher initially modeled the activity with the students. Only one initiation to the total group was recorded and the remaining interactions occurred between the student and student F.

The third week marked an increase in the student's initiations (40) and responses (35) over those recorded during week 1. The increased interaction was most often between the student and the teacher. In addition to interacting with the teacher, she engaged in discussion with all other group members except for student E. Student C self-responded three times.

Week 5 marked a decrease in participation as striking as the increase recorded for week 3. Although both the initiations and responses decreased, the student interacted with every group member, except student E. Most initiations were directed to student F and most responses were directed to student D.

Although this student fluctuated greatly in amount and type of interaction, she was successful at being involved with the majority of the group.

This student was not solicited by the teacher as frequently as others during week 5. However, the teacher may have initiated interactions and the student simply did not respond.

Target Students' Comprehension Performance

Target students' comprehension performances varied, as did their discussion participation (see Table 2). Students' comprehension performance was comparable to their discussion participation. Student A contributed frequently to the group discussion and performed well on both assessment measures. Student B engaged in a moderate amount of interaction and performed moderately on the two comprehension tests. Student C's participation fluctuated greatly. This student obtained the lowest score on both assessments.

It is interesting to note that the two measures assess different aspects of text comprehension. The multiple-choice quiz was narrow and required knowledge of text-bound vocabulary and concepts, administered as a recall task. In contrast, written summaries were broadly based on relevant personal knowledge, application of ideas, and text concepts. This structure allowed more freedom for expression of knowledge than did the quiz and was a production task. A dictation measure rather than the written summary may have documented greater success considering that students with reading disabilities often experience problems with written language production.

All target students obtained better performance during follow-up administrations of both measures. This may be an outcome of the integration of text-based knowledge and students' prior and relevant background knowledge, resulting in long-term understanding of larger concepts rather than the recollection of text-based details.

DISCUSSION

The interactive semantic mapping activity prompted student use of prior knowledge that facilitated comprehension of unfamiliar social studies concepts. Specifically, collective data documented success in two ways: (1) student strategy implementation improved, demonstrated by their increased use of interactive discussion prompts, and (2) social studies content comprehension increased. The holistic scores awarded to written summaries indicated a qualitative increase in ability to express understanding of text concepts over time. Comprehension was largely maintained, as illustrated by the written summaries collected at follow-up (only one student's performance dropped).

An analysis of case studies suggested the distinctiveness of group members. Students varied in the amount and nature of their involvement in discussion. For example, student A successfully engaged in interactions, soliciting aid and providing information with several group members. In contrast, student C was less involved in the activity and several times coped with the situation by participating in off-task conversations.

The interaction patterns revealed diverse discussion roles and responsibilities, illustrating a struggle for balance between personal *independent* knowledge and *interdependent* obligation to the group. Student A balanced the roles of both information provider and information seeker, a reflected by her initiation and response contributions to the discussion. Student B also performed as informant and information seeker. However, she more often sought information from others. Initiations regarding the procedure depicted student B's tentative confidence in her ability to perform the task, possibly as a result of her absence. Student C vacillated in her involvement, often interacting with the teacher or participating in off-task conversations. Students B and C occasionally directed comments to themselves, essentially self-monitoring their comprehension by "talking to themselves."

These distinct patterns suggested that students interacted with group members according to emerging or established classroom roles. For example, students may have based their interaction choices on their perceptions of academic or nonacademic expertise of other group members (i.e., social studies content knowledge, organizational skills, group leader, information strategies, popularity, or teacher's pet). Future research, especially research conducted in a complex setting such as a classroom, investigating group interaction must address and accommodate the existing relationships among its members. In this case, individual interviews with all participants may have provided insight regarding formal and informal networks.

In addition to participant roles, established interaction rules were also influential in involvement in group discussion. Discourse rules are strong and tenacious and are not readily changed (Anders & Gallego, 1989; Gallego, 1989). The enormity of the task is stated succinctly by Alvermann & Hayes (1989): "Oral language establishes the classroom culture, therefore attempts to modify classroom discussion amount to nothing less than attempts to modify the very culture of the classroom." (p. 307)

In summary, support was shown here for (1) the use of group discussion to aid students' content comprehension, and (2) the use of multiple comprehension tools to appraise individual student achievement. For instance, our findings supplement the growing literature supportive of restructured classroom interaction. However, the study does not address the influence of group dynamics in aiding *collective cognition* (Wertsch, 1987). Collective cognition refers to "shared mental contexts" from which teachers and children develop joint understandings, enabling them to engage together in educational discourse (Edwards, 1987). Developing joint understandings requires students' interdependent participation in discussion, arriving at knowledge unique to the group that could not have been generated independently. How such dynamic interchange can be documented is a complex issue. It is critical to do so, however, especially since instruction involving group discussion is flourishing (Cohen, 1986; Johnson & Johnson, 1987; Slavin, 1980).

Current research has identified two essential principles for restructured classroom interaction: (1) teacher support and (2) increased student participation in classroom discussion. A third principle crucial to the livelihood of collaborative endeavors is the use of appropriate assessment measures for documenting collective knowledge that do not reduce group performance into individual parts whose sum does not equal the whole. The general research approach used here could profitably be applied to analyses of instruction in such groups. Of course, this study is just a first step in what is expected to be a long program of research.

REFERENCES

Au, K. H. (1979). Using the experience–text–relationship method with minority children. *Reading Teacher, 32,* 677–679.

Au, K. H. (1980). Participation structures in reading lessons with Hawaiian children: Analysis of a culturally appropriate instructional event. *Anthropology and Education Quarterly, 11,* 91–115.

Alvermann, D., and Hayes, D. (1989). Classroom discussion of content area reading assignments: An intervention study. *Reading Research Quarterly, 24,* 305–335.

Alvermann, D., O'Brien, D. G., and Dillon, D. R. (1990). What teachers do when they say they're having discussions of content reading assignments: A qualitative analysis. *Reading Research Quarterly, 25,* 296–322.

Anders, P. L., and Gallego, M. A. (1989). Adoption of theoretically linked vocabulary-reading comprehension practices. In S. Mccormick and J. Zutell (Eds.), *Cognitive and social prespectives for literacy research and instruction: Thirty-eighth yearbook of the National Reading Conference* (pp. 481–487). Chicago, Illinois: National Reading Conference.

Anderson, R. C. (1984). Some reflections on acquisition of knowledge. *Educational Researcher, 13,* 5–10.

Armbruster, B. B., and Anderson, T. H. (1980). *The effect of mapping on the free recall of expository text.* (Technical Report No. 55). Urbana-Champaign: Center for the Study of Reading, University of Illinois.

Bos, C. S., and Anders, P. L. (1987). Semantic feature analysis: An interactive teaching strategy for facilitating learning from text. *LD Focus, 3*(1), 55–59.

Bos, C. S., and Filip, D. (1984). Comprehension monitoring in learning disabled and average students. *Journal of Learning Disabilities, 17*(4), 229–233.

Brown, A. (1982). Learning how to learn from reading. In J. Langer and T. Smith-Burke (Eds.), *Reader meets author, bridging the gap: A psycholinguistic and social linguistic perspective* (pp. 26–54). Newark, Delaware: International Reading Association, Deli Publishing.

Bryan, T., Wheeler, R., Felcan, J., and Henek, T. (1976). "Come on dummy": An observational study of children's communications. *Journal of Learning Disabilities, 9,* 53–61.

Cazden, C. (1981). Performance before competence: Assistance to child discourse in the zone of proximal development. *The Quarterly Newsletter of the Laboratory of Comparative Human Cognition, 3*(1), 5–8.

Cazden, C. (1986). Classroom discourse. In M. C. Wittrock (Ed.), *Handbook of research on teaching* (3rd ed., pp. 432–463). New York: MacMillan.

Cohen, E. (1986). *Designing groupwork: Strategies for the heterogeneous classroom.* New York: Teachers College Press.

Cross, D. R., and Paris, S. G. (1988). Developmental and instructional analysis of children's metacognition and reading comprehension. *Journal of Educational Psychology, 80,* 131–142.

Dillon, J. T. (1981). Duration of response to teacher questions and statements. *Contemporary Educational Psychology, 6,* 1–11.

Durkin, D. (1979). What classroom observations reveal about reading comprehension instruction. *Reading Research Quarterly, 14,* 481–533.

Edwards, A. D., and Furlong, J. J. (1978). *The language of teaching: Meaning in classroom interaction.* London: Heinemann.

Edwards, D. (1987). Educational knowledge and collective memory. *The Quarterly Newsletter of the Laboratory of Comparative Human Cognition, 9,* (1) p. 38–47.

Gallego, M. A. (1989). *Verbal interaction among teachers and elementary learning disabled students engaged in directive and interactive prereading strategies.* Unpublished doctoral dissertation. Tucson: University of Arizona.

Gallego, M. A., and Anders, P. L. (1988). *Comparison of the quality and quantity of communication during interactive and directive instructional practices.* Paper presented at the meeting of the National Reading Conference, Tucson, Arizona.

Gallego, M. A., Duran, G. Z., and Scanlon, D. J. (1990). Interactive teaching and learning: Facilitating learning disabled students' transition from novice and expert. *Thirty-ninth Yearbook of the National Reading Conference.*

Gallimore, R., and Tharp, R. G. (1983). *The regulatory functions of teacher questions: A microanalysis of reading comprehension lessons* (Technical Report No. 109). Honolulu: The Kamehameha Schools, Kamehameha Educational Research Institute.

Gambrell, L. (1987). Children's oral language during teacher-directed reading instruction. In J. E. Readence and R. S. Baldwin (Eds.), *Thirty-sixth yearbook of the National Reading Conference.* Chicago, Illinois: National Reading Conference.

Green, J. (1983). Research on teaching as a linguistic process: A state of the art. In E. W. Gorden (Ed.), *Review of research in education* (Vol. 10, pp. 151–252). Washington, D.C.: American Education Research Association.

Hagan, J. E. (1980). The effects of selected pre-reading vocabulary building activities on literal comprehension, vocabulary understanding, and attitudes of fourth and fifth grade students with reading problems. Ph.D. Thesis. University of Wisconsin. Madison. *Dissertation Abstracts International, 40,* 6216A.

Heath, S. B. (1983). *Ways with words: Language, life, and word in communities.* New York: Cambridge University Press.

Holdaway, D. (1979). *The foundations of literacy.* Sydney, Australia: Ashton Scholastic.

Irwin, P., and Mitchell, J. N. (1983). A procedure for assessing the richness of retellings. *Journal of Reading, 26,* 391–396.

Johnson, D. W., and Johnson, R. W. (1987). *Learning together and alone: Cooperative, competitive, and individualistic learning.* Englewood Cliffs, New Jersey: Prentice Hall.

Johnson, D., Toms-Bronowski, S., and Pittleman, S. (1982). *An investigation of the effectiveness of semantic mapping and semantic feature analysis with intermediate grade level children* (Program Report 83-3). Madison: Wisconsin Center for Education Research, University of Wisconsin.

Johnson, D., Pittleman, S., Toms-Bronowski, S., and Levin, K. M. (1984). *An investigation of the effects of prior knowledge and vocabulary acquisition on passage comprehension* (Program Report 84-5). Madison: Wisconsin Center for Education Research, University of Wisconsin.

Jones, S. T. (1984). The effect of semantic mapping on vocabulary acquisition and reading comprehension of black inter-city students. Unpublished paper, University of Wisconsin, Madison.

Langer, J. (1992). A sociolinguistic perspective on literacy. In J. Langer (Ed.), *Language, literacy and culture: Issues of society and schooling.* Norwood, New Jersey: Ablex.

Locke, E. Q. (1975). *A guide to effective study.* New York: Springer-Verlag.

Mehan, H. (1979). *Learning lessons.* Cambridge: Harvard University Press.

Moll, L., and Diaz, S. (1985). Ethnographic pedagogy: Promoting effective bilingual instruction. In E. Garcia and R. Padilla (Eds.), *Advances in bilingual education research* (pp. 127–149). Tucson: University of Arizona Press.

Myklebust, H. R., Boshes, B., Olson, D., and Cole, C. (1969). *Minimal brain damage in children.* Final Report, USPHS Contract 108-65-142. Evanston, Illinois: Northwestern University Publications.

O'Flahaven, J. F., Hartman, D. K., and P. D. Pearson (1988). Teacher questioning and feedback practices: A twenty-year retrospective. In J. E. Readence and R. J. Baldwin (Eds.), *Thirty-seventh yearbook of the National Reading Conference* (pp. 183–228). Chicago; National Reading Conference.

Palincsar, A. S., and Brown, A. L. (1984). Reciprocal teaching of comprehension-fostering and comprehension-monitoring activities. *Cognition and Instruction, 1,* 117–175.

Quarterly Newsletter of the Laboratory of Comparative Human Cognition, 9(1), January.

Reyes, E. I., Gallego, M. A., Duran, G. Z., and Scanlon, D. J. (1989). Integration of internal concepts and external factors: Extending the knowledge of learning disabled adolescents. *Journal of Early Adolescence, 9*(1–2), 112–124.

Rumelhart, D. E. (1980). Schemata: The building blocks of cognition. In R. J. Spiro, B. C. Bruce, and W. F. Brewer (Eds.), *Theoretical issues in reading comprehension* (pp. 33–58). Hillsdale, New Jersey: Erlbaum.

Sacks, H., Schegloff, E. A., and Jefferson, G. (1974). A simplest systematics for the organization of turn-taking in conversation. *Language, 50,* 696–735.

Salomon, G., and Perkins, D. N. (1989). Rocky roads to transfer: Rethinking mechanisms of a neglected phenomenon. *Educational Psychologist, 24,* 113–142.

Scanlon, D. J. (1992b). *Combining collaborative learning and interactive semantic mapping to enhance learning disabled adolescents' content area comprehension.* Unpublished doctoral dissertation. Tucson: University of Arizona, in press.

Scanlon, D. J., Duran, G. Z., Reyes, E. I., and Gallego, M. A. (1992a). *Interactive semantic mapping. LD Focus,* in press.

Sinclair, J., and Coulthard, R. M. (1975). *Towards an analysis of discourse: The English used by teachers and pupils.* London: Oxford University Press.

Sirotnik, K. (1983). What you see is what you get: Consistency, persistency and mediocrity in the classroom. *Harvard Educational Review, 53,* 16–31.

Slavin, R. (1980). Cooperative learning. *Review of Educational Research, 50,* 315–342.

Smith, F. (1975). *Comprehension and learning: A conceptual framework for teachers.* New York: Holt, Reinhart, & Winston.

Stahl, S. A., and Vancil, S. J. (1986). Discussion is what makes semantic maps work in vocabulary instruction. *The Reading Teacher, 40,* 62–67.

Stubbs, M. (1983). *Language, schools, classrooms.* New York: Methuen.

Torgeson, J. K., and Licht, B. G. (1983). The learning disabled child as an inactive learner: Retrospect and prospects. In J. D. McKinney and L. Feagens (Eds.), *Current topics in learning disabilities* (pp. 3–31). Norwood, New Jersey: Ablex.

Vygotsky, L. S. (1978). *Mind in society: The development of higher psychological processes.* Cambridge: Harvard University Press.

Wechsler, D. (1974). *Wechsler intelligence scale for children—Revised.* New York: Psychological Corporation.

Wells, G. (1986). *The meaning makers: Children learning language and using language to learn.* Portsmouth, New Hampshire: Heinemann Educational Books.

Wertsch. J. (1987). Collective memory: Issues from a sociohistorical perspective. *The Quarterly Newsletter of the Laboratory of Comparative Human Cognition, 9,* (1).

Wong, B. Y. L. (1980). Activating the inactive learner: Use of questions/prompts to enhance comprehension and retention of implied information in learning disabled children. *Learning Disabilities Quarterly, 3,* 29–37.

Woodcock, D. (1977). *The Woodcock-Johnson psychoeducational battery.* Allen, Texas: DLM/Teaching Resources.

8

Guiding Students' Cognitive Processing of Scientific Information in Text

Richard E. Mayer

INTRODUCTION

Between the ages of 5 and 18, children spend approximately 12,000 hours in schools as well as many more hours in academic work at home. For these students, learning from teachers and books becomes the dominant activity in their lives. In essence, we expect our children to become professional learners; however, we provide them with surprisingly little guidance in how to learn (Norman, 1980; Mayer, 1987; Weinstein & Mayer, 1985). In this chapter, I am concerned with a deceptively straightforward question. How can we maximize the effectiveness of students' academic learning? In particular, I focus on techniques for guiding students' learning of scientific information. This chapter, therefore, is part of the growing research literature on design of textbooks and teaching of learning strategies (Britton & Black, 1985; Britton & Glynn, 1987; Chambliss & Calfee, 1989; Duffy & Waller, 1985; Harris, 1990; Pressley, 1990; Pressley & Levin, 1983a,b; Weinstein, Goetz, & Alexander, 1988; Woodward & Britton, 1992).

How one attempts to improve students' academic learning depends, in part, on one's view of learning and teaching. Sternberg (1990) has shown how various metaphors of mind affect research and theory in one field of cognitive psychology. Table 1 lists three metaphors of learning that are

Table 1
Metaphors of Learning and Teaching

		Implications for instruction and learning outcomes	
Learning	Teaching	Instructional focus	Learning outcomes focus
Response acquisition	Dispensing feedback	Curriculum-centered (correct behaviors)	Quantitative/how much (strength of associations)
Knowledge acquisition	Disseminating information	Curriculum-centered (appropriate information)	Quantitative/how much (amount of information)
Meaning construction	Guiding cognitive processing	Student-centered (useful processing)	Qualitative/what kind (structure of knowledge)

relevant to educational psychology: learning as response acquisition, learning as knowledge acquisition, and learning as meaning construction. These three metaphors can be viewed as characters in a three-act play that summarizes the history of the psychology of learning and instruction.

As the curtain opens on psychology during the first half of this century, the learning-as-response-acquisition metaphor takes center stage. Based on animal research interpreted within behaviorist theory, the learner becomes a plastic being whose repertoire of behaviors is determined by experience. The learner is a blank slate on which the environment must leave an impression, a passive being for whom successful responses are automatically strengthened and unsuccessful responses are automatically weakened. Dewey (1902, p. 8) described the passive learner: "The child is simply the immature being who is to be matured; he is the superficial being who is to be deepened . . . It is his to receive, to accept." Correspondingly, in traditional behaviorism the teacher is viewed as a dispenser of feedback, giving rewards for appropriate responses and punishments for inappropriate responses. The teacher's role is to create and shape the behavior of the student by dispensing a reward here and punishment there.

It follows that instruction focuses on creating situations in which the learner must respond and on providing appropriate reinforcement for each response. The drill-and-practice method exemplifies the instructional focus of the learning-as-response-acquisition metaphor. For example, arithmetic learning involves learning to give the correct answer for each basic arithmetic problem such as $5 + 4 =$ _____, $6 + 2 =$ _____, and $3 + 8 =$ _____. It also follows that learning outcomes are evaluated in terms of the quantity of behavior change, for example, asking how many correct answers the student gave on an addition fact test.

This view of learning does not leave much room for increasing the effectiveness of students' academic learning. According to the learning-as-response-acquisition view, the mechanisms of learning are innate and are not subject to conscious control. Therefore, it does not make sense to teach students to be more effective learners or to talk about learning strategies. Although the curtain has dropped on the learning-as-response-acquisition metaphor, it is too early to declare it officially dead. For example, recent theories of skill learning have once again placed automatization of response in a key role in the psychology of learning (Anderson, 1983; Singley & Anderson, 1989).

The next act in our three-act play stars the learning-as-knowledge-acquisition metaphor, which dominated the stage during the 1950s and 1960s. The shift from response acquisition to knowledge acquisition occurred as research on learning began to move from the animal laboratory to the human laboratory and behaviorist psychology gave way to the cognitive revolution. In Act II, the learner becomes more cognitive; the learner is now a processor of information. Correspondingly, the teacher becomes a disseminator of information.

The focus of instruction is information. How can we get the information specified in the curriculum into the student's memory? Ninety years ago, Dewey (1902, p. 8) referred to this approach as curriculum centered. "Subdivide each topic into studies; each study into lessons; each lesson into specific facts and formulae. Let the child proceed step by step to master each one of these separate parts, and at last he will have covered the entire ground." The focus of evaluation is on the quantity of knowledge learned. How much does the student know?

Although the learner becomes more active in Act II, he or she is still not in control of the learning process. Although the purge of behaviorism allows the learner to engage in cognitive processes during the course of learning, the conscious control of those processes is not spotlighted. As the curtain falls on Act II, the view of the learner is changing from passive to active but the cognitive revolution is slow to attack the problems of learning and transfer.

By the 1970s and 1980s, the third act of our play, researchers who move from the laboratory to more realistic learning situations find a much more active and inventive learner—a learner who seeks to construct meaning out of the fragments of information in her or his environment. In the third act, the role of the learner is played by an autonomous being who has conscious control of her or his own learning process. This new learner possesses skills that are called metacognitive or metacomponential—knowledge of one's own cognitive processes or one's own knowledge-acquisition processes (Flavell, 1970; Flavell & Wellman, 1977; Sternberg, 1985, 1988). Dewey (1902, p. 9) described active learning: "Learning is active. It involves reaching out of one's mind. It involves organic assimilation from within." Instead of acquiring knowledge, the learner constructs it using prior experience to understand and shape new learning. Instead of providing knowledge, the teacher participates in the processes of shared cognition, of constructing knowledge with the student.

The implication for instruction, articulated 90 years ago by Dewey (1902, p. 9), is that it must be child centered. "The child is the starting point, the center, and the end. His development, his growth is the ideal." Consistent with the child-centered approach, the evaluation of learning is qualitative. Instead of asking how much knowledge is acquired, we ask about the structure and quality of the knowledge and the processes the learner uses to answer questions.

As the curtain falls on the third act, we are left with an active learner who uses what Wittrock (1974) called generative learning processes. Although this learner-as-meaning-constructor claims to be a new character, he or she has been lurking in the shadows throughout this century (Ausubel, 1968; Bartlett, 1932; Piaget, 1954; Wittrock, 1974). The curtain is down for the third time but the play is incomplete. A comprehensive cognitive theory of learning is still evolving.

FRAMEWORK FOR GUIDING STUDENTS' COGNITIVE PROCESSING

For the purposes of this chapter, I adopt the learning-as-meaning-construction metaphor. In particular, I view learners as active information processors who guide the processing of information presented in lectures and books. In order to maximize students' academic learning, we need to identify some basic information processes for prose learning and to understand how control of these processes affects the quality of learning.

Figure 1 shows a simplified model of the human information processing

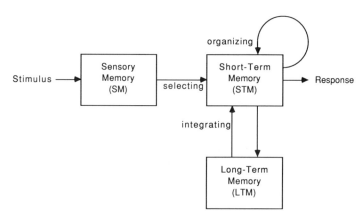

Fig. 1   An information processing system.

system. The boxes represent memory stores. *Sensory memory* (SM) holds a rapidly decaying, exact image of what the eye sees on the page. *Short-term memory* (STM) holds a few pieces of information that are transferred from SM; information in STM (sometimes called working memory) can decay within seconds unless it is actively rehearsed or manipulated. This is where connections are made among pieces of information. *Long-term memory* (LTM) is a person's store of permanent knowledge; it is organized, meaningful, and unlimited in capacity.

The arrows in Figure 1 represent cognitive processes. *Selecting* is the process of paying attention to some of the information in SM and transferring it to STM. *Organizing* is the process of combining the newly transferred information in STM. *Integrating* is the process of building connections between the incoming information and existing knowledge from long-term memory. Although these are the three major processes in the system, Figure 1 includes a fourth arrow from STM to LTM representing the process of *storing* the knowledge that was constructed in STM. Active learners exercise control over processes such as selecting, organizing, integrating, and storing.

Let us take a closer look at how these processes are involved in meaningful learning. I define meaningful learning as learning in which the learner engages in selecting relevant information, organizing that information into a coherent whole, and integrating that information with an appropriate existing knowledge structure. Accordingly, I predict that the outcome of meaningful learning will be characterized by retention of relevant information and problem-solving transfer.

Figure 2 summarizes the cognitive conditions for meaningful learning as proposed by Mayer (1984, 1987, 1989a), that is, the learning processes that must take place for the learner to construct meaning out of the presented information. These three cognitive conditions correspond to the knowledge-acquisition components identified by Sternberg (1985, p. 107), "processes used in gaining new knowledge."

The first process is what Mayer calls selecting and Sternberg calls selective encoding: focusing conscious attention on relevant pieces of information. Selecting involves "selecting information from the text and adding that information to working memory" (Mayer, 1984, p. 32) as is indicated by the arrow from SM to STM. Selective encoding involves "sifting out of relevant from irrelevant information." (Sternberg, 1985, p. 107)

The second process is what Mayer calls organizing and what Sternberg calls selective combination: building internal connections among the selected pieces of information. Mayer (1984, p. 32) refers to this process as "organizing the selected information in working memory into a coherent whole" as indicated by the arrow from STM to STM. Selective combination involves "combining selectively encoded information in such a way as to

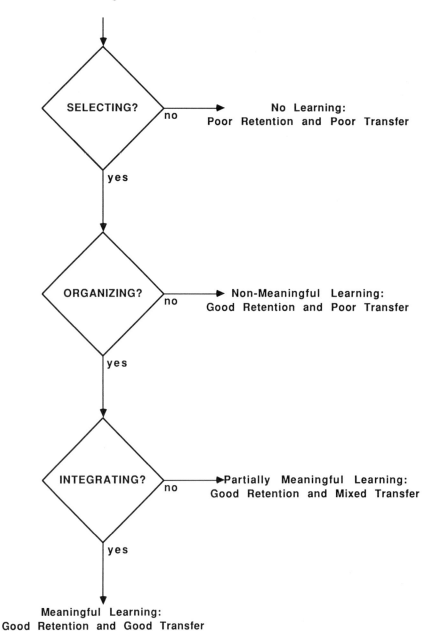

Fig. 2   Three cognitive conditions for meaningful learning.

form an integrated . . . internally connected whole." (Sternberg, 1985, p. 107)

The third process is called integrating by Mayer and selective comparison by Sternberg: the processes of building external connections between the organized new knowledge and organized existing knowledge. Integrating is "connecting the organized information to other familiar knowledge structures already in memory" (Mayer, 1984, p. 33) as indicated by the arrow from LTM to STM. Selective comparison is the process of "relating newly acquired or retrieved information . . . to old knowledge so as to form an externally connected whole." (Sternberg, 1985, p. 107)

How do effective and ineffective learners differ? The answer lies partly in the way that learners employ learning strategies, behaviors of the learner during learning that are intended to control her or his information processes (Weinstein & Mayer, 1985). Effective learners have appropriate learning strategies available, that is, they possess the strategy in long-term memory, and they are able to produce the appropriate strategy for the appropriate situation, that is, they apply the strategy to improve their learning. Flavell (1970; Flavell & Wellman, 1977) suggests that ineffective learners may fail to guide their cognitive processes either because they lack the appropriate learning strategies (i.e., availability deficiency) or because they do not know when to apply an appropriate strategy (i.e., production deficiency). Difficulties in knowing when to apply a learning strategy include failure to recognize that a problem exists.

How can we help learners control the three crucial processes summarized in Table 2? Two major ways of helping students control their learning processes are text-based guidance of processing and learner-based guidance of processing. Text-based guides are embedded in a text and are intended to encourage the learner to engage in various processes. Text-

Table 2
A Framework for Promoting Academic Competence

Cognitive process	Knowledge acquisition component	Description of cognitive process	Test-based guidance of processing	Learner-based guidance of processing
Selecting	Selective encoding	Focusing attention (arrow from SM to STM)	Headings	Underlining or copying
Organizing	Selective combination	Building internal connections (arrow from STM to STM)	Signaling	Outlining
Integrating	Selective comparison	Building external connections (arrow from LTM to STM)	Concrete advance organizers	Elaborating

based guidance is appropriate for counteracting production deficiencies, that is, situations in which the learner needs to be reminded to process the incoming information in a certain way. For example, Table 2 suggests that headings may encourage the learner to use the selecting process, signaling may affect selecting and organizing, and advance organizers may affect all three processes (Loman & Mayer, 1983; Mayer, 1979, 1984, 1992).

Learner-based guidance of cognitive processing is based on direct instruction of learning strategies, that is, teaching the student how to learn. Learner-based guidance is an appropriate remedy for availability deficiencies, that is, situations in which the learner needs instruction on how to control her or his cognitive processes for specific learning tasks. For example, Table 2 suggests that student underlining may affect the selecting process, student outlining may affect selecting and organizing, and elaborative note taking may affect all three processes (Peper & Mayer, 1986; Shrager & Mayer, 1989; Weinstein & Mayer, 1985). The following sections respectively examine research on text-based guides, such as advance organizers, and learner-based guides, such as note taking, that are intended to foster all three crucial learning processes.

TEXT-BASED GUIDANCE OF COGNITIVE PROCESSING

Textbooks, lectures, and other prose instruction contain information to be learned and cues for how to process that information. Not all students are aware of how text-based cues can be used to guide their processing of information, and not all text-based manipulations have the same effects on the learner's cognitive processing. In this section, I focus on concrete advance organizers because they exemplify text-based guidance of the three crucial processes of selecting, organizing, and integrating. In short, advance organizers can help the learner select relevant information from the text, connect that information into a cause-and-effect chain, and relate that chain to existing knowledge about analogous systems.

A concrete advance organizer is verbal or visual information presented prior to the lesson that is intended to help the learner select relevant information, build internal connections, and build external connections. A concrete advance organizer (1) depicts a familiar system that is analogous to or a simplified version of a to-be-learned system that is described in the lesson; (2) contains a few major parts with each part corresponding to a part in the to-be-learned system and (3) contains a few cause-and-effect relationships with each relationship corresponding to a relationship in the to-be-learned system.

For example, for a lesson on radar a concrete advance organizer could describe a system in which a pulse is sent, bounces off an object, returns to the sender, and the distance of the object can be determined by measuring the time taken for the pulse to return. The advance organizer could consist of a one-sheet introduction that lists five steps along with corresponding pictures of a bouncing ball.

1. Transmission: A pulse travels from an antenna.
2. Reflection: The pulse bounces off a remote object.
3. Reception: The pulse returns to the receiver.
4. Measurement: The difference between the time out and the time back tells the total time traveled.
5. Conversion: The time can be converted to a measure of distance, since the pulse travels at a constant speed.

This advance organizer presents a cause-and-effect system that is analogous to a radar system, as described in various parts of an actual lesson. ". . . Radar involves simply measuring the time between transmission of the waves and their subsequent return . . . and then converting that to a distance measure . . . To send out the radio waves . . . a directional antenna . . . sends out a stream of short pulses . . . Any object in the path of the transmitted beam reflects some of the energy back to the radio receiver . . ." As you can see, the advance organizer cues the learner to focus on information in the lesson about transmission, reflection, reception, measurement, and conversion; cues the learner to build causal relationships between events, such as the distance of the remote object from the source and the time it takes for the pulse to return; and cues the learner to connect the radar system to his or her knowledge of how bouncing balls or echoes work.

In order to examine the effects of a concrete advance organizer, Mayer (1983) asked science-naive students to read a passage about how radar works. Before the passage, some students received the one-page introduction just described, whereas other students read the lesson without the introduction. If the introduction helps the learner focus on the relevant information in the text, we can predict that the organizer group will recall more relevant information but not more irrelevant information than the control group. The results clearly support this prediction: the advance organizer group recalled approximately 50% more relevant information but slightly less of the other information than the control group. If the introduction helps guide the learner's building of internal and external connections, then we can predict that the organizer group will outperform the control group on tests of problem-solving transfer such as determining how to invent an improved radar system. As predicted, the organizer group produced approximately twice as many creative solutions for transfer problems as the control group. Similar results were obtained in a long series of experiments involving scientific and technical text (Mayer, 1989a).

Apparently, the cues provided in the concrete advance organizer helped learners to engage appropriate learning strategies by selecting information in the radar passage that was most relevant to how the system works, by integrating that information into a coherent cause-and-effect chain, and by relating that chain to familiar experiences with bouncing balls or echoes.

The success of concrete advance organizers suggests that certain kinds of illustrations in text offer a potentially powerful guide to readers for how to process instructional information. Interestingly, different kinds of illustrations may serve to prompt different kinds of cognitive processing in readers, ranging from selecting to organizing to integrating. For example, consider how illustrations can guide a reader's processing of a text on "how brakes work."

Levin's (1981, 1989; Levin & Mayer, 1992) taxonomy of illustrations includes five types of illustrations. *Decorational illustrations* are unrelated to the text, for example, a photo of a brake service garage, and thus do not elicit any of the three major cognitive processes. *Representational illustrations* show a picture of an item described in the text, for example, a photo of a drum brake, and thus may have a mild effect on the selecting process. *Transformational illustrations* provide a visual mnemonic to help the reader remember specific facts and thus strongly affect the selecting process. *Organizational illustrations* provide structure, for example, a diagram of a drum brake with labels for each part, and may affect both selecting and organizing processes. Finally, *interpretational illustrations* improve the comprehensibility of text, for example, a series of frames showing the status of each part in the drum braking system when the brake pedal is up and when it is down; interpretational illustrations (also called explanative illustrations) may affect selecting, organizing, and integrating processes and therefore have become the focus of a recent program of research.

In order to examine the effects of explanative illustrations in helping students to process text, Mayer (1989b) conducted a series of experiments in which science-naive college students read a passage about how brakes work. For each of three types of braking systems described in the passage, the text included an interpretational illustration (showing the state of each of six parts in the braking system when the pedal is up and when the pedal is down) or no illustration. For example, the interpretational illustration for drum brakes consisted of two frames. One frame showed that when the brake pedal is up, the piston in the master cylinder is back, the hydraulic fluid is not compressed, the piston in the wheel cylinder is back, and the brake shoe is not pressed against the spinning drum. The other frame showed that when the brake pedal is down, the piston in the master cylinder is forward, the hydraulic fluid is compressed, the piston in the wheel cylinder is pushed forward, and the brake shoe is pushed against the spinning drum. The text included a brief explanation of the cause-and-effect chain of events, which we refer to as the explanative information.

When the driver steps on the car's brake pedal, a piston moves forward inside the master cylinder. The piston forces the brake fluid out of the master cylinder and through the tubes to the wheel cylinders. In the wheel cylinders, the increase in fluid pressure makes a set of smaller pistons move. These smaller pistons activate . . . drum brakes . . . When the brake shoes press against the drum, both the drum and the wheel stop or slow down.

On a subsequent posttest, students were asked to recall the passage (including both explanative and other information) and to answer questions (including creative problem solving and verbatim retention). For example, some of the problem-solving questions asked the student to suggest improvements in braking systems or to suggest reasons why a braking system might fail.

Our hypothesis is that interpretational illustrations can help the reader process the explanative text in a way that leads to the selection of relevant information (selecting process) and the construction of a mental model of the system (organizing and integrating processes). First, if interpretational illustrations serve to guide the reader's attention toward the portion of the text that describes the causal chain (i.e., explanative text), then the interpretational-illustrations group should recall more explanative information but not more of other kinds of information from the text than the control group. As predicted, students who read the text with interpretational illustrations recalled approximately 50% more explanative information and slightly less of other material than students who read text only.

Second, if interpretational illustrations encourage students to build connections among the events described in the text, then the interpretational-illustrations group should perform better on problem-solving questions but not on verbatim retention than the control group. As predicted, students who read the text with interpretational illustrations generated more than 50% more creative solutions to problem-solving transfer questions but performed slightly worse on a verbatim recognition test than students who read text only.

These results suggest that the illustrations provided cues concerning how to process the information in the passage. The illustrations contained pointer lines from phrases in the text to the parts of the illustrations. If these pointers serve as guides to students for how to process the words, then eliminating the pointers should greatly reduce the effectiveness of the interpretational illustrations. As expected, a third group that read the text with unlabeled illustrations performed relatively poorly on recall of explanative information and on problem-solving transfer.

In a subsequent series of three experiments, Mayer and Gallini (1990) replicated the previous results for passages on brakes, pumps, and electrical generators; interpretational illustrations served to improve explanative recall and problem-solving performance. However, the effects were not produced for other types of illustrations, demonstrating that interpretational illustrations are more effective than other types in guiding readers' selecting, organizing, and integrating processes. In addition, the effects were not produced in readers who were highly knowledgeable about mechanical systems, demonstrating that interpretational illustrations are effective mainly for students who would not otherwise be able to make sense of the explanative information in the passage.

The next step in this program of research was to examine the effects of animations on learning from computer-based instructional systems. In a preliminary series of experiments, Mayer and Anderson (1991) asked college students to listen to a computer-generated verbal description of how a bicycle tire pump works, either before or while viewing a computer-presented animation of the pump (showing the changes in the state of five major parts as the handle is pulled up and pushed down). If the animation guides the student in selecting, organizing, and integrating the incoming information, then it would be crucial for the animation and speech to be presented concurrently rather than successively. As expected, although all students received identical information, students who heard the narration as they viewed the animation generated approximately 50% more answers on a subsequent problem-solving test than students who received the animation and narration successively. The crucial relationship between saying and doing has also been demonstrated in cognitive-behavior modification programs with exceptional children (Harris, 1982, 1990).

This series of studies provides new information concerning the role of visual cues in guiding the learning process. Visual cues (such as concrete organizers, illustrations, and animations) appear to affect the information that readers select and how they organize and integrate that information under certain conditions (see Levin & Mayer, 1992; Mayer, 1989a; Mayer & Gallini, 1990). First, the to-be-learned material must be potentially meaningful, for example, a passage on some cause-and-effect system. Second, the visual cues must serve an interpretational function, such as showing a sequence of frames. Levin & Mayer (1992) and Mayer (1989a) have noted that all visual cues are not equally useful and have described the characteristics of effective visual cues. One particularly important feature of effective visual cues is that they must be closely connected with the text, for example, by pointers between text and pictures or concurrent presentation of narration and animation; Mayer and Anderson (1991) have shown how this feature is consistent with Paivio's (1971, 1990) dual coding theory. Third, the effectiveness of visual cues depends on the characteristics of the learners. In particular, students who lack prior knowledge but possess basic reading skills are more likely to benefit than students who possess prior knowledge and adequate reading skills. Fourth, assessment of the effectiveness of visual cues requires multilevel tests. If overall amount remembered or overall percentage correct on a comprehension test is the only dependent measure, then effects are unlikely to be detected. Instead, visual cues that elicit selecting, organizing, and integrating processes affect recall of explanative but not other information and affect answering of problem-solving transfer but not verbatim questions. More research is needed to examine the process of learning in more detail, with particular focus on how students select, organize, and integrate information during learning.

LEARNER-BASED GUIDANCE OF COGNITIVE PROCESSING

Even when a text or lecture contains clear and appropriate processing cues, some students may fail to benefit from them. Presumably these students need instruction in how to learn from prose, that is, in how to process the information effectively. In this section, I focus on generative note-taking training as a prime example of learner-based guidance of the three crucial processes of selecting, organizing, and integrating. In short, effective note taking can help the learner select relevant information from the text, connect that information into a coherent structure, and relate that structure to existing knowledge.

Generative note taking occurs when, in the course of reading or listening to a lesson, the learner generates written notes that contain the relevant information organized into a coherent outline, including elaborations. Generative note taking involves selecting relevant information, fitting it into an appropriate structure, and adding any needed elaborations based on past experience.

For example, for a lesson on how the human ear works, students need to recognize that the lesson describes a five-step process. In their own words, students need to be able to complete "The first step is ____, the second step is ____, the third step is ____, the fourth step is ____, and the fifth step is ____." This is a generative process that requires selection of relevant information (i.e., information about each step), building internal connections (i.e., listing the information as a cause-and-effect chain of five steps), and building external connections (i.e., stating the steps in one's own words).

Cook and Mayer (1988) developed a two-part training program in generative note taking for science-naive students. First, students learned to recognize basic prose structures such as generalization (a main idea followed by supporting evidence), enumeration (a list of facts or properties all pertaining to the same topic), and sequence (steps in a cause-and-effect process). Then, students learned to take notes for each type of structure by writing the generalization and supporting evidence for a generalization paragraph, by listing the facts and the topic for an enumeration paragraph, and by listing the cause-and-effect chain for a sequence paragraph. A teacher modeled her note-taking strategies and then students compared their approach to that of the teacher.

In order to test the effectiveness of training in generative note taking, Cook & Mayer (1988) gave pretests and posttests to science-naive students who either received the training or did not. The tests involved reading short lessons and taking retention and transfer tests on the material. If the training helps the learners focus on the relevant information in the text, we can predict that the trained group will recall more relevant information but not more irrelevant information than the control group. The results support this prediction: the trained group showed an 11% pretest-to-posttest gain in recall of relevant information compared with no change for the control group, and showed a 4% decrease in recall of less important information compared with a 3% gain for the control group. If the training helps guide the learner's building of internal and external connections, then we can predict that the trained group will outperform the control group on tests of problem-solving transfer such as determining how to invent a hearing aid. As predicted, the trained group produced a 24% pretest-to-posttest gain in problem-solving transfer compared with a slight pretest-to-posttest decline for the control group.

Apparently, the training in how to generate notes helped learners to engage appropriate learning strategies by selecting relevant information, fitting it into an appropriate text structure, and describing the ideas in their own words. As for research on text-based guides, additional research is needed to examine how students select, organize, and integrate information during learning. The present results suggest that training specifically related to the subject domain, rather than domain-free general strategies, can be effective in maximizing cognitive processing during learning.

CONCLUSION

Academic learning involves more than acquiring information presented by the teacher or by books. At the core of academic learning is the ability to control one's learning processes, to focus attention on relevant information, to build connections among the relevant pieces of information, and to build connections between old and new knowledge. Therefore, teaching for academic competence and literacy must involve teaching in ways that help students to process information effectively. In this chapter, I have presented examples of text-based and learner-based guidance of learning processes.

Educational psychologists have progressed from viewing learning as response acquisition to knowledge acquisition to meaning construction. Correspondingly, our focus has moved from analysis of student behavior to curriculum to cognitive processes. As psychologists and educators become more interested in the cognitive processes of effective learners, they progress toward Dewey's (1902) vision of child-centered education. The resulting theory of learning and instruction will provide new insights into how instructional events affect cognitive events in the learner. These analyses can form the basis for promoting academic competence.

REFERENCES

Anderson, J. R. (1983). *The architecture of cognition.* Cambridge: Harvard University Press.

Ausubel, D. P. (1968). *Educational psychology: A cognitive view.* New York: Holt, Rinehart and Winston.

Bartlett, F. C. (1932). *Remembering.* Cambridge: Cambridge University Press.

Britton, B. K., and Black, J. B. (Eds.) (1985). *Understanding expository text.* Hillsdale, New Jersey: Erlbaum.

Britton, B. K., and Glynn, S. M. (Eds.) (1987). *Executive control processes in reading.* Hillsdale, New Jersey: Erlbaum.

Chambliss, M. J., and Calfee, R. C. (1989). Designing science textbooks to enhance student understanding. *Educational Psychologist, 24,* 307–322.

Cook, L. K., and Mayer, R. E. (1988). Teaching readers about the structure of scientific text. *Journal of Educational Psychology, 80,* 448–456.

Dewey, J. (1902). *The child and the curriculum.* Chicago University of Chicago Press.

Duffy, T. M., and Waller, R. (1985). *Designing usable texts.* Orlando, Florida: Academic Press.

Flavell, J. H. (1970). Developmental studies of mediated memory. In H. W. Reese and L. P. Lipsitt (Eds.), *Advances in child development and behavior* (Vol. 5). New York: Academic Press.

Flavell, J. H., and Wellman, H. M. (1977). Metamemory. In R. V. Kail and J. W. Hagen (Eds.), *Perspectives on the development of memory and cognition.* Hillsdale, New Jersey: Erlbaum.

Harris, K. R. (1982). Cognitive-behavior modification: Application with exceptional students. *Focus on Exceptional Children, 15,* 1–16.

Harris, K. R. (1990). Developing self-regulated learners: The role of private speech and self-instructions. *Educational Psychologist, 25,* 35–49.

Levin, J. R. (1981). On functions of pictures in prose. In F. J. Pirozzolo and M. C. Wittrock (Eds.), *Neuropsychological and cognitive processes in reading* (pp. 203–228). New York: Academic Press.

Levin, J. R. (1989). A transfer-appropriate processing perspective of pictures in prose. In H. Mandl and J. R. Levin (Eds.), *Knowledge acquisition from text and pictures* (pp. 83–100). Amsterdam: Elsevier.

Levin, J. R., and Mayer, R. E. (1992). Understanding illustrations in text. In A. Woodward and B. K. Britton (Eds.), *Learning from textbooks: Theory and practice.* Hillsdale, New Jersey: Erlbaum.

Loman, N. L., and Mayer, R. E. (1983). Signaling techniques that increase the understandability of expository prose. *Journal of Educational Psychology, 75,* 402–412.

Mayer, R. E. (1979). Can advance organizers influence meaningful learning? *Review of Educational Research, 49,* 371–383.

Mayer, R. E. (1983). Can you repeat that? Quantitative and qualitative effects of repetition and advance organizers on learning from science prose. *Journal of Educational Psychology, 75,* 40–49.

Mayer, R. E. (1984). Aids to text comprehension. *Educational Psychologist, 19,* 30–42.

Mayer, R. E. (1987). *Educational psychology: A cognitive approach.* Boston: Little, Brown.

Mayer, R. E. (1989a). Models for understanding. *Review of Educational Research, 59,* 43–64.

Mayer, R. E. (1989b). Systematic thinking fostered by illustrations in scientific text. *Journal of Educational Psychology, 81,* 240–246.

Mayer, R. E. (1992). Problem-solving principles. In M. Fleming and C. Reigeluth (Eds.), *Instructional design: Processes and principles.* Englewood Cliffs, New Jersey: Educational Technology Press.

Mayer, R. E., and Anderson, R. B. (1991). Animations need narrations: An experimental test of a dual-coding hypothesis. *Journal of Educational Psychology, 83,* 484–490.

Mayer, R. E., and Gallini, J. K. (1990). When is an illustration worth ten thousand words? *Journal of Educational Psychology, 82,* 715–726.

Norman, D. A. (1980). Cognitive engineering and education. In D. T. Tuma and F. Reif (Eds.), *Problem-solving and education.* Hillsdale, New Jersey: Erlbaum.

Paivio, A. (1971). *Imagery and cognitive processes.* New York: Holt, Rinehart and Winston.

Paivio, A. (1990). *Mental representations: A dual coding approach.* New York: Oxford University Press.

Peper, R. J., and Mayer, R. E. (1986). Generative effects of notetaking during science lectures. *Journal of Educational Psychology, 78,* 23–28.

Piaget, J. (1954). *The construction of reality in the child.* New York: Ballantine Books.

Pressley, M. (1990). *Cognitive strategy instruction that really improves children's academic performance.* Cambridge, Massachusetts: Brookline.

Pressley, M., and Levin, J. R. (Eds.) (1983a). *Cognitive strategy research: Educational applications.* New York: Springer-Verlag.

Pressley, M., and Levin, J. R. (Eds.) (1983b). *Cognitive strategy research: Psychological foundations.* New York: Springer-Verlag.

Shrager, L., and Mayer, R. E. (1989). Notetaking fosters generative learning strategies in novices. *Journal of Educational Psychology, 81,* 263–264.

Singley, M. K., and Anderson, J. R. (1989). *The transfer of cognitive skill.* Cambridge: Harvard University Press.

Sternberg, R. J. (1985). *Beyond IQ: A triarchic theory of human intelligence.* Cambridge: Cambridge University Press.

Sternberg, R. J. (1988). *The triarchic mind: A new theory of human intelligence.* New York: Penguin Books.

Sternberg, R. J. (1990). *Metaphors of mind: Conceptions of the nature of intelligence.* Cambridge: Cambridge University Press.

Weinstein, C. E., and Mayer, R. E. (1985). The teaching of learning strategies. In M. C. Wittrock (Eds.), *Handbook of research on teaching* (3rd ed) (pp. 315–327). New York: Macmillan.

Weinstein, C. E., Goetz, E. T., and Alexander, P. A. (Eds.) (1988). *Learning and study strategies.* Orlando, Florida: Academic Press.

Wittrock, M. C. (1974). Learning as a generative activity. *Educational Psychologist, 11,* 87–95.

Woodward, A., and Britton, B. K. (Eds.) (1992). *Learning from textbooks: Theory and practice.* Hillsdale, New Jersey: Erlbaum.

Part III

WRITING

All the chapters in this section provide important commentary about contemporary theories that address the nature and determinants of good writing. All also provide summaries of instructional programs designed to develop writing processes and skills.

Montague and Graves provide an overview of contemporary thinking on the nature of skilled writing; they detail the schematic (e.g., knowledge of story grammar), planning, and interpretive (e.g., knowledge of people and their motives) understandings that are essential for authoring. They also discuss how models of writing skill inform theories of instruction targeted at writing, particularly with learning disabled students. Montague and Graves discuss their own research and that of others on procedural (e.g., providing an aid reminding students of the various story grammar elements that should be included in a story) and substantive (e.g., providing extensive instruction, as occurs during a writer's workshop) facilitation of writing. Their view is decidedly that the type of writing instruction provided to the student will vary with the competencies of the student (e.g., procedural facilitation may be sufficient for students who know a great deal about story structure but do not use that knowledge in constructing stories).

Harris and Graham provide additional information about the writing deficiencies of learning disabled students compared with the techniques of skilled writers. They detail how strategy instruction in writing processes can increase student writing competency, highlighting their own research in this problem area. Their long-term goal is the development of self-regulated writers, and they present a detailed conception of how writing instruction can be planned to foster this goal. This instructional model complements and extends well the ideas presented by Montague and Graves and, indeed, is an elaborate and sophisticated version of what they referred to as substantive facilitation. Harris and Graham's conclusions about the challenges involved with this type of instruction leave no doubt about how difficult the development of skilled writing can be. At the same time, the chapter as a whole, especially when read in conjunction with the one by Montague and Graves, provides powerful testimony about the efficacy of explicit collaborative instruction in writing processes.

All models of skilled writing and the instructional development of competent writing include evaluation and revision as critical components to such an extent they have been targets of important research in recent years. Both the chapter by McCormick, Busching, and Potter and the contribution by Fitzgerald review how evaluation has been implemented in models of writing; both consider the role of evaluation in information-processing and problem-solving conceptions of writing. These models inspired McCormick and her colleagues to study carefully the development of children's evaluative competence in longitudinal research. Data accumulated over two years are summarized in their chapter. McCormick and co-workers, who were initially motivated by information-processing analyses but ultimately came to understand how critical social interactions can be to the development of competent evaluation and revision of writing, anticipate the main themes in Fitzgerald's chapter. After reviewing the more mechanistic conceptions of writing and revising, Fitzgerald develops in detail her thoughts about social-interactive processes during revision, carefully highlighting how the social-interactive perspective complements information-processing theories of writing. These two chapters provide comprehensive discussion of current knowledge of revision.

As a whole, these four chapters clearly delineate powerful and innovative approaches to teaching and learning. These are the products of the authors' integrative understanding of differing theories, models, and classroom approaches to learning and to writing in particular.

9

Teaching Narrative Composition to Students with Learning Disabilities

Marjorie Montague and Anne Graves

This chapter focuses on teaching narrative composition to students with learning disabilities. First, a brief overview of cognitive theory as it pertains to both comprehension and production of narrative text is provided, as background for a discussion of how writers plan and generate stories. Then, research on narrative text production by students with learning disabilities is reviewed. Finally, research on various techniques and procedures that appear to facilitate narrative composing for these students is presented, and the implications of this research for classroom teaching are discussed.

COGNITIVE THEORY AND NARRATIVE TEXT

Learning, from a developmental perspective, is perhaps best understood as active construction of knowledge. Learners continuously interact with the environment and, as they pass through the developmental stages, acquire, assimilate, and accommodate new information into cognitive frameworks or structures that are continually forming and expanding. An interactive view of reading and writing processes assumes that learners interact with the text as they accumulate evidence and test hypotheses about its meaning or generate ideas that spring from existing knowledge (Mason, 1984). Effective and efficient reading and writing require coordination of a variety of knowledge types. For comprehension of text, Mason (1984) indicated that schematic knowledge, planning knowledge, and interpretive knowledge are essential. These three knowledge types also are critical for production of text and, thus, serve as the framework for the following discussion of the role of knowledge in reading and writing narrative text.

Schematic Knowledge

To understand the role that schematic knowledge plays in the comprehension and production of narrative text, a brief review of schema theory is necessary. Schema theory, the foundation for much of the research in narrative text, postulates a mental processing mechanism that guides comprehension and production of textual material. The theoretical premise is that story schema, one of many structures represented in the cognitive system, constitutes an "organized set of knowledge used during the encoding, representation, and retrieval of information from stories." (Stein, 1982, p. 326) Story schema has been operationalized as hierarchical frameworks or sets of rules generic to narrative structure. Commonly referred to as story grammars, these frameworks specify parts or elements of a story and their temporal and causal relationships (Mandler & Johnson, 1977; Rumelhart, 1975; Stein & Glenn, 1979; Thorndyke, 1977).

It is particularly critical to understand story grammar in this context, since such knowledge is one of the fundamental cognitive bases for narrative production (Anderson, 1978; Rentel & King, 1983; Scardamalia & Bereiter, 1986). Stein and Glenn (1979) proposed the following seven categories as representative of an individual's schematic knowledge of narrative text. (1) *Major setting* introduces the protagonist. (2) *Minor setting* describes the time and place of the story. (3) *Initiating event* changes the state of affairs in the environment and causes a response from the protagonist. (4) *Internal response* includes affective or emotional responses, goals, desires, or thoughts. (5) *Attempt* represents the protagonist's goal-related actions. (6) *Direct consequence* indicates whether or not the goal is attained and signifies changes that resulted from the attempt. (7) *Reaction* includes a character's feelings or thoughts relating to the outcome and how the character is affected by the outcome. These elements are divided between two primary units: settings, which include information from both the major and minor settings, and episodes, which include the other five categories and their temporal and causal connections. To be considered an episode, the behavioral sequence must meet these criteria: (1) be an initiating event or internal response causing a character to formulate a goal-directed behavioral sequence, (2) be an action that is either an attempt or a consequence, and (3) be a direct consequence marking the attainment or nonattainment of the goal.

As readers and writers mature linguistically and develop knowledge of

narrative structure and conventions, their ability to comprehend and produce text improves. Many individuals acquire this knowledge naturally as
they mature; however, less proficient readers and writers usually require
instruction to develop schematic knowledge further or to gain access to
story schema knowledge as they read and write narratives. For example,
stories retold or produced by students with learning disabilities often are
incomplete or undeveloped when compared with stories of nondisabled
peers (Barenbaum, Newcomer, & Nodine, 1987; Laughton & Morris, 1989;
Montague, Maddux, & Dereshiwsky, 1990). These students may not possess
a fully developed schema for narratives or may not be using the knowledge
they have. Instruction that assists students in acquiring or further developing schematic knowledge or gives students techniques to facilitate knowledge application during text production seems to be necessary for these
students (Graham, Harris, MacArthur, & Schwartz, 1991a).

Planning Knowledge

Planning is an integral part of the composing process. Narrative composing, like other types of genre-based writing, depends in large measure on a
writer's ability to develop coherent plans prior to and during production.
Using a problem-solving model of writing, Flower and Hayes (1980) defined
planning as a broad cognitive process that involves basic operations such
as generating and organizing information and setting goals. Plans may be
interpreted as a series of personal schemata for solving problems. This
interpretation is not as simplistic as it appears, however. Scardamalia,
Bereiter, and Goelman (1982) warned against the idea of a "neat-high-level
plan sitting there and quietly directing activities." (p. 208) Rather, they
suggested that "when writers are engaged in high-level planning, they draw
on a representation that consists of goals, central ideas, structural decisions, and the like." (p. 203)

Instruction in planning appears to benefit older learners by assisting in
idea formation and organization, whereas planning instruction for younger
learners usually leads to simple content generation or knowledge telling
(Graham et al., 1991a; Haas, 1988). The main advantage that older learners
seem to have over younger learners is their ability to activate metacognitive processes that come into play during composing. By adolescence,
students become more conscious of the cognitive activities needed to
complete tasks. Sometime between Grades 4 and 10, students can be expected to begin making the transition from simple content generation as a
planning strategy to a form of planning that is more conceptual in nature.
Taking notes and outlining are examples of such conceptual planning. For
students who take notes, transformations from notes to text have been
observed. One study found that by age 14, students did not incorporate

notes into text without some major change occurring in the form of elaboration, reordering, combination, or addition (Burtis, Bereiter, Scardamalia, & Tetroe, 1983). It seems that, by secondary school, students are more flexible in their thinking, are better equipped to juggle thoughts and ideas, and are able to operate at a more abstract level when tapping their memory and when forming and organizing ideas.

There is a definite development over the elementary school years of planning activities as distinct from text-generation activities (Bereiter & Scardamalia, 1987). For the mature writer, planning appears to be a central process that interacts at all levels of text production. Initially, as part of the writing process, the author selects a topic, generates ideas, and organizes these ideas into a developing framework. Most mature writers make notes, develop outlines, or draw representations of their ideas to help them generate words, sentences, and paragraphs. Comparing the plan to the written text and then planning content revision before revising is another dimension of planning in which mature writers engage.

Planning appears to be qualitatively different for skilled and unskilled writers, that is, good writers spend more time in global planning than in the local sentence- and word-level planning that is characteristic of unskilled writers (Bereiter & Scardamalia, 1987). They also appear to plan both before and during text generation; most of the planning actually occurs while they compose (Humes, 1983). Furthermore, good writers continue to develop and modify their goals as they write. In comparison, poor writers only infrequently alter their original approach to the task (Flower & Hayes, 1980).

Students with learning disabilities experience moderate to severe problems in planning (Graham *et al.*, 1991a; see also Chapter 10). They appropriate virtually no time for planning in advance of writing (MacArthur & Graham, 1987) and rely on an associative technique wherein they simply write whatever comes to mind (Thomas, Englert, & Gregg, 1987). Although normally achieving children 10 years of age and younger seem to equate planning with production and use planning time to generate first drafts, by the age of 12 they usually are able to make and revise notes as they plan stories (Burtis *et al.*, 1983). In contrast, when given time to plan stories, middle-school students with learning disabilities typically write all or part of their stories and then recopy them for the final draft (Montague, Graves, & Leavell, 1991a). Students with learning disabilities seem not to know what to do when they are given time to plan and behave in a manner similar to younger normally achieving students who use planning time as an opportunity to write first drafts of stories (Burtis *et al.*, 1983). Techniques to facilitate planning for these students as they compose stories are discussed later in this chapter.

Interpretive Knowledge

Narrative comprehension and production are related directly to an ability to understand people's intentions, goals, plans, and social interactions, as well as interrelationships and interactions of characters (Bruce & Newman, 1978). According to Mason (1984), world knowledge or knowledge of people and their interactions in the real world is one of the bases for knowledge of actions. Mason's (1984) explanation of the process of constructing an interpretation of the fable "Stone Soup," as used in a study by Adams and Collins (1979), illustrates the importance of interpretive knowledge for comprehending narratives.

Stone Soup

A poor man came to a large house during a storm to beg for food. He was sent away with angry words, but he went back and asked, "May I at least dry my clothes by the fire, because I am wet from the rain?" The maid thought this would not cost anything, so she let him come in.

Inside he told the cook that if she would give him a pan, and let him fill it with water, he would make some stone soup. This was a new dish to the cook, so she agreed to let him make it. The man then got a stone from the road and put it in the pan. The cook gave him some salt, peas, mint, and all the scraps of meat that she could spare to throw in. Thus the poor man made a delicious stone soup and the cook said, "Well done! You have made a wonderful soup out of practically nothing."

Mason (1984) contended that the actions in the story (begging for food, sending the man away, asking to dry himself by the fire) operate in a bottom-up fashion to activate the reader to higher-level goals. Various interpretations of the actions are possible, depending on the orientation and interpretive knowledge of the reader. A good reader eventually will decide that the maid is only protecting her master's goods by sending the man away, because she later lets him in, and that the man asks to dry himself by the fire in order to get inside, because he later makes stone soup. The characters' goals become clear in this story as a result of interpreting the characters' actions. In many stories, however, not only must actions be interpreted, but characters' cognitions, beliefs, emotions, and decisions also must be interpreted. Thus, knowledge of how individuals think about and react to circumstances, problems, and other characters is vital when reading narratives.

Such knowledge varies with the developmental level of the child. In one of the classic narrative comprehension studies, Stein and Glenn (1979) were unable to detect developmental differences between first- and fifth-grade students, except in relation to recall of total units in a story and recall of internal responses; the older children recalled significantly more units and internal responses than the younger students. Nezworski, Stein, and Trabasso's (1982) results corroborated Stein and Glenn's (1979), showing that young children tended to transform cognitions to actions or end states.

What is critical here is that interpretive knowledge is necessary for the production as well as the comprehension of narratives. Compared with normally achieving students in elementary and secondary school, students with learning disabilities appear deficient in such knowledge (MacArthur & Graham, 1987; Montague *et al.,* 1990; Montague, Graves, & Leavell, 1991b; Ripich & Griffith, 1988; Vallecorsa & Garriss, 1990). In these studies, students with learning disabilities consistently recalled and produced significantly fewer internal responses, internal plans, and reactions of characters when reading and writing stories than did normally achieving students. In retelling stories they read, students with learning disabilities generally included less information about characters' motivations, emotions, and ideas than did normally achieving students. Also, their written stories contained fewer statements related to characters' cognitions and affective responses. Compared with normally achieving peers, students with learning disabilities also made fewer references to characters' problems and plans to solve them in their written narratives. To extend Mason's (1984) view, it seems that interpretive knowledge of characters is a more sophisticated approach to understanding or producing narrative text than interpretation of actions, and may need to be developed through explicit instruction, particularly for students who are deficient in this type of knowledge.

RESEARCH IN NARRATIVE WRITING AND LEARNING DISABILITIES

Students with learning disabilities produce substantially shorter and lower quality stories than normally achieving students (Barenbaum *et al.,* 1987; MacArthur & Graham, 1987; Montague *et al.,* 1990, 1991a; Nodine, Barenbaum, & Newcomer, 1985; Vallecorsa & Garriss, 1990). Their stories generally reflect narrative structure, but contain fewer initiating events, direct consequences, internal responses, and reactions than stories written by nondisabled peers (Graves, Montague, & Wong, 1990; Laughton & Morris, 1989; MacArthur & Graham, 1987; Montague *et al.,* 1990, 1991b). Additionally, their stories are less coherent and organized and contain fewer episodes than stories produced by nondisabled students.

Several different approaches have been investigated for ameliorating specific deficiencies as well as general narrative production problems manifested by students with learning disabilities. These approaches range from minimally intrusive and relatively short-term techniques (including story maps, story frameworks, and story grammar cue cards) to more extensive instructional programs such as writing process instruction, cognitive strategy instruction, and explicit instruction in character development. These approaches can be distinguished in terms of what Scardamalia and Bereiter (1986) call *procedural facilitation* and *substantive facilitation*. Procedural facilitation is help of a nonspecific sort that is related to cognitive processes, but is not responsive to the actual substance of students' writing. In contrast, substantive facilitation is a teaching–learning process wherein the cognitive burden is reduced by having the teacher assume part of it. In this approach, the teacher becomes an active collaborator and participant in students' composing. Substantive facilitation focuses on the content of students' writing.

Procedural Facilitation

Research in reading comprehension suggests that instructional supports such as networking, mapping, and flowcharting facilitate schema representation and understanding of text structure for both normal and low-achieving students (Anderson, 1978). These techniques emphasize the creation of diagrams to represent relationships among ideas presented in the text. In a classroom study of heterogeneous groups of third- and fourth-grade students, including five students with learning disabilities and low achievement, Idol (1987) used a story mapping procedure to improve reading comprehension with evidence of transfer to children's journal narratives. The procedural facilitator in this study was a worksheet on which appeared a set of boxes labeled setting (characters, time, place), problem, goal, action, and outcome. Students first completed their individual worksheets as part of a group activity. Later, they read stories and completed the story maps independently. After completing the maps, students then wrote answers to comprehension questions reflecting the various story elements. This technique exemplifies procedural facilitation because it is an activity that is nonspecific in nature. In other words, the procedure could be used to facilitate comprehension of stories generally and also could be used to facilitate narrative production. Consistent with Idol's (1987) findings, other studies using story grammar frameworks also have reported improvements in comprehension for normal and low-achieving students as well as for students with learning disabilities by teaching them to identify the elements of a story grammar and to use that knowledge in organizing and recalling information (Barenbaum *et al.,* 1987; Gordon & Braun, 1985; Idol & Croll, 1987).

Procedural facilitation also has been effective in improving narrative composition for these students. In a study by Graves and colleagues (1990), upper elementary students with learning disabilities were provided with a story grammar cue card during planning time to remind them of basic story grammar elements to include in their narrative compositions. These were setting, character, problem, plan, and ending (see Figure 1). Students were told to check off story parts as they incorporated them into their stories. This technique is an example of a procedural facilitator that serves to help students monitor their own performance. Students who used this prompt wrote longer and qualitatively better stories.

A follow-up study was conducted to determine whether or not checking off the story parts was an essential component of the procedure (Graves & Montague, 1991). Seventh- and eighth-grade students with learning disabilities were assigned randomly to one of three conditions. In the first condition, students were given time to plan but no additional support for writing stories. In the second condition, students were given planning time and a review of story grammar elements. The third condition combined planning time, story grammar review, and the cue card and check-off procedure. Checking off story grammar elements as they were used in a story seemed to improve story quality but not length, that is, students who received the three components (planning time, story grammar review, and check-off cards) wrote higher quality stories than students who received planning time and review or planning time only. Also, students who received the review wrote higher quality stories than students who received planning time only.

In a related investigation of the effects of procedural facilitation on story quality and length, compositions dictated or written by junior high school students with learning disabilities were compared with written compositions of normally achieving students (Montague *et al.*, 1991a). Three composing conditions were compared: no planning time, planning time only, and planning time plus procedural facilitation in the form of a story grammar cue card (see Figure 2). Although qualitative differences between normally achieving and learning disabled students were evident when students were not given time to plan, these differences were no longer apparent when time and structure for planning narratives were given. Additionally, a significant increase was found for the number of story grammar elements in written stories of students with learning disabilities when both planning time and procedural facilitation were provided. These studies

Story Parts

Place a check next to each story part as you include it in your story.

_____   Setting
_____   Character(s)
_____   Problem and Plan
_____   Ending

Fig. 1   Story grammar check-off card.

Create a Story

Place a check next to each story part as you include it in your story.

_____   Where and When
_____   Character(s): Have them tell their thoughts, feelings, emotions, and reasons
                           for doing what they do. Make them think and feel just as real
                           people do.
_____   Problem and Plan
_____   Story Ending

Fig. 2   Story grammar cue card.

highlight the importance of instructional supports in the form of procedural facilitators to help students activate story schema knowledge and direct themselves as they write narratives. Based on these studies, it appears that some students can improve the quality of their narrative compositions if they are given minimal supports such as time to plan; a basic review of story grammar elements in the form of a map, framework, or list; and a prompt such as a simple story element check-off card.

However, procedural facilitation may not provide enough support for some students to improve narrative production. In particular, students with limited schematic, planning, or interpretive knowledge may need more substantive support.

Substantive Facilitation

This approach to instruction is both more intensive and more extensive than procedural facilitation. Writing process instruction is an example of a substantive approach that is highly structured and predictable because students write daily at specified times in class, select their own topics, develop their compositions over extended periods of time, participate regularly in writing conferences with supportive and responsive instructors, learn skills in the context of their own writing, and interact frequently with peers about their writing (Graves, 1983). This approach is characterized by having students gradually take control over their writing and also by teaching writing processes such as planning and revising in the context of students' writing. Students and their teachers view writing as a social and collaborative activity during all phases of the writing process.

Writing process instruction has been used successfully with students with learning disabilities (Bos, 1988; Sunstein, 1990; Zaragoza, 1987). Zaragoza (1987) reported that her second-grade students with learning disabilities actively participated in story sharing and learned to give constructive feedback to their peers by using a simple strategy called TAG: (1) tell something you liked about the story, (2) ask questions, and (3) give a suggestion for making the story better. She also found that students' reading comprehension improved following writing process instruction.

According to Graham, Harris, MacArthur, and Schwartz (1991b), however, it may be unrealistic to assume that the quality of students' narrative writing will improve without systematic instruction in narrative structure and writing processes such as planning a story, generating ideas, editing, and revising. To improve narrative writing for students with learning disabilities, these authors recommend explicit instruction that is substantive in nature, or at least that procedural facilitation be incorporated into the writing process program (Graham *et al.,* 1991b). To illustrate, Danoff (1990) taught learning disabled children who had participated in a writing process program a cognitive strategy for remembering seven story elements. Following strategy instruction, stories were rated higher in quality, suggesting not only that explicit story grammar instruction benefitted the students but also that it could be effectively incorporated into writing process instruction.

Cognitive strategy instruction exemplifies substantive facilitation in its emphasis on sustained interaction and collaboration between teachers and students and active participation of students as they acquire and begin to apply strategies for planning, generating, and organizing ideas, or revising compositions. Strategy instruction has several distinct phases, including goal setting, cognitive modeling, strategy mastery, collaborative practice, and independent performance (Graham *et al.,* 1991b).

Focusing on fifth- and sixth-grade students with learning disabilities, Graham and Harris (1989) investigated the effects of strategy instruction and self-instructional training on narrative production. One group of students received strategy training only, whereas another group received strategy training and self-regulation training. Both groups first learned a mnemonic for seven story grammar questions (W-W-W, What = 2. How = 2). As an example, the first question was "Who is the main character; who else is in the story?" Then they practiced identifying the elements in stories. After students were informed about their pretest performance on story writing, they learned a strategy for writing using a picture prompt: (1) look at the picture; (2) let your mind be free, (3) write down the story part reminder using the mnemonic, (4) write down story part ideas for each part; and (5) write your story, use good parts, and make sense. Students generated self-statements reflecting these steps such as "Take my time, good parts will come to me." The instructor then modeled the story writing strategy and self-regulation statements as well as additional self-instructions for planning and evaluating stories and for self-reinforcement ("Good, I like these parts."). Students then thought aloud as they composed stories as part of a group activity. Following this activity, they wrote stories independently using the five-step strategy and self-instructional statements.

They were encouraged by the instructor to verbalize the steps covertly. Throughout the study, students shared what they were learning with teachers and parents and discussed with the instructors how they could use the strategies in their classes. The self-regulation group received additional instruction in self-monitoring (counting and graphing the number of story elements in their stories) and goal-setting (identifying the number of story elements they wished to include in a story).

Following strategy instruction, stories of students with learning disabilities were not only superior to those written prior to instruction but were also comparable to stories by normally achieving peers in quality and schematic structure. Moreover, the students with learning disabilities improved in self-efficacy, that is, they were more able to judge their ability to write stories following strategy instruction. Similar results were obtained in a replication study (Sawyer, Graham, & Harris, 1990). Graham and Harris (1989) contended that self-regulation procedures are inherent in systematic strategy instruction, and explicit instruction in self-regulation does not seem to improve writing of students beyond the improvement achieved through strategy instruction, that is, stories written by students who received strategy instruction in narrative structure and explicit self-regulation training were not superior in quality or schematic structure to stories by students who received only strategy instruction.

In some cases, more focused instruction may be needed, however. As mentioned earlier, several studies have noted a deficiency in characters' reactions and internal responses included in stories written by students with learning disabilities (MacArthur & Graham, 1987; Montague et al., 1990, 1991b; Ripich & Griffith, 1988). An explanation for this deficiency may relate to the ability of these students to process affective information and express characters' motives, thoughts, feelings, and emotions. Problems in this aspect of narrative text comprehension and production could reflect a lack of expertise in the interpretation of human intention, social interaction, and problem solving, knowledge that is necessary for story schema development (Mandler, 1982; Stein, 1982).

Some evidence suggests that children can be taught techniques to improve this aspect of narrative text processing (Dunning, 1987; Montague, Leavell, & Graves, 1991b). As an example, a recent pilot study conducted with nine students with learning disabilities focused on explicit instruction in character development (Montague et al., 1991b). In this study, both procedural facilitation and instruction in developing fictional characters were investigated. Two levels of treatment were included. For the first level, students were given only a story grammar cue card and instructions to check off story parts as they used them (see Figure 2). The second level of treatment, which lasted 3 days, included a review of story grammar elements, lessons focusing on internal responses and plans of characters,

Story Evaluation

Below are some questions that will help you tell if a story is well written. Read the story you wrote and see if it answers the questions. If it DOES answer the question, put a 1 on the line. If it DOES NOT answer the question, put a 0 on the line. When you have completed the questions, add the numbers on the lines and put a total score at the bottom.

1. Does the reader (you) know what the main character(s) is thinking?   1. _____
2. Does the reader know what the main character(s) is feeling?   2. _____
3. Does the reader know what the main character(s) will do to solve the problem? Does the reader know the character's plan?   3. _____
4. Does the reader know if the main character knows what the other characters are thinking and feeling?   4. _____
5. Does the reader know what the characters are saying in the different parts of the story?   5. _____
6. Does the reader know what the other characters are thinking and feeling?   6. _____
7. Do you think the characters in this story seem real and come alive?   7. _____

Total Score   _____

Fig. 3   Story evaluation form.

group story reading and writing, and story evalutation techniques (see Figure 3.

The first day of instruction centered on a discussion of the importance of characters to a story, the identities that characters can assume in stories, what motivates characters to act the way they do, the problems that characters encounter, and specific attributes of characters that help readers visualize and "get to know" characters. At the end of this lesson, students read a story along with the instructor and then underlined words in the story that described the characters and their actions, ideas, and emotions. The second day's lesson dealt with ways to make characters in stories act like real people and express thoughts and feelings the way real people do. As part of this lesson, students wrote a group story using the story grammar cue card as the framework. Students brainstormed ideas for the story and were prompted with questions to elicit responses about the affective qualities of characters. As students brainstormed, the instructor took notes on poster paper. Using the ideas they had formulated, students then dictated a story, which was written on poster paper and audiotaped. For the final lesson, two versions of the story were typed for evaluation by students. The story in its original form and a version with all words and phrases reflecting characters' cognitions and emotions deleted were typed. Using the evaluation form depicted in Figure 3, students first evaluated the story with the deletions and then evaluated the story as originally written. After assigning scores of 1 or 0 in response to questions regarding characterization, students tallied the scores for both versions of the story and then discussed why the original version was given a higher score. They concluded that the original story was more interesting and better because they had incorporated characters' thoughts and feelings into the story and, as a result, the characters seemed more like real people. Analyses of stories written by these students over a period of 2 months indicated substantial increases in story length and mild to moderate increases in story quality and the number of internal responses and plans of characters. Still, the researchers concluded that 3 days of instruction may be insufficient for most students to make substantial and lasting changes in producing characterizations. They acknowledged the day-to-day variability of student performance and the important role that motivation played in performance.

The findings reviewed thus far should make obvious the fact that "one-size" instruction does not "fit all students." The skills and knowledge students bring to instruction are critical determinants of the type of instruction that should be provided to them, a theme we develop additionally as we close this chapter.

INSTRUCTIONAL IMPLICATIONS AND RECOMMENDATIONS

The selection of procedural or substantive facilitation is a critical concern when considering individual needs of students with learning disabilities. Procedural facilitation seems appropriate only if students have requisite writing skills and schematic knowledge. When the organizational framework for narrative writing is not readily accessible by a writer, procedural facilitation can be used to free students' executive retrieval system to allow greater concentration on content (Scardamalia & Bereiter, 1986). For example, to facilitate the inclusion of story grammar elements in students' compositions, teachers could provide a brief review of the elements and a prompt such as the check-off procedure that appears in Figure 1. If students do not possess schematic knowledge of narrative structure, then substantive facilitation would be the appropriate instructional choice. In this instance, students would receive explicit and systematic instruction in story grammar elements.

Students' planning knowledge, that is, their ability to set goals and develop plans, also most be considered. Generally, students with learning disabilities need explicit instruction and practice in this writing process. Graham and colleagues (1991b) highlighted several effective strategies for developing students' planning knowledge. These included strategies typically designed to be used prior to writing, such as brainstorming ideas, generating and organizing content by posing and answering questions, and setting goals, as well as determining what needs to be done to achieve the writing goals. An effective writing process instructional program will address development of planning strategies for students with learning disabilities. Finally, techniques for teaching students to interpret actions, goals, and intentions of characters in their own stories as well as in stories written by others are important. Interpretive knowledge, similar to planning knowledge, develops and is refined over time. Instruction that focuses on the development of these knowledge types should be embedded in a long-term whole-language instructional program.

In conclusion, narrative writing is an enjoyable experience for most students if they possess or are provided with strategies to facilitate the process. Both procedural and substantive facilitation have been found to be effective and, it seems, teachers can implement these instructional approaches easily in their classrooms. The challenge, however, is to determine the most practical, yet effective and efficient, application for individual students in their writing programs.

REFERENCES

Adams, J., and Collins, A. (1979). A schema-theoretic view of reading. In R. Freedle (Ed.), *New directions in discourse processing* (pp. 188–205). New Jersey: Ablex.

Anderson, R. C. (1978). Schema directed processes in language comprehension. In A. Lesgold, J. Pellegrino, S. Fokhema, and R. Glaser (Eds.), *Cognitive psychology and instruction* (pp. 67–82). New York: Plenum.

Barenbaum, E., Newcomer, P., and Nodine, B. (1987). Children's ability to write stories as a function of variation in task, age, and developmental level. *Learning Disability Quarterly, 7,* 175–188.

Bereiter, C., and Scardamalia, M. (1987). *The psychology of written expression.* Hillsdale, New Jersey: Erlbaum.

Bos, C. (1988). Process-oriented writing: Instructional implications for mildly handicapped students. *Exceptional Children, 54,* 521–527.

Bruce, B., and Newman, D. (1978). Interacting plans. *Cognitive Science, 2,* 195–233.

Burtis, P., Bereiter, C., Scardamalia, M., and Tetroe, J. (1983). The development of planning in writing. In G. Wells and B. Kroll (Eds.), *Explorations in the development of writing* (pp. 153–174). Chichester, England: John Wiley.

Danoff, B. (1990). *Implementing a writing program with youngsters with learning problems.* Paper presented at the ICSEMM Third Annual Instructional Methods Forum, Washington, D.C.

Dunning, D. (1987). *The effects of instruction clarifying story characters' internal state on primary students' story comprehension.* Paper presented at the National Reading Conference, St. Petersburg, Florida.

Flower, L., and Hayes, J. (1980). The dynamics of composing: Making plans and juggling constraints. In L. Gregg and E. Steinberg (Eds.), *Cognitive processes in writing* (pp. 31–50). Hillsdale, New Jersey: Erlbaum.

Gordon, C., and Braun, C. (1985). Metacognitive processes: Reading and writing narrative discourse. In D. L. Forrest-Pressley, G. MacKinnon, and T. Waller (Eds.), *Metacognition, cognition, and human performance.* (Vol. 2, pp. 1–76). Orlando, Florida: Academic Press.

Graham, S., and Harris, K. (1989). A components analysis of cognitive strategy instruction:

Effects on learning disabled students' compositions and self-efficacy. *Journal of Educational Psychology, 81,* 353–361.

Graham, S., Harris, K., MacArthur, C., and Schwartz, S. (1991a). Writing instruction. In B. Wong (Ed.), *Learning about learning disabilities* (pp. 310–343). San Diego: Academic Press.

Graham, S., Harris, K., MacArthur, C., and Schwartz, S. (1991b). Writing and writing instruction for students with learning disabilities: Review of a research program. *Learning Disability Quarterly, 14,* 89–114.

Graves, A., and Montague, M. (1991). *The effects of cognitive and metacognitive cues on story composition of learning disabled students.* Paper presented at the Annual Meeting of the American Educational Research Association, Chicago, Illinois.

Graves, A., Montague, M., and Wong, Y. (1990). The effects of procedural facilitation on the story composition of learning disabled students. *Learning Disabilities Research, 5,* 88–93.

Graves, D. (1983). *Writing: Teachers and children at work.* Portsmouth, New Hampshire: Heinemann.

Haas, C. (1988). *How word processing affects planning in writing: The impact of technology.* Paper presented at the American Educational Research Association, New Orleans.

Humes, A. (1983). Putting writing research into practice. *The Elementary School Journal, 81,* 3–17.

Idol, L. (1987). Group story mapping: A comprehension strategy for both skilled and unskilled readers. *Journal of Learning Disabilities, 20,* 196–205.

Idol, L., and Croll, V. (1987). Story-mapping as a means of improving reading comprehension. *Learning Disability Quarterly, 10,* 214–230.

Laughton, J., and Morris, N. (1989). Story grammar knowledge of learning disabled students. *Learning Disabilities Research, 4,* 87–95.

MacArthur, C., and Graham, S. (1987). Learning disabled students' composing with three methods: Handwriting, dictation, and word processing. *Journal of Special Education, 21,* 22–42.

Mandler, J. (1982). Some uses and abuses of story grammar. *Discourse Processes, 5,* 305–318.

Mandler, J., and Johnson, N. (1977). Remembrance of things parsed: Story structure and recall. *Cognitive Psychology, 9,* 111–151.

Mason, J. N. (1984). A schema-theoretic view of the reading process as a basis for comprehension instruction. In G. Duffy, L. Roehler, and J. Mason (Eds.), *Comprehension instruction: Perspectives and suggestions* (pp. 26–38). New York: Longman.

Montague, M., Maddux, C., and Dereshiwsky, M. (1990). Story grammar and comprehension and production of narrative prose by students with learning disabilities. *Journal of Learning Disabilities, 23,* 190–197.

Montague, M., Graves, A., and Leavell, A. (1991b). *Character development in stories written by students with learning disabilities.* Unpublished raw data.

Montague, M., Leavell, A., and Graves, A. (1991c). *The effects of procedural and substantive facilitation on narrative writing of students with learning disabilities.* Manuscript submitted for publication.

Montague, M., Graves, A., and Leavell, A. (1991a). Planning, procedural facilitation, and narrative composition of junior high students with learning disabilities. *Learning Disabilities Research and Practice, 6,* 219–224.

Nezworski, T., Stein, N., and Trabasso, T. (1982). Story structure versus content in children's recall. *Journal of Verbal Learning and Verbal Behavior, 21,* 196–206.

Nodine, B., Barenbaum, E., and Newcomer, P. (1985). Story compositions by learning disabled, reading disabled, and normal children. *Learning Disability Quarterly, 8,* 167–179.

Rentel, V., and King, M. (1983). Present at the beginning. In P. Mosenthal, L. Tamor, and S. Walmsley (Eds.), *Research on writing: Principles and methods* (pp. 139–176). New York: Longman.

Ripich, D., and Griffith, P. (1988). Narrative abilities of children with learning disabilities and nondisabled children: Story structure, cohesion, and propositions. *Journal of Learning Disabilities, 21,* 165–173.

Rumelhart, D. (1975). Notes on a schema for stories. In D. Bobrow and A. Collins (Eds.), *Representation and understanding: Studies in cognitive science* (pp. 211–2360. New York: Academic Press.

Sawyer, R., Graham, S., and Harris, K. (1990). *Improving learning disabled students' composition skills with story grammar strategy training: A further components analysis of self-instructional strategy training.* Unpublished raw data.

Scardamalia, M., and Bereiter, C. (1986). Research on written composition. In M. Wittrock (Ed.), *Handbook of research on teaching* (3rd ed., pp. 778–803). New York: Longman.

Scardamalia, M., Bereiter, C., and Goelman, H. (1982). The role of production factors in writing ability. In M. Nystrand (Ed.), *What writers know: The language, process, and structure of written discourse* (pp. 173–210). New York: Academic Press.

Stein, N. (1982). What's in a story: Interpreting the interpretations of story grammars. *Discourse Processes, 5,* 319–335.

Stein, N., and Glenn, G. (1979). An analysis of story comprehension in elementary school children. In R. Freedle (Ed.), *New directions in discourse processing* (Vol. 2, pp. 53–120). Norwood, New Jersey: Ablex.

Sunstein, B. (1990). *Learning disabilities and the writing process approach.* Paper presented at the ICSEMM Third Annual Instructional Methods Forum, Washington, D.C.

Thomas, C., Englert, C., and Gregg, S. (1987). An analysis of errors and strategies in the expository writing of learning disabled students. *Remedial and Special Education, 8,* 21–30.

Thorndyke, P. (1977). Cognitive structures in comprehension and memory of narrative discourse. *Cognitive psychology, 9,* 77–110.

Vallecorsa, A., and Garriss, E. (1990). Story composition skills of middle-grade students with learning disabilities. *Exceptional Children, 57,* 48–54.

Zaragoza, N. (1987). Process writing for high-risk and learning disabled students. *Reading Research and Instruction, 26,* 290–301.

10

Self-Regulated Strategy Development: A Part of the Writing Process

Karen R. Harris and Steve Graham

Writing is one of the most difficult academic areas for students to master. This fact is not surprising, since writing is a highly complex process that places multiple demands on students and teachers. The writer must negotiate the rules and mechanics of writing, while maintaining a focus on factors such as organization, form and features, purposes and goals, audience perspectives and needs, and evaluation of communicative intent and efficacy (Bereiter & Scardamalia, 1982; Scheid, 1991). Recent students, such as those conducted as part of the National Assessment of Educational Progress, indicate that many students in our schools evidence poor composition skills and abilities (cf. Applebee, Langer, Jenkins, Mullis, & Foertsch, 1990). For students with learning disabilities or other severe learning problems, writing is especially problematic (Graham & Harris, 1988).

Since 1980, we have been involved in a program of research addressing the written language needs of students with learning problems and their teachers (cf. Graham, Harris, MacArthur, & Schwartz, 1991). Our research program has involved four interrelated, ongoing strands. One strand includes investigations of how students with learning problems compose and what they know about the process of writing (cf. Graham, 1990; Graham *et al.*, 1991). A second strand has focused on validating and evaluating a theoretically and empirically based instructional approach for developing writing and self-regulation strategies among students with learning problems, an approach we refer to as self-regulated strategy development[1] (cf. Danoff, Harris, & Graham, 1991; Graham & Harris, 1989a; Sawyer, Graham, & Harris, 1991). Studies in the third strand have been conducted to examine empirically multiple effects of teaching writing strategies to students with learning problems and to normally achieving students, using our self-regulated strategy development approach. We have developed and validated a variety of strategies in differing genres and processes, including planning, revising, regulating text production, and fostering the development of the mechanics of writing (cf. Graham & Harris, 1992; Graham *et al.*, 1991; Harris & Graham, 1992). The fourth strand has included studies of the role of self-regulation strategies and processes in writing (cf. Graham & Harris, 1989a; Harris, 1986a; Reid & Harris, 1991; Voth & Graham, 1991).

In this chapter we integrate information from each of these sets while highlighting our instructional approach. We begin by examining research and practices in writing and instruction that have informed our approach. The goals, characteristics, and components of self-regulated strategy development are discussed next. We then take an in-depth look at how one teacher incorporated self-regulated strategy development within the process approach to writing in her classroom, and describe the outcomes for normally achieving students and students with learning problems in this classroom. We conclude by noting several of the issues that have currently captured our attention.

WRITTEN LANGUAGE: RESEARCH AND PRACTICES

Scardamalia and Bereiter (1986) identified five areas of competence that are particularly problematic for developing writing in the general school population: (1) generation of content, (2) creating an organizing structure for compositions, (3) formulating goals and higher level plans, (4) quickly and efficiently executing the mechanical aspects of writing, and (5) revising text and reformulating goals. It is not surprising, therefore, that difficulties with narrative, informative, and persuasive writing have been well documented among students in American schools (Applebee *et al.*, 1990; Scheid, 1991). In addition, children in our schools frequently experience a deteriorating attitude toward writing, although they typically begin school with a positive attitude toward composing (Applebee, Langer, & Mullis,

---

[1]As our instructional approach has evolved over the years, so has the label, from self-control strategy training, to self-instructional strategy development, to self-regulated strategy development. We use the term self-regulated strategy development to more clearly indicate the multiple self-regulation strategies students assimilate throughout instruction, including self-instructions, goal-setting, self-assessment, self-recording, and self-reinforcement.

1986; Graves, 1983, 1985). Although these problems have been studied more frequently among the general school population, researchers have recently begun addressing the writing of students with learning problems.

Students with Learning Problems

Much of the early research on the writing of students with learning problems focused on comparisons of the writing products of these students and those of normally achieving students, to document the strengths and difficulties experienced by students with learning problems (Graham *et al.,* 1991). Generally speaking, these parametric data have indicated that the writing of students with learning problems is less polished, expansive, coherent, and effective than that of their normally achieving peers.

The utility of such parametric data, however, is relatively limited. Product data tend to be situation specific (i.e., what is written may depend on the writer's familiarity with and interest in the topic), provide the researcher with very little insight into the processes students employ while writing, and are often difficult to evaluate in terms of constructs such as quality (Bereiter & Scardamalia, 1982; Graham *et al.,* 1991a). Thus, a number of researchers have turned their attention to developing a model of the composing process among students with learning problems. These researchers have addressed such issues as what students with learning problems know about the act of writing, what writing means to them, what processes they employ when producing text, how these processes interact in ways that enhance or impede performance, how the conditions under which text is produced influence what and how they write, and how competence in writing is acquired. Answers to these questions indicate that students with learning problems

1. lack important knowledge about writing and the writing process, and are less aware than their normally achieving peers of how to write (cf. Englert, Raphael, Fear, & Anderson, 1988; Graham *et al.,* 1991; Wong, Wong, & Blenkisop, 1989)
2. experience difficulties generating ideas for written compositions and selecting topics (cf. Morocco & Neuman, 1986)
3. often do little advanced planning (cf. MacArthur & Graham, 1987)
4. engage in knowledge telling (simply writing whatever they know) rather than planning during writing (cf. Englert & Raphael, 1988; Graham, 1990; Thomas, Englert, & Gregg, 1987)
5. have difficulty accessing, generating, and organizing the knowledge they possess, at least in part because they do not have effective strategies for carrying out these processes (cf. Englert & Raphael, 1988; Graham & Harris, 1989b; Graham *et al.,* 1991; Morocco & Neuman, 1986)

6. experience significant difficulties with the lower-level, "secretarial" skills involved in getting language onto paper; these difficulties interfere with writing processes such as planning (cf. Graham, 1990; Isaacson, 1989; MacArthur & Graham, 1987)

7. engage in little revision, primarily addressing mechanics or making superficial changes such as changing a single word rather than substantially modifying organization or ideas; however, when acting as editor for another student, these students can make some substantive recommendations (cf. MacArthur & Graham, 1987; MacArthur, Graham, & Schwartz, 1991)

8. tend to overemphasize the role of mechanics in what constitutes good writing and revising (Graham, Schwartz, & MacArthur, 1991)

9. frequently overestimate their writing capabilities; multiple reasons for this may exist (cf. Graham & Harris, 1989a; Harris, 1989; Sawyer *et al.,* 1991)

Expertise in Writing

Studies of competence and expertise provide critical information for cognitive strategy instruction (cf. Chapter 1). As expertise develops, students exhibit a knowledge base that is increasingly coherent, principled, useful, and goal oriented (Glaser, 1991). Research on expertise has indicated that critical aspects of expert performance include "the organization of knowledge for quick retrieval from memory; the imposition of meaningful patterns in problem solving; the proceduralization of knowledge for problem solution; and the utilization of self-monitoring skills to secure effective performance." (Wittrock and Baker, 1991, p. 17) Expertise is also characterized by domain specificity, representational capabilities, a rich store of interrelated knowledge, task sensitivity, and effective self-regulation (Glaser, 1991).

Good strategy instruction is aimed at the development of expertise. Students are assisted to construct powerful cognitive and metacognitive strategies that empower learning and performance (Harris & Pressley, 1991; Pressley, Borkowski, & Schneider, 1987). Examining the composing behaviors of skilled writers (among both children and adults) has been helpful to us in determining both self-regulation and composition strategies to be developed as well as aspects of our instructional approach (Graham & Harris, 1989c; Harris & Graham, 1992). Although space limitation precludes a thorough discussion, the literature provides a great deal of useful information about expertise in writing (cf. Glaser, 1991; Graves, 1978, 1985; Harris & Graham, 1992; Scardamalia & Bereiter, 1986; Wallace & Pear, 1977).

For skilled writers, the process of writing is goal directed; they organize their goals and subgoals and can switch flexibly from simple to complex goals. To achieve their goals, skilled writers draw upon a rich store of cognitive processes and strategies for planning, text production, and revision. They also draw upon their knowledge of the patterns or schemas that are evident in different writing genres or models, and develop novel or modified frameworks as the writing task becomes more complex. Skilled writers are sensitive to the functions their writing is intended to serve and to the needs and perspectives of their audience. They use effective self-regulation procedures throughout the recursive writing process. Finally, they evidence knowledge of their topic, motivation, and persistence. Emerging practices in writing instruction, including strategy instruction, promote the development of expertise among all students.

Emerging Practices

Although multiple factors are involved in the difficulties that both normally achieving and low achieving students have with writing, the instructional practices that have predominated in American schools until the last decade are a critical factor for consideration. Until recently, a product-oriented model of writing prevailed in the public schools (Newcomer, Nodine, & Barenbaum, 1988). Under this model, writing instruction emphasized mechanics and grammar, not composition. Further, limited time and attention was given to writing, and few of the writing activities pursued in classrooms required sustained writing (Applebee *et al.,* 1990; Graham & Harris, 1988; Graves, 1978; Isaacson, 1987; Langer & Applebee, 1986). Students were taught little about the processes and strategies involved in writing, and little was done to promote their development. Students were expected to learn to write in isolation, typically by reading the work of others and completing similar types of compositions (Newcomer *et al.,* 1988). First drafts were commonly final drafts and were read only by the teacher, who primarily marked errors in mechanics and assigned grades (Applebee *et al.,* 1990; Scheid, 1991). Writing was not promoted as a means of either communicating or learning. Although characteristics such as these certainly do not describe all teachers and classrooms or the best of instruction, they have been far too common.

The predominance of this product-oriented model can be related to several other factors. Many teachers report either little knowledge of and poor preparation in the teaching of writing or negative attitudes about writing (Graham, 1982; Scheid, 1991). Crowded curricula and the relatively stronger emphasis placed on reading and math have also been noted (Graves, 1978; Scheid, 1991). In addition, both the back-to-basics movement and the notion that skills such as handwriting and spelling must be mastered before complex processes and advanced activities are introduced have strongly influenced instructional practices (Graves, 1978; Isaacson, 1987; Means & Knapp, 1991). Some special education teachers, perhaps partly in an attempt to prepare students for entry into the regular classroom, may have emphasized basic skill instruction even more strongly than their regular education counterparts.

Instructional practices in writing today, however, are beginning to evidence change in both regular and special education (Applebee *et al.*, 1990; Scheid, 1991; Wong, 1991). Emphasis on a process-oriented approach to writing has emerged in conjunction with an emphasis on critical literacy. Critical literacy refers to "a conception of reading and writing as high-level competency in using language as a tool to solve problems and to communicate" as the core curriculum at the elementary level for all students (Calfee, 1991, p. 71). These movements emphasize school as a community of learners and, similar to the concept behind special education, the importance of all students realizing their full potential. In addition, these movements highlight the importance of students and teachers actively collaborating and sharing responsibility for learning.

As we have elaborated elsewhere (Harris, 1982; Harris & Pressley, 1991; Harris & Graham, 1992; Pressley, Harris, & Marks, 1992), we support the shift away from the product-oriented model toward a model that emphasizes interactive learning among teachers and students and focuses on the meaning of students' writing. Skills and mechanics should be developed in the context of meaningful composition activities. Allocating adequate time for writing on a daily basis, facilitating student choice of writing topic, establishing a community of learners (including such activities as writing conferences and peer writing groups), immersing students in literature, integrating writing into the curriculum, responding to student meaning, and helping students see their first draft as just that are all important components of effective writing instruction (and are typical components of the process model; cf. Graves, 1978, 1985; Scardamalia & Bereiter, 1985). The creative process of writing should be encouraged as fear of writing is diminished. Students should come to see writing as a means of communication for themselves and others; as a tool for self-expression, learning, and the generation of new thoughts; and as a process that at times is difficult and frustrating, yet is also challenging and enjoyable (Graves, 1985; Harris & Graham, 1992).

EFFECTIVE TEACHING AND LEARNING

Changes in the conceptualization of effective writing instruction have been accompanied by changes in models of effective teaching and learning. As do all students, students with learning problems profit when teachers exhibit warmth, enthusiasm, involvement, organization and planfulness, patience, knowledge, and feedback and reinforcement (Ryans, 1960). These aspects have long been recognized as a part of effective instruction in both regular and special education (although teachers who are not actively implementing process or literacy models are sometimes mistakenly cast as devoid of these characteristics). Since the 1960s, however, increased attention has been given to the role of cognitive processes in the acquisition of knowledge and learning abilities (Harris, 1982, 1985). Models of effective instruction have been informed by research in such areas as teaching thinking (cf. Resnick, 1987), fostering "learning-to-learn" abilities (cf. Glaser, 1977), informed instruction and metacognitive development (cf. Brown & Campione, 1990), and the epistomology of the mind (cf. Wolf, Bixby, Glenn, & Gardner, 1991).

As Wolf and colleagues (1991) noted, recognition of the importance of thinking and the mind in the field of education can be traced at least as far back as the 1800s. The relatively recent emphasis on cognition and metacognition in teaching and learning, however, has had an important impact on the conceptualization of effective instruction. Models of effective instruction emphasize the student as an inherently active, self-regulating learner, intelligently acting on a perceived world rather than passively responding to the environment (Harris & Pressley, 1991). Learning is seen as occurring in qualitative and uneven shifts in understanding, rather than in small linear increments or in gradually accruing basic skills (Wolf *et al.,* 1991). Further, learning does not refer simply to the amount of knowledge acquired, but to the organization and structuring of knowledge in a functional system that allows for productive thinking, problem solving, and creative invention (Messick, 1984).

These views of learning and instruction set the stage for the development of instructional practices that "allow children to construct accurate knowledge and powerful procedures" (Harris & Pressley, 1991, p. 393). Dialogue, scaffolding, collaboration, interactive learning, reflection, and meaningful learning activities and environments are seen as critical components of effective instruction, and can be found in many new instructional approaches (including our own) for both normally achieving students and those with learning problems (cf. Brown & Campione, 1990; Englert *et al.,* 1991; Harris, 1982; Harris & Graham, 1992; Meichenbaum, 1977; Pressley *et al.,* 1992). It should be noted, however, that researchers did not "invent" these characteristics and components. Rather, they have been used by effective teachers and parents for quite some time (cf. Greenfield, 1984). What researchers have done is create models and alternative approaches to instruction that help communicate and operationalize these aspects of instruction for teachers, parents, and children.

Students with Learning Problems

In addition to the characteristics and components of instruction just noted, researchers have suggested that additional factors are important in the education of students with learning problems. Although students with learning problems represent a heterogeneous population, research indicates that the significant difficulties these students face are often the result of multiple problems of an affective, behavioral, and cognitive nature. In addition, ecological variables, including the situational, educational, cultural, and systems network of which the child is a part, are also critical concerns (Gabarino & Sherman, 1980; Harris, Graham, & Pressley, 1992; Turkewitz, 1984).

Recent research indicates that poor academic performance among students with learning problems may frequently be the result of problems in self-regulation of organized strategic behaviors, behaviors they have the ability to acquire and use given appropriate scaffolded instruction (Bjorklund, 1990; Harris, 1986b, 1990; Hughes & Hall, 1989; Zimmerman & Schunk, 1989). These children may not make use of effective verbal mediation processes or may not have developed an effective linguistic control system; thus, they may experience difficulties establishing correspondence between saying and doing or in using verbalizations to guide behavior (Englert *et al.,* 1991; Harris, 1986a, 1990). In addition, they may have difficulty in the comprehension of task demands, in the production of effective task strategies, and in the use of strategies to mediate performance (Flavell & Wellman, 1977; Harris, 1982; Meichenbaum, 1977).

Reciprocal relationships among academic failure, self-doubts, learned helplessness, negative attributions, unrealistic pretask expectancies, and poor motivation have received a great deal of attention in research on students with learning problems (Garner & Alexander, 1989; Licht, 1983; Sawyer *et al.,* 1991). Impulsivity, difficulties with memory or other aspects of information processing, low task engagement and persistence, devaluation of learning, and low productivity may also be experienced by some students. Thus, transactional relationships among affect, behavior, cognition, and social and ecological variables need to be considered (Kendall & Braswell, 1982; Meichenbaum, 1977; Meichenbaum & Asarnow, 1979).

An Integrated Approach

For students who face significant and often debilitating difficulties, we believe that a purposeful integrated approach to instruction that directly addresses affective, behavioral, cognitive, and social and ecological processes of change and outcomes is particularly appropriate (Harris, 1985; Harris & Graham, 1992; Harris *et al.,* 1992). Such a multicomponent approach, however, must be flexible and modifiable to meet the needs of both teachers and students. Further, such an approach must remain dynamic and open to change based on emerging issues and knowledge. It was based on this perspective that we initially developed our approach: self-regulated strategy development (Harris, 1982; Harris & Graham, 1985).

Explicitness

In addition to an integrated approach, researchers and educators have identified other aspects of instruction important for students with learning problems. These students may require more extensive, structured, and explicit instruction to learn skills and processes that other students learn more easily (Newcomer *et al.,* 1988; Palincsar & Brown, 1987; Reeve & Brown, 1985), and often profit from structured approaches and at least initial teacher direction (Hallahan, Lloyd, Kauffman, & Loper, 1983; Harris & Pressley, 1991). As learners' problems become more severe, explicitness becomes a more important aspect of instruction (Brown, Campione, & Day, 1981; Harris, 1982). As Brown and Campione (1990) noted, a considerable amount of research indicates that less capable students do not acquire a variety of cognitive and metacognitive strategies unless detailed and explicit instruction is provided. Further, the more complex the strategy to be learned, the more explicit instruction needs to be, even for more capable students.

Thus, for problem learners, "explicit instruction in understanding is particularly necessary" (Brown & Campione, 1990). Explicitness and structure, however, do not necessarily equate with isolated skill training, decontextualized learning of subskills, passive learning, and the teaching of gradually accruing basic skills (cf. Dole, Duffy, Roehler, & Pearson, 1991). Rather, what must be taught is the reflective flexible use of empowering strategies (strategies that students will make their own through modifying and personalizing them) within appropriate meaningful contexts and environments. Therefore, once again, an instructional model that is flexible and modifiable is necessary. Our strategy instruction model, as well as many others, allows for the level of explicitness to be adjusted to student needs (Harris & Graham, 1992; Harris & Pressley, 1991; Pressley *et al.,* 1992). Thus, teachers can use self-regulated strategy development procedures to explicitly teach single or complex strategies, or can modify these procedures to assist students in deducing or inducing a strategy, guide students in the discovery of a predetermined strategy, or assist them in creating their own strategy (Harris & Graham, 1992).

Further, as we have emphasized elsewhere, this perspective requires that the same strategies are *not* taught to all students, and that some students will not need full-blown strategy instruction at all (Graham, Harris, & Sawyer, 1987; Harris, 1982; Harris & Pressley, 1991; Pressley & Harris, 1990). Modeling, explaining, or facilitating discovery of a composition or self-regulation strategy may be all that is needed when a composition process or task is within the student's grasp and relatively minor support is needed. Some students may not need even these simple forms of support, or may need them only occasionally. As the writer's goals become more involved, however, and the student's difficulties more significant, strategy instruction becomes appropriate and more complex, involving multiple learning tasks, components, and stages. We turn now to a discussion of the strategy instruction approach we have developed for use when such complex instruction is appropriate.

SELF-REGULATED STRATEGY DEVELOPMENT

We begin the discussion of our approach to strategy instruction with four important caveats. First, academic competence and literacy represent a complexity of skills, strategies, processes, and attributes. Certainly, a single instructional approach can neither affect all aspects of performance nor address the complex nature of school success or failure (Harris, 1982; Harris & Pressley, 1991). Used appropriately, however, strategy instruction, including self-regulated strategy development, is a viable contribution to the repertoires of both regular and special educators (cf. Joyce & Weil, 1986). Second, strategy instruction is an emerging approach, one neither fully constructed nor fully understood at this time (Harris & Pressley, 1991). Thus, our approach has undergone and will continue to undergo changes. Third, there is no set of "cure-all" strategies. Finally, fourth, meeting the goals of strategy instruction in writing requires a carefully thought out combination of components, characteristics, and procedures, enacted in a meaningful environment.

Environment

As we have argued elsewhere (Graham, 1992; Graham *et al.,* 1987; Harris & Pressley, 1991), strategy instruction should not supplant or supplement the existing curriculum. Rather, strategy instruction should be an integral part of the curriculum. As Brown and Campione (1990) noted, learning environments that enhance students' conceptual understanding of strategies they adopt are an essential part of effective instruction. Students are encouraged to reflect on their level of understanding through activities such as discussion and group problem solving. Thus, we as well as other researchers have argued that strategy instruction complements the process approach to writing (Danoff *et al.,* 1991; Harris & Graham, 1992; Scheid, 1991). The establishment of a community of writers in the process classroom facilitates discussion and group problem solving. Theme-based instruction, in which students use writing and reading to explore a particular problem or theme (cf. Walmsley & Walp, 1990), also complements strategy instruction and shares many similarities with the process approach, among them the creation of a meaningful environment for writing.

Goals and Components

The major goals of our approach, which was designed for students in the upper elementary grades and above, include (1) assisting students in mastering the higher level cognitive processes involved in composing; (2) helping students further develop the autonomous, reflective, self-regulated use of effective strategies; and (3) supporting students in the development of positive attitudes about writing and about themselves as writers. (See Table 1 for an overview of the features of the research we have conducted.)

To meet these goals, the development of our approach over a decade ago began with the three major components that theorists considered critical to effective strategy instruction: skillful use of effective strategies; understanding of the use, significance, and limitations of those strategies; and self-regulation of strategic performance (including any combination of goal setting, self-monitoring, self-recording, self-assessment, and self-reinforcement) (Brown *et al.,* 1981; Harris & Graham, 1985; Palincsar, 1986; Palincsar & Brown, 1987). A large body of research indicates that these components are important in helping students understand how and when to apply a strategy; independently produce, evaluate, and modify a strategy effectively; recognize meaningful improvement in skills, processes, and products; gain new insights into strategies and their own strategic performance; improve their attitudes toward writing and toward themselves as writers; and facilitate maintenance and generalization of strategic performance. In addition to these basic components, however, our components analysis research (Graham & Harris, 1989a; Sawyer *et al.,* 1991) and work with teachers indicates that consideration must also be given to the characteristics of strategy instruction.

Characteristics

Our work with teachers and students has led us to identify six characteristics critical to the effective implementation of self-regulated strategy development in schools and classrooms (Harris & Graham, 1992).

Individualization

By individualization we do not mean students working alone or one-to-one instruction, necessarily. Teachers have used our approach successfully both with individual students (for example, during individual conferences

Table 1

Study Features of Self-regulated Strategy Development Research

Study	Process	Subjects	Grade	Design	Strategy	Length of instruction[a]	Instructor	Dependent measures	Social validation[b]	Transfer of strategy	Maintenance of strategy
Sawyer, Graham, & Harris (1991)	Planning: writing	43 S with LD[c]; 10 NA[d]	5 & 6	Pretest–post test control group	Prior to writing students answered questions based on story grammars.	Average of 8, 45 min sessions	4 preservice teachers in students' schools	Schematic structure / Story quality / Self-efficacy / Strategy use	Subjects / Subjects' special teachers	To different setting and teacher	2 wk; 4 wk
Graham & Harris (1989a)	Planning: writing	22 S with LD[e]; 11 NA	5 & 6	Pretest–posttest control group	Prior to writing students answered questions based on story grammars.	4–6.5 hrs	6 preservice teachers in students' schools	Schematic structure / Story quality / Self-efficacy / Strategy use	Subjects / Subjects' special teachers	To different setting and teacher	2 wk
Danoff, Harris, & Graham (1991)	Planning: writing	3 S with LD; 3 NA	4 & 5	Multiple-baseline across subjects with multiple probes during baseline	Prior to writing students answered questions based on story grammars.	6 wks, 3 times a wk, 45 min sessions	Students' special teacher delivered instruction to the regular class during Writer's Workshops[f]	Schematic structure / Story quality / Number of words / Self-efficacy / Strategy use	Subjects / Subjects' regular teacher	To different teacher	Up to 4 wk
Graham, MacArthur, Schwartz, & Voth (1992)	Planning: writing	4 S with LD	5	Multiple-baseline across subjects with multiple probes during baseline	Set goals for what paper would accomplish; determined how goals were met; generated and organized notes; evaluated success in obtaining goals once paper was written	4–6 hr	2 preservice teachers in students' school	Schematic structure / Writing quality / Number of words / Prewriting time / Total writing time / Knowledge of writing / Self-efficacy / Attitudes toward writing / Strategy use	Subjects / Subjects' special teacher	To second writing genre	Up to 15 wk

Study	Strategy/Focus	Subjects	N	Design	Procedure	Duration	Setting/Trainer	Dependent measures	Generalization assessors	Generalization	Maintenance
Graham & Harris (1989b)	Planning: writing	3 S with LD	6	Multiple-baseline across subjects with multiple probes during baseline	Considered purpose and audience; generated and organized content using text structure prompts; continued planning during writing	3.5–6 hr	1 preservice teacher in students' school	Schematic structure / Writing quality / Coherence / Number of words / Prewriting time / Self-efficacy / Strategy use	Subjects / Subjects' special teacher	To different setting and teacher / To second writing genre	Up to 12 wk
Harris & Graham (1985)	Planning: writing	2 S with LD	6	Multiple-baseline across behaviors nested in multiple-baseline across subjects	Brainstormed story topic and words to use in story	Average of 12, 45 min sessions	2 preservice teachers in students' school	Story quality / Number of words / Number of verbs / Number of adjectives / Number of adverbs	Subject / Subjects' special teacher	To different setting and teacher	Up to 16 wk
MacArthur, Schwartz, & Graham (1991b)	Revising: writing	29 S with LDg	4–6	Quasi-experimental	Peers provided structured feedback on the substance and form of each other's papers	6–8 wks during 50 min writing periods	Students' teachers taught strategy in context of Writers' Workshop/	Revisions / Writing quality / Number of words / Spelling, capitalization, and punctuation errors / Knowledge of writing / Strategy	—	—	—
Graham & MacArthur (1988)	Revising: writing	3 S with LD	5 & 6	Multiple-baseline across subject with multiple probes during baseline	Prompted students to add detail, examine clarity and cohesiveness and fix mechanical errors	5.5 hr	2 preservice teachers in students' schools	Revisions / Writing quality / Number of words / Spelling, capitalizationn, and punctuation errors / Self-efficacy / Strategy	Subjects	From computer to paper and pencil	Up to 9 wk

(continued)

Table 1 (*Continued*)

Study	Process	Subjects	Grade	Design	Strategy	Length of instruction[a]	Instructor	Dependent measures	Social validation[b]	Transfer of strategy	Maintenance of strategy
Bednarczyk, Harris, & Graham (1991)	Comprehension: reading	5 S with LD	5 & 6	Multiple-baseline across subjects with multiple probes during baseline	Located and made notes on important parts of a passage using prompts based on story grammar	8–10, 45–60 min sessions	Researcher and preservice teacher in students' school	Retelling; Number of story grammar components; Number of main ideas and supporting details recalled; Reading time; Strategy use	Subjects; Subjects' special teacher	To different setting and teacher; To a writing task	Up to 7 wk
Case, Harris, & Graham (1992)	Problem solving: mathematics	4 S with LD	5 & 6	Multiple-baseline across subjects with multiple probes during baseline	Solved math word problems by locating key words drawing a schematic picture and generating an equation	4.5–5.5 hr	2 preservice teachers in students' school	Number of correct equations and answers on addition and subtraction word problems; Strategy use	Subjects; Subjects' special teacher	To different setting and teacher	Up to 13 wk

[a] Instruction was criterion based; students, either individually or in groups, proceeded at their own pace rather than through a predetermined number of sessions.
[b] Based on interviews with, or comments made by, participants and their teachers.
[c] Students with learning disabilities (LD) assigned to three different versions of SRSD or a control group.
[d] NA, normally achieving students completed a posttest only.
[e] Students with LD assigned to two different versions of SRSD.
[f] A process approach to writing instruction.
[g] Thirteen students were taught the strategy: 16 students were in classrooms randomly assigned to control conditions.

within a process approach) and groups (including entire classes when appropriate). Regardless of the number of students and teachers working together, the preskills, skills, strategies, and self-regulation procedures to be developed should be responsive to a thorough understanding of the learner and the task, and tailored to individual students' capabilities. When the self-regulation and composition strategies to be learned are appropriate to a group of students, aspects of instruction can be individualized (i.e., the nature and content of self-instructions, process and product goals, affective goals, feedback and reinforcement, etc.). The demands for individualization are another area in which strategy instruction fits well with the process approach. The community of learners in the process classroom makes it possible for teachers to work with different groups or individuals as necessary, and for students to provide assistance to each other as well. Ongoing self-evaluation, using techniques such as self-monitoring or portfolio assessment, can also foster individualization (Harris & Graham, 1992).

Collaboration

Self-regulated strategy development emphasizes interactive learning between teachers and students. The teacher initially provides whatever degree of scaffolding is needed. Students gradually assume responsibility for recruiting, applying, monitoring, and evaluating strategies. We have found that the areas and ways in which students and teachers can collaborate during strategy instruction are limited only by their imaginations and willingness. For example, students can act as collaborators in determining the goals of instruction (we believe students should participate in strategy instruction only when they do so by choice); completing the task; and implementing, evaluating, and modifying the strategy, strategy acquisition procedures, and self-regulation procedures. Collaboration can also occur through Socratic dialogue, defined by Meichenbaum (1977) as a give-and-take exchange in which the teacher asks the student how he or she would do the task and then provides feedback and builds on that advice.

Mastery-Based Instruction

As we will explain shortly, the framework for our instructional approach consists of several stages. We believe that students should proceed through the stages at their own pace and should not proceed to later stages until they have met at least initial criteria for doing so. This does not imply, however, complete mastery at each stage before proceeding to the next. Rather, the stages (which may be reordered or combined) are recursive; criteria for progression become higher as students recycle through the stages. For example, preskill development is an early stage in our instructional model. However, students need not fully master preskills before going on to the next stages. Preskill development can continue throughout the early stages until mastery is reached. However, students should achieve a high level of preskill development before the later stages, such as collaborative practice or independent performance.

Anticipatory Instruction

Multiple aspects of strategy instruction need to be well thought out and planned in advance. For example, generalization and maintenance should be planned for and initiated from the very beginning of instruction (Harris & Graham, 1992). In addition, we also do what we call "anticipating glitches." We and the teachers with whom we work brainstorm as we plan about what could go wrong or prove difficult, particularly in light of our understanding of the students and the composition process or task involved. This helps us avoid or be ready for difficulties as they arise, even if they are not the difficulties we anticipated. As students become involved in the planning and implementation of strategy instruction, we also involve them in anticipating glitches and in problem solving. Thus, we are attempting to anticipate and subsume difficulties and failures into the instructional program (cf. Meichenbaum, 1977). We have found that routine review of earlier stages of instruction, as well as booster sessions aimed at maintenance or generalization once formal strategy instruction is complete, is particularly helpful.

Enthusiasm and a Support Network

Strategy instruction demands a great deal from teachers, including enthusiastic responsive teaching. Teachers must establish the credibility of strategies, and serve as models of self-regulated, strategic performance in a collaborative supportive environment for strategy development and autonomous reflective learning. Although classes are frequently large, a great deal of individualization is necessary. Regular education teachers may find this particularly challenging given the tendency among these teachers to plan for groups rather than to anticipate special needs and vary instructional approaches accordingly (Borko & Shavelson, 1990; Morocco, Gordon, & Riley, 1991). Given the complexity of such instruction, it is not surprising that, in our experience, teachers who operate from a sound support base are more successful in implementing and sustaining strategy instruction (cf. Harris & Graham, 1992; Harris *et al.,* 1992). Working together with other teachers to learn about and attempt strategy instruction not only makes this easier, but provides opportunities to share successes and failures. Further, a group of teachers in the same school or district can work together to maintain and generalize strategic performance across the curriculum and grade levels (cf. Harris *et al.,* 1992). In addition, organizational support is an important factor, since principals, learning specialists, and other school administrators can play a critical role in providing support and leadership in the nurturing of an instructional environment geared toward self-directed learning.

Developmental Enhancement

Teaching a strategy well demands a great deal of strategy and metastrategy knowledge on the teacher's part. The teacher must help students see the meaning and significance of the strategy, as well as its strengths and weaknesses. The teacher, therefore, needs an understanding of where the strategy fits in the larger scheme of things in terms of the student's development both as a writer and as a self-directed learner. Further, in order to help students take full advantage of the tool they are developing, the teacher needs to understand the many ways in which a strategy can empower the writer. As we have noted before (Harris & Graham, 1992), the skillful writer employs strategies and conventions of the craft the way a jazz musician uses a melody, profiting from the variations, the riffs, the twists, and ultimately the meaning of strategies and conventions in writing. Teachers can support the mature use of strategies by collaboratively planning for the developmental enhancement of strategies and strategic performance over time. For instance, a teacher and her students might begin by working with a planning strategy involving story grammar. Once this strategy might begin by working with a planning strategy involving story grammar. Once this strategy is learned, however, they may move on to other story telling structures such as those used by African tribal storytellers, or they might expand on the story grammar strategy by working on writing stories that have a moral. The strengths and weaknesses of different strategies can be compared, and additional strategies can be identified or developed.

Our goal now is to work on the developmental enhancement of strategic performance across the school years (cf. Harris *et al.,* 1992a). For instance, suppose the teacher just noted has engaged in cooperative curriculum and strategy instruction planning with the students' previous and future teachers. This teacher would know that not only will the strategies her students are learning be enhanced over time, but additional strategies (i.e., brainstorming strategies, creative writing strategies) will be created, developed, and mastered by these students and their teachers as the students mature. This knowledge allows these teachers to create powerful links between and among the strategies that students master, not only writing but across the curriculum.

Design of Instruction

As the preceding discussion indicates, the design of self-regulated strategy development should be done in an individualized, flexible, and collaborative manner. In our work with teachers, we emphasize a series of interrelated recursive stages for planning, implementing, and evaluating strategy instruction (see Figure 1). Students can act as collaborators in this process through discussions of the topic and genre of their writing, and their goals both for their work and their development as writers (Harris & Graham, 1992).

A thorough understanding of both the learner and the composition process or task is especially important for students with severe learning problems. Numerous considerations regarding the learner can influence the goals of instruction and thus affect the characteristics, components, and processes of instruction. These characteristics include age; cognitive development; beliefs, attitudes, attributions, and expectancies; motivation; writing anxiety; current metacognitive and self-regulation capabilities; initial knowledge state; tolerance for frustration, errors, ambiguity, and difficulty; and oral and written language style and development (cf. Garner & Alexander, 1989; Harris & Graham, 1992). Similarly, understanding the composition process or task requires consideration of the affective, behavioral,

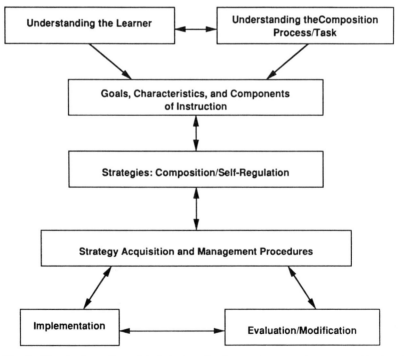

Fig. 1 Planning for self-regulated strategy development: a recursive process. Reprinted, by permission, from K. R. Harris and S. Graham, *Helping young writers master the craft: Strategy instruction and self-regulation in the writing process.* Copyright © 1992, by Brookline Books.

and cognitive demands it places on the learner; preskills; and link to the larger context and content of learning (Harris, 1982; Harris & Graham, 1992). The goals and components of our approach were noted previously. We turn now to a discussion of the stages of instruction.

Stages of Instruction

Throughout the stages of instruction, teachers and students collaborate on the acquisition, implementation, evaluation, and modification of strategies. The stages are not meant to be followed in a "cookbook" fashion; rather, they represent a "metascript," providing a general format and guidelines (cf. Gallimore & Tharp, 1983). The seven stages include (1) preskill development, (2) initial conference (instructional goals and significance), (3) discussion of the composition strategy, (4) modeling of the strategy and self-instructions, (5) mastery of the strategy, (6) collaborative practice (composition and self-regulation strategies), and (7) independent performance.

As noted previously, the stages are meant to be recursive, and may be reordered, combined, or modified as appropriate. For instance, Stage 1, preskill development, may not be needed at all for some students. Similarly, Stage 5, mastery of the strategy, is included in our model because of the memory problems encountered by so many students with severe learning problems, and may not be necessary for other students or may be combined with Stage 3 (discussion of the strategy). One of the teachers we work with recently used an innovative approach. A group of middle school students was working on a strategy (developed and validated by a local group of teachers) that was a developmental extension of one they had mastered previously. While working with this group, the teacher decided to combine Stages 4 (modeling) and 6 (collaborative practice). Given the students' prior knowledge and success with strategies, she felt this combination would work and be more efficient. After discussion of the new strategy, she modeled using the strategy to first plan and then create, with the students' help, her own composition (a persuasive essay) while the students followed the same strategy steps but planned their own essay on the same topic. Each student then wrote his or her own essay. Although this combination might sound awkward, and was not one we would have recommended beforehand, our observations of her lesson and her students' essays indicated that it worked quite well.

Teachers have made many other effective modifications as well. For instance, one upper elementary teacher was not comfortable with modeling in front of the class. She taperecorded her self-talk while writing an actual story. She then listened to the tape with her class, using overheads and soliciting their help with the parts as they worked together. The students designed and made their own bulletin board about the strategy before going on. Another teacher believed that the story grammar concept could prove very useful to his first-graders with severe reading problems. He modified the strategy and the instruction to fit story retelling, starting with *The Three Billy Goats Gruff.* Initially, the story parts who, when, and where were identified. Other story parts were added later. The students in his class did art work related to the retelling and the story components (e.g., dioramas). When they were able to retell the story, using all of the parts, they wrote and produced a play.

Barbara's Class: An Illustration

Rather than discuss each stage of self-regulated strategy development, we illustrate them here with a description of how one teacher, Barbara Danoff, implemented them to help her students master a story grammar strategy designed to enhance advanced planning and content generation (see Table 2). Barbara was working with a fifth-grade class during Writer's Workshop, a process approach used throughout the school. Students were used to choosing their own topics and genre, determining the content and purpose of their writing, selecting pieces for completion and publication, using the writing community as a resource, and peer editing. Barbara planned to incorporate strategy instruction in this process approach. Before beginning

Table 2
Story Grammar Strategy Steps and Mnemonic[a]

Strategy
   1. Think of a story you would like to share with others
   2. Let your mind be free
   3. Write down the story part reminder (mnemonic)
      W-W-W
      What = 2
      How = 2
   4. Make notes of your ideas for each part
   5. Write your story—use good parts; add, elaborate, or revise as you go; make sense
Mnemonic
   Who is the main character; who else is in the story?
   When does the story take place?
   Where does the story take place?
   What does the main character do or want to do; what do other characters do?
   What happens when the main character does or tries to do it? What happens with other
      characters?
   How does the story end?
   How does the main character feel; how do other characters feel?

---

[a]This strategy is not meant to be used to order story content; where, when, and how the story parts are introduced, used, and developed is up to the author.

instruction, she carefully considered both the learners in this class and story writing as a composition task. The students' portfolios indicated that most of the students commonly neglected two or more of the seven parts of a story and that all the students could improve their story writing by including greater detail and elaboration, as well as more goals and actions.

Barbara also considered the affective and cognitive characteristics of the individual students in the group. She had worked with most of the students for 2 years and knew them well. Most of the students enjoyed writing. A few students, however, evidenced anxiety about composing as well as difficulty writing (several, but not all, of these students had been identified as learning disabled). Barbara wanted to help these students establish a stronger sense of motivation, enhanced self-efficacy, and more internal attributions (what she termed an overall "I can do this if I try" attitude). Finally, she felt that knowledge and use of the story grammar strategy could benefit some of the students in terms of reading comprehension and would be of use to all the students in middle school the following year, where they would face increased demands for specific writing products, such as book reports and biographies. Thus, Barbara decided to offer the strategy instruction to all the students and work with those who elected to pursue the strategy. She planned her instruction using the seven stages, with a few modifications. In terms of self-regulation, she decided to incorporate proximal goal setting (on an individual basis), self monitoring (including self-assessment and self-recording), and self-reinforcement into strategy instruction. How she and her students worked together is described in the subsequent text.

Stage 1: Initial Conference

Barbara decided to begin with a conference with the entire class in order to offer instruction in the strategy to all the students and then work with those who chose to learn it. The group discussed the common parts of a story, the goal of story grammar strategy instruction (to write better stories, ones that are more fun for you to write and more fun for others to read), and how including and expanding story parts can improve a story. Barbara also briefly outlined how the students would learn the strategy, stressing their roles as collaborators (including the possibility of acting as a peer tutor for other students who wished to learn the strategy in the future) and the importance of effort in strategy mastery. All the students opted to learn the strategy.

Stage 2: Preskill Development

Knowing that her students were comfortable with the vocabulary involved in the story grammar strategy, Barbara decided to focus on the story parts and the mnemonic. The group discussed the meaning of each story part and then identified story grammar elements in literature they were currently reading. To promote linkages to reading, the group also discussed how, when we read the writing of others, we can use our knowledge of story grammar to help us get their meaning. The different ways in which authors developed or used story parts were highlighted as well. Next, the group spent some time generating ideas for story parts, using differing story origins. Then the students worked on memorizing the story parts mnemonic in several ways. Finally, each student selected two or three stories he or she had written previously, and determined which story elements were present in each story. Barbara met individually or in small groups with the students to explain and demonstrate graphing of the number of story parts in each story and how they would continue to use the graph for self-recording. With those students whose graphs indicated that they typically used all of the story parts, Barbara discussed with them how they could improve their parts with detail, elaboration, and more action.

Stage 3: Discussion of the Composition Strategy

Now Barbara introduced the 5-step story grammar strategy: each student had a small chart listing the 5 steps and the mnemonic. Barbara asked the students what they thought the reason for each step might be. The group then discussed how and when to use the strategy. In addition to writing stories, linkages to writing book reports, biographies, and other compositions, and to reading were discussed. Discussion also centered around the importance of student effort in mastering the strategy, since a strategy cannot work if it has not been mastered (this was meant to serve both goal setting and attributional functions). Finally, Barbara decided to introduce creativity self-statements. She modeled statements she often used to free her mind and think of good story ideas and parts. After discussing how these statements were helpful, each student determined their own preferred creativity self-statements, recorded them on paper, and practiced using them.

Stage 4: Modeling

Barbara shared a story idea with her students that she had been thinking about using, and began modeling by planning a story while "thinking out loud." The group helped her as she planned and made notes for each story part and as she wrote the first draft of her story (changes or additions to her plans were made several times as she wrote). While composing, Barbara modeled five additional types of self-instructions: problem definition, planning, self-evaluation, self-reinforcement, and coping (cf. Meichenbaum, 1977; Graham *et al.,* 1987). After completing the story, the group again discussed the importance of what we say to ourselves while we work (students volunteered examples of personal positive, and sometimes negative, self-statements they used while writing) and identified the functions and types of self-statements Barbara had used. Students then generated and recorded their own self-statements of each type. Finally, Barbara asked the students to consider the strategy steps and mnemonic and suggest any changes they thought were needed to make the strategy more effective or efficient. No changes were suggested at this point. Barbara asked the students to continue considering this as they worked with the strategy (Barbara had taught the strategy for several years; changes had been made in the strategy and instructional procedures in earlier years. No further changes were made by this group).

Stage 5: Memorization of the Strategy and Mnemonic

Barbara asked her students to practice the 5-step strategy alone or with a partner in any way they liked, and noted the importance of memorizing the strategy and mnemonic as well as examples of each type of self-statement from their lists. Some students memorized the strategy, mnemonic, and self-statements easily, whereas others needed more practice (some students continued to work on memorizing these as they began collaborative practice). At this point, instruction continued on an individual, or sometimes small group, basis; all aspects of the process approach (i.e., use of peers as a resource, peer editing) continued. Barbara moved into collaborative practice with each student when she and the student determined they were read to do so. Use of self-statements was prompted as appropriate during writing and at other times; this continued throughout instruction and afterward as well.

Stage 6: Collaborative Practice

Barbara initiated goal-setting, self-monitoring (continuing use of the graphs), and self-reinforcement during conferences with individual students as collaborative practice began. The goal for each student was to include all the story parts. Barbara believed this to be a proximal goal for all students; otherwise smaller initial goals would have been set. During this stage, whenever a student completed a story (or sooner if he or she preferred), Barbara and the student identified the story parts independently, compared counts, filled in the student's graph, and then compared this number with the goal. Barbara collaboratively planned a story with each student who needed her assistance at the beginning of this stage, and made sure each student was using the strategy steps and mnemonic. She modified her input and support to meet the individual needs of students (sometimes the students provided assistance to each other, as well). In some cases she helped students determine self-statements that were especially helpful to them or provided prompting and guidance. Re-explanations and modeling were provided as necessary. With some students, she focused on planning for greater detail and elaboration, or incorporating more goals and actions on the part of the characters. Scaffolding, including use of the charts and self-statements lists, was faded individually, and Barbara began encouraging students to use covert self-speech if they weren't already doing so. Barbara found that collaborative practice took less time than she had anticipated; most of the students who had been experiencing difficulty were ready for independent performance after two or three collaborative experiences. Students went on to independent performance when they were ready.

During this stage, one conference was held with the entire group to discuss and plan strategy maintenance and generalization. The students decided on review and booster sessions for maintenance, and discussed opportunities they might have for generalization (one student reported using the strategy in English class when they read stories; another reported using it to help write outlines).

Stage 7: Independent Performance

Students now planned and wrote stories independently: Barbara provided positive and constructive feedback as appropriate. Some students continued using the charts and lists of self-statements; they were encouraged to try working without them. The use of planning paper, with the mnemonic written at the top, was encouraged. Some students no longer wrote out ideas for all the story parts. These students told Barbara this was because they had the parts in their heads and were ready to write (this was not seen as a problem unless the student then left out story parts). Students continued the goal setting and self-monitoring (graphing) procedures independently for two more stories, and then were told that using these in the future was up to them.

Once again, a group conference was held to evaluate the strategy and instruction. The students were pleased with the strategy and their use of it. Barbara initiated a discussion of the strategy's weaknesses at this point as well as discussions of other story structures. Students indicated an interest in learning other story structures in the future. The plans for maintenance were reviewed and generalization was discussed again. Several students explained how they had used the strategy for reading or for other writing assignments. One student, for instance, reported using the strategy to write a "tall tale" in another class, while other students mentioned using it for journal writing or writing for the school newspaper. These reports were confirmed by the observations of other teachers (in fact, one fourth-grade teacher adopted the strategy for use during both reading and writing in her classroom); use of self-statements in other classes was also noted. Barbara planned to continue to prompt and discuss generalization.

Evaluation

Formal data were collected on several students (both learning disabled and normally achieving) throughout instruction; pre and post data were collected for all students (Danoff *et al.,* 1991; Graham *et al.,* 1991). Self-regulated strategy development had a significant impact on the structure of students' stories; the number of story parts increased meaningfully (the learning disabled and some normally achieving students doubled the number of story parts they were using). Scores for the quality of included parts nearly tripled among those students followed throughout instruction. Holistic quality ratings also showed improvement for these students. Maintenance checks at 2 and 4 wks indicated that these effects were maintained. Generalization across teachers was also obtained. Finally, data collected throughout instruction indicated that students' writing improved across the stages of instruction; the greatest improvements resulted after Stages 6 and 7.

Barbara and her students also engaged in less formal methods of evaluation throughout instruction and at the end of instruction (as can be seen in previous text), through the use of the graphs and by looking through students' portfolios and discussing the changes occurring in their writing. Barbara informally assessed students' attributions, attitudes toward writing and the use of strategies, and attitudes toward themselves as writers through individual and group discussions. She believed positive changes were occurring in these areas for nearly all her students, particularly those who had been anxious about writing. When Barbara interviewed each of the students at the end of formal instruction, the mnemonic was most frequently nominated by students as the most enjoyable aspect of instruction. One student commented, "The W-W-W, What = 2, How = 2 builds up your resources." None of the students indicated any problems in incorporating strategy instruction into the process approach used in their school. Another teacher who worked with Barbara during Writers' Workshop commented that she could see "light bulbs going off" as the students worked to master the strategy. As one student remarked to her, "Now this story writing makes sense." In short, although most of the students were already familiar with the parts of a story, mastery of the strategy helped them to understand, use, and extend what they already knew.

Research Base

At this point we have completed 10 empirical studies of self-regulated strategy development in the classroom (see Table 1). These studies indicate that self-regulated strategy development is a productive method of improving what and how students write, for students with severe learning problems and for normally achieving students (Graham *et al.*, 1991; Graham & Harris, 1992). Across a variety of strategies, the quality and, usually, the length and structure of the compositions has improved. In several studies, improvements have been quite pronounced among students with learning disabilities. These students, following instruction, did as well as their normally achieving peers (Danoff *et al.*, 1991; Graham & Harris, 1989a).

Our research has also indicated changes in how students go about the task of composing. For instance, depending on the strategy, students have spent more time planning in advance of writing or have modified their revising processes, expanding to address substantive as well as mechanical concerns. Their metacognitive knowledge has also improved, including shifts in their conceptualizations of what constitutes good writing. Self-efficacy has typically improved, and social validity has been demonstrated through interviews and anecdotal evidence. Both teachers and students find self-regulated strategy development effective and recommend it for others. Several of the teachers we have worked with have continued using this approach for several years now.

We have consistently found that the effects of self-regulated strategy development are maintained over short periods of time, and that generalization across settings, persons, and writing medium (word processor to paper and pencil) are obtained. However, long-term maintenance was not investigated in several studies (usually due to the end of the school year). In our experience, booster sessions frequently have been necessary for long-term maintenance. Students' abilities to adapt a writing strategy they have learned to differing genres or writing tasks have been more varied. This form of generalization is more challenging, since it requires identifying necessary changes or adaptations in the original strategy. Some students with learning problems were able to do so with only minor assistance (brief discussion and suggestions). Thus, learning time required to acquire a strategy for a new genre is reduced. Other students have required more intense scaffolding to use a strategy effectively with a new writing task.

ISSUES AND CHALLENGES

As is typically the case, our research continues to present us with questions, challenges, and issues to address. Many of these issues are the same as those being addressed by other researchers, as can be seen in this volume. For example, maintenance and generalization remain a challenge, although our understanding of these processes has increased and progress has been made (Harris & Pressley, 1991; Harris *et al.*, 1992a; Reeve & Brown, 1985). As can be seen in this chapter, the full self-regulated strategy development model includes several commonly recommended procedures for promoting generalization and maintenance, including informed learning, modeling of effort and strategy attributions, recognition of gains following strategy execution, knowledge about when and where the strategy can and cannot be used, sufficient practice to allow automatization and personalization of the strategy, diverse practice, encouraging and prompting generalization and maintenance, self-regulation of strategy use, and collaboration and scaffolding. As we noted earlier, however, long-term maintenance is not achieved with all students.

We are particularly interested in investigating effects of various follow-up procedures on long-term maintenance, for example, long-term goal-setting and self-monitoring of strategy use, periodic review and practice, peer support, proactive planning, homework assignments, problem-solving sessions, and the embedding of strategy instruction in the child's larger systems network (cf. Deshler & Schumaker, 1986; Kendall, 1989; Sawyer *et al.,* 1991). In addition, we believe that a great deal remains to be learned about the breadth, depth, and course of the development of maintenance and generalization capabilities in children (Harris & Pressley, 1991; Harris *et al.,* 1992). Relatively few descriptive, developmental studies of maintenance and generalization are available (cf. Brown & Kane, 1988; Garner & Alexander, 1989); thus, we have little but intuition to guide us in setting reasonable criteria and evaluating outcomes in our research (Harris, 1985).

The multicomponent nature of emerging strategy interventions (including our own) has brought our attention to a number of issues in the area of intervention integrity (Harris, 1990). The concept of intervention integrity parallels and expands on the treatment integrity concept. First, it parallels treatment integrity by requiring that each component or characteristic or procedure in a multicomponent strategy intervention is both delivered and carried out as intended and recommended. This is particularly important in replications and in comparisons of different instructional approaches (Harris, 1985). For instance, at a recent conference, a study was presented comparing three approaches to strategy instruction. Unfortunately, as became obvious in a videotape of the three instructional conditions, the teacher in one condition was markedly less warm, enthusiastic, and responsive to students and kept a great deal more distance between herself and her students. These differences in the characteristics of instruction confound any differential outcomes that may have been due to planned differences in the interventions. Second, the concept of intervention integrity expands on treatment integrity by requiring assessment of the processes of change as related to both intentions and outcomes. Specification and assessment of intervention processes will allow us to test and expand the theoretical basis of strategy interventions (Harris, 1990).

We are also interested in issues pertaining to teacher implementation of strategy approaches, as are a number of other researchers (for example, see Chapter 15). Cognitive strategy instruction in the classroom creates many demands on teachers. How these demands can be met in order to facilitate strategy instruction demands our attention, as does preservice and in-service preparation of teachers to prepare them for integrated responsive forms of instruction (Harris, Preller, & Graham, 1990). Finally, our work has led us to appreciate the many ways in which interactive strategy instruction provides rich informative assessment data (Harris & Pressley, 1991; Harris *et al.,* 1992a). Research is needed to establish the role and functions of such assessment information for teachers, students, parents, and administrators. As researchers address these and other issues, we continue to find that researchers, teachers, and students are constructing important new knowledge during strategy instruction.

ACKNOWLEDGMENTS

We would like to thank Barbara Danoff, as well as the students, teachers, and principal at Georgian Forest Elementary School, for this illustration (adapted from Harris & Graham, 1992) and for her work with us over the past few years in the development and refinement of the story grammar strategy. Barbara is a special education teacher; she developed a "plug in" program for her school in which she works collaboratively with regular educators and with all students in the regular classroom, rather than in a separate resource room. Thus, Barbara and the regular education teachers work together to offer strategy instruction to all students. We would also like to thank the participating teachers and students in Charles County, Maryland, for the other illustrations used here.

REFERENCES

Applebee, A., Langer, J., and Mullis, I. (1986). *The writing report card: Writing achievement in American schools.* Princeton, New Jersey: Educational Testing Service.

Applebee, A., Langer, J., Jenkins, L., Mullis, I., and Foertsch, M. (1990). *Learning to write in our nation's schools.* Princeton, New Jersey: Educational Testing Service.

Bednarczyk, A., Harris, K. R., and Graham, S. (1990). *Story grammar instruction to improve reading comprehension.* Unpublished raw data.

Bereiter, C., and Scardamalia, M. (1982). From conversation to composition: The role of instruction in a developmental process. In R. Glaser (Ed.), *Advances in instructional psychology.* (Vol. 2, pp. 1–64). Hillsdale, New Jersey: Erlbaum.

Bjorklund, D. (1990). *Children's strategies: Contemporary views of cognitive development.* Hillsdale, New Jersey: Erlbaum.

Borko, H., and Shavelson, R. (1990). Teacher decision making. In B. Jones and L. Idol (Eds.),

Dimensions of thinking and cognitive instruction (pp. 311–346). Hillsdale, New Jersey: Erlbaum.

Brown, A. L., and Campione, J. C. (1990). Interactive learning environments and the teaching of science and mathematics. In M. Gardner, J. Greens, F. Reif, A. Schoenfeld, A. di Sessa, and E. Stage (Eds.), *Toward a scientific practice of science education* (pp. 111–139). Hillsdale, New Jersey: Erlbaum.

Brown, A. L., and Kane, M. (1988). Preschool children can learn to transfer: Learning to learn and learning from example. *Cognitive Psychology, 20,* 493–523.

Brown, A. L., Campione, J. C., and Day, J. D. (1981). Learning to learn: On training students to learn from texts. *Educational Researcher, 10,* 14–21.

Calfee, R. (1991). Schoolwide programs to improve literacy instruction for students at risk. In B. Means and M. Knapp (Eds.), *Teaching advance skills to educationally disadvantaged students* (pp. 71–92). Washington, D.C.: U.S. Department of Education.

Case, L., Harris, K. R., and Graham, S. (1992). Improving the mathematical problem solving skills of students with learning disabilities: Self-instructional strategy development. *Journal of Special Education.*

Danoff, B., Harris, K. R., and Graham, S. (1990). *Cognitive strategy instruction and the process approach: Effects on composition among learning disabled and normally achieving students.* Unpublished raw data.

Deshler, D. D., and Schumaker, J. B. (1986). Learning strategies: An instructional alternative for low-achieving adolescents. *Exceptional Children, 52,* 583–590.

Dole, J. A., Duffy, G. G., Roehler, L. R., and Pearson, P. D. (1991). Moving from the old to the new: Research on reading comprehension instruction. *Review of Educational Research, 61,* 239–264.

Englert, C., and Raphael, T. (1988). Constructing well-formed prose: Process, structure, and metacognitive knowledge. *Exceptional Children, 54,* 513–520.

Englert, C., Raphael, T., Fear, K., and Anderson, L. (1988). Students' metacognitive knowledge about how to write informational texts. *Learning Disability Quarterly, 11,* 18–46.

Englert, C., Raphael, T., Anderson, L., Anthony, H., Stevens, D., and Fear, K. (1991). Making writing strategies and self-talk visible: Cognitive strategy instruction in writing in regular and special education classrooms. *American Educational Research Journal, 28,* 337–373.

Flavell, J., and Wellman, H. (1977). Metamemory. In R. Kail and J. Hagen (Eds.), *Perspectives on the development of memory and cognition* (pp. 3–33). Hillsdale, New Jersey: Erlbaum.

Gabarino, J., and Sherman, D. (1980). High-risk neighborhoods and high-risk families: The human ecology of child maltreatment. *Child Development, 51,* 188–198.

Gallimore, R., and Tharp, R. (1983). *The regulatory functions of teachers questions: A microanalysis of reading comprehension lessons* (Technical Report No. 109). Honolulu: Kamehameha Educational Research Institute, The Kamehameha Schools.

Garner, R., and Alexander, P. A. (1989). Metacognition: Answered and unanswered questions. *Educational Psychologist, 24,* 143–158.

Glaser, R. (1977). *Adaptive education: Individual diversity and learning.* New York: Holt.

Glaser, R. (1991). Expertise and assessment. In M. Wittrock and E. Baker (Eds.), *Testing and cognition* (pp. 17–30). Englewood Cliffs, New Jersey: Prentice Hall.

Graham, S. (1982). Composition research and practice. A unified approach. *Focus on Exceptional Children, 14,* 1–16.

Graham, S. (1990). The role of production factors in learning disabled students' compositions. *Journal of Educational Psychology, 82,* 781–791.

Graham, S. (1992). Helping students with learning disabilities progress as writers. *Interventions.*

Graham, S., and Harris, K. R. (1988). Instructional recommendations for teaching writing to exceptional students. *Exceptional Children, 54,* 506–512.

Graham, S., and Harris, K. R. (1989a). A components analysis of cognitive strategy instruction: Effects on learning disabled students' compositions and self-efficacy. *Journal of Educational Psychology, 81,* 353–361.

Graham, S., and Harris, K. R. (1989b). Improving learning disabled students' skills at composing essays: Self-instructional strategy training. *Exceptional Children, 56,* 201–214.

Graham, S., and Harris, K. R. (1989c). Cognitive training: Implications for written language. In J. Hughes and R. Hall (Eds.), *Cognitive behavioral psychology in the schools: A comprehensive handbook* (pp. 247–279). New York: Guilford Publishing.

Graham, S., and Harris, K. R. (1992). Self-instructional strategy development: Programmatic research in writing. In B. Wong (Ed.), *Intervention research with students with learning disabilities: An international perspective.* New York: Springer-Verlag.

Graham, S., Harris, K. R., MacArthur, C., and Schwartz, S. (1991). Writing and writing instruction with students with learning disabilities: A review of a program of research. *Learning Disability Quarterly, 14,* 89–114.

Graham, S., Harris, K. R., and Sawyer, R. (1987). Composition instruction with learning disabled students: Self-instructional strategy training. *Focus on Exceptional Children, 20,* 1–11.

Graham, S., and MacArthur, C. (1988). Improving learning disabled students' skills at revising essays produced on a word processor: Self-instructional strategy training. *Journal of Special Education, 22,* 133–152.

Graham, S., MacArthur, C., Schwartz, S., and Voth, T. (1992). Improving LD students' compositions using a strategy involving product and process goal-setting. *Exceptional Children.*

Graham, S., Schwartz, S., and MacArthur, C. (1991b). *Learning disabled and normally achieving students' knowledge of the writing process, attitudes toward writing, and self-efficacy.* Unpublished manuscript.

Graves, D. H. (1978). *Balance the basics: Let them write.* New York: Ford Foundation.

Graves, D. H. (1983). *Writing: Teachers and children at work.* Portsmouth, New Hampshire: Heinemann.

Graves, D. H. (1985). All children can write. *Learning Disability Focus, 1,* 36–43.

Greenfield, P. (1984). A theory of the teacher in the learning activities of everyday life. In B. Rogoff and J. Lave (Eds.), *Everyday cognition: Its development in social context* (pp. 117–138). Cambridge: Harvard University Press.

Hallahan, D., Lloyd, J., Kauffman, J., and Loper, A. (1983). Academic problems. In R. Morris and T. Kratchowill (Eds.), *Practice of child therapy: A textbook of methods* (pp. 113–141). New York: Pergammon Press.

Harris, K. R. (1982). Cognitive-behavior modification: Application with exceptional students. *Focus on Exceptional Children, 15,* 1–16.

Harris, K. R. (1985). Conceptual, methodological, and clinical issues in cognitive-behavioral assessment. *Journal of Abnormal Child Psychology, 13,* 373–390.

Harris, K. R. (1986a). Self-monitoring of attentional behavior vs. self-monitoring of productivity: Effects on on-task behavior and academic response rate among learning disabled children. *Journal of Applied Behavior Analysis, 19,* 417–423.

Harris, K. R. (1986b). The effects of cognitive-behavior modification on private speech and task performance during problem solving among learning disabled and normally achieving children. *Journal of Abnormal Child Psychology, 14,* 63–76.

Harris, K. R. (1989). *The role of self-efficacy in self-instructional strategy training and the development of self-regulated learning among learning disabled children.* Paper presented at the Annual Meeting of the American Educational Research Association.

Harris, K. R. (1990). Developing self-regulated learners: The role of private speech and self-instructions. *Educational Psychologist, 25,* 35–50.

Harris, K. R., and Graham, S. (1985). Improving learning disabled students' composition skills: Self-control strategy training. *Learning Disability Quarterly, 8,* 27–36.

Harris, K. R., and Graham, S. (1992). *Helping young writers master the craft: Strategy instruction and self-regulation in the writing process.* Cambridge, Massachusetts. Brookline Press.

Harris, K. R., and Pressley, M. (1991). The nature of cognitive strategy instruction: Interactive strategy construction. *Exceptional Children, 57,* 392–404.

Harris, K. R., Preller, D., and Graham, S. (1990). Acceptability of cognitive-behavioral and behavioral interventions among teachers. *Cognitive Therapy and Research, 14,* 573–587.

Harris, K. R., Graham, S., and Pressley, M. (1992). Cognitive behavioral approaches in reading and written language: Developing self-regulated learners. In N. N. Singh and I. L. Beale (Eds.), *Current perspectives in learning disabilities: Nature, theory, and treatment.* New York: Springer-Verlag.

Harris, K. R., Higdon, J., Liebow, H., Bennof, A., Metheny, L., Nelson, V., Packman, S., and Strause, C. (1992). The Charles County academic self-management consortium: S.C.O.R.E.ing across the grades. *LD Forum.*

Hughes, J., and Hall, R. (1989). *Cognitive behavioral psychology in the schools: A comprehensive handbook.* New York: Guilford Publishing.

Isaacson, S. (1987). Effective instruction in written language. *Focus on Exceptional Children, 19,* 1–12.

Isaacson, S. (1989). Role of secretary vs. author: Resolving the conflict in writing instruction. *Learning Disability Quarterly, 12,* 209–217.

Joyce, B., and Weil, M. (1986). *Models of teaching* (3rd ed.). Englewood Cliffs, New Jersey: Prentice Hall.

Kendall, P. (1989). The generalization and maintenance of behavior change: Comments, considerations, and the "no-cure" criticism. *Behavior Therapy, 20,* 357–364.

Kendall, P., and Braswell, L. (1982). On cognitive-behavioral assessment: Model, measures, and madness. In C. Speilberger and J. Butcher (Eds.), *Advances in personality assessment* (Vol. 1, pp. 35–82). Hillsdale, New Jersey: Erlbaum.

Langer, J., and Applebee, A. (1986). Reading and writing instruction: Toward a theory of teaching and learning. In E. Rothkopf (Ed.), *Review of research in education* (Vol. 13, pp. 171–194). Washington, D.C.: American Educational Research Association.

Licht, B. (1983). Cognitive-motivational factors that contribute to the achievement of learning-disabled children. *Journal of Learning Disabilities, 16,* 483–490.

MacArthur, C., and Graham, S. (1987). Learning disabled students' composing with three methods: Handwriting, dictation, and word processing. *Journal of Special Education, 21,* 22–42.

MacArthur, C., Graham, S., and Schwartz, S. (1991a). Knowledge of revision and revising behavior among learning disabled students. *Learning Disability Quarterly, 14,* 61–73.

MacArthur, C., Schwartz, S., and Graham, S. (1991b). Effects of a reciprocal peer revision strategy in a special education classroom. *Learning Disabilities Research and Practice, 6,* 201–210.

Means, B., and Knapp, M. (1991). Models for teaching skills to educationally disadvantaged students. In B. Means and M. Knapp (Eds.), *Teaching advance skills to educationally disadvantaged students* (pp. 1–20). Washington, D.C.: U.S. Department of Education.

Meichenbaum, D. (1977). *Cognitive behavior modification: An integrative approach.* New York: Plenum Press.

Meichenbaum, D., and Asarnow, J. (1979). Cognitive-behavioral modification and metacognitive development: Implications for the classroom. In P. Kendall and S. Hollon (Eds.), *Cognitive-behavioral interventions: Theory, research, and procedures* (pp. 11–35). New York: Academic Press.

Messick, S. (1984). Abilities and knowledge in educational achievement testing: An assessment of dynamic cognitive structures. In B. Blake (Ed.), *Social and technical issues in testing: Implications for test construction and usage* (pp. 155–172). Hillsdale, New Jersey: Erlbaum.

Morocco, C., and Neuman, S. (1986). Word processors and the acquisition of writing strategies. *Journal of Learning Disabilities, 19,* 243–247.

Morocco, C., Gordon, S., and Riley, M. (1991). *Designing classroom activities for diverse language needs.* Paper presented at the Annual Meeting of the American Educational Research Association, Chicago, Illinois.

Mosenthal, J., and Englert, C. (1987). The beginning capacity to teach. *Remedial and Special Education, 8,* 38–47.

Newcomer, P., Nodine, B., and Barenbaum, E. (1988). Teaching writing to exceptional children: Reaction and recommendations. *Exceptional Children, 54,* 559–564.

Palincsar, A. S. (1986). The role of dialogue in providing scaffolded instruction. *Educational Psychologist, 21,* 73–98.

Palincsar, A. S. and Brown, D. A. (1987). Enhancing instructional time through attention to metacognition. *Journal of Learning Disabilities, 20,* 66–75.

Pressley, M., and Harris, K. R. (1990). What is really known about cognitive strategy instruction. *Educational Leadership, 48,* 31–34.

Pressley, M., Borkowski, J. G., and Schneider, W. (1987). Cognitive strategies: Good strategy users coordinate metacognition and knowledge. In R. Vasta and G. Whitehurst (Eds.), *Annals of child development* (Vol. 4, pp. 89–129). Greenwich, Connecticut: JAI Press.

Pressley, M., Harris, K. R., and Marks, M. (1992). But good strategy instructions are constructivists! *Educational Psychology Review.*

Reeve, R., and Brown, A. (1985). Metacognition reconsidered: Implications for intervention research. *Journal of Abnormal Child Psychology, 13,* 343–356.

Reid, B., and Harris, K. R. (1991). *A comparison of self-monitoring of productivity with self-monitoring of attention on LD students' on-task behavior, study behavior, and spelling achievement.* Unpublished manuscript.

Resnick, L. (1987). *Education and learning to think.* Washington, D.C.: National Academy Press.

Ryans, D. (1960). *Characteristics of teachers.* Washington, D.C.: American Council of Education.

Sawyer, R., Graham, S., and Harris, K. R. (1991). *Theoretically based effects of strategy instruction on learning disabled students' acquisition, maintenance, and generalization of composition skills and self-efficacy.* Unpublished manuscript.

Scardamalia, M., and Bereiter, C. (1985). Fostering the development of self-regulation in children's knowledge processing. In S. Chipman, J. Segal, and R. Glaser (Eds.), *Thinking and learning skills: Current research and open questions* (Vol. 2, pp. 563–577). Hillsdale, New Jersey: Erlbaum.

Scardamalia, M., and Bereiter, C. (1986). Written composition. In M. Wittrock (Ed.), *Handbook of research on teaching.* (3rd ed., pp. 778–803). New York: MacMillan.

Scheid, K. (1991). *Effective writing instruction for students with learning problems.* Columbus, Ohio: LINC Resources.

Thomas, C., Englert, C., and Gregg, S. (1987). An analysis of errors and strategies in the expository writing of learning disabled students. *Remedial and Special Education, 8,* 21–30.

Turkewitz, H. (1984). Family systems: Conceptualizing child problems within the family context. In A. Meyers and E. Craighead (Eds.), *Cognitive behavior therapy with children* (pp. 69–98). New York: Plenum Press.

Voth, T., and Graham, S. (1990). *The effects of goal setting and strategy facilitation on the expository writing performance of junior high students with learning disabilities.* Unpublished raw data.

Wallace, L., and Pear, J. (1977). Self-control techniques of famous novelists. *Journal of Applied Behavioral Analysis, 10,* 515–525.

Walmsley, S., and Walp, T. (1991). Integrating literature and composing into the language arts curriculum: Philosophy and practice. *Elementary School Journal, 90,* 251–273.

Wittrock, M., and Baker, E. (1991). *Testing and cognition.* Englewood Cliffs, New Jersey: Prentice Hall.

Wolf, D., Bixby, J., Glenn, J., and Gardner, H. (1991). To use their minds well: Investigating new forms of student assessment. In G. Grant (Ed.), *Review of Research in Education* (Vol. 17, pp. 31–74). Washington, D.C.: American Educational Research Association.

Wong, B. (1991). Three conceptual perspectives on the connections between reading and writing processes. In J. Lampart and A. McKeogh (Eds.), *Toward the practice of theory-based instruction: Current cognitive theories and their educational promise* (pp. 66–90). Hillsdale, New Jersey: Erlbaum.

Wong, B., Wong, R., and Blenkinsop, J. (1989). Cognitive and metacognitive aspects of learning disabled adolescents' composing problems. *Learning Disability Quarterly, 12,* 330–323.

Zimmerman, B., and Schunk, D. (1989). *Self-regulated learning and academic achievement: Theory, research, and practice.* New York: Springer-Verlag.

11

Children's Knowledge about Writing: The Development and Use of Evaluative Criteria

Christine B. McCormick, Beverly A. Busching, and Ellen F. Potter

The predominant themes in writing research and instruction have evolved considerably over the last few decades. Early research mirrored the traditional instructional approaches that focused on providing student writers with direct instruction in rules for good writing supplemented by models of completed "good" writing. Students' correct use of the rules and successful approximation of the models was determined by teacher evaluation, which was communicated to students primarily by teacher correction of texts. It was assumed that, through exposure to these rules, models, and teacher corrections, students would develop and make use of schemata of good writing. This instructional approach, however, proved not to be particularly effective. A few students did become good writers, but the inadequate efforts of the rest have been well documented (Beach, 1976; Emig, 1971; Shaughnessy, 1977). In particular, this approach was unable to generate methods to help average and low achieving students (Perl, 1979).

Dissatisfied with what Hillocks (1986) later called the "presentational" mode of instruction, leaders in the field at all levels of schooling proclaimed a new vision of writing instruction that moved the teacher from the role of assigner and corrector of writing to the role of coach of writing processes. Murray (1968) pointed out that meaning is not thought up and then written down afterward. The act of writing itself is an act of thought. Murray explained how college instructors could guide students through these processes of thought. At the core of this new process approach was the notion that it is not enough for inexperienced writers to be shown the qualities of a finished product; they need both instruction and guided practice in creating such a product. As more voices (Donald Graves and Lucy Calkins, for example) joined the new movement, teachers at all grade levels began to change, and researchers began to study the effects of these instructional innovations on student writing.

In his meta-analysis of methods of writing instruction, Hillocks (1984, 1986) pointed out both the advantages and the limitations of the process approach. Although emphasis on teaching the processes of creating a piece of writing did result in better writing than did the traditional "presentational" approach, a process emphasis alone was not as effective as a combination of process emphasis and explicit attention to the qualities of good writing through the use of criteria lists, group discussion, and student self-evaluation conferences. Recent observational studies of student writers in classroom contexts provide additional support for Hillocks' conclusions. These descriptions reveal the importance of teachers helping students verbalize their growing understanding of their writing processes and also their growing sense of what constitutes good writing (Atwell, 1988; Calkins, 1983; Graves, 1983; Perl & Wilson, 1986).

Although the young writers in these classrooms draw upon many sources of knowledge as they write, much current research focuses on children's writing processes. Stein (1986) expressed concern that this overemphasis on process has turned the attention of researchers away from other kinds of knowledge that are important to writers. She questioned whether poor writing results primarily from a lack of metacognitive knowledge, and proposed a re-evaluation of conceptualizations of the nature and development of writing ability in light of a more accurate description of the many types of knowledge (about writing as well as about the writing context) used during the writing process. This chapter will focus on a type of knowledge that has not received close attention from researchers, students' available knowledge about good writing, and how this knowledge is transformed into criteria in the act of evaluating actual texts. First, we will consider the role of evaluation and evaluation criteria in theoretical models of the writing process. Then, we will summarize studies that describe students as they apply personal criteria to writing. Next, we will describe the contributions of our longitudinal study of the evaluation criteria used by older elementary school children to this knowledge base. Finally, we will conclude with implications for instructional support of students' construction of usable evaluative criteria. Emphasis will be placed on the later elementary school years, because this understudied period in a writer's life provides the crucial bridge between the intuitive understanding of writing of early childhood and the more sophisticated abilities of the mature writer.

THE ROLE OF EVALUATION IN MODELS OF WRITING

The process of evaluation plays an important role in theories of writing, especially in the study of revision. As Hilgers (1984, p. 366) noted, "Neither revising nor generating is likely to occur except in response to evaluation. Evaluation, then, would seem to take precedence over all segments of the writing process except perhaps motor operations." How do current models of writing incorporate the kinds of knowledge used in the evaluation process?

Flower and Hayes and their colleagues (1981, 1984) have developed an influential model of the composing process that recognizes the role of different kinds of knowledge used in the subprocesses that writers orchestrate during writing. The act of writing is assumed to be a goal-directed thinking process, guided by the writer's own growing network of goals. In order to create text, the writer engages in four kinds of mental processes: *planning, translating* mental images into words, *reviewing* what has been written, and *monitoring* the entire process. Knowledge of topic (specific domain knowledge), knowledge of audience (readers' background, beliefs, and values), and the availability of writing plans (a generalized sense of how to produce the text) are stored in the writer's long-term memory. The specific writing task creates additional kinds of knowledge: the writer's concept of the "rhetorical problem" at hand and the writer's concept of the "text produced so far."

In order to shed light on our understanding of children's knowledge of good writing, the "reviewing" portion of this model is of special interest. The evaluative act of reviewing involves a comparison of two mental representations. Writers compare not the text itself, but the text as they read it to the set of diverse constructs that can be called the "intended text." During the reviewing process, the writer negotiates between the knowledge that resides in long-term memory ("what you know") and the knowledge that is activated by the immediate task environment ("what you use"), which includes an understanding of both the rhetorical problem at hand and the text so far. These mental representations exist in an implicit "language of thought," often intermingling relatively vague with exact constructs in a fluid manner (Flower & Hayes, 1981). When students apply criteria to a text, these multiple and often confusing representations must be "instantiated" or embodied in the specific instance and translated to the explicit language of writing. Thus, the application of criteria to an actual text is a result of stored knowledge of many kinds combined with current intentions.

Much of the process of moving between mental representations and text is automatic; some of it is available for introspection and verbalization. An important component of this process is the nature and availability of knowledge of criteria and the ability to apply this knowledge. Calkins (1986) points out the power of verbalizing criteria to make them more available to clarification and alteration and, thus, more usable for the writer. Alternatively, Graves (1984) notes that students' ability to make use of what they understand about writing can precede their ability to verbalize, and that the verbalizations of students often represent the growing edge of their learning.

The nature of the criteria used during this reviewing process also depends on the evaluative stance of the writer. As Flower, Hayes, Carey, Schriver, and Stratman (1986) have noted, initial evaluation is primarily based on the process of reading for comprehension. In reading for comprehension, the writer sets certain goals a text must meet, such as truthfulness or logical consistency, and then detects the failure of the text to meet these goals. When the writer reads to evaluate the text as a piece of writing, the writer "raises the ante" and entertains a larger, more inclusive set of constraints, such as interesting a specified audience. The stringency of the criteria used is also determined by the goals of writing.

Scardamalia and Bereiter (1986; Bereiter & Scardamalia, 1987) have developed a model of writing expertise that distinguishes between more and less mature young writers by describing the different ways they apply available knowledge to a piece of writing. They described two broad strategies of composing: knowledge telling and knowledge transforming. In knowledge telling, a strategy used more often by novice writers, what is known about a topic is presented in the paper until the supply of knowledge is exhausted. This composing strategy would likely elicit very different levels of evaluative criteria (e.g., "Have I said it all?") than the more sophisticated knowledge transforming strategy. In knowledge transforming, the writer actively reworks the text in order to meet the demands of far reaching criteria such as interest, persuasive power, appropriateness to genre, and so forth. Thus, growth in the availability and use of knowledge of evaluative criteria is a critical component in the development of a skilled writer.

In summary, the evaluation of a particular piece of writing involves the conversion of multiple kinds of knowledge into specific criteria. Generalized notions of good writing, audience, and content are available with differing degrees of specificity depending on the sophistication of the writer. A specific writing task triggers not all stored knowledge, but only the knowledge that the writer feels is appropriate and is related to the focus of his or her attention. We are interested in learning more about the development of this usable knowledge as reflected in the criteria used to evaluate writing.

In order to support students' continuing struggle to become more effective writers, teachers must know more about how students articulate and apply personal evaluative schemata. Although teachers' requirements for school writing assignments are an important influence on students, each writer constructs personal criteria that will guide his or her efforts at composing text. These criteria may be more or less appropriate, accessible, or clear. The difficult task of the teacher is to encourage students continually to clarify, refine, and enlarge their internal vision so they can develop a felt sense of "good writing" to help them make decisions as they write. First, however, teachers must understand the general nature of the criteria their students use and understand. Unfortunately, our current understanding of the development of students' personal criteria for writing is inadequate, and is unable to provide such assistance to teachers. We will now examine the few studies that have described how students apply criteria to writing.

THE DEVELOPMENT OF VERBALIZED EVALUATIVE CRITERIA OF WRITING

Research on children's verbalized evaluations of texts shows that young writers choose a variety of criteria, some of which are similar to those used by their teachers and other adults and some of which differ in important ways (Applebee, 1978; Galda, 1990; Graves, 1984; Hilgers, 1984, 1986; Newkirk, 1982). Although they vary greatly in research perspective, task, and setting, these studies concur on a general developmental trend away from the global, affectively based, idiosyncratic judgments of 5–7-year-olds toward multifaceted comparisons of actual and ideal text by an adolescent. A variety of classification systems has been designed to capture the essential features of this development.

Newkirk (1982) analyzed transcripts of writing conferences and interviews of first and second graders collected by Graves and provided examples of individual children who demonstrated a developmental progression in general approach to evaluation from *protocritical* judgments (based on reactions to elements embedded in or associated with the text, such as drawings, spelling, and handwriting, and any associated meanings or experiences, rather than to the text) to *critical* judgments. Children in the critical stage evaluate texts as autonomous entities that exist apart from their associations to them, and apply criteria such as truthfulness, elaboration, and focus, either singly or serially. Newkirk also described one second grader who was able to juggle multiple criteria.

Taking a different approach, Applebee (1978) described children's approaches to story evaluation from the perspective of readers rather than that of writers. He asked children ages 6–17 to justify why they did or did not like specific stories, and classified their responses as *unintegrated* (a global general evaluation of the story often justified by restating a salient portion of it), *categoric* (which evaluated the story as an example of a genre the child liked or disliked or in terms of a perceived characteristic of the story, for example, "boring"), *analytic* (evaluation based on a structural quality of the story that justified the child's personal response), and *generalizing* (in which the evaluation was based on the story's contribution to the child's personal understanding or growth). Applebee noted the relationship between these approaches and Piagetian stages of cognitive development. Children do not abandon their earlier modes of response as their abilities grow, but "integrate their older structures into a new and more systematic representation of experience." (p. 125) Using Applebee's categories of evaluative criteria in an investigation of the development of story responses of elementary and middle school age children, Galda (1990) found a similar general developmental trend.

In contrast to these generalized stage-based conceptualizations of response to text, Hilgers (1984, 1986) attempted to group into meaningful categories the specific criteria children used to evaluate their own and others' writing. He used interview and case study methodologies to determine the criteria children in Grades 2–6 applied when he asked them to rank several texts (their own and those written by other children) in order of preference and to justify their rankings. The most common basis for evaluation was a general affective response to the subject matter of the text, similar to Applebee's unintegrated and Newkirk's protocritical evaluation. Next most often used were criteria related to a surface feature of the text, such as neatness, length, or spelling. Criteria related to clarity of the text and criteria of craftsmanship (word choice, organization, and integration) were also salient in the children's responses.

Hilgers' investigation corroborated Newkirk's progression from the use of a single criterion to the juggling of multiple criteria in formulating an evaluation. He noted the individuality of each child's "evaluation lexicon," relating it to the particular current focus of the child's writing skill development or the salient feedback of a particular audience. Hilgers reported that his informants at times appeared to use criteria in their evaluations that they could not yet articulate, an observation that suggests the ambiguity present as students struggle to express (and researchers struggle to categorize) evaluative criteria.

What understandings about student use of evaluative criteria in the middle years of schooling can be drawn from these studies? First, some types of criteria have emerged across studies: personal affective response, surface features, text coherence, aspects of craft such as word choice, and the meaning or significance of the work. Other criteria appear idiosyncratically, perhaps reflecting individual student perspectives or researcher influence. Additionally, these studies suggest that the upper elementary school years may be a period of transition. Students move from affective to objective responses, from simple to multiple criteria, and from individual criteria to integrated evaluations. Although the category systems are descriptive to some extent, their developmental focus has resulted in a confounding of evaluative criteria with a style or an approach to evaluation that is specific to a stage or to an individual. Disparate criteria have been grouped together in an effort to capture the developmental gestalt of the stage. Additionally, small numbers of students and diverse loosely controlled contexts make it difficult to understand trends in the growth of children's constructs about good writing.

A LONGITUDINAL STUDY OF CHILDREN'S EVALUATIVE CRITERIA

Our goal was to pursue a detailed study of the constructs that older elementary students applied to the evaluation of writing, preserving the strengths of Hilgers' exploratory work, but specifying more systematically the context and child characteristics and preserving the actual content of students' criteria in a detailed nonoverlapping category system (Potter, Busching, & McCormick, 1987). In this way, relationships between variables can be examined in conjunction with qualitative analysis, and the research can be extended to other contexts and samples to provide a more complete picture of evaluative knowledge at this age.

We used two kinds of text: three or four samples of the students' own writing and four researcher-constructed texts. The constructed texts (see Table 1), attributed to a fictional peer, were written to vary on the dimensions of student interest in the topic (determined through pilot testing) and writing craftsmanship (operationally defined by the features of information, precise language, style, clarity, and story structure). Second, we used a semistructured rather than a completely naturalistic interview; interviewers were trained to provide similar nonintrusive prompts to guard against uncontrolled researcher influence. After reading each group of stories aloud (own and constructed), students were asked to designate the best, next best, third best, and last. They were then asked to give the

Table 1
Constructed Stories

	High craft	Low craft
High topic	A Terrible Snake When I was five years old, my grandma chopped off the head of a snake with a hoe. She saved my life! I was walking up to the back porch when I saw the terrible snake right in front of me. It hissed. "Help! Help!" I called. Grandma came running. When she saw the big snake, she took the hoe and chopped its head right off. I was shaking and crying because I was so scared. Grandma hugged me, and we watched the snake's long brown body wiggle on the ground. My grandma is the greatest.	Space Adventure I'm going into space. Whoom! I can go far. I went out in space on the space ship. There are lots of places to go in space, and we went very far past many stars. He was a big creature, and he was in space, too. The space ship was great. I know how to go into space. You go in the ship out in space. I saw stars and galaxies as we flew. The stars were very nice to see and interesting. I liked the stars. I saw stars on T.V. They were nice.
Low topic	Waiting while My Mother Shops When my mother takes me to the furniture store with her, I pretend that I can buy anything in the store. I look for furniture for my room. Last time I found a blue velvet chair with big fluffy pillows. "This is like sitting on a cloud," I said, as I sank into the soft chair. Then I saw a crazy lamp. The light bulb was a coconut. Two monkeys climbed up to get it. "What a crazy lamp!" Just then I heard my mom calling, "Get over here. We're going to look at tables now." I didn't want to do it, but sometimes you have to do what your mother says.	School You need books, pencils, and other supplies and other things. I am not late to school because I always get ready on time. I am always on time for school. School is nice for learning all the things. It has six grades, and then you go to another school. Children learn about what you need in life, like things you need to know in reading and in math. I am good in math, and I get good grades. I had a good paper today. My sister has good papers, too.

reasons for their rankings for only the best, next best, and last stories in turn (because of time limitations). This task was familiar because of its similarity to classroom evaluation conferences.

We segmented the stream of student responses into recognizably separate evaluative statements. Then began a long process of building a category system based on student statements, in which we established intercoder reliability of the categories to which the statements were assigned. The methods we used were consistent with the grounded theoretical approach described by Glaser and Strauss (1967).

A relatively large sample (27 fifth graders) that was representative of a defined ability range allowed us to explore differences within age groups. Achievement ranged from the first to the tenth decile on the California Test of Basic Skills language subtest. Students scoring in the upper five deciles were designated high achievers (n = 12) and those scoring in the lower five deciles were designated low achievers (n = 15). Almost half our sample was male and approximately 25% was black. The size and diversity of our sample allowed us to capture a broad sampling of criteria that are characteristic of this age.

The school attended by these students is situated at the rural edge of a medium-sized urban area in a southeastern state. All the students were taught writing for a class period each day by the same teacher, who emphasized recursive steps in the process of writing, peer and teacher responses to drafts, and discussion of the qualities of good writing. The low achievers, in addition, were part of this teacher's special language arts/reading program, based on reading and writing about student-selected children's literature, which used similar instructional approaches. The high achievers had experienced one previous year of process writing instruction; the low achievers had little previous experience with composing.

In order to provide a means for describing the schemata that students apply to writing when they make evaluations, the resulting system categorizes the student comments into five broad criteria areas; multiple criteria are specified for each area (see Table 2). The classification system is applicable at different levels of student expertise or development, allowing comparisons between selected groups of students as well as providing a relatively detailed descriptive profile of individual student responses. This system is more detailed and fine-grained than previous systems; thus, we believe it has allowed us to avoid the confounding of an individual's style of evaluation with the criteria that he or she uses. Although our category system is not based on preconceived theoretical notions, it does reflect instructional concerns and therefore should prove sensitive to teacher emphasis (e.g., children's use of specific criteria stressed by an individual teacher) and useful in suggesting points for instructional intervention.

As indicated in the summary of categories in Table 2, the five criteria areas are Text-based, Topic, Nontext Association, Process, and Surface Qualities. Each criteria area represents a different direction of the student's focus of attention. In the *Text-based* criteria, students focus on aspects of the writer's manipulation of words to achieve rhetorical and content goals. For example, these comments refer to the clearness of the text, the kind and sufficiency of information, the interest level of the text, or the language

Table 2
Categories of Student Evaluative Responses

Text-based	Topic
General	General
Repeats text	Importance
Information	Interest level
General	Other
Elaboration	
Reasons	Nontext association
Other	General
Makes sense	Personal experience
General	Nonpersonal events
Clarity	Other
Repetitiveness	
Relevance	Process
Organization	General
Other	Effort
Features to create interest	Audience reaction
General	Steps in process
Creativity	Self as writer
Emotions	Other
Humor	
Action	Surface qualities
Characterization	General
Style	Neatness
Other	Spacing
Reality	Handwriting
General	Mechanics
Credibility	Usage
Real life	Length
Other	Art work
Identification	Other
Language features	
Word choice	Not interpretable
Sentences and paragraphs	
Other	
Literary features	
Plot	
Characters	
Forms/genres	
Matches requirement	
Other	
Moral lesson	
Age appropriateness	
Other	

choices themselves. The *Topic* criteria focus solely on the subject of the composition, but not on how the topic is developed in the text. When the student evaluates the text based on aspects of his or her own life that are related to but not included in the text, these criteria are categorized as *Nontext Association.* When the students based their evaluation of events in the creation or sharing of the text, such as whether it was a first or final draft, or whether effort had been expended on it, the comments were categorized as *Process.* Finally, comments about mechanics or appearance of the written product were grouped in the criteria area of *Surface Qualities.* Complete descriptions and examples of the five criteria areas and subcategories are provided in Table 3.

In addition to classifying responses according to the categories just described, each response was analyzed for other qualities of the students' evaluations. All criteria were categorized as positive, negative, mixed, or neutral in evaluative stance. For the Text-based criteria, all statements were also classified according to whether the student appeared to be taking a reader's viewpoint or a writer's viewpoint when examining the work.

What Have We Learned about Children's Use of Evaluative Criteria?

Most students used three or more criteria areas, rather than focusing on one area, to justify their rankings. No differences in criteria used were observed as a function of gender or race. As shown in Table 4, nearly 70% of the statements children made in their evaluation of the texts were text-based. Three of the criteria areas, specifically, Surface Qualities, Nontext Association, and Process, were understandably applied more frequently to the students' own writing rather than to the constructed stories. Within the Text-based criteria area (see Table 5), the six most frequently used evaluative criteria were Features to Create Interest, Repeats Text, Identification, Makes Sense, Information, and General. The number of different text-based evaluative criteria per child ranged from two to eight.

Students also applied to the stories an array of other criteria that were used less frequently but were indicative of the range of available criteria. Students referred to the credibility or "reality match" of a story and to a variety of language and literary features. It should be noted that some categories that these students might be expected to use appeared noticeably infrequently. Surface qualities as a whole were relatively rare as the basis for evaluating even their own stories. It was also striking that few students referred to teacher judgments or teacher rules in their evaluations.

Students' use of the five criteria areas varied as a function of achievement level. Although text-based comments were of high incidence for both low

Table 3
Criteria Categories, Definitions, and Examples for the Five Criteria Areas

Text-based	Refers to characteristics, qualities, and content of the text itself (other than topic or surface features)
	General: States only general feeling, tone, or preference for the text as a whole without reference to any specific text characteristics
	That just isn't a very good story to me; it's all right but it's not my favorite one.
	Repeats text: Refers to parts of the text without reasons for the choice; repeats the text, either verbatim or in paraphrase
	Um (long pause) I like the part where it says I am not late to school because I always get up on time (uh huh) and school is nice for learning all things . . .
	Information: Focuses on the presence, sufficiency, and adequacy of the information present in the text
	It just, it tells more things about what the story is about.
	Makes sense: Refers to disruptions in the meaning of the text or whether the text is easy or difficult to understand
	I really didn't understand it cuz . . . where it says there are lots of places to go in space and we went very far past many stars. They don't tell when they seen the big creature and everything.
	Features to create interest: Refers to interest level of the text or describes qualities that are commonly assumed to create this interest
	It's just dull, . . . you don't think, The pencil's all mine! What next!
	Reality: Focuses on whether or not the text is true, believable, or a fantasy
	Cuz um it's true. And it tells the story of what happened to my dog . . .
	Identification: Refers to personal similarities (or dissimilarities) with characters, situations or events described in the text
	I'd probably do the same thing. I wouldn't stand there watching the snake's head.
	Language features: Refers to words, sentences or other linguistic features without giving the detail or reasons required for "Features to create interest" or "Makes sense" categories
	Because . . . this story didn't have . . . that much good words in it.
	Age appropriateness: Refers to whether the text or part of the text is appropriate for the author's (or the reader's) age, grade, or ability level
	It sounds like a little kid wrote it.
	Literary features: Refers to types of literature or literary features such as characters, plots, or endings without giving reasons for the choice
	It kinda took after a . . . nursery rhyme or story.
Topic	Refers to the subject or topic of the text but not to events, characters, or other specific features of the text
	General: The student states only feeling tone or preference for the topic
	'Cause I'm not crazy about space.

Table 3   (*Continued*)

	Importance: Cites the topic of the text for its importance
	A lot of people should know about it (diabetes).
	Interest level: Cites the subject of the text as interesting or exciting, or not
	Other: Cites qualities of the topic other than those specified as criteria
Nontext association	Students evaluate the text based on events and ideas from their own experiences which are suggested by or loosely related to the context of the text.
	General: Is not possible to distinguish between subcategories
	Personal experience: Refers to events/happenings in student's own life or in the life of family and friends
	'Cause I love my dog . . . I like to help my dog and he likes to help me. . . . he almost stepped on a rattlesnake. He went and jumped XXX and grabbed it . . . He live on a farm. (None of the events mentioned appear in the text.)
	Nonpersonal events: Refers to events or people that student has heard about or read about (books, TV shows, movies, historical incidents)
	(based on *James and the Giant Peach*) When he saw in the . . . but I ain't, I ain't put this in the story, but when he saw . . . the white thing come XXX like monsters and all like clouds, cloud men and stuff, they have a rainbow . . .
Process	Evaluates text based on references to processes of creating and sharing/publishing text
	General: Process-related statement too vague to be further categorized
	Effort: Refers to amount of difficulty or ease demanded by the writing task or to time required
	I just kind of threw it down so that's why I put it last.
	Audience reaction: Refers to an actual or projected audience response to the text
	I guess because the class liked it.
	Steps in process: Refers explicitly to steps in the process of creating and sharing/publishing text, such as selecting topic, writing or revising drafts, reading to an audience, and copying over
	I pretty much wrote it down the way it is but I put in two, some more drafts . . . and stuff to see if that was the best
	Self as writer: Refers to own thoughts about personal experiences, ambitions, or development as a writer
	Because I'm not a big poem writer, and when I do I'm usually proud of them.
Surface qualities	Refers to mechanics, spelling, or another aspect of the linguistic correctness or to its image on paper
	General: Doesn't give sufficient information to categorize further
	Well, I made a lot of obvious mistakes in that one.
	Neatness: Refers to the appearance of the text or to a specific part
	And it's neat and everything, to me it is.
	Spacing: Refers to how the writing is organized or placed on the page

(*continued*)

Table 3 (*Continued*)

	Handwriting: Refers to the quality of handwriting
	I can't read some of my writing
	Mechanics: Refers to spelling, punctuation, or capitalization
	And it got periods. It got quotation marks.
	Usage: Refers to correctness of word usage, form, or sentence construction
	Length: Refers to whether the text is of the correct or desired length
	And it was supposed to be a page, one page and a half a page, but I didn't write that much.
	Art work: Refers to artistic embellishments not part of text or handwriting
	I drew a picture of the little martian and I cut it out.
Not interpretable	Statement does not provide enough information to understand the category applied
	I thought so . . . For, for something that short . . . I don't know . . . I can think about it, yeah

and high achievers, high achievers used text-based comments more frequently, whereas low achievers used three presumably less mature criteria areas (Topic, Nontext Association, and Surface Qualities) more frequently than did high achievers. For example, when Teara was asked why her story about her dog was best, she replied with a personal association ("Because I used to like the dog . . . when my brother had it. And I never did want it to die and it died."). When asked if anything else made this story best, she continued to refer back to her love for this dog ("I'll never forget him . . . forget her."). High achievers were more likely to convert their caring relationships into other text-based criteria, for example, identification with a character or features to create interest, thereby integrating affective and objective responses.

Both high and low achievers devoted equal numbers of their comments

Table 4
Mean Proportion of Fifth-Grade Student
Statements in the Five Criteria Areas[a]

Criteria area	Mean
Text-based	.69
Topic	.09
Nontext association	.09
Process	.08
Surface qualities	.05

[a]Proportions were first computed for each child and then averaged across the 27 children.

Table 5
Mean Proportion of Fifth-Grade Student
Statements within Text-based Criteria[a]

Text-based criteria	Mean
General	.12
Repeats text	.20
Information	.12
Makes sense	.13
Features to create interest	.27
Identification	.15

[a]Proportions were first computed for each child and then averaged across the 27 children.

to their own stories and to the constructed stories, but there were differences in how the two groups of students applied criteria to the two types of stories. Mainly, the high achievers applied Topic criteria more frequently to their own stories, whereas low achievers were more likely to apply Topic criteria to the constructed stories. Low achievers' opinions about topic were often stated with strong feeling. (Kip's sole comment about his first ranked constructed story, *Space Adventure,* was "Because I . . . always like space. I like spaceships . . . that's all.").

Use of Positive and Negative Stance in Children's Evaluation

These data helped us shed light on another important controversy in text evaluation, the differential use of positive and negative comments. The well-documented traditional negative emphasis of teachers—from 94% to 89.4% in six studies of teachers' text comments (Daiker, 1983, 1989; Dragga, 1986; Harris, 1977; McCarthy, 1987)—has been viewed as a major barrier to the production of text (Rose, 1985). Even revision, often characterized as a search for text weaknesses, may depend on the identification of strengths in text. As Murray (1985) advises, ". . . the most successful revision comes when we identify something that works—a strong voice, a pace that moves the reader right along, a structure that clarifies a complicated subject— and build on that strength." (p. 59) The importance of positive feedback is supported by motivational literature, which indicates that excessively negative feedback may cause children to feel that they are unable to perform successfully and to manifest declines in achievement motivation and effortful task-engaged behavior (Schunk, 1990). At all stages in the process of creating text, writers must believe in their potential to meet internal and external standards.

Little is known about how students themselves use positive and negative evaluations, and how they are associated with writing processes, products, and specific criteria. Newkirk (1984) found college-age students to be much more positive than their instructors, particularly when the content was close to the student's experience. In peer response groups, students in Grades 5–12 were observed making negative as well as positive comments, even when instructed to make only positive comments (Gere & Stevens, 1985). Finally, according to our informal examination of examples in the interview studies reviewed earlier, elementary students gave positive or negative responses that corresponded to high and low rankings.

In our analysis of positive and negative stance (Busching, Potter, & Mc-Cormick, 1990), we also found that positive comments were generally associated with high rankings and negative comments with low rankings, a pattern true for both high and low achievers. Surprisingly, students were as positive about their own stories as they were about the constructed stories. Students were not particularly defensive of, or overly critical of, their own stories; there appeared to be no differences in overall response patterns by achievement level, gender, or race.

As a group, these children displayed the tendency to use some categories consistently, either positively or negatively. Qualitative analysis revealed this pattern in the behavior of individual students as well as the group. For example, when students commented on Surface Qualities (almost always in reference to their own stories), their comments tended to be negative ("I can't read some of my own writing."), perhaps reflecting the years of predominantly negative teacher comments about punctuation, spelling, and handwriting. On the other hand, Nontext Association comments (almost exclusively used by low achievers evaluating their own writing) were infrequently used for negative evaluations. Of the Text-based criteria, comments categorized as Repeats Text, Identification, and Features to Create Interest tended to be used positively.

Low achievers especially exhibited a strong tendency to repeat portions of the text that they appreciated; they apparently have difficulty verbalizing specific positive criteria, whereas their negative comments are almost always in the form of specific criteria. For example, Teara pointed out several specific weaknesses in the texts, noting that the constructed story, *Space Adventure,* didn't make sense ("He said he was a big creature and didn't put what the big creature was.") and that her own last-ranked text did not exhibit good word choice ("This story doesn't have that much good words in it."). In contrast, only one of her 10 positive text comments was specific; the other nine comments just repeated parts of the stories that she valued.

High achievers, on the other hand, were better able to specify the positive esthetic qualities of the stories, as evidenced by their relatively high proportion of positive criteria in the category Features to Create Interest. (For example, Jessie commented about *A Terrible Snake,* ". . . they saw this terrible snake right in front of 'em, you know, and it seems to make you think, Oh no, what happened? and that makes you want to read on."). Jessie made eight comments categorized as Features to Create Interest, representing a wide array of rhetorical features: lively action, suspense, emotional impact, creative details, unexpected connections, "grossness" (a positive quality), and humor. Interestingly, the students found it easier to comment on positive features that create interest in the constructed stories than in their own stories.

"Makes Sense" was the category most frequently used for negative comments by high and low achievers alike. In particular, low achievers dwelt on this category, using it for 40% of their negative comments. The use of this category primarily for criticism may reflect Grice's (1975) "Cooperativeness Principle" that, in conversation, the obvious need not be stated. Thus, students may have felt that only violations of basic characteristics of written discourse (e.g., lack of text coherence) were appropriate for comment.

When the students verbalized an author of a story (themselves or an imagined author), they, particularly low achievers, were more negative than when they discussed the story as an impersonal text. This result may reflect students' general tendency to be more critical when they see texts as human creations rather than as impersonal finished products. It may also reflect the teacher's tendency to couch praise of writing in impersonal terms ("This is a well-organized piece of writing.") and to verbalize the student as agent when offering criticism and suggestions ("You need to be more clear here.") The relatively critical nature of the low achievers' author awareness may reflect their more frequent experience with teacher criticism.

Influence of Text Characteristics on Children's Evaluative Criteria

Although it is widely recognized that writers do not use evaluative criteria directly, but use it as mediated through their intentions and their interpretation of the specific text and context at hand, little research attention has been given to the relationship of text differences to evaluation. Students' application of criteria to a particular text is influenced by their previous experience with writing and written texts, both in terms of their internalized evaluative representations and in terms of how they define the appropriate use of internalized criteria with a particular text in a particular situation. Our manipulation of craftsmanship in the constructed texts is shown in Table 1; using these features we had the opportunity to analyze the effect of relatively subtle differences in text characteristics on children's evaluative criteria (Busching, McCormick, & Potter, 1989).

Each of the four texts successfully stimulated similar levels of student interest, as indicated by roughly equivalent amounts of student talk overall. In general, students did recognize the better written stories, as indicated by story rankings.

Although all stories elicited high levels of Text-based comments, students differentiated among stories in terms of specific features of text. For example, the two high-craft stories, *A Terrible Snake* and *Waiting while My Mother Shops,* received three times as many comments in the Features to Create Interest category than did the low-craft stories. This result suggests that students recognized at least some of the specific characteristics that created the effectiveness of these stories. In addition, the students justified their rankings with positive Repeats Text comments twice as often for the two high-craft stories as for the low-craft stories. This result is consistent with the other evidence that some students appreciate the strong qualities of texts, but find it difficult to articulate criteria. The low frequency of positive comments in the categories representing clarity and sufficiency of information (Makes Sense and Information), although these high-craft stories were high in these dimensions, supports other indications in our data that students choose to note these qualities only when they are absent.

The two low-craft stories, *Space Adventure* and *School,* both received criticisms for not making sense, but twice as many comments dealt with the interruptions in *Space Adventure.* In fact, half the comments about *Space Adventure* focused on this apparently overriding problem in the story. *School* was a controversial story, differentiating between the high and low achievers in terms of both rankings and comments. Although *School* was constructed to be a dull story limited to generalized information that would be obvious for an upper elementary audience, some low achievers articulated their appreciation of the information given in the story (perhaps in a desire to communicate their positive attitude toward school); they were able to project their identification with an imagined character although the story was not in the first person ("I always . . . buy supplies on time, and I always have good papers . . .").

Each text elicited a different pattern of evaluative criteria. Most students did not attempt to apply a uniform set of criteria to each text by putting each through the same "evaluative screen;" instead they accessed from their available criteria those that applied to the dimensions of the text that were most salient to them at that time. Assessment of students' understanding of writing must consider that student comments about a single text provide a narrow sampling of a student's range of available knowledge. For example, if *School* had been the only text used in this study, it might have been concluded that low achieving students do not use clarity as an evaluative criterion.

Development of Children's Evaluative Criteria: The Second Year

As an initial follow-up in a planned longitudinal study, we interviewed 25 of the original fifth graders one year later, when they were students in the sixth grade (Potter, Busching, & McCormick, 1991). Once again, these students ranked own texts (written within 5 wk of the interview) and constructed texts (the same as in the initial study) and gave a rationale for their rankings. Interviews with the four sixth-grade teachers indicate that writing instruction this year focused on basic writing skills (e.g., clarity, word usage, mechanics, sentence structure, elaboration) as defined by the state writing essay examination. Writing was less frequent, and teacher-selected topics and essay examination prompts guided many writing assignments.

We found approximately the same total number of criteria per child across both years. In the sixth grade, however, high achievers offered more criteria than low achievers. Also, when they were discussing their own stories, older students were more likely to speak from the stance of an author. This finding suggests a growing sense of authorship for their own work, but no change in their tendency to infer an author for the work of others.

Two changes in the focus of comments by the low achievers suggest that they may have been slower in their developmental progress than their more academically successful peers, but were moving along a developmental curve believed to be characteristic of all writers (Hilgers, 1986; Newkirk, 1982). First, low achievers tended to evaluate stories less on the basis of Nontext Association in the sixth grade. In the fifth grade, these low achievers, unlike the high achievers, had frequently used the immature evaluative strategy of personal associations as criteria for evaluation, but markedly reduced their use of this strategy in the sixth grade.

Also, as shown in Table 6, low achievers made fewer Repeats Text statements in the sixth grade. We believe that Repeats Text comments, in which students express their response (typically positive) to a text by repeating portions of it without articulating specific criteria, indicate the cutting edge of the development of evaluative criteria. Students who repeat text appear to be trying to express the sense that a certain part of the text has positive qualities, but are unable to translate this appreciation into words that will explain the nature of these qualities. It appears that, by sixth grade, the students were better able to verbalize internalized criteria.

The tendency of both high and low achievers in the second year, how-

Table 6

Mean Proportion of Student Statements within Text-Based Criteria
as a Function of Grade and Achievement Level

Text-based criteria	Fifth grade		Sixth grade	
	Low achievers	High achievers	Low achievers	High achievers
General	.10	.15	.14	.26
Repeats text	.29	.08	.18	.05
Information	.15	.09	.32	.18
Makes sense	.11	.14	.23	.34
Features to create interest	.15	.46	.13	.17
Identification	.19	.09	0	0

[a]Proportions were first computed for each child and then averaged across the 12 high achievers and 12 low achievers who used these text-based criteria in both years.

ever, to make more frequent use of the Information and Makes Sense criteria categories, combined with an extreme reduction in Identification statements, might reflect increased school pressures toward a utilitarian view of writing (see Table 6). It is possible that this instructional emphasis resulted in more pedestrian student texts. Support for this possibility emerges when differences in criteria associated with type of text are examined. High achievers exhibited a sharp decline in Features to Create Interest in their own work (but only a slight decrease in the constructed stories). When they did mention these qualities in their own work, they frequently criticized their absence. In light of these trends, it is interesting to contrast the sixth-grade teachers' emphasis on basic writing with the fifth-grade writing teacher's emphasis on a wide variety of forms and purposes for writing and on classroom discussions about responses to writing. At this point one can only speculate whether trends represent developmental changes, instructionally influenced changes, or changes in the qualities of student texts. Whatever the source of the change, it can be viewed as possible progress for the low achievers, who were able to articulate at least the basic requirements of writing more completely, but as perhaps a step backward for high achievers, who had already demonstrated the ability to articulate multiple criteria (utilitarian as well as rhetorically demanding) in the previous year.

Summary of Students' Use of Evaluative Criteria

How the students evaluated the writing varied widely; the concepts used differed by student, text, and, to a smaller extent, by students' achievement level. (See Table 7 for a summary of students' use of criteria.) Our data support the general shape of the work of Hilgers (1984, 1986), Newkirk (1982), and Applebee (1978) since students mixed a personal and evaluative orientation and generally used separate specific criteria rather than integrated criteria. Some of our low achievers responded in ways similar to those of younger children in these studies, focusing on personal associations and surface features. They were, however, able to mix objective and affective responses and made considerable progress between fifth and sixth grade. Our findings differ from previous research because students dis-

Table 7
Summary of Findings by Criteria Area

Text-based
  predominant category of criteria
  linked to characteristics of specific texts
  Six most frequent text-based criteria:
    General
      trend for increased use in sixth grade
    Repeats text
      used primarily by low achievers
      tended to be positive
      decreased use in sixth grade
    Information
      increased use in sixth grade
    Makes sense
      most common type of negative criterion
      increased use in sixth grade
    Features to create interest
      in fifth grade, tended to be positive and applied to high craft constructed texts, especially by high achievers
      in sixth grade, decreased use and more negative for high achievers for own writing
    Identification
      tended to be positive
      not used in sixth grade
Topic
  used more frequently by low achievers, especially for constructed texts
  high achievers used more for own writing
Nontext association
  used primarily by low achievers for own writing
  tended to be positive
  decreased use by low achievers in sixth grade
Process
  relatively stable use in fifth and sixth grades
Surface qualities
  relatively low incidence
  tended to be negative

---

played a wider variety of criteria in their evaluations. In addition, some categories, such as surface qualities, were not mentioned frequently.

Although our data show a range of criteria that reflect a substantial portion of those that writing instructors would include in a set of criteria of good writing, many of the children worked within a very limited set of criteria. Some struggled to articulate any criteria. Some were distracted from objective evaluation by personal associations.

By looking at the responses of our high achieving students, we can provide some partial answers to the question "What should skilled older elementary evaluators be doing?". Our high achievers don't apply a "teacher's grid" (the same set of criteria to each story). They seem to generate an unstated vision for each new story, as suggested in Flower and Hayes's model; their evaluations play off that particular vision. They mix personal and objective reactions as they reach for more mature integrated evaluations. They struggle to articulate their growing sense of the artistry or craft of writing, assessing the text according to the standards of "good literature" as well as those of basic writing. In Scardamalia and Bereiter's terms, the language students use during evaluation indicates a "knowledge transforming" approach. Their comments are permeated with a growing sense of a writer at work, crafting words to create desired effects. They tie their judgments about language use and rhetorical devices to a sense of purpose. They concentrate on what strikes them about each separate story; almost always these are multiple criteria, not a single criterion. Although students are somewhat susceptible to the influence of context (teacher and text), they display a certain stability in their accumulated evaluative concepts about writing.

SUPPORTING STUDENT CONSTRUCTION OF CRITERIA: INSTRUCTIONAL IMPLICATIONS

Our findings support the use of a teaching strategy that relies on frequent conversations about writing among students as a way of helping them construct useful criteria. We believe that the potential for success of such a strategy is good, because there clearly exists among the entire class a pool of knowledge about writing that is both broad and deep. The teacher's job of helping students access this pool of knowledge requires awareness of and sensitivity to the language and purposes of students. Often, students' criteria are couched in colloquial language that is very difficult to decode in the midst of a busy classroom. Moreover, teachers and students often use different criteria, as Gere and Stevens (1985) noted; these differences are based, perhaps most importantly, on their different views of the functions of text. Teachers tend to hold a "formal semantics" view of text, in which meaning is conventionalized in the sentences of a text; a good student text is one that conforms to a prototype. Students, on the other hand, respond to a specific text; they see an opportunity to inform the author about how they interpret the text in order to help the author more effectively communicate the intended meaning to the audience.

When students make statements that repeat text or give other unintelligible hints at criteria (e.g., "It's got more stuff in it."), they are telling us that they are presently reaching for the growing edge of learning. Students need teachers to be attentive listeners to these inarticulate expressions of understanding; they need to have teacher support when moving to more articulate and mature criteria. We believe that these expressions reveal the critical edge of learning that Vygotsky (1978) called "the zone of proximal development." What a child can do with the help of others at one point is what he can do by himself soon after. Such learning can be supported by current instructional approaches that take the classroom in the direction of the "artist's studio," in which each student member is working to create products representing an individual style and meaning. Each student strives to grow in understanding of the craft of the esthetic so he or she can create these personal meanings; the community is available to support this growth.

If young writers grow through support of their personally constructed understanding of writing, questions can be raised about the use of lists of criteria, even high quality lists that attempt to capture the range of choices available to a writer. Since these middle years may represent a stage of individual criteria, followed by the next stage of integrated evaluations that embed multiple criteria, the *overuse* of criteria lists could have the effect of stunting young writers' growth, leaving them in an immature stage of evaluation.

The complexity of the process involved in moving from received knowledge to used knowledge is exemplified in Scardamalia and Bereiter's investigation of a procedure they termed "Compare, Diagnose, and Operate." These researchers (Bereiter & Scardamalia, 1987; Scardamalia & Bereiter, 1983) constructed a list of statements that included evaluative criteria and directed fourth through eighth graders to apply these criteria systematically to their writing in a sentence-by-sentence comparison procedure. Although students reported that this procedure facilitated their detailed evaluation of their writing and they did increase their revisions, ultimately the technique did not produce better writing performance. Mechanical use of adult-provided criteria without well-developed understandings apparently is not an effective shortcut to excellence in writing.

Our data support the value of instructional programs that provide frequent class time for student reflection on their own writing processes and the purposes and qualities they are striving for in their writing. Such programs, recommended by leading spokespeople for writing instruction (Atwell, 1988; Calkins, 1983; Graves, 1983; Harste, Short, & Burke, 1988), recognize that literacy is a "socio-psycholinguistic" event (Harste, Woodward, & Burke, 1984). A supportive context for student learning can be provided by a workshop time several times a week in which students work at different phases of completion of a piece and are free to consult with the teacher or other students as needed. During formal and informal conferences at different times in the process of writing, teachers can help students articulate their questions, purposes, satisfactions, and frustrations. Brief sessions (sometimes called "minilessons"), in which information about writing form and function is taught in a way that ties closely to actual work in progress, help increase the salience of essential qualities of good writing in the minds of students. Other recommended procedures that are useful in helping children share and reflect on criteria are the Writer's Circle, to which students bring a piece of writing in progress for comments by their peers that will help them make better decisions about revisions, and the Author's Chair, where completed pieces of writing are brought for real audience reaction, positive evaluative comment, and questions that reflect what the audience would like to know.

In addition, ways in which the goals and purposes of writing and any school-required evaluations are handled can assist children in the development of their criteria. For example, the goal-directed evaluations that our best students exhibited can flourish when students have authentic purposes and audiences for writing. Students should write, not to show that they can write, but to use the craft of writing for a purpose they choose: to share their ideas with significant others, to discover what they know and believe, and to accomplish something in the world. An evaluative technique called Portfolio Assessment (Tierney, Carter, & Desai, 1991) takes students a step beyond the evaluative conference. In building a portfolio, students reflect on their criteria as they make decisions about what items to include, and they defend their own assessment of the portfolio.

CONCLUSION

If writing programs are to be effective in these crucial middle childhood years, it is important for teachers and students to hold many conversations in which they articulate criteria at all times during the writing process. Since the used criteria are sensitive to the social, rhetorical, and linguistic context of a particular writing task, these conversations must range across a variety of topics, purposes, and forms of writing. Research, theory, and teacher experience are in agreement that a single prescribed set of criteria for good writing is unlikely to have much effect on student growth in writing ability. Criteria must, instead, arise from group reflection on purposeful writing tasks, as students struggle to find and articulate coherent criteria on which they base their sense of a job well done. Once verbalized, these perhaps vague and inarticulate expressions of standards can be examined, refined, and altered, as the teacher and students move together toward an ever-growing shared "felt sense" of writing quality based on accessible and clear criteria that can guide drafting and revising decisions on each new writing assignment.

REFERENCES

Applebee, A. N. (1978). *The child's concept of story: Ages two to seventeen.* Chicago: University of Chicago Press.

Atwell, N. (1988). *In the middle.* Portsmouth, New Hampshire: Heinemann.

Beach, R. (1976). Self-evaluation strategies of extensive revisers and nonrevisers. *College Composition and Communication, 27,* 160–164.

Bereiter, C., and Scardamalia, M. (1987). *The psychology of written composition.* Hillsdale, New Jersey: Erlbaum.

Busching, B. A., McCormick, C. B., and Potter, E. F. (1989). *The influence of text characteristics on elementary students' use of criteria to evaluate writing.* Paper presented at the American Educational Research Association meeting, San Francisco.

Busching, B. A., Potter, E. F., and McCormick, C. B. (1990). *"It's got humor and stuff": Positive and negative stance in elementary students' postwriting evaluations.* Paper presented at the American Educational Research Association meeting, Boston.

Calkins, L. (1983). *Lessons from a child.* Portsmouth, New Hampshire: Heinemann.

Calkins, L. (1986). *The art of teaching writing.* Portsmouth, New Hampshire: Heinemann.

Daiker, D. (1983). *The teacher's options in responding to student writing.* Paper presented at the Conference on College Composition and Communication, Washington, D.C.

Daiker, D. (1989). Learning to praise. In C. M. Anson (Ed.), *Writing and response: Theory, practice, and research* (pp. 103–113). Urbana, Illinois: National Council of Teachers of English.

Dragga, S. (1986). *Praiseworthy grading: A teacher's alternative to editing error.* Paper presented at the Conference on College Composition and Communication, New Orleans.

Emig, J. (1971). *The composition process of twelfth graders,* Urbana, Illinois: National Council of Teachers of English.

Flower, L., and Hayes, J. R. (1981). A cognitive process theory of writing. *College Composition and Communication, 32,* 365–387.

Flower, L., and Hayes, J. R. (1984). Images, plans, and prose: The representation of meaning in writing. *Written Communication, 1,* 120–160.

Flower, L., Hayes, J. R., Carey, L., Schriver, K., and Stratman, J. (1986). Detection, diagnosis, and the strategies of revision. *College Composition and Communication, 37,* 16–55.

Galda, L. (1990). A longitudinal study of the spectator stance as a function of age and genre. *Research in the Teaching of English, 24,* 261–278.

Gere, A., and Stevens, R. S. (1985). The language of writing groups: How oral response shapes revision. In S. W. Freedman (Ed.), *The acquisition of written language: Response and revision* (pp. 85–105). Norwood, New Jersey: Ablex.

Glaser, B. G., and Strauss, A. L. (1967). *The discovery of grounded theory.* Chicago: Aldine.

Graves, D. H. (1983). *Writing: Teachers and children at work.* Exeter, New Hampshire: Heinemann.

Graves, D. H. (1984). *A researcher learns to write.* Portsmouth, New Hampshire: Heinemann.

Grice, H. P. (1975). Logic and conversation. In P. Cole and J. L. Morgan (Eds.), *Syntax and semantics* (Vol. 3, pp. 41–58). New York: Academic Press.

Harris, W. H. (1977). Teacher response to student writing: A study of the response pattern of high school teachers to determine the basis for teacher judgment of student writing. *Research in the Teaching of English, 11,* 175–85.

Harste, J. C., Woodward, V. A., and Burke, C. L. (1984). *Language stories and literacy lessons.* Portsmouth, New Hampshire: Heinemann.

Harste, J. C., Short, K. G., and Burke, C. (1988). *Creating classrooms for authors: The reading–writing connection.* Portsmouth, New Hampshire: Heinemann.

Hilgers, T. H. (1984). Toward a taxonomy of beginning writers' evaluative statements on written compositions. *Written Communication, 1,* 365–384.

Hilgers, T. H. (1986). How children change as critical evaluators of writing: Four three-year case studies. *Research in the Teaching of English, 20,* 36–55.

Hillocks, G. (1984). What works in teaching composition: A meta-analysis of experimental treatment studies. *American Journal of Education, 93,* 133–170.

Hillocks, G. (1986). *Research on written composition.* Urbana, Illinois: National Council of Teachers of English.

McCarthy, L. P. (1987). A stranger in strange lands: A college student writing across the curriculum. *Research in the Teaching of English, 21,* 233–265.

Murray, D. (1968). *A writer teaches writing.* Boston: Houghton Mifflin.

Murray, D. (1985). *A writer teachers writing* (2nd ed.). Boston: Houghton Mifflin.

Newkirk, T. (1982). Young writers as critical readers. *Language Arts, 59,* 451–457.

Newkirk, T. (1984). How students read student papers. *Written Communication, 1,* 283–305.

Perl, S. (1979). The composing processes of unskilled college writers. *Research in the Teaching of English, 13,* 314–336.

Perl, S., and Wilson, N. (1986). *Through teachers' eyes: Portraits of writing teachers at work.* Portsmouth, New Hampshire: Heinemann.

Potter, E. F., Busching, B. A., and McCormick, C. B. (1987). *Criteria children use to evaluate their own and others' writing.* Paper presented at the American Educational Research Association meeting, Washington, D.C.

Potter, E. F., Busching, B. A., and McCormick, C. B. (1991). *Developmental trends in middle school students' criteria for evaluating writing.* Paper presented at the American Educational Research Association meeting, Chicago.

Rose, M. (Ed.) (1985). *When a writer can't write: Studies in writer's block and other composing-process problems.* New York: Guilford Press.

Scardamalia, M., and Bereiter, C. (1983). The development of evaluative, diagnostic, and re-medial capabilities in children's composing. In M. Martlew (Ed.), *The psychology of written language: Developmental and educational perspectives* (pp. 67–95). New York: John Wiley.

Scardamalia, M., and Bereiter, C. (1986). Writing. In R. F. Dillon and R. J. Sternberg (Eds.), *Cognition and instruction* (pp. 59–81). Orlando, Florida: Academic Press.

Schunk, D. H. (1990). Goal setting and self-efficacy during self-regulated learning. *Educational Psychologist, 25,* 71–86.

Shaughnessy, M. P. (1977). *Errors and expectations.* New York: Oxford University Press.

Stein, N. (1986). Knowledge and process in the acquisition of writing skills. *Review of Research in Education* (pp. 225–258). Washington, D.C.: American Educational Research Association.

Tierney, R. J., Carter, M. A., and Desai, L. E. (1991). *Portfolio assessment in the reading-writing classroom.* Norwood, Massachusetts: Gordon.

Vygotsky, L. S. (1978). *Mind in society.* Cambridge: Harvard University Press.

12

Variant Views about Good Thinking during Composing: Focus on Revision

Jill Fitzgerald

In this chapter, I will try to show that different positions on good thinking in composing, and specifically in revision, arise from theoretically variant views on composing and revision. First, a global view of writing (and reading) is presented as a framework within which divergent views on writing and revision can be placed. Then, three major models of composing are briefly sketched; their similarities and differences are discussed in reference to what constitutes good thinking. Next, to provide a detailed example of how variant views of writing lead to different positions on good thinking, three models of revision (each associated with one of the three major models of writing) and accompanying tenets about good thinking are explained. After a brief summary of research findings on good thinking in revision, implications for classroom teachers are given.

A GLOBAL VIEW OF WRITING AND READING

Over the last two decades, a grand scheme has emerged in my mind that shows what is involved in reading and writing and ways in which the two are interrelated. The experience of the development of the scheme might be described as gradual, shadowy, and continually more distanced. In the beginning, I felt I was up close, looking through a microscope at the features that make up reading, especially from the perspective of isolated readers. Gradually, results of investigations began to shed more and more light on ways in which readers access texts; authors of the pieces became more prominent. Taking a step back, I enlarged the scheme to include authors, primarily as contextual necessities for understanding reading. Eventually, as a fuller sense of composing took shape, it became clear that an even more distanced perspective was necessary—one in which writers and readers were not merely contexts for each other, but were interactive in ways that affected many other aspects of the grand scheme.

Although the grand scheme in my mind is fuzzy at best—it clearly lacks detail—most literacy scholars would probably accept it as a reasonable global representation of major aspects of literate events. The current version of the scheme is shown in Figure 1. There are three worlds in the universe of reading and writing—the writer's, the reader's, and the printed text. Enveloping and permeating the universe are writers' and readers' knowledge and skills; their sentiments, or feelings and emotions; and their spirit or disposition to participate in the universe. A brief description of each of these elements follows (cf. Fitzgerald, 1990, 1992):

1. *Sentiments* are the urge, the motivation, the purpose, and the reason(s) to read and write. They are the overarching driving forces of the universe.

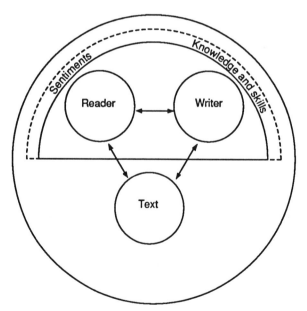

Fig. 1 Model of the universe of reading and writing. (Reprinted from Fitzgerald, 1990, p. 83, with permission.)

2. *Knowledge and skills* can be classified in four ways. First, what Hillocks (1986) called declarative knowledge is knowledge of the text attributes of both substance and form. Second is what Hillocks (1986) called procedural knowledge, that is, knowledge about how to access, use, or create content. Third is procedural skill and ability to negotiate the universe. Fourth is "metaknowledge," or knowledge about knowledge. Included in this category is knowledge of the interactive motives of the universe and knowledge that authors and readers seek each other within a system of common understandings.
3. *Text attributes* are the substantive, formal, and stylistic features of text.

MAJOR MODELS OF COMPOSING AND GOOD THINKING

Although scholars would most likely accept the grand scheme of the universe of literacy as a general depiction of reading and writing, significant differences of opinion abound with respect to which aspects of the universe are focal or most critical and, therefore, with respect to what is good thinking in composition. The differences of opinion are related to differences among three major models of composing—a stage model, a problem-solving model, and a social-interactive model. In the following sections, each of the three models will be described briefly and placed in relation to the grand scheme of the universe of reading and writing just depicted. [For a detailed explanation of epistemological similarities and differences among the models, see Fitzgerald (1992).] The qualities of good thinking projected by each model will be discussed.

A Stage Model of Writing

Before the 1980s, the stage model was a predominant model of writing. Well-known illustrations of a stage model of writing include the Prewrite/ Write/Rewrite model of Rohman (1965) and the Conception/Incubation/ Production model of Britton, Burgess, Martin, McLeod, and Rosen (1975). In such views, writing is described as a linear series of stages, separated in time. The first stage is prewriting—an idea-generation period; the second stage is actual writing, during which pen is put to paper; the third stage is rewriting—final editing and reworking of the text.

In a stage model of writing, the constructive powers of the mind are given credence; ideas are incubated, and text is created. However, because the model basically describes the growth of the written product, its focus is external to thinking; it focuses on the world of the printed text. It is a model of *composition.* In the universe of reading and writing depicted in Figure 1, the stage model focuses on the text world. Thinking processes are not really highlighted in the stage view of writing. Rather, knowing what makes a text good, that is (as described earlier for Figure 1), knowledge of universal text attributes, is most important. Further, the ways in which writers acquire the necessary knowledge to produce good compositions would be primarily through prescriptions proffered by scholars, teachers, and handbooks on "correct" forms and styles.

A Problem-Solving Model of Writing

The problem-solving view of writing, most fully depicted by Flower and Hayes (1981), focuses more on the thinking involved in composing. In fact, the development of the problem-solving model was revolutionary *because* it put the cognitive processes of composing in the spotlight. It is a model of *composing.* In the model, writing is seen as a process of solving problems, in which writers have goals and purposes and act to achieve those goals. Problems occur when there are discrepancies between desired goal states and text content.

The Flower and Hayes model is an information-processing one that describes inputs and outputs to the mind. Main components of the model are:

1. *Task environment:* the rhetorical problem (topic, audience, exigency) and the text produced so far
2. *Writer's long-term memory:* knowledge of topic, audience, and writing plans
3. *Writing processes:* planning, translating, reviewing, and monitoring

An important characteristic of the model (that distinguishes it greatly from the stage model) is that interactions among the components and subprocesses are recursive. Elements of the model do not necessarily occur one after the other; instead, one may be embedded in another or recur at various times during writing.

The Flower and Hayes model is more like a production-systems information-processing model than a constructivist one (as the two types of information-processing models are described by Cobb, 1987). First, although the model does attribute constructive powers to the mind, it has a production orientation; authors start with purposes or ideas and translate them into products (Nystrand, 1986). This view of composing is sometimes referred to as monologic because authors "will" text and "act on readers" to achieve the desired product (Nystrand, 1986, p. 26). Second, like production-system information-processing theories, the model portrays writers as working through "rule-following" behaviors that are talked about as strategies for making decisions and choices.

Although it is important to emphasize that the problem-solving model of composing refers to or takes into account virtually *all* the major elements of the universe of reading and writing shown in Figure 1, it focuses on, and particularly tries to explain, certain mental *processes* of authors. Therefore, this model is centered on the world of the writer. The major targeted knowledge is procedural knowledge and skill and ability to negotiate the universe.

Good thinking mainly entails careful implementation of logical steps in solving problems. It requires knowing one's goals, careful identification of problems (discrepancies between what is wanted and what is available from the author's perspective), precise location of problem sources, generation of alternatives to address the problem, and ability to carry out desired operations.

Finally, a strong inference of the model (and one borne out in research on writing from the problem-solving perspective) is that writers would largely acquire the knowledge central to thinking during composing through explicit instruction by expert others or through some type of explicit facilitation of the process directed by expert others (for example, procedural facilitation, which is explained in subsequent text). Because the cognitive processes are spotlighted, it seems possible that the processes could be taught, to some degree, out of the context of the other elements in the model.

A Social-Interactive Model of Writing

Nystrand's (1986, 1989) social-interactive model of writing is the most fully developed representation of the social-interactive view. The work of Graves (e.g., Graves, 1978, 1983), Odell and Goswami (1982), and Rommetveit (1974) might be considered among the forerunners of his articulation. Also, work on social constructionism by Bartholomae (1985), Bizzel (1982), and Bruffee (1986) is highly related to the social-interactive model, although Nystrand (1990) notes distinctions between social constructionism and his own views.

In the social-interactive model, writing is ". . . a fiduciary act for both writers and readers in which they continuously seek to orient themselves to a projected state of convergence between them" (Nystrand, 1989, p. 75). Writing is likened to a series of moves and states in a game (cf. Fillmore, 1985) in which writers do three things. (1) They *initiate written discourse.* That is, they try to fashion the beginning of a text so it sets up a mutual frame of reference between writer and reader, or what Nystrand (1989) calls a shared social reality. (2) Writers *sustain written discourse.* While writing, new information is tested for reciprocity, so when reciprocity is threatened and "trouble sources" occur, "choice points" for text changes are precipitated. (3) Writers *employ options or elaborations* to clarify the communication.

Whereas the social-interactive model focuses on mental and constructive aspects of composing, it also portrays the process and product of composing as an interaction of minds. Whereas the stage model de-emphasizes the mind and the problem-solving model focuses on the individual mind of the author, the social-interactive model focuses on the interaction of minds. Composing happens as a social construct whereas, in the problem-solving model, composing happens in a social context (cf. Bruffee, 1986, p. 184, on a similar point with regard to social constructionist and cognitive work in composition). In the universe of reading and writing, as depicted in Figure 1, this model focuses on the threads (represented in the arrow) that link readers to writers and, to some extent, on the threads that link readers and writers to texts. Far more than the two other models, the social-interactive one reflects concern for readers' and writers' sentiments and their metaknowledge.

In the social-interactive model of writing, good thinking entails the ability to see into the hypothetical or real reader's mind. It requires the ability to think from the reader's perspective, to perceive potential trouble sources, and to think as the reader would think.

Finally, a strong inference embedded in the social-interactive model is that writers acquire the necessary good thinking in social contexts, that is, in the context of communities of writers and readers. Further, inherent in the model is the belief that the elements of writing are best learned in the social contexts of natural acts of writing. Cognitions and procedural skills are subordinate to, and grow out of, practice in social settings. In classrooms, the background and knowledge of individual writers should be given preeminence, discovery should be emphasized, and interaction with peers and adults is necessary.

MAJOR MODELS OF REVISION AND GOOD THINKING

To illustrate in more detail how variant views of writing lead to different positions on good thinking, I will now narrow the discussion to one aspect of writing—revision. In this section, three models of revision, each associated with one of the three models of writing just presented, will be described and the accompanying beliefs about good thinking explained.

Revision as Final-Stage Editing

Historically, practitioners and theoreticians have believed that revision is an important part of writing (Hodges, 1982; Lyman, 1929; Tressler, 1912).

Until fairly recently, revision has been conceived as word- and sentence-level polishing, that is, error correction or editing. The view of revision as final-stage editing is linked to the linear stage model of writing.

As in the stage model of writing, in the revision-as-final-stage-editing view there is little focus on the thinking involved in revision. Instead, the spotlight is on the marks on the written page, the world of the text in Figure 1, and on revision as change or product. Good thinking in revision in the final-stage-editing view requires knowledge of good text features in order to make needed changes on the paper to improve the quality of the draft.

The reviser acquires knowledge about needed revisions mainly by reading handbooks on good writing or listening to teachers' remarks. Practice in editing also helps develop the needed knowledge. The peer-editing group that was somewhat popular in the 1970s is an example of an effort to develop the knowledge needed for revision.

Revision as Problem Solving

The problem-solving model of writing that emerged during the 1970s and 1980s affected a shift in conceptions of revision. If subprocesses could be embedded in one another, then revision could occur at any time during composing—before, during, or after pen met paper. Also, if revision could be embedded in other subprocesses of writing (e.g., planning), then it could consist of more than editing. The notion of recursiveness in the problem-solving model of writing paved the way for thinking about revision as a way of reseeing, rethinking, and changing the substance of the text. Finally, the focus on mental processes in the problem-solving model led to more interest in the *process* of revision, especially in the mental cognitions involved in revision.

Although there has not always been a consensus about whether actual changes to written texts (that is, the products or the marks on the texts themselves) ought to be included in models of the mental process of revision (cf. Scardamalia & Bereiter, 1983) or about the kinds of evaluations that are part of revision (cf. Hayes, Flower, Schriver, Stratman, & Carey, 1987), a new view of revision evolved (cf. Beach, 1984; Bridwell, 1980; Flower & Hayes, 1981; Flower, Hayes, Carey, Schriver, & Stratman, 1986; Hayes & Flower, 1980a,b, 1983; Scardamalia & Bereiter, 1983). In the problem-solving view of revision

1. Writers identify discrepancies between what they want and what is instantiated in the text. They establish goals and monitor their texts for consistency with the goals.
2. Writers diagnose. When problems are located, revisers make decisions about needed changes and about alternative ways of addressing the changes.
3. Writers carry out the actual changes. (cf. Fitzgerald, 1987, 1992)

The model focuses on the world of the writer (cf. Figure 1) and, specifically, on the mind of the writer. The rule-following aspects of revision are central. The emphasis is on cognitions; the applicable knowledge a reviser needs is procedural. Good thinking entails some knowledge of textual attributes and some knowledge of what readers expect in and from texts. More pointedly, however, the model spotlights the routine of thinking involved in solving problems. Good thinking in revision is monitoring texts and identifying problems (differences between an initial state and a goal state, cf. Carter, 1988, p. 552), determining where problems are located and how to solve them; and maneuvering the text to finally resolve problems.

Revision is a routine. It is a process of solving problems that can be described in a generic, universal way, complete with subelements or steps. Consequently, the good thinking involved in revision can be taught through some form of instruction from others. Further, the elements can be isolated to some extent, so instruction can be componential.

An example of such instruction in good thinking is explicit instruction in the revision routine. A brief account follows of explicit instruction in revision used in a recent study (Fitzgerald & Markham, 1987). Fifteen sixth graders participated in four 3-day cycles of 45-min lessons and a thirteenth summary lesson, all conducted over a period of 1 month. Each of the four cycles focused on one kind of revision: addition, deletion, substitution, or rearrangement. [Faigley and Witte's (1981, 1984) definitions were used for each kind of revision.] On Day 1 of each cycle, a review and overview were done using charts. For example, the teacher pointed to a chart describing aspects of the revision process and, on Day 1 of Cycle 1, she also used charts to define and talk about additions. Next, the teacher modeled the problem-solving thinking process of revision by voicing her thoughts aloud and pointing to a chart describing the problem-solving process, while making revisions on a transparency. Finally, she helped the group of students revise an example. On Day 2, there was again a review and overview. Then, in pairs, the students practiced revising part of a text by using a handout that led them through the problem-solving process of revision. Finally, they wrote a story. On Day 3, review and overview were repeated. Next, the children individually revised a section of a story supplied by the teacher. Finally, they were given a chance to revise the story they had written the day before.

Revision as Social-Interactive Process

Nystrand's recent articulation of writing as social interaction implies a model of revision:

> The author continuously monitors her text . . . sensing, as best she can, the
> 'moves and states,' as Fillmore puts it, that her text will make in the here-and-

now of the reader's encounter, that is, in the *context of eventual use* (see Nystrand, 1983). And she treats as a *trouble source* each point in her text where she suspects her convergence with her readers may fail. These potential trouble sources for readers define *choice* points for her, for it is at these points that she must fashion elaborations that will restore balance between herself and her readers . . . When writers fail to elaborate trouble sources, the results are *misconstraints,* that is, mismatches between the writer's expression and her reader's comprehension . . . a misconstraint results only when there is a mismatch between what the writer has to say and what the reader needs to know. (Nystrand, 1989, pp. 78–80; cf. Nystrand & Brandt, 1989)

The implied model is:

1. Writers monitor their texts and find potential trouble sources, that is potential threats to reciprocity with readers.
2. Writers make choices about how to address trouble sources.
3. Writers make needed elaborations.

The social-interactive model of revision is similar to the problem-solving one because it does address problems and problem solving. Trouble sources are problems, making choices is decision making, and elaborating is operating or making changes in the text itself. There is, however, an important difference in perspectives between the two models that revolves around which part of the universe of reading and writing is highlighted. In the social-interactive model, revision occurs in response to potential disruption of links between readers and writers, shown in Figure 1 in the arrow between readers' and writers' worlds. The "other" is always fully in view.

Further, goals or purposes and solutions are seen differently (cf. Carter, 1988). All goals can be traced in one way or another to the grand purpose of achieving shared reality with readers. The definition of "problem" is, therefore, different from that in the problem-solving model. In this model, a "problem" is an incongruity between reader and writer. Also, actual solutions, that is, the revision marks on the paper themselves, are not fixed in an absolute sense. They are tentative text *hypotheses* proffered by the author (Nystrand, 1986).

Whereas good thinking in the problem-solving model of revision was more restricted to the writer's world and, specifically, to the writer's mind, good thinking in the social-interactive model of revision requires reaching out to the reader on the part of the writer, and vice versa. Targeted knowledge is the "howness of mind meeting," the feeling and sensing of others' expectations and needs (metaknowledge and sentiments, as described earlier in relation to Figure 1). As in the problem-solving model, good thinking in the social-interactive model of revision entails making decisions about how to address potential problems, as well as making changes in the text.

However, good decisions and changes are contingent on careful sensing and intuiting of the reader's reaction.

The good thinking involved in revision is most likely to be acquired in situations in which revisers learn about the needs and expectations of their readers. Good thinking is likely to arise from the interactions of minds of readers and writers. Thus, practicing writing and revising in communities of readers and writers is optimal (cf. Bruffee, 1984, on knowledge as socially constructed artifact and on collaborative learning).

Also, because knowledge about needed revision arises from the interaction of minds, good thinking in revision tends to be situation dependent. To some extent, good thinking in one situation may be different from good thinking in another.

Finally, from the social-interactive perspective, the various elements of good thinking work in concert. Good thinking is likely to be best acquired in situations that attend to writing and revision from a holistic perspective, rather than in ones that isolate and teach components.

Teachers who hold the social-interactive perspective of revision are likely to set up classrooms in which students write and revise regularly, and in which settings such as peer consultation and teacher or peer conferences provide continual interactions among readers and writers. An example of an instructional setting consistent with the social-interactive model of revision is given in the following situation used in a recent study of first-grade writing conferences (Fitzgerald & Stamm, 1990). Eight first graders met with their classroom teacher once every other week starting in February and continuing through the end of the school year. The conferences involved both teacher and student participation. In each conference, the children took turns reading their work aloud. After each author read his or her piece aloud, the teacher asked three questions: What was the piece about? What did you like about it? and What comments, questions, or suggestions do you have for the author? Children were encouraged to discuss anything except spelling and punctuation.

Summary: The Compatibility
of the Three Models

The three models of revision are not necessarily incompatible. Rather, each model of revision targets somewhat different locations in the universe of reading and writing shown in Figure 1. The revision-as-final-stage-editing model focuses on the text itself, the problem-solving model on the world of the writer, and the social-interactive model on the links between readers and writers.

The revision-as-final-stage-editing model zeroes in on knowledge that writers need about universal text attributes. The problem-solving model spotlights the kind of thinking related to procedural knowledge and skill and ability to solve problems. The social-interactive model focuses more on the thinking that goes on between and among readers' and writers' minds, especially targeting sentiments and metaknowledge.

RESEARCH FINDINGS ON GOOD THINKING IN REVISION

Central findings relevant to good thinking in revision will be summarized briefly in this section. Table 1 shows an outline of the major concepts. [For a detailed review of revision research, see Fitzgerald (1987).] Findings more closely linked to the problem-solving view of revision will be presented first; those more closely tied to the social-interactive view follow. (Since

Table 1
Summary of Two Research Perspectives and Findings Relevant to Good Thinking in Revision

	Revision as problem solving	Revision as social interaction
Focus	Components of the problem-solving process and revisers' internal cognitions	Revision development in classrooms
Main methods	Process tracing	Case study, observation, interview
	Explicit instruction; procedural support	Conferences
Findings	Revisers use a goal-directed process	Revision development moves from representations of ideas without attention to readers to more careful consideration of readers' needs
	Experts' revision happens iteratively using a collection of processes	Revision thinking cannot be separated from the social contexts of writing
	Explicit instruction can enhance ability to use a problem-solving revision process; amount of revision; amount of substantive revision; and quality of compositions	Conferences can positively affect knowledge about revision and revision activity; and quality of compositions
	Procedural support can enhance writers' evaluations of their work; problem identification; higher-level revisions; and quality of revisions and of text	Effectiveness of conferences may be mediated by characteristics of the conferences or participants

the *process* of revision is not highlighted in the revision-as-final-stage-editing model, there is no research that examines good thinking associated with it.)

Revisers' Internal Cognitions

Research on revision as problem solving has tended to focus on the components of the problem-solving process and on the internal cognitions of revisers. Such investigations have tried to specify writers' goals, decisions, and the procedures they use as they revise.

One of the main methods used in research on revision as problem solving is a process-tracing method in which think-aloud protocols are procured from writers as they compose. As described by Hayes and Flower (1980b), typically, subjects are assigned a topic and asked to write an essay and to think aloud while writing. A tape recording of the whole session is then transcribed. The transcription is called a protocol. An elaborate system is used to analyze the protocols (cf. Perl, 1979).

One finding from studies on revisers' internal cognitions is that revisers use a goal-directed process that can take precedence over and interrupt other writing processes at any time (Hayes & Flower, 1980a,b; Perl, 1979). Some other tentative conclusions may be drawn about the good revision thinking of expert writers. (The conclusions should be interpreted cautiously because they are based on a small number of studies spanning a wide range of individuals from competent twelfth-grade writers to professional authors.) Experts' revision happens as "a collection of . . . processes that must be approached iteratively in successive passes" (Hayes *et al.,* 1987; Monohan, 1984). Their cognitions can be described aptly by the problem-solving model of revision. First, they tend to consider the gist of the text and the readers' needs (cf. Berkenkotter & Murray, 1983; Hayes *et al.,* 1987). Sometimes they have intricate style goals (Berkenkotter & Murray, 1983; Graves *et al.,* 1988) and evaluate their own thinking plans considerably (Berkenkotter & Murray, 1983). Second, they detect problems, especially ones above the sentence level, and represent the problems in rich ways (Hayes *et al.,* 1987). Third, experts use a wide array of diagnostic strategies—comparing texts with authors' intentions, comparing text to universal rules for grammar or spelling, and using maxim-based guidelines, such as "use parallel structure" or "avoid wordy prose" (Hayes *et al.,* 1987; Hull, 1987). Fourth, experts tend to have a large repertoire of strategies for addressing problems (Hayes *et al.,* 1987).

Associated work on ways to enhance cognitions involved in revision in classrooms has primarily used directive means, such as explicit instruction and procedural support. Feedback from "distanced" teachers or peers and telling students to revise are other directive means that have been used to enhance revision. For the most part, however, the targeted outcomes of the studies have focused on products of revision, rather than on the thinking involved in revision. The number of such studies is relatively small.

Regarding explicit instruction in the cognitive process of revision, the numbers of subjects in studies have been relatively small. Subjects have included sixth graders and learning disabled students from fifth through twelfth grade. Students have been explicitly taught the compare-diagnose-operate problem-solving way of thinking of revision (Fitzgerald & Markham, 1987), a six-step revision strategy (Graham & MacArthur, 1988), a strategy for monitoring mechanical errors (Schumaker *et al.,* 1982), and a peer-editing strategy (MacArthur & Stoddard, 1990).

To give a fuller sense of the studies' explicit instruction, here is a summary of the instruction in one study. Graham and MacArthur (1988) instructed three students with learning disabilities, age 10 and 11, using a seven-element procedure. In element 1, the students were taught the components of a good essay using charts and explanation. They then practiced identifying the parts in essays. Next, they practiced memorizing the parts. Finally, the students were asked to name the essay parts from memory and to identify each part in a test essay. In element 2, the teacher and each student met to review the student's baseline revision performance. They talked about the goal of training (to make more and better revisions and write better essays) and its importance. Each student also wrote a goal indicating commitment to learn a way to revise. In element 3, a six-step strategy for revising essays was introduced using a chart and explanation. The steps were (1) reading the essay; (2) locating a specific sentence that told what the student believed; (3) adding two reasons for the belief; (4) scanning each sentence; (5) making changes on the computer; and (6) rereading and making final changes. In element 4, the teacher modeled the six-step revision strategy, using a chart to point out each step as it was done. The teacher also modeled four kinds of self-instruction as she revised, for example, defining the problem (What is it I have to do?) In element 5, students practiced memorizing the six-step revision strategy. In element 6, students practiced using the strategy while revising a previously written story (at a word processor). Practice was repeated until each student was able to use the strategy proficiently. In element 7, activities were done to promote generalization and maintenance of the strategy. For example, students were asked to share what they were learning with their resource room teacher and parents.

Results of explicit instruction in the cognitive process of revision have been quite positive. The various explicit instruction procedures have enhanced ability to identify problems, knowledge of how to make changes, and ability to carry out desired changes (Fitzgerald & Markham, 1987). Further, they have increased the amount of revision (Fitzgerald & Markham,

1987; Graham & MacArthur, 1988; MacArthur & Stoddard, 1990; Schumaker *et al.,* 1982) and the amount of substantive (as opposed to surface) revision (Graham & MacArthur, 1988; MacArthur & Stoddard, 1990). Also, quality of compositions has sometimes been enhanced as a result of the explicit instruction (Fitzgerald & Markham, 1987; Graham & MacArthur, 1988; Mac-Arthur & Stoddard, 1990).

Procedural support, such as procedural facilitation and student self-assessment, has also produced positive outcomes. An example of procedural facilitation is Scardamalia and Bereiter's (1983, 1985) "card selection" technique, designed to help writers think of revision as a problem-solving process in which authors compare intentions and goals to actual text, diagnose the problem by specifying it, and operate on the text to solve the problem. Writers were required to implement the compare/diagnose/operate process, but the process was simplified. Writers were shown sets of standard evaluative and diagnostic statements (for example, "People won't see why this is important," "I think this could be said more clearly," and "I'd better say more"). Students wrote and were stopped occasionally, shown a set of cards, asked to select cards that reflected evaluations, diagnoses, and tactics, and then asked to carry out any desired revisions. An example of self-assessment used as procedural support is Beach and Eaton's (1984) Guided Self-Assessing Form. Students were asked to reread their drafts, answer questions in writing (for example, What is your goal in this paper? and, for each paragraph, List the questions or problems someone else might have when reading it), and then think about how they might improve their drafts.

Procedural support has affected revisers' thinking in at least two ways. (1) It has helped elementary-grade children make appropriate evaluations of their work (compared with professionals' evaluations) (Scardamalia & Bereiter, 1983, 1985). (2) It has helped college freshmen to better judge problems (Beach & Eaton, 1984). However, student self-assessment has not affected college freshmen's ability to describe revision strategies (Beach & Eaton, 1984). Procedural support has also led to higher-level revisions than normal by elementary-grade children (Scardamalia & Bereiter, 1983, 1985) and enhanced quality of children's texts, as well as quality of individual revisions (Cohen & Scardamalia, 1983).

Revisers' Thinking as They Work in Communities of Readers and Writers

Far fewer studies have been done on revision as social interaction. This section is divided into two parts. First, major findings related to good thinking in revision are presented from studies that focused on describing the development of young beginning writers' thinking about revision as they write in classroom settings. Second, major results are given from investigations that centered more exclusively on influences of group or peer interaction (primarily in conferences) on revision.

In a sense, the studies on the development of revision in classrooms represent a transition between the studies of revision as problem solving and those of revision as social interaction, sometimes combining elements of the two views (as the following example shows). At the very least, these studies seem to have been forerunners of the second group of studies described next. They did not regularly specifically describe the social interactions among writers and readers. They often focused on single cases, but were carried out in the context of looking at writers' development in communities of writers, always with the assumption that writers and readers in communities influence each other. As such, these studies clearly are more aligned with views of revision as social interaction than are the others discussed so far.

The investigations aimed at describing revision development in classrooms primarily have used case study, observation, and interview procedures (e.g., Calkins, 1979, 1980a,b; Graves, 1979). The research methods and designs used in the studies tended to differ from those used by investigators who are more aligned with a view of revision as problem solving. An example of one of these studies is Calkins (1980b). For a year, Calkins (1980b) daily observed four third graders while they wrote. While she observed, the children were encouraged to think aloud, but the procedure and analysis of the data were not carried out using the same formal systems that investigators used for think-aloud protocols in revision as problem-solving studies. Calkins, using a self-devised system, took notes about student comments and behaviors during writing and revision. Sometimes she interviewed the children about their writing and revision (e.g., "Why'd you make this change?"). Calkins also observed other children throughout the year, but not as often. In her report, Calkins (1980b) delineates a simulated rewriting exercise in which the children were given a paragraph about a classroom experience and were prompted with questions to elicit further information that might be incorporated in the paragraph if the children chose to do so. The simulated rewriting exercise has not been widely used in other studies focusing on revision as social interaction, and today might even be termed "artificial" by some investigators that hold social-interactionist beliefs. Results of the studies were reported primarily through delineation of the investigators' inferences and conclusions from the data and analyses, supported by anecdotes and examples using the children's own words and writing.

A pattern of development can be inferred from the relatively small number of studies. The development appears to involve movement from representations of ideas and thoughts in print without attention to the needs of readers to more careful consideration of readers' expectations (cf. Calkins, 1979, 1980a,b; Graves, 1979). For example, Calkins (1980b, p. 333) has described early revision as random drafting, during which authors

> write successive drafts without looking back to earlier drafts. Because they do not reread and reconsider what they have written, there is no comparison or weighing of options. Changes between drafts seem arbitrary. Rewriting appears to be a random, undirected process of continually moving on.

She has characterized later revisers as interactive.

> Revision results from interaction between writer and draft, between writer and internalized audience, between writer and evolving subject. Children reread to see what they have said and to discover what they want to say. There is a constant vying between intended meaning and discovered meaning, between the forward motion of making and backward motion of assessing. (Calkins, 1980b, p. 334)

Most importantly, investigators who have studied the development of revision in classroom writing communities suggest that the thinking cannot be described solely as internal cognition because the cognitions cannot be separated from their contexts (cf. Graves, 1979). In classrooms, for example, the presence of teachers and peers impinges on, and is part of, the revision thinking process.

Associated studies on revision enhancement in the classroom mainly have addressed ways in which revision might be influenced through conferences. Again the number of studies is limited.

The procedures used in studies of conferences have varied considerably. Some are studies of individual conferences with a teacher (e.g., Walker & Elias, 1987); some are of group conferences without a teacher present (Nystrand & Brandt, 1989). Most researchers (e.g., Gere & Stevens, 1985) have transcribed tape-recorded conferences and then coded the transcriptions for information such as who talked and what was the content of the information. Others have included additional procedures. For example, procedural details of the Fitzgerald and Stamm (1990) study (mentioned in an earlier section) follow. In February, two groups of eight children each began conferences and met every other week through the end of the school year. Three baseline data collection points (done before conferences started) and seven conference data collection points were done. Several things happened at each conference data collection point. (1) Children wrote (using blue pens). (2) One or two days later, conference groups met (for about an hour) and discussed at least four of the papers. (3) One or two days later, each child was interviewed about changes he or she might make in the paper (e.g., "Is there anything that could or should be changed in your story?" "Why do you want to make that change?"). (4) The next day, students received their original papers and could make desired changes on the original papers (using black pen). They also received clean paper to make new drafts if they wished (using black pen). (Using different colored pens allowed study of revision at different stages of writing.) At baseline points, the same events occurred except that no conferences happened. All conferences and interviews were taped and transcribed.

As in other studies of conferences, the transcriptions of conference talk were coded. Percentages of statements that fell into each category were then calculated (e.g., percentage of all statements that identified problems in the piece; percentage of all statements that addressed how to correct a problem). Additionally, a system was worked out to determine the extent to which conference suggestions and problems identified in interviews were carried out. Further, quantitative variables were formed for students' knowledge of revision, revision activity, and quality of writing. These quantitative variables were used in graphs for each student, showing development over time from baseline to the end of the year.

Tentatively, from the aggregated reports, it appears that conferences that involved interactions of writers and readers, either in groups or one-on-one, with teachers or peers (with first graders, and with fifth graders through college students), can have positive effects on knowledge about revision and revision activity (Benson, 1979; Fitzgerald & Stamm, 1989; Gere & Stevens, 1985; Karegianes, Pascarella, & Pflaum, 1980; Nystrand, 1986, 1990; Nystrand & Brandt, 1989; Walker & Elias, 1987). Further, in some instances, quality of writing was enhanced (Benson, 1979; Karegianes *et al.,* 1980; Nystrand & Brandt, 1989).

There is some evidence that conference effectiveness may be mediated by characteristics of either the conference itself or of the participants. For example, in one case, conferences judged more successful by college students were ones that focused on principles of good writing (Walker & Elias, 1987). In another study; conferences were more influential for first graders who initially had low levels of knowledge about revision (Fitzgerald & Stamm, 1990).

CLOSING STATEMENTS

In summary, good thinking in writing and revision is described differently in various models. However, the models and perspectives on good thinking need not be considered incompatible. Rather, when viewed within the framework of the universe of reading and writing shown in Figure 1, each perspective seems to target different, but important, terrains in the universe. Consequently, each of the kinds of good thinking targeted in the variant models of writing is probably necessary to good writing. Also, limited research supports the kinds of thinking implied in both the problem-solving and the social-interactive models.

The good thinking implied in the model of revision-as-final-stage-editing is product-oriented and targets the world of the text in Figure 1. A writer thinks well if he or she has knowledge of universal text attributes that make good compositions. The good thinking implied in the problem-solving model of revision targets the world of the writer in Figure 1. It is primarily cognitive and internally focused. A writer thinks well if he or she sets goals, detects problems, considers alternatives for fix-ups, and carefully executes the changes. The good thinking implied in the social-interactive model of revision highlights the link between readers' and writers' worlds, represented by an arrow in Figure 1. This good thinking is more focused on sustaining reciprocity with readers and is more externally directed than the thinking involved in the problem-solving model. A writer thinks well if he or she senses threats to sustained reciprocity with readers and then considers alternatives for changes and elaborates on them.

By taking a distanced view of the universe of reading and writing, and of the research conducted on variant aspects of the universe, points made in Chapter 3 by Pressley, Beard, and Brown about reading comprehension are echoed here with regard to writing. At its best, writing is an exceptionally complex activity, particularly since good writing does not occur without regard to readers. Most individuals would agree, and research tends to support the view, that the complexity of the act, or the entirety of the universe, should be attended to in the classroom.

However, exactly what good writing instruction should consist of is not, to date, clear—largely because the variant models of writing, each of which has accrued some research support, are associated with different perspectives on how writing should be taught. One perspective suggests that writers need to learn about the qualities that make good texts by listening to teachers and by reading handbooks. Another adheres to the view that the necessary cognitions and strategies can be learned best through methods such as explicit instruction. Yet another disavows explicit instruction, purporting that the necessary cognitive knowledge and strategies can be garnered best through social interactions with readers in real writing settings. Further, research tends to support aspects of each of the positions on instruction.

It seems most likely that each of the various instructional scenarios does, in fact, develop some of the attendant knowledge, skills, and motivations in the universe of reading and writing. Further, if the whole universe of reading and writing is addressed in classrooms, then a kind of amalgam of instructional approaches might be easily envisioned. One approach might be best for developing certain kinds of knowledge about writing, whereas another might be best for enhancing development of other knowledge. Motivations might be piqued by one instructional arrangement; selected procedural ability might be acquired best using another arrangement.

Although a combination of scenarios can be hypothetically envisioned, we have little data to help us construct such combinations. How do various instructional approaches distinguish themselves with regard to outcomes? What is learned through explicit instruction that is not learned through instruction devised around social interaction and vice versa? What do writers learn when taught in isolation that they do not learn when they interact in groups and vice versa? When outcomes from variant instructional approaches are identical, which approaches are more efficient?

In short, we are only just beginning to probe the effects of various forms of instruction in writing and revision. More importantly, we know virtually nothing about the benefits and disadvantages of selected forms of instruction when the forms are compared with one another. Large-scale research is needed to examine interrelationships between or among two or more of the worlds in the universe of reading and writing, that is, to simultaneously consider various models of writing and revision. Similar research on so-called competing instructional methods would help us learn about the compatibility of the methods and how they might be arranged in classrooms to result in students' best writing and revision.

Significantly, if various sectors of the universe of reading and writing (as portrayed in Figure 1) and their interrelationships are investigated, combining methods in studies will likely need to be considered. To study the cognitive processes of writing and revision in relation to social considerations, such an anticipating readers' effects on authors' revisions, for example, will likely require a special sort of blending of "ways of looking" or perhaps a new way of looking not yet conceived.

REFERENCES

Bartholomae, D. (1985). Inventing the university. In M. Rose (Ed.), *When a writer can't write* (pp. 134–165). New York: Guilford.

Beach, R. (1984). *The effect of reading ability on seventh graders' narrative writing.* Paper presented at the annual meeting of the American Educational Research Association, New Orleans.

Beach, R., and Eaton, S. (1984). Factors influencing self-assessing and revising by college freshmen. In R. Beach and L. Bridwell (Eds.), *New directions in composition research* (pp. 149–170). New York: Guilford.

Benson, N. L. (1979). The effects of peer feedback during the writing process on writing performance, revision behavior, and attitude toward writing. *Dissertation Abstracts, 40*(04), 1987A.

Berkenkotter, C., and Murray, D. (1983). Decisions and revisions: The planning strategies of a publishing writer, and responses of a laboratory rat—or being protocoled. *College Composition and Communication, 34,* 156–172.

Bizzel, P. (1982). Cognition, convention, and certainty: What we need to know about writing. *PRE/TEXT, 3,* 213–243.

Bridwell, L. (1980). Revising strategies in twelfth grade students' transactional writing. *Research in the Teaching of English, 14,* 197–222.

Britton, J., Burgess, T., Martin, M., McLeod, A., and Rosen, H. (1975). *The development of writing abilities: 11–18.* London: MacMillan.

Bruffee, K. (1984). Collaborative learning and the "conversation of mankind." *College English, 34,* 634–643.

Bruffee, K. A. (1986). Social construction, language, and the authority of knowledge: A bibliographical essay. *College English, 48,* 773–790.

Calkins, L. M. (1979). Andrea learns to make writing hard. *Language Arts, 56,* 569–576.

Calkins, L. M. (1980a). The craft of writing. *Teacher, 98,* 41–44.

Calkins, L. M. (1980b). Notes and comments: Children's rewriting strategies. *Research in the Teaching of English, 14,* 331–341.

Carter, M. (1988). Problem solving reconsidered: A pluralistic theory of problems. *College English, 50,* 551–565.

Cobb, P. (1987). Information-processing psychology and mathematics education—A constructivist perspective. *Journal of Mathematical Behavior, 6,* 3–40.

Cohen, E., and Scardamalia, M. (1983). *The effects of instructional intervention in the revision of essays by grade six children.* Paper presented at the annual meeting of the American Educational Research Association, Montreal.

Faigley, L., and Witte, S. (1981). Analyzing revision. *College Composition and Communication, 32,* 400–414.

Faigley, L., and Witte, S. (1984). Measuring the effects of revisions on text structure. In R. Beach and L. Bridwell (Eds.), *New directions in composition research* (pp. 95–108). New York: Guilford.

Fillmore, C. (1985). Linguistics as a tool for discourse analysis. In T. van Dijk (Ed.), *Handbook of discourse analysis* (Vol. 1) London: Academic Press.

Fitzgerald, J. (1987). Research on revision in writing. *Review of Educational Research, 57,* 481–506.

Fitzgerald, J. (1990). Reading and writing as "mind meeting." In T. Shanahan (Ed.), *Reading and writing together: New perspectives for the classroom* (pp. 81–97). Norwood, Massachusetts: Gordon.

Fitzgerald, J. (1992). *Towards knowledge in writing: Illustrations from revision studies.* New York: Springer-Verlag.

Fitzgerald, J., and Markham, L. (1987). Teaching children about revision in writing. *Cognition and Instruction, 4,* 3–24.

Fitzgerald, J., and Stamm, C. (1990). Effects of group conferences on first graders' revision in writing. *Written Communication, 7,* 96–135.

Flower, L., and Hayes, J. A. (1981). A cognitive process theory of writing. *College Composition and Communication, 32,* 365–387.

Flower, L., Hayes, J. R., Carey, L., Schriver, K., and Stratman, J. (1986). Detection, diagnosis, and the strategies of revision. *College Composition and Communication, 37,* 16–55.

Gere, A. R., and Stevens, R. S. (1985). The language of writing groups: How oral response shapes revision. In S. W. Freedman (Ed.), *The acquisition of written language: Response and revision* (pp. 85–105). Norwood, New Jersey: Ablex.

Graham, S., and MacArthur, C. (1988). Improving learning disabled students' skills at revising essays produced on a word processor: Self-instructional strategy training. *Journal of Special Education, 22,* 133–152.

Graves, D. H. (1978). *Balance the basics: Let them write.* New York: Ford Foundation.

Graves, D. H. (1979). What children show us about revision. *Language Arts, 56,* 197–206.

Graves, D. H. (1983). *Writing: Teachers and children at work.* Exeter, New Hampshire: Heinemann.

Graves, M., Slater, W. H., Roen, D., Redd-Boyd, T., Duin, A. H., Furniss, D. W., and Hazeltine, P. (1988). Some characteristics of memorable expository writing: Effects of revisions by writers with different backgrounds. *Research in the Teaching of English, 22,* 242–265.

Hayes, J. R., and Flower, L. S. (1980a). Identifying the organization of writing processes. In L. W. Gregg and E. R. Steinberg (Eds.), *Cognitive processes in writing* (pp. 4–30). Hillsdale, New Jersey: Erlbaum.

Hayes, J. R., and Flower, L. S. (1980b). Writing as problem solving. *Visible Language, 14,* 388–399.

Hayes, J. R., and Flower, L. S. (1983). Uncovering cognitive processes in writing: An introduction to protocol analysis. In P. Mosenthal, L. Tamor, and S. A. Walmsley (Eds.), *Research on writing: Principles and methods* (pp. 207–220). New York: Longman.

Hayes, J. R., Flower, L., Schriver, K., Stratman, J., and Carey, L. (1987). Cognitive processes in revision. In S. Rosenberg (Ed.), *Advances in applied psycholinguistics, Volume 2, Reading, writing, and language learning* (pp. 176–240). New York: Cambridge University Press.

Hillocks, G., Jr. (1986). The writer's knowledge: Theory, research, and implications for practice. In A. R. Petrosky and D. Bartholomae (Eds.), *The teaching of writing: Eighty-fifth yearbook of the National Society for the Study of Education:* Part II, (pp. 71–94). Chicago: National Society for the Study of Education.

Hodges, K. (1982). A history of revision: Theory versus practice. In R. A. Sudol (Ed.), *Revising: New essays for teachers of writing* (pp. 24–42). Urbana, Illinois: ERIC Clearinghouse on Reading and Communication Skills, National Institute of Education and National Council of Teachers of English.

Hull, G. A. (1987). The editing process in writing: A performance study of more skilled and less skilled writers. *Research in the Teaching of English, 21,* 8–29.

Karegianes, M. L., Pascarella, E. T., and Pflaum, S. W. (1980). The effects of peer editing on the writing proficiency of low-achieving tenth grade students. *Journal of Educational Research, 73,* 203–207.

Lyman, R. L. (1929). *Summary of investigations relating to grammar, language, and composition.* Chicago: The University of Chicago.

MacArthur, C., and Stoddard, B. (1990). *Teaching learning disabled students to revise: A peer editor strategy.* Paper presented at the annual meeting of the American Educational Research Association, Boston.

Monohan, B. D. (1984). Revision strategies of basic and competent writers as they write for different audiences. *Research in the Teaching of English, 18,* 288–304.

Nystrand, M. (1983). The context of written communication. *The Nottingham Linguistic Circular, 12,* 55–65.

Nystrand, M. (1986). *The structure of written communication: Studies in reciprocity between writers and readers.* Orlando, Florida: Academic Press.

Nystrand, M. (1989). A social-interactive model of writing. *Written Communication, 6,* 66–85.

Nystrand, M. (1990). Sharing words. *Written Communication, 7,* 3–24.

Nystrand, M., and Brandt, D. (1989). Response to writing as a context for learning to write. In C. Anson (Ed.), *Writing and response: Theory, practice, and research* (pp. 209–230). Urbana, Illinois: National Council of Teachers of English.

Odell, L., and Goswami, D. (1982). Writing in a non-academic setting. *Research in the Teaching of English, 16,* 201–223.

Perl, S. (1979). The composing processes of unskilled college writers. *Research in the Teaching of English, 13,* 317–336.

Rohman, G. (1965). Pre-writing: The stage of discovery in the writing process. *College Composition and Communication, 29,* 209–211.

Rommetveit, R. (1974). *On message structure: A framework for the study of language and communication.* London: Wiley.

Scardamalia, M., and Bereiter, C. (1983). The development of evaluative, diagnostic, and remedial capabilities in children's composing. In M. Martlew (Ed.), *The psychology of written language: A developmental approach* (pp. 67–95). London: Wiley.

Scardamalia, M., and Bereiter, C. (1985). The development of dialectical processes in composition. In D. Olson, N. Torrance, and A. Hildyard (Eds.), *Literacy, language and learning: The nature and consequences of reading and writing* (pp. 307–329). Cambridge: Cambridge University Press.

Schumaker, J. B., Deshler, D. D., Alley, G. R., Warner, M. M., Clark, F. L., and Nolan, S. (1982). Error monitoring: A learning strategy for improving adolescent performance. In W. M. Cruickshank and J. Lerner (Eds.), *Best of ACLD* (Vol. 3, pp. 170–183). Syracuse, New York: Syracuse University Press.

Tressler, J. C. (1912). The efficiency of student correction of composition. *English Journal, 1,* 405–411.

Walker, C. P., and Elias, D. (1987). Writing conference talk: Factors associated with high- and low-rated writing conferences. *Research in the Teaching of English, 21,* 266–285.

Part IV

DEVELOPMENT OF TEACHERS WHO PROMOTE ACADEMIC COMPETENCE, SKILLED READING, AND GOOD WRITING

For researchers to determine how academic competence and literacy can be promoted is one thing. For researcher-developed instruction to be translated into classroom practice is quite another. Four of the chapters in this section are presentations by experienced educators about the challenges involved in translating cognitive-instructional theory and research into practice. The Kansas group, represented here by Kline, Deshler, and Schumaker, has almost two decades of experience providing teacher training across North America, specifically with respect to delivery of strategies instruction to learning-disabled students. Gaskins, Cunicelli, and Satlow present the Benchmark School story, informed by 20 years of experience providing cognitive-based intervention, including intensive efforts to do so across their entire school in recent years. Roehler, Anders, and Bos are leading teacher educators who have been studying how to deliver information about cognitively inspired instruction to teachers in the field. Both Roehler's contribution and the chapter by Anders and Bos present new longitudinal data on teacher change as teachers introduce strategies in their classrooms. The best available information about the challenges associated with the professional development of cognitive process teachers is represented in the first four chapters of this section.

Borkowski and Muthukrishna conclude the section with a theoretical discussion of teacher understandings that probably change as a result of becoming a strategies teacher. This chapter provides a fitting conclusion to the book, reiterating the nature of good information processing and discussing how teachers can come to understand such thinking, as well as why they must understand it if they are to succeed as cognitive strategies teachers. The strategic, knowledge, metacognitive, and motivational components highlighted throughout the book are present in this chapter, as is consideration of the explicit collaborative instructional models that are featured in this volume. Most importantly, however, for this section of the volume, Borkowski and Muthukrishna demonstrate that it is critical to develop a particular type of model of mind in teachers, if they are to be successful teaching efficient processing to their students. They must be "thinking teachers," ones who think about their students and their instructional practices in terms of strategies, knowledge, metacognition, and motivation.

Thus, the volume ends with both good news and challenges with respect to teacher development. It is possible to develop teachers who encourage academic competence and literacy using the methods reviewed in this volume. This development is occurring in schools using the Kansas model, at Benchmark School, and in Michigan and Arizona schools, but the changes necessary are not easy. Developing strategies and cognitive process approaches will never be sufficient, without the development of teachers who can teach them.

13

Implementing Learning Strategy Instruction in Class Settings: A Research Perspective

Frank M. Kline, Donald D. Deshler,
and Jean B. Schumaker

THE LEARNING STRATEGIES INSTRUCTIONAL APPROACH

During the last decade, the learning strategies instructional approach has been emphasized as a means of increasing the academic performance of normally achieving students (e.g., Gagne, 1985; Jones, 1986; Mayer, 1987; Pressley, Borkowski, & Schneider, 1990) as well as of students who are at risk for academic failure (e.g., Deshler & Schumaker, 1988; Ellis & Lenz, 1987; Graham & Harris, 1987; Swanson, 1989). This instructional approach, in which the focus is teaching students "how to learn and how to solve problems," has strong validity because of its logical relationship to the increasing societal demands of teaching students how to think, how to solve problems, and how to process large and diverse bodies of information. Indeed, learning strategy instruction has been touted as an appropriate and potentially powerful response to these demands. The validity of this instructional approach is enhanced by the mounting empirical evidence that learning strategies can be taught to students who can, in turn, use these strategies to become more efficient and effective learners (e.g., Borkowski, Weyhing, & Turner, 1986; Duffy & Roehler, 1987; Graham &

Harris, 1989; Pressley, Johnson, & Symons, 1987; Schumaker & Deshler, 1992; Wong, 1985).

Although learning strategy instructional protocols have been developed by researchers and program developers in a variety of fields (e.g., general education, cognitive psychology), a number of common features characterize the instructional programs of many of these individuals. First, learning strategy instruction often includes (1) a description of the strategy and the covert processes involved in using the strategy; (2) a description of the conditions under which the strategy should be used (i.e., when, where, and why); (3) a model of the strategy that includes demonstration of the covert processes involved in using the strategy; (4) multiple practice opportunities (including guided and independent trials) to apply the strategy to academic tasks; (5) encouragement to use self-regulation processes during strategy application (e.g., self-instruction, self-assessment, self-reinforcement); (6) ample interactions between the teacher and the student for the purpose of providing feedback to students about their practice attempts; and (7) deliberately programmed opportunities for students to transfer and generalize the strategy to other situations and settings.

Second, the focus of the instruction is on teaching the student to use a new approach to the task of learning: a learning strategy. Learning strategies have been defined as "goal-directed cognitive operations employed to facilitate performance" (Pressley, Harris, & Marks, 1991b, p. 2). Although the structure of different learning strategies may vary, a learning strategy typically comprises a series of steps the student uses in a certain order to complete a learning task. Each of the steps might involve the use of cognitive, metacognitive, or other behaviors by the student (Ellis, Deshler, Lenz, Schumaker, & Clark, 1991).

Third, the instructional approach represents a new instructional paradigm for teachers and students because instructional control is shifted during the instructional process from the teacher to the student. Learning strategy instruction generally progresses from teacher-mediated instruction in the initial instructional phases to increased student-mediated instruction later in the learning process. This shift is operationalized in a variety of ways. In the early phases of instruction, students may have a major voice in choosing the strategies they will learn and in setting their own instructional goals. They may participate in teacher-led discussions and guided practice activities. Later in the instruction, they may assume responsibility for evaluating the quality of their performance on independent practice activities or for adapting and combining strategies for their own purposes. Involving students in such facets of the instructional process is seen as central to teaching students to take a proactive posture toward the learning process and, in turn, to become independent learners and performers.

Fourth, learning strategy instruction requires mastery on the part of students. That is, students must master a learning strategy if they are to be expected to apply it to academic tasks in a way that will improve their performance on such tasks. Thus, instruction in the strategy must provide students with an opportunity to achieve proficiency.

Fifth, learning strategy instruction appears to be an intensive as well as a long-term endeavor (Pressley, Goodchild, Fleet, Zajchowski, & Evans, 1989). In other words, for students to become "good information processors" (Pressley *et al.,* 1990), they must be immersed in strategy instruction for relatively long periods of time (see Chapter 14). Learning strategy instruction is not seen as something that can take place every Friday for half an hour; the instruction for one strategy must take place daily over an extended period of time (Slavin, 1990). Additionally, students must learn several strategies so they have a "menu" of strategies from which to choose each time they face a new learning task.

Finally, the developers of learning strategy instructional protocols usually emphasize the importance of not teaching students in a "cookbook" fashion. Instead, they encourage teachers to reflect on the dynamic characteristics of a given instructional situation and to fashion their instruction accordingly. Thus, teaching students to be strategic learners is seen as being largely dependent on the teacher's ability to understand and integrate a host of variables into the instructional setting (e.g., the demands of the mainstream curriculum, the motivational level of the student, the student's willingness to take risks in a learning situation, the complexity of the strategy being taught) and to respond accordingly by tailoring learning strategy instruction to meet the unique requirements of the situation.

Thus, learning strategy instruction represents a new approach to instruction that is significantly different from the instruction that has traditionally taken place in our nation's schools. It includes a sequence of instructional methods different from what teachers typically use. It focuses on a type of content that has rarely been taught. It is based on constructs that are abstract in nature. It requires the student to master the strategy if benefits are to be achieved. It must be intensive as well as extensive. It requires the student to assume control as instruction proceeds. Finally, it requires the teacher to be reflective, inventive, and flexible while conducting the instruction.

To the credit of a number of researchers, a significant amount of research on this new and distinctly different instructional approach has been completed in recent years. Indeed, a great deal has been learned about powerful methods of teaching strategies, optimal design of learning strategies, and motivational elements that increase student participation in strategy instruction. However, most of this work has been conducted in single classrooms or in laboratories. Although this work has been both essential and productive, it has left unanswered a very pressing question: Can strategy instruction be incorporated into educational practices in thousands of schools throughout the nation?

Although demonstrating the effectiveness of instruction in a given learning strategy in a specific classroom with one teacher is important, whether or not instruction in that same learning strategy and other learning strategies can be implemented in a broad array of classrooms across multiple schools, teachers, and districts over a sustained period of time is more important. In short, the robustness of learning strategy instruction relative to broad-scale implementation has not been addressed in the literature. Can teachers and administrators readily adapt and adjust to this new type of instruction?

In response to these concerns, the staff of the University of Kansas Institute for Research in Learning Disabilities (KU-IRLD) has recently conducted research to (1) identify barriers that prevent the broad-scale implementation of learning strategy instruction and (2) evaluate the effects of various interventions designed to overcome these barriers. This chapter describes that research. First, as an introduction, background information is presented on how the KU-IRLD staff operationalizes learning strategies, the instructional methodology used to teach learning strategies, and the dissemination process that has been followed. Second, descriptive information common to many of the studies presented in this chapter will be reviewed. Third, the studies conducted to identify the major barriers to broad-scale implementation will be described and the identified barriers will be specified. Fourth, intervention studies that have been conducted to evaluate methods of reducing barriers will be presented. Finally, a set of conclusions will be presented about the actions required of school personnel if the broad-scale implementation of learning strategy instruction is to be successful.

THE KU-IRLD APPROACH TO LEARNING STRATEGY INSTRUCTION

The Strategies Intervention Model

Since the institute's inception in 1977, the KU-IRLD staff's major research agenda has been the design and validation of an intervention model for improving the academic success and life adjustment of adolescents and young adults who are experiencing problems associated with low achievement, for example, learning disabilities (LD). Emerging out of this work has been a comprehensive intervention model called the Strategies Intervention Model (SIM) (Deshler & Schumaker, 1988). The SIM has been developed to respond to the broad array of academic, social, and motivational needs of students who are at risk for school failure. The major goal of the model is to teach students to be strategic in their approach to curriculum and other setting demands. Instruction, therefore, is focused on teaching students how to learn and how to perform. Students are taught strategies for meeting the demands of various school and out-of-school settings. For the purposes of this instructional model, a strategy has been defined as "an individual's approach to a task; it includes how a person thinks and acts when planning, executing, and evaluating performance on a task and its outcomes" (Lenz, Clark, Deshler, Schumaker, & Rademacher, 1990). Since students face a variety of academic, social, and motivational tasks in secondary and postsecondary settings, strategies that help students respond to these kinds of tasks are the main content taught in the SIM.

The Learning Strategies Curriculum

A major component of the SIM, the *Learning Strategies Curriculum,* was designed to help students respond to academic task demands (cf. Deshler & Schumaker, 1988). This curriculum consists of strategy interventions designed and field-tested for use in public school settings (Schumaker & Deshler, 1992). Each unit of the curriculum includes instructional procedures to facilitate students' acquisition and generalization of a given learning strategy. The *Learning Strategies Curriculum* is organized into three major strands corresponding to three major academic demands: acquisition, storage, and expression of information.

To determine which learning strategy(ies) to teach to a student from the *Learning Strategies Curriculum,* teachers analyze the setting demands that the student is expected to meet. This differs from traditional remedial interventions, which emphasize understanding the attributes of the learner as the primary basis for designing an instructional program. The *Learning Strategies Curriculum* is founded on the notion that the strategies taught must be sufficiently powerful to improve performance markedly in the mainstream environment. Therefore, the *Learning Strategies Curriculum* focuses on "strategy systems" used to approach the complex learning tasks encountered in mainstream settings. Each strategy system is a collection of cognitive and metacognitive strategies as well as other behaviors integrated into a routine used by a student to meet a given curriculum demand (Deshler & Lenz, 1989).

Throughout this chapter, several strategies from the *Learning Strategies Curriculum* will be mentioned. From the acquisition strand of the curriculum, the Word Identification Strategy (Lenz, Schumaker, Deshler, & Beals,

1984) is designed to enable students to decode multisyllabic words, whereas the Paraphrasing Strategy (Schumaker, Denton, & Deshler, 1984) is designed to assist students in the transformation of main ideas and important details into their own words. From the storage strand, the FIRST-Letter Mnemonic Strategy (Nagel, Schumaker, & Deshler, 1986) enables students to organize, memorize, and use stored information to answer test questions. Finally, from the expression strand, the Sentence Writing Strategy (Schumaker & Sheldon, 1985) provides students with a means of writing a broad array of well-structured sentences. These strategies are representative of the types of strategies needed by at-risk students to cope successfully with the demands of secondary school settings.

The Instructional Methodology

Each of the task-specific strategies in the *Learning Strategies Curriculum* is taught to students using an eight-stage instructional methodology that has been the focus of KU-IRLD research efforts for over a decade (Ellis *et al.,* 1991). This instructional methodology is characterized as a "working model" because ideas regarding the instruction of learning strategies continue to evolve. This working model includes a set of procedures for promoting the acquisition and generalization of a learning strategy. In general, the instructional process involves systematic and intensive instruction in which the teaching emphasis gradually shifts from teacher-mediated to student-mediated instruction as students pass through the instructional stages of acquisition to those of generalization.

Briefly, the instructional methodology consists of seven acquisition stages and one generalization stage. In the Pretest and Make Commitments stage, students are tested to determine their current learning habits regarding a particular setting demand. If the pretest shows a need to learn the strategy, students are asked to make a personal commitment, in the form of a written goal, to learn that strategy. In the second stage, the Describe stage, a description of the strategy is provided by the teacher, including where, when, how, and why the strategy should be used. In the Model stage, the teacher demonstrates all aspects of the strategy for the students by thinking aloud. As the Model stage progresses, the teacher prompts student involvement in the demonstration, checks understanding of the underlying strategic processes, shapes and corrects student responses, and engineers student success. The purpose of the fourth stage, Verbal Practice, is to enhance student understanding and mastery of the processes underlying the strategy and the memory system used to facilitate memory of the strategy steps. During this stage, students progress to a level of proficiency at which they can fluently name and explain each of the steps of the strategy and the underlying cognitive processes. Then, in the Controlled Practice and Feedback stage of instruction, students practice applying the new strategy to materials in which the complexity, length, and difficulty levels have been controlled until the students reach a predetermined mastery level. During the sixth instructional phase, Advanced Practice and Feedback, students are given a variety of opportunities to practice using the strategy with materials and in situations that closely approximate the demands placed on them in mainstream educational and out-of-school settings. The provision of feedback after each practice attempt in the practice stages is an important opportunity to individualize the instruction so students make rapid progress toward mastery (Kline, Schumaker, & Deshler, 1991). During the seventh stage of the instructional process, the Post test and Make Commitments stage, students are tested to determine if they have mastered the strategy. The teacher and student take time in this stage to reflect on progress and to celebrate the achievement of the original goal. Also during this stage, students are asked to make a commitment to generalize their use of the strategy to other settings and situations.

During the final stage of the instructional methodology, the Generalization stage, teachers focus their energies on engineering situations that will afford students with multiple opportunities to generalize the strategy across tasks, situations, and settings. Although this stage explicitly targets generalization, instruction for generalization is emphasized throughoutthe entire instructional sequence by (1) enlisting student commitment in the Pretest and Posttest stages; (2) incorporating multiple examples in the Describe and Model stages; and (3) emphasizing generalization as students apply the strategy in the practice stages (Ellis, Lenz, & Sabornie, 1987a,b).

Although generalization can be emphasized throughout strategy acquisition, the Generalization stage itself has been shown to be critical for insuring that all students actually generalize the strategy (Schmidt, Deshler, Schumaker, & Alley, 1989). During the first phase of the Generalization stage, Orientation, teachers make students aware of the various contexts in which the learning strategy can be applied. During the second phase, Activation, students are given opportunities to practice the strategy with new materials and in a variety of settings. In the Adaptation phase, the teacher prompts students to modify and combine the strategy with other strategies to meet different setting demands. The final generalization phase, Maintenance, involves the use of periodic probes to determine whether the student is continuing to use the strategy. These probes enable the teacher to determine whether additional instruction in the strategy is needed.

This eight-stage instructional methodology has been empirically validated through a series of research studies showing that students who are at risk for school failure can (1) learn to use these strategies; (2) apply them to tasks resembling those assigned in mainstream classrooms; and (3) generalize the strategies across materials and settings (Schumaker & Deshler, 1992).

The KU-IRLD Dissemination Process

Once the instructional methodology for teaching learning strategies was validated, the attention of the KU-IRLD staff turned to the challenge of disseminating strategy instruction to school settings throughout the nation. Initially, a traditional model of inservice was used, that is, the training[1] typically consisted of a single session in which a trainer visited a district for at most a day. Teachers were required by administrators to attend the session. The information was presented, the trainer departed, and the teachers were left without incentives or support for implementing the new instruction. The administrators did not require teachers to implement the new instruction, nor did they check to determine whether the new instruction had been implemented. Implementation activities within and across schools in a district were typically not coordinated.

Not surprisingly, this traditional inservice model resulted in a very low rate of implementation. The KU-IRLD staff realized that several significant changes in the dissemination process were needed to increase the implementation of strategy instruction. The first step in improving the dissemination process was to translate the field-test versions of the units in the *Learning Strategies Curriculum* into a set of instructional materials that were "teacher friendly." Teachers provided suggestions about how the materials could be revised and formated. Following their recommendations, several of the learning strategies packets have been transformed into commercially produced manuals. Each manual includes the necessary teaching instructions, worksheet masters, scoring instructions, and teaching scripts for implementing instruction in one strategy (e.g., Hughes, Schumaker, Deshler, & Mercer, 1988; Lenz *et al.,* 1984; Nagel *et al.,* 1986; Schumaker & Lyerla, 1991; Schumaker *et al.,* 1984; Schumaker & Sheldon, 1985; Schumaker, Nolan, & Deshler, 1985).

Although teachers reported a high level of satisfaction with the newly produced instructional packets, a relatively low rate of strategy implementation was still observed when the traditional inservice training model was used (Deshler, Schumaker, & Clark, 1985). Thus, the KU-IRLD staff realized that significant additional steps beyond merely translating the materials into "cleaned-up" versions had to be taken in order to affect a higher rate of

---

[1]When referencing *student* learning, the terms, "instruction" and "instructor," are used in this chapter. When referencing *teacher* learning, the terms, "training" and "trainer," are used. The purpose for using different terms is merely to avoid confusion when the teacher becomes the learner. No disrespect toward teachers is intended.

implementation for a complex educational innovation such as strategy instruction.

Simultaneous with the publication of the first set of instructional materials was the formation of a national network of qualified inservice trainers to be associated with the KU-IRLD. The purpose of this network is to provide training of a consistently high quality about instructional innovations developed at the KU-IRLD to educators across the nation. Over the past 6 years, this network has grown from about 15 founding members to more than 600 professionals in 40 states, in four provinces in Canada, and in Germany. Preparation for these trainers has been available at the KU-IRLD, through several state-sponsored projects associated with state departments of education, and through other smaller local efforts in several states. In all cases, however, each of the trainers has been required to meet an extensive list of qualifications, including demonstrated competence in teaching various learning strategies to students and in providing inservice training for teachers.

In an attempt to improve traditional inservice practice, the KU-IRLD staff has developed a system of "best practices" relative to staff development and system change. This system is based on those practices that have been reported as successful in the literature, as well as on practices recommended and followed by network trainers. The system includes a flexible training sequence that can be adjusted to meet the needs of different schools or educational agencies. The sequence consists of four major phases: Needs Assessment, Initial Training, Program Integration, and Institutionalization (Schumaker & Clark, 1990).

The Needs Assessment phase is initiated in response to a request for training from an educational site. During this phase, a trainer presents information in the form of an overview of SIM, filmstrips (Deshler & Schumaker, 1984; Schumaker & Deshler, 1985), or videotapes (e.g., Clark, Deshler, Schumaker, & Rademacher, 1988) to enable school personnel to make an informed choice about committing to learning strategy training. As a result, school personnel understand the trade-offs necessary to implement the instruction and support the program long term. Before formal training begins, written commitments are made by teachers and administrators regarding a long-term training sequence that spans several years. This phase also produces an articulation of the perceived needs of the school or agency that can be used as a basis for designing the training sequence.

The Initial Training phase begins after the Needs Assessment phase has been completed. During this phase, teachers are presented with information that helps them understand how strategies instruction is different from other instruction, the instructional principles that underlie the teaching process, the educational outcomes expected for students, and the way in which strategies should be taught to insure effective and generalized use of the strategy. This initial training session (3–6 hr) also includes training in one task-specific strategy. Such training consists of suggestions on how to teach and manage instruction of the specific strategy in a classroom.

After the initial training session, teachers are expected to begin implementing the strategy immediately. They are encouraged to begin implementation on a small scale (with 2 to 5 students) to build up their familiarity and confidence with the strategy. As problems are encountered, they are encouraged to call their trainer. Formal meetings may also be held for the purpose of problem solving and sharing information among teachers. After a period of time has elapsed and teachers have had an opportunity to teach the first strategy, the trainer returns and provides training in a new strategy. During the course of one academic year, teachers may be trained in the use of one to three task-specific learning strategies. The rate of introducing new strategies is tied to the successful implementation of previously taught strategies.

The third phase, Program Integration, is designed to help teachers integrate strategies that they have learned separately into a cohesive program. Issues such as scope and sequence of instruction, cooperative planning with other teachers, implementing an evaluation system, insuring generalization across settings, and integrating strategies instruction with other ongoing instructional efforts are addressed. During the final phase, Institutionalization, the emphasis is on making the district self-sufficient. In this phase, policies and procedures are formalized within and across schools. An on-site trainer is prepared and provisions are made for staff turnover, so the longevity of strategy instruction can be insured.

The sequence of training activities outlined here is founded on a set of principles that has been specified in the literature on staff development and the change process (Schumaker & Clark, 1990). The first principle, obtaining broad-based support and commitment, is based on the notion that all stakeholders must understand the nature of the innovation, the costs of implementation, and the necessity of long-term training and support for teachers. Prior to beginning any formal training, participants are asked to make a group decision to adopt SIM and to make individual commitments to participate in the training.

The second principle is to view training broadly. This principle underscores the fact that effective training must be conceptualized on several levels that include awareness, practice, and application experiences. Traditional inservice efforts focus solely on awareness-level experiences for teachers. Thus, this principle is based on the notion that, in order for teachers to become strategic instructors, they must have ample opportunities to practice using their newly learned skills and they must receive feedback on their performance (Joyce & Showers, 1980, 1981, 1982). As a result, KU-IRLD training activities encourage such procedures as peer coaching and the use of meetings in which teachers are given an opportunity to share their successes and generate ideas for solving common problems.

The third principle, requiring active and continued participation by key participants, underscores the fact that representatives of all stakeholders must be involved in both decision making and actual training. For example, the development of policies and procedures to support the instructional program and the attendance of key administrators at training sessions can do much to communicate its importance to other staff members.

The final principle, adopting a change perspective, is founded on the notion that the adoption of an innovation usually involves a significant amount of change at both a personal and a system level. Trade-offs are often required, and priorities may need to be altered. Under such circumstances, sacrificing the innovation is sometimes easier than working through the necessary changes. Nevertheless, if participants are aware that change can be an uncomfortable process, they will be more likely to stay the course.

In summary, the work of the KU-IRLD staff and associates not only has focused on the specification and validation of a set of learning strategy interventions but has involved significant efforts to translate these interventions into packages that can be readily used by teachers. In addition, it has focused on the establishment of a dissemination system based on known principles of change. As new elements of the dissemination process have been added, increased rates of implementation have been noted. However, these actions alone appeared to be insufficient to overcome several barriers that seemed to be impeding the progress of broad-scale institutionalization of strategy instruction. Thus, the need to understand these barriers and to take the necessary steps to circumvent them became the thrust of a programmatic line of research.

AN OVERVIEW OF A MAJORITY OF THE STUDIES

Except where otherwise noted, most of the KU-IRLD work on barriers was conducted in a school district located in southern Kansas. The district serves 47,500 students in 7 comprehensive high school, 14 middle schools, and 65 elementary schools. There are about 3000 teachers employed in the district; 100 of these teachers are responsible for serving students with learning disabilities. During the 3 years in which this research was conducted, there was no formal district policy regarding the implementation of strategy instruction for mildly handicapped students or any other students.[2]

All the teachers involved in the studies were certified special education teachers who were responsible for serving students formally identified as learning disabled in their resource classrooms. All teachers, except one, were female. Some of the teachers served elementary students in Grades 4–6 and others served secondary students in Grades 6–8 or Grades 9–12. The elementary teachers provided instruction for their students in language arts and math. The secondary teachers were responsible for providing instruction in English, social studies, and science. All these teachers held master's degrees or were working toward master's degrees; most who held master's degrees had been involved in additional graduate training past their master's degree work.

The training the teachers received followed the recommended sequence described earlier. The training experience was described to all the teachers as a long-term endeavor in which they could participate if they wished to volunteer. All committed to at least 1 year's participation in the training sequence. They received training about strategy instruction from a member of the KU-IRLD training network. All the teachers received a 3-hr overview of strategy instruction and SIM before receiving instruction on a particular strategy. The teachers received instruction on a minimum of two strategies per school year. Each strategy training session included descriptions of the strategy and how to teach it, demonstrations, scoring practice, and individual planning for implementation. About 20 teachers per year volunteered to initiate the training sequence. The training took place during school hours; substitute teachers covered for participating teachers.

After each workshop session on a given strategy, the teachers were required to complete a Weekly Report Form (Kline, 1988) for each group of students they instructed. On the form, they communicated the name of the strategy being taught, the names of students being taught the strategy, the days of the week that strategy instruction took place, and a brief description of the instructional activities that took place during each hour of strategy instruction during the week. Thus, the Weekly Report Form served as a method of gathering self-report data on the teachers' implementation of strategy instruction. The reliability of the teachers' reports was established by randomly visiting the classrooms and comparing student products and progress to the reports. In all cases, teachers were found to be accurately reporting their implementation.

Finally, the students of each teacher had been formally identified as

[2]Since the completion of this research, the district has included a learning strategies course in the secondary curriculum and has added a half-time supervisory position over strategy instruction.

learning disabled according to Kansas guidelines. In general, strategy instruction was provided to students in their deficit areas (e.g., a student having a deficit in writing was included in instruction on the Sentence Writing Strategy). The students were selected for participation in instruction for a particular strategy by their teachers after the students had taken a pretest for the strategy and failed to meet the mastery criteria. All students participated in some mainstream educational experiences each day.

THE BARRIER IDENTIFICATION STUDIES

The barrier-identification process involved several independent efforts. First, individuals who had participated in strategy instruction and in training others to implement strategy instruction were asked to identify the barriers they had encountered or had observed others encountering as they tried to implement strategy instruction. Second, a study was conducted to analyze the teaching skills of special education teachers after participating in a strategy workshop (Kea, 1987). Third, a study of the fidelity with which teachers implemented the instructional sequence was conducted to identify points in the instructional sequence where barriers appeared to be present. Fourth, a study of the time teachers spent providing strategy instruction was conducted. Finally, a study of teacher use of instructor's manuals was completed to identify problems with the manuals that might impede instruction.

Barrier Survey

To obtain a national perspective on the problem, qualified strategy trainers who attended a national meeting of the Network of Strategy Trainers sponsored by the KU-IRLD were asked to identify barriers to the implementation of strategy instruction. The participants at the meeting were asked to volunteer to complete a survey and were offered a 5-dollar incentive for participation in the survey. The questionnaire was open-ended in format. The respondents were asked to list the two or three most critical barriers they had witnessed that impeded the implementation of learning strategies instruction. Twenty-eight trainers responded to the survey. These individuals all had experience teaching learning strategies to students and had experience training teachers to teach learning strategies. About half the group (15) was currently teaching in classrooms whereas the remainder was serving in supervisory or training capacities.

The respondents' perceptions of critical barriers are summarized in Table 1. Their responses were related to seven major categories. By far the most frequently mentioned barrier was related to the teacher's "mind set."

Table 1
Barrier Categories and Responses from the Barrier Survey

Barrier	Number of responses
Mind set	21
Overall plan	16
Support	11
Start-up costs	10
Management problems	9
Student problems	4
Poor teaching skills	2

The trainers noted that critical barriers were present when teachers were struggling with releasing old beliefs, were unwilling to make a commitment to something new, were hesitant, lacked confidence, held low expectations for their students, were concerned that this might be just another "fad," and were uncomfortable with accepting a new way of thinking about instruction.

The next most frequently mentioned barrier related to the lack of an overall plan for strategy instruction. The trainers noted that teachers often lacked a common vision or a coherent philosophy, were unsure about how to integrate strategy instruction into their ongoing curriculum, often allowed their instruction to be interrupted, and had no idea how to prioritize the kinds of instruction they could deliver. Another relatively frequently mentioned barrier related to the support teachers were getting for their efforts in strategy instruction. The trainers noted that teachers often did not receive any support, that their administrators did not become involved, that administrators did not require accountability with regard to strategy instruction, that administrators did not have an understanding of the change process required while someone was in the process of becoming a strategic teacher, and that administrators did not communicate a clear vision of what kind of instruction should be taking place.

Another barrier related to start-up costs. The trainers reported that obtaining the required materials, copying handouts or worksheets for students, and finding the necessary equipment (e.g., tape recorders) were all time-consuming tasks and that teachers often delayed starting instruction because of the preparation time involved in getting ready.

Another barrier frequently reported by the trainers was management trouble. They reported that teachers had difficulty scheduling groups of students, grouping students, managing their time, coordinating their efforts with other teachers, and setting up their physical environments for strategy instruction.

Two barriers that were mentioned less frequently by the trainers were student problems and poor teaching skills. They reported that student resistance to strategy instruction and failure of students to progress were barriers to strategy instruction. These student problems seemed highly related to the skills of teachers. One might surmise that teachers who were skilled in instructional techniques would be able to "sell" their students on strategy instruction and insure that their students reach mastery. Two of the trainers felt that poor teaching skills were often detrimental to the implementation of strategy instruction.

An Analysis of Teachers' Skills

Since the KU-IRLD staff suspected that poor teaching skills might be a major barrier to strategy instruction, although only a few trainers mentioned this barrier, a study was conducted to analyze special education teachers' skills in detail after they participated in a strategy workshop. For the study, Kea (1987) asked special education teachers participating in a series of strategy workshops in a southwestern state to volunteer to have an observer visit their classrooms. She also asked another group of special education teachers residing in a midwestern state who were not participating in the workshops to volunteer to be observed. Fifteen workshop participants constituted the experimental group, and fifteen nonparticipants constituted the comparison group.

All the teachers taught students in Grades 6–12. Teachers in the experimental group ranged in age from 27 to 59 years ($M = 41$ years), whereas the comparison teachers ranged in age from 23 to 54 years ($M = 34$ years). With the exception of one male in the experimental group, all teachers were female. The teachers in the experimental group and in the comparison group had been special education teachers for a mean of 11 years (range = 4–19 yr) and 7 years (range = 1–15 yr), respectively. All the teachers in the experimental group held master's degrees; 31% of the teachers in the comparison group held master's degrees. None of the teachers in the experimental group had participated in courses about learning strategies prior to the study. Two teachers in the comparison group reported that they had had some exposure to learning strategies while in college. All the teachers received $10 for participating in the study.

The experimental group teachers attended a training series that took place between March and May, 1985. All were enrolled in a college course for which they received credit hours at a local university. They met six times with the trainer, who was a qualified KU-IRLD trainer and held a Ph.D. in Special Education.

At the first meeting, the teachers received an overview on strategy instruction. In subsequent sessions, they received manuals and training on how to instruct two learning strategies: the Paraphrasing Strategy and the

Word Identification Strategy. Additionally, in the second session, nine critical teaching behaviors that had been identified through the literature on effective teaching (giving rationales, communicating expectations, using organizers, using reviews and checks, facilitating independence, insuring intensity of instruction, monitoring, providing feedback, requiring mastery) were defined. Examples of how each behavior should be used in strategy instruction were provided, and examples of the teaching behaviors that appear in the manual for the Paraphrasing Strategy were identified. The research that supported the use of the behaviors was described. The teachers also watched a videotape of strategy instruction and were asked to identify each of the critical teaching behaviors that they witnessed on the tape. At several points, the tape was stopped and the critical teaching behaviors were discussed.

In the fourth session, the critical teaching behaviors were reviewed with the group for about 30 min before training in the second learning strategy began. Thus, the experimental group teachers received a total of about 2 hr of training at the awareness level on the critical teaching behaviors.

All the participating teachers were required to teach each learning strategy to at least three students and to document each student's mastery of each strategy through the use of student progress charts in order to receive credit for the course. Teachers in the experimental group were observed before and after the training series for one 45-min class period. Teachers in the comparison group were observed once, after the training series had been terminated. All the teachers were asked to use direct instruction to teach a skill of their choice to a group of four or more students for 20 min and to facilitate their practice of the skill for the remainder of the class period. In each classroom, Kea observed whether or not strategy instruction was taking place and the extent to which each teacher engaged in each of the nine critical teaching behaviors. To collect data on the latter measure, Kea used a time-sample recording system through which the teachers were observed for 10-sec intervals and their behavior was recorded. She also used a checklist to record behaviors related to each of the nine critical teaching behaviors.

Kea found that seven experimental teachers engaged in strategy instruction when she visited their classrooms whereas none of the comparison teachers engaged in strategy instruction. Thus, following the workshop series, only 47% of the participants were engaging in strategy instruction although they knew that a person associated with the workshop series was coming to visit and observe in their classrooms. Kea found almost no differences between the two groups of teachers with regard to the percentage of intervals in which they engaged in the critical teaching behaviors. Most of the behaviors were engaged in very infrequently. For example, Kea found that the experimental teachers spent only 4% of the intervals providing feedback to students. Although all the teachers in Kea's study provided "brief feedback" (i.e., a simple acknowledgement regarding the correct or incorrect nature of a response, such as "Good!"), only 67% of the experimental teachers provided what she called "sustaining feedback" (e.g., probing for another answer, repeating the question, giving a clue, or allowing more time after an incorrect response) after training. Only 20% of the experimental teachers used specific descriptive corrective feedback in the case of incorrect responses, and none of the experimental teachers used specific descriptive positive feedback for correct responses or remodeled or retaught a skill as necessary after the strategy training. Requiring mastery (i.e., making statements that mastery is required and making statements regarding whether mastery was reached) was not observed at all. According to the checklist data, the comparison group teachers used more of the critical teaching behaviors than did the experimental group teachers after the strategy training.

When Kea reviewed the materials handed in at the end of the course by the experimental teachers, she found that 10 of the 15 teachers had taught a learning strategy to a total of 40 students. The time span between the training session and the onset of strategy instruction ranged from 2 to 6 weeks. Of the students in the study, 21 reached mastery at the Verbal Practice stage, 14 at the Controlled Practice stage, 3 at the Advanced Practice stage, and 2 at the Posttest stage. When Kea correlated the teachers' scores on the Checklist with the progress of their students using the Kendall Correlation Coefficient, she found that the correlation was .57 ($p <$ .038). In summary, teachers can participate in strategy training and be provided with materials that carefully describe what they are to do (e.g., guidelines for providing specific feedback to students) and still not teach strategies, in spite of ample evidence that students can profit from them.

An Analysis of the Implementation of the Instructional Sequence

In light of Kea's results regarding the poor progress of students through the stages of strategy instruction, another study was conducted to gather data on more teachers and to look more closely at how teachers and students progress through the eight instructional stages of the instructional sequence. Twenty teachers volunteered to participate in the study. The mean age of the teachers was 36 years. They averaged 9.9 years of general education teaching experience and 8.8 years of experience teaching special education. They received an overview of strategy instruction and were trained to teach two learning strategies: the Word Identification Strategy and the Paraphrasing Strategy. The inservice sessions on the two strategies were held 3 months apart to give the teachers ample time to complete the training in one strategy before being trained in the next strategy. All the teachers made a commitment to teach the strategies in which they had been trained to at least three students in at least one class period per day. As the teachers implemented strategy instruction in their classes, they completed a Weekly Report Form. On the form, they reported the stage of instruction and the instructional activity for each day of the week for each student.

At the end of the school year, the number of students mastering each step as reported on the Weekly Report Forms for the Word Identification Strategy instruction was analyzed. The results parallel Kea's outcomes. The number of students completing each stage of instruction decreased as instruction across the instructional stages progressed. The teachers began the instruction with an average of 4.8 (sd = 2.19) students. This number of students remained fairly stable through the Pretest, Describe, and Model stages of instruction. When the students reached the first stage of instruction at which mastery was required, the Verbal Practice stage, the number of students began to drop. An average of 3.65 (sd = 2.76) students completed instruction in this stage. The average number of students completing instruction in the Controlled Practice stage of instruction decreased dramatically to 1.8 (sd = 1.58) whereas an average of 1.25 (sd = 1.48) students completed the Advanced Practice stage. An average of only 0.9 (sd = 1.41) students completed the Posttest stage. Although data were not collected on the number of students completing the formal generalization activities in the Generalization stage, not more than an average of 0.9 students could have completed them.

These outcomes, in combination with Kea's results, indicate that students of first-time strategy teachers may not proceed through the instructional stages the way students did in the original validation studies. When the teachers were asked why the later stages of instruction were not implemented with the majority of the students, they indicated that the students were not reaching mastery on earlier stages and that they were hampered by student absences, interruptions, and other demands on their time. These results are cause for concern because the entire instructional sequence needs to be implemented if all students are to be expected to generalize the strategies to other learning situations (e.g., Schmidt *et al.,* 1989).

Analysis of Time Spent on Strategy Instruction

Since the teachers in the previous study and the strategy trainers had mentioned that strategy instruction is often interrupted (e.g., by other school activities, absenteeism of students) and the trainers had indicated that teachers had difficulty managing their instructional time, a study was conducted to determine how teachers were spending their instructional time. Volunteers to participate in the study consisted of 57 special education teachers who had participated in an overview session on strategy instruction and at least one workshop session on how to teach a learning strategy. All the teachers were serving students with learning disabilities in their classrooms. All the teachers made a commitment to teach a given strategy to at least three students in at least one class period per day for a given length of time. (Each teacher was free to choose the length of time that strategy instruction would take place.) As the teachers implemented strategy instruction in their classes, they completed a Weekly Report Form. On the form, they reported the instructional activity for each day of the week. If they did not provide strategy instruction on a given day, they were asked to supply a reason for not giving the instruction. They also reported student absences on the form.

At the end of the school year, the Weekly Report Forms were reviewed, and five categories of interruptions were created: no school on that day, inservice activities, other curriculum demands that had to be met, other school activities (e.g., assemblies, spirit rallies), testing (e.g., administering and taking standardized tests), conferences, teacher absences, and miscellaneous interruptions (e.g., unreported reasons or reasons that did not fit the other categories). For each teacher, the number of days for which he or she planned strategy instruction was counted. In addition, the number of days on which strategy instruction actually occurred and the number of each type of interruption occurred were counted. Thus, for each teacher, the number of days planned for strategy instruction, the number of days actually spent on strategy instruction, and the number of days that each type of interruption occurred were available. In addition, the number of student absences was also counted.

According to the results gathered from the Weekly Report Forms, the 5070 periods allotted for strategy instruction by the teachers represented 49% of the total periods available for the year for the targeted classes. Of the 5070 class periods allotted by the 57 teachers for strategy instruction, 1754 (35%) were interrupted so severely that strategy instruction did not take place. Thus, 3316 periods (or 32% of the total periods available across the year) were actually spent on strategy instruction. Of the interrupted periods, 18% were spent on other curriculum demands, 3% on other school activities, 3% on testing, 6% on conferences, and 3% involved miscellaneous interruptions. On 3% of the days, there was no school. Across the 3316 periods of actual strategy instruction, there were 2139 student absences. Thus, the teachers were experiencing a total average of 65 absences per day or 1.2 absences per day per teacher in the targeted class. Since the teachers were teaching small groups of students, these results indicate that they were often missing a significant part of their class on a daily basis. These data are cause for concern, since students with learning disabilities need intensive daily instruction if they are to master learning strategies (Ellis *et al.*, 1991).

Analysis of the Instructor Manuals as a Barrier

Professionals in the field of strategy instruction voiced a concern that the scripts provided in the instructor's manuals for the *Learning Strategies Curriculum* might serve as a barrier for some teachers who might feel that they are restricted from using their own teaching styles and words as they implement the instruction. As a result of this feedback, a study was conducted to determine how teachers were using the instructor's manuals. The goal was to determine whether the teachers were restricting their instruction to the words scripted in the manuals or whether they were using the script as a model for what they were to say as they provided instruction using their own words and teaching styles.

Fifteen teachers volunteered for the study. All the teachers had received at least an overview of strategy instruction and inservice instruction in how to teach the Word Identification Strategy. They had an average of 9 years of experience in special education and 12 years total teaching experiencing. Their mean age was 38 years, and all had master's degrees. Eight of the teachers were first-year implementors of strategy instruction whereas seven had 2 or 3 years of experience. The eight first-year implementors were teaching the Word Identification Strategy for the first time. The seven teachers that were experienced in strategy instruction all had taught the Word Identification Strategy previously at least once.

To measure the teachers' adherence to the script in the instructor's manual, a checklist was developed that was based on the organization of the script in *The Word Identification Strategy: Instructor's Manual* (Lenz *et al.*, 1984). (This manual was chosen because of the relatively short script for the Describe stage of instruction, which enabled observation of the whole Describe stage in two or three class periods.) The script in the manual was organized according to boldfaced headings in an outline format. Thus, the checklist included all the boldfaced headings to represent the information covered under the heading (hereafter referred to as instructional steps). It also included spaces next to each instructional step for the observer to indicate (1) the sequence in which the step was covered relative to the other items in the list, (2) whether the information subsumed under the step was covered verbatim, (3) whether the teacher expanded on the information presented in the manual for the step, or (4) whether the teacher omitted information presented in the manual for the step. It also included spaces next to each step for the observer to indicate whether the teacher read from the manual constantly, whether the teacher referred to the manual occasionally, or whether the teacher did not refer to the manual at all during the instruction of the step. Finally, it included spaces for the observer to note whether interaction occurred between the teacher and students during the presentation of each step.

Each teacher informed the research staff of the date on which instruction for the Describe stage would begin. The teachers were informed that the Describe stage was being observed for the purpose of judging the effectiveness of the instruction in the Describe stage for the Word Identification Strategy. Although every effort was made to observe each teacher's instruction for the entire stage, scheduling problems occasionally occurred. At the minimum, for all teachers, the first day of instruction was observed. During each observation, the observer referred to a copy of the script and completed a checklist. All sessions were tape recorded for later reference and reliability assessment.

To evaluate the interobserver reliability of the scoring, a second observer listened to a randomly selected samples of 13% of the tapes and recorded observations on the checklist. Observers' responses were compared item-by-item. The total percentage of agreement was 91%.

Four of the teachers (27%) presented the instruction in such a way that the observation checklist could not be used, that is, there was no discernible relationship between the script and the way instruction was presented by these teachers. These teachers' responses are not included in the percentages discussed here. (Two of the teachers had adapted the instruction in appropriate ways for their elementary students. Although they purported to be teaching the Word Identification Strategy, the other two teachers significantly departed from the recommended sequence and content of instruction.) For the remaining teachers, the results showed that, of the instructional steps observed, 79% were covered in the sequence suggested by the manual. In 17 of 35 classes (48%), the sequence of instruction exceeded a 90% match between how the steps were actually presented and how they were recommended to be presented in the manual. In 13 of the 35 classes (37%), the teachers matched the sequence exactly.

Although a majority of the teachers was, generally, following the sequence of instruction, only 8% of the instructional steps was presented verbatim. For 59% of the steps covered, the teachers expanded on the information in the manual. They added examples, prompted student responses, added personal information, or added additional material of some type. For 18% of the steps, the teachers omitted information. For 14% of the steps, some of the information was expanded on and some of the information was omitted. The teachers referred constantly to the manual during only 14% of the instructional steps. During the majority of the steps (85%), the teachers occasionally glanced at the manual for reference. During 1% of the steps, the teachers did not refer to the manual at all.

Student involvement in the instruction was frequent. The teachers involved students in the instruction during 76% of the instructional steps, a level higher than that called for in the script. Thus, one way the teachers expanded on the scripted instruction was by asking additional questions or prompting some kind of student response.

In summary, four of the teachers (about 25%) were not restricted by the manuals at all; their instruction was so dissimilar to the instruction specified in the manual that observers could not use the observation checklist. The remaining teachers did not use the script verbatim, although they followed the basic sequence of instruction as recommended in the script. They involved students frequently, and they transformed the information in a large majority of the instructional steps in some way. They used the manual as a guide for instruction in such a way that they could ensure that the majority of information was covered and that they could monitor the students while they were presenting the instruction. These results were obtained when the teachers were told that they would be observed presenting the Describe stage of instruction for the Word Identification Strategy. Whether they would have followed the sequence of instruction in the manual this closely when an observer was not present is not known. Additionally, whether the instruction as presented by the manuals is so formidable to some teachers that they never begin the instruction is not known. All the teachers in this study began the instruction and implemented it for several weeks.

Summary

To summarize the barrier identification studies, the sequence of studies that was conducted indicated that teachers might be hampered by lack of an overall instructional plan, their own mind set toward instruction, the preparation time required to begin strategy instruction, a lack of support, their own skills as teachers and managers, and interruptions in the instruction. The data from Kea's study were cause for concern because the teachers observed were using few of the teaching behaviors validated in the literature as critical for producing learning gains. The results of the study of the implementation of the instructional stages indicate that few students were reaching mastery on the strategies and that instruction for the majority of students often did not proceed beyond the Controlled Practice stage of instruction. These findings are not surprising if special education teachers are not using the teaching skills that are critical for insuring learning gains and if strategy instruction is often interrupted.

THE INTERVENTION STUDIES

Several studies have been conducted to evaluate ways of reducing some of the identified barriers to strategy instruction. This line of programmatic research is ongoing, and several additional studies are either currently being completed or being planned. The studies that have been completed already relate to the preparation time required to begin strategy instruction, the lack of support for teachers, the interruption of strategy instruction, lack of teacher skills, and the tendency of teachers not to reinitiate strategy instruction in subsequent school years.

The Materials Study

Since teachers and trainers had mentioned that the gathering of materials and equipment for strategy instruction can be a daunting task, a study was conducted to determine the effects of providing needed materials and equipment to the teachers at the inservice workshop. Conceivably, the provision of needed materials might serve as a gesture of administrative support for the implementation of strategy instruction as well as reduce the time demands outside of class for strategy instruction. Additionally, the provision of materials and equipment from a central source might save the district money. For example, by copying all needed handouts at a central source, copying costs can be reduced. Valuable teacher time can be spent planning for instruction and presenting instruction instead of searching for equipment and copying handouts for students.

Twenty teachers volunteered to participate in the study. They were serving students with learning disabilities at the elementary, junior-high, and high-school levels. They were randomly assigned to two groups. The groups were stratified by school level so both groups had teachers teaching elementary, junior-high, and high-school students represented in approximately the same numbers. Teachers assigned to the same school building were assigned to the same group. With the exception of one teacher in Group 1 (age = 58 years), both groups were very comparable in age (mean age: Group 1 = 37 years; Group 2 = 35 years), the number of years teaching students with learning disabilities (mean: Group 1 = 8.4 years; Group 2 = 9.3 years), their total years of teaching experience (mean: Group 1 = 10.5 years; Group 2 = 9.4 years), and the amount of education they had (all teachers except one in each group held master's degrees).

For each learning strategy to be taught, a list of the necessary materials and equipment was developed. These lists included such items as copies of any worksheets needed (enough for 10 students), overhead transparencies of the cue cards and an overhead projector for use in describing and modeling the strategy, reading materials for the Controlled Practice stage of instruction, blank note cards for the students to use in making their own cue cards, a large calendar for use in setting goals, and tape recorders and audiotapes for recording student practice attempts. The consumable materials were prepared and organized for each targeted teacher, and necessary equipment was found within the district.

The two groups of teachers attended separate inservice training sessions. Both groups received a 3-hr overview of strategy instruction and separate 3-hr sessions on instructing the Word Identification Strategy and the Paraphrasing Strategy. (These two strategies were selected because the types of materials and equipment needed to teach them are roughly equivalent.) Inservice sessions were held on school days and substitute teachers were provided for the teachers. These separate sessions were scheduled 12 weeks apart to insure that teachers had plenty of time to implement instruction in the Word Identification Strategy before receiving training in the Paraphrasing Strategy. For the Word Identification Strategy, teachers in Group 1 received the instructor's manual and all the materials and equipment needed for teaching the strategy; teachers in Group 2 received the instructor's manual, which included detailed lists of the materials and equipment needed. For the Paraphrasing Strategy, teachers in Group 2 received all the needed materials and equipment; teachers in Group 1 received the instructor's manual. During the training sessions, all the teachers were invited to attend monthly 1-hr support-group meetings (see "Support Group Study" for a description of these meetings). These meetings were held at the teachers' convenience outside the regular school day. After the sessions, all the teachers had access to the staff member employed by the district for providing consultation, support, and encouragement to the teachers. Both groups could also access needed equipment through this person.

Two measures were examined in this study. At the end of each strategy training session, each teacher filled out an Implementation Planning Form (Clark, 1990). On the form, the teacher indicated the date on which he or she intended to begin the strategy instruction. From the teachers' responses on this form, the number of days between the inservice session and the planned date of implementation could be determined for each teacher. Additionally, the teachers completed a Weekly Report Form each week indicating the names of students involved in strategy instruction that week, the strategy being taught, and the stage(s) of instruction that had been presented. From the teachers' responses on this form, the number of days before each teacher started instruction and the number of students involved in strategy instruction with each teacher during each week of the semester was determined.

The mean days of preparation time anticipated by the teachers varied according to whether or not they received the materials and equipment for the strategy instruction. Teachers who received the materials and equipment planned a mean of 6.7 days between the training session and the onset of instruction; teachers who did not receive the materials and equipment planned a mean of 8 days. This pattern was seen regardless of whether Group 1 or Group 2 received the material support. The differences between the means approached statistical significance, as indicated by separate t tests for independent group means ($t = 1.3597$, $df = 16$, $p < .10$ for the comparison in which Group 1 received the materials; $t = 1.2814$, df 16, $p < .10$ for the comparison in which Group 2 received the materials).

When the number of students served on a weekly basis was averaged for each group, the pattern shown in Figure 1 emerged. The teachers who received the materials and equipment taught the strategy to more students. The direction of the differences between the two groups is consistently in favor of the group that received the materials except for the one week immediately following the second training session. The differences for the first strategy are smaller than those for the second strategy, which was taught at the end of the school year during the months of April and May. Whether or not this difference is caused by the rush of activities at the end of the school year or by the fact that teachers were adding the second learning strategy to their program is not known at this time.

Consequently, the provision of material support may have an effect on teachers' planning for instruction. The teachers receiving the support in this study anticipated fewer days of preparation before starting instruction and served more students. Whether this phenomenon is restricted to the strategies trained, to the end of the school year, or to the addition of

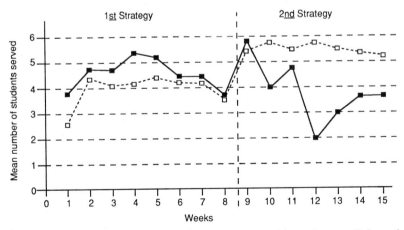

Fig. 1 The average number of students served per week by each group. ■ Group 1: First strategy, with materials; second strategy, without materials. □ Group 2: First strategy, without materials; second strategy, with materials.

subsequent strategies to a program is unclear. Since instruction in many of the other strategies requires more materials and worksheets than the two strategies trained in this study, one might assume that assembling the materials would be an even more formidable barrier for instruction in those strategies.

Support Team Study

The results of the barrier survey indicated that teachers feel a lack of support for strategy instruction. This finding is not surprising in light of many authors' descriptions of the teacher's job (e.g., Duffy and Roehler, 1985; Sarason, Davidson, & Blatt, 1986; Skrtic, 1988) in which teachers are typically described as isolated from each other. This isolation is particularly evident for special education teachers who work in buildings separated from other special education teachers and special education administrators. This isolation is cause for concern, especially when a teacher is attempting to learn to implement new instructional procedures. Thus, a study was conducted to determine the effects of providing interpersonal support to teachers learning to implement strategy instruction.

Twenty-four teachers volunteered for the study. They taught students with learning disabilities at the elementary, junior-high, and high-school levels. They were randomly assigned to two groups. The groups were stratified by school level so each group contained approximately the same number of teachers at each school level. Teachers from the same school building were assigned to the same group. This process resulted in 11 teachers in the experimental group and 13 teachers in the control group. The experimental group teachers were older (M = 45.7 years) than the control group teachers (M = 37.4 years), had fewer years of experience teaching students with learning disabilities (mean: experimental group = 5.7 years; control group = 9.4 years), and had slightly more years of teaching experience (mean: experimental group = 12.5 years; control group = 10.8 years). All the teachers except two in the experimental group and one in the control group held master's degrees. All the teachers agreed to teach a learning strategy to at least three students during at least one class period per day.

All the teachers had received a 3-hour overview of strategy instruction and previous training in at least two other strategies. For this study, they received an additional 6-hr training session in how to teach the FIRST-Letter Mnemonic Strategy. The teachers in the two groups were trained in separate training sessions on consecutive days. The two training sessions were equivalent, except the final minutes of the training session for the experimental group were spent in assigning the teachers to one of two support teams (one group had five members, and the other had six members), explaining the purpose of the support team meetings, setting the time and place for the first support group meeting, and telling the teachers what to bring to the support group session (stories of successes, concerns, and challenges, and copies of their students' pretests).

Each support team met for 60–90 min once a month, except for the last month of the school year, at a location and time convenient for the teachers. All meetings took place outside school time. Attending the meetings were the teachers and the administrative staff person responsible for organizing the strategy training and insuring the implementation of strategy instruction. All support team meetings were led by this administrator. An eight-element agenda was used to guide the content of the meetings. First, the teachers were encouraged to share stories of successes and progress in strategy instruction. Next, their concerns and challenges were elicited. Third, the teachers were asked to select the concerns and challenges that they wished to discuss further. Fourth, for each challenge, the teachers brainstormed potential solutions for the selected concerns and challenges. After a list of potential solutions had been generated for a given challenge, the teachers evaluated the solutions for potential application. Next, the teacher(s) who had identified the challenge were encouraged to use one of the solutions, and were prompted to set goals orally about when and how they would implement the solutions. Next, the content of the session was summarized. Finally, the next meeting time and place were set. Each support group met three times over the course of the study (one semester).

The teachers in the Control Group were not assigned to support teams. They had unlimited access to the administrator responsible for organizing strategy instruction and insuring its implementation. The last few minutes of their training session was devoted to additional scoring practice to insure that they experienced training time equivalent to the experimental group in the initial training session.

All the teachers submitted a Weekly Report Form each week for the duration of the study. On the form, they named the students receiving instruction in the FIRST-Letter Mnemonic Strategy and the instructional stage presented each day to each student. From the teachers' responses on this form, the number of days between the inservice session and the onset of strategy instruction, the number of students receiving instruction each week, and the amount of progress made through the instructional stages were determined.

All the teachers (100%) in the experimental group began the strategy instruction. Only 7 teachers (49%) of the 13 in the control group did so. For the teachers who actually implemented the instruction, the average number of days before starting instruction was 9.36 for the experimental group and 13.4 for the control group. A one-way analysis of variance established this as a statistically significant difference ($F = 9.440$, df $= 1, p <$ .010).

The number of students served by the two groups of teachers also varied significantly. The experimental group taught an average of 5.18 students, whereas the control teachers averaged 2.15 students. (The teachers who did not implement the instruction were treated as if they served 0 students.) This difference was found to be significant at the .01 level ($F = 9.459$, df $= 1$) when a one-way analysis of variance was computed.

When the last stage of instruction to which the teachers had progressed by the end of the semester was compared across the two groups, some differences were apparent. The students of teachers in the experimental group had, as a whole, progressed farther through the instructional stages than the students of teachers in the control group, although the differences were not large ($p < .10$).

The Intensity of Instruction Study

Since the instructional time that was lost to a variety of interruptions was cause for concern, a case study was conducted to determine whether the generation of new policies and management procedures by the teachers in cooperation with a consultant could increase the amount of instructional time spent on learning strategy instruction. This study took place during two school years in two school districts in eastern Kansas. During the first year, two resource room programs (Programs A and B) were involved in the study. After the first year, Program B's school district built a second high school. One of the teachers from Program B was transferred to this new school. She became affiliated with Program C, which was included in the second year of this study. All three schools were located in middle class communities. The student populations of the schools in the first year were approximately 1700 and 1600 for Programs A and B, respectively. The student populations were approximately 1700, 1000, and 700 in the second year of the study for Programs A, B, and C, respectively. During the first year, Program A had 44 students with learning disabilities and Program B had 39 students with learning disabilities enrolled in the program. Both programs had four special education teachers. Program A's teachers had an average of 6.1 years and Program B's teachers had an average of 4.0 years of teaching experience in special education. All the teachers had master's degrees. During the second year, Program A had 32 students, Program B had 29 students, and Program C had 19 students enrolled. The teachers in Program A had had extensive training in learning strategy instruction over several years. They were able to teach 4–10 strategies apiece. Teachers in Programs B and C had had no formal training in learning strategy instruction.

A time-sample observation system was used to record the activities in each of the programs including each of the student's and teacher's activities, the instructional or noninstructional nature of the activities, and the instructional approach being used. Each person in the room was observed for 30 sec, and all items regarding that person's behavior were recorded before moving on to the next person. Everyone in the room was observed once before a new observation "loop" was initiated. An average of six "loops" were watched in a 50-min class period, but this number varied according to the number of students and teachers present in the room at a given time. During each school year, sufficient class periods to constitute at least 6 full days were observed in each program. The observations were spaced over the school year, and each class period was observed at least six times. Only class periods that followed the program's typical routine were observed, that is, field trips, special movies, and class periods interrupted by assemblies were not observed.

The interobserver reliability of the measurement system was determined by having two observers independently, but simultaneously, observe each of the resource room programs during at least 10% of the class periods. Their records were compared item-by-item, and the percentage of agreement was calculated. During the first school year, the agreement was 96.7%; during the second year, agreement 92.1%.

At the end of the first school year, the data gathered with the observation system were shown to the teachers in Program A. They were asked to discuss the data and to design a set of policies and management procedures that would insure that their program was a "learning strategies" program. Assistance was provided to the teachers by the experimenters when it was requested. The resulting set of policies and procedures was aimed at providing guidelines for making decisions about students' educational programs and tracking each student's progress. The goals adopted by the teachers included (1) insuring that the students in the program would participate in learning strategy instruction as appropriate for their skill levels, (2) insuring that the students would be involved in strategy instruction for more than 70% of the time they spent in the resource room, (3) insuring that student time in the room would be spent on instructional tasks, and (4) insuring that decisions that might deviate from fulfilling these goals would be made according to a set of guidelines. The teachers divided the class period into two 25-min periods and planned instruction for two learning strategies for each student in each class. They specified a goal that each student would master three to four learning strategies per school year. They also specified what kinds of interruptions would be allowed, how chronic absences would be handled, what students and teachers would be expected to do at the beginning and end of the class period and during the transition from one period of strategy instruction to another to reduce the loss of instructional time, and how students' needs for tutoring in mainstream classes would be handled.

The data from the first year were also shared with the teachers in Program B and their principal. The data were explained and discussed, but there were no discussions of how improvements might be made in the presence of the researchers.

Table 2 shows the proportions of time the students and teachers spent in instructional activities in each program in Years 1 and 2. The students in both Programs A and B were spending comparable amounts of time in instructional activities. The percentage of time spent in instructional activities substantially increased in both Programs A and B from Year 1 to Year 2 for both teachers and students. Both teachers and students in Program A were spending about 82% of their time in instructional activities in Year 2.

During Year 1, the instructional time for students and teachers in Program A was almost equally divided among the learning strategy, remedial, and tutorial approaches, although the program had been labeled by the teachers as a "learning strategy" program (see Table 3). The large majority of instructional time for students in Program B was devoted to the remedial approach. Instructional time for teachers in Program B was largely devoted to the remedial approach; about one-fifth of their time was devoted to the tutorial approach.

During Year 2, the pattern changed substantially for Program A; more than 70% of teacher and student was time spent in learning strategy instruction. Some time was still being spent in other types of instruction, but this time was less than one-fourth of the instructional time. Students and teachers in Programs B and C were spending about two-thirds of their instructional time in tutorial instruction and about one-third of their time in remedial instruction. The learning strategies approach was used infrequently in these two programs (less than 1% of the time).

In summary, the development of policies and procedures by teachers specifying how learning strategy instruction was to take place in a program affected the intensity of learning strategy instruction. Program A students,

Table 2

Percentage of Intervals Spent in Instructional Activities during the Intensity-of-Instruction Study

| | Program A | | Program B | | Program C |
	Year 1	Year 2	Year 1	Year 2	Year 2
Teachers	55	82	38	66	49
Students	69	82	66	83	87

Table 3

Percentage of Instructional Intervals Spent in Different Instructional Approaches during the Intesity-of-Instruction Study

Approach	Teachers					Students				
	Program A		Program B		Program C	Program A		Program B		Program C
	Year 1	Year 2	Year 1	Year 2	Year 2	Year 1	Year 2	Year 1	Year 2	Year 2
Learning strategies	36.0	76.7	1.0	0.0	0.0	35.0	73.7	0.0	0.3	0.1
Tutorial	30.0	12.0	18.0	65.5	65.5	30.0	16.7	4.0	67.1	59.7
Remedial	30.0	8.7	69.0	34.5	29.5	31.0	7.8	82	29.3	39.3
Career–vocational	1.0	0.0	1.0	0.0	0.0	2.0	0.3	6.0	0.4	0.4
Functional	2.0	2.6	7.0	0.0	2.0	1.0	1.5	8.0	2.8	0.5
Compensatory	0.0	0.0	0.0	0.0	0.0	0.0	0.0	0.0	0.0	0.0
Memory/thinking	0.0	0.0	0.0	0.0	0.0	0.5	0.0	0.0	0.0	0.0
Unidentifiable other approach	1.0	0.0	4.0	0.0	0.0	0.5	0.0	0.0	0.0	0.0

who were spending an average of 12 min per day in learning strategies instruction in a program that was labeled a "learning strategy" program in Year 1, were able to experience an average of 31.4 min of learning strategies instruction per day in Year 2. Thus, the teachers, through their development of a set of policies to guide their decision making, were able to increase the time spent in learning strategy instruction by 162%. This change in instructional emphasis resulted in most of the students mastering an average of three learning strategies in Year 2, compared with an average of 1 learning strategy in Year 1.

The Feedback Study

Since special education teachers do not give substantial feedback to students (Kea, 1987), and students often fail to reach mastery, a study was conducted to determine whether teachers' feedback skills could be enhanced and whether their use of specialized feedback routines could improve their students' learning (Kline *et al.*, 1991). The hypothesis was that enhancing teachers' skills would reduce a barrier to strategy instruction. The study had two parts. In Part 1, special education teachers were taught to provide feedback to their students. The effect of this training on their ability to provide feedback in simulated and real feedback sessions was determined. In Part 2, the effects of teacher use of feedback routines on student performance were measured.

Eighteen teachers participated in Part 1 of the study. They all volunteered to participate in inservice training for the Sentence Writing Strategy and to participate in this study. They were randomly assigned to one of the three groups: a group to receive training in a special feedback routine (the feedback group); a group to receive training in the special feedback routine and training in how to teach students a feedback-acceptance routine (the feedback-plus-acceptance group); and a comparison group. The six teachers in the feedback group ranged in age from 31 to 58 (M = 41.8). Their total years of teaching ranged from 6 to 30 years (M = 15.3), and their years of teaching with students with learning disabilities ranged from 5 to 10 years (M = 9.6). The six teachers in the feedback-plus-acceptance group ranged in age from 28 to 41 years (M = 35.3). Their total years of teaching experience ranged from 3 to 18 years (M = 6.8), and their years of teaching students with learning disabilities ranged from 3 to 18 years (M = 6.6). The age of the six teachers in the comparison group ranged from 29 to 51 years (M = 41). Their years of teaching experience ranged from 7 to 15 years (M = 12.1), whereas their years of experience teaching students with learning disabilities ranged from 7 to 10 years (M = 8.3). All 18 teachers received an overview of strategy instruction and a 6-hr inservice session on how to teach the Sentence Writing Strategy.

A checklist of the steps of the Feedback Routine (for the Feedback-Acceptance Routine) was used to measure the teachers' delivery of feedback in simulated feedback sessions (test probes) and in the natural environment of the classroom (generalization probes.). The interobserver reliability of this measurement system was determined by having a second independent observer score a randomly selected sample of teacher performances (21% of the test probes and 13% of the generalization probes). Observers' checklists were compared item-by-item and the percentage of agreement was calculated as for previous studies. The agreement for test probes was 94% and for generalization probes was 95%.

A variation of the multiple-baseline-across-teachers design (a multiple-probe design) was used to evaluate the effects of teacher training. In brief, teacher training consisted of describing the Feedback Routine (or the Feedback-Acceptance Routine), modeling it, and having the teacher practice the routine in simulated feedback sessions. Additional instruction and feedback was provided to the teacher as needed until he or she met a specified criterion of performance.

The six teachers in the feedback group and the six teachers in the feedback–acceptance group learned the routine they were taught to criterion levels. During baseline, their performance often included scoring a paper correctly, using a pleasant voice tone, and making positive remarks to the student. Infrequently, they pointed out error categories to the student. On the average, during test probes, they performed about 20% of the steps of the feedback routine before training. After training, the teachers categorized the student's errors, explained to the student the category of error being made, provided suggestions on how to avoid the error in the future, designed a ministrategy to help the student avoid the error, modeled the ministrategy, had the student practice applying the ministrategy, and prompted the student to summarize the feedback. On average, during test probes, they performed about 80% of the steps of the feedback routine after training. Improvement in teacher performance on test probes occurred only after learning the feedback routine in each teacher's case. The teachers generalized their use of the feedback routine to their classrooms and applied it when giving feedback to their students at levels comparable to the levels they achieved in the simulated sessions. The performance of the comparison group teachers was comparable to the performance of the teachers in the other two groups during baseline and remained stable throughout the remainder of the study.

In Part 2 of the study, the performance of these teachers' students on lessons was monitored. Two measures were used: the trials required for mastery and the repetition of errors. These measures were derived from student worksheets completed while learning the Sentence Writing Strategy (Sheldon & Schumaker, 1985). Interscorer reliability was determined by having a second scorer independently score the students' worksheets, comparing the score item-by-item, and calculating the percentage of agreement. The agreement for a 10% random sample of the trials to mastery scores was 100%, and the agreement for a 10% random sample of error repetitions was also 100%.

The results of Part 2 of the study showed significant differences between the performance of students of teachers who used one of the feedback routines and the performance of students of the comparison teachers. The students of the feedback group teachers and the feedback-plus-acceptance group teachers completed significantly fewer worksheets before reaching mastery and repeated significantly fewer errors on subsequent trials when the students of comparison teachers. These results were replicated across several lesson sets. The results for high school students were the most dramatic: when given the specialized feedback by their teachers, high school students had to complete half as many worksheets as comparison students before reaching mastery. Such a reduction in instructional time is critical for students who have very little time left for learning important skills. In short, special education teachers' critical teaching skills were enhanced in this study, resulting in improved performance by their students.

An additional finding of the study relates to the reinitiation of strategy instruction. When the teachers who had participated in this study were interviewed in the subsequent school year, they were asked whether they were continuing to teach the Sentence Writing Strategy. Seven of the eleven teachers in the feedback groups who were still teachers in the district were still teaching the Sentence Writing Strategy. None of the comparison teachers had reinitiated instruction in the strategy.

The Reinitiation Study

Because some of the teachers whose skills had improved in the study just discussed did not reinitiate instruction the second year, additional means of insuring that teachers reimplement instruction appeared necessary. Thus, another study was conducted to determine whether a relatively inexpensive intervention could be developed that would have an effect on the rate of reinitiation of strategy instruction.

Seventeen teachers volunteered for additional strategy training after their first year of strategy training was completed. They were randomly assigned to one of two groups. As in the previous studies, the groups were stratified by school level, and teachers in the same school building were assigned to the same group. This selection process resulted in an experimental group with 8 teachers and a comparison group with 9 teachers. The mean age of the groups was similar (37.7 years for the comparison group; 39.3 years for the experimental group. The experimental group had more experience teaching students with learning disabilities (mean: experimental group = 12.1 years; comparison group = 9.6 years), but on average the groups had about the same total years of teaching experience (mean: experimental group = 12 years; comparison group = 13 years). The amount of education the two groups had was similar; all the teachers in the study, except two in the experimental group, had master's degrees.

The intervention for the experimental group consisted of a 3-hour inservice session at the beginning of the school year. The agenda for the session was designed with three goals in mind: (1) to remind the teachers of the successes they had experienced in the previous year in teaching the two strategies they had learned; (2) to review the instructional procedures for those strategies; and (3) to help the teachers integrate instruction in the strategies learned in the previous year with instruction in new strategies. Thus, during the inservice session, the teachers were first asked to share stories of their successes in the previous year while teaching strategies. They also shared with each other sample student products from before and after strategy instruction. Next, the teachers reviewed the instructional procedures with each other. Each of the instructional stages was reviewed, and teacher questions were solicited and answered. New activities related to each of the strategies were presented for the teachers to use in the coming year. Concerns of the teachers were addressed through a group problem-solving process. Third, information was presented about how the teachers might integrate strategy instruction into each student's Individualized Education Program and about how they might manage teaching more than one strategy at one time.

Teachers in the comparison group also received a 3-hour inservice session at the beginning of the school year on the same day that the teachers in the experimental group received training. During this session, they were given information about math instruction for their students. Both groups of teachers received training in a new learning strategy on the next day.

Three dependent measures were employed. The first measure was whether or not the teachers reinitiated instruction in each of the strategies learned the previous year. The second measure was the number of days between the start of the school year and the day on which instruction was initiated for each of the strategies learned in the previous year. The third measure was the number of students the teachers included in the instruction. This information was gathered through the use of the Weekly Report Form described earlier.

Six of the eight teachers in the experimental group (75%) and three of the nine teachers in the comparison group (33%) reinitiated instruction of the Word Identification Strategy. Teachers who did not reinitiate instruction in a strategy were considered to have started instruction on the last day of the study (they received a score of 150 days) for the purposes of the statistical analyses involving separate independent sample t tests. The experimental teachers began the instruction in a mean of 64.5 days, and the comparison teachers began the instruction in a mean of 126.8 days. The difference between the means was significant at the .05 level. The experimental group teachers served a mean of 5.37 students; the control group served a mean of 1.44 students. This difference was also significant at the .05 level.

None of the teachers reinitiated instruction in the Paraphrasing Strategy. When a researcher inquired why they had not, they responded that they wanted their students to master the Word Identification Strategy before receiving instruction in the Paraphrasing Strategy. They had not planned to teach both strategies during the same school year because they were devoting their time to learning how to teach a third and a fourth strategy.

DISCUSSION AND CONCLUSIONS

To summarize, teaching students to use learning strategies as a means of improving their overall performance on school-related tasks has gained increased attention from researchers, product developers, and teachers over the past decade. Studies have shown that students can, in fact, master and use a broad array of learning strategies in dealing with the problems they are expected to solve and the academic tasks they are expected to complete. Many of the investigations, however, either have been conducted in laboratory settings, or have involved instruction that was provided by teachers who were not necessarily representative of the overall teaching corps in today's schools. Strategy instruction has often been provided by seasoned teachers who were sought out because of their highly regarded teaching repertoires and who volunteered to implement the new interventions or by preservice teachers who did not have the same level of responsibility as inservice teachers, or the instruction was provided in atypical school settings (e.g., a private school with an extraordinarily talented and seasoned staff, administrative support for strategy instruction, and extremely favorable teacher/student ratios). The question of whether learning strategy interventions can impact educational practice in a broad array of educational settings when introduced to a cross section of teachers representing a variety of backgrounds and levels of expertise needs to be addressed if learning strategy instruction is to be viewed as a viable and central part of the instructional process in all the nation's schools.

The line of research reported here represents a programmatic effort to address this question through two phases of research. One phase focused on the identification of barriers that might negatively impact the implementation of learning strategy instruction with students who are at risk for school failure. The findings that emerged from this phase enabled the delineation of an interesting array of potential barriers including those related to setting factors (e.g., lack of administrative support and high start-up costs), teacher factors (e.g., a poor mind set and failure to use critical teaching skills), programmatic factors (e.g., lack of overall plans that specify how strategy instruction will be incorporated into ongoing instruction, and competing role expectations for resource room teachers), and instructional factors (e.g., high rates of interruptions during strategy instruction, bogging down during the instructional process, and not insuring that students demonstrate mastery and generalization of the strategy). Although each of these barriers has been described separately, in all likelihood they probably operate in combination, thus presenting a complex array of potentially interfering factors to the newly trained practitioner.

As these barriers were identified, a host of tactics was studied to determine methods of overcoming certain barriers and promoting the implementation of learning strategy instruction. Among the factors that were found to be effective in facilitating implementation were (1) providing teachers with the materials needed to support strategy instruction (e.g., progress charts, supplementary reading books, work sheets) to reduce start-up costs, (2) affording teachers an opportunity to meet regularly as support teams for the purpose of interacting with other teachers to share ideas and to solve problems, (3) having teachers develop a set of policies and procedures for insuring the efficient operation of the classroom relative to the intensive delivery of strategy instruction, (4) training teachers in the use of a feedback routine that enhances the speed with which students reach mastery on a given strategy as well as increases the probability that strategy instruction will be reinitiated by the teacher, and (5) providing teachers with a refresher training session at the beginning of an academic year for the purpose of encouraging the reinitiation of strategy instruction during the upcoming school year. Although the power of each of these procedures varied, each was shown to contribute to improved implementation in some way. Logically, the combination of all or several of these tactics should have an even greater impact on the implementation of strategy instruction than the use of each in isolation.

Several issues and questions arise that warrant further discussion. The first is a very basic one: What constitutes successful implementation of strategy instruction? The field of learning strategy instruction is relatively young; thus, data on initial and repeated implementation attempts by teachers working in a variety of settings generally have not been reported. Consequently, program designers and evaluators are uncertain about the standard to use to determine whether the adoption of strategy instruction is acceptable. Clearly, the implementation of any educational innovation will vary considerably depending on the complexity of the innovation, the target population, and the background and commitment of the staff, among a host of other factors (Heck, Stiegelbauer, Hall, & Louks, 1981). Until the literature contains a database on the implementation that can be expected, making evaluative statements about whether a given implementation level for learning strategy instruction is successful or unsuccessful depends on arbitrary criteria.

Related to this issue is the question of the dimensions that should be considered in implementation research. When the present line of research was initially conceived, the goal was to measure only the percentage of trained teachers who initially implemented learning strategy instruction after training. Once the research was underway, the necessity of gathering information on additional implementation measures became apparent. For example, we realized the initial implementation of instruction in a strategy must be differentiated from reinitiation of that instruction with new groups of students and across subsequent school years when we witnessed some teachers immediately reinitiating instruction in a variety of ways and other teachers not doing so. In addition, we realized that the quality of implementation must also be measured when we observed some teachers not completing all the stages of instruction. Clearly, additional measures of the quality of strategic teaching are needed in addition to those reported here.

We also realized that implementation of instruction in the first strategy must be differentiated from implementation of instruction in subsequent strategies. In several of the studies reported here, 100% of the teachers initially implemented instruction for the first and second learning strategies in which they were trained. However, when they were trained to instruct a third and fourth strategy in subsequent studies, the implementation rates for these later strategies reflected a significant drop. The reasons for this drop are unclear. Possible explanations include the following. The novelty of the new instruction may have worn off. Integrating instruction in more than two strategies into an instructional plan may required organizational and management skills beyond those required for instruction in one or two strategies. Teachers may need special training for incorporating a complex array of learning strategies into a program for at-risk students, and the expectations for teachers to perform a host of other instructional roles (e.g., tutoring students in academic content subjects such as science) in addition to teaching learning strategies to students may create a limit for the number of strategies that can be taught.

A third issue related to the implementation of strategy instruction concerns the context of the instruction. As data on the implementation of strategy instruction are described in the literature and discussed among professionals, the context within which the instruction has taken place is critical and should also be described, along with the intervention itself. In short, the type of student, the educational setting in which instruction occurs, the background of the teacher, and the commitment of the administration and school district may individually or collectively affect the outcomes of an effort to infuse strategy instruction.

Whether the results obtained in the studies reported here would be similar to those obtained with other strategy interventions in other contexts is unknown at this time. We suspect that they would not be similar, given the various reports from around the nation regarding the implementation of strategy instruction that has been achieved in other contexts. For example, in states like Florida where state department support, district support, and supervisory support are present for the implementation of learning strategy instruction, the rate and quality of implementation appear to be better than in the studies reported here. Many other sites report poorer rates and qualities of implementation. Additional research delineating the impact of contextual factors on the rate and quality of implementation is certainly needed.

A fourth issue regarding implementation research relates to the importance of determining the relative strength of the variables that have been identified as affecting implementation. For example, Kline and colleagues' (1991) research clearly underscored the importance of the skill level of teachers regarding the fluent use of feedback. The follow-up measures in this study indicated that a high percentage of teachers (64%) who were trained to give effective feedback to students while teaching a strategy retaught the strategy the following year, whereas none of the teachers who did not receive the special feedback training continued to implement the strategy instruction during the following school year. This finding clearly implies that training activities that focus on improving the technical teaching skills of teachers may be as important in enhancing implementation as those that focus on training teachers to teach a given strategy.

Once the pertinent variables have been weighted, administrative functioning and training and staff development efforts can be altered accordingly. For example, if teacher skill level turns out to be one of the more heavily weighted barriers to implementation, training agendas can be altered to include an emphasis on the critical prerequisite skills. Although Pressley and co-workers (1991b) and Schumaker and Clark (1990) have emphasized the importance of the intensity of teacher-training activities, few studies in this area have allowed for the fact that many teachers may not have the prerequisite skills needed for strategy instruction. Thus, the planning of training experiences for teachers in the area of strategy instruction may need to account for, among other things, instruction in the use of key technical teaching skills that facilitate the instruction of learning strategies as well as the provision of information on the content of the targeted strategy and the methodology for teaching that strategy. Additional research appears warranted with regard to providing teachers the skills they need for teaching strategies to students.

Another issue related to the implementation of strategy instruction is whether the most salient factors or variables have been studied with regard to improving implementation. Although variables such as use of certain teaching behaviors, administrative support, and start-up costs may be related to low implementation rates, they may not be the most critical factors. Variables related to the teacher's "mind set," such as a teacher's willingness to take risks, a teacher's beliefs about his or her own abilities, a teacher's beliefs about his or her students' abilities, a teacher's ability to conceptually integrate an educational innovation within ongoing instructional activities, or a teacher's cognitive or emotional ability to make the major paradigm shift required when adopting a new model of instruction, may be representative of classes of variables that more effectively explain why teachers fail to implementing learning strategy interventions than the variables studied here do.

Indeed, learning strategy instruction requires the adoption of a significantly different paradigm of instruction than paradigms traditionally adopted by most teachers of at-risk populations. Specifically, strategy instruction is theoretically grounded in information processing. Pressley and colleagues (1989) have indicated that few teachers have been exposed to information-processing models during their educational experiences. The importance of analyzing student performance in light of information-processing demands and designing instructional experiences to enable students to become more effective information processors—one of the overriding goals associated with learning strategy instruction—requires a markedly different approach to the teaching process than teachers have been prepared to use. Pressley and others (1991a) reported that the introduction of this new paradigm causes significant discomfort among teachers, in part because of the control they are required to give up to students when actively involving them in the learning process.

This instructional approach is not only significantly different for teachers, but is very demanding of them because of the complexity of good strategy use and the amount of work required to promote generalized strategy use in at-risk students. In describing the dynamics of classroom settings in which strategies instruction is successfully delivered, Pressley and co-workers (1992) indicated that these classrooms are exceedingly well-organized, and instruction is carefully orchestrated to provide students with a high degree of exposure to strategic approaches for most academic learning tasks. Most instructional routines in these classrooms are geared toward engaging students in strategic problem solving. This type of instruction may be perceived by teachers as very demanding to establish and maintain over an extended period of time. In short, learning strategy instruction may be perceived as demanding extraordinary levels of commitment, hard work, and high teaching skill levels for successful implementation. As a result, many teachers may not even start the process because of the amount of perceived change that is required.

Although such variables as teachers' mind set and the amount change perceived to be necessary by a given teacher logically appear to be important, they tend to be more difficult to measure and alter than some of the variables studied in this research effort. Additional research is needed to more clearly identify these critical variables, develop reliable means of measuring them, and create methods of impacting them.

A sixth issue related to the implementation of strategy instruction concerns the design of learning strategy interventions, including the strategies and the methodology used in teaching the strategies. The learning strategy interventions used in the studies reported here were a part of the SIM and the *Learning Strategies Curriculum;* a specific set of design features characterizes them (Deshler & Lenz, 1989). Because these interventions were developed for use with students with learning disabilities and other at-risk students, they have been designed with a high degree of specificity and instructional detail for the teacher to insure that students are exposed to the strategy content in a controlled, logical, and systematic fashion. Additionally, since both the strategies and the instructional methodology have been carefully tailored to meet the learning needs of adolescents who are at risk for school failure, they are relatively complex in nature. For example, the strategies in the *Learning Strategies Curriculum* have been characterized as being "complex learning strategy systems" rather than simple learning strategies (Ellis *et al.,* 1991). Such strategy systems were deemed necessary to enable adolescents to meet the demands present in their secondary school. Although the instructional methodology designed for teaching these strategy systems has been shown to be extremely effective with at-risk populations (Schumaker & Deshler, 1992), the detailed and relatively complex nature of the overall program may be negatively viewed by teachers. Such initial negative impressions of strategy instruction may negatively impact broad-scale implementation. Perhaps methods are needed for introducing strategy instruction to preservice teachers in such a way that the teachers develop the required "mind set" for strategy instruction before they begin teaching and to inservice teachers in a simplified way so they "get hooked" on using the approach before they are expected to implement more complex forms of the instruction. Clearly future research needs to explore new ways of training strategic teachers so they are open to teaching a variety of strategies and to using a variety of methodologies with their students.

A seventh issue related to the success of the implementation of strategy instruction is how strategy instruction is generally viewed in education, today and in the future. On the surface, learning strategy instruction may not appear to result in the immediate changes in student behavior that correspond to the current emphases in education today and that can be measured by the kinds of assessment tools traditionally used by school personnel to determine the efficacy of instructional programs. Although some authors have claimed that students who have been taught strategies can make substantial gains in achievement when compared with students who have not learned strategies (e.g., Schumaker, Deshler, Alley, & Warner, 1983), such growth may not be expected or apparent. When immediate and direct changes are not predicted or realized on such measures, administrators may decide to deny or withdraw support for such instruction. Given the increased emphasis on such models as the outcome-based paradigm (e.g., Spady, 1988), in which student mastery of certain elements of a knowledge domain (e.g., history) is valued over proficiency in attacking an academic task (e.g., reading a history chapter in a strategic fashion), strategy researchers and developers can expect continued skepticism from educators.

The problem of "fitting in" with current educational values is exacerbated by the difficulty inherent in measuring strategic competence. Clearly, assessing student competence in memory and understanding of a given set of history content is relatively easy compared with assessing competence in how strategic learners approach a history task. Such assessment often requires that inferences be made because of the covert nature of the learning activity. Glasser (1990) has argued that, because of the growing and widespread concern that all that is taught must be measured, teachers are often pressured to limit what they teach in order to prepare their students for state- or district-made minimal competency tests. Such tests often fail to measure whether students really have become effective learners and not merely receptacles of fragments of measurable knowledge. A key element in promoting the broad-scale adoption of learning strategy instruction may be the development of evaluation models that allow teachers and administrators to demonstrate that students exposed to learning strategy instruction not only show increased knowledge acquisition but also showed increased proficiency as learners. There is some indication that process-oriented assessments such as those being explored in Michigan, Illinois, and California have promise as strategy assessment tools.

Significant refinements may be required in both the content and methods associated with learning strategy instruction, as well as in administrative functioning and teacher-training efforts, if successful implementation is to be expected in a cross section of the national teacher corps. Nevertheless, some caution is in order. Although there may be a need to create some simple strategies and streamlined instructional manuals to increase the "palatability" of strategy instruction for teachers new to the approach, such innovations should not be created at the expense of those features of strategy instruction central to producing changes in the performance of at-risk learners. Strides may need to be made in refining strategy instruction, but such changes cannot compromise the integrity and strength of the interventions for the populations for whom they were initially intended.

Refinements in the structure of strategies and strategy instruction may be helpful. However, the most fruitful developments for the implementation of strategy instruction might come when education finds a place for strategy instruction, and administrative policies and teacher-training efforts are structured accordingly. Strategy instruction and the prerequisite skills associated with strategy instruction must be integrated into preservice instruction for teachers, and successful cost-effective means of training inservice teachers to implement strategy instruction must be developed.

Thus, the results reported here are viewed as a starting point: the beginning of a new realm of research. We view these research results as a positive addition to the experiential results gathered through eight years of training and dissemination efforts conducted by KU-IRLD affiliates in more than 600 school districts across the nation. These efforts have indicated that learning strategy interventions can be adopted on a broad-scale basis (Schumaker & Clark, 1990). The work completed in the states of California, Florida, Iowa, Kentucky, Nebraska, and North Carolina, for example, is evidence that the interventions can be successfully implemented across a broad array of school settings when the state department of education becomes involved in the effort. Indeed, personnel in some of the school districts in these states have been implementing strategy instruction for as many as eight years. A recent report from Florida indicates that 800 teachers are currently implementing strategy instruction and that 24 districts in the state have established demonstration classrooms (M. Mazzarino, personal communication).

To more thoroughly understand the factors that account for full-scale adoption and institutionalization of strategy instruction, future research efforts might focus on those schools and teachers at the extremes of the implementation continuum. Researchers might study, at one end of the continuum, teachers who have implemented instruction extensively and with high fidelity and, at the other end of the continuum, those who have totally rejected strategy instruction. An analysis of the variables that differentiate these two groups and their contexts may shed a good deal of light on the issue of strategy implementation.

Finally, as future research is conducted in this area, teachers as well as researchers must be highly involved. We are convinced that the research paradigm that the KU-IRLD staff has followed for the past 14 years has been productive because it has required researchers and teachers to team up in the specification of research questions as well as in the formulation and validation of instructional routines. We see this partnership as central in tasks that lie ahead relative to the refinement of strategy instruction and the broad-scale implementation of that instruction. The commitment of teachers and researchers to work together better to understand the complex interactions and dynamics that are at play in teaching students how to become strategic learners is central to the resolution of a myriad of instructional issues. Some of the most productive work conducted in this area to date has resulted from efforts that have pooled the perspectives and expertise of professionals from both the teaching and research ranks (e.g., see the work conducted by Pressley and his colleagues, Gaskins and her colleagues, and the KU-IRLD staff and its associates). An exciting synergy has been demonstrated through these efforts; it holds promise for producing significant advancements in the years ahead.

ACKNOWLEDGMENTS

This research was supported by Grant G008730148 from the U.S. Department of Education (Office of Special Education Programs). The authors would like to express their appreciation to the teachers, administrators, and staff of the Wichita School District (USD #259) for their unwavering cooperation and support during all aspects of the research effort. We also want to express appreciation to Frances L. Clark and B. Keith Lenz, who played key roles in conceptualizing and critiquing many of the studies in this effort.

REFERENCES

Borkowski, J. G., Weyhing, R., and Turner, L. (1986). Attributional retraining and the teaching of strategies. *Exceptional Children, 53,* 130–137.

Clark, F. L. (1990). Strategies intervention model training implementation plan. In F. L. Clark, J. B. Schumaker, B. K. Lenz, D. D. Deshler, B. A. Duchardt, and J. A. Rademacher (Eds.), *SIM training library: Strategies instruction—inservice training issues.* Lawrence: University of Kansas Institute for Research in Learning Disabilities.

Clark, F. L., Deshler, D. D. Schumaker, J. B., and Rademacher, J. (1988). *Making a difference: From those who know* (Videotape). Lawrence: University of Kansas Institute for Research in Learning Disabilities.

Deshler, D. D., and Lenz, B. K. (1989). The strategies instructional approach. *Journal of Disability, Development and Education, 36*(3), 203–224.

Deshler, D. D., and Schumaker, J. B. (1984). *Strategies instruction: A new way to teach* (Filmstrip) Salt Lake City: Worldwide Media.

Deshler, D. D., and Schumaker, J. B. (1988). An instructional model for teaching students how to learn. In J. L. Garden, J. E. Zins, and M. J. Curtis (Eds.), *Alternative educational delivery systems: Enhancing instructional options for all students* (pp. 391–411). Washington, D.C.: NASP.

Deshler, D. D., Schumaker, J. B., and Clark, F. L. (1985). *An inservice training model to increase the likelihood of implementing innovations with handicapped students in secondary schools* (G008630046). Washington, D.C.: Office of Special Education Programs.

Duffy, G. G., and Roehler, L. R. (1985). *Constraints on teacher change.* Unpublished manuscript. Michigan State University, The Institute for Research on Teaching, Lansing.

Duffy, G. G., & Roehler, L. R. (1987). Improving reading instruction through the use of responsive elaboration. *Reading Teacher, 40,* 514–520.

Ellis, E. S., and Lenz, B. K. (1987). Effective learning strategies for hearing disabled students. *LD Focus, (Spring),* 97–114.

Ellis, E. S., Lenz, B. K., and Sabornie, E. J. (1987a). Generalization and adaptation of learning strategies to natural environments. Part 1: Critical agents. *Remedial and Special Education, 8*(1), 6–20.

Ellis, E. S., Lenz, B. K., & Sabornie, E. J. (1987b). Generalization and adaptation of learning strategies to natural environments. Part 2: Research into practice. *Remedial and Special Equation, 8*(2), 6–20.

Ellis, E. S., Deshler, D. D., Lenz, B. K., Schumaker, J. B., and Clark, F. L. (1991). An instructional model for teaching learning strategies. *Focus on Exceptional Children, 23*(6), 2–24.

Gagne, E. D. (1985). *The cognitive psychology of school learning.* Boston: Little, Brown.

Glasser, W. (1990). *The quality school: Managing students without coercion.* New York: Harper & Row.

Graham, S., and Harris, K. R. (1987). Improving composition skills of inefficient learners with self-instruction strategy training. *Topics in Language Disorders, 7,* 66–77.

Graham, S., and Harris, K. R. (1989). Improving learning disabled students' skills at composing essays: Self-instructional strategy training. *Exceptional Children, 56,* 201–214.

Heck, S., Steigelbauer, S. M., Hall, G. E., and Louks, S. F. (1981). Measuring innovation configurations: Procedures and applications. Austin: The University of Texas Press.

Hughes, C. A., Schumaker, J. B. Deshler, D. D., and Mercer, C. D. (1988). *The test-taking strategy: Instructor's manual.* Lawrence, Kansas: Edge Enterprises.

Jones, B. F. (1986). Quality and equality through cognitive instruction. *Educational Leadership, 43*(7), 4–11.

Joyce, B. R., and Showers, B. (1980). Improving inservice training: The message of research. *Educational Leadership, 37,* 379–385.

Joyce, B. R., and Showers, B. (1981). Improving inservice training. In B. R. Joyce, C. C. Brown, and L. Peck (Eds.), *Flexibility in teaching: An excursion into the nature of teaching and training.* New York: Longman.

Joyce, B. R., and Showers, B. (1982). The coaching of teaching. *Educational Leadership, 40*(1) 4–8.

Kea, C. D. (1987). *An analysis of critical teaching behaviors employed by teachers of students with mild handicaps.* Unpublished doctoral dissertation. University of Kansas, Lawrence.

Kline, F. M . (1988). *Weekly report form.* Unpublished form (Available from Frank Kline, 745 Litchfield, Wichita, Kansas 67203).

Kline, F. M., Schumaker, J. B., & Deshler, D. D. (1991). The development and validation of feedback routines for learning disabled students. *Learning Disabilities Quarterly, 14,* 191–207.

Lenz, B. K., Clark, F. L., Deshler, D. D., Schumaker, J. B., and Rademacher, J. A. (1990). *SIM training library: Ensuring strategic instruction.* Lawrence: The University of Kansas Institute for Research in Learning Disabilities.

Lenz, B. K., Schumaker, J. B., Deshler, D. D., and Beals, V. L. (1984). *The word identification strategy: Instructor's manual.* Lawrence: University of Kansas Institute for Research in Learning Disabilities.

Mayer, R. E. (1987). *Educational psychology: A cognitive approach.* Boston: Little, Brown.

Nagel, D. R., Schumaker, J. B., and Deshler, D. D. (1986). *The FIRST-letter mnemonic strategy: Instructor's manual.* Lawrence, Kansas: Edge Enterprises.

Pressley, M. (1990). *Cognitive strategy instruction that really improves children's academic performance.* Cambridge, Massachusetts: Brookline Books.

Pressley, M., Johnson, C. J., and Symons, S. (1987). Elaborating to learn and learning to elaborate. *Journal of Learning Disabilities, 20,* 76–91.

Pressley, M., Goodchild, F., Fleet, J., Zajchowski, R., and Evans, E. D. (1989). The challenges of classroom strategy instruction. *Elementary School Journal, 89,* 301–342.

Pressley, M., Borkowski, J. G., and Schneider, W. (1990). Good information processing: What it is and how education can promote it. *International Journal of Educational Research, 2,* 857–867.

Pressley, M., Gaskins, I. W., Cunicelli, E. A., Bordick, N. J., Schaub-Matt, M., Lee, D. S., and Powell, N. (1991a). Strategy instruction at Benchmark School: A faculty interview study. *Leaning Disability Quarterly, 14,* 19–48.

Pressley, M., El-Dinary, P. B., Gaskins, I. W., Schuder, T., Bergman, J. L., Almasi, J., and Brown, R. (1992). Beyond direct explanation: Transactional instruction of reading comprehension strategies. *Elementary School Journal.*

Pressley, M., Harris, K. R., and Marks, M. B. (1991b). But good strategy instructors are constructivists! *Educational Psychology Review.*

Sarason, S. B., Davidson, K. S., and Blatt, B. (1986). *The preparation of teachers: An unstudied problem.* Cambridge, Massachusetts: Brookline Books.

Schmidt, J. L., Deshler, D. D., Schumaker, J. B., and Alley, G. R. (1989). Effects of generalization instruction on the written language performance of adolescents with learning disabilities in the mainstream classroom. *Journal of Reading, Writing, and Learning Disabilities, 4*(4), 291–309.

Schumaker, J. B., and Clark, F. L. (1990). Achieving implementation of strategy instruction through effective inservice education. *Teacher Education and Special Education, 13*(2), 105–116.

Schumaker, J. B., and Deshler, D. D. (1985). *Learning strategies: A new way to learn* (Filmstrip). Salt Lake City: Worldwide Media.

Schumaker, J. B., and Deshler, D. D. (1992). Validation of learning strategy interventions for students with LD: Results of a programmatic research effort. In B. Y. L. Wong (Ed.), *Intervention research with students with learning disabilities: An international perspective.* New York: Springer-Verlag.

Schumaker, J. B., and Lyerla, K. D. (1991). *The paragraph writing strategy: Instructor's manual.* Lawrence: The University of Kansas Institute for Research in Learning Disabilities.

Schumaker, J. B., and Sheldon, J. (1985). *The sentence writing strategy: Instructor's manual.* Lawrence: The University of Kansas Institute for Research in Learning Disabilities.

Schumaker, J. B., Deshler, D. D., Alley, G. R., and Warner, M. M. (1983). Toward the development of an intervention model for learning disabled adolescents. *Exceptional Education Quarterly, 4*(1), 45–74.

Schumaker, J. B., Denton, P. H., and Deshler, D. D. (1984). *The paraphrasing strategy: Instructor's manual.* Lawrence: The University of Kansas Institute for Research in Learning Disabilities.

Schumaker, J. B., Nolan, S. M., and Deshler, D. D. (1985). *The error monitoring strategy: Instructor's manual.* Lawrence: The University of Kansas Institute for Research in Learning Disabilities.

Sheldon, J., and Schumaker, J. B. (1988). *The sentence writing strategy: Student lessons.* Lawrence, Kansas: Edge Enterprises.

Skrtic, T. (1988). The crisis in special education knowledge. In E. Meyen and T. Skrtic (Eds.), *Exceptional children and youth: An introduction* (3rd ed. pp. 415–448). Denver: Love.

Slavin, R. E. (1990). General education under the regular education initiative: How must it change. *Remedial and Special Education, 11,* 40–50.

Spady, W. G. (1988). Organizing for results: The basics of authentic restructuring and reform. *Educational Leadership, 46*(2), 4–8.

Swanson, H. L. (1989). Strategy instruction: Overview of principles and procedures for effective use. *Learning Disability Quarterly, 12*(1), 3–16.

Wong, B. L. (1985). Potential means of enhancing content skill acquisition in learning disabled adolescents. *Focus on Exceptional Children, 17,* 1–8.

14

Implementing an Across-the-Curriculum Strategies Program: Teachers' Reactions to Change

Irene W. Gaskins, Elizabeth A. Cunicelli, and Eric Satlow

Few teachers would dispute the merit of making instructional changes that appear to have a high likelihood of fostering increased student learning, thinking, and problem solving, especially in a school for poor readers. Certainly the Benchmark staff did not. Beginning in the 1988–1989 school year, the staff embarked on a 3-year research and development project to change instruction. The goal was to implement an across-the-curriculum strategy program. The impetus for this project was teacher concern about their students' lack of active involvement in learning. Thus, when asked whether they would like to see the school implement strategy instruction across the curriculum, the faculty was enthused about the prospect of creating more responsive students. In this chapter, we sketch the 3-year process of instructional change at Benchmark School, and give particular attention to the responses and reactions of the teachers involved.

Benchmark is a school for bright underachievers between the ages of 6 and 14 whose primary problem is significant underachievement in reading. The 167 children who attend the school have average or above average intelligence and no primary emotional or neurological problems. The average duration of a child's enrollment at the school is 4 years and the ratio of boys to girls is 4 to 1. Follow-up data on the school's graduates suggest that the vast majority of the students are mainstreamed to regular classrooms when they leave Benchmark, function in the top half of their classes, and go on to college after graduating from high school.

When teachers and their supervisors (33 faculty members, 6 of whom were supervisors) made the commitment to an across-the-curriculum strategy project, no one was certain what changes might be needed. Some thought a course for students on how to think might be sufficient. Others thought that the instruction that was necessary would probably take place during the time allocated for reading and language arts; carryover to other areas of the curriculum would be the responsibility of the students. It soon became obvious that each of us viewed the school's goal and the need for change through idiosyncratic lenses reflecting personal needs, attitudes, goals, and circumstances, as well as unique beliefs and understandings about cognition (Peterson, Clark, & Dickson, 1990; Richardson, 1990). Based on past experiences with change projects (Gaskins, 1988; Gaskins & Elliot, 1991; see Chapter 11), we knew that this change project could not be rushed and that teachers' concerns and anxiety about implementing change needed to be heard, respected, and addressed. We also knew that an investment in the knowledge and tools teachers need to grow professionally would be an investment in both the success of the project (Darling-Hammond, 1990) and the future of our students.

Data presented here regarding teachers' reactions to and interpretations of the project were gathered from several sources. These include transcripts of interviews with teachers, supervisors' notes, notes from sharing meetings, and informal conversations with teachers. In order to confirm the accuracy of the author's interpretations, all 33 staff members responded anonymously to an earlier draft of this chapter. Alterations were made so the chapter would accurately reflect staff responses.

The across-the-curriculum learning, thinking, and problem-solving research and development project took place during 3 school years, beginning in 1988–1989 and was preceded by a pilot project in 1987–1988. During the pilot year, an effort was made to integrate process and content in one middle-school class. The first year of the actual project, which included 11 volunteer teachers and their supervisors, was devoted to developing guidelines for teaching strategies. In the second year, with tentative guidelines to follow that had been developed in the first year, more teachers joined the project. During the third and final year of the development project, the entire teaching staff was asked to participate in teaching strategies across the curriculum. This chapter presents teachers' reactions to this change project.

THE PILOT YEAR

Establishing a Social Context for Change

Although the staff wholeheartedly supported the goal of creating better learners, thinkers, and problem solvers across the curriculum, and was excited about our receipt of a Cognitive Sciences in Education grant from the James S. McDonnell Foundation to support the project, individual enthusiasm for involvement in the project varied. In fact, for a few teachers, the reaction to receipt of the grant was one of panic. The unspoken question was "What are you going to *make* us do?" This question underscored the need for the faculty to play an active role in the change process (Richardson, 1990; Tyack, 1990).

Receiving the grant in December, 1987, allowed 6 months before the start of a new school year to explore with teachers the research base on which instruction might be built, and to collaborate with them about how to implement these ideas. It also provided time to listen to and address teachers' concerns. Unlike the developers of many change projects, we would not be satisfied with implementing the innovation in a few, or even most, classrooms. We wanted all 33 teachers and supervisors of academic subjects ultimately to enlist in the project. Together we would construct the standards of "warranted practice" (Richardson, 1990), integrating our practical knowledge and value premises with empirical premises derived from research. The social context we established would be a critical factor for the success of the project.

Creating a Model and Learning from One Teacher's Reactions

Change in educational practice usually comes about through the adoption of models (Slavin, 1990). Therefore, during the school year prior to the beginning of the strategy project, a pilot program was conducted. Instructional practices designed through staff collaboration and informed by current research were implemented in a middle-school social studies class. The course was taught jointly by the director of the school and a young historian with no prior teacher training or teaching experience. Our goal was to develop a model that could serve as a starting point for developing a strategy program across the curriculum. As the model began to take shape, teachers were invited to observe the social studies lessons to develop a sense of what instruction might look like when teachers endeavor to blend content and process. (See Gaskins and Elliot, 1991, for the story of this pilot program.)

Although this was a project involving change, the historian (Jim) confided right from the start that he would leave the "process stuff" to his co-teacher (Irene) and that he would concentrate on what he knew best—history. Because he loved history himself, he was convinced that he could make Colonial America come alive for even the most passive students. Jim was given several articles to read about cognitive and metacognitive strategies, but as a first-year teacher he had his hands full just preparing to teach the content.

Jim's job was to facilitate discussions about history. He easily captured the students' interest with entertaining stories that seemed to make history come alive. Although the students were attentive, they remained passive in their approach to learning. Irene's job was to teach the students the cognitive and metacognitive processes that would enable them to actively construct an understanding of the history discussed. Jim's expertise enabled Irene to develop and mediate for the students a more complex understanding of history. As this occurred, she shared with the class the processes that she was using to construct understandings about history, revealing that many years earlier she had merely memorized facts in order to get good grades. The students appreciated being let in on "cognitive secrets" and began calling Irene's portion of the lesson "Psych 101." Jim frequently commented on how much more actively involved the students were when they were being guided to apply strategies to processing the material in the text than when he taught. Gradually, as Jim witnessed the success of students who were becoming strategic, he began to incorporate into his teaching explicit strategy instruction.

A number of theories about implementing a new program in a school resulted from the pilot project. One was the idea that a beginning teacher might accept a new program more readily than someone with years of experience teaching another way. We suspected that this opportunity to watch the day by day development of a new teacher was not representative of the change process for an experienced teacher. For example, we suspected that Jim was more flexible about his convictions than an experienced teacher, or even than a novice teacher who had completed a teacher education program. In addition, experienced teachers are often guarded in revealing their feelings about programs that claim to be research-based, but run contrary to their practices. Jim, however, was quite candid in sharing his thoughts about teaching, providing an opportunity to gain a glimpse of what one teacher thought when faced with instructional procedures that did not fit the teaching schema he had developed from his own 18 years of experience as a student.

It was clear that, initially, Jim did not fully accept the idea of devoting the better part of the instructional time to teaching students how to process the content. His reluctance was for understandable reasons: (1) teaching strategies did not fit his schema for history instruction, (2) he had only a very vague idea about what strategies should be taught and no idea how to teach them, and (3) as a new teacher, he felt he had his hands full learning to manage a class and preparing lessons about the content of social studies, without trying to add something that he did not understand or see as part of content instruction. These reasons only substantiate the point made by Tozer, Anderson, and Armbruster (1990) that we must pay attention to "practical contexts of teaching as a guide to integration of research knowledge and theory" (p. 296) and to construct with teachers the "theory and knowledge in the form of tools they can use in practice" (p. 298). However, with a great deal of reflection, support, and an increasing understanding of the process used to construct meaning, Jim created a new vision of what instruction might be like. The result was the development of an expert strategy teacher over the 3 years of the project.

The apparent success of this pilot year, both in developing students who were actively involved in strategically processing information and in training a teacher to teach strategies, convinced us that a research and development project held great promise for training teachers and for developing students who were actively involved in their learning. It appeared that, for the change project to be successful, we would need to structure the project in such a way that teachers gained both knowledge and experience regarding teaching strategies and had the opportunity for reflection about both. Teachers would need to be supported in their endeavors to integrate knowledge and experience in light of the belief systems that currently guided their thinking. Clearly, the focus had to be not only on what teachers did in the classroom, but also on what they thought.

YEAR ONE

Beginning with Volunteers

In order for the initial year of the research and development project to have the best possible chance of being both successful and manageable, we decided that it should involve only a limited number of teachers who volunteered. It was our belief that, with fewer teachers, we would be able to nurture more carefully the expertise of these volunteers (Anderson & Armbruster, 1990). Eleven teachers volunteered, representing most grade levels and subject areas.

We learned from our interviews with teachers and their reactions to the initial draft of this chapter that there were various reasons for volunteering and not volunteering. The most common reason for volunteering was that the teacher, usually through regular attendance at the weekly research seminars, was convinced that involvement in the project was in the best interest of his or her students. Nevertheless, these teachers were nervous about the commitment they were making for reasons such as time constraints, inexperience in teaching strategies, and lack of confidence. In addition to believing this project was in the best interest of the students, other reasons for volunteering included becoming a better teacher, being part of a dynamic social group, being in on shaping a program from its inception, pleasing the school's director, earning extra money, and pleasing a supervisor who was strongly urging involvement. For the most part, the volunteers exemplified the Carnegie Forum Task Force and Holmes Group's vision of thoughtful teachers, "ones who are engaged continuously in the process of learning; who are able to learn all the time; and who view learning and development as a lifelong process for themselves and their students." (Peterson *et al.,* 1990, p. 336)

Reasons for not volunteering were also varied. The most common reasons related to time constraints. Many of the teachers were already over-committed. They had family obligations, were enrolled in graduate courses, or traveled long distances. Other teachers seemed fearful or apprehensive, although these reasons usually were not stated explicitly. Some seemed to have an unspoken fear that they were not as good at teaching as others on the staff thought they were or as good as they thought they should be. Aware of the observations and audiotaping that were part of the project, some confided that they feared they would be found wanting or would not measure up to the other volunteers. Several teachers expressed the concern that they would be forced into a mold and would lose their individuality, that opportunities for creativity would disappear. Another reason for not volunteering was that teachers wanted to wait until the guidelines for the program were more clearly outlined.

Other concerns were expressed in terms of the students. Some felt that a strategy emphasis would result in less content being covered; thus, the students would not have the background they needed for higher-level content classes. Other teachers were concerned that involvement in a research project would disrupt the normal flow of their classrooms and, as a result, not be in the best interest of their students. Yet another reason was expressed by a teacher of beginning readers. She felt that, considering the needs of the children she taught, there were other more pressing priorities on which she needed to concentrate with her students, such as breaking the code, acquiring a sight vocabulary, and realizing that reading must make sense. A second teacher expressed a similar concern.

Providing Direction

During the 6 months prior to the opening of the first school year of the project, several meetings were held to address concerns, solicit ideas, discuss research and theory, and keep teachers apprised of progress regarding the project. Strategy teaching was the topic of weekly research seminars at which teachers wrestled with reconciling personal beliefs and understandings with the theoretical research-based framework we were building collaboratively. We all benefitted from the opportunity to talk about how theoretical premises agreed or disagreed with personal premises about how children learn new information. The result was an ever evolving view of warranted practice developed by the staff. In addition to meetings, memos were regularly distributed to share findings from the research literature, propose possible formats for strategy teaching, and solicit continued dialogue about the application of research to classroom practice. Outside consultants (e.g., Richard Anderson, Jonathan Baron, Gerald Duffy, Scott Paris, Michael Pressley, Laura Roehler, and Peter Winograd) met with the faculty to share ideas, as well as to react to our ideas, for teaching cognitive and metacognitive strategies. Planning sessions were held to decide which strategies might prove most beneficial to our students. All these methods of communication, dialogue, and training were used in the belief that understanding and discussing the integration of research and experience "produces teachers with knowledge without reducing them to puppets manipulated by policymakers or researchers." (Floden & Klinzing, 1990, p. 17) We believe that collaborative action research promotes teachers' intellectual development (Baird, Fensham, Gunstone, & White, 1991) and that effective teaching depends on the extent and quality of teacher training (Darling-Hammond, 1990).

During the summer after the pilot program was implemented, a manual was written and given to the volunteer teachers outlining a rationale, based on how the mind works, to be shared with students regarding the need to employ strategies for constructing meaning (see Gaskins and Elliot, 1991). Directions for instructing students, derived from the 6 months of preparation for the project, were elaborated at the back-to-school inservice in early September. At this time, the volunteer teachers agreed on a tentative format to guide the teaching of the cognitive and metacognitive strategies for processing the content of the regular school day. The model included telling students *what* strategy they might employ, *why* the strategy would be helpful, *when* it might be used, and *how* to use it. These explanations would be followed by the teacher modeling the reasoning used when implementing the strategy. Students then would be given opportunities to use the strategy while receiving teacher feedback and elaboration. Teachers decided to experiment with this format for several weeks prior to attending school-sponsored weekend retreats in October at which they would share successes, work out problems, and plan future lessons.

A "minicourse" in psychology was developed for the middle school to support both student and teachers in their understanding of how the mind works. The impetus for the course resulted from the success students experienced during the pilot co-teaching of social studies described earlier and took the name given to it by the students: Psych 101. Irene and Jim continued to co-teach, only now they taught daily 20-min lessons in a separate course about the workings of the mind. The course was an attempt to put research-based variables together into a possible prototype for explaining cognition to young people. Classes were also designed to aid the oldest (Grades 6–8) and often least flexible students in understanding the new lesson format being implemented by teachers. During Psych 101 classes, classroom teachers remained in the rooms to observe. They were then able to use and reinforce concepts presented in Psych 101 as they taught reading, language arts, and social studies. Thus, a common language of the mind was introduced to both students and teachers. (See Gaskins and Elliot, 1991, for an overview of Psych 101.)

For most of our volunteer teachers, the fall weekend retreats cemented their commitment to teaching strategies. One group of teachers met from 8:30 one Saturday morning until 9:30 in the evening, brainstorming ideas and planning strategy lessons to mesh with their content objectives. Another group met all day on Sunday. A few weekends later, many of the same teachers met again. There was a great deal of learning from one another and a sense of being part of an exciting project. Although teachers were paid for attending the retreats and for the lesson plans they wrote and shared with the staff, it was clear that they were there to learn and grow professionally. The dialogues that were begun on these weekends continued informally throughout the year.

Teacher Reactions to the First Year of Change

Responses of the teachers who had volunteered to be part of the project were varied. Some expressed feeling energized, having a sense of exhilaration about teaching that they had never experienced before. They, like Baird and co-workers (1991), stressed the importance of reflection and collaboration. Some, however, were overly self-critical in their reflections and at times expressed concern that they were not yet presenting lessons that met their own high standards.

A few who initially volunteered, but were unable to take full advantage of the ongoing opportunities for collaboration due to time constraints, tended to return to familiar patterns of teaching once the lessons planned during the retreats had been taught. Observers noted that, despite the intent of these teachers to combine process and content and despite their ability to verbalize how they thought the process of teaching strategies should be implemented, their instruction more closely resembled facts and skills transmitted from teacher to students than the development of student expertise through mediating (verbally guiding student thinking processes) and encouraging dialogue between students about their use of strategies to construct meaning. They seemed unable to project themselves into the alternative vision they described as ideal or to create new role metaphors for themselves to guide instruction (Briscoe, 1991). Their old images of instruction seemed to be too powerful to put in the background, suggesting that individual commitment to change is not sufficient to induce the desired changes (Briscoe, 1991). If change is to occur in practice, "teachers must examine their beliefs, judgments, and thoughts regarding what they do and how they do it." (Briscoe, 1991, p. 197) Anderson (1989) has suggested several other possible explanations for teachers that return to familiar ways of instruction: teachers may not agree with or understand the model; they may feel there are more important goals that take priority, such as covering the content; or they may fear that the innovation will cause them to lose control of the class, with nothing to show for the lesson. The few teachers who shared the fact that they did not totally identify with the goals of the project provided confirmation for the powerful role played by prior beliefs about teaching and learning and the fact that real change can occur only when there are changes in practical knowledge and cognitions (Richardson, 1990).

All the volunteers admitted that, at least initially, the change in the way they taught meant spending more time reflecting and planning, time that some did not feel they always had. One first-year teacher who had taken a preservice course that emphasized strategy teaching shared her discovery that a good preservice background in strategy teaching was helpful, but not sufficient, for successful strategy teaching.

> I hadn't learned the concepts well enough in preservice to actually implement them. I thought I understood the concepts and was ready to teach them but found that doing it is different from knowing. A person needs to internalize the process somewhat before she or he can teach it.

The volunteer teachers all agreed that they enjoyed working in a school culture characterized by collaboration, professional inquiry, and reflection. One of these teachers wrote:

> I agree that at the beginning of teaching a strategy it takes more planning time, but experience and increasing comfort seem to lessen that. Reflection, in addition to helping me as a teacher think about and improve my teaching methods, is an invaluable tool for assessing student growth and change, thus enabling me to meet them where they are in their understanding. Reading about student responses/behaviors in observers' journals is a tremendous help in triggering that reflection on the way individual students are responding to instruction.

There were responses, too, from the teachers who had not volunteered to be involved in the project during its first year. Some wanted assurances that they were not going to be forced to change the way they taught or that they would not receive poor performance evaluations because they had not volunteered for the project. One felt that:

> in some ways the research project caused a division among the faculty since it seemed that those who immediately tried new ideas and volunteered to take part in the study were the "favored ones."

Another nonparticipant expressed frustration regarding the nature of a development project in which teachers construct the program together. He suggested that:

> It was very stressful among those who did not participate—information about the project was limited and direction was poor, at first, creating even more stress.

It appears that, for some, the process of developing the program together made strategy teaching seem ambiguous. We were concerned about this seeming lack of direction, yet it was our belief that we should not dictate how strategies should be taught; instead, each teacher should develop his or her own instructional processes by wrestling with the theories and research being shared in the school and applying them to instruction that met the needs of the students. We felt that to dictate a program would be to invite mindless teaching by dissatisfied teachers. We saw the development project as a collaborative venture.

Some of the nonparticipants grew increasingly concerned about the amount of time the volunteer teachers were devoting to the project. Even if the nonparticipants were convinced that strategy instruction was in the best interest of their students, they wondered where they would find the time to teach that way. On the other hand, a few of the nonparticipants attended most of the inservice and sharing meetings and experimented on their own with some of the ideas that the volunteer teachers were implementing. They liked being able to move into the project at their own pace, and some of them expressed delight in not having participant observers in their classrooms with journals and tape recorders. As one teacher said:

> I must admit I felt threatened, but only for a very brief time. I quickly came to view the taping and journals as a way to help me analyze my teaching style and my effectiveness in the classroom, as well as an invaluable aid in meeting students' needs. Feedback from a supervisor through an interactive journal was much more valuable than from a researcher because my supervisor knew the students and was able to help analyze why a particular lesson did not work or why a strategy was meeting a particular groups' immediate needs.

The theme that a support structure is necessary to create and sustain change was prevalent in the teachers' notes and comments (Tikunoff & Ward, 1983). The teachers clearly appreciated assistance in the reflection process, as well as the many other forms of support that were available.

YEAR TWO

Continuing Support

During the summer of 1989, Gaskins and Elliot wrote a guidebook for teachers describing what the staff had learned about a theoretically sound implementation of cognitive strategy instruction. This guidebook included a review of the literature and a rationale for teaching strategies, a description of specific cognitive and metacognitive strategies and suggestions for teaching them, and numerous case studies outlining how teachers had implemented a strategy program. Staff members were given copies of the guidebook and asked to provide the authors with feedback regarding how to make the guidebook more helpful. After moving through several rounds of staff editing, the guidebook was published (Gaskins & Elliot, 1991).

Knowing that there is more to promoting change in classrooms than the design of theoretically sound guidelines for instruction, the director and supervisors made plans to work in classrooms in order to continue to build their own understanding of classroom environments, as well as to collaborate with teachers about strategy instruction. During the summer and early fall, Benchmark supervisors encouraged the nonvolunteer teachers to make a commitment to become involved in the strategy project in some way. Most agreed to collaborate with a supervisor on a short-term strategy teaching project. The roles that each supervisor played varied. Some collaborated with the teacher to plan a unit of instruction; then the teacher taught the lessons while the supervisor took notes and provided feedback. In other cases, the supervisor planned and taught the lessons and the teacher wrote reactions in an interactive journal. In still other cases, the teacher did all the planning and teaching and the supervisor provided an extra pair of hands, sometimes leading a small group discussion or providing feedback to students as they applied the strategy being taught. Whatever role the supervisors played, they learned that, to manage the development of instructional expertise, they had to learn to think in ways that were responsive to the social details of particular problem situations and to integrate that knowledge into an action plan (Lampert & Clark, 1990).

Psych 101 continued for the middle-school students; the lower-school teachers requested a similar course for their students in which the rationale for being actively involved in learning would be presented. The director began teaching a 12-session course called LAT (Learning and Thinking) to eight of the lower-school classes (Grades 3–5). The content of this course consisted of miniexperiments designed to demonstrate to the students in a powerful, experiential manner the effectiveness of strategy use. During each class session, half the class (the experimental group) was involved actively in the content of the lesson and half the class (the controls) was designated "eyes only." The experimental group was taught a strategy for learning the content of the lesson while the "eyes only" group was allowed to use only their eyes—no writing notes, discussing with classmates, or asking for clarification. At the conclusion of each miniexperiment, those in the experimental group would explain to the control group why they were able to learn the lesson content so easily. The answer was always the same—because they were actively involved and were implementing strategies.

As in the previous year, there were weekly meetings at which the staff discussed research and classroom applications, monthly inservice meetings featuring experts in strategy teaching, several retreats, and regular memos about strategy teaching. Teachers' reactions to and concerns about the project continued to be actively solicited and addressed.

Teacher Reactions

As one part of our research, we conducted an interview study to gather information about the staff's background regarding strategy teaching, as well as their reactions to the project (Pressley *et al.,* 1990). We were particularly interested in factors they cited that influenced their understanding of strategy teaching. The factors (and the percentage of the teachers citing each factor) were interacting with other teachers (97%), reading and reacting to Benchmark manuscripts (87%), reading professional articles (87%), attending monthly inservice with outside experts (81%), interacting with supervisor (81%), interacting with school director (81%), observing other teachers (74%), attending team meetings and other sharing meetings (68%), attending research seminar (65%), reading professional books (42%), observing the director teach (35%), and observing one's supervisor teach (26%).

Beyond *understanding* strategy teaching, reactions of teachers during the second year suggested that most particularly enjoyed the aspects of the project that involved personal support from a supervisor or the director, for example, demonstration lessons, collaborative teaching projects, LAT, interactive journals, and regular meetings with their supervisors and the director. One teacher commented:

> Support from the supervisors and the director is the key to change. I think most teachers are reluctant to take the risk of changing unless they are absolutely sure they have support from above. Change is stressful enough without the worry of being chastised for failure.

On the other hand, a small minority saw the active involvement of the director and supervisors as pressure. All the teachers appreciated being allowed to move into strategy teaching at their own pace, yet a few expressed feeling that they were not part of the "in" group because they had not initially volunteered for the project.

Some continued to express concern that in the third year of the project they might be forced to become strategy teachers. This reaction was based primarily on worries about time. Teachers viewed both learning to be a strategy teacher and planning strategy lessons as requiring more time than their present way of teaching. They were also concerned about the amount of time strategy teaching would take away from covering content. This concern was present despite the fact that supervisors stressed that "less is better." The overriding concern seemed to be that in a short time these students would be returning to the mainstream, where knowing the facts might allow them to feel more successful than knowing how to learn, think, and solve problems. This is a concern that has frequently been expressed regarding curriculum reform aimed at problem solving and the development of higher-order thinking skills (Darling-Hammond, 1990).

Another growing concern was that if a teacher did not volunteer to be part of the strategies-across-the-curriculum project, he or she might be regarded as a bad teacher. The tape recording of lessons also continued to be a concern despite the fact that lessons were only observed or taped with a teacher's permission.

YEAR THREE

Training Teachers Using Interactive Journals

Our goal had been that, by the end of the third year of the project, all academic teachers voluntarily would be teaching students strategies for becoming better learners, thinkers, and problem solvers. Now that we were seeing the difference in student learning made by strategy teaching, we did not want to settle for the original goal that every teacher have some knowledge of strategy teaching and occasionally include strategy instruction as part of a lesson. We wanted all teachers to be at the level of expertise in strategy teaching achieved by some of our early volunteers.

By the outset of the third year, the way we talked about instruction had changed. We wanted teachers to teach not only strategies, but to mediate strategy use through questioning and through sharing how they thought through the process of constructing knowledge. The key to this construction of knowledge was the way teachers initiated and supported a transaction involving students, the teacher, and the task (Gaskins, Anderson, Pressley, Cunicelli, & Satlow, in press; Pressley *et al.*, 1992).

We dealt with this dilemma of increasing expertise in strategy teaching among the staff in two ways: by providing novice strategy teachers with opportunities to co-teach with teachers who were already expert in strategy teaching and by providing opportunities to observe supervisors and teachers present a series of strategy lessons. There was very little staff turnover during the first two years of the project; nevertheless, we did have a few new teachers to train. The selection of the new teachers had been based partially on teacher applicants' enthusiasm about and commitment to strategy teaching. Thus, we faced a much easier task in training the new teachers than in training a staff of teachers who had not begun their careers at Benchmark expecting to become strategy teachers. As one new teacher remarked:

> It may have been easier for me to change or adapt since I am new to Benchmark and wasn't set in my ways. I also think that as a new teacher I got a lot of guidelines and support from supervisors and staff members. I am hopeful the guidelines will continue since I have tons to learn.

Teachers who were new to their positions attended a 2-wk new-teacher inservice program during August and, in addition, prior to the opening of school, read several manuscripts and books about teaching at Benchmark. Once school began, new teachers collaborated with their supervisor on a daily basis about teaching one aspect of the curriculum. For example, the focus of attention for using strategies to construct meaning might be reading, writing, or social studies instruction. The supervisor was present in the classroom each day. During this time she might write reflections, questions, or comments in the interactive journal as the teacher taught or she might teach and the teacher would take notes and write reflections. This provided daily written dialogue about strategy teaching between the teacher and the supervisor; both the teacher and the supervisor were writing questions, reflecting, and responding. Teachers discovered that interactive journal writing enabled them to see more clearly what they knew and to rethink the assumptions that guided their instructional practices (Gitlin, 1990). As one teacher noted:

> Reacting to daily journal notes about lessons forces us to rethink our approaches and assumptions—something we would otherwise put off because of the other demands of teaching.

During the third year of the project, three new teachers were trained using the interactive dialogue journal as a vehicle for professional growth.

In addition, several veteran Benchmark teachers were engaged in similar collaborative projects with their supervisors or the school's director. For example, the director co-taught social studies with a teacher who was teaching middle-school social studies for the first time, and co-taught science for several months with a science teacher. Planning and teaching with these teachers on a daily basis, as well as writing daily reflections, gave those in the school who were responsible for the direction of classroom instruction a greater understanding of the concerns expressed by teachers. One teacher's response to co-teaching with the director follows.

> It was, for me, a tremendously encouraging experience to co-teach with Irene. Having the opportunity to bounce ideas off her before trying them gave me the confidence to try many things I would probably never have attempted on my own. It was also very important for me to be able to check my feelings/reactions against those of a pro. Since neither of us was "married" to the content, it seemed very natural and right to digress from plans to spend more time meeting students' needs for ways to construct meaning. Because we were learning with the kids, we could more clearly see the strategies needed to help them construct meaning. Some days we were only a day ahead of them, so our experiences were fresh in our minds. While I was a little nervous about teaching with the director in the beginning, I was anxious to cement my understanding of strategy instruction more carefully and also to try something new. I love a challenge, and teaching social studies certainly represented that challenge! Because I joined Benchmark's staff when the strategy teaching program was in effect, I was a "believer" from the beginning, and was very anxious to try new ways to teach strategies in my reading groups—so in effect I was able to ease in without the accompanying fears that experienced teachers had. It then seemed very natural to carry this over to social studies.

Teacher and Administrator Reactions

The director and supervisors who were teaching classes worried as much as teachers in previous years when they realized that, in some instances, they were spending twice as long as usual on a particular unit of study because allowing students to construct their own knowledge can be more time consuming than simply telling them what you want them to know. We also discovered that, at least in the initial stages, planning strategy instruction that is embedded in content is more time consuming than planning content lessons. In addition, we learned, as Shulman (1986) has pointed out, that to teach well the teacher must know the subject matter well, and that it is uncomfortable and difficult to be flexible in teaching a topic about which you may have a little background knowledge as the students. We solved the problem of lack of expertise by reading a great deal about each topic prior to teaching it.

We were encouraged by the fact that students in some classes expressed increased enjoyment of school when instruction was structured so that every student could be involved and supported in the application of strategies to what they were reading or learning. On the other hand, a few students seemed to resist teachers' efforts to change their instructional roles. The teachers' new roles as mediators of the construction of knowledge were incongruent with the students' understandings of how school is supposed to run (Anderson, 1989). For example, we discovered during the first 2 years of the project that we had to guide students to understand their restructured roles as constructors of knowledge rather than recipients. In addition, we now needed to deal with students' concepts of the noncompetitive accountability system set up in a few classrooms. Some students seemed baffled by a new system that fostered daily self-assessments that students corrected or evaluated themselves and could study and rework until satisfied with the results. Questions had many "correct" responses; a student's explanation of the reasoning behind an answer was valued as much as the answer. Tests, too, could be retaken, and only the final test would be included in the student's portfolio. This system made it possible for all students to earn As so collaboration between students was encouraged. As one teacher wrote in response to this chapter:

> Our social studies class certainly seems to be proof that this can work. They share knowledge and help one another willingly and are excited when they all understand. They are really learning to think!

Initially, students found it foreign to regard their classmates as cognitive resources rather than impediments to learning or competitors. A few students insisted they liked the old system better. For some the old way seemed like less work, whereas for others the competitive aspect was appealing because it allowed them to be at the top. It was clear that if we were to be successful in creating learners, thinkers, and problem solvers, we needed to attend not only to teachers' beliefs and schemata, but also to those beliefs and schemata that students brought to the classroom.

SUMMARY OF REACTIONS TO CHANGE

Reactions to, as well as results of, implementing new instructional practices across the curriculum differed before, during, and toward the end of the 3-year strategies project. At each stage of the project, significant factors either facilitated or impeded change. Although the experience of individual teachers varied, all agreed that the summary that follows includes their point of view and accurately represents essential characteristics of their experience with the strategies-across-the-curriculum change project.

For some teachers, the commencement of the project precipitated immediate concerns, some of which were cited as reasons for not participating in the early stages of the project. These concerns included (1) a fear that they would be forced to change the way that they taught, (2) worries about the time commitment required by the innovation, (3) a preference for applying the innovation at their own pace, (4) a dislike for the research trappings of the project, (5) a worry about a decrease in content coverage that would result in students' not having the content background they needed when they left Benchmark, and (6) uneasiness about the effect that not participating in the project would have on how they would be evaluated as teachers.

During the initial stages of becoming a part of the strategies-across-the-curriculum project, most teachers felt an increase in the demands made on them. New teachers in particular found they had a lot to keep in mind just in applying concepts learned in preservice training and in Benchmark's new-teacher inservice; thus, some experienced stress when encouraged to be part of the project. Even the veteran teachers who volunteered for the project, although they usually did not identify the process as stressful, reported an initial increase in the reflection and planning time required to prepare strategy lessons.

A few of the teachers who initially did not volunteer approached the project cautiously, yet over the 3 years, and at their own pace, they did begin teaching strategies. Other initial nonvolunteers expressed a willingness to become involved once they understood the theory and rationale behind the instructional practices; many of these individuals began teaching strategies in the second year. Still other nonvolunteers continued during the second year to resist implementing the new instructional practices, generally for the same reasons listed earlier.

Those teachers involved in the project tended to express new-found enthusiasm for and satisfaction with their work. By integrating process and content, they were meeting the needs of the students in a new way. Not only were they teaching content, they also were providing students with strategies for understanding and remembering the content. One temporary roadblock that teachers encountered was winning students over to recognizing the value of being strategic, especially when the students perceived the new instructional approach as incongruent with their view of how school was supposed to run. Most teachers, however, saw winning students over to recognizing the value of being strategic as a challenge they were determined to meet.

Throughout the course of the project, there were actions that supported change. Teachers reported enjoying the emphasis on collegiality and professional inquiry that characterized the culture of the school. In particular, teachers identified sharing and collaborating with peers (other teachers, supervisors, and the director), ongoing inservice, and professional reading as factors that influenced their strategy teaching. In addition, they felt supported by their supervisors and the director.

Toward the end of the project it was possible to assess the effects of the time individuals committed to the project. It appeared that those teachers who were able to make the most substantial time commitments to grow professionally were also the teachers who were most likely to make lasting instructional changes. Those who intended to change, but who were unable to avail themselves of the opportunities for professional growth, reflection, and collaboration, tended to assume previous patterns of instruction. This may have resulted from teachers' unconscious adoption of the instructional patterns they had experienced when they were students. In addition to time constraints, other reasons for reverting to old practices included (1) finding that he or she did not agree with or understand the new model of instruction, (2) feeling that other instructional goals were a priority, or (3) for a number of reasons regarding the innovation as risky, or not in the best interest of the students.

The attempt to fully integrate strategy instruction into an existing curriculum required change and professional growth from all those involved— teachers, supervisors, and the director. These individuals concurred that adherence to the following principles regarding the school's social context fostered instructional change.

1. Teachers are encouraged to be active partners in the process of change and are provided with opportunities to construct theories about instruction and to determine the premises and standards of instruction. The result is the construction of a model of instruction, based on research and real-world experience, that provides a vision of the instructional practice.
2. Teachers are allowed to volunteer to take part in the change project and are provided with ongoing support, both in and out of the classroom. As these volunteer teachers increase in expertise and refine the program, other teachers become interested in participating based on the positive results they see in the students of the volunteer teachers.
3. Collaborative methods are employed that provide teachers with opportunities for supportive feedback and reflection. These collaborative methods may include joint planning of lesson units and daily oral and written dialogue between teachers and supervisors as well as other methods that provide teachers with support and stimulation.

The Benchmark School 3-year research and development project to create better learners, thinkers, and problem solvers across the curriculum resulted in instruction that fostered the transactional construction of knowledge among both students and teachers (Gaskins *et al.*, in press) and produced significant changes in the way students handled many school tasks (Gaskins *et al.,* in preparation). The most significant results tended to be in curriculum areas that coincided with the most teacher training, reflection, and collaboration. Thus, our goals for our next 3-year research and development project include more training, reflection, and collaboration, now emphasizing mathematics and science. We also plan to continue systematic study of the change process among both teachers and students.

ACKNOWLEDGMENTS

This project was funded by the James S. McDonnell Foundation whom we gratefully acknowledge. We also appreciate the support of the 33 teachers who made this project a success. The first author is particularly appreciative of the opportunity to learn from and with her coteachers during the past four years: James Benedict, Frances Boehnlein, Eleanor Gensemer, Eric MacDonald, and Warren Young.

REFERENCES

Anderson, L. (1989). Implementing instructional programs to promote meaningful, self-regulating learning. In J. Brophy (Ed.), *Advances in research on teaching* (Vol. 1, pp. 311–343). Greenwich, Connecticut: JAI Press.

Anderson, R. C., and Armbruster, B. B. (1990). Some maxims for learning and instruction. *Teachers College Record, 91,* 396–408.

Baird, J. R., Fensham, P. J., Gunstone, R. F., and White, R. T. (1991). The importance of reflection in improving science teaching and learning. *Journal of Research in Science Teaching, 28,* 163–182.

Briscoe, C. (1991). The dynamic interactions among beliefs, role metaphors, and teaching practices: A case study of teacher change. *Science Education, 75,* 185–199.

Darling-Hammond, L. (1990). Achieving our goals: Superficial or structural reforms? *Phi Delta Kappan, 72,* 286–295.

Floden, R. E., and Klinzing, H. G. (1990). What can research on teacher thinking contribute to teacher preparation? A second opinion. *Educational Researcher, 19,* 15–20.

Gaskins, I. W. (1988). Helping teachers adapt to the needs of students with learning problems. In S. J. Samuels and P. D. Pearson (Eds.), *Changing school reading programs* (pp. 143–159). Newark, Delaware: International Reading Association.

Gaskins, I. W., and Elliot, T. T. (1991). *Implementing cognitive strategy instruction across the school: The Benchmark manual for teachers.* Cambridge, Massachusetts: Brookline Books.

Gaskins, I. W., Anderson, R. C., Pressley, M., Cunicelli, E. A., and Satlow, E. (1992). Six teachers' dialogue during cognitive process instruction. *Elementary School Journal,* in press.

Gaskins, I. W., Benedict, J., Boehnlein, F., Cunicelli, E. A., and Satlow, E. (1992). *A naturalistic assessment of a three-year strategy program.* Unpublished manuscript.

Gitlin, A. (1990). Understanding teaching dialogically. *Teachers College Record, 91,* 537–563.

Lampert, M., and Clark, C. M. (1990). Expert knowledge and expert thinking in teaching: A response to Floden and Klinzing. *Educational Researcher, 19,* 21–23.

Leithwood, K. A. (1990). The principal's role in teacher development. In B. Joyce (Ed.), *Changing school culture through staff development* (pp. 71–90). Alexandria, Virginia: Association for Supervision and Curriculum Development.

Peterson, P. L., Clark, C. M., and Dickson, W. P. (1990). Educational psychology as a foundation in teacher education: Reforming an old notion. *Teachers College Record, 91,* 322–346.

Pressley, M., El-Dinary, P. B., Gaskins, I. W., Schuder, T., Bergman, J. L., Almasi, J., and Brown, R. (1992). Beyond direct explanation: Transactional instruction of reading comprehension strategies. *Elementary School Journal.*

Pressley, M., Gaskins, I. W., Cunicelli, E. A., Burdick, N. A., Schaub-Matt, M., Lee, D. S., and Powell, N. (1990). Perceptions of Benchmark School's experienced strategy teachers and strategy researchers about the nature of effective long-term strategy instruction. *Learning Disability Quarterly, 14,* 19–48.

Richardson, V. (1990). Significant and worthwhile change in teaching practice. *Educational Researcher, 19,* 10–18.

Shulman, L. S. (1986). Paradigms and research programs in the study of teaching: A contemporary perspective. In M. C. Wittrock (Ed.), *Handbook of research on teaching* (3rd ed., pp. 3–36). New York: Macmillan.

Slavin, R. E. (1990). On making a difference. *Educational Researcher, 19,* 30–34.

Tikunoff, W. J., and Ward, B. A. (1983). Collaborative research on teaching. *The Elementary School Journal, 83,* 453–468.

Tozer, S., Anderson, T. H., and Armbruster, B. B. (1990). Psychological and social foundations in teacher education: A thematic introduction. *Teachers College Record, 91,* 293–299.

Tyack, D. (1990). Restructuring in historical perspective: Tinkering toward Utopia. *Teachers College Record, 92,* 170–191.

15

Embracing the Instructional Complexities of Reading Instruction

Laura R. Roehler

Skills and strategies are often taught in reductionistic ways, that is, they are simplified for ease of learning. Gagné (1985), for instance, suggests three phases of teaching. In the first phase, students learn a declarative representation for each step in the procedure; this often involves the memorization of rules. In the second phase, the learning moves from a step-by-step declarative understanding to a step-by-step performance-based understanding. In the third phase, students are taught to combine the pieces to create larger efficient-action sequences of declarative and procedural knowledge. Complex tasks are simplified first; then the pieces are combined for application. The assumption that a complex task such as reading instruction initially should be simplified and later should be integrated is deeply rooted in classroom practice.

Recently, researchers (e.g., Feltovich, Spiro, & Coulson, 1989) have begun to question the reductionistic approach to instruction. The argument is that initially breaking the process into small units is detrimental when learning involves complex multiple interrelated goals. Rather than limiting knowledge to the simplification of declarative and procedural variables at the beginning of reading instruction and learning and subsequently combining these strategies with content for later use, it may be better to begin with the development of a vision for larger conceptual understandings about reading and how this vision is integratable into literacy and subsequently move to sets of strategies that develop not only declarative and

PROMOTING ACADEMIC COMPETENCE AND LITERACY IN SCHOOLS

procedural knowledge, but also situational and conditional knowledge. This developed knowledge about strategies then must be combined with emerging conceptual framework of what reading is, when to use it, and why to use it. The development of strategic understandings finally must be combined with multiple opportunities for using strategies in relevant situations for which making sense is the goal. This type of approach embraces the complexities of classroom instruction, acknowledges the importance of the learners having conceptual frameworks from the beginning, builds on the wealth of classroom learning opportunities in cognitively, metacognitively, and motivationally sound ways, and advances the possibilities that students will become enthusiastic strategic sense makers when they read.

BACKGROUND

Interest in strategies and strategy instruction developed simultaneously in educational psychology and teacher education. In educational psychology, carefully crafted laboratory experiments developed in the 1970s led to an extensive knowledge base about what strategies are and when, why, and how they should be used. Knowledge about memory strategies, cognitive strategies, and metacognitive strategies soon promised a wealth of information for classroom teachers. In the 1980s, researchers moved into classroom settings and began to teach all types of strategy lessons to various grade levels, continuing the development of understandings about strategies. As the wealth of information about strategy instruction grew, a major problem emerged. When teachers were asked to do what the researchers did, they had more difficulties teaching strategies during classroom instruction. This concern has led a number of researchers to rethink classroom strategy instruction.

During the same time period in teacher education, naturalistic classroom studies were being conducted in which regular teachers, not researchers, taught strategies. The researchers worked with the teachers, helping them develop expertise in strategic instruction (see Au & Kawakami, 1984; Duffy *et al.,* 1987; Palincsar & Brown, 1984; Paris, Cross, & Lipson, 1984; Stevens, Madden, Slavin, & Farnish, 1987, as examples of classroom strategy instruction). For instance, Duffy and Roehler and associates (Duffy *et al.,* 1987) have been investigating classroom reading strategy instruction. This work began in the mid-1970s when process–product studies were showing that the actions of teachers during instruction have a positive and significant effect on student achievement (Brophy & Good, 1986). Building on this research and the findings of information processing studies, they (Duffy *et al.,* 1987) showed in naturalistic experimental studies taught by classroom teachers that explicitness in instruction had a significant and positive effect on students' awareness of the content covered in class and on the use of reading strategies that had been taught. In addition, strategy-instructed students were more likely than control students to have conceptual understandings that reading is a self-directed activity, that reading involves problem solving, that skills and rules aid comprehension, and that the purpose of reading involves the selection of strategies for appropriate use. These teachers created instructional opportunities in which students developed reading understandings in ways that encouraged them to use strategies metacognitively when sense-making was disrupted.

As the researchers conducting these studies continued to study lesson transcripts generated during the research, it became apparent that some teachers were using slightly different instructional actions that affected learning. Thus, a correlational analysis of teacher statements during instruction revealed high correlations between teacher motivational statements about what a strategy is, how it is used, and when it will be used and student achievement, thereby adding to the importance of teacher talk as a determinant of student learning (Sivan & Roehler, 1986). What students come to know, are aware of, and can talk about has a strong relationship with instructional actions. Teachers can learn to engage in instructional talk about the cognitive and metacognitive processes of reading. When this occurs, student performance improves.

Although the results of the direct explanation studies were enlightening and useful, some perplexing problems about teacher effectiveness regarding reading strategies remained. For instance, as the lesson transcripts, the teacher interviews, and the student interviews were examined, it became apparent that some teachers had students who were becoming strategic and other teachers had students who simply possessed a set of strategies. Strategic students were able to recognize that sense-making had been disrupted, could select and apply appropriate strategies until sense-making was regained, and then continue reading. Students who simply possessed a set of strategies could use them in isolated situations only. Drawing on cognitive psychology studies and the naturalistic classroom studies, research was conducted in which students were taught to connect conceptual understandings to strategic actions. When teachers taught lessons reflecting these connections, learning appeared to increase and students appeared to have broader conceptual understandings and be strategic in their approach to reading for sense-making (Roehler, Duffy, & Tiezzi, 1987). Explicit awareness of the complexities of strategic reading instruction seemed to make a difference.

These studies led to a current set of studies that is exploring the relationships among teacher thinking, teacher actions, and student outcomes.

The particular study described in this chapter examines how teachers develop strategic readers in terms of their understandings, actions, awareness of lesson content, and motivation for reading. The measure of success for the teachers in this study was whether the students moved toward literacy in terms of developing (1) conceptual understandings about reading, (2) strategic actions of reading, (3) awareness of strategic actions in reading, and (4) motivation. Questions were developed regarding the manner in which reading instruction occurred and whether reading instruction that embraced the complexities of literacy acquisition was related to better student learning. The overall question was "Do teachers whose instructional thinking and instructional actions reflect an embracing of the complexities of reading instruction have more impact on learning as their students move toward expertise in strategic reading than teachers who do not?"

The specific questions that guided the study were:

1. How did the teachers' instructional understandings about reading outcomes change over the year?
2. How did teachers' instructional actions for the reading outcomes change over the year?
3. How did students' understandings about strategic reading change over the year?
4. How did students' awareness of lesson content change over the year?
5. How did students' strategic actions for reading change over the year?
6. How did students' motivational attributions toward reading change over the year?
7. What is the relationship between teachers' instructional understandings and actions for reading and students' growth toward reading expertise?

METHOD

Participants

The participants for this study were three teachers selected from 18 teachers who participated with their principals in the first year of a 5-yr reading instructional study involving four rural school districts in the Midwest. The selected teachers included a first-grade teacher, a third-grade teacher, and a sixth-grade teacher from one school. Each teacher designated the lowest achieving reading group to participate in the study; five of these low-group students were randomly selected to participate in the research.

Teacher A taught 24 first graders in a school from which the principal and several other teachers participated in the study. She had 12 years of experience. Her September classroom environment included a blending of the basal reader approach and the literature-based approach. She was extremely interested in learning about the mental processes that helped her and her students to be strategic. She was well read in current research, having recently completed several reading methods courses at the Master's degree level. Teacher A was highly motivated to learn how and when to employ empowered decision making that moved students toward literacy.

Teacher B taught 24 sixth graders in the same school. This was the first time she had taught at the sixth-grade level, although she had been teaching for 8 years. Teacher B was interested in incorporating strategies into her instructional program, but expressed concerns initially about her ability to do so since it was her first attempt at sixth grade. She cautiously moved into new types of instruction, simplifying the instructional complexities by making certain she understood the new concepts before adding them to her instruction.

Teacher C, who had been teaching for 25 years, taught 27 third-grade students in the same school. She relied heavily on a basal text program, carefully following the teacher's guide, but expressed interest in learning to teach without a basal reader. She strongly believed in surrounding students with love and care, creating unusual and different ways to present basal text content whenever possible.

The principal for these three teachers had 7 years of administration experience at the elementary level. He attended all sessions with the teachers, observed a reading lesson once a month for each teacher, and met with all participating teachers once a month to discuss reading issues and concerns.

Context of the Study

Certain instructional principles were built into this project. Of prime importance was the development of the understanding that reading instruction has multiple outcomes and that teaching should involve opportunities for students to develop in all outcomes. Teachers were not expected to follow prescriptions faithfully. Instead, they were to be strategic in taking knowledge and flexibly adapting it to their situations. Teachers were to feel empowered about their reading instruction: they were to provide adaptive, adjusted, instructional actions. Teachers were to develop an understanding of the importance of in-depth teaching of a few useful strategies embedded in a network of strategic thinking. Teachers were to understand the importance of teaching metacognitive awareness of the mental processes being used during strategic actions. Teachers were to instruct in ways that enhanced motivation in terms of enthusiasm and self-efficacy for students. Finally, teachers were to develop an understanding of how and when to increase students' awareness and use of the mental processes that support strategic understandings and actions in meaningful and useful lessons that started with a vision and ended with that vision being realized. These strategic mental processes were not to be taught separately, but were to be integrated into set of well-situated lessons using texts that have value for students.

What really counted for teachers who participated in the study was the students' growth toward literacy in ways that increased their strategic actions, conceptual understandings about reading, metacognitive awareness of lesson content, and positive attitudes as reflected in measures of motivation.

In order to help teachers instruct in this way, their principal became an instructional facilitator and created opportunities for collegial interactions with other teachers in the school. The principal's instructional role was critical for three reasons. First, he needed to support the professional growth efforts of these teachers. Second, teachers needed feedback from a significant individual about the appropriateness of their instructional understandings and actions on an ongoing and immediate basis. Third, when he participated in the development of the mental processes and shared language of these teachers and their students about literacy, the complexity of literary instruction and learning was better understood by all participants.

Thus, the principal was asked to show active support by participating in professional growth sessions that occurred throughout the year. He provided feedback to teachers about effectiveness of lessons in monthly observations and helped the three teachers develop understandings about instruction through interactive reflection and participation designed to help students move toward literacy.

The second type of on-site support, collegial interactions, was created for all teachers by the principal. Because the three teachers in this study and two other teachers who also participated in the larger reading instructional study were from this school, they were able to develop their understandings further through scheduled and impromptu discussions. Developing understandings were explored, refined, and restructured through multiple collegial interactions throughout the school year. All three teachers participated equally in these experiences.

MEASURES, DATA COLLECTION, AND DATA ANALYSIS PROCEDURES

Each of the pre-, mid-, and postmeasures; pre- and postmeasures; and ongoing measures for teachers and then students is described. Analyses of these data are taken up as well.

The Teacher Instructional Understandings Measure

The measure of teacher instructional understandings examined thinking about the reading instructional outcomes of strategic processes, routine skills, positive responses, conceptual understandings, and content knowledge. Observers interviewed teachers at the beginning of the school year, the middle of the school year, and the end of the school year. Seven questions were asked. (1) What do you think reading is? (2) What is the role of literate activities in reading instruction? (3) What is the purpose (or goal) of the reading instruction you provide for your students? (4) What do you do to promote students' movement toward reading expertise? (5) What is the students' role in the development of reading expertise? (6) How do you assess your students' success in reading? Why do you assess in this way? (7) In your classroom, what kinds of things help your students become more literate? All three sets of interview responses were noted on protocols and audiotaped for later transcription. For this study, the baseline and end-of-year interviews were used.

Raters determined which of the five outcomes were included in the teachers' responses. For each question, raters looked for evidence that teachers understood that reading involves gaining knowledge in (1) strategic processes, (2) routine skills, (3) positive attitudes, (4) conceptual understandings, and (5) content. The maximum obtainable score for each interview was 35; each of the five outcomes potentially receives a score of one for each of the seven questions.

Two raters, a researcher and a graduate student in teacher education, rated the lessons. When interrater reliability of 80% was reached and maintained, the ratings for instructional understandings were completed.

When rating transcripts, raters (1) independently read and rated all transcripts and recorded the scores; (2) conferred with each other, compared the various assigned ratings for instructional understandings, and reconciled any differences to arrive at scores for each protocol; and (3) submitted the jointly determined scores as final ratings.

After the protocols were rated, each teacher's pre- and postyear ratings were converted to percentages, including the overall scores and each separate outcome score. Both converted scores were examined for evidence of growth.

The Teacher Adaptive Actions Measure

The adaptive action measure represented instances of transformed information. Transformed information was defined as information designed by the teacher to fit students' emerging levels of understanding. This instrument, used in an earlier study (Johnson & Roehler, 1989), was designed to examine teacher talk during reading lessons that transformed reading knowledge in ways that helped students move toward literacy. The instrument was organized into a matrix that displayed the types of knowledge—declarative, procedural, conditional, and situational—along the horizontal axis and the outcomes of literacy instruction—content knowledge, routine skills, strategic processes, conceptual understandings, and positive attitudes—along the vertical axis. The matrix was used to determine the amounts and types of adaptive actions and the degree of metacognitive awareness of the adaptive actions.

Data were collected on an ongoing basis throughout the school year. Roughly every month, a researcher or principal observed a lesson, taking field notes and noting anomalies. Six reading lessons were transcribed for each teacher. For this study, two lessons were selected for the three teachers: the baseline lesson and an end-of-year lesson.

Data were analyzed in three ways. Amounts of adaptive actions were recorded by counting the instances of adaptive actions and the number of lines classified as adaptive in each instance. The noted adaptive-actions segments were then placed in the matrix in terms of the five outcomes of reading instruction and the types of knowledge. Finally, each instance of adaptive action was rated in terms of the development of metacognitive awareness on a scale of 0 to 4, 0 being the absence of the criterion, 1 and 2 being the presence of awareness but the absence of metacognition, 3 being the presence of metacognitive awareness, and 4 being an exemplary instance of metacognitive awareness.

Two raters were trained to score typed transcripts of the lessons using the matrix format for amounts, types, and awareness of the adaptive actions. The raters were a researcher and a graduate student in the College of Education at Michigan State University. When an inter rater reliability of 80% was reached and maintained, the ratings for adaptive actions were completed following the format established with the instructional understandings interview.

After adaptive actions were rated, the numbers of adaptive actions designated by lines of lesson transcripts were converted to percentages in order to examine growth through the year. Also, types of adaptive actions were examined in terms of the five outcomes to see if the types of lessons broadened over the year. Finally, quality of adaptive actions was converted to percentages to explore growth in metacognitive awareness over the year.

The Student Reading Understandings Measure

The student reading understandings interview, similar to the teacher understandings interview, measured students' thinking about the reading outcomes of strategic processes, routine skills, positive attitudes, conceptual understandings, and content knowledge. Observers interviewed four or five target students from the low reading group of the three participating teachers at the beginning of the year, the middle of the year, and the end of the year. Four questions were asked. (1) What do you think reading is? (2) Think about a person you know who is a good reader. Why do you think that person is a good reader? (3) What does this person do when she or he is reading? (4) What did this person have to learn to become a good reader? All interview responses were noted on protocols and audiotaped for later transcription. For this study, the baseline and end-of-year interviews were used.

Raters determined if the five outcomes were included in the students' answers to the five questions. For each question, raters looked for evidence that reading involves (1) strategic processes, (2) routine skills, (3) positive attitudes, (4) conceptual understandings, and (5) content knowledge. The maximum obtainable score was 25 for each interview; each of the five outcomes potentially received a score of 1 for each of the five questions. Two raters, having established interrater reliability of 80%, scored each student's answers.

After student protocols were rated, each student's pre- and postyear ratings were converted to percentages, including the overall scores and each separate score. Both converted scores were examined for evidence of growth.

The Student Awareness Measure

To determine whether students were consciously aware of what the teacher taught in individual lessons (declarative knowledge) when to use it (conditional knowledge) and how to use it (procedural knowledge; Paris *et al.,* 1984), observers (principals or researchers) individually interviewed four or five target students immediately after observed lessons in an ongoing manner throughout the year. The observer interviewed students separately in the hallway or a conference room. All students were asked three questions. (1) What were you learning in the lesson I just saw? (2) When would you use what the teacher was teaching you? (3) How do you do what you were taught to do? Probing follow-up questions were used with all students. All interview responses were noted on protocols and audiotaped. Interviews were transcribed for analysis. The baseline and end-of-year interviews were selected for this study.

Lesson interviews were rated using an instrument developed previously (Duffy *et al.,* 1987). Scores were assigned for students' verbal statements about (1) what strategy was taught, (2) the situation or conditions when the strategy should be used, and (3) how one employs the strategy. Students received a rating of 0 to 4 for each of the three questions, a score of 0 being an absence of awareness and a score of 4 being exemplary metacognitive awareness. The highest possible score was 12 for each student.

Two researchers scored the typed transcript with the procedures described for the teachers' understandings interviews. Interrater reliability was 80%. After the awareness protocols were rated, the scores were converted to percentages in order to examine growth over the year.

The Student Strategic Actions Measure

Student strategic actions while reading were measured using a modified graded oral reading paragraph (GORP) technique adapted from the *Qualitative Reading Inventory* (Leslie and Caldwell, 1989). The modified GORP examined the students' ability to (1) predict the content of the passage and explain the reasoning for that process, (2) self-correct reading errors and explain the reasoning for the self-corrections, and (3) increase content knowledge about concepts developed in the passage and explain the reasoning used to gain that new knowledge. Passages for the oral readings were selected from Leslie and Caldwell's (1989) assessment device, with two university professors trained as researchers. In September and again in May, they administered the 30-min test individually to each of the randomly selected low-reading-group target students. Each student's performance was tape recorded and noted on protocols.

Each testing session proceeded as follows. A preliminary test of sight word recognition involving 20 words for each grade level (provided by the Leslie and Caldwell device) preceded the actual reading of the passage and served as a determiner of the level of the passage to be read. Passages that were difficult were selected so students would have greater opportunities to be strategic as they read. The researcher showed the title of the passage to each student and asked for predictions about the selection's content and about the reasoning for the prediction. Following predictions, the student was asked to give a definition for three to five concepts that would be developed in the passage. The lowest rated concepts were noted for examination after the passage had been read. The student read the passage aloud as the researcher noted all self-corrections. After the passage was read, the researcher asked the student to answer six to eight questions designed to measure explicitly and implicitly gained knowledge. Then the student was asked to verify the accuracy of the prediction and the reasoning involved with the prediction. After predictions were explained, the student was asked to provide additional meanings for the lowest-rated pre-reading concept explanation and the reasoning for changes in the meaning. Finally, the researcher elicited the student's self-report about self-correction while reading. The researcher asked each student about the self-corrections noted during the oral reading and how it was accomplished. Two self-correction explanations were asked for each student. The highest scored response was used for the study.

Using audiotapes and written protocols completed during testing, two researchers noted the presence or absence of metacognitive awareness for this pre- and postyear measure regarding predictions, development of concept understanding through content knowledge acquisition, and self-corrections. Using a 0 to 4 rating (0 being the absence of the criterion, 1 and 2 being the presence of awareness but the absence of metacognition, 3 being the presence of metacognitive awareness, and 4 being an exemplary instance of the metacognitive awareness criterion), researchers established and maintained an 80% interrater reliability when determining scores for strategic actions in the three categories. After the ratings were determined, the scores were converted to percentages in order to examine growth across the year.

The Student Motivation Measure

Student motivation was measured using a pre- and postyear questionnaire designed to capture students' self-perceptions of enthusiasm and self-efficacy about reading. This measure was adapted for this study from the Raphael, Englert, and Anderson studies (Raphael, Englert, & Anderson, 1987). Using a 5-point Likert scale, students were asked to respond to 15 statements about enthusiasm and 20 statements about self-efficacy. Classroom teachers administered the motivation questionnaire in September and again in May to the low-reading-group students. A total possible score was 175. Each student's protocol was scored, and percentages were established for both pretest and posttest measures. Changes in enthusiasm and self-efficacy were examined for growth.

RESULTS

Results are organized by the research questions. First, the two questions about teacher understandings and actions are addressed. Then, the four questions about student understandings about reading, strategic actions, awareness of lesson content, and motivation are addressed.

Evidence of Change in Teacher Instructional Understandings

The instructional understandings interview that assessed knowledge about the five outcomes yielded scores that showed varying amounts of increase for each of the three teachers.

Teacher A started with a score of 15 (of 35) and ended the school year with a score of 28, for a growth of 86% in instructional understandings about the outcomes of reading (see Figure 1). For both test points, the specific outcome measures of strategic processes, routine skills, positive responses, conceptual understandings, and content knowledge showed reconfigurations of amounts of understanding. Strategic processes received a score of 0 for the preyear test and ended with 21% at the time of the postyear test. Conceptual understandings increased from 13 to 25%, routine skills moved from 6 to 14%, and content knowledge moved from 20 to 21%. Positive responses decreased slightly over the year, moving from 27 to 18%. Teacher A started the year with knowledge that emphasized the development of positive responses and ended the year with a balance for the five outcomes of reading instruction. Teacher A had begun to embrace the instructional complexities of reading instruction by increasing her knowledge about instructional understandings and showing balanced knowledge about the outcomes of reading instruction.

Teacher B initially scored 12 (of 35) and ended the year with a score of 22, showing a growth of 83% in instructional understandings (as shown in Figure 1). For both test points, the specific outcome measures showed reconfiguration. Strategic processes initially received a score of 0 and ended with a score of 4%; content knowledge also received an initial score

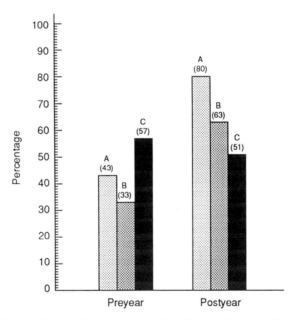

Fig. 1 Teachers' instructional understandings. Teacher A, teacher B, teacher C.

of 0 but moved to a score of 23%. Conceptual understandings changed very little, moving from 25 to 27%. Routine skill dropped slightly, from 25 to 23%, and positive responses dropped considerably from 50 to 23%. Teacher B started the year with instructional understandings that emphasized the outcome of positive responses and excluded any reference to strategic processes and content knowledge. By the end of the year, the strategic processes outcome had increased slightly and the content knowledge outcome had increased considerably. Teacher B showed growth in the overall measure of instructional understandings, but balanced knowledge about the five outcomes did not occur.

Teacher C showed a decrease in her scores (as seen in Figure 1). She began the year with a score of 20 (of 35), and ended the year with a score of 18. For both test points, the submeasures showed little reconfiguration. Strategic processes received a score of 0 for the preyear test and increased slightly to 2.9% at postyear test time. Content knowledge increased from 11.4 to 14.3%, whereas routine skills remained the same at 8.6%. Conceptual understandings decreased from 20 to 14.3%, as did positive responses, decreasing from 17.1 to 11.4%. Teacher C started the year with understandings that primarily emphasized the development of conceptual understandings and positive responses and ended the year with understandings that emphasized positive responses and content knowledge. There was little evidence for understandings of strategic processes. Teacher C did not show evidence of balanced understandings for all outcomes.

Evidence of Change in Teacher's Instructional Actions

The adaptive actions measure for reading lessons was used to examine evidence of change in instruction for each of the three teachers in the amounts and types of adaptive actions and the degree of metacognitive awareness.

Teacher A's growth in adaptive actions is seen in Figure 2. At the preyear time point, her ratings showed that 2.9% of her instruction was adaptive, increasing to 25.1% at the end of the year, showing growth of 766%. Teacher A's adaptive actions began with a lesson designed only to develop understandings about content knowledge and routine skill outcomes. The year ended with a lesson emphasizing integrated strategic processes and content knowledge. Teacher A expanded her adaptive actions in instruction from a lesson on routine skills and content knowledge to a lesson where strategic processes and content knowledge were purposefully integrated.

The preyear ratings for amounts of metacognitive awareness in Teacher A's lesson showed three instances of adaptive actions with a range of ratings from 1 to 3 of a possible score of 4. At the end of the year, there were

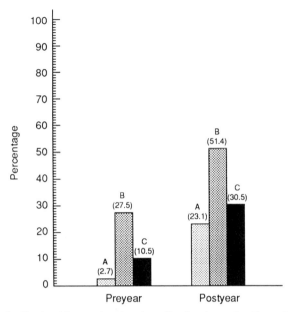

Fig. 2 Teachers' instructional actions. Teacher A, teacher B, teacher C.

seven instances of adaptive actions, with a range of 1 to 3. Three adaptive actions received metacognitive ratings. Teacher A embraced the instructional complexities in terms of amounts and types of adaptive actions and degrees of metacognitive awareness as she moved toward expertise in strategic reading instruction.

Teacher B's adaptive actions in lessons began with a rating of 27.5% and ended with a rating of 51.4%, showing a growth of 87%. Her adaptive actions began with a lesson designed to develop understandings about content knowledge outcomes and concluded the year with a lesson focusing on the integrated development of understandings about strategic processes and content knowledge.

Teacher B's preyear ratings showed five instances of adaptive actions with range of ratings from 1 to 3 of a possible score of 4, with an adaptive action receiving a metacognitive rating. At the end of the year, variance in awareness ratings dropped to 1 to 2 for 17 instances of adaptive actions when Teacher B attempted integrated strategic processes and content knowledge lessons. No metacognitive awareness was present. Teacher B attempted to embrace the complexities of instructional actions in terms of the types of lessons and amounts of adaptive actions, but these attempts appeared to be related to a loss of metacognitive awareness developed during lessons.

Teacher C's adaptive actions during lessons began with a rating of 10.5%

and ended with a rating of 30.5%, showing a growth of 191%. Her adaptive actions began with a lesson designed to develop understandings about content knowledge and routine skill outcomes and ended the year with continued development of routine skills and content knowledge outcomes. Teacher C did not expand her adaptive actions in instruction beyond routine skills and content knowledge outcomes.

The beginning of the year ratings for Teacher C's adaptive actions showed six instances with a range of 1 to 3 of a possible score of 4; three instances of adaptive actions received metacognitive ratings. At the end of the year, there were five adaptive actions with a range of 1 to 2 of a possible score of 4 and no instances of metacognitive awareness in the lesson. Teacher C increased the amounts of adaptive actions but did not increase the types of adaptive actions. Loss of metacognition occurred across the year. Teacher C did not embrace the complexities of instructional actions.

Evidence of Change in Student's Reading Understandings

The reading understandings interview was used to explore the growth of selected students' knowledge about the reading outcomes in each of the three teachers' classrooms. As seen in Table 1, growth occurred in Teacher A's classroom, but no growth occurred in Teacher B's or Teacher C's classroom. In order to get an accurate growth measure, the pretest score was subtracted from the posttest score resulting in net change. The net change was then divided by the pretest score to give a numerical improvement or decline. Finally, this value was converted to percentages for discussion purposes.

At the preyear time point, Teacher A's first-grade students scored 3.2 and then 6.6 of a possible score of 25, showing growth of 106%. For both time points, specific outcomes were reconfigured. The students' scores at the preyear time point showed no knowledge for the importance of strategic processes; this knowledge increased over the year to 50%. The positive response, conceptual understandings, and content knowledge outcome scores also started at 0 and increased over the year to 11, 12, and 12%. Knowledge of routine skill outcomes decreased slightly across the year from 64 to 56%. These first-grade students had begun to reconfigure their reading understandings, showing more balanced knowledge about all the outcomes of reading.

Teacher B's sixth-grade students initially scored 3.8 of 25 and again scored 3.8 of 25, showing no growth. For both time points, some reconfiguration occurred. The students' scores at the pretest time showed no knowledge about strategic processes; this knowledge increased to 12% at the end of the year. For content knowledge, the students increased their

Table 1
Student Reading Understandings[a]

	Teacher A		Teacher B		Teacher C	
	Pre	Post	Pre	Post	Pre	Post
Student 1						
SP	0	3	0	1	0	0
CU	0	1	0	0	0	1
PA	0	1	0	0	0	1
CK	0	1	0	1	1	0
RS	2	3	3	2	1	1
Student 2						
SP	0	4	0	0	0	0
CU	0	0	0	0	0	0
PA	0	2	0	0	0	1
CK	0	1	0	0	1	0
RS	3	2	2	2	1	1
Student 3						
SP	0	1	0	0	0	0
CU	0	1	0	0	0	0
PA	0	0	0	0	0	0
CK	0	1	0	0	1	0
RS	3	3	3	2	1	1
Student 4						
SP	0	1	0	0	0	0
CU	0	0	1	1	1	1
PA	0	0	0	0	0	1
CK	0	0	0	0	1	0
RS	5	4	5	3	1	1
Student 5						
SP	0	1	0	2	0	0
CU	0	1	1	1	0	0
PA	0	0	0	0	0	0
CK	0	0	0	0	1	1
RS	3	2	4	4	1	1

[a]SP, strategic processes; CU, conceptual understandings; PA, positive attitude; CK, content knowledge; RS, routine skills. Range is 0–5; total possible score for any one student is 25.

understandings slightly, moving from 0 to 4%. For positive responses and conceptual understandings, students did not change their knowledge; scores remained at 0 and 8%. For routine skills, students' knowledge began with a score of 68%, which decreased to 52% at the postyear time point. These sixth-grade students started the year with knowledge about mostly routine skills and began to increase their knowledge in the areas of strategic processes and content knowledge. Knowledge about positive response outcomes did not change at all. A balance of knowledge about all outcomes did not occur.

Teacher C's third-grade students initially scored 2.2 of 25 and remained at that score at the postyear time point. For each time point, some reconfiguration occurred. Students showed no knowledge of strategic processes; this continued at the postyear time point. Some knowledge growth occurred for positive response and conceptual understanding; scores moved from 0 to 12% and 4 to 8%. Content knowledge dropped over the year from 20 to 4%. Knowledge of routine skills remained at 20% across the year. Some reconfiguration occurred, but knowledge about content and conceptual understandings remained low; strategic processes remained at 0 for these third-grade students. No balance of knowledge about the outcomes occurred.

Evidence of Change in Students' Metacognitive Awareness

The student awareness interview conducted immediately after an observed lesson was used to explore metacognitive awareness of lesson content in terms of declarative, procedural, and conditional knowledge. Growth occurred in all three classrooms across the year. The same conclusion procedures that were used with the student's reading understandings were used with this measure.

Teacher A's first-grade students showed an overall average of .33 of a possible score of 4 at the preyear time point (see Table 2). At the postyear time point, students' awareness of lesson content increased to 2.27. These first-grade students grew 588% in their awareness of lesson content during the school year; 5 of the 12 instances showed metacognitive awareness.

Teacher B's sixth-grade students had an overall average of .75 of 4 at the preyear time point, as seen in Table 2. None of the 12 instances showed metacognitive awareness. At the postyear time point, students' awareness of lesson content showed an overall average of 2.8 of 4. These students grew 273% in their awareness of lesson content during the school year. Two of the 12 instances showed metacognitive awareness.

Teacher C's third-grade students showed preyear scores of 1.07 of 4 (see Table 2). At the postyear time point, students' awareness of lesson content was 1.53 of 4. These third-grade students increased 43% in their awareness of lesson content during the school year. There were no instances of metacognitive awareness at either time point.

When awareness of the submeasures of declarative, procedural, and conditional knowledge were explored, additional patterns of growth were found. Teacher A's students moved from mostly declarative awareness to awareness of all three types of knowledge. For the preyear time point, these

Table 2
Student Metacognitive Awareness of Lesson Content[a]

	Teacher A		Teacher B		Teacher C	
	Pre	Post	Pre	Post	Pre	Post
Student 1						
declarative	1	2	0	3	1	1
procedural	0	3	2	2	0	2
conditional	1	4	1	2	0	1
Student 2						
declarative	1	2	1	1	1	2
procedural	0	1	0	3	0	2
conditional	0	2	0	2	1	0
Student 3						
declarative	1	2	2	2	2	1
procedural	0	3	1	2	1	2
conditional	0	3	1	2	0	2
Student 4						
declarative	0	1	1	1	2	1
procedural	0	1	0	3	1	2
conditional	0	3	0	2	1	2
Student 5						
declarative	—	—	—	—	2	1
procedural	—	—	—	—	2	2
conditional	—	—	—	—	2	2

[a]Range is 0–4; total possible score for any one student is 12. Ratings of 3 and 4 signal metacognitive levels.

students received nonmetacognitive scores that were primarily in the declarative knowledge area. At the postyear time point, the students had grown, showing awareness that was at metacognitive levels in all three knowledge areas. Similar to results in the Teacher Explanation Study (Duffy *et al.*, 1987), Teacher A's first-grade students showed increases in amounts and types of awareness.

Teacher B's students showed preyear patterns indicating awareness in all three areas, but showed no instances of metacognitive awareness. At the postyear time point, all students showed awareness in declarative, procedural, and conditional knowledge; only two of the students showed metacognitive awareness levels for only procedural knowledge.

Teacher C's students also showed preyear patterns indicating awareness in all three knowledge areas. As for Teacher A's and Teacher B's students, there were no levels of metacognitive awareness at the preyear time point. At the postyear time point, the pattern changed slightly. All but one of the students showed awareness of declarative, procedural, and conditional knowledge, but none of the students had metacognitive levels for any of the three knowledge areas.

In summary, Teacher A's students increased their awareness of lesson content in all three knowledge areas across the year; metacognitive ratings appeared for three of the four first-grade students. These students seemed to show balanced growth in metacognitive awareness as Teacher A embraced the instructional complexities regarding understandings and actions. Teacher B's students also increased their amounts of awareness, but only two increased their awareness of metacognitive levels in procedural knowledge. These students grew slightly in metacognitive awareness as Teacher B grew in her knowledge of adaptive actions but not in her knowledge of instructional understandings. Teacher C's students increased their awareness slightly, but metacognitive levels were never acquired. Teacher C increased her adaptive actions but, like Teacher B, did not increase her instructional understandings across the year.

Evidence of Change in Students' Strategic Actions

The modified GORP technique adapted from Leslie and Caldwell (1989) was used to examine students' growth in strategic actions while reading. This technique measured students' self-reports about the reasoning used to (1) predict and verify predictions, (2) self-correct reading errors, and (3) gain understandings about concepts as a result of reading content information in texts. The same conversion procedures for growth were used for this measure. As seen in Table 3, growth occurred for most students across the year. Teacher A's first-grade students averaged a score of 0 of a possible score of 4 for the preyear measure. For the postyear measure, the students averaged a score of 1.73 of 4. Growth also occurred in each of the three submeasures. Regarding the reasoning used in predicting before reading, the students averaged a score of 0 at preyear, which grew to 2.6 of 4 at postyear. Regarding the reasoning used in self-corrections when reading, the students averaged a score of 0, which grew to 1.20 of 4 for the postyear time point. On the final submeasure of reasoning used when gaining knowledge about concepts from text, the students moved from 0 to 1.4 of 4. All students increased their knowledge about all areas of strategic actions; four students received metacognitive awareness ratings in at least one of the submeasure areas.

Teacher B's sixth-grade students scored 1.3 of 4 for the preyear time point. They scored 1.9 of 4 for the postyear time point, showing growth of 46%. Growth also occurred in each of the three submeasures. Regarding the reasoning used in predictions and verifications of those predictions, the students scored 1.0 of 4 for the preyear time point, which grew to 1.8 of 4,

Table 3
Student Strategic Actions[a]

	Teacher A		Teacher B		Teacher C	
	Pre	Post	Pre	Post	Pre	Post
Student 1						
predicting	0	3	0	1	1	1
self-correcting	0	1	1	2	1	1
concepts	0	0	0	1	1	1
Student 2						
predicting	0	1	1	2	1	1
self-correcting	0	1	1	2	0	0
concepts	0	1	1	1	0	1
Student 3						
predicting	0	3	2	2	1	1
self-correcting	0	1	2	2	1	1
concepts	0	3	1	2	0	1
Student 4						
predicting	0	3	1	2	1	2
self-correcting	0	2	1	3	1	1
concepts	0	0	0	1	0	0
Student 5						
predicting	0	3	1	2	1	1
self-correcting	0	1	1	2	1	2
concepts	0	3	0	3	0	0

[a]Range is 0–4; total possible score for any one studet is 12. Ratings of 3 or 4 signal metacognitive levels.

for a growth of 80%. Regarding the reasoning used in self-corrections when reading, the students scored 1.8, which moved to 2.2 of 4 at the postyear time point, for a growth of 22%. On the final submeasure of reasoning used when gaining knowledge about concepts from text, the students scored 1 initially, which increased to 1.6 of 4, showing a growth of 60%. All sixth-grade students increased their knowledge about the strategic actions in at least one of the submeasures. Only one student gained in all three submeasures of strategic actions. No students received metacognitive awareness ratings in any of the submeasure areas.

Teacher C's third-grade students scored .6 of 4 for the preyear time point. They scored .93 of 4 for the postyear time point, showing a growth of 55%. Growth in each of the three submeasures varied. Regarding the reasoning used in predictions and verifications of predictions, students scored 1, moving to 1.2 of 4, showing a growth of 20%. Regarding the reasoning used in self-corrections when reading, students scored .8, moving to 1 of 4, showing a growth of 25%. On the final submeasure of the reasoning used when gaining content knowledge about text concepts, students scored .2, moving to .6 of 4 at the postyear time point, showing a growth of 200%. There were no instances of metacognitive awareness in any of the submeasures of strategic actions.

In summary, Teacher A's first-grade students increased the amounts of knowledge about strategic actions in all three submeasures. Four of the five students reached metacognitive awareness levels about strategic actions in at least one of the submeasures. These students showed balanced growth about strategic actions as they grew substantially in their ability to use and explain the three types of reasoning involved in the application of strategic actions as they read. Teacher B's sixth-grade students all increased their knowledge about strategic actions in at least one of the submeasures. Only two of the five students reached metacognitive awareness levels in procedural knowledge as they used strategic actions. Teacher B's students grew slightly in strategic actions. Teacher C's third-grade students increased their strategic actions slightly, four of the five students showed some growth in at least one of the subareas. None of the students reached metacognitive awareness levels about strategic actions.

Evidence of Change in Student Motivation

A student motivation measure was used to examine amounts of enthusiasm and self-efficacy for preyear and postyear time points. Little growth occurred across the year, since motivation remained high. Students' growth in motivation was converted using the procedures explained for student growth in reading understandings.

In Teacher A's classroom, the students' motivation scores ranged from 102 to 162 of 175 with an average score of 137 at the preyear time point and ranged from 134 to 169 with an average score of 152 at the postyear time point, showing an overall growth of about 11% in motivation across the year. In the motivation measure, enthusiasm scores moved from 60 to 63 of 75. Slightly more growth occurred in the self-efficacy measure. For the preyear measure, students scored 77, and moved to 88 of 100 for the postyear measure. These students showed high levels of motivation at the beginning of the year and maintained this motivation throughout the year.

In Teacher B's classroom, motivation scores ranged from 93 to 129 of 175, with an average score of 105 at the preyear time point. For the postyear time point, students' scores ranged from 86 to 125 of 175, with an average score of 102, showing a decrease of 2% in motivation across the year. In the motivation measure, the enthusiasm scores moved from 42 to 44 of 75. In the self-efficacy measure, a slight decrease occurred. For self-efficacy, the students scored 62.8 of 100 for the preyear measure and scored 58 for the postyear measure. These students showed moderate levels of motivation at the beginning of the year, and maintained that level throughout the year. In the motivation measure, students increased slightly in enthusiasm and decreased slightly in self-efficacy.

In Teacher C's classroom, motivation score originally ranged from 111 to 159 of 175 with an average score of 133. For the postyear time point, students' scores ranged from 119 to 166 of 175, with an average score of 139, showing an overall growth of 5% in motivation across the year. In the motivation measure, the enthusiasm scores moved from 58 to 60 of 75. The increase in self-efficacy was slightly lower. At the preyear time point, students scored 76 of a possible score of 100, which moved to 79 at the postyear time point. These students showed high levels of motivation at the beginning of the year, and maintained this motivation throughout the year with a slight increase for enthusiasm and efficiency at the end of the school year.

Evidence of Relationships between Teacher Understandings and Actions and Student Growth

When the relationships between teacher understandings and actions and student growth in conceptual understandings, strategic actions, lesson-content awareness, and motivation were explored, different patterns emerged for the three teachers and their students.

Teacher A increased her instructional understandings by 86%. Her understandings increased from primarily one outcome to a more balanced understanding about all outcomes. The amount of her adaptive actions during lessons grew almost 766% over the year. The types of lessons grew from an emphasis on either routine skills or content knowledge to integrated strategic processes and content knowledge. These lessons improved in quality; the early lesson showed only one instance of metacognitive awareness and the postyear lesson showed more instances of metacognition awareness. At the year's end, Teacher A had embraced the complexities, showing both balanced understandings about all the reading outcomes and increased amounts and types of adaptive actions that reflected metacognitive awareness.

Students showed similar patterns of growth in their reading understandings, awareness of lesson content, strategic actions, and motivation. Students grew in their reading understandings by 106%. Understandings increased from primarily one outcome to a more equitable balance across all outcomes. For awareness of lesson content, these first-grade students showed an increase of 588%. Awareness of lesson content was rated low at the beginning of the year, but increased to metacognitive awareness of mental processes by the postyear time point. Regarding strategic actions while reading, Teacher A's students showed an overall increase from 0 to 2.2

of 4. In this measure, the ability to predict and explain the reasoning for the prediction, the ability to self-correct errors and explain that reasoning, and the ability to gain knowledge of concepts as a result of reading and explain that reasoning all increased. Finally, this trend continued with motivation because the students maintained their high levels of motivation and even grew slightly. As Teacher A embraced instructional complexities, her students moved toward expertise in multiple areas of reading.

Teacher B increased her overall instructional understandings 83%. Little change occurred in her understandings of the five outcomes. Understandings about content knowledge outcomes increased, concern for positive response and conceptual understandings outcomes decreased, and concerns for strategic processes changed slightly, remaining very low. Teacher B did not achieve a balanced set of understandings about reading outcomes. Second, the amounts of Teacher B's adaptive actions grew 87% over the year. The types of lessons grew from content knowledge outcomes to content knowledge and strategic processes outcomes that were integrated into the same lesson. Metacognitive awareness disappeared when the teacher attempted to increase the complexity by integrating two outcomes. At the end of the year, Teacher B had begun to integrate multiple reading outcomes into her adaptive actions in a lesson, but she did not embrace the instructional complexities associated with instructional understandings and she did not achieve metacognitive awareness for adaptive actions during lessons.

Students showed patterns of change that reflected Teacher B's changes. For reading understandings, no increase occurred. Little reconfiguration occurred in the understandings of the five outcomes. The sixth-grade students started and ended the year with understandings mostly about routine skills. Understandings about strategic processes, positive responses, and content knowledge increased slightly. For awareness of lesson content, these sixth grade students showed an increase of 273%. Two of the students reached metacognitive awareness levels for procedural knowledge by the end of the year. Regarding strategic actions while reading, Teacher B's students also showed an overall increase of 46%. In this measure, the ability to predict and explain the reasoning for the prediction, the ability to self-correct errors and explain that reasoning, and the ability to gain knowledge of concepts as a result of reading and explain that reasoning all increased. The students decreased slightly in their motivation scores, increasing slightly in enthusiasm and decreasing slightly in efficacy. The students gained in measures that reflected specific lesson growth, but did not gain in measures that reflected year-long growth.

Teacher C decreased her instructional understandings. Her understandings of the reading outcomes altered little over the year with little evidence of understandings about strategic processes. Second, the amounts of

Teacher C's adaptive actions grew 196%. The types of lessons did not change, remaining with content knowledge and routine skills outcomes throughout the year. The beginning lessons had instances of metacognitive awareness that disappeared by the end of the year. Teacher C's adaptive actions increase in amounts only.

Students showed similar patterns of change in their reading understandings, awareness of lesson content, strategic actions, and motivation. The students showed no growth in their reading understandings. For each of the outcomes, little reconfiguration occurred. The strategic processes rating remained unchanged at 0. The conceptual understandings and positive response outcomes increased slightly, with a decrease in understandings about content knowledge. For awareness of lesson content, these third-grade students showed an increase of 20%. There were no instances of metacognitive awareness at either time point. Regarding strategic actions while reading, Teacher C's students showed an overall increase of 55%. Within this measure, the ability to predict and explain their reasoning for the prediction, the ability to self-correct errors and explain that reasoning, and the ability to gain conceptual knowledge as a result of reading and then explain that reasoning all increased. For motivation, students maintained high ratings across the year, improving slightly by the end of the year in both enthusiasm and efficacy. These students showed growth in actions but not in understandings about reading.

DISCUSSION

This study begins to illustrate the complexities of reading instruction and the connections between teacher thought and action and student growth. When the growth of low-group students in the classrooms of these three teachers was examined, it was evident that the sets of students moved in varying amounts along the path toward literacy. Teacher A's students increased their understandings about reading and showed balanced growth in the types of understandings. They also grew in their abilities to reason and use strategic actions while reading. Lesson awareness for all students increased; that awareness reached metacognitive levels by the end of the year. Motivation increased slightly; high levels of motivation were maintained across the year. Teacher A's students showed growth in all measures of reading acquisition.

Teacher B's students did not increase their understandings about reading and showed some reconfiguration of understandings about the various outcomes. A balanced set of understandings did not occur. These sixth-grade students grew considerably in awareness of lesson content but grew very little in strategic actions and decreased in motivation. Teacher B's students showed growth in areas related to instructional actions connected to specific lessons but showed little or no growth in areas connected to longitudinal strategic reading and understandings.

Teacher C's students also did not increase their understandings about reading, showing little reconfiguration of understandings about the various outcomes. A balanced set of understandings did not occur. However, these third-grade students did grow in awareness of lesson content. This growth was reflected to a lesser degree in strategic actions and motivation. Teacher C's students showed growth in areas related to instructional actions, but showed little growth in areas related to instructional understandings.

When the results for the three teachers were examined for evidence that they might be embracing the complexities of reading instruction, some interesting findings emerged. Teacher A appeared to view the outcomes of reading as multiple and complex. Although her baseline lesson contained adaptive actions geared only to develop understandings about the outcomes of routine skills and content knowledge, her end-of-year lesson contained adaptive actions geared to develop understandings about the outcomes of integrated strategic processes and content knowledge. In addition, Teacher A's adaptive actions increased in instances of awareness to metacognitive levels.

Although Teacher A illustrated both understandings and actions reflecting the complexities of instruction, Teacher B did not. Teacher B appeared to simplify the complexities by focusing on adaptive actions and not focusing on understandings about the outcomes of reading instruction. No balance occurred across the five outcomes. As the year ended, she had increased in terms of amounts and types of adaptive actions but had not yet reached metacognitive levels of awareness during adaptive actions.

Teacher B seemed to display an initial simplification of the instructional complexities and a later movement toward including more of the complexities, but Teacher C did not. She initially simplified the reading instruction complexities, which remained at the simplified level throughout the year. Teacher C had reading outcome understandings that were less complex, routine skills and content knowledge were most important. Her lessons contained adaptive actions geared only to develop routine skills and content knowledge outcomes, with no adaptive actions present for strategic reasoning, positive responses, or conceptual understandings. When evidence of instructional understandings about reading were examined, Teacher C showed a slight increase over the year, but her reconfiguration of outcomes did not show a balance across the five outcomes. Understanding about strategic processes was very low.

When end-of-year interviews were examined, further evidence was found that Teacher A was trying to embrace the complexities of reading instruction, Teacher B was initially simplifying the complexities, and Teacher C was simplifying the complexities throughout the year. Teacher A's view was illustrated in the following when she responded to the question of her outcomes for reading. She said,

> My goal is to have motivated, self-regulated strategic readers. Last year, I was so worried about getting the children through the basal. This year I didn't worry about it. When I think back to September, I've really expanded on what I think reading is. It is not just the ability to decode and comprehend; it is for information and for pleasure. I really emphasized decoding and comprehension in the fall, and I still want them to decode and comprehend; but now it's different. I want them to have strategies, and I want them to appreciate reading. Last year, I had them sound words. I never really taught them strategies. Now I do.

Teacher B's view was also illustrated in an end-of-year interview. She said,

> I don't mind trying new things; I just want to take it slow and understand things first. I don't think anything I did this year is that radical or that different. More importantly, I never feel like someone was saying "You should do it this way." When *I* thought something was successful, *I* planned to continue it. Then I thought about something else. I moved at my pace.

Teacher C's final interview yielded data that showed that she seemed to view the outcomes of reading in a reductionist way. She said,

> The more I reflect, I begin to wonder if indeed that there isn't a trick of the trade to help a child make sense of what was just read. Just one way to evaluate and understand the parts that make up the whole. I would feel more comfortable with a prescribed list of strategies which I could then monitor and adjust to my style. There are too many things to think about.

It appears that the instructional understandings and actions that teachers have about developing reading may be a productive way to explore problems of classroom implementation of research when the outcomes are as complex as they are in classroom reading instruction.

The results of this study support the need for teachers initially and continually to embrace the complexities of classroom reading instruction, in terms of both their instructional understandings and their instructional actions. In addition, two other insights emerged. First, classroom instruction that has complex outcomes requires time. Although Teacher A embraced the complexities and spent most of the school year developing balanced opportunities for all outcomes, she was just beginning to control the instruction as the year ended. It takes time for teachers to understand these complexities and to teach in ways that develop all outcomes. Second, teachers need a broad vision about reading instruction that allows them to more easily access and use all the new information as they plan and implement lessons. It seems that Teacher A had a vision about reading instruction that included understandings and actions about all the outcomes that guided her use of the new information as she planned, implemented, and evaluated lessons. It also appears that Teacher B's view of instruction was "one step at a time" until new information was understood. Finally, Teacher C's view of instruction was a search for simplification.

As interesting as these findings are, it must be kept in mind that this study only begins to explore the connections between teacher understandings and actions and student outcomes. Many questions remain. Why were Teacher A's understandings and actions more closely related to positive student outcomes? What roles do age and experience play in teacher change? Do students' strategic actions and understandings generalize from reading to other subject areas? Studies are currently underway to examine these and other issues.

Although these findings are tentative, and substantiation is needed, they do suggest that teacher educators and researchers need to examine the assistance and interventions they provide for teachers. When the desired student outcomes involve complex understandings, strategic actions, high motivation, and awareness of lesson content, it appears that initial simplification or continual simplification that reduces the complexities of the instructional intervention may be detrimental. Simplification seems to lead to the possibility of mind sets that exclude acknowledgment of the complexities for later use and solidifies keeping the process simple. This simplification appears to lead to less student growth toward literacy. It may be that researchers and teacher educators should stop simplifying and reducing the content of reading instruction interventions initially for teachers and, instead, develop ways to help them embrace and work comfortably with the complexities from the onset of professional development.

CONCLUSIONS

Our society is moving from the industrial era, in which we needed large numbers of people who could repetitively complete a task that was an isolated part of a larger product, to the knowledge era, in which large numbers of people are needed who can reason through problems in flexible and adaptive ways. These changes are bringing new instructional complexities to the classrooms. These complexities require changes in educational practices that typically have been taught in reductionist ways. What is needed in educational practices is instruction in which the collection of the parts is preceded with an explicit vision of the whole. Instructions must begin with a vision of the outcomes, which then guides the instruction as desired patterns and pieces of understanding emerge and become integral parts of the vision. Rather than using the instructional approach of initially breaking reading into various strategies for ease of instruction and learning and then combining those strategies with content for later use, this study indicates that it may be better to start with a vision for what the strategies are, how the strategies should be used, when they should be used, and why they should be used while reading worthwhile content. The specific cognitive strategies that support the vision are then taught with worthwhile content, as learners gradually gain cognitive and metacognitive control of the strategies (Palincsar & Brown, 1984). Declarative, procedural, situational, and conditional knowledge is developed in conscious ways, as is the knowledge of how all parts fit into the vision.

It may be that teachers need to create instructional opportunities for student learning that are somewhat like the creation of a tapestry. The weaver starts with a mental image of the finished product and painstakingly lays the foundations of the patterns that give substance and warp to the tapestry. The weaver carefully follows the patterns, expanding on patterns when needed, adding in new patterns when needed, and dropping patterns when needed. The specific patterns are carefully attended to in the message of the overall tapestry. As the finished product emerges, it is generally the whole tapestry that is enjoyed, understood, and used. The combined specific patterns become a way for the whole tapestry to be understood. The weaver embraces the complexities of creating a tapestry just as teachers may need to embrace the complexities of reading instruction. It appears that students can be better helped in their movement toward literacy when teachers embrace instructional complexities. Teachers need to start with a vision that includes the development of all five outcomes and carefully attend to the specific patterns that make up the whole of reading instruction, always remembering that the concept of moving toward literacy is what counts.

This type of instruction embraces the complexities of classroom instruction, acknowledges the importance of having a vision from the beginning, builds on the wealth of classroom learning opportunities in cognitively, metacognitively, and motivationally sound ways, and advances the possibilities of learners becoming enthusiastic strategic sense makers when they read. Embracing the complexities becomes the way of instruction.

REFERENCES

Au, K., and Kawa Kami, A. (1984). Vygotskian perspectives on discussion processes in small-group reading lessons. In P. L. Peterson, L. C. Wilkinson, and M. Hallivan (Eds.), *The Social Context of Instruction* (pp. 209–225), Orlando, FL: Academic Press.

Brophy, J., and Good, T. (1986). Teacher behavior and student achievement. In M. Wittrock (Ed.), *Handbook of research on teaching* (3rd ed., pp. 328–375). New York: Macmillan.

Duffy, G., Roehler, L., and Rackliffe, G. (1986). How teachers' instructional talk influences students' understandings of lesson content. *Elementary School Journal, 87*(1), 357–366.

Duffy, G., Roehler, L., Sivan, E., Rackliffe, G., Book, C., Meloth, M., Vavrus, L., Wesselman, R., Putnam, J., and Bassiri, D. (1987). Effects of explaining the reasoning associated with using reading strategies. *Reading Research Quarterly, 22,* 347–368.

Feltovich, P., Spiro, R., and Coulson, R. (1989). The nature of conceptual understanding in biomedicine: The deep structure of complex ideas and the development of misconceptions. In D. Evans and V. Patel (Eds.), *The cognitive sciences in medicine* (pp. 113–172). Cambridge: MIT Press.

Gagné, R. (1985). *The cognitive psychology of school learning.* Boston: Little, Brown.

Johnson, J., and Roehler, L. (1989). *Teachers' rationale and their instructional actions: The reasons teachers give for doing what they do.* Paper presented at the annual conference of the National Reading Conference, Austin, Texas.

Leslie, L., and Caldwell, J. (1989). *Qualitative reading inventory.* Glenview, Illinois: Scott Foresman/Little, Brown Higher Education.

Palincsar, A., and Brown, A. (1984). Reciprocal teaching of comprehension-fostering and monitoring activities. *Cognition and Instruction, 1,* 117–175.

Paris, S., Cross, D., and Lipson, M. (1984). Informed strategies for learning: A program to improve children's reading awareness and comprehension. *Journal of Educational Psychology, 76*(6), 1239–1252.

Raphael, T., Englert, C., and Anderson, L. (1987, December). What is effective instructional talk? A comparison of two writing lessons. Paper presented at the annual meeting of the National Reading Conference, St. Petersburg Beach, FL.

Roehler, L., Duffy, G., and Tiezzi, L. (1987). *Teachers' instructional expertise and the role of situational knowledge.* Paper presented at the National Reading Conference, St. Petersburg Beach, Florida.

Roehler, L., Duffy, G., and Warren, S. (1987). *Characteristics of instructional responsiveness associated with effective teaching of reading strategies.* Paper presented at the National Reading Conference, St. Petersburg Beach, Florida.

Sivan, E., and Roehler, L. (1986). Motivational statements in explicit teacher explanations and their relationship to students' metacognition in reading. In J. A. Niles and R. V. Lalik (Eds.), *Solving problems in literacy: Learners, teachers, and researchers* (pp. 178–184). Thirty-fifth yearbook of the National Reading Conference. Rochester, New York: National Reading Conference 1.

Stevens, R., Madden, N., Slavin, R., and Farnish, A. (1987). Cooperative integrated reading and composition: Two field experiments. *Reading Research Quarterly, 22,* 433–454.

16

Dimensions of Professional Development: Weaving Teacher Beliefs and Strategic Content

Patricia L. Anders and Candace S. Bos

When asked to contribute a chapter to this volume, the authors were in the midst of collecting and analyzing data from two research projects, both with intensive and comprehensive professional development components.[1] The purpose for each of these projects was to introduce cognitive processing possibilities for instruction. In the first project, the cognitive strategies to be taught were explicit, whereas in the second project many research-based cognitive strategies were available and their presentation depended on teachers' questions and concerns. This chapter is being written at the "conclusion" of those projects—at least the financial support for those projects has ended, but our thinking, analyzing, and ruminating about what we have learned continues. Our interpretation of the findings from these projects has underscored our commitment to continue a quest to better understand professional development and, specifically, to better understand how a teacher continues to elaborate on, refine, and improve practice.

[1]We are using the term professional development in the title rather than staff development or in-service. We choose professional because teachers possess great skill and experience that they use to conduct their work; in contrast, staff members are in the role of supporting and helping a leader or an employer. The term in-service has not been used in the recent literature because it connotes short term, often ineffective staff development. However, in the chapter we use the term staff development because this was the term used during these projects.

This chapter briefly describes the research projects, elaborates on the nature of the professional development component of each of the projects, presents data to support what we believe we have learned, and relates those findings and interpretations to what the future may hold for professional development specifically and teacher education generally. The purpose of this chapter is to argue that although progress has been made toward offering theoretically sound programs of professional development, further study of the processes of teacher reflection and development is needed to refine the nature of support provided to teachers as they progress through their professional careers.

Typical professional development takes one of two forms.[2] The first is driven by an intention to teach teachers how to implement a new program or use a new strategy that someone outside the classroom—usually an administrator or a researcher—believes will improve student learning. The literature describing professional development programs that best reflects this model was produced during the days of the process–product movement (Campbell, 1989). For example, Gage (1978) sought to identify the teaching style, method, model, or strategies that best contributed to increased student achievement and improved student attitudes. Basically, his goal was to develop a model or formula whereby the teacher would do a specific behavior and a specific achievement would increase. The teacher educators' role, then, was perceived as transmitter of this knowledge to teachers.

The second form of professional development emanates from those who study the development and influences of the organization on behavior, issues, and outcomes (Deal & Derr, 1980). Programs with this emphasis usually procure the services of an outside consultant who helps a group of teachers and other school personnel identify problems in a school or district and develop solutions to the problem.

These two forms differ both in purpose and in method of delivery. The first tends to be didactic: content drives delivery and the goal is to pass on or transmit research-based knowledge to the consumer. Success is measured by student outcomes, usually in terms of achievement scores on a standardized measure. The second is not content driven; instead group processes of problem identification and solution development are emphasized. The project is judged successful if the participants perceive a change in the identified problem.

Recently, a new generation of staff development programs has evolved that attempts to bring together concern for content with an understanding that the process must attend to what is known about how and why teachers

---

[2]The authors are indebted to Virginia Richardson for conceptualizing the literature related to staff development in this way.

change their practices (for example, Au, 1990; Carpenter, Fennema, Peterson, Chiang, & Loef, 1989; Peterman, 1991; Richardson & Anders, 1990). This form of staff development is framed cognitively: (1) it recognizes the importance of teachers' beliefs and prior knowledge; (2) it provides ways of helping teachers explore their beliefs and knowledge; (3) it creates an environment for the social construction of meaning through dialogues and conversations (Campbell, 1989); and (4) it introduces new understandings and practices into participants' classrooms. The two projects described here represent this new generation, but take on different emphases. The first project emphasizes content—the researchers needed to present specific content and teachers were expected to learn and use the content, but the process of presentation took into account socio-cognitive principles of learning. The second project emphasizes teacher beliefs. Although the researchers wanted to present specific content, it would only be presented in response to meaningful teacher-asked questions that emanated from their experience and were embedded in a classroom context.

INTERACTIVE TEACHING PROJECT STAFF DEVELOPMENT

We approached staff development for the Interactive Teaching Project[3] with a set goal and agenda. The staff development occurred during the second year of a multiple-year research project (Anders & Bos, 1991) and had a goal of determining the effectiveness of interactive teaching strategies on the content learning and reading comprehension of students with learning disabilities.

First Year of Project

During the first year of the project, three interactive teaching strategies—semantic mapping, semantic feature analysis, and semantic/syntactic feature analysis—were compared with definition instruction. The theoretical grounding for the interactive teaching strategies was based on principles that engage students in active cognitive processing of information related to the content and provide opportunities for students to develop cognitively oriented reading comprehension strategies (Bos & Anders, 1990). Assumptions for interactive teaching strategies are derived from (1) schema theory (e.g., Rumelhart, 1980), (2) concept learning and development theory (e.g., Klausmeier & Sipple, 1980), (3) the psycholinguistic model of

[3]This research was funded in part by the U.S. Department of Education, Office of Special Education and Rehabilitation Services (G008630125).

reading (e.g., Goodman, 1984), and (4) a socio-cultural theory of cognitive development (e.g., Vygotsky, 1978).

Schema theory highlights the importance of activating background knowledge relevant to the new information being learned. Schema theory explains how knowledge is structured in memory. Instructionally, schema theory addresses the importance of activating the learner's background knowledge and highlighting the relationships among concepts. It also emphasizes the importance of analyzing the semantic features of a concept to ensure a rich understanding (Anderson & Freebody, 1981).

The theory of *concept learning and development* advanced by Klausmeier and his colleagues (e.g., Klausmeier & Sipple, 1980) specifies four levels of concept attainment: concrete, identity, classification, and formal. Concepts are learned more completely when all four levels are engaged and the hierarchical organization of concepts (i.e., superordinate, coordinate, and subordinate) is explained during instruction. Concepts found in content disciplines are organized in hierarchical structures that may serve as metaphors for schemata.

The *psycholinguistic theory of reading* (Goodman, 1984) highlights the importance of using cognitive strategies to construct meaning. Key among the cognitive strategies are sampling or selecting, predicting, confirming, integrating, and justifying. The degree to which instruction explicates these cognitive strategies affects the quality of comprehension and content learning.

The *socio-cultural theory of cognitive development* assumes that cognitive functioning grows out of social interactions during problem solving and practical activity (Vygotsky, 1978). Learning occurs when experts and novices interact to move the level of learning from a socially guided, mediated learning experience to an individual experience. Key to this theory is the use of interactive dialogues related to content and strategy instruction. Initially, the expert guides the novice using self-talk and language related to the content and cognitive processes. However, as the novice become adept at the content and cognitive processes, he or she assumes increasing responsibility. Instructionally, this theory highlights the social nature of learning and the importance of teaching within a context of respect and acceptance of each others' knowledge and experiences that are related to the content and cognitive strategies.

To provide instruction that contrasted theoretically with the interactive teaching strategies, definition instruction was chosen. This type of instruction emphasizes direct teaching of concise content-related definitions of conceptual vocabulary. In this instruction, the teacher engages students in oral recitation of definitions and monitors students for correctness, providing corrective feedback (Engelmann & Carnine, 1982).

The concepts that were selected for instruction in the interactive and definition instruction were the same. However, students participated in one of four different prereading and postreading activities, depending on their instructional group: (1) learning the definitions (definition instruction), (2) constructing a map by predicting the meanings and relationships among the concepts (semantic mapping), (3) completing a relationship chart by predicting the meanings and relationships using a matrix format (semantic feature analysis), or (4) completing a relationship chart and completing cloze-type sentences using the chart (semantic/syntactic feature analysis). After the prereading activity, students read the chapter and, as a group, reviewed the definitions, map, chart, or chart and sentence, depending on the type of instruction.

Comparisons of interactive teaching and definition learning were made across several studies, one of which involved upper-elementary bilingual students with learning disabilities who were learning social studies content (Bos, Allen, & Scanlon, 1989). During the first year of the project, the instructional interventions were conducted by the researcher, who served as a teacher.

Effectiveness for content learning was measured with a multiple choice test over key concepts in the chapter that was read. Students who participated in the interactive teaching strategies had better understanding of the concepts and better overall comprehension of the text than students who participated in the definition instruction, both immediately after instruction and one month after instruction.

Second Year of Project

During the second year of the project, we focused on whether or not teachers could implement these interactive teaching strategies in their classrooms with good results. The staff development was based on the same theories and assumptions that guided development of the interactive teaching strategies during the first year of the project. The eight components of interactive teaching in the classroom include (1) providing an overview and scaffold, (2) activating background knowledge, (3) tying new knowledge to old knowledge, (4) providing opportunities for learners to predict relationships among concepts, (5) using cooperative knowledge sharing, (6) teaching conceptual vocabulary in relation to the content to be learned, (7) providing opportunities for learners to justify relationships among concepts, and (8) encouraging learners to confirm their understandings (Bos & Anders, 1990). This instruction occurred in teacher–student dialogues and discussions with opportunities to reflect on learning.

The teachers participated in a 5-wk staff development program designed to teach them how to use the interactive and definition instructional strategies. After the staff development, teachers used one of the strategies in their classroom using materials and tests provided by the research project. Thus, a purpose of the second year of the study was to compare the quality and quantity of learning that took place when teachers taught rather than researchers using the theoretically based instructional strategies.

During the first day of staff development, an overview of the purpose and a rationale of the project were discussed. This discussion provided a twofold opportunity for teachers to: (1) activate their background knowledge about teaching reading comprehension and content subjects and (2) tie those prior ideas to the new concepts presented as part of the staff development (Anders & Gallego, 1989). Through modeling, the researchers enacted how they envisioned the interactive and definition-emphasis strategies being used. Teachers were encouraged to share their expertise by providing suggestions regarding procedures and strategies that would best enlist students' active participation and enhance student learning. This open arena encouraged discussion and provided the foundation for a collaborative endeavor between teachers and researchers.

Teachers then participated in three 40-min, small group simulations in which a researcher introduced the teachers to one strategy. Using procedural and cognitive modeling and materials similar to those used in the study, the researcher demonstrated the strategy. Throughout the sessions, teachers and researchers engaged in interactive dialogues designed to assist teachers in understanding the strategy both theoretically and practically. Included was anticipating possible classroom situations that might arise when they used the strategies with their students. Experimenting with the strategy by role playing also allowed teachers to question and confirm their understanding of the strategy.

This exercise was followed by a 4-wk period during which teachers were asked to practice their assigned strategy with their students in the classroom using materials developed for the project. As teachers practiced their strategy, a researcher observed and served as a coach. At least one session was videotaped and served as the focus for the second day of staff development.

The teachers then returned for a second day of staff development, again meeting in groups to discuss, evaluate, and reflect on their use of the strategies. To prepare for the second day of staff development, the researchers reviewed the teachers' videotapes and selected examples of each of the interactive components as they were enacted for each interactive strategy. These examples were edited onto a single videotape for each strategy and used to stimulate interactive dialogue. The same process was used to develop a videotape for definition instruction. During this second day of staff development, teachers met in groups, according to their assigned instructional strategy, to work collaboratively. They reviewed the components that related to their assigned instruction by viewing the exemplary videotape and sharing constructive comments, personal experiences, and concerns. Teachers were asked to draw relationships between their teaching and the components and to justify and confirm their understanding of the strategy they were to use in the experiment. Teachers also studied the content of the chapters to be used during the study and engaged in a content-oriented discussion with others planning to teach the same content and use the same instructional materials.

Four data sources were used to gain an understanding of the effects of the staff development on teacher and student learning. One source was the videotapes produced when the teachers implemented the study after participating in the initial staff development meeting. These videotapes were analyzed using an observational scoring system that was designed to measure the frequency and quality of each interactive component (e.g., activate prior knowledge, tie old knowledge to new, predict relationships) as the teacher taught the content (Anders & Gallego, 1989).

A second source was a survey completed by each teacher at the conclusion of the project. The survey (Miller, 1987) was designed to ascertain the relationship between the teachers' evaluation of the effectiveness and usability of empirically based vocabulary strategies including interactive strategies as opposed to more direct instruction procedures such as definition instruction. On the survey, each vocabulary strategy was described; the teacher was asked to rate the strategy for effectiveness and usability on a 5-point Likert scale.

A third source was a structured interview designed to ascertain the language that teachers use when discussing the strategies employed in the project. For the interview, teachers reported on (1) background information concerning previously used strategies, (2) how well their assigned strategy helped students understand and remember what they read, (3) the strengths and weaknesses of each strategy used, and (4) how the strategies might be generalized for nonexperimental use by teachers and students. Each interview was audiotaped and transcribed. The transcriptions were analyzed by generating a list of stated empirical premises about the teaching of content area concepts and reading comprehension strategies. An empirical premise was considered an observable and testable explanation of a phenomenon (e.g., "The chart made students pull their prior experiences into their reading. . . "). The proportion of empirical statements related to interactive teaching strategies was computed.

The fourth source was student learning as measured by a researcher-developed multiple-choice test covering the concepts and overall content of the chapter.

Evidence for the Effects of Second Year Staff Development

Seven teachers of upper-elementary bilingual students with learning disabilities participated in the staff development, completed the survey, conducted one or more interactive strategies during the experimental study, and completed the interview. All but one of the teachers were female and ranged in experience from 2 to 22 years, with an average of 11 years teaching experience. Two teachers had a bachelor's degree, four had completed master's degrees, and one had an educational specialist degree. All were certified in special education–learning disabilities. In addition, one had a reading endorsement and two had bilingual or ESL endorsements.

Teachers' Use of the Interactive Strategies

Teachers' use of the interactive strategies was documented by analysis of the videotapes. The percentage of teacher utterances reflecting the use of the interactive components ranged from 48 to 75% per teacher. Analysis of the different components indicated that the teachers focused more on activating background knowledge and helping students make connections among ideas than on other components.

Teachers' Evaluation of the Practices

The teachers evaluated the effectiveness and usability of the interactive teaching strategies as opposed to traditional definition instruction for building content vocabulary and concepts. They rated the interactive strategies as more effective (mean = 4.2) and usable (mean = 4.1) than practices aligned with definition-type instruction (effectiveness mean = 2.5; usability mean = 2.5).

Teachers' Language about the Interactive Strategies

The analysis of the interviews revealed 58 empirical premises about content learning and reading comprehension instruction by the seven teachers. Of the statements, 50 could be categorized according to the eight components of interactive teaching. Teachers placed the greatest importance on the components of interactive teaching that highlight activating background knowledge (18% of the statements), tying old knowledge to new, predicting relationships, and teaching concepts in relation to content (15% of the statements for each of these categories). In contrast, teachers said little about justifying and confirming relationships and using cooperative knowledge sharing.

Student Comprehension and Content Learning

Students' learning was evaluated using the multiple-choice test. First and second year results were compared, that is, achievement when researchers served as teachers was compared with achievement when teachers worked with their own students. The three interactive teaching strategies—semantic mapping, semantic feature analysis, and semantic/syntactic feature analysis—were compared with definition instruction. When comparing the three interactive strategies with definition instruction, simple effect sizes (effect size for concepts = 1.28; for comprehension = 1.46) indicate that the teachers were at least as successful as the researchers (effect size for concepts = .50; for comprehension = .81) in using the interactive strategies.

Questions That Still Remain

Overall, this interactive model of staff development appeared to be effective in facilitating teachers' use of interactive teaching strategies when teaching content information using texts. Although teachers used the interactive strategies when support in terms of prepared materials and instructional guidance was provided, it is unknown whether or not this staff development changed the teachers' general teaching practices and the beliefs associated with content teaching and learning. The next section describes a staff development process that attempted to account for the relationship between teacher's beliefs and practices and change.

THE READING INSTRUCTION STUDY

This 3-year project[4] was designed to investigate the barriers that prohibit teachers from using research-based reading comprehension practices in their classrooms.

Research Questions and Design

We focus on three of the main questions addressed in this study.

1. What are the barriers to the use of research-based practices?

[4]This research was funded in part by the U.S. Department of Education, Office of Educational Research and Improvement (G008710014).

2. Can a school-based staff development model affect teachers' use of research-based instruction of reading comprehension?
3. Does the use of research-based teaching of reading practices affect student reading achievement in a positive direction?

All 38 Grade 4, 5, and 6 teachers in seven schools representing two school districts in an urban area in the Southwest participated in the study. Three schools were designated "experimental;"[5] these schools participated in the staff development described here. Two schools were designated "control." In these schools, we interviewed teachers, observed them teaching, and collected reading achievement data from their students. We provided staff development for the control schools during the third year, but it was a typical model of staff development: we delivered content on topics of interest. The seventh school was designated as a "pilot" school. We spent time with these teachers testing our planned methodology and inviting their criticism.

The heart of this project and the focus of this chapter lay in questions 1 and 2. Two types of barriers that prevent teachers from using research-based practices were explored: (1) potential school-level factors and (2) teachers' beliefs and knowledge about reading and the teaching of reading. Three procedures were used to provide a description of school factors that could contribute to the use or nonuse of research-based reading comprehension practices and to predict the degree to which teachers would be willing to change their existing practices: (1) a teacher questionnaire concerning organizational context, (2) a principal interview on beliefs concerning teacher practice and change, and (3) qualitative descriptions of the school climate, organization, and reading curriculum. Data were summarized across schools and case studies were developed for each school (Placier, 1989).

The second potential barrier, teacher beliefs, was examined by interviewing teachers concerning their beliefs about the reading process and the teaching of reading. An ethnographic approach (Spradley, 1979) to the belief interviews was used, and the interviews were analyzed using categories that emerged from the data. The interviews also provided baseline data against which change could be measured since interviews were also conducted and analyzed at the conclusion of the project.

The study of school-level factors and the interviews helped shape the staff development program, which consisted of an individual component

---

[5]Data from the third school have not yet been analyzed. The circumstances surrounding their participation was problematic. The school was built on a landfill, and both students and teachers became very ill during the research. The school was closed and students and teachers were moved to several schools throughout the district, thereby compromising the collection of data from this school.

and a group-level component. The focus of the individual component was the practical argument (Fenstermacher, 1986). Each teacher was video-taped while teaching reading comprehension. The researchers and the teacher then viewed and analyzed the tape together, discussing the activities, the rationale for each activity, and alternative practices and reasoning. The practical argument discussion concluded with the teacher formulating a goal to try new practices or to improve existing practices. For example, in one case the videotape showed a basal story introduced with minimal attention paid to students' prior knowledge that related to the story. After discussing the importance of activating and instantiating background knowledge for reading comprehension, the teacher decided to try practices that would provide students the opportunity to elaborate and expand on their prior knowledge related to stories before reading. These teacher-generated goals were integrated into the group-level meetings because teachers would discuss with the group any practices that they were trying, and questions about those practices, because of the practical arguments discussion.

The school-level group component of the staff development process lasted for 11 sessions in one school and 8 sessions in the second school. Each group decided when they would meet, where the meetings would take place, and the compensation they wished to receive. The first school agreed to meet after school in the library and to receive university credit for their participation. The second group agreed to meet in the home of one of the staff developers and to have substitutes teach their classes on those afternoons.

The agenda for each group was similar. The first activity was sharing of the interviews discussed earlier. Each interview was transcribed and analyzed for empirical premises, statements made by the teacher that could be verified. These statements were highlighted on each teacher's interview transcript and returned to the teacher at the first staff development meeting. The empirical premises for all teachers in each school were also summarized by the categories that emerged. For example, one category was "students at this school;" another was "definitions of reading comprehension." Discussion of teachers' reactions and reflections about their individual interviews and the composite of those interviews was the basis for the first and second group-level staff development meetings. At the conclusion of the second meeting, a handout summarizing 16 theoretical foci (see Table 1) and related instructional practices from the literature review was distributed. These were generated from a comprehensive literature review conducted by the researchers. Teachers were asked to look over the list and to consider which of the practices they were most interested in learning more about. During the third meeting, the foci and practices were explained by relating them to theories of the reading process. The agenda

Table 1
Theoretically Related Foci and Categorized Practices

Foci	Pratices
Background knowledge	Providing background knowledge statements; teaching/using analogies; reading conceptually related text; using advanced organizers; confronting misconceptions; previewing stories; reading headings; predicting story events; using concrete advanced organizers; probing background knowledge
Text characteristics	Story mapping; mapping expository text; teach lexical ties; pattern guides; cloze exercises; sentence anagrams; structured overviews; teach expository text structures; structured overview and cloze; reorder information; identify and eliminate extraneous information; identify main idea; concept relationship matrix; links, studying maps of expository test; completing graphic organizer based on text structure; idea mapping; revising inconsiderate text; synonym drills; decoding drill
Vocabulary	Asking questions to determine meaning from context; using familiar content to teach word meanings; semantic maps and networks; reading text with explicit context cues; teach definitions; concept method; discussion to relate words to prior knowledge; teach the concept of definition; rich and varied vocabulary instruction; mnemonic aids

Independent study strategies	Survey, question, read, recite, review; summarize each paragraph; study guides; post-questioning
Visualization	Visual imagery; drawing; provide pictures; mimetic maps
Self-monitoring/metacognition	Learning strategies; underlining interesting words; strategic approach; informed strategies for learning; reciprocal teaching; inference awareness
Teacher/text-generated questions	Question–answer relationships; story characters; inferential question; reflective questions; interspersed post-questions; text look-back strategy; WH questions
Self-generated questions	Predictive questions; knowledge, want to know; learned; important points; higher-order questions; reciprocal post-questions; self-questions plus underlining
Modality	Dramatizing stories; oral reading; silent reading
Oral reading accuracy	No corrections during oral reading; corrections during oral reading
Reading and writing	Summarizing; sentence combining; reflective questions; writing after listening to stories; creative writing after reading; journals
Critical reading	Direct instruction
Attention/selection	Provide purpose; provide behavioral objectives; advance organizer
Memory and retrieval	Elaboration training
Literature groups	Student-selected literature groups; text sets
Lesson frameworks	Guided reading procedure; directed reading–thinking activity; directed reading activity; experience–text relationship; revised basal lesson

for the rest of the meetings was driven by interests, questions, and issues raised by the teachers.

An ethnography of the process was conducted by Hamilton (1989), providing the following description:

> The staff developers obviously brought their own beliefs and personal theories into the staff development process. Having designed the project, they had ideas and plans for the staff development program and directions for the practices they employed in that staff development. Doubtless the biases and beliefs of the staff developers affected their entry into the project, but importantly, these biases and beliefs did not appear to greatly affect the directions and topics that the teachers chose to focus upon in the staff development programs.
>
> As the staff development programs progressed, the staff developers seemed less inclined to talk about their ideas and more inclined to ask, "Well, what do you think?" even as the teachers pleaded for information about the "right way" to teach reading. Of course, their beliefs were apparent and acknowledged, but they did not attempt to sell the teachers on their ideas. Rather, they took great efforts to listen carefully to what the teachers said. Moreover, they brought in and examined topics of concern expressed by the teachers, and veered away from discussions about their own beliefs. (p. 198)

The staff development was planned this way to provide a context for integrating teacher beliefs and content regarding research-based strategies. Articulation of the teachers' beliefs and related practices seemed critical to the acceptance and use of practices that either elaborated on existing beliefs or called for a change in existing beliefs.

Results of Staff Development

Transcribed videotapes of the staff development meetings provided opportunities for analyzing both the process and results of the program. In terms of process, we learned that the program appeared to follow three specific stages (Hamilton, 1989). The first stage was identified as introductory, the second as breakthrough, and the third as empowerment.

During the introductory stage, teachers familiarized themselves with each other, their philosophies, and their ways of thinking. During this time, they did not ask questions of each other; rather, they politely listened to the conversation. The staff developers talked about general practices and pressed the teachers to describe their classroom practices. In the first school, the introductory stage lasted for 8 of the 11 meetings. In contrast, the second school moved quickly out of the introductory stage during the middle of the second meeting.

The second stage, the breakthrough stage, occurred when a person or persons moved from one line of thinking, or way of doing things, to a new way of thinking about the topic. Sometimes there were hesitations and concerns as a result of the newness of the experience, yet recognition of that newness served as an affirmation of change. At this stage teachers asked "do you" questions ("Do you do literature groups?" or "When do you do skills?"). When these questions were asked, teachers began to offer their options and suggestions. At the same time, the staff developers participated less. This is not to say they were not engaged; instead, they became participants rather than leaders.

The final stage of empowerment was when teachers claimed ownership of the staff development itself. In this stage, teachers dominated the conversation. They arranged agendas, asked questions, and proposed answers to each other's questions. The first school reached the empowerment stage at their last meeting; in contrast, the second school entered this stage during its sixth meeting. Analyses of the discourse suggest that teachers were engaged in cognitive strategic thinking when in this stage. For example, a theme running through discussions in the first school was the issue of where meaning resides—in the book, in the mind of the teacher, or somewhere between—but during the last session, this issue was talked about in a very different way. During this session, both teachers and researchers moved beyond their "roles" and began to justify their beliefs in terms of empirical evidence and generalized experience. Another finding was that presentation styles during the meetings could be categorized into five different types: sharing, show and tell, lecture 1, lecture 2, and a new suggestion. The difference between lecture 1 and lecture 2 was that the former was a prepared presentation about an activity extracted from the literature and the latter was a formal presentation that had not been prepared but added to the discussion at hand. The content of the sessions was studied by creating topic maps for each section. Although research-based reading comprehension strategies constituted the anticipated content of the staff development, the conversation often moved away from reading comprehension practices and their justifications into two additional areas: (1) writing and other language arts and (2) testing/assessment and grading. The time spent on the latter was quite surprising. At both schools, approximately 20% of the discourse time was devoted to issues surrounding grading, testing, and assessment (Anders, Richardson, & Morgan, 1989).

Teachers resisted using the list of practices they received at the second meeting. When asked to select from the list, their answer was that we, "the experts from the University," should choose. We resisted making the choice because we believed that teacher's choice and interest were necessary for acceptance of the practices and for the requisite change in beliefs that using such practices would entail. A tally of the practices discussed revealed that the teachers shared and presented more practices than we did. In the first school, teachers presented 40 practices and we presented 17; in the second school teachers presented 26 practices and we presented 16.

The outcome of the staff development process in terms of changes in beliefs and practices was equally interesting. By analyzing and comparing the empirical premises teachers made during the interviews conducted before and after staff development, we learned that all but one of the seven teachers in one school, and all the teachers in the second school, changed in their theoretical orientation toward the reading process. The one teacher who did not change was absent from several of the group meetings. During the initial interviews, most teachers were described as believing that meaning lies in the text and that reading is a matter of decoding and knowing words. In contrast, after the staff development process, most teachers moved from that orientation to a position of defining reading as engaging text; however, there was less consistency among teachers about whether meaning was in the text, in the reader, or in some interaction of the two (Richardson & Anders, 1990, pp. 80–81).

Teachers elaborated extensively on their definition of reading during the interviews. Many moved from a short definition in the first interview, which implied that reading comprehension was being able to answer comprehension check questions accurately, to a much broader and deeper, more cognitively oriented definition. For example, one teacher responded to the question concerning reading comprehension in the final interview in this manner.

> It is understanding what you read. And like I said, when you read different novels or different materials it depends on what you read before, so I think it would be really important to talk to kids about what they already know and have read . . . in the past I always taught in terms of reading the book and then answering the questions and giving the kids a quiz. Now I think one of the big things is if they can take what they have read and apply it to something else.

There was also a change toward a sense of multiple purposes for reading, and that purpose affects the definition. In her first interview, one teacher defined reading in a very short and straightforward statement: "Well, first thing that came to my mind was: understanding what is read. Also, it is being able to give it back." In contrast, the following dialogue occurred during her final interview.

Interviewer: How do you see reading comprehension now?

Teacher: Well, I see it on different levels. I see it as facts, reading facts and coming back with answers and I see it as a different . . . its different in different subjects. Literature is more a feeling you get, whereas comprehension in social studies or science is more facts. And yet as I say that, I've even gotten away from emphasizing facts and more into studying of feelings about the war . . . about slavery . . . about fighting.

These quotes are indicative of an increased elaboration on the teachers' understanding of what might constitute reading comprehension and the teaching of reading. A teacher from the first school said it well:

> I think I'm formulating strong beliefs about reading that I maybe had before . . . see in the (initial) belief interview I don't think I stated anything very strongly . . . yet, I know I have strong beliefs. Getting them articulated and meshed is another thing . . . I think I have been a lot stronger today (exit interview) about positions and about what I think is important.

These teachers also changed their practices. The evidence for this change comes both from their self reports and from videotapes of their instruction after the staff development process. Changes in practice included (1) less reliance on the basal reader; (2) increased use of prereading activities such as semantic mapping to activate and build background knowledge; (3) increased integration of literature across the curriculum in subjects such as social studies and science; (4) less acceptance of imposed methods of assessment and more interest in methods that better reflect current research on the reading process; (5) an increased concern for networking with colleagues toward creating an environment for critical analysis of practice; (6) more attention to drawing out students' background knowledge and making connections between what was already known and what was to be learned; (7) increased sharing of children's literature, both with each other and with their students; (8) use of intentional strategic instruction encouraging students to ask their own questions about what was being read; and (9) increased use of journal writing to react to what was read both in content subjects and literature.

Finally, teachers were asked what the staff development program had been like for them. The faculty from the first school provided many "quotable quotes," but one said it best:

> It was like doing calisthenics and sometimes I just wasn't in that frame of mind and it was just too tiring. But yet I knew it was good for me. Kind of like eating bran, you know. You don't always want to do it, but you know you should.

The teachers in the second school quickly took over the direction of the process and openly discussed practices and beliefs. One quote, representative of several, reflects the process:

> . . . when we came here we didn't have to necessarily follow any kind of format . . . everybody was able to speak freely and I think that's important. I think that allowed everybody a lot in the area of growth and those people who

were thinking about changing had the opportunity to ask for the help that they needed. For me, personally, as I said the first few meetings I felt real defensive . . . speaking and noticing my defensiveness allowed me to share my convictions. And when you're sharing your convictions, you don't have to be defensive.

CONCLUSION

These two staff development programs, the Interactive Teaching Project and the Reading Instruction Study, offer important lessons to those of us who are trying to affect change in schools. It seems that accepting, acknowledging, and helping teachers elaborate on their beliefs as related both to old and new practices is critical for change. In both cases, the researchers were interested in helping teachers become more strategic teachers of reading comprehension. To do so, the teachers were invited to participate in programs that were based on cognitively oriented principles of learning, with plenty of opportunities to talk about what they were learning and doing. For example, these programs recognized that, just as children need to relate their prior knowledge to new information, teachers need to relate their prior knowledge and experience of teaching and learning to new ideas and practices. The accommodation of new ideas requires that old experiences be seen from different perspectives. Seeing old and new ideas from new perspectives is difficult. It takes time, reflection, and opportunities to talk, write, and critically analyze in a safe and supportive atmosphere.

One fallacy of the transmission approach to professional development is that it is often delivered in a locked-step didactic fashion that fails to model the very principles of instruction that are targeted. The adage "Do as I say, not as I do" may be an apt description of what often occurs in these programs. Without concrete experience with the principles being taught, teachers are unlikely to challenge their personal experiences or see the distinction between new theories and practices and what they have always believed and done.

The projects described in this chapter are examples of how professional development sensitive to social and cognitive principles of learning might be organized. However, two specific questions remain as we consider our future work in this area. First, we wonder about the role of the person "in charge" of the professional development sessions. In a Vygotskian sense (1978), the "expert" would be capable of playing different roles as needed, but we know little about the processes involved in playing those roles. Second, neither of these projects had the luxury of examining long-term change on the teachers' parts. The norms of schools (Lortie, 1975) are strong and may limit the extent that any one person can sustain change. Future research should examine the qualities of professional development that support maintenance and continued change in practice.

To continue this inquiry, the following tenets may serve as guidelines.

1. The results of experimental studies are not transferable to a particular classroom; even the best research-based practices must be transformed by teachers.
2. The transformation of practices requires reflection, that is, practices must be viewed according to teacher's perceptions of the experience.
3. The transformation is supported or limited by the social climate in which the teacher thinks, learns, and teaches. Administrators, policy makers, researchers, and teacher educators need to examine their contributions to that climate.

Finally, when norms, expectations, and the system of rewards change so that teachers are reflective, articulate, and critical about what they do and why they do it, many of the secrets of teaching and learning that have eluded researchers and teachers alike may come to light. Our work, along with the work of others, will attempt to contribute to the revelation of those secrets.

REFERENCES

Anders, P. L., and Bos, C. S. (1991). *The interactive teaching project: Final report* (G008630125). Tucson: College of Education, University of Arizona.

Anders, P. L., and Gallego, M. A. (1989). Adoption of theoretically linked vocabulary-reading comprehension practices. In S. McCormick and J. Zutell (Eds.), *Cognitive and social perspectives for literacy research and instruction* (Thirty-eighth yearbook, pp. 481–487). Chicago: The National Reading Conference.

Anders, P. L., Richardson, V., and Morgan, B. (1989). *Influences on reading instruction: The testing and instruction connection.* Paper presented at the annual meeting of the National Reading Conference, Austin, Texas.

Anderson, R. C., and Freebody, P. (1981). Vocabulary knowledge. in J. T. Guthrie (Ed.), *Comprehension and teaching: Research reviews* (pp. 77–117). Newark, Delaware: International Reading Association.

Au, K. (1990). Changes in a teacher's views of interactive comprehension instruction. In L. C. Moll (Ed.), *Vygotsky and education* (pp. 271–286). New York: Cambridge University Press.

Bos, C. S., and Anders, P. L. (1990). Interactive teaching and learning: Instructional practices for teaching content and strategic knowledge. In B. Y. L. Wong and T. E. Scruggs (Eds.), *Intervention research in learning disabilities* (pp. 166–185). New York: Springer Verlag.

Bos, C. S., Allen, A. A., and Scanlon, D. J. (1989). Vocabulary instruction and reading comprehension with bilingual learning disabled students. In S. McCormick and J. Zutell (Eds.), *Cognitive and social perspectives for literacy research and instruction* (Thirty-eighth yearbook, pp. 173–180). Chicago: The National Reading Conference.

Campbell, G. B. (1989). *Staff development through dialogue: A case study in educational problem solving.* Unpublished doctoral dissertation, University of Pennsylvania, Graduate School of Education, Philadelphia.

Carpenter, T. P., Fennema, E., Peterson, P., Chiang, C. P., and Loef, L. (1989). Using knowledge of children's mathematics thinking in classroom teaching: An experimental study. *American Educational Research Journal, 26,* 499–532.

Deal, T., and Derr, C. B. (1980). Toward a contingency theory of organizational change in education: Structure, processes and symbolism. In C. S. Benson, M. Kirst, S. Abromowitz, W. Hartman, and L. Stoll (Eds.). *Educational finance and organization: Research perspectives for the future.* Washington, D.C.: National Institute of Education.

Engelmann, S., and Carnine, D. W. (1982). *Theory of instruction: Principles and applications.* New York: Irvington.

Fenstermacher, G. D. (1986). A philosophy of research on teaching: Three aspects. In M. C. Wittrock, (Ed.), *Handbook of research on teaching* (3rd ed., pp. 37–49). New York: MacMillan.

Gage, N. (1978). *The scientific basis of the art of teaching.* Columbia University: Teacher's College Press.

Goodman, K. S. (1984). Unity in reading. In A. C. Purves and O. Niles (Eds.), *Becoming readers in a complex society* (Eighty-third yearbook, pp. 79–114). Chicago: The National Society for the Study of Education.

Hamilton, M. L. (1989). *The practical argument staff development process, school culture and their effects on teachers' beliefs and classroom practice.* Unpublished doctoral dissertation. University of Arizona, Tucson.

Klausmeier, J. H., and Sipple, T. S. (1980). *Learning and teaching process concepts: A strategy for testing applications for theory.* New York: Academic Press.

Lortie, D. (1975). *Schoolteacher.* Chicago, Illinois: University of Chicago Press.

Miller, A. (1987). *What reported literature, classroom observations and a teacher survey reveal about vocabulary instruction.* Unpublished master's thesis. University of Arizona, Tucson.

Peterman, F. (1991). *A teacher changing beliefs about teaching and learning.* Unpublished doctoral dissertation. University of Arizona, Tucson.

Placier, P. (1989). *School level influences on adoption of instructional practices in reading.* Paper presented at the National Reading Conference, Tucson, Arizona.

Richardson, V., and Anders, P. L. (1990). *Final report of the reading instruction study.* Tucson: University of Arizona. ERIC Documentation No. ED 312 359.

Rumelhart, D. E. (1980). Schemata: The building blocks of cognition. In R. J. Spiro, B. C. Bruce, and W. F. Brewer (Eds.), *Theoretical issues in reading comprehension* (pp. 33–58). Hillsdale, New Jersey: Erlbaum.

Spradley, J. P. (1979). *The ethnographic interview.* New York: Holt, Rinehart & Winston.

Vygotsky, L. S. (1978). *Mind in society.* Cambridge, Massachusetts: Harvard University Press.

17

Moving Metacognition into the Classroom: "Working Models" and Effective Strategy Teaching

John G. Borkowski and Nithi Muthukrishna

Over the last three decades, a great deal of research has focused on teaching individual strategies to enhance learning and elevate performance (cf. Borkowski & Cavanaugh, 1979; Paris, 1988; Pressley, Goodchild, Fleet, Zajchowski, & Evans, 1989a; Pressley, Johnson, Symons, McGoldrick & Kurita, 1989b). For instance, an inordinately large number of studies has aimed to perfect elementary study strategies such as rehearsal, categorization, and associative elaboration (Pressley, 1982; Pressley, Cariglia-Bull, Deane, & Schneider, 1987b; Torgeson, 1980). Although this phase of instructional research has been informative—we now know that most children can be taught to execute many strategies after rather simple explanations and that their performance improves accordingly—failures in strategy maintenance and generalization have been commonplace (Borkowski & Cavanaugh, 1979; Garner, 1990; Resnick, 1987). Straightforward direct instruction is generally not followed by persistent and widespread strategy use. Further, narrowly focused strategy instruction often does not result in self-regulated learning and, generally, has no appreciable influence on classroom performance (Belmont & Butterfield, 1977; Borkowski, Carr, & Pressley, 1987; Schunk & Rice, 1987).

Cognitive strategy instruction also has been criticized for teaching individual strategies, often out of context, rather than producing strategic learners. For instance, Duffy (1990) has stressed that strategy instruction should not help students merely acquire discrete strategies but should teach them how to become active and thoughtful learners. From this perspective, simply possessing a repertoire of strategies is not sufficient to guarantee self-regulated learning in which flexible, rather than rote, strategy use characterizes overt and covert cognitive actions. It seems clear that self-regulated learning needs to be carefully nurtured—in the home and school—to develop fully. The goal of this chapter is to outline ways in which self-regulated learning can become the focus of classroom instruction. More specifically, we argue that a "working model" of metacognitive development is a prerequisite for strategy-based teaching that aims to produce self-regulated learners. Working models of metacognition help teachers mold and maintain an instructional framework for initiating interactive learning that is guided and direct, as well as transactional and constructive. We turn now to a discussion of working models, their importance in teaching flexible strategy use, and the potential role of the Good Information Processing model and, more generally, metacognitive theory in their formation and function.

STRATEGIC FLEXIBLE LEARNING AND ITS INSTRUCTION

Pressley and colleagues (1989a) offered the concept of the "good strategy user" to portray the culmination of effective strategy teaching. This concept emphasizes the importance of acquiring sets of strategies, coordinating multiple strategies, and switching strategies when a desired outcome is not obtained (Pressley, Borkowski, & Schneider, 1987a; Pressley *et al.,* 1989a; Pressley, Snyder, & Cariglia-Bull, 1987c; see also Chapters 3 & 4). Such higher-order regulatory skills produce flexibility and innovation in strategy use, and are at the heart of metacognitive theory (Weinert & Kluwe, 1987).

Duffy (1990) has outlined several ways in which young students can be taught to behave flexibly, rather than merely to repeat discrete strategies in rote fashion. Basically, teachers themselves must develop broad conceptual knowledge, or internal models, of what it means to be strategic. According to Duffy, teachers themselves must become knowledgeable about what good information processing involves (see Chapter 15). For example, strategies should be seen as sets of interdependent mental operations that are interchangeable and can be modified in response to different situations; hence, strategies should never be taught out of context. Instead, they need to be introduced and practiced as part of an ongoing curriculum, such as reading, mathematics, and content-related instruction. Teachers need to "situate strategies" so children have immediate feedback that the use of strategies is indeed improving performance; thus, students must constantly be encouraged to monitor carefully their use of strategies and the corresponding performance outcomes. Pressley, Harris, and Marks (1992b) stress that, in a good strategy teaching model, "teachers encourage habitual reflecting and planning by students." They model planfulness and provide opportunities for students to think through problems. In short, they foster an environment in which such reflection is valued more than the completion of assignments or the production of correct answers. In proper context, metacognitive development flourishes because students have rich, diverse opportunities for planfulness and reflection, and are active deliberate participants in the learning process.

We have found, on repeated occasions, that a major problem in developing strategy-oriented teachers, in Duffy's (1990) sense, is their lack of understanding about why strategies should be explicit targets for instruction. Many teachers do not have a working model or framework about children's metacognitive development that guides their formation of classroom goals and learning activities. A metacognitive framework seems useful, and perhaps necessary, for acquiring, modifying, and deploying teaching methods to instruct flexible strategy use and to persevere until the use of strategies is commonplace in the classroom.

In short, we believe that metacognitive theory has considerable potential for aiding teachers as they strive to construct classroom environments that focus on strategic learning that is both flexible and creative. Our hypothesis is that teachers who possess a "working model" of children's metacognitive development are more likely to become, and remain, strategy-oriented teachers. The goal of this chapter is to present a working model of metacognitive development that teachers might find plausible as a conceptual framework within which to become strategy-oriented, and also to suggest methods for reducing obstacles that impede metacognitive instruction.

"WORKING MODELS" OF METACOGNITION

When a strategy-based instructional curriculum, for example, the many new strategy-oriented basal reading series, is introduced to novice or even experienced teachers, we have frequently encountered bewilderment, confusion, and sometimes resentment. Often, the initial set of questions is: "But what is a strategy? Do I teach one or two? How do I know they'll work? What about phonics? Won't students be restless, and parents dissatisfied, if I focus on strategies instead of content?" All of these questions suggest a strong, and perhaps universal, need on the part of teachers for assistance in their development as strategy-oriented instructors.

By forming and continually updating their "working models" of children's metacognitive development, teachers make a commitment to the importance and intricacies of strategy-based approaches to instruction. The development of a working model during a teacher's initial exposure to strategy instruction seems especially important. Each model needs to evolve gradually and be carefully fitted to the unique disposition and history of the teacher. Although there are undoubtedly many useful plausible working models of strategic teaching, we have found that the components of metacognitive theory, as taught from a developmental perspective, represent an extremely efficient and useful starting point.

It should be emphasized that, to operate properly, each teacher needs to challenge the components of our preferred metacognitive model—rejecting some, accepting others—and then, over time, to add components that meet situational needs and that flow from the teacher's own experiences in fostering mental development. Before we present a sequence for training teachers in good information processing and metacognitive models, a clarification of the concept of "working model" is needed.

Working Models

We have stated previously that it is important for teachers to develop "working models" of metacognitive development in order to deliver inventive, flexible, strategy-oriented curricula. Our hypothesis is built on the rationale developed in other fields of inquiry about the importance of working models in guiding human decision making (Craik, 1943), as well as on the observations of seasoned effective teachers, most of whom display a rich perspective on, and interest in, theories about children's mental development (Pressley *et al.,* 1991).

A working model provides a schema for organizing knowledge, a framework in which to incorporate new information, and a springboard for launching future actions. Craik (1943) provided an important operational definition for the concept of a working model.

> If the organism carries a small-scale model of external reality and of its own possible actions within its head, it is able to try out various alternatives, conclude which is the best of them, react to future situations before they arise, utilize the knowledge of past events in dealing with the present and future, and in every way to react in a much fuller, safer and more competent manner to the emergencies which face it (p. 61).

It is Craik's (1943) final function of a working model—reacting to opportunities and challenges—that is perhaps its most essential characteristic, especially as applied to teachers' adoption, modification, and consistent use of a strategy-based curriculum.

Bretherton (1985), in her discussion of the role of "working models" in the formation of secure attachment in infants, outlined two advantages of this conceptual metaphor. Both have relevance to the extension of "working models" to strategy-based teaching. The adjective "working" emphasizes the dynamic nature of the concept. The concept helps provide interpretations of present situations and determines a range of alternative future actions. In the hands of a strategic teacher, a working model assists in decisions about the next course of action for a class, a small group, or a particular student.

The noun "model" implies an active personal construction of one's own theory, as well as its inevitable change in content and function with experience (Bretherton, 1985). Hence, there is ownership of a teacher's model since it has been carefully crafted, reshaped, and groomed through successes and failures. Teacher training should provide a broad framework and practical suggestions about potential components in the general model, but each individual must accept, reject, and invent components based on his or her personal observations and the unique demands of the classroom context.

The model we develop in the next section should be viewed, in this light, as a starting point, an "initial working model of metacognitive development." The function of the model is not so much to aid in curriculum planning as it is to assist in forming what McCutcheon (1980) called mental dialogues and Morine-Dershimer (1979) referred to as "mental plans or lesson images." The function of global plans is to direct more detailed curriculum planning and, perhaps more importantly, to direct the process of interactive guided discovery.

In order for our model of metacognition, or any similar conceptualization of strategy-based learning, to function properly it must be "internalized and personalized." It must be owned rather than borrowed. To "own" a model, in this sense, implies that a teacher must practice its major components, receive guidance in modifying techniques and goals, adopt the model's characteristics to the unique circumstances of the classroom, and update the model based on personal experiences and observations of teaching successes and failures. In short, an externally imposed model will do little to enhance flexible, transactional, constructively oriented teaching.

"The Good Information Processor" and Metacognitive Development

Over the last few years, the goals and prerequisites for strategy-based learning have evolved (Pressley *et al.,* 1987a; Pressley, Borkowski, & Schneider, 1990; see also Chapter 3). These goals include the teaching of strategies per se, the processes necessary for their implementation, and the self-system (and motivational beliefs) that is their consequence as well as their inspiration (Borkowski, Carr, Rellinger, & Pressley, 1990). Since teachers must understand the complex interactive nature of metacognitive development, they must understand what a strategy is, observe a variety of strategies in operation, and appreciate the personal–motivational contexts in which flexibly used strategies operate.

We believe three steps in the teacher training process are necessary (but perhaps not sufficient) to introduce strategy-based instruction successfully: (1) Learn what strategies are, see first hand how they function, and observe their effectiveness. (2) Understand the complex characteristics that define the ultimate goal of teaching: producing good information processors. (3) Develop a "working model" of metacognitive development that places the act of strategy use into broad information processing, motivational, and personal perspectives.

Defining and Observing Strategies

Pressley, Forrest-Pressley, Elliot-Faust, and Miller (1985b) have provided us with a reasonable definition of a strategy.

> [Strategies] . . . are composed of cognitive operations over and above the processes that are a natural consequence of carrying out [a] task, ranging from one such operation to a sequence of interdependent operations. Strategies achieve cognitive purposes (e.g., memorizing) and are potentially conscious and controllable activities.

From this perspective, strategies are not necessarily conscious, only "potentially conscious." Their function is to assist the learner in carrying out essential cognitive operations that produce efficient insightful learning.

More important than the definition of strategy, however, is observing strategies in operation. Videotapes of elementary strategies, such as rehearsal and organization, as well as more complex strategies, such as elaboration, paraphrasing, and summarization, help emphasize the fact that strategies are an integral part of good information processing. Visualizing multiple strategies in operation, and assessing their relative effectiveness, serves to dramatize a key point. Strategy-based learning is deliberate, effortful, and usually produces a higher level of performance than nonstrategic learning.

Characteristics of Good Information Processing

Since working models of metacognition will inevitably be multifaceted, it may be best to begin with the final goal: a rich, accurate, and complete description of the child or adolescent who is a good information processor. Although somewhere, someday, a teacher may discover the child who actually mirrors our hypothetical conceptualization of good information processing, it probably has not occurred yet. Thus, the vision we espouse serves as an ultimate goal to strive for in facilitating children's learning. The unique feature of the good information processor is the successful *integration* of the main components of the metacognitive system, including cognitive, motivational, personal, and situational characteristics. There are 10 major characteristics that seem essential. Most of these components are developed, or reshaped, by classroom experiences. The child

1. *knows* a large number of learning strategies.
2. *understands* when, where, and why these strategies are important.
3. *selects* and *monitors* strategies wisely, and is extremely *reflective* and *planful.*
4. adheres to an *incremental* view regarding the growth of mind.
5. *believes* in carefully deployed *effort.*
6. is *intrinsically motivated, task-oriented,* and has *mastery goals.*
7. does not *fear failure,* in fact, realizes that failure is essential for success, hence, is not *anxious* about tests but sees then as learning opportunities.
8. has concrete, multiple images of *"possible selves,"* both hoped-for and feared selves in the near and distant future.
9. *knows* a great deal about many topics and has rapid *access* to that knowledge.
10. has a history of being *supported* in all of these characteristics by *parents, schools,* and *society at large.*

Each of these characteristics needs to be discussed fully with teachers, with emphasis on the reasons why they are important. We prefer to present the characteristics as goals or objectives, without a great deal of discussion, and then to explain each characteristic more fully as we outline metacognitive development (see the next section). Background literature and diverse rationale for most of the 10 characteristics can be found in Ames and Archer (1988), Borkowski *et al.* (1990), Borkowski, Schneider, and Pressley (1989b), Deci (1975), Markus and Nurius (1986), Nicholls (1989), and Pressley *et al.* (1991).

Although space constraints do not permit a thorough review of the literature surrounding each characteristic, several are particularly important and deserve highlighting: (1) Strategies learned out of context, or in the rote fashion, will prove transient (Characteristic 2 suggests that developing an in-depth awareness of how each strategy works is critical). (2) Executive functioning is the most important process in the system (Characteristic 3 emphasizes the need for task analyses, planfulness, and reflectivity in decisions to select a strategy and to monitor its effectiveness). (3) Beliefs about hard work in analyzing tasks and selecting strategies and an orientation toward solving the task at hand rather than pleasing others energize self-regulation (thus, Characteristics 5 and 6 are related to Characteristic 3). (4)

Students need to visualize themselves in short- and long-term time frames in order to develop goals that drive the entire metacognitive system (Characteristic 8). (5) Consistency in strategy instruction—across time and settings (Characteristic 10)—seems useful, perhaps essential, for instructional success.

An Approach to Instructing Metacognitive Theory

After understanding the characteristics of good information processing, it is generally helpful to illustrate to teachers how these characteristics become interrelated by focusing on a simplified scenario of how the essential components might develop. Borkowski and colleagues (1992) have recently traced metacognitive development in terms of what happens to a child who receives high quality interactive strategy instruction.

1. The child is initially taught to use a learning strategy and, with repetition, comes to learn about the attributes of that strategy (this is called *specific strategy knowledge*). These attributes include the effectiveness of the strategy, the range of its appropriate applications, and how to use it with a variety of tasks. Figure 1 shows how a simple strategy (such as repetition), in isolation from the rest of the system, can be expected to produce an improvement in performance.
2. Next, the child learns other strategies and repeats them in multiple contexts. In this way, specific strategy knowledge is enlarged and enriched. Figure 2 presents a schematic showing the emergence of a number of specific strategies. The child comes to understand when, where, and how to deploy each strategy.
3. The child gradually develops the capacity to select strategies appropriate for some tasks (but not others), and to fill in knowledge gaps by monitoring performance, especially when essential strategy components have not been adequately learned. At this stage, higher-order executive processes emerge. This is the beginning of self-regulation,

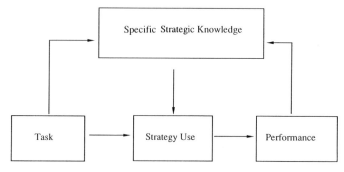

Fig. 1 Primitive view of the strategy use–performance relationship.

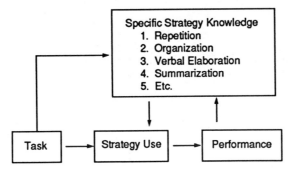

Fig. 2 Multiple strategies and their attributes.

the basis for adaptive planful learning and thinking. Figure 3 shows the relationship of executive processes to specific strategies. Initially, the function of the executive is to analyze the task at hand and to select an appropriate strategy; later during the course of learning, its role shifts to strategy monitoring and revision.

4. As strategic and executive processes become refined, the child comes to recognize the general utility and importance of being strategic (*general strategy knowledge*) and beliefs about self-efficacy develop. Children learn to attribute successful (and unsuccessful) learning outcomes to effort expended in strategy deployment rather than to luck, and to understand that mental competencies can be enhanced through self-directed action. In this way, the metacognitive model integrates cognitive acts (in the form of strategy use) with their motivational causes and consequences.

A sense of self-efficacy and an enjoyment of learning flow from individual strategic events and eventually return to energize strategy selection and monitoring decisions (i.e., executive processes). This latter connection—the association between the learners' reasons for

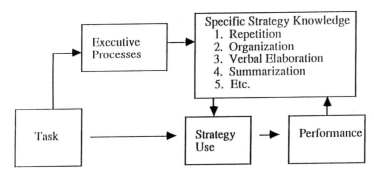

Fig. 3 Executive functioning and strategy use.

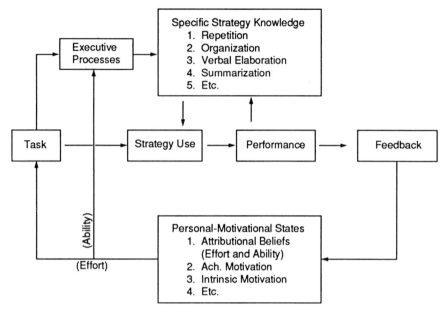

Fig. 4 Motivational correlates and causes of strategy use.

learning and the deployment of self-regulation—has been absent from most instructional programs. This theme is at the heart of our most recent extensions of metacognitive theory (Borkowski *et al.,* 1990, 1992). Figure 4 suggests that, after cognition acts, the child is provided with or infers feedback about the successfulness of performance and its specific cause(s). This feedback is essential for shaping personal–motivational states that in turn energize the executive processes necessary for strategy selection.

5. *General knowledge about the world* as well as *domain-specific knowledge* (e.g., math) accumulate. Such knowledge is often sufficient to solve problems, even without the aid of strategies. In these situations, metacognitive processes such as strategy selection are unnecessary, although some motivational components may remain functional and important (see Figure 5).

6. Crystallized visions into the future help the child form a number of "hoped-for" and "feared" possible selves (Markus & Nurius, 1986), providing the impetus for achieving important short-term as well as long-term goals, such as becoming a "competent student" in order to eventually become a "successful lawyer" (cf. Day, Borkowski, Dietmeyer, Howsepian, & Saenz, 1992). In this way, the self-system takes on a futuristic perspective, providing goals and incentives that simu-

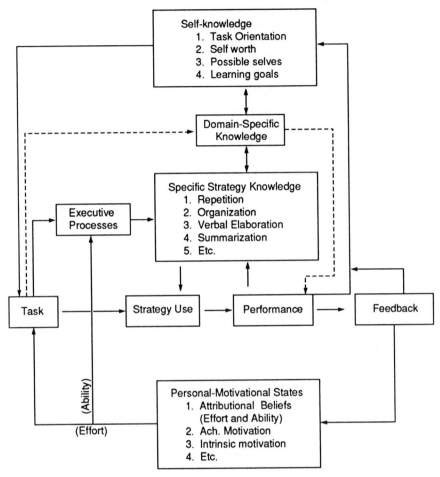

Fig. 5 Cognitive, motivational, and self-system components of metacognition: the complete model.

late the operation of the entire metacognitive system. The complete metacognitive model, including the self-system and the domain-specific knowledge "bypass," is presented in Figure 5.

Metacognitive theory serves as a potential working model that teachers can use and modify to understand better the richness and complexities of strategy-based instruction. There are several advantages in presenting the model from a developmental perspective. (1) The full model is sufficiently complex to overwhelm even experienced teachers. Building gradually from an elementary starting point (Figure 1) helps overcome apprehension and stimulates conversations about relevant examples and experiences. (2) Since metacognitive development occurs at different rates and at different levels, each child should be initially located at a different point in the instructional sequence. A step-by-step analysis of the build-up and integration of metacognition components aids the diagnosis, assessment, and planning process for children with diverse skills.

In summary, the centerpiece of metacognitive theory is strategy selection and use. Not only are specific strategies essential for effective learning and problem solving, they provide the context for presenting higher-level planning and executive skills as well as represent the basis for restructuring attributional beliefs and enhancing self-efficacy. As such connections are formed and ingrained, instructional emphasis can shift to their interface with domain-specific knowledge and the explicit incorporation of "possible selves" training into individualized curricula. Hopefully, the net result of integrating and instructing these central and peripheral components of metacognition will be the production of more effective and efficient students, who share many of the characteristics of the good information processor.

THE COMPLEXITIES OF GOOD STRATEGY INSTRUCTION: TRANSACTIONAL CONSTRUCTIVE TEACHING

Direct Explicit Teaching Is Effective

Most recent perspectives on strategic teaching have emphasized extensive instructional involvement by the teacher (Duffy & Roehler, 1989; see also Parts II and III). These new approaches stand in contrast to the simple explanations of strategies prevalent in most early instructional research. For instance, the teaching of a strategy such as summarization is very explicit, containing a great deal of direct explanation about the type of strategic processing involved (i.e., showing how to format the strategy to a given task), information about where and when to use a strategy, and feedback about its effectiveness (i.e., observing changes in performance after strategy use) (Duffy & Roehler, 1989; Deshler & Schumaker, 1988; Pressley *et al.,* 1989a). To accomplish these objectives, direct explanation involves the use of feedback, modeling, and teacher-guided student practice. Teacher guidance often includes hints, cues, elaborations of student responses, verbal explanations, and re-explanations of the thinking process. In short, explicit instruction makes strategies overt, sensible, and purposeful.

The essence of strategy instruction lies in *explanation* followed by challenging and extensive practice. For instance, Duffy and co-workers (1987) found that students' understanding of strategies increased after detailed explanations. Although prompting children to be more strategic and to value strategies enhances the production and use of strategies (Borkowski & Cavanaugh, 1979), students also need to experience success in actually using recently acquired strategies. This experience can be achieved by providing guided practice with appropriately difficult tasks, carefully monitored successes, and focused assistance when students experience failure and difficulties. In addition, it is essential that failures occur and that each failure occasion be used as an opportunity to repair or perfect an incomplete strategy (Clifford, 1991).

Direct explanation, with teacher modeling, helps children acquire metacognitive knowledge; that is, explicit instruction with feedback during strategy training is superior to asking students to infer or abstract a strategy's characteristics (Elliot-Faust, Pressley, & Dalecki, 1986). Students have the opportunity to learn the value of strategy use by means of explanations and practice. They realize that strategies usually have a facilitating effect on learning and understand when and how to use them effectively (Pressley & Van Meter, 1992; Pressley, Borkowski, & O'Sullivan, 1985a).

Teaching a few strategies at a time, intensively and with metacognitive understanding, is an important feature of direct strategy instruction. To accomplish understanding, strategies are extensively modeled by the teacher with verbal explanations of the complete strategic sequence and with information (and concrete examples) about the utility of the strategy being taught. The "modeling is not rigidly algorithmic, however, but reflects sensible adaptation and use of the procedures with the continuous message that personalization and modification of the procedures to meet particular needs and personal preferences is important" (Pressley *et al.,* 1992b).

It is essential that teachers cue students to generalize the strategies they are acquiring to new situations. Prompting generalization has the effect of encouraging reflective and planful processing. This approach to strategy instruction probably plays a critical role in the eventual autonomous use of strategies (O'Sullivan & Pressley, 1984; Pressley *et al.,* 1990; Ringel & Springer, 1980). Thus, a properly taught strategy will continue to be used on subsequent tasks, often in modified form.

Transactional Instruction

Pressley and colleagues (1992a) have stressed that students' affect, interests, responses, and interpretations are critical for effective strategy instruction. Good strategy instruction always stresses that teachers be responsive to the instructional needs of students who have varying cognitive capacities, depths of conceptual knowledge, and types of motivational beliefs (Borkowski, Estrada, Milstead, & Hale, 1989a; Pressley *et al.*, 1990). It is clear that good strategy instruction does not condone teaching strategies that students do not fully appreciate, or teaching the same tightly prescribed strategies to all children. On the contrary, good strategy instruction allows for unique dialogues about the thinking and learning process and promotes teacher-directed activities that are interactive in nature (Duffy & Roehler, 1989; Pressley, 1986).

Students should be, at all times, actively engaged in evaluating and managing their own learning. This orientation to transaction-based instruction encourages students to modify strategies modeled by peers and teachers and to construct strategies to fit their own learning styles. In this way, good strategy instruction incorporates, but goes beyond, the direct explanation approach because the instruction is transactional in nature.

Pressley and colleagues (1992b) have observed that competent students engage in "substantial collaborative discussions" with teachers as they try out strategies. In turn, teachers constantly initiate discussions and provide re-explanations to address student difficulties. According to Pressley and co-workers (1992b), these re-explanations take the form of dialogues; students and teachers collaborate to work out an understanding of the strategies. The teacher does not provide "canned, standardized input."

In the teaching of reading, for example, teachers and students are both learners who jointly determine the kinds of exchanges that occur during instruction (although the teacher has an explicit agenda to accomplish). The meaning of the text is co-determined by teacher and students. Children are encouraged to bring to the reading situation their diverse background knowledge and interpretations of relevant events and phenomena. Teacher and students decide what strategies to apply, when to apply them, and whether to modify or reject interpretations of the text. Alternative perspectives are generated by the students and clarified by the teacher (Pressley *et al.*, 1992a). In the long term, this kind of instruction likely produces autonomous comprehenders, who display self-regulated strategy use in selected situations, especially when rapid encoding or responding is inappropriate.

Good Strategy Instruction Is Also Constructivist

A major criticism of strategy instruction has been that it does not place sufficient emphasis on the active construction of metacognitive knowledge by the learner. If strategy instruction views the learner as a passive participant, with the teacher as simply a manager, then children will work on highly specified strategies that have little meaning to them (Poplin, 1988a,b). Children will merely be drilled on what strategy to apply, and asked to memorize and reproduce strategy sequences. The resulting effects will be minimal and short lived.

Radical constructivists would describe direct teaching as incorporating features of behavioral instruction; hence, they would call it mechanical in nature. According to Pressley and associates (1992b), good strategy instruction is, in fact, *constructivist.* These authors argue that characteristics of constructivist instruction cited by Poplin (1988a,b) are consistent with the principles of good strategy instruction. Their conclusions are based on 2 years of qualitative research in school settings that practice good strategy instruction (see Pressley *et al.,* 1992a, for a review).

The purpose of explaining and modeling is to provide a conceptual foundation on which students can expand and build. From this framework, students are stimulated to explore new strategies; good teachers guide their students to discover the effectiveness of each strategic sequence. Thus, students' understanding is constructed through interactions with the more competent problem solvers.

The net result is that strategies evolve through a process of "guided discovery." An important component of good strategy instruction is scaffolding. The teacher assumes control in promoting attention to the task and to appropriate strategies, controls frustration, decreases the risk inherent in problem solving by reducing the number of steps in the process, and makes overt any discrepancies between the child's response and ideal strategy use. Pressley and colleagues (1992b) explain that the teacher does not merely deliver content to students but models strategic processing. During extensive practice sessions, teachers discuss and illustrate how content can be understood using study strategies. A critical aspect of this process is that the students' responses have substantial impact on the course of student–teacher interactions. Strategy instruction, including the kind of scaffolding provided to a particular student, is, therefore, unique because the components of teacher–student interactions are not scripted but develop as instruction unfolds. The nature and content of student–teacher interactions are determined by the teacher's perception of student progress in acquiring each strategy. The ultimate goal of scaffolding is to develop student independence through the gradual internalization of the processes that are encouraged during scaffolded instruction.

Good strategy instruction involves substantial teaching and practice over a long period of time and across multiple tasks. This sequence permits maximum exploration of strategies and provides ample opportunities for students to discover when and where to use particular strategies and to adapt these procedures to new situations. Teachers and students explore each learning situation for its potential transfer implications. Then they practice adapting strategies to new tasks. The long-term goal is the student's construction of knowledge about the appropriateness of each particular strategy to a variety of new tasks and problem-solving challenges.

Harris and Pressley (1991) conceded that some researchers and educators did view strategy instruction as "imposing static, prescriptive routines on passive learners." We believe, however, that good strategy instruction develops active learners, involved in meaningful, planful, and reflective processing. Descriptive data, provided by Pressley and co-workers (1992a), revealed that effective teachers generally promote a view of reading as an interactive task of "constructing meaning." Students come to realize that comprehension depends on a combination of their own personal effort and strategy use in searching for understanding. In short, the aim of good strategy instruction is to provide opportunities for students to personalize strategies.

Finally, Harris and Pressley (1991) argued that constructivism is not synonymous with discovery learning. Teachers do not have to choose between constructed and instructed orientations to instruction. By incorporating the concept of guided discovery, strategy instruction provides ample opportunities for constructive processes to develop and operate effectively.

Transactional Classroom Behaviors

Pressley and colleagues (1992a) have collected qualitative inductive data that is typical of teachers who practice effective strategy instruction. The aim of Pressley's observations was, in part, to document the transactional nature of strategy instruction. During the transaction-based instruction of reading strategies, students were generally guided by the teacher in the learning and application of strategies as they (1) developed and practiced the use of strategies, (2) discussed metacognitive information, such as the rationales for various strategies and examples of situations in which they might be fruitfully applied, (3) built a nonstrategic knowledge base, and (4) participated in learning tasks that were designed to maximize motivation.

Effective teachers seemed to possess a clear understanding of their mission and how they planned to achieve it, that is, they appeared to have formed a broad conceptual framework (or internal model) in which strategic teaching occurred. For instance, strategy-oriented teachers prompted the use of particular comprehension strategies appropriate to the demands of the contents being studied. They used a "think-aloud" technique to make comprehension strategies explicit, encourage children to activate prior knowledge, and generate predictions about the story (Pressley *et al.*, 1992a).

During such lessons, children were frequently encouraged to offer interpretive remarks both in response to the teacher's comments and in reactions to the comments of other students. Children were actively involved with the text as they search for meaning. In transactional learning, teachers encourage predictions that are relevant to the context of the story, yet sensitive to particular students. Predictions are not scripted but generated during lessons, as part of naturally occurring teacher–student interactions. Sometimes students point out new information as they read that either confirms or discredits a prediction or interpretation made earlier (Pressley *et al.,* 1992a).

In essence, students and teachers interact cooperatively as they develop an awareness of the importance of the strategic skills they are acquiring. Teachers help students be flexible and selective in their deployment of reading strategies, depending on the nature of the text and the purpose of the assignment (Pressley *et al.,* 1992a). The interactive nature of instruction likely promotes self-regulating learning. In summary, transactional interactions are metacognitive in nature. They prompt students to evaluate, plan, and regulate their own reading. The goal is for students to come to manage their own reading activities.

One of the criticisms of strategy instruction has been that it is often most effective with individuals or in small-group situations. Therefore, Pressley and coworkers (1992c) observed a large classroom in a public elementary school in Maryland. In the lessons observed, the teacher was able to promote strategy use effectively during the reading lessons. One session, for example, began with the teacher setting a purpose for reading the text. As she read, she was able to stop frequently to assess comprehension, stimulate discussion, and guide and model strategy use. She prompted students to check and validate their own reading behavior and use "fix-up" strategies (such as re-reading). Throughout the lesson, the teacher employed the text as a cue to strategy use, and encouraged students in the meaning-construction process. Pressley and colleagues (1992c) noted that a common teaching pattern was used. Teachers consistently modeled and encouraged the coordinated flexible use of strategies. This activity likely was practiced by teachers who understood the importance of self-regulated learning and possessed flexible working models of children's metacognitive development. Hence, in large classrooms as well as in small group settings, transactional learning and teaching are the trademarks of effective strategy-based instruction.

Gaskins, Anderson, Pressley, Cunicelli, and Satlow (1991) conducted a detailed analysis of the cycles of student–teacher interactions at Benchmark School near Philadelphia. Their observations of skilled strategy teachers revealed a startling fact: 88% of the lesson time was spent on interactive cycles. A typical transactional cycle involved the following components: (1) The teacher initiated the interaction, for example, through a question intended to stimulate the use of a strategy (e.g., can you summarize what was just read?). (2) Several students usually reacted to the teacher's initiation, usually one at a time. (3) The teacher sometimes responded to student comments. (4) Students responded to one another. (5) Students questioned their teacher and peers. (6) The teacher continued prompting until the strategic goal that stimulated the initial question was fulfilled (e.g., a good summary was produced). It was evident that most students engaged in social role-taking and communication as they acquired strategic skills. Thus, in the transactional approach, much of the responsibility for learning is shifted from the teacher to the students. This transfer of responsibility, in turn, apparently enhances feelings of self-efficacy as students learned to attribute success to their own efforts and hard work in deploying strategies.

Pressley and co-workers (1992a) have argued that the transactional approach stimulates critical components of strategy-based instruction such as self-regulation, metacognitive knowledge about those strategies, general prior knowledge, academic self-esteem, and intrinsic motivation. As we have claimed, these components are the essence of metacognition and are at the heart of "working models" possessed by skilled teachers. In this vein, Pressley and his colleagues have made a number of astute observations. Students with metacognitively knowledgeable teachers were often prompted to model and explain the strategies they were learning. Throughout instruction, the utility of strategies was stressed. Teachers modeled and discussed flexible strategy use. Teachers conveyed messages that the students' thought processes were more important than the content material. Teachers also attempted to transfer control by promoting collaboration among students. In short, effective teachers attempted to foster personal ownership of strategies by guiding students through authentic activities with powerful strategies.

From our vantage point, recent observations of transactional learning imply that strategy-oriented teachers possess rather well-developed views and perspectives of how children's understandings of strategy-based learning can be facilitated. Many (if not all) effective teachers have constructed, often on their own, "implicit working models of mental development." If this assumption is correct, then providing unskilled teachers with a model of metacognitive development—along with methods to enhance transactional learning—may help overcome the obstacles that often inhibit the effective teaching of strategies.

OBSTACLES TO STRATEGIC TEACHING: POORLY FORMED MENTAL MODELS

Duffy (1990) believes that, to develop strategic readers, their instruction of readers must involve subtle distinctions that go beyond individual techniques such as direct instruction (Rosenshine & Stevens, 1984), direct explanation (Duffy & Roehler, 1989), or reciprocal teaching (Palincsar & Brown, 1984). In his staff development project, conducted in 10 rural school districts in northern Michigan, Duffy focuses on helping teachers develop strategic readers. The approach requires instructional flexibility and responsiveness by the teachers. Teachers are taught how to provide reading experiences that assist children in developing conceptions and beliefs that view reading as a purposeful activity. An additional goal is to train teachers to develop metacognitive readers who understand why reading is important and know the processes necessary to read effectively.

An important aspect of Duffy's staff development project is to help teachers assume control of their own instructional techniques within a conceptual framework about reading, that is, knowing what good readers do when they read and what strategic processes a teacher might strive to develop in her or his students. Teachers are encouraged to be reflectively analytical and adaptive, and to modify materials to meet the needs of strategy-based instruction. The teacher's control of his or her own professional development is stressed. In a sense, the key to empowerment is in becoming a metacognitively oriented teacher (Duffy, 1990).

Recently, Duffy (1990) conducted a descriptive study based on four teachers who were involved in his staff development project. Informal qualitative assessments of their teaching were made to ascertain their beliefs and conceptions about what students know about the nature of strategy-based reading. Analysis of the interviews and observations revealed interesting obstacles to becoming a metacognitively oriented teacher: Teachers often had difficulty presenting strategies as unitary sets of interdependent mental operations that are interchangeable and can be modified to fit different situations.

During lessons, teachers frequently talked about strategies and required answers to questions about strategies. At the same time, however, they conveyed misconceptions about what strategic readers actually do. For example, one teacher taught a lesson on main ideas in which the objective was for children to pick central topics out of expository paragraphs, as is common in most achievement tests. The teachers, however, failed to create the broad conceptualization that thinking about the main idea can also be useful in determining critical story events and learning major supporting details. Thus, children did not come to understand the flexible nature of the strategy. Similarly, another teacher prepared a lesson on expository and narrative texts in which students were required to give definitions of two major kinds of texts, rather than reflections on how to think strategically when encountering these different texts. Hence, teachers themselves sometimes lack metacognitive understanding and flexibility.

Teachers had difficulty developing techniques that promote metacognitive growth (Duffy, 1990). For example, they often failed to provide students with background information about how good readers process texts. More importantly, they did only a minimum amount of modeling. Teachers frequently required students to give answers based entirely on content rather than on describing the processes involved in constructing meaning from a text. For instance, a lesson on monitoring focused exclusively on the content of the story rather than on the monitoring the children actually did as they read. In short, the teacher conveyed the wrong message about what was important in the lesson. The teaching of strategies had taken second place to performance objectives.

Teachers also tended to teach strategies as independent entities rather than as processes activated in conjunction with monitoring. The interdependence among strategies that is associated with high quality reading was not stressed. Teachers required answers and conceptual routes that made children think of reading as a matter of naming and identifying specific strategies. Thus, they conveyed incorrect messages about the thinking routes required in metacognitively based reading. Answers required during strategy lessons often emphasized procedural memory-based teaching rather than reasoning about strategies. In short, "working models of metacognition" often seemed impoverished and narrowly focused (Duffy, 1990) and may have constituted the most serious obstacle to effective teaching.

Duffy (1990) found that using authentic rather than contrived materials did not automatically guarantee that information about a strategy's usefulness was conveyed to children. Teachers needed to guide children's thinking explicitly so that they could see the purposefulness of their reading and the strategies associated with it. Teachers and children needed to construct a "conceptual model" for strategic learning and thinking jointly, that is, they needed a shared understanding of what it means to be strategic. What seems crucial in strategy instruction is the "totality of experiences" which teachers provide to children and the "messages" that are conveyed to children about what it means to be strategic as a result of these experiences (Duffy, 1990).

Garner (1990) contends that traditional classroom goals frequently do not support the instruction of strategies. Relatedly, Ames and Archer (1988) cautioned researchers and educators that training strategies and modifying attributional beliefs may not have lasting effects if classroom goals are antithetical to, and fail to support, children's strategy use. They describe classrooms as either performance oriented (in which students are competitive, are concerned about the products of learning, and hope for success with little effort) or mastery oriented (in which students are interested in acquiring new skills, are focused on the processes of learning, and are willing to expend effort in search of problem solutions). Ames and Archer (1988) found that high school students who rated their classrooms as mastery oriented used more learning strategies than students from classrooms rated as performance oriented. It is doubtful that even excellent strategy instruction can be influential in a performance-oriented environment. Students will be unlikely to invoke strategies if they do not believe that strategy use will enhance performance, if the classroom environment does not value effort and mastery goals, and if they feel frightened or helpless when tasks become challenging.

Pressley and Gaskin's observations of expert teachers at Benchmark School (see Chapter 14) and Duffy's reports of obstacles to successful strategy instruction share a common emphasis: the necessity of establishing "working models of metacognitive development" to instruct novice teachers and to perfect experienced teachers in the art of strategic instruction.

CONCLUSION

The last 10 years have witnessed a rebirth of interest in the rationale underlying good teaching. A review by Clark and Peterson (1986) of over 40 studies of "teacher thinking" paints a sweeping portrait of the competent teacher.

> The emerging picture of the teacher as a reflective professional is a developmental one that begins during undergraduate teacher education and continues to grow and change with professional experience. The teacher education majors who would become professionals in this sense are firmly grounded in the disciplines and subject matters that they will teach. Their study of subject matter focuses on both content and on the cognitive organization of that content in ways useful to themselves and their future students. They have had both supervised practice in using the behavioral skills and strategies of teaching and have also been initiated into the less visible aspects of teaching, including the full variety of types of planning and interactive decision making. The maturing professional teacher is one who has taken some steps toward *making explicit his or her implicit theories and beliefs about learners, curriculum, subject matter, and the teacher's role.* This teacher has developed a style of planning for instruction that includes several interrelated types of planning and that has become more streamlined and automatic with experience. Much of this teacher's interactive teaching consists of routines familiar to the students, thus decreasing the collective information-processing load. During teaching, the teacher attends to and intently processes academic and nonacademic events and cues. These experienced teachers have developed the confidence to depart from a planned course of action when they judge that to be appropriate. *They reflect on and analyze the apparent effects of their own teaching and apply the results of these reflections to their future plans and actions.* In short, they have *become researchers on their own teaching effectiveness* (Clark & Peterson, 1986, pp. 292–293).

This perspective on the "thinking teacher" is validated by a recent interview study by Pressley and colleagues (1991). A group of classroom teachers, all of whom were identified as experienced strategy instructors, and a

group of seasoned strategy researchers were asked to describe their understandings and beliefs about strategy instruction. The two groups generally
had similar and consistent beliefs about the major components of strategy
instruction as well as when and how to include such components in teaching. Teachers and researchers agreed on issues such as the importance of
motivation, attributional beliefs, the nature of strategy maintenance and
transfer, what specific strategies should be taught and to which students,
and the specific focus of strategy instruction in the curriculum. These
results suggest that experienced teachers usually develop sophisticated
models of effective strategy instruction. Rich models serve to organize
existing knowledge of teaching, to facilitate specific and global planning,
and to guide moment-to-moment decision making in contexts in which
automatic responding is inappropriate. We believe that the metacognitive
model will supplement, by providing greater content specificity, general
models of classroom interactive decision making, such as that of Shavelson
and Stern (1981).

If the goals of teacher training are to encourage the development of
active, reflective, and independent learners, to view teaching as a collaborative process, and to incorporate instructional methods based on information-processing theory into their planning activities and teaching styles,
then teachers must be supported fully and consistently during training. The
working model developed in this chapter, which conceptualizes students as
metacognitively, motivationally, and behaviorally active participants in
their own learning, should be a useful source of support. It not only has
profound implications for the way in which teachers interact with students
but also for the way they organize their long- and short-range classroom
activities. Since the focus of instruction is always on the student's personally initiated learning process, the teacher becomes adept at hypothesizing
how the learner is processing information at any moment and at modifying
the teaching strategy to alter the course of the student's learning. Hence,
the model, when used correctly, provides instructional flexibility and insight.

The metacognitive model emphasizes the teacher's role as a thinker and
as an instructional agent for each student. Clark and Peterson (1986) and
Brophy (1984) found that limited conscious decision making and minimal
on-line instructional adjustments are made by most teachers because of
their inability to process the wide variety of information that emerges
during ongoing classroom interactions. The working model we have outlined should reduce this complexity and enable teachers to adopt a more
active approach to responding and interacting with individual students
during instruction, instead of being bound by pre-established rigid teaching
routines.

We believe that the concept of "working models of metacognition" will serve to help teachers develop richer and more useful implicit theories of children's learning, to use internal models to form classroom plans and facilitate decision making, and to provide a structured context in which they can conduct meaningful private research on their own teaching experiences. The net result of adopting "working models" should be the continuous refinement of strategy-based teaching by those in charge of classroom environments—teachers themselves.

REFERENCES

Ames, C., and Archer, J. (1988). Achievement goals in the classroom: Students' learning strategies and motivational processes. *Journal of Educational Psychology, 76,* 588–597.

Belmont, J. M., and Butterfield, G. C. (1977). The instructional approach to developmental cognitive research. In R. Kail and J. Hagen (Eds.), *Perspectives on the development of memory and cognition* (pp. 437–481). Hillsdale, New Jersey: Erlbaum.

Borkowski, J. G., Carr, M., and Pressley, M. (1987). Spontaneous strategy use. Perspectives from metacognitive theory. *Intelligence, 11,* 61-75.

Borkowski, J. G., and Cavanaugh, J. (1979). Maintenance and generalization of skills and strategies by the retarded. In N. Ellis (Ed.), *Handbook of mental deficiency* (2nd ed., pp. 569–617). Hillsdale, New Jersey: Erlbaum.

Borkowski, J. G., Estrada, T. M., Milstead, M., and Hale, C. A. (1989a). General problem-solving skills: Relations between metacognition and strategic processing. *Learning Disabilities Quarterly, 12,* 57–70.

Borkowski, J. G., Schneider, W., and Pressley, M. (1989b). The challenges of teaching good information processing to learning disabled students. *International Journal of Disability, Development and Education, 36,* 169–185.

Borkowski, J. G., Carr, M., Rellinger, L., and Pressley, M. (1990). Self-regulated cognition: Interdependence of metacognition, attributions and self-esteem. In B. Jones and L. Idol (Eds.), *Dimensions of thinking and cognitive instruction.* Vol. 1, pp. 53–92). Hillsdale, New Jersey: Erlbaum.

Borkowski, J. G., Day, J. D., Saenz, D. S., Dietmeyer, D., Estrada, T., and Groteluschen, A. (1992). Expanding the boundaries of cognitive interventions. In B. Wong (Ed.), *Intervention research with students with learning disabilities* (pp. 1–21). New York: Springer-Verlag.

Bretherton, J. (1985). Attachment theory: Retrospect and prospect. *SRCD Monographs, 50,* 32–35.

Brophy, J. (1984). The teacher as a thinker. In G. G. Duffy, L. A. Roehler, and J. Mason (Eds.), *Comprehension instruction: Perspectives and suggestions* (pp. 173–204). New York: Longman.

Cavanaugh, J. C., and Borkowski, J. G. (1979). The metamemory–memory "connection": Effects of strategy training and transfer. *Journal of General Psychology, 101,* 161–174.

Clark, C. M., and Peterson, P. L. (1986). Teachers' thought processes. In M. C. Wittrock (Ed.), *Handbook of research on teaching* (3rd ed., pp. 255–296). New York: Macmillan.

Clifford, M. M. (1991). *Strategy: Oversights, advantages, determinants, and obstacles.* Paper presented at the annual meeting of the American Education Research Association, Chicago, Illinois.

Craik, K. (1943). *The nature of explanation.* Cambridge: Cambridge University Press.

Day, J. D., Borkowski, J. G., Dietmeyer, D., Howsepian, B. A., and Saenz, D. S. (1992). Possible selves and academic achievement. In L. Winegar and J. Valsiner (Eds.), *Children's develop-*

ment within social contexts: Metatheoretical, theoretical, and methodological issues. Hillsdale, New Jersey: Erlbaum.

Deci, E. L. 91975). *Intrinsic motivation.* New York: Plenum.

Deshler, D. D., and Schumaker, J. R. (1988). An instructional model for teaching students how to learn. In J. L. Graden, J. E. Zins, and M. J. Curtis (Eds.), *Alternative educational outcomes for all students* (pp. 391–411). Washington, D.C.: National Association of School Psychologists.

Duffy, G. G. (1990). *Reading strategy instruction: Rethinking what's really basic.* Paper presented at the conference of the American Education Research Association, Boston.

Duffy, G. G., and Roehler, L. (1989). *Improving classroom reading instruction: A decision-making approach* (2nd ed.). New York: Random House.

Duffy, G., Roehler, L., Sivan, E., Rackliffe, G., Book, C., Melmoth, M., Vavrus, L., Wesselman, R., Putman, J., and Bassiri, D. (1987). Effects of explaining the reasoning associated with using reading strategies. *Reading Research Quarterly, 22,* 347–368.

Elliott-Faust, D. J., Pressley, M., and Dalecki, L. B. (1986). Process training to improve children's referential communication: Asher and Wigfield (1981) revisited. *Journal of Educational Psychology, 78,* 22–26.

Garner, R. (1990). When children and adults do not use learning strategies: Towards a theory of settings. *Review of Educational Research, 60,* 517–529.

Gaskins, I. W., Anderson, R. C., Pressley, M., Cunicelli, E. A., and Satlow, E. (1991). *Cognitive strategy instruction at Benchmark School: The instructional moves good strategy instruction teachers make.* Media, Pennsylvania: Benchmark School Technical Report.

Harris, K. R., and Pressley, M. (1991). The constructivistic nature of cognitive strategy instruction. *Exceptional Children, 57,* 392–404.

McCutcheon, G. (1980). How do elementary school teachers plan? The nature of planning and influences on it. *Elementary School Journal, 81,* 4–23.

Markus, H., and Nurius, P. (1986). Possible selves. *American Psychologist, 41,* 954–969.

Morine-Dershimer, G. (1979). Planning and classroom reality: An in-depth look. *Educational Research Quarterly, 3,* 83–99.

Nicholls, J. G. (1989). *The competitive ethics and democratic education.* Cambridge: Harvard University Press.

O'Sullivan, J. T., and Pressley, M. (1984). Completeness of instruction and strategy transfer. *Journal of Experimental Child Psychology, 38,* 275–288.

Palincsar, A. S., and Brown, A. L. (1984). Reciprocal teaching of comprehension-fostering and monitoring activities. *Cognition and Instruction, 1,* 117–175.

Paris, S. G. (1988). Models and metaphors of learning strategies. In C. E. Weinstein, E. T. Goetz, and P. A. Alexander (Eds.), *Learning and study strategies: Issues in assessment, instruction and evaluation* (pp. 299–321). San Diego: Academic Press.

Poplin, M. S. (1988a). Holistic/constructivist principles of the teaching/learning process: Implications for the field of learning disabilities. *Journal of Learning Disabilities, 21,* 401–416.

Poplin, M. S. (1988b). The reductionist fallacy in learning disabilities: Replicating the past by reducing the present. *Journal of Learning Disabilities, 21*(7), 389–400.

Pressley, M. (1982). Elaboration and memory development. *Child Development, 53,* 296–309.

Pressley, M. (1986). The relevance of the good strategy user model to the teaching of mathematics. *Educational Psychologist, 21,* 139–161.

Pressley, M., and Van Meter, P. F. (1992). Memory strategies: Natural development and use following instruction. In R. Pasnak and M. Howe (Eds.), *Emerging themes in cognitive development (Vol. 2,* New York: Springer-Verlag.

Pressley, M., Borkowski, J. G., and O'Sullivan, J. T. (1984). Memory strategy instruction is made of this: Metamemory and durable strategy use. *Educational Psychology, 19,* 94–107.

Pressley, M., Borkowski, J. G., and O'Sullivan, J. T. (1985a). Children's metamemory and the teaching of memory strategies. In D. L. Forrest-Pressley, G. E. MacKinnon, and T. G. Waller

(Eds.), *Metacognition, cognition and human performance* (pp. 111–153). Orlando, Florida: Academic Press.

Pressley, M., Forrest-Pressley, D. L., Elliott-Faust, D. J., and Miller, G. E. (1985b). Children's use of cognitive strategies, how to teach strategies, and what to do if they can't be taught. In M. Pressley and C. J. Brainerd (Eds.), *Cognitive learning and memory in children* (pp. 1–47). New York: Springer-Verlag.

Pressley, M., Borkowski, J. G., and Schneider, W. (1987a). Cognitive strategies: Good strategy users coordinate metacognition and knowledge. In R. Vasta and G. Whitehurst (Eds.), *Annals of child development* (Vol. 4, pp. 89–129). Greenwich, Connecticut: JAI Press.

Pressley, M., Cariglia-Bull, T., Deane, S., and Schneider, W. (1987b). Short-term memory, verbal competence, and age as predictors of imagery instructional effectiveness. *Journal of Experimental Child Psychology, 43,* 194–211.

Pressley, M., Snyder, B. L., and Cariglia-Bull, T. (1987c). How can good strategy use be taught to children? Evaluation of six alternative approaches. In S. Cosmier and J. Hagman (Eds.), *Transfer of learning: Contemporary research and applications* (pp. 81–121). Orlando, Florida: Academic Press.

Pressley, M., Goodchild, F., Fleet, J., Zajchowski, R., and Evans, E. D. (1989a). The challenge of classroom strategy instruction. *Elementary School Journal, 89,* 301–342.

Pressley, M., Johnson, C. J., Symons, S., McGoldrick, J. A., and Kurita, J. A. (1989b). Strategies that improve memory and comprehension of what is read. *Elementary School Journal, 90,* 3–32.

Pressley, M., Borkowski, J. G., and Schneider, W. (1990). Good information processing: What it is and how education can promote it. *International Journal of Educational Research, 2,* 857–867.

Pressley, M., Gaskins, I. W., Cunicelli, E. A., Burdick, N. J., Schaub-Matt, M., Lee, D. S., and Powell, H. (1991). Strategy instruction at Benchmark School. A faculty interview study. *Learning Disability Quarterly, 14,* 19–48.

Pressley, M., El-Dinary, P. B., Gaskins, I. W., Schuder, T., Bergman, J., Almasi, J., and Brown, R. (1992a). Direct explanation done well: Transactional instruction of reading comprehension strategies. *Elementary School Journal.*

Pressley, M., Harris, K. R., and Marks, M. B. (1992b). But good strategy instructors are constructivist. *Educational Psychology Review.*

Pressley, M., Faculty and Administration of Summit Hall School, Almasi, J., Schuder, T., Bergman, J., Hite, S., El-Dinasy, P. B., and Brown, R. (1992c). Transactional instruction of comprehension strategies in the Montgomery County, Maryland, SAIL program. *Reading and Writing Quarterly,* in press.

Resnick, L. B. (1987). *Education and learning to think.* Washington, D.C.: National Academy Press.

Ringel, B. A., and Springer, C. J. (1980). On knowing how well one is remembering: The persistence of strategy use during transfer. *Journal of Experimental Child Psychology, 29,* 322–333.

Rosenshine, B., and Stevens, R. (1984). Classroom instruction in reading. In P. D. Peason (Ed.), *Handbook of reading research* (pp. 745–798) New York: Longman.

Shavelson, R. J., and Stern, P. (1981). Research on teacher's pedagogical thoughts, judgments, decisions, and behavior. *Review of Educational Research, 51,* 455–498.

Schunk, D. H., and Rice, J. H. (1987). Enhancing comprehension skill and self-efficacy with strategy value information. *Journal of Reading Behavior, 3,* 285–302.

Torgeson, S. K. (1980). Conceptual and educational implications of the use of efficient task strategies by learning disabled children. *Journal of Learning Disabilities, 13,* 364–371.

Weinert, F., and Kluwe, R. (1987). *Metacognition, motivation, and performance.* Hillsdale, New Jersey: Erlbaum.

Index